PITTSBURGH THEOLOGICAL MONOGRAPH SERIES

General Editor

Dikran Y. Hadidian

15

The Hellenistic Mystery-Religions:
Their Basic Ideas and Significance

HELLENISTIC MYSTERY-RELIGIONS

THEIR BASIC IDEAS and SIGNIFICANCE

By

RICHARD REITZENSTEIN

Translated by

JOHN E. STEELY

The Pickwick Press
Pittsburgh, Pennsylvania
1978

Library of Congress Cataloging in Publication Data

Reitzenstein, Richard, 1861-1931.
Hellenistic mystery-religions.

(Pittsburgh theological monograph series ; 18)
Translation of Die hellenistischen Mysterienreligionen.
Includes indexes.
1. Greece--Religion. 2. Mysteries, Religious.
3. Religions. I. Title. II. Series.
BL785.R413 200'.938 77-12980
ISBN 0-915138-20-4

THE PICKWICK PRESS
5001 Baum Boulevard
Pittsburgh, PA 15213

Dedicated to the memory of

Albrecht Dieterich

and

Wilhelm Bousset

TRANSLATOR'S PREFACE

For philologists, historians of religion, church historians, and New Testament scholars the importance of this book will not need to be described; it will already be known to these, at least second-hand, or will quickly become evident. Participation in the work of making it available to the English-reading public, therefore, is a welcome opportunity.

Equally evident will be the author's massive learning. For a translator who does not share the author's specific field of labor or his erudition, the book poses difficulties and sets pitfalls on every page. I must ask for understanding and indulgence from the reader, especially from the specialist, who no doubt will note infelicities of expression and less-than-appropriate renderings of terms in some instances.

Although it is not the translator's privilege to dedicate a book, I should like to dedicate my labor in this translation to my wife Donnie, who has assisted and encouraged me from start to finish, and whose own contribution to the completed work is far greater than can be described here.

John E. Steely

Wake Forest, North Carolina
January 1977

FOREWORD TO THE THIRD EDITION

I began in the second edition to adapt this book to the expanded body of information that had come to me since its first appearance, partly through the kind help of various Orientalists and partly from my own labors as well. For this reason an unaltered reprint is no longer possible, however much I might have desired it for various reasons. Unfortunately a complete rewriting is likewise impossible. The material does not allow a systematic presentation in the chapters and sections of a textbook; we still stand at the beginning of the work and perhaps shall never arrive at a clean, sharp delineation of the various individual religions and mysteries. Such a form also would inevitably rob the book of what is its most distinctive quality, its very soul, by relegating the insights into the history of our own religion to a concluding chapter. The book marked for me the climax of my own teaching activity at the German university at Strassburg, to which I devoted the best energies of my adult life for more than seventeen years, and it was an outward expression of that rewarding sense of a commonality of interest with a theology that may be called "liberal" in the noblest sense of that word, and that was, following the experiences of my childhood and youth, the need of my heart. I cannot eliminate from the main body of the book the outward form of the lecture which was once given in the little church on Niklasstaden to a group of theologians and laymen who were interested in questions of religion. Nor can I renounce the liberty of selecting, for presentation in the explanatory part of the book, in arbitrary sequence, what

appears to me to be helpful in interpretation and important as well. It is hoped that indulgent readers will detect a certain unity. Anyone who has too strong an impression of incomplete work may excuse it with the recognition that the author's knowledge and labors have remained partial and imperfect, and he desires only to enlist collaboration and completion.

I have sought to the best of my ability to make use of the abundant literature which has grown up in the fifteen years since the first edition, and I ask for forgiveness if there is much that has eluded me. Anyone who has come belatedly into such related studies on the boundaries of his real area of specialization will have to take it upon himself to survey a great deal if he wishes to offer anything that is at all his own. So of what is new here, still more goes back to the personal instruction and help which I have found among many friends and colleagues; I mention in particular Fr. C. Andreas, W. Bang, W. Bousset, A. v. Le Coq, Heinr. Junker, M. Lidzbarski, F. W. K. Müller, H. H. Schaeder, K. Sethe, W. Spiegelberg, H. Thiersch, L. Troje, and H. Zimmern. For myself I may claim only the modest merit of having taken in hand a task which at the time could not be fulfilled by a single person, so that young theologians and Orientalists or classical theologians might see what they must learn in order more fully and more satisfactorily to discharge this task, and to open the way for collaboration in this area. The writings in which I have attempted this since the first appearance of this little book may be mentioned briefly here because, in order not to be burdensome, I must refer to them

frequently. They are the three essays: "Die Göttin Psyche in der hellenistischen und frühchristlichen Literatur," *Sitzungsbericht der Heidelberger Akademie* for 1917, Abh. 10; "Das mandäische Buch des Herrn der Grösse und die Evangelienüberlieferung," *ibid.* for 1919, Abh. 12; and finally "Weltuntergangsvorstellungen, eine Studie zur vergleichenden Religionsgeschichte," *Kyrkohistorisk Årsskrift Uppsala*, 1924, pp. 129-212 (also available in a separate printing in Uppsala from the Lundquistska Bokhandelen). There are also two books: *Das* ix *iranische Erlösungsmysterium* (Bonn, 1921), and the work done jointly with Prof. Schaeder, *Studien zum antiken Synkretismus, Aus Iran und Griechenland* (Leipzig, 1926). As to form, the greatest change in this present edition lies in my decision to make the "Explications" less tedious and more independent by inserting as footnotes in the "Lecture" my references to literature and the text of brief passages for documentation. The fate of books like this one to become more and more detailed and thus less usable could not be avoided entirely, nor could some repetitions, in such a fragmented arrangement.

Hermann Usener and Albrecht Dieterich have shown the way and pointed to the goal for every researcher in these areas; however, they were not granted a closer, more intimate feel for Oriental studies, though Christianity in its origins is an Oriental religion. When we here expand and revise what they did, it is done, as I know from both of them, in harmony with their intention. But the guide for this expansion has been Wilhelm Bousset. Hence the new edition of this little

book also is meant to pay my thanks to the departed friends, the philologist and the theologian.

Göttingen, August 8, 1926 R. Reitzenstein

CONTENTS

LECTURE

It is with a sense of sincere gratitude, but also of mild anxiety, that I respond to the invitation to speak as a philologist in a theological circle on a topic in the history of religions. Every philologist, when he finds it necessary to subject the major issues of primitive Christianity to his scrutiny, is always gratefully aware that all his work issues from the ground that has been won for us by liberal Protestant theology and that without the preliminary work and collaboration of that discipline his work would be inconceivable. Unfortunately, however, it is similarly inevitable that at the very outset he will have to defend himself against a notion, which is being fostered in word and in print by eminent theologians and philologists, that when he deals with questions that are and must be treated by theologians also, he is moving into an alien territory as an unauthorized person, to a certain degree as an invader. If it is the task of the philologist to gain a lively perspective of the intellectual and spiritual development of the whole of antiquity, and thus not least of all of its closing stages, he will not be able to avoid dealing with the earliest development of Christianity. Further, even if he wished arbitrarily to confine himself to paganism, there is much therein that he could not understand without taking into consideration the early Christian literature, its language and the development of its concepts, the life of feeling, and the cultus of the churches as well. Thus the work of the two disciplines must in fact often run parallel, even where each stays strictly within its own area, though to be sure the goals are different. One approach will place the major emphasis on the unity of the total development

2 of the period, will particularly stress the similarities and points of contact between Christianity and paganism, and will easily be in danger of allowing what is the distinctive element in the former to recede into the background, or of underestimating it; conversely, a way of treating the same questions which makes Christianity the sole object of its study and must set what is peculiar to Christianity or is borrowed from Judaism in a central position will prefer to limit those points of similarity to externals and will want to concede influences only for that time in which Christianity already was in existence as a complete entity. Both ways of treating the material appear to me to be as intrinsically justified and suited to complement each other as--to use a different figure which to be sure is not entirely appropriate--in historical studies the emphasis on the milieu or on the personality. The only problem with this is that the immense scope of both bodies of literature, which it is no longer possible for anyone fully to survey, makes this complementing work difficult for the individual and can easily produce personal conflicts, which of course should be relieved by the awareness of equally grave sin committed on both sides.

It has been my intention to deal with some basic perspectives of Hellenistic religions which are not unknown but perhaps not adequately stressed; perspectives, indeed, which are common to these religions, not the special property of a particular one.[1] In this treatment I use the word "Hellenistic" to identify religious forms in which Oriental and Greek elements are mingled, even though the Greek part may consist only of the fact that it has provided the language and concepts or the philosophical interpretation and justification. On the other hand, conceptions which now press in from the

Orient may be shown already to have been present in a very early epoch of Greek experience, and indeed in many cases the Orient may only have provided the impetus for a revival of something that in the early period had penetrated the Orient

3 from the Greek world.[2] Greek religion indeed had very early, through its artistic and therefore anthropomorphic delineation, individualized and propagated Oriental stimuli, but precisely through these also had lost its power to resist the speculation and *Aufklärung* that would soon set in. In that artistic portrayal it was taken up by the city-state of the fifth and fourth centuries and made into a political structure, for which the faith of the individual citizen did not have much significance. Polis-religion on the one hand and *Aufklärung* on the other hand then pushed the elements of popular or mystically deeper piety into the background in most places. It is true that Plato early drew from it some strong stimuli and later, in the *Timaeus*, even blended Oriental ideas, which were imparted to him by Eudoxos, with Greek philosophy, to produce a "natural teaching on religion" (*naturalis theologia*) which to be sure was not meant to do away with the polis-religion but to minimize it for the thinking person; however, neither he nor his closest followers, who to a degree were committed to the popular faith, at first exerted much influence in the area of religion. Plato's religious language continued to have an influence only as it was transferred to artistic production. It was only with the

4 rise of the monarchies that there begins a deliberate taking-into-account of the religious feelings of the wider masses, which in fact was a political necessity in the Oriental area from the very outset. The Stoic philosophy adapts itself to this effort, seeks to combine the "natural teaching on reli-

gion" with the polis-religion, and creates the literary category of apologetic. By interpreting the gods as concepts or as forces of nature and explaining the myths allegorically, it achieved, at first for the Greek religions but soon for the Oriental religions as well, a *tolerari posse*, a proof which appealed to the reason, that popular belief and the scientific knowledge of the educated person need not be at odds. Since in the great Oriental religions, which are guarded and speculatively developed by an established priestly caste, a reinterpretation of the deities as forces of nature or as concepts had already begun, the primary contribution of the Stoa in this regard was to provide the vocabulary for the Hellenistic re-formation of those religions and in a certain sense to produce the religious κοινή. In itself, its apologetic was as ineffective religiously as an apologetic usually is, and as it remained, at least for the Greeks, for the ruler-cult, in which the new monarchies sought to combine their Greek and Oriental subjects and to create, as had been done in the city-state, a divine representation of the political structure. But it is true that in the course of the third and second centuries B.C., philosophy acquired for the Greek an almost religious significance. Now in essence oriented to ethics, philosophy would render him independent of the blind play of external event and the struggle with his own passions and would give him a fixed point within himself, and with his freedom, peace. To what extent it now also captures people of an utterly non-theoretical bent and to what nobility of soul it trains and educates even at its periphery may be attested by as sober a man of practical life as Polybius; and a teacher such as Panaitios can show to what heights of intellectual development and what ideal level of most authen-

5 tic humanity it can elevate one. Religion plays no role in this. It was only the collapse of his aristocratic ideal of humanity, which his pupil, the Syrian Poseidonios, experienced in advance, at least in the moral sphere, that produced the yearning for a new, stronger grounding of ethical ideals; the Oriental sense of an indissoluble connection between God and man also helped to lead him back to Plato's religiously fruitful philosophy. A universal knowledge, such as no one else in antiquity after him gathered, seeks its ultimate crown in mystical vision; the philosopher becomes a prophet, and the strength of his discourse and the ardor of his imagination influence pagan as well as Christian religious literature down to the close of antiquity and carry an abundance of Platonic conceptions and terms over into the Orient. A remolding of Hellenism has begun, which was remarkably hastened under the pressure of terrible times and an ever more general sense of sin and guilt; soon, in Neo-Pythagoreanism, we see Oriental belief in magic combined with presumably ancient Greek wisdom; later, in the gradual remolding of Platonism into Neo-Platonism, we see a purely Oriental form of ecstasy become the climax and goal of the philosophical life. The principle is always maintained: in Hellenism only Greek philosophy and Oriental religion or religiosity possess the strength of conquest and practice a missionary activity.

If we turn our attention first to these, we must keep in view a fundamental difference within the religion of western Asia and, in connection with this, in some way define the concept with which we shall be concerned in the following pages.

Two essentially different types of religion collide quite early in western Asia, types in which we may see not only peculiarities of the two major races, but, even more, various

stages of the general religious development. At one stage, the more sober one, the connection of God with man remains more ex-
6 ternal:[3] God has created or chosen for himself a particular tribe and cares for it and especially for its representative, the king, so long as they remain faithful to him; but his rule is related only to the earthly life; no community of essence or hope of the hereafter connects men with God. This type is probably most purely exhibited by the Babylonian and the earlier Israelite religion. At another stage, the soul, at least the soul of the adherent of the true (i.e., the tribal) religion, is akin to God in essence, and thus is, like God, immortal. Man and God are infinitely close to each other. We may identify Iranian and Indian religions as examples. It is clear that the concept of the soul must be more strongly developed here. A development is in fact evident. The really essential, the person or the self, is at first always the body, even where a contrast of sensual and suprasensual is felt. The world itself, as a body filled with life, is regarded as the deity and at the same time, at least in the religions mentioned, as a human being, indeed, as the man. Further reflection sets the suprasensual vitality of life and mind apart from the material; that vitality is the deity, both in the world and in the individual man. The soul, as the breath of life as well as the vitality of spirit, therefore remains the general, non-individual; the I or Self still is bound to the body, and yet the very placing of the spiritual aspect on a higher level will constantly demand that the real essence, the true I of man, be seen in it, the I which then necessarily becomes a part of the deity, or the deity itself. This connection of essence between man and deity can be conceived in various forms; it everywhere affects the conception of immortality, but by no means neces-

sarily the idea of the immortal individual soul which has come
7 from God and returns to God. This is opposed by the fact that
at first the concept "man" is everywhere restricted to the
tribe; the enemy, or the person of a different belief, is not
a man; he does not have a soul, because he does not have the
deity, knowledge of the deity, religion.[4]

Of course neither of these two types remains pure; they
constantly exert reciprocal influence. Within the former
type, nature myths of a dying and rising God[5] can produce the
idea that the individual man can be connected with him by
means of *magic*, that is, by sacred actions, and hence can
share his lot, or there arises the belief that the king is
begotten directly by God and hence is, like God, immortal;
the imitation of the consecration or anointing of the king
thus can here become a kind of immortality-magic.[6] This involves the immortality of the individual man; Egyptian religion provides the earliest and clearest documentation. It
gradually becomes a general possession and a general belief.
The idea, developed within the second type, of a common soul
of all believers or members of the nation, which is divine and
immortal, can likewise have a wider and continuing effect, as
we see in Judaism in the awakening of the belief in immortality. But also within the second type, the need to individual-
ize, which besets all religious experience, and the understanding of religion as the true knowledge of the deity, demand a
distinction of degrees in this knowledge and cultic actions
which will accomplish one's ascent in these degrees. We see
on Indian soil in the building of the altar of fire (see be-
8 low, p. 197) a primeval cult of magic which makes the lord of
the sacrifice into Agni (the fire-god as the world-soul). In
the Persian realm, already in the earliest version of the ad-

mittedly *late* Bahman-Yasht, the prophet is given omniscience (the vision of the universe) through a cup of water that he is to drink; he possesses it as long as the water remains in his body. The same rite, thrice repeated, enables Arda Viraf to walk through heaven in the spirit and to bring down the true knowledge of religion; in the mysteries of Mithras, Persian belief is combined with initiation that is divided into seven stages, and in Manichaeism the distinction between warriors (hearers) and perfect ones (elect) itself shows the existence at least of a mystery, of which unfortunately we do not know anything more specific. It is self-evident that in this connection, the admission of foreign-born people into the religion or the tribe would require such cultic actions particularly, and even here different grades or degrees are distinguished: it is only the third initiation that makes the believer in Mithras into a warrior, and only the fifth makes him a full-fledged member of the tribe of the souls (a Mandaean designation), a Persian. And yet each preceding level had already offered him revelation, heavenly vision, which, because it enriches his knowledge about God, has a deifying effect on his nature. As best I can see, the two elements are combined in the Greek concept *mysterion*, in the pagan as well as in New Testament usage; when Paul says, "I tell you a mysterion", underlying this is the fact that he has been granted the vision of Christ and later visions as well, and once was even lifted up to the third heaven. It lies in the very nature of the case that as a rule cultic practices are supposed to render such a vision possible, that they are related to ancient practices which have become incomprehensible to the layman and which have the appearance of magic--particularly practices of the early cult of the dead--and, like magical practices, mi-

grate from one people to another. In spite of the already-mentioned fundamental distinctions among the religions of western Asia, for the Hellenistic period one may see and posit once again a kind of unity in these actions which al-
9 ways place the participant in relationship with the deity in extraordinary fashion, particularly in a survey the aim of which is to show the impact of the environment on the language and felt experience of infant Christianity.

What is involved in the actually religious part of these mysteries is always immortality, and thus, in the broadest sense, "redemption", and it is clear that in the second type it must be cosmologically grounded; cosmology and eschatology here belong indissolubly together; it is a mistake to try to consider them separately. Thus I may emphasize here at once that at least for one of these religions we may now somewhat more clearly survey the development, since a brilliant discovery by Albrecht Goetze[7] allows us to date in the fifth century B.C. a copy of the Persian Avesta, preserved in scraps and in later imitations, the Damdaδ-Nask. The last being created by the Most High God here bears the name Gaya maretan, "mortal life". The distinguishing adjective shows that according to the original intention life had to be immortal, that it belongs to the very nature of deity. Submerged in the material world, it is subject to death, to the anti-godly, but by its being dissolved, its flowing into matter, it causes men to emerge from matter; upon the collapse of the material world, or rather upon the world's absorption into the deity and the expulsion of mortality from it, life returns to the deity, and along with it all its descendants or parts, individual men. The idea that that "mortal life" at the same time has brought to the world the powers of the seven guides of the spheres

(planets), represented as the world's metals, and movement (i.e., freedom) already has wholly receded. We sense that the idea of a world-god or a world-soul which in the transient individual manifestations still prevails is already suppressed by the interest in the fate of the individual man.

10 Another, not necessarily later, stage of the development is represented by the twenty-second Yasht, which in itself is in fact later. Here the association with cosmology is dissolved; the soul of the individual man is the only thing at issue. After death the soul of the devout man meets its heavenly counterpart, which consists of its good thoughts, words, and deeds--thus of its religion--and this heavenly counterpart leads the soul upwards through three heavens. The latter has become like the god Ohrmazd and will be given reverence, as is the deity. It is important that this ascent of the soul, in which a redeemer appears, had already been set forth also in the Damdaδ-Nask, in spite of the internal contradiction between this view and the idea of the resurrection of the body at the final judgment.

One consequence appears to me to be the teaching offering in later writings, that Gayomard himself, that is, mortal life, signifies the essence of true religion. It is the presupposition for a Greek revision of the Damdaδ-Nask, which we meet in the Hermetic writing Poimandres from about the beginning of the Christian era.[8] Only the ascent of the soul here forms the end of the presentation, which however still is altogether cosmologically structured. The role of the redeemer emerges more strongly. He is the "Good Mind", the counterpart and the emissary of the "Wise Lord", Ohrmazd, and thus once again religious knowledge. During the lifetime of the pious person he appears to that person, in whom however he already resides

as his innermost self, shows him the god of the world, teaches him the ascent of the soul and its union with God, who like the primal man and every devout person is light and life, and then, because thus he has received all knowledge of God, sends him forth as proclaimer, to save mankind by means of this teaching. We shall hardly be able here to speak of a mystery; a purely inward experience, similar to the one in Buddhism which makes 11 one "perfect",[9] is set forth here. But it includes in itself the missionary commandment; we are in the Diaspora.

Here we encounter at least a basic feature of Indo-Persian thought which in the concern with the Persian tradition otherwise can easily escape one's view, namely the profound drive for a unified view of the world and God.[10] It can no longer be purely mythological, and even less can it be purely scientific; it is traditional, dogmatically inhibited, and yet it demands an inward experience, an actual "vision" of the great mystery. "I desire to come to know that which is, to understand its essence, and to become acquainted with God," says the prophet.[11] And the understanding of the Persian priestly knowledge is similar in the same period in Philo;[12] as we shall see later, he understands it as fuller than what we now call "Gnosis", but the less worthy, indeed corrupt, imitation, its counterpart, is magic.

In the second type of religion we are able to recognize the development only with some uncertainty. It seems to me to be important that at least for later understanding, gods like Osiris, Attis, and Adonis were for a long time men; they had died but had risen again. If we are somehow united with these 12 gods, as by putting on their clothing or by employing the means by which the god was awakened from the dead, or in some other way share his lot and become the god himself, we too may hope

for a continuing life. Here the magical means provides the basis for the confidence or the mystery. The portrayals of the experience of the god, the struggles over Osiris, the searching of Isis, the lament for the deceased Adonis, and the hailing of the resurrected one, the major themes of the Attis-faith--all these sacred actions (whether old or newly introduced) appear to have become, in the Hellenistic cult, parts of an artistically arranged worship and to be entirely public, or at least open to the community. It does not matter much whether we still want to call them mysteries--they are indeed also continued in the mystery-communities--and whether they ever were such in the full sense, so long as we sharply distinguish them from those purely personal mysteries which are accessible only to the individual.

But more about these later. First we must consider a document which shows us the uniting of these hopes, by their nature diverse, of the hereafter and which fortunately allows us to fix its place in time. It is the so-called Naassene Preaching,[13] which was composed about A.D. 100, and thus a century after the Poimandres, by a completely hellenized Oriental for a Phrygian-Jewish community; it probably is the most important document for ancient syncretism. A universally developed mystery-movement is presupposed; but the mysteries of all religion only tell of the one primal man, who here is called Adam. He appears in dual form. Non-individualized, he holds sway as the soul of the universe, and as individual soul he resides in the individual man, the first corporeal Adam and his offspring. Of course, since they are slumbering, he lies in them unconscious. Only when as the heavenly Adam he has awakened these counterparts that have sunk down in matter can he lead them into the kingdom of God, to which he himself belongs. The Persian doctrine of the primal man is

13

meant to give a certain measure of metaphysical justification to the magical hopes of immortality; but in the cult the magical elements apparently continue to function.

We recognize that this purely pagan doctrine could and must be christianized. We find one quite similar to it as a folk religion among the Mandaeans, a Semitic tribe which originally lived in the vicinity of the Jordan, and thus in the neighborhood of Judaism and under its influence, but later migrated to the lower reaches of the Euphrates. The fact that the tribe once changed its faith is shown in the designation for God; the generally Semitic *ilah* comes to be used only for the false gods, while for the true God they use the Iranian designation for a being, *haije* ("Life"). The cult of the dead and the hymns for the dead, that is, the hymns of the ascent of the soul, show, through their close connection with the twenty-second Yasht and later Persian sources, as has long been recognized, their dependence on Iranian religion. The concept of rising from the dead, which we have already encountered in the Naassene Preaching, utterly dominates religious thought. The primal man, who is identified as the knowledge of the deity (*Manda d'Haije*),[14] as the perfect man, the first man, the righteous, the pure one, as the head of generations, as Adam or even as Enosh (Man), slumbers as "hidden Adam" (Adakas) in every individual person, but he is also wandering, unknown or even invisible, as an emissary through the earth, "to test the hearts and to weigh and test all minds, to see in what heart he himself dwells, in what mind he resides".[15] He sounds the call to awaken, for he is a word[16] and a son of word, indeed is called Adakas Malala (Adam the Word) as well as Adakas Mana (Adam the divine being). Returning, then, at the death of the body he leads

14

the soul--or, more properly speaking, that part of it that is divine--heavenward. Thus even the ascending soul itself can be called Adam, particularly since those hymns of the dead originally, as a kind of analogy-magic, pictured the ascent of a cosmic divine being, Adam as the world-soul. Even when according to ancient tradition from western Asia four world-epochs are assumed and the divine being ascends to heaven four times, each time he is followed in his ascent by the entire host of his own people who have died during this epoch, now released from an interregnum; this resembles the procession of the dead in Gayomard's train in the Persian Damdaδ-Nask. Just as later on in the Naassene Preaching this Adam is called the world-soul (Psyche), so we also find among the Mandaeans the concept of the "great Nitufta", the *monuhmed vuzurg*[17]

15 of the Manichaean Turfan texts, used for the same purpose, and beside it stand the individual souls; even the individual has a Nitufta or *monuhmed*. Here we can even follow the formation of the concept. Nitufta originally means "a drop", and in the early Persian Damdaδ-Nask (Gr. Bundahisn, ch. 28, Goetze, *Zeitschrift für Indologie und Iranistik*, II, 60) the comparison of the microcosm with the (divine) macrocosm begins with the sentences: In the holy books (the Avesta) it is said, "The human body is an exact image of the world." For the world is made from a drop of water, as it is said, "This creation is, in its totality, a drop of water; even man himself has developed out of a drop of water." Just as the world is as wide as it is

16 long, so also is man, every individual man, as tall as the span of his arms. For the first man Gayomard this then is explicitly emphasized in the account of creation. Hence for him the designation Nitufta also can emerge.[18] Here too, as with the Naassenes, a mystery, the sacrament of baptism, cul-

tically speaking stands in the foreground; it determines the status of belonging to the tribe of the souls, and thus of religion.[19]

Thus has been confirmed what Eduard Meyer had asserted in his *Geschichte des Altertums*:[20] in spite of the religious toleration shown by the Persian government, the faith of the ruling class influences all of western Asia.[21] What Meyer himself set forth only for the Jewish religion can be pursued much further by individual observations. The views within the individual religions are expanded and deepened, even where the cult does not undergo any changes; further possibilities are opened up for individualism. This standardizing and internalizing feature reaches from Egypt to southern Russia
17
and eastward to the borders of China, in many places at least advanced by the speculation of the established priestly orders. Thus already at the beginning of this epoch the Orient stands over against the religiously impoverished Greek world. Its religions supposedly offer age-old traditions and continuously operative revelations of God, divine protection, and the certainty of eternal salvation. It is no wonder that they had to spread.

Infant Christianity grew up between two thought-worlds which had begun to intermingle, the Greek and the Oriental; it is obvious that both of them exerted an influence on it. The impact of philosophy on Christianity, which modern researchers in Hellenism at first emphasized, certainly has not yet been set forth with adequate thoroughness, but it has been stated often enough that I can leave it aside here. My task can only be to focus precisely on the second, really Oriental part of Hellenistic religions. It may not simply be equated with the ancient folk-religions. The interchange of ideas in

the Persian period, already referred to, and the growth and advancement of this Oriental part had to bring to it the penetration of the Greek universal language, the substitution of Greek words, by no means always adequate, for the concepts of the various priestly speculations. Quite apart from this, however, in propaganda and Diaspora any religion must become different, infinitely more personal than it is within a self-contained national constituency in which participation in it is taken for granted and no personal decision is placed upon the individual, and yet again it also must become more universal, intended for the whole of humanity, not for a single nation alone. Like the primitive religion each one will have to admit the temptation, and even be compelled, to establish definite forms and symbols, as distinctive as possible, for belonging to it--similar in this respect to the sects that are formed within the individual national religions. This end is served above all by the mysteries.

Of course for that very reason the material for our knowl-
18 edge of the re-shaping of old national and nature religions in the Hellenistic propaganda is small. For the Egyptian religion, the existence of Hellenistic rites, accessible also to the Egyptian, can be demonstrated at least by linguistic observations,[22] and for these Egyptian-Hellenistic mysteries--but also only for them--the description of the Isis-religion in Apuleius lets us somewhat more precisely recognize the cult, language, and life of experience; for the Phrygian religion, we have, in addition to the already mentioned Naassene Preaching, which must be used with caution, two portrayals of the cult.[23] For the Persian religion we have the testimony, in itself not very fruitful, of theophoric names,[24] and in addition to the aforementioned only the brief references, not to be used without care, to the later mysteries of Mithras and

the documents, to be taken more seriously, of the Manichaean sects and reflections in magical practice. For the Babylonian religion, since we are concerned with the Hellenistic and Roman periods, we have nothing, and for other periods only a few scattered allusions. We must undertake, by means of comparisons, to imbue these religions with vitality for our own perspective, and this is all the more possible since the same tendency, already earlier operative, on the one hand to view the deities as forces of nature and on the other hand to ethicize religion, applies everywhere. Only if the soul has become like God can it return to him as its origin. Thus even where the basic outlook had to demand a restoration of all souls, intermediate stages and differentiations slip in; for its return home the soul requires enlightenment and divine
19
assistance; specific actions must be taken to assure the soul of these aids. But the mere word also can exert the miraculous influence; the images used in this connection show us the perspectives which once were set forth in the actions. A consideration of the basic ideas of the mystery religions must not be kept within the narrow limits which our modern doctrine of the sacraments gives to the concept of mystery, but must take into account the breadth of meaning of the word in the Hellenistic usage.[25]

Apuleius gives us some information about the organization of a Diaspora-community of the Isis-faith[26] which at that time was spread over the entire known world. To this community belonged "affiliated persons" of various degrees, believers or proselytes, *advenae*, as they are also called here. They participate in worship and visit the temple; in fact, they may even reside in the sacred precincts. Nevertheless they are separated from those who have been *betrothed* to the deity and

have *given* their lives to the deity as its very own, the *mystai*, even when these latter live in the world. These 20 have "*taken the yoke upon themselves*" and--as it is said here, in other mysteries to which Livy refers, and in the Mithras cult--have committed themselves to *service in the holy war*.[27] An oath, *sacramentum*, obligates them for lifelong service. The service is demanding, a strict asceticism is bound up with it, and many shrink from it. For the Isiscult's openness to the proselytes is matched by its strict demand that the initiates observe, even in external matters, the ritual prescriptions which in the homeland applied to the priest. In the Diaspora, where the insistence upon priestly lineage and the installation at the hands of the king had to be abandoned from the very first, the mystery itself was what created the priestly status. From among those initiated, then, the god called--in practice that meant the cooptation of the priest actually then functioning--the individual, to a position for a specific period of time or for life, depending on the relative influence of the Roman practice of arranging *collegia*. A priestly ancestry is created for this person by means of the fiction that by giving him instruction, the one who performs the initiation becomes the father of the one being initiated. The initiation itself is in two parts, separated by a period of strict asceticism. First there is a baptism, which in its ritual corresponds exactly to the old Egyptian baptism of the dead and the baptism of the king upon his ascending the throne. This is adequately explained by the statement of Apuleius that in the entire celebration the idea is that of a voluntary death and a new life bestowed by grace. Even the agreement of the king's baptism with the baptism of the dead can be understood. It is true that the king is be-

gotten by God; but this sonship to God is generally acknowledged only at the actual assumption of the throne and at that time is solemnly proclaimed by God.[28] Thus for the king also 21 this act signifies the beginning of a new life, and such (for example, the recognition of manhood and one's admission to the tribe) is represented, as is well known, among many peoples by a burial and reawakening. Since the priest too, at least insofar as he acts as representative of the king, has divine power and is God, it is in fact conceivable that the national cult had a corresponding consecration of priests, at least for the higher levels, who in fact, according to later views, were the ones usually who opened up access to secret knowledge. But since witnesses to this seem to be lacking, we shall be more correct to turn our attention more to the baptism of the dead. It will suffice to explain in some measure the second part of the action. It should be evident that a heavenly journey is described; only on such a journey can a man present his veneration to the heavenly gods in direct, immediate relationship. This is demonstrated by such antitypes as the heavenly journey of Nechepso[29] and the so-called Mithras liturgy.[30] The consecration of the king also provides, in the circumambulation of the temple, which in fact for the Egyptian symbolizes heaven, and in the veneration of the individual gods, a certain counterpart. Egyptian belief in the later time gives us the explanation of the journey or flight[31] through the elements: it too only symbolizes the ascent to heaven. On the other hand, other references point to the earlier belief, the entrance into the underworld and the twelve-hour duration of the migration through that world, in which the initiate must assume twelve different forms. How the two are combined in the ritual of Corinth remains uncertain.[32] The fact that alien elements have intruded is shown

by many traces and is expressed above all in the fact that at
22 the conclusion of the wandering, the deceased person does not become a reflection of Osiris, but a reflection of a sun-deity or a world-deity. For the internal development it seems to me to be significant that even in the Phrygian mystery, a sacrificial action, which at first was for the benefit of the cultic community and in which the priest of the highest rank participated, the Taurobolium, becomes the initiatory rite of the mystic, the bath of rebirth, which is preceded by a dying. The real mystics here too are a nation of perfect ones or of priests. The difference between these personal mysteries and the previously mentioned national or community mysteries is clear enough: the initiate no longer beholds what the deity has experienced, but he himself experiences it and thereby becomes the deity, just as in earlier Egypt the deceased person himself also becomes Osiris. When the high priest himself is called Attis, he must be understood to be the embodiment of the deity already in his own lifetime.

The tie between god and man cannot be thought of in closer and stronger terms, and they are joined by a feeling not only of lifelong gratitude but of personal love, which in its expression passes over into sensual terms.[33] Here, in the Diaspora, each of these deities has, so to speak, a definite message of salvation--philologists have spoken at least with some justification of a gospel of Isis whose text we still possess. Furthermore, collections of sacred writings intended for liturgical use, and indeed collections composed in the Greek language, appear.[34] Moreover, *faith* (πίστις, *fiducia*) in these deities is an act of personal will, a divine power which, based upon personal experience in the mystery, is explicitly set in contrast to any philosophical conviction.[35]

Preaching assumed definite forms--we know of prayers of thanks- 23 giving, expositions of sacred texts, and missionary sermons. Finally, fixed confessions bind the communities together, and a rich literature of miracle stories and accounts of visions contributes to revival and edification. When all these facts are taken into account, we understand the remarkable magnetic power which this Hellenistic form of Oriental faith was bound to exert upon the religiously impoverished West.

If we wish rightly to evaluate the distinctiveness of that faith, we must first take a look at the emergence of the communities. The transplanting of large masses of people, wrought within a world empire or cultural area by a ruler's decree or by the peaceful constraints of trade, to a certain extent dilutes the national character of the folk-religions and influences their nature. I may only remind you of the Jewish Diaspora and of that surprising discovery that already in the Persian period a Jewish military colony in Aswan had its own temple to Yahweh with a cultus that was not strictly monotheistic.[36] This was a colony that was consciously Jewish and was in contact with the leadership of the national cult in Jerusalem, but in conflict as well. When we now can prove for the early Ptolemaic period a Mithras shrine in Egypt, we will think of the successors and descendants of the Persian occupation troops, the Πέρσαι τῆς ἐπιγονῆς. The temple of Astarte in the sacred precincts of Sarapis at Memphis will make it believable that there was a temple of Sarapis in Babylon already in Alexander's time. Sarapis does not thereby become a Babylonian god (no more than does Astarte become Isis). We may not simply dismiss even Indian influences on Egypt, since in Pap. Oxyrh. 1380 a cult of the *Isis Latina* in India is attested for the Roman period, and for the Hellenistic period

a certain value will have to be attributed to the inscriptions of the Indian king Asoka. Similarities, particularly in the 24 cults transmitted through commercial contacts, are probable from the very outset. When Egyptian tradesmen in Athens early form an association of their countrymen and found an Isis-shrine as the cultic center of their association, both cult and perspective similarly are adapted first to the circumstances, and then soon to the environment also, and new shrines or cults, influenced by this one or founded from this center, will be still more strongly hellenized. Still more marked are the changes in the cults that are appropriated for political reasons. When the Hellenistic ruler of Egypt reorganized the Sarapis cult, had a specific theology worked out, and imported the cultic image, with the intention (as seems probable to me, in spite of Schubert's objection) of bringing the two classes of the population of his country closer together, he still had to hold as closely as possible to earlier ideas, concepts, and terms; he was aided in this by an Egyptian and a Greek specialist. However, the Greek cities, which, in order to honor him, immediately thereafter officially adopted the cult, needed neither to appropriate an Egyptian priestly caste--hardly even a single Egyptian appears as advisor to the Greek priest--nor to imitate the cult in all details. They did in fact *constitute* it anew, and the purely representative character of the *polis*-cult makes details appear hardly important. The relationship to the foreign religion was necessarily more inward in those private and free cultic associations which soon were transplanted even into the homeland of Egypt. Even if the individual made his choice in terms of worshiping a foreign god, there had to be an attraction exerted by what was new and set in contrast to the cult of his homeland. But then the indi-

viduality of the *founder* or the leader of the company also had to acquire a special importance, but a faithful imitation of the cultic patterns of an Oriental popular religion was bound to be impossible in many respects even for external reasons. At present, at least, I am unable to discern to what extent then in later times the private and public cults penetrated and influenced each other; we can only recognize or suspect that with the intensifying of religious need the Oriental element becomes stronger, and the magic of the mysterious, attested by age-old tradition, becomes even more compelling.

25

The rapid spread of those cults even in remote places hardly touched by commerce cannot be understood unless we focus sharply on the few notes about the activity of wandering servants of individual Oriental deities. I would not see them--and have never seen them--as official priests who were attached to a particular shrine in their homeland. But they represent themselves as priests and prophets and validate their proclamation by means of the ecstatic spirit of their discourse and by means of prediction and miracle. The famous passages in which Livy gives a detailed account, as instruction for his own time, of the rise and the suppression of an evidently Hellenistic orgiastic mystery-cult in Italy at the beginning of the second century seem to me to be especially instructive. The goal is σωτηρία. The rite of initiation puts in a form discernible to the physical senses a sexual union with the god; we hear of sacral meals, secret prayers, divinely inspired discourses (προφητεύειν), and nocturnal torchlight processions. A migrating Greek first brought the cult to Etruria; his *native* pupils, constantly forming new communities, quickly spread it over Italy; they even decisively reshaped it, "on the basis of

divine revelations".[37] Like that Greek, so also soon thereafter Magi and Chaldeans or Egyptian miracle-workers appear to move through Italy. Already in Cicero's time a prominent Roman named Nigidius Figulus practiced all those kinds of magic to which our papyri refer, and he did this in order to provide attestation, by means of miracles, for a Hellenistic teaching; he also even founded a kind of community. He had already had predecessors in the smaller cities of Italy; this is shown by the latest Italian comedy.[38] They are the men soon thereafter mentioned by Philodemus as the "so-called θεῖοι" through whom God speaks. The well-to-do Roman of the time had in his entourage, along with or in addition to a philosopher, as a spiritual guide, this kind of Oriental prophet--that Sergius Paulus of the book of Acts much like Memmius, the companion of Lucretius. A general conception of the θεῖος ἄνθρωπος begins to prevail, according to which such a divine man combines within himself, on the basis of a higher nature and personal holiness, the profoundest knowledge, vision, and the power to work miracles. Without this conception, phenomena such as the preacher and wonder-worker Apollonius of Tyana, or the seer and religious founder Alexander of Abonoteichos, remain incomprehensible; indeed, the same is true even of the ideas attached to the Cynic Peregrinus Proteus. In the narrative literature it is regarded as self-evident that such men have foreknowledge of the future, can read the thoughts of the people they meet, heal the sick, and even revive the dead for a moment or for a longer time. In life, the "prophet" is the title of honor for them, "sorcerer" the contemptuous one. The explanation apparently is offered by the character of Oriental religion. For the Stoic Chairemon, the teacher of Nero, Egyptian religion consists in an astrologically applied nature-

cult and in magical incantations, the means of breaking the compulsion exercised by the stars. This becomes comprehensible when we see in the daily cultus of the Egyptian priest how every cultic action really is a bit of magic, and when we consider the fact that the indissoluble connection between supernatural knowledge and miraculous powers, which now is regarded in Hellenism as self-evident, finds its simplest explanation in that basic perspective of the mysteries that they unite one with God and deify one. Indeed, everywhere we encounter the theme that only by means of this union does the magician perform his wonders and the seer or teaching prophet behold the future or the divine secrets; in fact, we hear that this union has a retroactive effect and that by the practice of magic and by experiencing the future, one becomes immortal.[39] It is not surprising that the practice of magic constantly imitates the mysteries and only clothes the same ideas in ever new forms, individually, because they are dissociated from any community cult. Thus the numerous magical texts which were found in Egypt and which in the main probably were produced there show how great the importance of those personal mysteries became here in the late Hellenistic period. It is the natural impact of the Diaspora back upon the homeland.

27

It is true that when they moved out into other countries, neither the Egyptian nor the Phrygian nor even the Persian religion had a fixed doctrinal system; we can affirm this with certainty, in spite of the fact that these religions were cultivated in closed priestly companies. The local diversity which is affected thereby is intensified still further by the nature of the translation and by the selection of deities afforded at least by the Egyptian religion. First one deity and then another moves into the central position,

dictated even more by the philosophical education of the time than by the needs of the cult.[40] Martial ridicules, as common knowledge in Rome, a message of salvation which climaxes in the confession of Hermes as the triune god of the world: *Hermes omnia solus et ter unus*. Imitating this and yet set in contrast to it is another confessional formula which is preserved for us in an inscription: *Isis, una quae es omnia*.
28 These are the two greatest revelational deities of Hellenistic mystical literature. Plutarch speaks of a secret teaching of those who worshiped Anubis, and a confessional inscription from the Diaspora shows us this deity, who in fact elsewhere is called the servant of all the gods, installed in place of Horus as ruler of the world.[41] In fact, even communities of one and the same deity diverge from each other as to detailed forms and appear not to be closely related; when Apuleius, who was initiated in Corinth, came to Rome, he was a proselyte, "not in the religion, to be sure, but in this temple". When the goddess commanded that his first initiation be repeated, he could not receive this in Rome, but only in Corinth.

Still more unusual is a second feature. When the initiate of Isis offers his whole life as a vow and joins her army as thanksgiving for the σωτηρία that is attained, he must, consistent with this commitment, renounce the cult and the mysteries at least of the non-Egyptian gods. Precisely the opposite of this feature is exhibited by the Egyptian mystery-prayers and those of Phrygia, which rarely are in agreement with the Egyptian. In the Hellenistic period all the mystery religions of antiquity are presented as intended for *all* men, but they all acknowledge each other. Each one purports to offer the *original religion* which was taught the first men by God; but all other men have appropriated this original religion from this

beginning; all peoples worship the same deity under different names and cults.[42] Thus the particular mystery-cult, which always is supposed to issue from the place where the first men

29 appeared, still can only claim to offer the most correct and effectual name and ritual. But is this after all fully acknowledged? Can a man decide among the various claims to sacred traditions? It appears to me to be not unimportant that this doubt is expressed even in the prayers. The imperceptible change in feeling in the empire also was at work. "We must all revere the gods in common (κοινοί)," says Plutarch when he is attempting to render the message of Isis comprehensible to the educated Greek; that is, to interpret it philosophically. "We must not rob mankind by emphasizing the externals in the myth and its interpretation and thus making so powerful a religion a national thing and the sole possession of the Egyptians." It is true that the argument still is Stoic in essence. "Just as the sun and the moon remain the same and are only given different names by the various peoples, so also the all-governing Logos and Providence remain everywhere the same, even though names and cultus vary. The symbols under which the various religions conceal these realities may in one case be stated more sharply and in another case less clearly, but they all have the intention only to lead the spirit to God, and they *all*, when viewed superficially, contain the danger of superstition or of godlessness."[43] But we readily sense that these principles would never provide the justification for the esteem accorded the individual religions, an esteem which is expressed in the admonition not to rob mankind. Underlying this admonition is a profound awareness of the *vigor* of the particular religion, whose beneficial effects, by no means limited to the lower classes, may not be confined

by national boundaries. The more symbols a person compares and 30 correctly interprets, the more certain he will become of the kernel that is common to all. Plutarch does not explicitly say here that this kernel is most clearly disclosed in the mysteries, yet that is the general view, which has its strongest support in the concepts of the "secrets of God", and of the "initiated" or the "perfect", and even Plutarch believes that in the mysteries a divine power is imparted, one which assists toward knowledge of the truth. Thus that reciprocal recognition of the various mysteries, which must at first glance seem so strange to us, is supported just as much by the belief in magic among the lower classes as by the philosophical deepening of religion among the loftier spirits. Both are affected by the conviction that in the sacred act the initiate acquires a divine power of action or of knowing; thus he himself may make a decision or rather settle matters for himself.

It is recognized that this is entirely in harmony with life itself. Godfearing men seize every opportunity to be initiated into a new mystery, and they combine within themselves the most diverse Oriental initiatory rites with the revived Greek rites. What they expected from these rituals is of course widely varied: many did relate the σωτηρία which is promised in all of them, primarily to the outward aspects of life, to deliverance from dangers, success in business, protection against illness--it is characteristic that even as early as the Italian bacchanalia, as also later quite generally in the Hellenistic cult, a vow was made for a sick person promising initiation after recovery from the illness; but even then, as Apuleius shows, a promise of life hereafter is bound up with the assistance in external matters. From very early times, the more serious persons sought in the mystery a new

knowledge and a heightening of the divinity of their own selves. Any and every new union with God was bound to enhance that divinity. In this way the religion of the individual and particularly of the devout person becomes syncretistic and thereby at the same time individualistic as well; it becomes *sui generis*.[44]

31 Magic naturally presents the opposite picture. It becomes a general practice to name the name of the same god in Egyptian, Syriac, Phrygian, Persian, and even Hebrew, and the effort to press one's way back to an original mystical religion is exhibited in the attempt to add also the language of the "angels" or of the divine powers or of other specific primal powers. Further, there is an infrequent but readily understandable combination with these names of the formulas of address which have been employed and taught by a particular man of the recent past or the present, one who is especially gifted and attested by miraculous powers; perhaps an especially effective language had been revealed to him. When the book of Acts has the pagans say of Paul that "he is proclaiming new names of the gods", or when in the same book Simon Magus lets himself be baptized by Peter and wants to purchase his magic, this is entirely in harmony with the picture preserved by the papyri. Furthermore, it is in keeping with the secret literature which begins long before the beginning of the Christian era: theological, astrological, alchemistic, and other writings mix Egyptian, Persian, Syrian, Phoenician, and even Jewish teachings, which are always presented as *revelations* of a god who in some instances speaks to us directly, perhaps in the form of instruction to a younger god, and in other instances has revealed his secrets to one of the kings or wonder-workers of earlier times who

now is introduced as the one speaking or writing. Of course 32 it is not unusual for the actual author to speak to us in his own name, to offer us his teaching and to legitimate it by prefacing it with an account of how he has been united with God or God with him; in fact, even where gods are introduced as speaking, they sometimes seek to validate their knowledge through their mystical union with the primal deity. As a rule, however, whether they refer to man or to deity, the forms of this union closely correspond to the images and rites of the *mysteries*.

We readily recognize another no less important basic feature of these religions: alongside the appeal to an original revelation and tradition there stands, as a second source of faith, a steadily ongoing direct revelation of the deity to his servants. The climactic point of the religious life is formed by the ecstasy which reaches its fullest and most unerring form in the mystery. When man is united with God in the mystery, he must thereby attain a direct, non-mediated knowledge that is independent of all earlier knowledge, and from this time on, God speaks through the servant who is consecrated to him; thus for the believer this new message stands alongside the earlier one with equal validity, or even above it. We moderns cannot quite take this in, but it is a common Oriental belief. The Pharaoh is God's Son and himself God, and hence no one knows the gods as he does. Akhnaton prays, "Thou art in my heart, and no one but thy son Akhnaton knows thee; thou hast initiated him into thy thoughts and into thy power." On the basis of this belief he changes the religion of his people, just as Ptolemy changes the Sarapis-cultus on the basis of his sacral position and the divine revelation that issues from it. But in many religions, at

least, even for the priest, revelation and the non-mediated vision continued, down to the last gasp of paganism, to be the outcome and the climactic point of the true cultus; he beholds God, and God speaks through him; only thus could the Greek designation of *prophet* have been chosen for the highest class of priests. Similarly, every magician asserts that he alone knows the names, the form, and the secrets of his God, and on 33 the strength of that devises new formulas. The same perspective is the source particularly of the theological literature in which each new author quite freely supplements or changes the earlier revelation even on the most important issues, on the basis of his own revelation. In that context the polemic often is extraordinarily sharp; only when according to the story the gods themselves speak and correct each other this is done in the polite form, saying that the primal deity could not reveal *everything* to the rival because the latter had been too young or had not yet been initiated into the supreme mysteries. By rights every person granted union with God must be *autonomous*. He may deny anyone else, especially the uninitiated, the right to pass judgment on what he has seen; on the other hand, he himself can and must sit in judgment on everything. *Revelation liberates*.

The contradiction into which the two principles of belief in an original revelation and tradition and in a continuing revelation and one's own vision *must* necessarily fall will be less obvious within a *single* community's cultus; what is offered to the novice by way of sensuous observations to direct his stimulated imagination is always the same, and a preceding course of instruction, or better, a promise of what he will behold--we now have in the Mithras liturgy a literary account--insures that he will rightly interpret the light-

phenomena, visages, and voices. It is easily understandable that one community cannot regard the initiatory rites performed in another community as fully valid for its own purposes and that only on the basis of *its own* rites does it elevate the person in question to priestly status.

The individual inevitably gains still more freedom once the cultic action in worship and even in this its loftiest expression diminishes or disappears and the entire experience is transposed into the excited religious imagination. It is the final and, for us, most important stage of the mystery-faith of antiquity. An example, which may at the same time be a warning against transposing to the ancient setting the distinctions that are common in our theological discussions of the doctrine of the sacraments, may offer a brief explanation of what I mean.

34

Necessarily included among the forms in which the primitive peoples conceived of religious initiation, union with God (the ὁμιλεῖν θεοῦ) is that of a sexual union whereby the man receives the inner-most essence and power of a god, his seed.[45] This idea, at first held in fully physical terms, leads, in the most widely diverse passages independent of each other, to sacred acts in which the god is represented by human deputies or by a symbol, the phallus. Very early, then, the sacred act was crystallized in one place into the uncomprehended representation of a wedding, while in another place it was given a re-interpretation according to which only the soul was deemed worthy of such mixing with the deity, and in still another a strained over-stimulation of the imagination was supposed to have brought about a kind of inward and yet corporeal experience. The various stages exist side-by-side in the Hellenistic cults almost at the same time. From those frequently

mentioned bacchanalia down to the end of Christian gnosticism, in some cults sexual union with a servant of the god constitutes the initiation which elevates one to heaven and there unites one with the god. A little story incidentally preserved in the life of Apollonius of Tyana teaches us that among the pagan Cilicians the same formulas were common as were found in Christian-gnostic communities that were far removed from the former in space and in time.

We recognize the same basic idea when in late Egyptian texts it is said, as explanation of the skill or excellence of a man, that he bears within himself the seed of all the gods,[46] or when in the practice of magic the adept must furnish a bridal chamber, a bed, and a table with food and wine, in order there to await the πάρεδρος δαίμων and to attract it to the bed. The result is knowledge of the future, miraculous powers, and *immortality*.[47] Closely akin to this is the equally widespread idea that the god unites thus only with a pure virgin, that she must remain faithful to him, and that so long as she does so, she receives his *pneuma* and prophesies through it. According to still another view, the god only requires of the maiden a kind of firstfruit offering; he must open and consecrate her womb. We find this idea in Roman marriage customs in an obscure version, and it is found also in further development and in instructive detail in the old Egyptian idea of the begetting of the Pharaoh in the sexual union of the deity with the queen; by this sacred act she herself becomes a goddess. But alongside her there appear other women also in a kind of sacral status as secondary wives or lovers of the god. When theological writings of Egyptian priests, written in Greek, in a more recent time attempt to provide theoretical justification for the fact that there is no

sexual intercourse between a mortal man and a goddess, though there is between a mortal woman and a god, their intention of course is not to justify old Egyptian conceptions of royalty, but rather a mystery which can be shown to have existed in the

36 Diaspora, but also in Egypt itself down to the demise of paganism: the god invites married women to marriage with himself. It is worthy of note that Philo of Alexandria is acquainted with these ideas and employs them in his allegorical expositions.[48] The primary idea originally was apparently the endowment of the expected child with special powers; but the mother too was sanctified thereby.[49] I shall refrain from tracing out here how strongly the cultic rules of the Gnostics and the legends of the Oriental peoples were influenced by this idea. I may mention at least in passing the re-shaping which was brought about with the increasing tendency toward asceticism. It refers to the idea that the deity only approaches a pure virgin and that she must remain faithful to him. The two views appear together in the second part of the Acts of Thomas. There the apostle has come to the wedding of a king's daughter and is suddenly seized with desire for her as a bride for himself or rather for his Lord. Since he is accredited by a miracle, *the king willingly agrees, leads him into the bridal chamber, and asks him to pray over the newly wedded pair.* The apostle does so, but as soon as he has left and the door to the chamber is closed, Christ is suddenly there with them, and by means of his teaching, which sows "life" in her, he consummates for her a divine marriage with the "true man". It is a union (ἕνωσις) with himself, which delivers her from perish-

37 ability (matter) and elevates them to the "Greatness" (God). The various individual expressions here are altogether in harmony with the ancient idea of an actual sexual union with

the deity. The necessary inference is that they must avoid human sexual intercourse. It is also in keeping with this widely held idea when Jerome expresses serious doubt whether God can at all forgive the misstep of a nun, adultery against himself. The originally physical idea then becomes purely figurative: every sin is an imperiling of the divine seed within us, an act of unfaithfulness against the heavenly bridegroom of the soul or the community. This literature exhibits every level, from the crudest physical interpretation to the mystical feeling of the marriage of the soul or the figure of speech that has become totally devoid of meaning; from the actual δρώμενον with external events or symbols of such to the fleeting awakening of an idea; and from the intervention of a consecrating prophet or wonder-worker to the effect of the written word. But even where the entire mystery appears to have paled into a mere figure, as in the Christian church at large, the figure still exerts an uncanny force, exercising a manifold influence upon life. The exhortations of Jerome (Ep. 22) about how the nun is to exchange words of love with the bridegroom upon her bed and what she should expect to receive from him are distinguished from the prescriptions of pagan magical texts only by the more thoroughgoing and more specifically physical description and the use of the Song of Solomon.

That omission of the sacred action and the transposition of the entire process into the inner experience of the initiate had to arise for various reasons and with varying degrees of rapidity, in the various conceptions of the mysteries. In some cases it was the offensiveness of individual actions adopted from a primitive nature-cult that provided the occasion; in others perhaps it was purely external reasons such

38 as the lack of a temple and such a complicated apparatus as is required for the cult, for example, by the mystery of the heavenly pilgrimage described by Apuleius. Even where the reasons for the re-shaping lie only in the spiritualizing of the religion, various factors could be at work. The important thing about the sacrifice was not the gift but lifting the heart up to God; this was recognized in the Orient by pious minds in various places and was repeatedly emphasized by Greek philosophy independent of the Orient. It is utterly impossible to trace back exclusively to a *single source* the general Hellenistic view that true worship is unceasing praise of God, and that the proper sacrifice is a prayer of thanksgiving. If even before Paul's time the λογικὴ λατρεία or λογικὴ θυσία had become a formal expression of Hellenistic theology[50] and was only utilized by him, ancient prayer-formulas and the equation of the word and the reality in magical practice can be cited as explanation of its emergence in Egyptian-Hellenistic worship. However, it is not general considerations alone that argue for the view that that spiritualizing of religion and internalizing of the cultus found its chief support and encouragement in Greek thought. The history of a formula like λογικὴ θυσία can make the intervention of Greek philosophy or rather its popular re-shaping clear. In the spiritualizing of the mysteries also it unmistakably played a crucial role.

In order to pursue this inevitable and general development of the mystery-conceptions, we must first turn our gaze once again to Apuleius, the only source that affords us a description, at least by allusion, of a cultic mystery.[51]

He has already enlisted in the "military service of the 39 goddess" and resides in the temple area as a kind of κάτοχος (cf. Appendix III), as it were, blessed with constant dream-

visions and participating in the daily cultus of the priests. He burns with longing and yet he is unable to attain the initiation; the goddess must *call* both the novice and the initiating priest in a dream; for they both must ascend into her ἄδυτον, and anyone who does this *without being called* must die. Pausanias, who is acquainted with this same view from the Egyptian as well as from the Phocian Isis-cult, explains quite correctly: anyone who beholds the deity dies.[52] As the priest informs Apuleius, the initiation is a voluntarily chosen death and a new life bestowed by grace (χαριζομένη σωτηρία). The goddess rules the gates of the realm of the dead and of *salus*. The expression repeatedly recurs, and the meaning fluctuates between "preservation of the earthly life" and "bestowal of a new, higher life". Would we not do well, in our theological explanations of the concept of the σωτήρ, once again to give a little more emphasis to the latter meaning even in the cultic designations *salutaris dea*, Ἶσις σώτειρα, and Σάραπις σωτήρ?[53] This meaning for Apuleius is confirmed by the rationale offered for the principle just cited: "for the old life has run its course; but the goddess calls the one who is worthy and discreet back from the threshold of the underworld and *transplants him into a new life of* σωτηρία." Thus he is, "as it were, born again". This rebirth is a transformation of essence, the assumption of a new form; *renasci* alternates with *reformari*,[54] and even the transformation from the form of an ass into human form means for the community a part of that divinely wrought rebirth. The word παλιγγενεσία is in fact

40 also used in Hellenistic literature for the "migration of souls", the assumption of a new form. Underlying it is the view that in that migration through the twelve hours of the night which is reenacted in the mystery the deceased person,

like the deity, assumes twelve different forms, the forms of animals, before he attains or regains the divine form. A *transfiguration*, a μεταμορφοῦσθαι or μεταβάλλεσθαι, is for this conception indissolubly bound up with the rebirth, the παλιγγενεσία; hence the account can form the conclusion of a book of "Metamorphoses"; this also explains the fact that in the Mithras mystery the unusual word μεταγεννηθῆναι, "to be 'trans-born'", also appears in place of ἀναγεννηθῆναι. Here too it is explicitly stated in this connection that through God's miraculous power the initiate is elevated into a better nature.

In a nocturnal vision both Apuleius and an initiate chosen by the goddess receive the *call* (καλεῖται). The obligation of the latter in this connection consists of sacral actions and teachings; by means of these teachings he becomes the *father* of the novice. We find the term πατήρ as a fixed title in the Isis-cult at Delos, in the Phrygian mystery-communities, in the Mithras-cult, among those who worship the θεὸς ὕψιστος, and elsewhere. Yet in the Phrygian cult it is also here and there emphasized that one and the same man has performed the functions of the ἱερεύς and of the πατήρ in the initiation, as happened in the case of Apuleius. We must keep in mind the fact that in the major religions of the Orient the priesthood was hereditary and at least in the time of Hellenism it was a matter evoking special amazement that here the son receives the teaching from the father.[55] It is from this that there arose, in the Diaspora, in the mission communities, 41 the insistence that the initiate must receive the teaching from his "spiritual father". All the instruction in magic and the secret literature of Hellenism is represented as the teaching of the father to the son; this is based upon the

claim of the mystery communities and later also of the Christians that instruction, even where it is received in written form, *makes one a son.* It further follows that where there is an established teacher and father for all the novices, the latter become brothers to each other. Since they all have received the initiation, naturally they all are also ὅσιοι or ἅγιοι. When Paul considers his churches as his children because he has taught them, and yet forbids them to call themselves by his name, as Hellenistic communities identify themselves by their ἱερεύς and πατήρ, he appeals to the fact that he has not baptized them, and thus has not appeared as their ἱερεύς; ἱερεύς evidently is at first the greater dignity, and πατήρ the lesser one. When the cultic practice fades or disappears entirely, of course this will have to change.

In the community which Apuleius joins the two positions are not separately established, but in every case are combined in a single person. Initial instruction from sacred books, written in hieroglyphs, about what is required for initiation, is followed by a bath of purification, and, as in magical practice distinguished from that bath, a baptism, a sprinkling with drops of a holy and sanctifying liquid. Since in the representations of the Egyptian royal baptism the individual drops are identified as symbols of life and power (?), it should not surprise us to see, in other Hellenistic documents, σωτηρία, i.e., salvation in this life as well as in the life beyond, already connected with the baptism with holy water. Various symbolic actions with similar meaning are early brought together in the mysteries; others are detached from the context of an artistically constructed action and become independent. After baptism a new secret instruction brings to Apuleius the inexpressibly blessed promise of what

he is about to see; then, after ten days of a rigorous program of ascetic discipline, there follows a solemn departure from the community, whose individual members present farewell gifts to him.[56] On the following morning the community is once again summoned to the concluding act of the mystery; in the corresponding Phrygian practice, which we shall consider presently, it plays a similar role. This suggests that this purely personal initiatory celebration is also the counterpart to an earlier community celebration in which the experiences of the deity were acted out by his priest. After the community is dismissed Apuleius is led by the high priest into the *adyton*, to the actual initiation, of which he tells only that he crossed over the threshold of the realm of the dead and, having been borne (or having traveled) through all the elements, returned to the light. Out of the darkness of midnight the illuminating sun shed its radiance upon him, he beheld the gods of the realm of the dead and of heaven, and paid homage to the latter in their immediate presence. We hear further that his body has been sanctified by twelve garments; by means of them the initiation is accomplished (he becomes *sacratus*: ἱερός; in the inscriptions the word is well known as designation for a status); this symbolizes his having assumed twelve different forms. When the morning appears, he then is clothed with the "heavenly garment" and thus, carrying a blazing torch in his right hand, wearing a garland of flowers upon his head, emerging from the palm branches that resembled rays, he was placed before the goddess upon a pulpit as an image of the sun-god and worshiped as god by the assembled community. The mention only of the sun-god, not of Osiris or Horus, as we should expect from the Egyptian cult,

43 shows, as does the description of the garb of the deity, that

the Corinthian community has taken over various particular details from the Semitic sun-cult and the Mithras-cult. It is true that according to Egyptian belief also the resurrected person bears on his head the ornamentation of the sun-god Ra and wears the light-colored garment of Osiris; but his garland is different--the bleached palm-leaves are Syrian--and that interweaving of the "celestial garment" with marvelous animal figures corresponds to the garb of the "lion" in the Mithras-ceremony.[57] When, moreover, the high priest of Isis at Corinth bears the name Mithras, as the priest of Attis himself is called Attis, we probably may conclude that Sarapis, the regular temple-companion of Isis (here according to the ancient confession "one is Sarapis, Helios, and Mithras"), was identified with the Persian god. As we mentioned earlier, in purely Egyptian form Apuleius would have been venerated as Osiris or Horus, the consort of Isis and the first of the resurrected ones.

A festive banquet then celebrates this divine birth festival,[58] and for a few days Apuleius may enjoy the unutterable bliss of being the image (εἰκών) of the god. Then he leaves the "celestial garment" in the temple, where it is kept for him; for the Egyptian the temple always symbolizes heaven. Although bonds of unending devotion would hold him, Apuleius goes back into the world, with the promise that he would keep the appearance and nature of the goddess in the innermost shrine of his heart and ever in view of his inward eye. We later learn that when the deity demands it, the mystery must be renewed, and can be renewed only by the putting-on of that celestial robe. The garment, or, as I might put it, the celestial body achieves the φωτίζεσθαι, which in one place signifies *bodily transfiguration*, and in another illumination through

44

knowledge--the νοῦς is in fact φῶς--and in still others appears simply as a term for being initiated, though of course with a clear reference to the brilliant light in a nocturnal ceremony.

Through Plutarch we hear from another community that after death the light-colored Osiris-garment is once again placed on the body of the elect person, who has earned it in the mystery; again, for others a simpler, black and white robe, which identifies them as the Logos, the Word of God. The robe is meant to indicate that the deceased person is united with God and that when he goes into the beyond he wears only the deity, nothing else.

The same perspective naturally prevails in Egyptian magical practice. There a *mystes*, to whom his deity has appeared, brings a thank-offering and prays: "I have come together with thy holy form, through thy name I have attained power, thy beneficent emanations (or radiance) I have received into myself, God, my Lord, and now may return home 'in possession of a godlike nature' (ἰσόθεος φύσις)." Then another prays in the often uttered words: "Come into me, Hermes, as children come into their mother's lap", and describes the result thus: "Thou art I and I am thou, what is thine is mine and what is mine is thine; for I am thy image (εἴδωλον)." And in another passage we read: "Enter into the soul of this child, that it may be formed (τυποῦσθαι) according to thy immortal form in the mighty, imperishable light."[59]--But back to the mysteries.

45 Apuleius makes only a brief reference to the dying of his old body, which must happen before he can assume the twelve transitional forms and finally the form of God: he was led even through the portals of the underworld. The idea is clarified by the Phrygian mystery of rebirth, the ἀναγέννησις,

which of course we know only in a revised form, which substitutes the sacrificial blood for the water. The initiate must descend into a *grave*, and a bull or a ram is slaughtered above him; its blood is conducted into the grave through a number of small tubes, and is sprinkled over him. Both the practice and the words closely correspond to the Egyptian baptism by sprinkling. Underlying all this is the ancient idea that the blood, in which in fact the soul resides, revivifies the dead person; thus in the ancient grave-cultus there are shafts that convey it down upon the dead body. The Phrygian *mystes* fills all his sense-organs with the blood, mouth, eyes, nose, and ears; a similar baptismal practice for Egypt is certain, for Hellenistic theology later thinks that the descending divine spirit *seals* the sense-organs against everything that is earthly.[60] Originally they naturally would thereby be awakened to new life.[61] Now in this act the Phrygian initiate also wears a wondrous festal robe and upon his head a garland. When his robe and garland are colored with the blood, he climbs out of the grave and is *venerated* by the community as *God*. Again the garment (his baptismal robe) is kept for him; after twenty years the initiation must be renewed; then he puts the robe on again, and through it once again becomes God. The close parallelism, especially in the concluding part of the ceremony, fully confirms the interpretation which Dieterich, more correctly than Hepding and Gruppe, has recognized. It is a burial of the man and the resurrection of a deity, not a ritual of expiation but actual rebirth, originally corresponding to a communal festival in which the high priest appears for the deity and is also celebrated as a vicarious sacrifice for others. Conceptions that were at least similar also appeared in the Mithras-cult; this is shown in the initiation

of the "lion" by the celestial garment, whose embroidered patterns appear to have been interpreted by some as the figures of the zodiac and by others to refer to metempsychosis or the assumption of particular animal forms.[62] Now we comprehend how in the only slightly egyptianized so-called Mithras-liturgy, which can be best understood from Manichaean and Mandaean texts, the initiate, who through a celestial pilgrimage wishes to be reborn and to become the son of God, addresses his own celestial body, which God himself has formed for him in the world of light as the terrestrial world.[63] He must put it on and leave behind the earthly body, to assume the latter again after the sacred activity is finished. It is a pneumatic body; only as πνεῦμα can man behold God. Here our thoughts might immediately turn to Paul, who also speaks of a heavenly or pneumatic body which God has laid up in heaven for him and which he desires to put on, either after he has put off the earthly body or as a garment put on over the earthly body. But it will be better first to pursue the matter of that internalizing and individualizing of the mysteries in the Hellenistic and late Oriental literature, and indeed in the doctrinal writings as well as in the community liturgies. Only these may be compared to some extent with the Pauline writings as to their character.

We find the types of doctrinal writings most fully repre-
47 sented in that Hellenistic theological literature that emerged in the first three Christian centuries in Egypt for readers with a Greek education. These writings are represented as revelations of Egyptian deities, Hermes (Thoth), Agathos Daimon, Asklepios (Imhotep), Tat (Thoth), or Isis, and others. However, they also, in keeping with the syncretistic piety of the time, have incorporated alien elements; thus our corpus

has three writings that exhibit significant Iranian influence: Book I, the so-called Poimandres (cf. above, p. 12), Book XI, and Book XIII.[64] A larger collection, which considerably predates our corpus, had distinguished in the writings of Hermes to his son Tat some general discourses (γενικοὶ λόγοι) from more specialized ones (διεξοδικοὶ λόγοι) which evidently were intended for the most narrowly restricted group; the latter corresponds to a work preserved in a corpus of writings addressed to Asklepios, the λόγος τέλειος, which, like the τελεία τελετή, the supreme mystery, was supposed to lead to perfection. We readily recognize the distinguishing of instructional material that is customary in the mystery communities. Included among the more specialized sections is a discourse of Hermes to Tat (Book XIII) which I single out here. It refers to three writings which evidently were included in the general discourses: the Poimandres (Book I); in Book XI, a teaching of the Νοῦς, or Poimandres, to Hermes; and finally a general discourse (now lost) delivered on a mountain and dealing with the nature of the deity, in which Hermes had said that no one could attain salvation, σωτηρία, without rebirth (παλιγγενεσία).[65]

Here the description takes up. At the very first Tat had prayed that he might experience the teaching of rebirth. At that time Hermes answered that he must first detach himself
8 from this world of deceit. Now he has done this, but he still does not know from what womb and from what seed "the man" is born. Hermes does not answer; he only discloses that the seed is the truly good, that what does the begetting is the will of God, that the divine son who is begotten is the All in All, consisting of all the powers of God. Things of this kind are not to be taught; when God wills it, the recollection is

aroused in the heart (the divine soul in man awakens). And yet there is an overseer of the rebirth, γενεσιουργὸς τῆς παλιγγενεσίας,[66] who is the Son of God, the one "Man" (and thus here, as in the Naassene Preaching, the very one that is already slumbering in man; thus also for the Mandaeans), according to the will of God. About his own rebirth Hermes can only relate that he suddenly beheld within himself a non-material vision, and through God's mercy was transported from his own body into an imperishable body.[67] He is no longer what he was, but is born in the Spirit (νοῦς); the earlier form of manifestation, composed of various parts, has disintegrated; the new form has neither color nor mass, nor can it be touched. It is true that the son still sees him with his earthly eyes, but what he sees is only an illusion; what Hermes is cannot be seen by anyone who uses the body and human powers of seeing. While these words are being uttered the transformation begins in the son; suddenly he no longer sees his own body; he still sees that of the father, but he is told that this is only an illusion; he must learn to behold what is

49

invisible, in order to attain birth in God. He suffers doubt, but the father admonishes him: draw him into yourself, and he will come; will it, and it will happen; cleanse yourself of the irrational (ἄλογος) evil spirits that rule over the material realm.

An inquiry of the son as to whether he then has such spirits within him leads now to a doctrinal passage: the father enumerates twelve evil inclinations (evil spirits) that torment the "inner man" (ἐνδιάθετος ἄνθρωπος--formed in imitation of ἐνδιάθετος λόγος) which resides in the body as in a prison; these tendencies disappear only gradually, one by one, expelled by the ten powers of God, which gradually and

member by member fit together the Logos.[68] The father sees these powers descend, one by one, and the corresponding vices disappear; he summons the former and commands the latter to flee. When the last three divine attributes, those that are particularly and peculiarly his, goodness, life, and light, have come *together*, any new approach by the evil spirits is impossible, and the birth in the spirit and as God is consummated (συνετέθη ἡ νοερὰ γένεσις καὶ ἐθεώθημεν[69] τῇ γενέσει). Now Tat is capable of non-material vision, and he cries: "I am in heaven, I am in the earth, in the water am I, am in the air"--we recall that according to Apuleius the Isis-initiate also felt himself to be in all the elements--"I am in the animals, in the plants, in the womb, before the womb, after the womb, everywhere." It is the feeling of being the Aion, the world-god,[70] who indeed is "the man" or "the soul". A brief doctrinal passage that now follows shows us that the author actually has this in mind. Tat must ask how it is that the twelve evil spirits (vices) can be expelled by only ten divine powers, and he learns that the twelve form a unity--that unity evidently signifies the body, which in fact according to Chaldean (and thus late Persian) doctrine is connected with the signs of the zodiac--but the number ten is soul-begetting (ψυχογόνος); the One (the πνεῦμα) is contained within it, and in the One the Ten.[71] Further, Tat must ascertain that this spiritual body cannot again be dissolved; thus he requests, referring to the earlier mentioned (p. 12) revelational writing that was borrowed from the Persian, that he might hear the song which the soul (here the νοῦς) of the deceased hears when, having pressed beyond the seven heavens, in the eighth, the ὀγδοάς, he hears the powers of God singing. It is the true "hymn of rebirth". The father grants his request. As the reborn or resurrected one, he is now the world-

god; the "powers" that are praising God are in him; in him God's Logos praises God and presents to him in the Word (λόγος) the universe as a spiritual offering (λογικὴ θυσία): "from thee thy will, to thee the whole universe!" As "the man of God" he sings God's praise through the five (Persian) elements; for his song stems from the aion of God, the content of these divine elements, and in the will of God he has found his rest.

It strikes us as rather stiff when now a second, very brief, and formal song is presented by the son in "his own words" and the father then enjoins him not to tell anyone else this teaching about the rebirth and summarizes the meaning of the whole in the words: "in the mind (νοερῶς) you have come to know yourself and our father", i.e., you have fully attained gnosis, the beginning of which is the knowledge of your own self and whose end is the knowledge of God. The whole matter becomes clear as soon as we look at the original 51 Persian writing to which the author refers. The soul that ascends after death must, after it is united with the powers of God in the eighth heaven, the Garoδman of the Persians, and has praised him with them, ascend still further, under their guidance, to the "eternal light", there to worship God himself and then to be absorbed into him. It is a celestial journey, corresponding to the celestial journey of the soul after death. The perspective here is that not only does the soul rid itself of an evil impulse in each of the seven lower spheres, but a positive power of God, a virtue, joins itself to the soul and suppresses that power of evil. These seven (after the entrance into the Ogdoad, ten) new powers now form the soul's Self and fit together to form the god in the soul. This is what is new and distinctive in this writing.[72] The similarity with the basic ideas of the Isis-mysteries on the

one hand and with the Mithras liturgy on the other hand is evident, as is also an overwhelming similarity with the funeral dirges of the Mandaeans and with a Manichaean liturgy which is preserved for us at least in part; and finally with certain conceptions of the Mithras mysteries. The fact that they too have seven stages will be significant for us.

But before I go into a comparison of content, just a word about the form of the Hermetic writing. It does not

52 present a mystery in the strict sense of the term, but rather the *description* of one, set forth in a succession of alternating discourses and mixed with a doctrinal writing. The author, who plays the role of the mystagogue and preserves the outward form of the mystery, can publish it in a book because the forms of the cult of the dead are well known anyway and because he hopes that, if God wills it and if the reader of the book has turned away from the world, his presentation will exert upon the reader the same effect as an actual mystery. The reader is to experience such a mystery in his imagination. The miraculous power which is connected with the action of the mystery can also be attached to the word, even the written word. We sense immediately that the detachment of the mystery from the outward activity significantly heightens the possibility of the individualizing and differentiating of religions. But at the same time this example shows the limitation to which that individualizing is always subject. One does not invent religions at the study-desk; they develop in the contact of different nationalities, because one complements the other and in one respect or another better serves to satisfy the religious needs of the individual. In this process the basic religious ideas and crucial images, whose number is remarkably small, are maintained with amazing vitality; only in

the selection of them and in details of their fleshing-out can individuality be expressed. We can indeed with some justification assert that at this stage of development the teacher and founder of a community has become almost as free as the magician, but in saying this we must not forget that it is precisely magic that most strikingly exhibits the peculiar capacity of original ideas to survive.

The explanation of the content of the afore-mentioned "literary mystery" will make this observation clearer. We can achieve the explanation only through comparisons. In the Naassene Preaching described above (p. 14) and in the Mandaean funeral songs, which now in fact are generally accessible, we find reappearing the perspective of that strange divine being that is called the son of God, the Logos, the "one" man (or primal man), and the All in All, and yet at the same time

53

arises within the individual man and appears in place of the individual man. In the same places we also find the view that this being is created, in a certain sense, by a divine being, the teacher of the religion, which is altogether like the one created. Most closely connected with this latter view, however, are the Manichaean ideas about the celestial journey of the soul. The escort that comes to meet the soul; the gifts that the escort brings; the guiding sage, who corresponds to the Manda d'Haije (the knowledge of God) and yet also appears as a virgin, who is like this soul and thus its prototype, as in the Persian Yasht 22--in essence everything is the same. Here we also have, as a cosmological and mythological counterpart, the liberation of Adam or of Ohrmazd or the world-god (the god of the five heavenly elements, or of the world-soul) from matter, and in fact this is found in the treatment by Theodore bar Konai as well as in the fragments

of Manichaean writings found in Turfan. Yet my attention here is drawn, not to this mythological counterpart, but to a major liturgy that presumably consisted of twelve parts. In a small part it has been preserved for us verbatim, and in a larger part in a selection, which like the Mandaean liturgies gives only the beginnings of the various hymns which are sung in responsive fashion and which constitute the various individual parts. Here also, as in that Hermetic writing from which I began, we have the description of an ongoing action which recurs in quite similar fashion in the Mandaean funeral hymns[73] and therefore can be reconstructed with some degree of probability.[74] In heaven the messenger is chosen, who is to awaken and to bring back that portion of the deity that is embedded 54 in matter, lying there in drunken sleep. He declares himself ready, chooses a heavenly escort, and sets sail in a lightship--it is well-known that both the sun and the moon are regarded as such--to descend to the earth. He awakens the soul with a salutation and summons it to a recollection of its ancestry and its original homeland. The soul then looks about itself, laments the horrors of death that surround it, and implores the messenger to take it away at once. The messenger, however, instructs the soul that this request is impossible; the soul must wait until he, when he comes once again, shall call it. In the meantime it must remain awake, constantly think of the last days, and pray to him; it has the assurance of redemption so long as it does not forget him. The soul acts accordingly, increasingly detaches itself from its body, the hateful prison, indeed bodily death, in which it is imprisoned, and constantly pleads for its redeemer to come soon. Then a loud cry sounds from heaven, saying that the world now is collapsing in unutterable disasters, and anyone who desires to be saved must cry to God. Then the one who uttered the cry

himself appears; it is Mani, who is introduced as God's emissary, in a brief hymn that perhaps was composed by Mani himself. From several other fragments we see that the deification of the founder,[75] which in Zoroastrianism had earlier been hinted at, also has transferred to him all the activity of the redeemer. It is hardly possible to say whether he also plays the role of the divine liberator and redeemer in the following part of the liturgy; in any case the portrayal is wholly connected with the mythological figure. The soul rejoices: "the friend of the light-beings has come to me". He greets the soul and addresses it as the pearl for which he has been sent, the soul (the πνεῦμα?) of man of the same kind; the one speaking is its very self, its being, its origin. In another song (though it is still altogether uncertain whether it belongs to this literature[76]), he says that he is its soul (*monuhmed*), and it is his body, the garment into which the "powers" have entered. The redeemer then announces in the liturgy to the soul that, in order to save it, the gods have destroyed destruction and have slain death; hence it is his intention now to heal it of all ills, liberate it from all evils, and lead it to eternal bliss with the divine father and the divine mother. He brings to it the garment of light and the laurel of victory (the "glory", or nimbus). Another part shows the soul ascending, under constant exhortations and calls from the emissary (usually beginning with "Ascend higher, O soul"), while all around it the world is collapsing and the stars are falling from heaven. The conclusion, none of which we have up till now, must have portrayed the union of the soul with God.

It is hardly possible to say whether this twelve-part whole, which is held together internally by a unitary conception, and externally by the unitary form of an ecclesiastical discourse, was originally bound up with a cultic activity.[77]

Mani, in fact, is acquainted with a purification of the soul in a pilgrimage through twelve aions, in each of which it acquires a virtue--the last aion is perfect light.[78] The birth or construction of the "new man", who is the full light, is accomplished for him in the "second day" and its twelve hours, in which the victorious redeemer (Jesus) gives to the light-soul twelve wonder-working garments and thereby makes it perfect.[79] In this connection it is explicitly emphasized that he causes it to ascend, to advance, and to be forever released from the earth--all these are ideas that recur in the fragments of the liturgy, but they are also referred to in the Hermetic text. We recall immediately that Apuleius is initiated (*sacratus*) and is made God by means of twelve actual robes.[80] On the other hand the Mandaean parallels suggest to us the cult of the dead. In both cases we are dealing with deification, as the Hermetic writing itself could show. More important, it seems to me, than the definition of the cultic significance is the fact that we gain such an extensive acquaintance with the ideas and the forms of presentation of pagan religious literature.

56

We are led still further by the origins of a hymn that treats of Zarathustra which, as I have already emphasized in the first publication, certainly does not belong to the earlier Iranian tradition; indeed, in its present form it must go back to a Manichaean author, perhaps to Mani himself, but yet it must give what at that time served as Zoroastrian teaching. Indeed, Mani wanted to blend with his own religion three others, the Zoroastrian, Buddhist, and Christian religions; he recognized their three founders as emissaries of God, whose teachings he only wished to purge of the distortions that had entered them early. We have long known that he revised Christian writings, and we are acquainted with fragments from his

gospel; the fact that he appropriated not only Zoroastrian doctrine but also a collection of "Zoroastrian prayers" has likewise been accessible to us for a considerable time.[81] A
57 collection of redemption-hymns cites, as a testimony of the earlier fathers, from among these prayers a hymn; Prof. Andreas
58 has translated for me the beginning of this hymn, which is preserved in a Turfan-fragment, and has edited to show the later expansions (here italicized):

Strophe 1 — If you wish, I shall instruct you
through [*the strong testimony of the*] earlier fathers.
The redeemer, the true Zorohusht,
as he consulted with himself:

Strophe 2 — Shake off[82] the drunkenness in which you slumber,
Awaken and look to me.
Salvation upon you from the world of joy,
from which I am sent for your sake. --

Strophe 3 — And that one answered [*(he,) Srosh*] the one who is free of passion:
I am I, the son of the gentle.[83]
I am mixed, and I behold lamentations,
lead me out of the clutches of death.

Zorohusht spoke to him, with a blessing, the age-old saying: (O) my body,

Strophe 4 — Power of the living and (*of the greatest world*) salvation
upon thee from thy homeland!

Follow after me, O son of meekness,
set the garland of light upon thy head.

[*Offspring of the mighty ones, thou who art given high esteem, so that thou bestowest recognition on all places.*][84]

This hymn appears not to have been composed for Manichaeans, but probably translated into their religious language.

59

Zarathustra's *daena* or Fravashi, his heavenly (or, as it is called in the terminology of this hymn, his living) Self, descends in order to awaken its counterpart[85] that is fettered in the body. It can hardly be determined whether it is only this instruction, which indeed later brings in its train the celestial journey, or the actual celestial journey after death --we may think of the twenty-second Yasht (above, p. 12)--that is meant. The glossator evidently interprets it to refer to the awakening and *calling of the prophet*;[86] the command to put on the garland of light, the divine triumphant power which the soul of the deceased receives, is not necessarily in contradiction with that interpretation. The Christian Gnostic also believes that he has already received immortality along with his awakening; for him the death of the body is without significance. I refer once again to the Hermetic writing. That garland of light can also signify, in connection with the prophet, the elevation into the new divine nature. The liturgical character of the hymn can readily be made still more evident by a comparison with the mythological accounts of the liberation of Ohrmazd or Adam. I do not know, and I am not asking, whether there was ever an actual cultic activity that corresponded to this liturgy. It is to be evoked in the hearer's imagination, and in the ancient sense which I am using here, it is a mystery.[87]

60 The Gnostic Justin offers an antitype with all the forms of mystery-literature:[88] The world-deity Elohim has ascended to heaven and to the highest God, "the Good", leaving his pneuma, his self, behind in the material realm; there, in matter, this pneuma is "bound"[89] in men and suffers torments at the hands of Edem, the female ruler of matter who has been abandoned by Elohim. In order to regain possession of it, he wants to destroy the world, but "the Good" prevents him. So he sends Baruch, the third emissary (thus the Mithras of the Manichaeans, the Enosh or Man of the Mandaeans); this emissary is to attempt, through Moses and the prophets, to persuade the pneuma that resides in men to flee from matter; but the souls resist those mediators, and it is only in Jesus that Baruch finds the proper one to proclaim his message. It is evident that this invention is not Christian. What has happened is that Baruch actually has been identified, in a Jewish-gnostic circle, with Zarathustra and has been viewed as "the emissary" and son of God.[90] Then a Jewish-Christian gnostic view appropriated these ideas, and only upon its being combined with Christianity was Jesus inserted into the schema. We can most clearly discern this when we compare another type of this literature. In the Acts of Thomas the apostle, who has been *cast into prison*, in order to encourage himself and his fellow-prisoners and to achieve their liberation sings a hymn that is embellished in the colorful splendor of Oriental fables; Cumont has already identified the Persian origin of this song. A king's son in the Orient relates that
61 while he was still a small child in the house of his parents, they had sent him to Egypt to seize from the dreadful serpent that lies there in the sea the pearl (it is, in the established language of these circles, "the soul"), and had promised him as his reward that he and his brother, now the second in

succession after them, would become heirs of the kingdom. He puts off his royal robes, undertakes the journey with two messengers through the hostile realm, and comes to Egypt. But while he tarries in the vicinity of the serpent, the unclean inhabitants of the land note that he is an alien, feed him some of their poisonous food, and thereby plunge him into sleep and forgetfulness. His parents hear of this and send him a letter--in the Mandaean dirges the emissary is sometimes represented by such a letter also--: the letter is signed by all the great ones of the kingdom and first of all brings greetings "From thy father, the king of kings, and from thy mother, who rules the East, to thee our son in Egypt, hail! Awake and arise from thy sleep. Remember that thou art a king's son; see whom thou hast served in thy slavery." His commission and the promises connected with it are then repeated. The letter, which is explicitly equated with an emissary, flies as an eagle and, having arrived, becomes a discourse that awakens the sleeping one. By invoking the name of his father, he puts the dreadful serpent to sleep, seizes the pearl, and prepares himself for his return home; he lays aside the filthy garments of the Egyptians, and the letter guides him and encourages him on the long journey. At the border of his homeland two treasurers bring him his royal garment, which in the meantime has been ornamented with his exploits; marvelous figures are woven into it and the motions of gnosis sparkle and flash in it. It appears to him altogether as a mirror-image; it hastens toward him and he hastens to receive it. Clothed with this garment, he ascends to the "gates of greeting and adoration" and worships the father, who has fulfilled 62 his promises (obviously the promises of aid) just as the son has fulfilled the father's commandments. The intention was to conclude the hymn here. But just as in the Hermetic writing

an appendix follows. Only one of his father's nobles governs here; this one now approaches with the royal son and leads him to the father's arms. A way leads from the Garoδman, the Persians' heaven of the gods, still higher into the eternal light, into God.

I shall not go into the numerous connections with Mandaean and Manichaean hymns here. The long-range impact of this text or of its purely religious prototype reaches much farther. In the Demotic magical papyrus of London and Leiden[91] we find a healing incantation with a mythological introduction: "I am a king's son, the chief noble of Anubis. My mother, Sechmet-Isis, followed me into the land of Syria, to the hill of the land of the millions (i.e., of the realm of the dead), into the territory of the consumer of men, and she said: 'Hasten, hasten, run, run, my son, son of the king, chief noble of Anubis,' and she said: 'Arise, come back to Egypt; for your father Osiris is king (Pharaoh) of Egypt, he is the great one of the whole land; all the gods of Egypt are gathered together to receive the diadem from his hand.'". Isis, who is represented as an eagle, brings the son a vivifying charm, but as he arises, he suffers still another wound, and Isis tells him to heal it by licking it (an addition of the magician). Such a religious text appears already to have been known to Greek historians in the imperial era.[92]

Hence it is not surprising that influences are also discernible even in the more strictly Jewish literature in the Baruch apocalypses. When in the Syriac Apocalypse of Baruch (77.20) Baruch summons home the lost part of the tribe of the souls (of Israel), he commissions an eagle to carry the letter; in the Ethiopic text the bird itself is the divine envoy and as such is itself able to awaken dead persons, and in the prayer of the martyr Kyrikos (Quiricus)[93] we recognize the whole

63

course of the hymn of the Acts of Thomas and the basic ideas of the Baruch literature as well. The prayer begins with the preparation of the travel garments by the mother, describes the bringing back of the tribe of the souls from the realm of the dead and ends with the worship in the royal palace. That the letter is given to the emissary at the very outset and performs all the deeds for him, including at last the slaying of the dragon of death, is easily understandable as an expansion. We should not be surprised that in Jewish circles there developed the polemical view that Baruch apostasized from Judaism and wrote the Avesta book for the Persians.[94] Little enough is preserved for us of this evidently one time widely disseminated literature; the same is true of the Jewish source-writing of the Ascension of Isaiah, which from the very first was closely connected with the martyrdom. Here mystery and revelation, and indeed even pure doctrinal writing, are inextricably woven together.[95] We possess an exhortation of Hermes to the soul, preserved in an Arabic translation;[96] in its major part it may stem from the first or the beginning of the second century A.D., and appears later to have been expanded by a Manichaean (?) author. The format and basic ideas are entirely in harmony with the recently discovered Manichaean liturgy, only all mythological and cosmological references are so completely eliminated that we believed we had nothing but a quite banal sermon in which a prominent philologist thought then that he could detect the influences of Greek philosophy.
64 And then again in other passages a brief and powerful exhortation corresponds to the situation portrayed in that liturgy and its views, like the anonymous quotation in Eph. 5:14: "Awake, thou that sleepest; arise from the dead, and then Christ will illumine thee" (make thee light); the ancient

pagan prototype of this quotation makes us suspect a very early alchemistic writing.[97]

The internal reason for the connection between teaching and vision when then is repeated in all the mysteries lies in a basic Oriental perspective, one which we can trace back to a very early age in India and Persia: revelation is achieved only in the vision--especially of the world-deity--but this vision is not self-explanatory; the deity himself or a teacher must interpret it.[98] But the vision also can be evoked in the soul even without a cultic representation.

This conviction and this experience form the basis of the literary mysteries, of which the Hermetic writing on rebirth affords us an example. Anyone who published these mysteries as books expected that the reader, if God chose to favor him, would, upon reading them, feel the same effect as Thoth felt upon hearing; the miraculous power of God's message functions even in the written word: the vision, the experience, occurs. But he also expected that the unbeliever into whose hand the book might fall would not understand it; indeed, for him it must remain dead, just because the vision does not occur. The admonitions or even adjurations not to betray these secrets, or the assertion that the divine power (ἐνέργεια) is associated only with the original barbarian text and a Greek translation offers only empty words, signify--particularly in such an alleged Greek translation as book XVI of the Hermetic corpus--only stylistic instruments to certify the source and to heighten the anticipation. It appears to me highly noteworthy that Philo, who claims to have taken his higher knowledge always from a direct communion of his soul with God, a ὁμιλεῖν θεοῦ, identifies quite similarly intended passages in his writings published through booksellers as mysteries which only the

initiated person is to read and which only such a person, in any case, can understand.[99] This cannot be, as Bousset still believed, merely conventional phrasing formed by a development out of Platonism; Philo evidently bases upon this his self-estimate, his claim to a particular religious position that validates his right to make allegorical interpretations of the Scripture; this kind of mysticism is an entirely essential part of his piety and the piety of his circle. But actual Judaism knows no such "initiated persons" and in the official structuring of its cult does not at all acknowledge any such ὁμιλεῖν θεοῦ. Now since Philo is familiar with the chief ideas of the mystery-religions and is constantly using their language, it may be said with certainty that he borrows that literary form from them. He is a classical witness for the antiquity and dissemination of that form, a witness that has been preserved for us by the interest of Christian authors, while his pagan counterparts, preachers, prophets, magicians, in short those θεῖοι ἄνθρωποι of whom we hear occasionally, are no longer accessible to us.[100]

66 It is characteristic that in the Hermetic literature that is extant, even in the purely doctrinal writing that feigns nothing of any sacred action and does not purport to evoke an inner experience in the *imagination* of the reader, the conclusion is formed by the hymn or the prayer of thanksgiving to God. This shows how firmly the author places his trust in the ἐνέργεια, the living power of the word of God that he is bringing. "We thank thee, Most High, that through thy grace we have received this light of γνῶσις; redeemed by thee (or: transposed into σωτηρία), we rejoice that thou hast shown thyself to us fully, we rejoice that thou *hast made us*, in our earthly body, *to be God through the vision of thee*. We have only one petition: let us remain preserved in thy γνῶσις and do not let

this new life in that γνῶσις be lost."[101] Throughout these writings the same note sounds: the vision of God, which is always described similarly as immediate vision and perception of the universe, deifies; it bestows σωτηρία. And this highest vision (θέα) is called γνῶναι θεόν. The γνῶσις is an immediate experience and perception, it is a gift of God's grace (χάρισμα), it illumines man (φωτίζει) and at the same time transforms his very substance; it draws him through the body up into the world of the suprasensuous, it is a kind of new life, the highest perfection of the soul, the liberation from the body, the way to heaven, the means of salvation, the true worship of God and piety, just as the ἀγνωσία θεοῦ is always love for the body and sin. Anyone who has γνῶσις or is in γνῶσις is already, as man, θεῖος. In this usage the word γνῶσις has a technical meaning, a meaning that it could not at all contain in an originally Greek development; this is most clearly shown by the two expressions just mentioned, οἱ

67 ἐν γνώσει ὄντες and ὁ γνῶσις ἐσχηκώς.[102] A sentence like the following, found in the earliest of these writings--τοῦτό ἐστι τὸ ἀγαθὸν τέλος τοῖς γνῶσιν ἐσχηκόσιν θεωθῆναι--would have been just as incomprehensible, in its strict wording, to a genuine Greek as would the much-discussed contrasting of a λόγος σοφίας and a λόγος γνώσεως in Paul or his curious gradation of divinely inspired discourse that was common in his congregations: γλώσσαις λαλῶν...ἢ ἐν ἀποκαλύψει ἢ ἐν γνώσει ἢ ἐν προφητείᾳ ἢ ἐν διδαχῇ, which apparently is arranged according to the degree of comprehensibility and the level of ecstasy. It should be clear from this that Paul is familiar with and imitates the technical usage of the word γνῶσις in Hellenism.

Still another observation is crucial for understanding this perspective. Already in the Isis-mystery of Apuleius

the goddess liberates the person who is deified from the power of the stars' compulsion, εἱμαρμένη, and in the mystery of regeneration the transfiguration of our nature liberates at least from their psychic effects. It is fully understandable that in other writings it is repeatedly stated that the revealing deity elevates those who belong to him above εἱμαρμένη and its domain; they already live, even now, in the Beyond, in σωτηρία, the αἰὼν μέλλων, or the βασιλεία θεοῦ. It is true that now and then it is still emphasized that the earthly body and its fate are still subject to εἱμαρμένη, but this does not trouble the *pneumatic* person (i.e., the Gnostic); indeed, it is even said that under that compulsion of the stars this earthly body still can sin, or that it can commit murder or adultery. The person who is blessed by God with his revelation however does not himself sin, but only appears to sin. He is no longer to be identified with his body; his real "I" stands above all things, above εἱμαρμένη and above the law.[103] One cannot possibly give sharper expression to the consciousness of a complete doubling of the personality of the one who has been favored by God.

58 In considering these excerpts from Persian or Egyptian-Greek writings all of you not only will have been reminded now and then of Paul; but particularly when you recall even a little of the exemplary and careful collections in Anrich's book about the ancient mysteries in their influence on Christianity, you will have sensed immediately that all this could be transferred word by word to that movement within Christianity that we call Gnosticism. In using this term we are admittedly expanding the range of a party label which some of the sects under consideration gave themselves, and we shall be able to do this without hesitation if among the sects which we add this γνῶσις, which appeared to those men to be their char-

acteristic mark, their most distinctive feature in contrast to the world around them, has the same significance. But we may not affirm this significance on the basis of our own concepts and then say something like the following: "γνῶσις means knowledge, and thus the gnostics are religious philosophers; whatever does not fit this definition is not true gnosticism, and thus not the gnosticism that we are considering." Such an approach would offer only arbitrary constructions and at best subjective value-judgments instead of a knowledge of the development. In so doing we would, moreover, be assuming that the name and concept first arose on Greek soil, while the self-designation of the Mandaeans (γνωστικοί) and the name of their revelation-deity Manda d'Haije (γνῶσις of life, i.e., of God) would from the very outset at least equally suggest that we think of an Oriental origin of this designation. We must unquestionably first determine from the usage of those γνωστικοὶ κατ' ἐξοχήν what meaning the times associated with the word that early became a technical term: immediate knowledge, drawn from direct commerce with the deity, of the deity's secrets that had to remain hidden from the natural man and his understanding, and at the same time a knowledge that exerts a crucial influence upon our relationship to God and even on our
69 own creaturely existence, our φύσις--in short, pretty much the exact opposite of philosophy or even of religious philosophy. As Minucius Felix correctly interpreted it (Chapter 6: *nosse familiarius*), the idea that is contained in this word is not an intellectual or even scientific knowledge, but a becoming-acquainted and being-familiar in a personal sense. From this perspective, it is precisely those fantastic systems, for the authentication of which one can only appeal to revelation, and the means of gaining this revelation, i.e., the immediate vision of God, that become the crucial characteristics by

which we then judge the other sects. The consequence is that precisely because this concept of γνῶσις is common, only a few sects give themselves a name based upon it. The customary terminology is proper, in essence, because for the individual person even in the most widely different sects and in spite of the most widely divergent systems, γνῶσις, in the narrower sense just defined, plays a crucial role. Any pupil can bring to the teachings of his master constantly new expansions and revisions; primitive popular views and the most highly individual imagination can penetrate, and Oriental mystery-belief and magic are reclothed in and mixed with Greek philosophy; but all this becomes understandable only when we relocate this movement, which we can demonstrate in the Egyptian, Phrygian, Iranian, Jewish, and Christian religions and in which Persian dualism and Babylonian belief in the stars play a crucial role, out of church history in an exclusive sense and place it in the broader context of the history of religion in general. It exhibits the inevitable development of Oriental religions in the Diaspora, the climactic point of their individualistic and at the same time universalistic development, the last stage of Hellenism, in a certain sense, and therefore it is just as universal as the latter. We should not even speak of gnostic religions. 70 Those Egyptian-Hellenistic writings with which I began, therefore, may safely be called gnostic only if we keep clearly in mind that the word "gnostic" signifies only a natural phase of development, not an alien element that is transferred from some remote development, and only when we concede that these writings too can instruct us about the rise and the nature of gnosticism.

The self-designation of γνωστικός in these circles significantly never produced a fixed term for its opposite, and in

the Latin part of the empire this word itself never formed a *terminus technicus*. More widespread as a self-designation, it is acknowledged, is πνευματικός, the "spiritual man", a word that was all the more widely used since a contrast to it, ψυχικός, the "psychical man", the purely natural man, was formed quite early. We need not concern ourselves here with a later development, which once again distinguished him from the σαρκικός, the "fleshly man". The psychical man does not have γνῶσις, and he lives in a lower world; the material, psychical world stands in contrast to the pneumatic world. There is a remarkable correspondence between this Christian-gnostic language usage, which is found in the epistles attributed to James and Jude, and the use of the word in that pagan introductory prayer of the Mithras liturgy (cf. Appendix II, pp. 200ff.). There the initiate, reborn, that is, elevated into his celestial body, desires to behold God by means of the πνεῦμα, while his human and psychical nature, the ἀνθρωπίνη καὶ ψυχικὴ φύσις, remains behind on earth; for what is only earth-born cannot behold God. It has been shown earlier that all the ideas in this prayer are purely pagan; yet one could not be blamed for imagining a strange transposal of this one word and concept out of Christian gnosticism. Of course this idea would be mistaken, as can easily be demonstrated.

71 It is well known that even Paul, in the two passages where he uses the word ψυχικός, assumes that it is familiar and understandable to the community without further elaboration and connects the same double concept with it: a person is psychical who does not have γνῶσις, and who is of earthly material. Corresponding to the contrasts of ψυχικός and πνευματικός are ἐπίγειος and οὐράνιος, ἐκ γῆς and ἐκ θεοῦ, ἄνθρωπος and θεός. In that context the word ψυχικός remained up to

that point utterly unexplainable; the fact that the technical meaning at first was connected only with the adjective made it impossible to think of any direct borrowing from the Semitic sphere. In the contrast with πνευματικός, a person who is πνεῦμα or who has πνεῦμα, ψυχικός can only mean a person who is ψυχή or who has ψυχή, but it can never mean a person who besides his ψυχή does not *also* have a πνεῦμα; in that case, in these sharp contrasts an ἀπνεύματος would have been set in opposition to the πνευματικός (cf. Appendix XVI, p. 435).

But further: it seems not yet to have been observed that all the various shades of meaning that the word πνεῦμα assumes in Paul are also to be found in the magical papyri in utterly classical examples. Paul did not construct a special psychology and a secret language properly belonging to it, but he spoke the Greek of his time. There πνεῦμα is sometimes a general designation for deity--the πνεῦμα Ἄμμωνος is in essence Ammon himself--, sometimes the innermost aspect of deity, sometimes a gift that is almost substantial, a *fluidum* that God places in our hearts, a power, and again, alongside all these, without any supernatural or extra-human meaning quite simply only our immaterial, spiritual part, contrasted with the σῶμα or σκῆνος, fully equated and interchangeable at will with the word ψυχή. Since it is not at all uncommon for Paul to follow this general Hellenistic usage, the question does *not* arise as to how he could use πνευματικός to mean "suprasensory"--that is explained by that usage first discussed, and the magician also speaks of a πνευματικὴ αἴσθησις, a spiritual perception of the divine secrets--; the question we confront is rather this: how could Paul get the idea of labeling what is sensuous, material, as ψυχικόν, when after all in a number of expressions the words ψυχή and πνεῦμα serve for him as identical?

72

The answer perhaps is offered by those Hellenistic mysteries of regeneration which we have already considered at such great length. Who actually is that new I that travels through the heavens and beholds God? It is evident that for the true Hellenes since Plato it can or could be only the soul, and indeed the individual soul.[104] For the Orient, at least for the Indo-Persian area, the question would have to be much more difficult. Let us take a Greek text like the Hermetic regeneration mystery: it carefully avoids the word ψυχή. The new I is constituted out of the powers of God, and when the Son asks, "Then is this new I of a different nature, and an altogether different being from myself?" the Father has no answer. An actual and specific God emerges, not an individual soul somehow deified; to what extent the person, the I, survives in this God is a mystery on which the thought of the author touches only hesitantly. In the Oriental texts we can do little with the individual word. Certainly there is a conception of the individual soul, once the ethical demand has come to require the idea of an individually diverse destiny in the hereafter. The Persian Yasht 22 speaks of the individual soul; its own thoughts, words, and deeds must have given it the divine beauty; but the conclusion connects it, in a way that is puzzling to us, with the God Ohrmazd, who once descended into matter. Ohrmazd and the "final God" are similarly connected 73 in Manichaean documents.[105] In the funeral hymns of the Mandaeans also what is involved apparently first of all is a mythological being (the Mana) that once came into the world, the primal man, Adam; in every human soul he ascends again. It is true that here there is also an individualizing: in the later hymns the particular individual soul is spoken of. The Indian conception that our innermost self is the world-self, the divine in the world, helps us to explain the idea that our

self that is bound within matter has a double, a heavenly or original self to which it corresponds; but this self is, in an entirely non-individual sense, the knowledge of God (religion), the divine νοῦς. Thus in the initiate of the Mithras liturgy there lives and breathes the *holy spirit*, no longer his ψυχή; he has left his person behind, on the earth. It is somewhat different, and yet again similar, in the religions in which a magical action unites one with the gods that have experienced a death and a resurrection. Here also it is not an immortal soul that survives, but the particular God arises again: "this Osiris", as the Egyptian says.

We must add the complementary idea which among most peoples alternates with and is permeated by the one just discussed, namely, that man is not elevated to deity, but God rather descends and enters into man. To begin with, I note the remarkable fact that the ideas of "entering into God" and of receiving into oneself God or the spirit or the *holy spirit* are just as readily alternated in the pagan literature, and indeed not in the mystical literature alone, as are the ideas of "being in Christ" and of having Christ in oneself in the thought of Paul. The poet, who likes to compare himself with the seer or the prophet, prefers to portray God's entering into a person. I shall cite a portrayal from Paul's time which apparently is based upon an earlier Hellenistic portrayal. The poet Lucan describes the rapturous trance of Pythia: the deity enters into her *mentemque priorem expulit atque hominem toto sibi cedere iussit pectore*; he expels from her breast her ψυχή, the actual person; he alone lives in her, and now she, detached from time and space, beholds all that happens, from the very beginning of the world to the very end. It is that miraculous vision (θέα) that only God has and that makes one God, the same vision that was pictured in the mys-

4

tery of rebirth; as was the case there, a dual being develops here.

In this perspective, which is shown to be Hellenistic and pre-Pauline, πνεῦμα and ψυχή form direct opposites: where the ψυχή is, the πνεῦμα can no longer be, and where the πνεῦμα is, the ψυχή can no longer be. Thus even before Paul there arose the pair of concepts "pneumatic" and "psychical"; it is also demonstrated from the lexicons that gnosticism in its basic perspectives was already present prior to Paul.

Now of course this was the conviction of many theologians engaged in scientific labors even when this present book first appeared. In his brilliant work *Hauptprobleme der Gnosis*, W. Bousset had insistently posed the question whether gnosticism belongs to the general history of religions or to church history alone. Soon thereafter M. Lidzbarski began to make available for use the documents of the Mandaean religion, while the publications of the Turfan finds by F. W. K. Müller, A. v. Le Coq, Chavannes, Pelliot, Bang, and others taught us a better understanding of the Manichaean documents; Cumont continued his brilliantly initiated studies of religions of western Asia; and Norden carried out his lexical observations on a broad scale and set forth the Oriental characteristics even of Christian sacred language. Further monuments of a purely pagan gnosticism were shown in Greek literature and analyzed, and their basic ideas and the nature of the piety they represented were pursued on into the earlier popular monastic literature.[106] Over against all this, there is the basi- 75 cally different work now of Eduard Meyer, *Ursprung und Anfänge des Christentums*, which by virtue of the compact unity of an amazing achievement is assured of a great impact. The attempt to interpret Christianity exclusively in its own terms or in those of Judaism and to trace parallel pagan phenomena to the

influence of Christianity has never been more forcefully and confidently made; it gains in persuasive force because the reader constantly senses that there is no dogmatic interest at work here and the author is entirely objective in dealing with his material.[107] One does, however, have the strong impression of the author's interest in setting limits to the immense amount of material and his tendency to settle by fiat those questions that would have to take him too far afield into areas that are foreign to him. This is manifest particularly in the treatment of gnosticism and the closely related question of the mystery religions. And yet, though one's view of the source of Christianity is not dependent upon one's view of gnosticism or upon where one places the latter in temporal sequence, the view of the beginnings of Christianity is thus dependent. Hence I should like now once more to attempt an exposition of the significance, for an understanding of the apostle's basic perspectives, of the assertion that Paul borrowed the pair of terms γνῶσις and πνεῦμα from predominantly Hellenistic religious language. I must leave to the theologian, as better equipped for the task, the further explication of the Jewish components of those perspectives, which earlier were somewhat one-sidedly stressed. I shall attempt *solely* to determine what the word πνευματικός signifies for Paul, as the earliest and most important witness, and to what extent then we can determine the original meaning in early Christian usage of the word γνῶσις, which was translated out of the Oriental world. For the present I shall leave aside those questions that are not immediately connected with these issues; I shall not attempt to offer a unitary and total picture of the apostle, but only a contribution to such a picture. The history of words, when it is carried to a deeper level, to the history of concepts, can always afford us rich information about prob-

76

lems which we are unable to approach in any other way; of course there is no other area where harmonious collaboration between theology and the various philologies is so vital as in that of such a history of religious language. Even in a writer like Paul the language itself, when rightly heard, must disclose to us at least a part of his evolution, which in fact is otherwise completely unknown, and of the intellectual forces that influenced him, and this goal is attractive enough to justify even a groping attempt. In this process at the outset a correct framing of the question is far more important than a conclusive answer. We shall begin with the two passages in I Corinthians where the word ψυχικός appears. I shall attempt later (cf. Appendix XVI) to justify the interpretation of the individual passage from the context, but here I shall point out the essentials.

Paul has received the pneuma from God, that pneuma that knows even the inmost depths of deity. Hence at every new infusion of the spirit he can compare what is pneumatic with what is pneumatic. But the *psychical* man cannot even receive the gifts of the spirit of God; he cannot discern them, for they must be judged pneumatically. The pneumatic can judge all and each and *himself can be judged by no one, at least not by any non-pneumatic person*. For who knows the spirit of the Lord? And Paul has received that spirit. Hence the Corinthians have no right to pass judgment on his teaching at all; for he has

77

not addressed them as pneumatics, and even now he is not addressing them as such; they are yet *men*, and the pneumatic person is no longer man. In the second place, as is known, he sets in contrast to the psychical body that is sown the pneumatic body that will be raised; for as we have borne the image of the first man, who became a living ψυχή, we must also bear the image of the second, who became a life-giving πνεῦμα.

It is, as is often mentioned, that *heavenly* body that God is keeping for him and that one day, when he puts it on, will make him fully πνεῦμα. And yet that heavenly body is already in a certain sense in him, because he has already received the earnest of the πνεῦμα. Because with unveiled face he reflects and beholds God, he experiences in this σῶμα ἀσώματον, as Hellenistic mysticism calls this reflection of the heavenly in the earthly, the transfiguration (μεταμόρφωσις) from one glory to another; the πνεῦμα accomplishes this. And as in Paul, so in every Christian Christ will gradually assume full form (μορφοῦσθαι), just as in the earlier mentioned magical incantation the soul assumes the form of the entering deity by means of the light that possesses the power to create and to transfigure.

It is on the vision of the *resurrected one* that he bases the apostolate of the *disciples*, like his own, and on this vision he bases his *freedom* in teaching.[108] He has not received or learned the content of his message from any man; thus it is not a εὐαγγέλιον κατὰ Πέτρον or κατ' ἄνθρωπον at all. After that conversion-miracle he did not consult "flesh and blood" at all (as did Apuleius, for example, in the case of the visions granted to him), nor did he, as one might expect, go to Jerusalem, to inquire of as many disciples as possible about the life and teachings of his Lord. What he had done earlier in this respect now appears to him as insignificant and immaterial; he does not even mention his baptism, in spite of the fact that otherwise he places such high value upon the effect of this mystery. According to the view of his communities and his own conviction, anyone who has *once* seen the Lord must not stand in need of any further tradition, but is in a position in and of himself to discern all things,

78

as is explicitly said of such a man in the Hermetic rebirth-mystery.[109]

He can be absolutely certain of this non-mediated knowledge, and only of it, and if an angel should descend from heaven and bring a different message, he can pronounce a curse upon that angel. Indeed, he is privy to the secrets that all the powers of the intermediate realm strive after in vain. And just as *this* knowledge of Christ alone has truth for him, so also *this* relationship to him alone has value. In fact, Paul lives in the suprasensory world and has died to the old world; for him no man can any longer exist according to the flesh, but rather stands in a special relationship to him. "And even though I had known Christ according to the flesh"--the idea evidently has reference to the other apostles, who could appeal to this connection between themselves and the living Master--"now I know him thus no longer. If anyone is 'in Christ', for him a new world is created; the old one has passed away, and all things have become new." In comparison with this very exalted sense of one's own autonomy and immediate knowledge, the Hellenistic (i.e., Hermetic) utterances--"Nothing in the world of the corporeal is true, and in the world of the non-corporeal everything is sure and certain", "In heaven nothing is unknowable, on earth nothing actually is known", and "In heaven nothing is unfree, and on earth nothing is free"--appear feeble and frivolous.[110]
79 Nevertheless they too make a contribution toward introducing us to the general attitude of the time in which a tremendous experience detached a religiously creative nature from its previous allegiance and focused that nature, that man, on itself.

I can only suggest my version of the individual sayings of the apostle, and I shall be glad later to attempt to justify

it, and shall even more gladly accept correction.[111] This version, however, explains to me as intentional and necessary what has often evoked amazement, namely that Paul does not appeal to Jesus' life and deeds and does not impress Jesus' words as such upon his communities. Echoes, which are so diligently sought for, as a rule prove nothing, and they completely vanish in the face of this remarkable fact. The three well known exceptions however are explained as soon as one seriously considers them: the authorization given to the apostles to make their living by the gospel, which Paul cannot deny them, while he himself does not take advantage of this permission and boasts of that fact; the prescription concerning marriage, which must have come up for discussion at the so-called apostolic council--thus two issues of order in the churches; and alongside these the solemn narration of the institution of the Lord's Supper, introduced as a recollection of what Paul has also shared with the community orally. The mystery naturally demands the formula. But Paul appears to be giving it out of a knowledge somehow received from the Lord, and he has added to the words which the gospels relate the command to repeat the event, and it is this command that renders the narrative the inauguration of a mystery; here one observation reinforces the other. When Paul in this reshaping adds the intention εἰς τὴν ἐμὴν ἀνάμνησιν, "in memory of me", of course I can never interpret these words simply to mean a memorial meal, such as is known in the Greek cult of the dead. This would be in contradiction to the sacramental doctrine which Paul gives immediately after this. One could rather interpret them in a mystical sense, somewhat corresponding to that narrative, from about the time of Paul, in a magical text in which Osiris gives to Isis and to Horus his blood to drink in a cup of wine, so that after his death they will not forget

80

him, but must search for him with longing and lamentation, until, brought back to life, he is re-united with them.[112] In fact, in the love magic and in friendship covenants of most peoples the potion of blood puts a magical spell upon the soul of the one who drinks it, and the idea is understandable that the Christians also, thanks to the effects of this draught, cannot forget the Lord's death, but must speak of 81 him--of course not in empty lamentations--until he himself shall re-appear. The return is connected with the proclamation throughout the world. A certain reference to the words of the gospel about re-uniting could be discernible in this point. Yet, unless a happy accident should give us new information about the practice and interpretation of the mystery-meals that were common in most of the cults, this remains only a matter of playing with possibilities; only baptism, not the Lord's Supper, can be compared, up to this point, with non-Christian counterparts. Only this much appears certain: precisely in this citation and this arrangement Paul entirely maintains his autonomy in relation to the tradition of the first community.

Paul found both sacraments already present in the community, and yet neither of them can be explained in terms of Judaism. It is a bit of arbitrary procedure or, more correctly said, a makeshift of the poorest kind, to derive even the baptism of John alone from the idea, mentioned in Ezekiel only once in passing (36:29, 33), of a purification, by somehow combining it with some general and pale pictures offered by Isaiah (4:4) and Jeremiah (4:14; 2:22), and in so doing to ignore its connection with the message of Hellenistic σωτῆρες about the imminent collapse of the world and the possibility of being rescued. In the work of Paul himself we may trace out the relationship to the mystery religions, not in the

sacraments in themselves, but only in the figurative language and in individual, unique words. Since the appearance of Dieterich's classic book, *Eine Mithrasliturgie*, there is hardly any need for new proof that Paul was familiar with the language of the mystery religions and constantly made use of this acquaintance in marvelously profound images. The reader will recall that "putting on" or "putting on over" (KJV: "being clothed upon") the heavenly body which was cultically represented in the mystery religions and was so common in their language that as in Paul, the verb is applied to the heavenly or earthly dwelling; he will also recall expressions such as "the body of death", which is found also among Mandaeans and Manichaeans and in their usage is anchored in the total outlook on the terrestrial world; and the famil-
82 iar images of "being baptized into Christ's death" or "being buried by baptism with Christ in death", which can also be found in all these religions, most clearly of course in the Phrygian baptism in blood. Another figure, which is introduced incidentally, can be explained in terms of Iranian perspectives. Christ has caused the fragrance of his γνῶσις to become manifest everywhere through Paul; thus the apostle himself is to a certain degree the sweet aroma of Christ for God to all those who are saved and for those who are perishing, for the one an aroma of life unto life, and for the other an aroma of death unto death. Similarly, among the Mandaeans the "emissary" relates concerning himself (Genza r., p. 58.23 Lidzbarski): "I am the emissary of the light; every one who smells its aroma receives life; and every one who accepts his discourses into himself, his eyes are filled with light....The adulterers scented me; then they quickly forsook their adultery...; they came and surrounded themselves with my aroma.

They said, 'When we were without knowledge (γνῶσις), we practiced adultery; now, since we have knowledge, we commit adultery no longer.'" An almost even closer connection with Paul is seen in a hymn sung on Tuesday (*Liturgien*, p. 199 Lidzbarski): "The aroma came from its place, the truth came from its place, the aroma came from its place, it came and settled in the house (the world). It calls and revives the dead, it shakes and brings hither those who were lying there, it awakens the souls that are zealous and are worthy of the place of light. This, this did the Good One (the emissary) and erected the signs of life." In the same hymns he is called the lofty emissary, the king of the Uthras. Even if it were intrinsically an utter impossibility for one who knows this literature to assume an influencing of the Mandaean text by Paul, still similar passages in the earliest Mandaean funeral texts, which also have counterparts in the Persian Avesta[113] and in a very

83 early, originally Aramaic alchemistic text, make it certain that the perspective is Iranian. The aroma of life (i.e., here the aroma of God) constantly announces the closeness of the divine emissary and the coming salvation, and the bad aroma announces the envoy of the evil one and the approaching condemnation; they constitute the very essence of the two contending powers. Hence it is not surprising that that pagan alchemistic writing attributes this bringing of life to a φάρμακον τῆς ἀθανασίας. This expression, which also recurs in later Egyptian literature, apparently had acquired the character of a formula, and for Ignatius, who in fact is close to the Syrian circle of thought, it can even signify the bread of the Lord's Supper, and thus the body of Christ. When one considers the capacity of such ideas to change, perhaps one may even be reminded of that earlier-mentioned Phrygian act of initiation in which, in the nocturnal celebration of the resurrection of the

deity, the throat of the believer was anointed with an aromatic ointment and the promise of σωτηρία was whispered to him. In the same cult, after the *rebirth* the initiate receives milk as nourishment. This has long been compared with Paul's proposing to offer milk instead of solid food to the Corinthians, to whom he could not say everything, because they were not yet πνευματικοί, but only children in Christ. The fact that later the first epistle of Peter employs the same cultic practice as a figure may only be cited as confirmation of this interpretation. But more important than all these individual features, which could easily be multiplied, is of course the question whether that entire distinctive train of thought, that in the one all die and are raised, the idea of being Christ, the understanding of vision as a power that transforms one's nature, indeed, even that idea of the vision of God and of the utter autonomy and freedom that it produces, --whether all these are related to the spirit of the Hellenistic mystery-religions. Individual images and ideas can indeed arise simultaneously and yet independently in different
84 places, but not a unitary train of ideas. This is why I have attempted to bring out in a little bit sharper focus than has previously been done the connections between the various ideas.

Of decisive significance to me in this context is a strange feeling, to us at first hardly comprehensible, of the duality of his own personality that appears to me not seldom to break through in Paul. By this I do not mean the sense of the conflict between a will to do good and a constraint to do evil in us; every sensitive person is familiar with this, and even Seneca could portray it without venturing far from the soil of ancient Greek feeling. Nor do I mean the contrast between a plain outward life and a rich inner life, which Plato had already sensed in his master and stressed. Of course at

certain times the feeling for this contrast increases to a particular strength, and it is not at all limited to the religious realm. Certainly millions of hearts, not in Christianity alone, have been comforted by the idea of being, outwardly, only a poor and wretched, perhaps crippled, child of man, and yet inwardly being the most elevated and blessed imaginable, a child of God. And it was somewhat similar when, in the time when our scholarship was still a matter of the heart, the wandering humanist or the starving schoolmaster in a miserable little room experienced the wealth of his inner life and his association with the greatest spirits of all ages as such a blessed thing that to those who were able to see only the externals he could proudly say, "You do not even know what I am." But such feelings, with which all of us can sense some sympathy, and which undoubtedly also had an impact upon Paul, do not suffice to explain a sentence like "I live, yet not I, but Christ lives in me." The fact that this is very familiar to us and has almost become a formula for us must not be allowed to dull our sensitivity to its uniqueness; we must attempt first to understand it word-by-word and then from it to interpret many another word that impresses us as being

85 strange and alien. It strikes me somewhat like that unique formulation of the highest vision, to which Paul appeals: "I know a man in Christ who--whether in the body or out of the body I do not know, God knows--was caught up...this man was taken up...this man heard...for this man I will boast, but of myself I will not boast, except of my weakness." Some interpreters label as affected and stilted this division, continuing even after the ecstatic experience, of two persons in one's own self, or they strive to get around it by attempting to impose an incorrect form of expression upon the simple and clear words, and thus they destroy the connection.[114] But the

same dual awareness of the weak man and the deity in him, from which alone these words can be explained easily and without forcing, can in my judgment itself be explained only by the remarkable combination in Paul of the sublime obstinacy and almost superhuman self-certainty of the pneumatic and the sighing and yearning of the miserable human heart for redemption from sin. Of course a person does not learn such an awareness or simply transfer it out of an alien religion into his own; nevertheless it becomes more comprehensible in particular if we can demonstrate that there is something similar existing in the attitudes of his own times. We find this feeling of a duality of being in the fullest sense of the term in the mystery-literature and the mystery-religions, and we find it also in the gnosticism that grew out of them. Here too the pneumatic is essentially a divine being and in spite of his earthly body is caught up into another world which alone has value and truth. The autonomy is ultimately in-

86

tensified to the point that the religious imagination is released from all restraints, and the more freely it develops the elements which at first were borrowed from the reinterpreted folk-religions and places them in ever new combinations, just so much more surely does it make the impression of inner truth upon its own times. Perhaps, if one wishes to compare small with great, one may recall that late blooming of romanticism in E. T. A. Hoffmann (cf. Appendix XVIII). The idea that besides the ordinary, everyday world there is another, a higher world, in which the child and the poet live, and that this other world not only also possesses a kind of truth, but that it alone is of value, gives rise, through an inner compulsion, to ever more tortuous and bizarre fantasies, whose appeal for their times lies precisely in the fact that they

appear to the ordinary man so strange and incomprehensible and appeal to more sophisticated persons.

It is true that a wide chasm separates Paul from this later development; but we encounter in him the beginnings of that basic Hellenistic consciousness, and the religio-historical way of considering these matters may place him in this course of development not as the first, but perhaps as the greatest of all the gnostics. But this way of viewing things will be able to understand that general basic consciousness in historical terms. Primitive popular belief had derived the initiation of the living from ideas of death and immortality; magical practices, whose meaning in their original setting were hardly understood any longer, originally served to set forth this belief. Now in the dissemination of the belief there came the encounter with a foreign populace and the compulsion to explain; religion had become personal, and the consecration of priests had become the basis of the believers' hope of salvation; Greek language and Greek thought required that concepts be formulated and interpretations sought. Contradictions were unavoidable here for the pagan, and they can easily be traced out in the Hermetic literature, for example. 87 Because of the profound moral earnestness of the Jewish religion, which was in flat opposition to the magical transformation of sinful man into a divine being, these contradictions became for Paul even sharper. He did not overcome them, but in the struggle to settle them he developed the profoundest religious feelings and understandings and created a language of the heart that served even the times in which the sense of that compulsion out of which they were born, and thus also the understanding for the individual word, had been lost.

The conflict between autonomy of the religious feeling and obligation to the tradition, which determines the develop-

ment of every higher religion, was greatly intensified for post-exilic Judaism, at first by the immediate influences of other Oriental religions, but soon also by the influence, which reinforced and in some measure renewed those earlier influences, of Hellenism, which according to our view in fact offered, in these areas, in essence Oriental metal in Greek coinage. We certainly must at least pose the question to what extent those two waves of the same flood made some impact upon Paul even through Jewish mediation. But the question must not be regarded as at all crucial, and it can never be completely answered. We see in the Corinthian epistles, and it would have to be self-evident, that Paul takes into account and concerns himself with the views of the communities to whom he is writing. To this extent a working together of indirect and direct (that is, at first Hellenistic-Jewish and later purely Hellenistic) influences is probable from the very outset. Only we may not derive what was innermost and most personal in the piety of Paul from the faith of his later communities. The preaching of John the Baptist, which is surprisingly explained and expanded by a slightly later Mandaean writing, shows that strong influences of other Oriental religions were already making themselves felt on the periphery of Palestinian Judaism. But what we know of the baptism of John still remains far removed from the Pauline understanding of the sacrament that unites one with Christ. That elsewhere in Judaism also symbolic actions like the bath of purification were becoming more highly valued and individual images reminiscent of Hellenism perhaps were already arising at that time; further, that a person who is converted from his sins receives a spirit of purity that impels him to walk the way of goodness,

38

and that he is to live as though he had just been born; or that the proselyte who has undergone baptism and circumcision, who is detached from his nationhood and from all other connections, is like a newborn child;--all this one can readily acknowledge and still regard it as much too little to justify deriving from Judaism the belief in the dying of the old man and the creation of the new man. Such religious influences are not exerted by whims, but only by vital convictions. Certainly it is important that, just as in the entire environment, so also in Judaism at that time, in spite of official rejection, the belief in the continuing "effects of the spirit", in prophetism, miraculous powers, and magic was once again on the increase. One may however ask where then on Jewish soil these "effects of the spirit" have similarly central significance for σωτηρία, that they signify a total transformation of the entire essence and nature. Where do we find anything corresponding to the Hellenistic mystery? Moreover, that vision that caught Paul, or his other "I", up into the third heaven certainly was "Jewishly" experienced. Instead of the "domain of truth", which the Hellenistic initiate seeks in his celestial wandering, that vision speaks of Paradise, and it may also be distinguished from the Hellenistic counterparts by the number of the heavens. In any case, there will already have existed Jewish apocalypses and ascensions, and ideas of that kind, though to be sure completely devoid of color and without any religious meaning, had made their way into the rabbinical literature. But *thanks to Hellenism*, ascensions and apocalypses

89 had become edifying literature and were being created or reshaped at the writing desk. It is something different when a Paul *experiences* such *visions*; this presupposes that he had already earlier been living entirely within these perspectives,

and the form of the narrative shows that his community also was familiar with these perspectives. And he can base his claim, not to stand beneath the original apostles but rather above them, upon this vision only if both he himself and his community are permeated with the Hellenistic (and thus originally Oriental), not the Jewish, evaluation of this non-mediated vision of God--and if the Petrine party at Corinth does not have something similar to relate about *their* chief.

But we have an absolutely certain proof and even a measure of the strength even of the direct impact of Hellenism upon the apostle; I refer to his language. The words that are used in a technical way in such a context, which is in doubt as to its origin, must be questioned; in our case this means such words as ψυχικός and πνευματικός, γνῶσις and ἀγνωσία, φωτίζειν and δόξα, μορφοῦσθαι and μεταμορφοῦσθαι, or μορφή, σῴζεσθαι and σωτηρία, or νοῦς in the sense of πνεῦμα as that divine *fluidum* that is bestowed upon the elect person as a gift of grace, a χάρισμα. The idea which the apostle connects with each of them cannot be drawn from modern speculation, but only from the usage of his times, and each of these words has in it its own history. Anyone who would explain for us, with a knowledge of both languages and literatures, the words and images of the diverse patterns of thought of Paul and his successors would be the first actually to introduce us to his thought,[115] and would *not* lose that powerful, religiously creative individuality if we recognized what he made his own and *reshaped* in himself out of the most profound feeling of *both* of the worlds that formed his environment.

The few facts that he relates to us from the history of his own development now can be somewhat more internally connected with each other (cf. Appendix XX). Having grown up in the Diaspora, thus thinking in the Greek world-language, with

the broad horizon that full membership in the world-empire bestows, participating in the world-culture with its unusual opposites and interconnections, he first seeks fulfillment in the religion of his fathers for an extraordinarily profound religious need. He strives in Jerusalem to become entirely a "Jew". It certainly is understandable that in this effort he joins the Pharisees, who in spite of their "zeal for the Law" had been strongly influenced by the Iranian belief in immortality and were the real bearers of the missionary idea in the homeland; the same influences in fact even more heavily affected Judaism in the Diaspora, here permeated with the elements of Hellenistic mysticism. Differently from Philo, whom one can compare but can never invoke for the purposes of genetic explanation, Paul gradually comes to sense the inner opposition of the two elements. A righteousness that could actually lead to union with God he can no longer find in the service of the Law in earlier Judaism; for in its fullest sense the Law cannot be fulfilled. It only awakens in him the sense of his sinfulness and his alienation from God. The battle against the newly emerging sect, in which he participates with zeal, compels further reflection. A powerful inner experience, a vision, about which we are never told anything more specific, brings with the full conviction of the resurrection also the break with his past, and his joining the side of the opponents against whom he previously had been fighting.
91 In the Hellenistic community he receives the first instruction; then in two years of solitary inner struggle over a new total religious outlook the Jewish messianic hope becomes for him the belief in an emissary of God who *redeems humanity*, who has appeared and continues to work in those who are his. That Paul had a point of contact and a kind of prototype for this

idea in an Oriental or Hellenistic belief I would have to presuppose, even if the history of religions did not demonstrate to me the possibility, and even the probability. Nevertheless, his connecting this idea with the Jesus who had been crucified as a blasphemer is a tremendous act of faith that can be comprehended only in terms of the conviction that that totally new interpretation of God and his relationship to men that Jesus proclaimed is the only true one, because only it brings peace to the soul. *Jesus* must have been "the emissary". But the form in which he makes his inner experience comprehensible is not connected with the Jewish conception of the prophet, but with a Hellenistic conception, and it is a Hellenistic community in which he gains a leading position and which then first sends him forth as a missionary. And the vision of that divine emissary acquires for him a significance altogether different from the significance for the five hundred in Jerusalem of their vision of the risen master. As he sees it, it gives him an entirely unique religious position and independence. With it he stands on an equal footing with the whole company of the apostles. If this estimate of his vision can be explained in terms of Hellenistic religion, then we are justified in saying that even though an immeasurable amount in Paul's thinking and feeling remained Jewish, he owes to Hellenism the belief in his apostleship and his liberty. Herein lies the greatest and the most significant impact for world history of the ancient mystery-religions.

NOTES

1. On what follows here cf. Appendix I.

2. Thus the Samothracian mysteries probably are connected with Phrygia, but continued to work their way toward Greece and influenced others there also (Kabeiro as mother of Kabeiros, for example, corresponds to Brimo as mother of Brimos in Eleusis). Nevertheless, in view of the scantiness of our knowledge, it seems best to exclude from consideration the older Greek mysteries. Even though after the revival of religion they once again acquire a certain significance, still that revival itself does not issue from them, and their impact in return upon the mystery-conceptions which were borrowed from the Orient (and thus are Hellenistic) cannot have been great. They lack the background of a particular religion and its presentation in the literature, but most of all, the promotional activity of the prophets.--In any case, the Orphic mystery shows strong Oriental influence, and partly through Orphism, partly through Greeks of Asia Minor as early as the beginning of the fifth century B.C., Oriental stimuli had penetrated Pythagoreanism (cf. Reitzenstein-Schaeder, I, 3). The task of tracing out Oriental influence among the pre-Socratics has been posed anew by A. Goetze (*Zeitschrift für Indologie und Iranistik* II, 1923, pp. 60 and 167).

3. I may only refer to Zimmern's splendid essay, "Babylonische Vorstufen der vorderasiatischen Mysterienreligionen," in *Zeitschrift der deutschen Morgenländischen Gesellschaft* LXXVI, 1922, pp. 36-37; I myself am completely lacking any information on this point.

4. It becomes something personal, a kind of tribal soul. On what follows, cf. Appendix II.

5. Of course, when we think of the primitive mind, grave injury or captivity is to be equated with the dying of the God. Whether a *death* of Marduk is attested in the Babylonian hymns does not matter for our purposes here. Yet Zimmern is correct in comparing the myth of his imprisonment in the mountain with myths of Ishtar-Tammuz and in emphasizing Babylon's importance for the Syrian-Phoenician cult of Adonis and other cults.

6. Thus admittedly in Egyptian religion; a transitional form is exhibited by Babylonian religion, which originally has the king adopted by God upon accession to the throne.

7. *Zeitschrift für Indologie und Iranistik* II, 1923, pp. 60 and 167-68.

8. Cf. Reitzenstein-Schaeder, I i and II i.

9. The little book by a Japanese spiritual leader, *Zen, Der lebendige Buddhismus in Japan* (translated by Schuej Ohasama, edited by A. Faust, 1925), was extremely instructive to me for gaining a feel of the movement.

10. Correctly stressed by Prof. Schaeder, in Reitzenstein-Schaeder, II, at the end of Chapter II.

11. The really untranslatable words (Poimandres I.3) read, in Greek: μαθεῖν θέλω τὰ ὄντα καὶ νοῆσαι τὴν τούτων φύσιν καὶ γνῶναι τὸν θεόν. This could have a philosophical ring to it, but the fulfillment of the petition is brought about by the vision and the God who interprets it.

12. De spec. leg. III 100: τὴν μὲν οὖν ἀληθῆ μαγικήν, ὀπτικὴν ἐπιστήμην οὖσαν, ᾗ τὰ τῆς φύσεως ἔργα τρανοτέραις φαντασίαις αὐγάζεται, σεμνὴν καὶ περιμάχητον δοκοῦσαν εἶναι, οὐκ ἰδιῶται μόνον, ἀλλὰ καὶ βασιλεῖς καὶ βασιλέων οἱ μέγιστοι καὶ μάλιστα οἱ Περσῶν διαπονοῦσιν οὕτως, ὥστ' οὐδένα φασὶν ἐπὶ βασιλείαν δύνασθαι παραπεμφθῆναι παρ' αὐτοῖς εἰ μὴ πρότερον τοῦ μάγων γένους κεκοινωνηκὼς τυγχάνοι. ἔστι δέ τι παράκομμα ταύτης, κυριώτατα φάναι κακοτεχνία, ἣν μηναγύρται καὶ βωμολόχοι μετίασι καὶ γυναίων καὶ ἀνδραπόδων τὰ φαυλότατα, περιμάττειν καὶ καθαίρειν κατεπαγγελλόμενα καὶ στέργοντας μὲν εἰς ἀνήκεστον ἔχθραν, μισοῦντας δὲ εἰς ὑπερβάλλουσαν εὔνοιαν ἄξειν ὑπισχνούμενα.

13. In my *Poimandres* (p. 83) I have determined the occasion and nature of this work and published the purely pagan part. I recognized later that the Jewish parts belonged to it from the very first; I have edited the text again (Reitzenstein-Schaeder, I, p. 161) and in the appendices (p. 191) published a hymn, extant in full, which corresponds to the Mandaean hymns for the dead and the Martyrdom of Isaiah. That divine being who as primal man is the Son of God, the All in All, the Soul, here also bears the name Aion. The philosophical justification appears to go back to Poseidonios; cf. Appendix I, at the end.

14. Thus he corresponds to the Persian concept *daēna* (religious knowledge) and to the Aramaic *achamoth* (σοφία), which is taken over into Gnosis.

15. Right Genza XVI 4, in Lidzbarski, p. 389, 23.

16. In the Iranian, the word of God also is a person, and the Adam of the Naassenes is the Logos.

17. I must maintain in substance this interpretation of the *monuhmed vuzurg* in spite of the objections which Waldschmidt and Lentz have recently raised against it (*Abhandlungen der Preussischen Akademie*, 1926). They place no weight on the adjective *vuzurg* (great, broad), leave unexplained the text which affixes this adjective to the noun *monuhmed*, and on their own part conclude, from the lists of the five parts of the soul or parts of the equipment of the primal man who is equated with the soul, that the word only means γνῶσις (Aramaic *manda*). I respond with the objection that this interpretation is inadequate even for the passage from which Prof. Andreas and I formerly began, the rendering of the Greek word δίψυχος by the Soghdian translator as "which stand in two *monuhmed*" (cf. Prof. Andreas in my essay, "Die Göttin Psyche," p. 4, n. 3); and of course it is even less adequate for most of the passages newly cited by Lentz and Waldschmidt. They show that along with that enumeration of five religious forms of thought or knowledge by the soul still another formula is at work, according to which one of them (the first *bom* or the second *monuhmed*) is added as a complement and counterpart to the word "soul", just as in the system of Poimandres the νοῦς is added to the ψυχή; it is the Self of the soul, and thus corresponds to its whole. The relationship of Achamoth (σοφία) to the soul among the Gnostics is similar. No Greek or German word can fully express such Oriental-religious concepts. Hence at least the scholarly investigator must start out from the functions which these concepts exercise in the individual passage, unconcerned about whether our language and psychology allow us to find an expression suitable for all passages (one may think for example of the Indian word *atman*). If in such a word personification prevails and allows myths to enter, the difficulties naturally increase, as for example with the Mandaean counterpart to the *monuhmed*, the *Manda* (*d'Haije*). In this term the connection with the primal man is just as clear as the equation with the awakening emissary. When he appears as the first man or the righteous, pure one, we sense the connection with the Gayomard idea, which is confirmed by consideration of the Nitufta-view as well as by the consideration of the Adakas (or Adam) speculations of the Mandaeans. The names of categories, such as Adam, "Ανθρωπος, Enosh, and the designations for concepts, such as λόγος, νοῦς, σοφία, and ψυχή, then are supplemented by secondary proper names (for

Adam his sons Hibil and Sitil, i.e., Abel and Seth); the final, purely speculative expansion is introduced with the intentional blending of religions. Thus the Naassene Preaching begins its expositions (Hippolytus, Ref., p. 81. 7 Wendland) with ψυχῆς γάρ, φασί, πᾶσα φύσις, ἄλλη δὲ ἄλλως ὀρέγεται, finds this divine nature in Attis, Adonis, Osiris, Hermes, Ἄνθρωπος, and others, and concludes (98.14): οὗτος (Attis), φησίν, ἐστὶν ὁ πολυώνυμος, μυριόμματος, ἀκατάληπτος, οὗ πᾶσα φύσις, ἄλλη δὲ ἄλλως ὀρέγεται. Thus Jesus is fitted into the Manichaean series as counterpart of our light-soul. It always involves the same basic religious perspective, the same divine being, which no name fully identifies. Therefore the consideration of this point in religio-historical terms must not fasten on the individual name--no more on the conceptual name *monuhmed* than on the proper name Jesus--but only on the basic idea.

18. Instructive for the connection of the Mandaean and Persian conceptions is the account, taken from the Avesta (the Damdaδ-Nask) in Hamza al-Isfahani's Annals (Reitzenstein-Schaeder, II, p. 234; cf. 215): "When he (Gayomard) died, a drop of seed (*nutfa*) came out of his loins and penetrated the earth." This equation of seed, man, and divine soul dominates the religious thought of the Mandaeans, but likewise that of the author of the Naassene Preaching, indeed of most Gnostics, who in fact claim to be of a different nature and descent from those of other men. Out of this there arises necessarily the idea of the tribe of souls, and from this position the idea of rebirth as well as that of awakening is influenced.

19. I have attempted to provide, in the essay on "Das mandäische Buch vom Herrn der Grösse", and later in my *Iranisches Erlösungsmysterium*, the proof that the Mandaean religion, the portrayals of which in their present version are relatively late, dates from before the time of the rise of Christianity and is not significantly influenced by the latter. The studies of W. Bauer, Bultmann, and most recently H. H. Schaeder (Reitzenstein-Schaeder, II, 4), which in their results are in full agreement, indeed suffice to disarm the doubts of Ed. Meyer, who has not been closely engaged with the material.

20. III, p. 167.

21. On this, cf. Appendix IV.

22. Sethe, *Nachrichten der Gesellschaft der Wissenschaften*, Göttingen, 1919, p. 158.

23. Prudentius, Peristephan. X 1006 f. and Incerti carm. contra paganos v. 57 f., Hepding, *Attis*, pp. 65 and 61 (not sufficiently sharp in the comparison of the two portrayals), as well as Firmicus Maternus, de errore prof. rel., ch. 22 (cf. infra, p. 510).

24. Cf. *Iran. Erlösungsmysterium*, p. 159. One might also refer to the presentation of Mithras as guide of souls on the monument to Antiochus IV of Commagene (cf. Julian Conv. 336c).

25. Cf. Appendix IX.

26. To be compared now with the lists of the cultic places of a god which are found in the earlier period in many of the Egyptian temples (Junker, *Die Onurislegenden,* p. 69) is the Greek hymn to Isis (Oxyrh. Pap. 1380), which in its major part sets forth her shrines throughout the entire οἰκουμένη. A similar list--though of course greatly abbreviated--is provided in prayers, preserved in the literature, which identify Isis with the most widely diverse goddesses. While that hymn provides us with more insight into the extent of the propaganda, the tractate of a believer in Imuthes, written on the reverse side (Oxyrh. Pap. 1381) opens up to us a no less surprising insight into the attitude of Hellenistic Egyptian circles and at the same times gives us an understanding of Hermetic religious literature. The author describes the aim of his Greek revisions of Egyptian religious writings (line 198): Ἑλληνὶς δὲ πᾶσα γλῶσσα τὴν σὴν λαλήσει ἱστορίαν καὶ πᾶς Ἕλλην ἀνὴρ τὸν τοῦ Φθᾶ σεβήσεται Ἰμούθην. It perhaps will make the missionary thrust of the Oriental religions even more comprehensible if I set beside this the words of Paul (Phil. 2:11): καὶ πᾶσα γλῶσσα ἐξομολογήσεται ὅτι κύριος Ἰησοῦς Χριστὸς εἰς δόξαν θεοῦ πατρός. The strength of admixture of philosophy in these writings, which in tendency were religious--even that believer in Imuthes boasts of having inserted it as a necessary component part in the old text of a world-creation--is determined by the level of education of the author and of the public which he has in view.

27. Cf. Appendix V.

28. Similarly in Babylon; cf. W. Stärk, *Die Schriften des Alten Testaments* III, 1 (Göttingen, 1901), on Psalm 2:7: υἱος

μου εἶ σύ, ἐγὼ σήμερον γεγέννηκά σε (Norden, *Die Geburt des Kindes*, p. 92.1).

29. Below, Appendix II.

30. Below, Appendices II and V.

31. Since the word *vectus* in Apuleius has caused some puzzlement, I refer to the Mithras liturgy 6.2 Diet.: ὄψει σεαυτὸν ἀνακουφιζόμενον καὶ ὑπερβαίνοντα εἰς ὕψος, or Genza, p. 208.2 Lidzb.: "Winds carry him away, storms drive him onward, leaders bear him up into the heights."

32. Cf. Appendix V (Apuleius' account).

33. One may think of the prayer of Apuleius upon leaving the temple (Met. XI.25).

34. Cf. Appendix IV; Reitzenstein, "Die Göttin Psyche," pp. 23-24.

35. Cf. Appendix VI.

36. Cf. Eduard Meyer, *Der Papyrusfund von Elephantine*, pp. 38-39.

37. Cf. Appendix I (p. 119).

38. Cf. Appendix VII.

39. Cf. the Mithras liturgy and the Nephotes-magic in the conclusion of Appendix I or the λῆψις παρέδρου in Parthey, *Abhandlungen der Preussischen Akademie* 1865, p. 125. About the πάρεδρος δαίμων, the God in us, it is said: τελευτήσαντός σου τὸ σῶμα περιστελεῖ ὡς πρέπον θεῷ, σοῦ δὲ τὸ πνεῦμα βαστάξας εἰς ἀέρα ἄξει σὺν αὐτῷ. εἰς γὰρ Ἅιδην οὐ χωρήσει ἀέριον πνεῦμα συσταθὲν κραταιῷ παρέδρῳ. τούτῳ γὰρ πάντα ὑπόκειται.

40. The Persian in fact offers a certain selection among Zurvan, Ahura Mazda, and even Mithras, while the Phrygian affords a choice among the various manifestations of the Great Mother and her consort (Attis or Sabazios, among others).

41. On Hermes see Martial V 24 (a Christian counterpart is offered by the Martyrium Petri [Lipsius-Bonnet, Acta apost. apocr. I 17.26]: *Christus,...qui est constitutus nobis sermo*

unus et solus); on Isis, C. I. Lat. X 3800: *te tibi, una quae es omnia* (in this saying, is Isis, since she is the All, symbolically offered to herself? Cf. Corp. Herm. XIII 18: δι' ἐμοῦ δέξαι τὸ πᾶν λογικὴν θυσίαν). Plutarch mentions (De Is. et Os. 44) Anubis communities (σεβόμενοι τὸν Ἄνυβιν), and Kaibel (Epigr. graec. 1029 = C. I. Gr. 3724) offers a kind of confession of Anubis. Pap. Oxyrh. 1382 offers a confessional formula as an acclamation of the community at the conclusion of the worship service.

42. See Appendix VIII.

43. Plutarch, De Is. et Os. c. 66-67. His source (cf. c. 33, οἱ σοφώτεροι τῶν ἱερέων) contests the interpretation (cited in c. 38) of Osiris as meaning the Nile and of Isis as meaning Egypt, and argues for the more general interpretation as meaning water and earth in general (for the Egyptian himself the two interpretations merge). The third explanation of Osiris as the halfway personally conceived λόγος θεοῦ (cf. 1-3; 58-61; 68) is connected with the Naassene Preaching and Aelian (Apion?); cf. Hist. an. X 29 with Plutarch, c. 2.

44. According to this view Christian gnosticism becomes the expression, not merely comprehensible but even necessary, of Hellenistic piety, even where it does not arise out of Judaism or paganism. When the devotee of Attis desires to attain for himself the powers and the revelations of the new religion as well, or when the Christian desires, by means of the addition of further mysteries, to quiet a thirst for knowledge which has not yet been satisfied or a religious yearning, according to the Hellenistic view this is a pious act. The only question is whether their religious force is strong enough to exert an influence upon others. They do not conceive of themselves at all as creating a new religion in this mixture; thus in most cases the Christian does not feel obliged to leave the church. Yet the whole idea of the church is not basically "Hellenistic". From the very first it sets Christianity apart from its pagan competitors, and a reasonable measure of understanding of its language and ideas can be gained only from the perspective afforded by Judaism.

45. On the following, cf. Appendix X.

46. Because of the passionate polemic that was once directed against Dieterich, I should mention explicitly that I too see the enigmatic saying of such an utterly Hellenistic bit of writing as I John is in all its particulars, "Whoso-

ever is born of God does not sin, because his seed remains in him" (3:9), as traceable essentially to this same perspective. The only difference is that I believe another idea has been mingled with it, one which hardly allows this origin any longer to be recognized by the writer; even the Word (λόγος) can be identified as seed--it is sown--and the Logos is understood as the seed of God in the full sense in the very circle of thought from which this writing comes. On this see further Appendices X and XVII.

47. Cf. Pap. Berol. II (above, p. 95, n. 39): esp. the words εἰς γὰρ Ἅιδην οὐ χωρήσει πνεῦμα ἀέριον συσταθὲν κραταιῷ παρέδρῳ. τούτῳ γὰρ πάντα ὑπόκειται. The religious concept would be the νοῦς (it appears in the Poimandres throughout as πάρεδρος δαίμων) or the second soul, the πνεῦμα θεοῦ. The word συνίστασθαι has become almost the technical expression for ὁμιλεῖν θεῷ.

48. Here it cannot be denied that he is influenced, not by ancient Greek views that have come down to him through the literature, but by Hellenistic mystery views. When he adds the idea that the deity through its contact with these married women makes them into virgins once again, this too is owed to the sources which he utilizes.

49. This appears very clearly in an alchemistic text which has been preserved in two versions (Berthelot, *Alchimistes grecs* 28-29 and 53-54): Isis tells her son Horus that she once entered a shrine in order to gain secret knowledge. The deity who appeared to her there demanded her love in exchange for the knowledge; she granted it to him and adjured him to reveal the knowledge only to the child which she would bear him, ἵνα ᾖ αὐτὸς σύ, καὶ σὺ αὐτός (imitation of a Hellenistic prayer-formula).

50. This will explain the fact that in the Christian revision of the Poimandres prayer (Pap. Berol. 9794) the colorless expression δέξαι λ[ιτανείας ἀγ]νάς is inserted in place of δέξαι λογικὰς θυσίας ἁγνάς.

51. Cf. Appendix V.

52. Cf. Appendix XI.

53. The common Oriental idea of the σωτήρ as the savior-king, which was also taken over into Judaism, hardly has any closer connection with the designation from the mysteries,

"the one who makes alive" (Syrian). Paul avoids the word, as he also avoids Ἅιδης, εἱμαρμένη, and others, but his usage of σῴζειν corresponds to the Hellenistic.

54. Cf. Appendix XII.

55. Diodorus II 29.4: παρὰ μὲν γὰρ τοῖς Χαλδαίοις ἐκ γένους ἡ τούτων φιλοσοφία παραδέδοται, καὶ παῖς παρὰ πατρὸς διαδέχεται τῶν ἄλλων λειτουργιῶν πασῶν ἀπολελυμένος. διὸ καὶ γονεῖς ἔχοντες διδασκάλους ἅμα μὲν ἀφθόνως ἅπαντα μανθάνουσιν, ἅμα δὲ τοῖς παραγγελλομένοις προσέχουσι πιστεύοντες βεβαιότερον (according to E. Schwartz probably from Poseidonios; Hecataeus is far more sober in what he says about the Egyptian priests, in Diodorus I 73.5). The statement appears to be applicable to the highest classes of the Babylonian priests, but among the Egyptians only to a certain degree. In other places it could be a matter of a family-cult (cf. the decree of the senate about the bacchanalia), and it is understandable that in the Diaspora there was a contrived imitation of the cult.

56. I would not take these to be gifts for the deceased; they are different.

57. Cf. Porphyry, De abst. IV 16, where the connection of the garment with the belief in the pilgrimage of the soul is due only to the scholarly reinterpretation by Pallas. The Osiris-garment is described by Plutarch, De Is. et Os. 77 (φωτοειδές), and that of the Ἰσιακοί in chapter 3. Heraiskos' garment of the deceased (Photios, Bibl. cod. 242 p. 343a 29 Bek.) will also be a mystery-garment; the Christian monk also in fact is buried in the robe that he wore at his reception into the order. Here I only refer to the garment in the hymn of the soul in the Acts of Thomas and in the funerary texts of the Mandaeans (and the Manichaeans).

58. A banquet for the soul that is exalted to heaven is represented in the tomb of Vibia (Maass, Orpheus 219). The *Septem pii* that appear there recur also in Manichaeism (Bang, Manich. Beichtspiegel, *Museon* 1924, p. 220). Similar is the idea in the martyrdom of Agathonike *et passim*. Yet the festal meal of the community also allows of another interpretation.

59. On the first passage cf. Appendix II, p. 217; on the second, Kenyon, *Greek Papyri* I, p. 116, and *Poimandres*, p. 20; on the third, Kenyon, *op. cit.*, I, p. 102: ἧκέ μοι, τὸ πνεῦμα τὸ ἀεροπετές, καλούμενον συμβόλοις καὶ ὀνόμασιν ἀφθέγκτοις ἐπὶ τὴν λυχνομαντίαν ταύτην, ἥν ποιῶ, καὶ ἔμβηθι αὐτοῦ εἰς τὴν

ψυχήν, ἵνα τυπώσηται τὴν ἀθάνατον μορφὴν ἐν φωτὶ κραταιῷ καὶ ἀφθάρτῳ.

60. Cf. Corp. herm. I 22; VII 3.

61. Thus in Egypt, touching one with the bloody shank of a bull once again opens the mouth of the deceased person; Wiedemann, *Archiv für Religionswissenschaft* XXII 1924, pp. 83-84.

62. Originally it is, as Indian parallels show, probably the garment of the world-deity, the Aion.

63. Cf. Appendices II and XIII.

64. In others, like the Asclepius or λόγος τέλειος, we find insertions like the Apocalypse, chapters 24-26; cf. Reitzenstein-Schaeder I 2, pp. 43-44.

65. Philo was already familiar with teachings about this rebirth; in his interpretation the ascent was achieved in seven stages. Cf. below, p. 343. The wording of the Hermetic passage is found in the appendix of my book, *Poimandres*.

66. The expression certainly is strange, but it should not be emended, as Scott does; alchemistic mysticism speaks of the act of creating the "new" man as καινουργεῖν; in the Mithras liturgy 4.3 the σῶμα τέλειον, our celestial Self, is described as διαπεπλασμένον ὑπὸ βραχίονος ἐντίμου. If it is thought of as the λόγος θεοῦ, one speaks of a συνάρθρωσις τοῦ λόγου (thus our tractate §8; then, in the description of the process §9 adds συνετέθη <ἡ> νοερὰ γένεσις; the birth is a fitting together of the various individual members that are already at hand. Immediately after this the "begetter" is mentioned.)

67. Cf. the Mithras liturgy below, Appendix II, pp. 204ff.

68. As according to Plutarch, De Is. et Os., chapter 2, Isis assembles the Logos in the heart of the initiate. On the mystery-conception cf. Appendix XIII.

69. Cf. τοῦτό ἐστι τὸ ἀγαθὸν τέλος τοῖς γνῶσιν ἐσχηκόσιν θεωθῆναι, in Corp. Herm. I (26), a tractate borrowed from the Persian.

70. Thus it is portrayed in the eleventh tractate (p. 97 Parthey). It should be observed that this tractate also dis-

plays an intrinsic connection with the first one, and appears to exhibit an Iranian influence.

71. The sign of the aion is the letter I, which can signify ten, but also one; cf. Monoimos in Hippolytus' Elenchos VIII 12-13, p. 232.20. He is also "the man". The comparison with the Hermetic writing and the Naassene Preaching is highly instructive. One can see here how a purely pagan speculation subsequently is christianized.

72. Fr. Bräuninger (in his Berlin dissertation, "Untersuchungen zu den Schriften des Hermes Trismegistos", 1926, pp. 14-15) rightly compares this writing with the fourth one (Κρατὴρ ἤ Μονάς, the designation for the πνεῦμα or the νοῦς). Underlying that fourth one too is a mystery-action (cf. Iamblichus, De myst. VIII 4, and with the latter, Porphyry, in Augustine, De civ. dei X 28), but as a figure, not an experience. But then in the words of IV 6, ἐὰν μὴ τὸ σῶμά σου (σου is lacking in M and a recent manuscript of Scott, but it is found in C A and in the excerpts of Neapolitanus) μισήσῃς, σαυτὸν φιλῆσαι οὐ δύνασαι, the subject is not so much the Aristotelian concept of φιλαυτία as it is the Oriental concept of the "self", which elsewhere is signified by πνεῦμα or νοῦς or τελεία φύσις (the spiritual and celestial counterpart). This concept, which Bräuninger could not yet know, makes it possible to demonstrate more connections with Oriental piety than he is willing to acknowledge, even in the second, more heavily hellenized group of Hermetic writings.

73. To be sure, in the only fully extant ritual (Right Ginza, Book II), the number of the parts is different (28, following the stages in the lunar cycle), as is the arrangement of the individual hymns (each one is a unit in itself, and this only more strongly emphasizes what each one offers that is new). The Manichaean number twelve surely is connected with the course of the sun through the signs of the zodiac, and thus with the two-hour blocks of a single day.

74. On the objections offered by Waldschmidt and Lentz, cf. Appendix XIV.

75. Plato (Alcib. I p. 121 c.) already had heard that Zarathustra was also identified as a son of God (son of Ohrmazd), as well as the primal man, who according to another view has reappeared in him and will appear again in the Saoshyant, the last redeemer. Since religion, knowledge about God, itself is a kind of divine being, this development is comprehensible.

76. [It certainly belongs to another hymnic cycle; cf. Appendix XIV.]

77. Later on it certainly was not connected thus with a cultic activity; the extant fragments are much too numerous and belong to entirely different manuscripts. Mysteries are expressly spoken of in the anathematisms published by Cotelier (cf. below, n. 81) and in Marius Victorinus, though it can hardly be ascertained how broadly or how narrowly they conceive the term.

78. It is the celestial migration through the twelve signs of the zodiac or gates. When the soul receives a gift in each of these, one is reminded of the Babylonian portrayal; see below, p. 193.

79. *Journal Asiatique* Sér. X, Tome 18, 1911, p. 566; below, p. 281; *Das iranische Erlösungsmysterium*, pp. 152-53.

80. In the twelve hours of the night, of course.

81. Windischmann (*Zoroastrische Studien*, p. 264) has printed, in an essay that is still useful, the crucial passage from the anathematisms of Parisinus Reg. 1818 which Cotelier (*Patrum Apost.*, op. I) published as a note on the Pseudo-Clementine Recogn. IV 27. Kessler (*Mani*, p. 430) says that he is printing them, but he offers only an excerpt in which the most important part is omitted. At the very beginning we read: ἀναθεματίζω Ζαράδην, ὄν ὁ Μάνης θεὸν ἔλεγε πρὸ αὐτοῦ φανέντα παρ' Ἰνδοῖς καὶ Πέρσαις καὶ Ἥηλιον ἀπεκάλει, σὺν αὐτῷ δὲ καὶ τὰς Ζαραδείους ὀνομαζομένας εὐχάς. ἀναθεματίζω πάντας οὕς ὁ Μάνης ἀνέπλασε θεούς (then these deities are enumerated). The reference here has been abridged; originally it read: Βουδδᾶν καὶ Ζαράδην, οὕς ὁ Μάνης θεοὺς ἔλεγε πρὸ αὐτοῦ φανέντας παρ' Ἰηδοῖς καὶ Πέρσαις καὶ Ἥλιον ἀπεκάλει κτλ. This passage does not contain an abjuration of Zoroastrianism; it deals exclusively with Manichaeism and with what survives in Manichaeism from Buddhism and Zoroastrianism. Hence it is impossible to connect the Ζαράδειοι εὐχαί with the Avesta or a part of it. It is a book-title, and only books used among the Manichaeans are mentioned. On the view of Manichaeism cf. Marius Victorinus, "Ad Iustinum Manichaeum" (Migne, P. L. VIII 1003; Gallandi, Bibl. patr. VIII 134): *Iam vidistine ergo, quot Manes, Zarades aut Buddas haec docendo deceperint?* This concerns exclusively a thesis of Mani which has nothing to do with Zarathustra or Buddha. Elsewhere also the little writing of Victorinus is most strangely

connected with the early part of the anathematisms. Only from these do we learn what is meant by the Manichaean assertion about the flesh of Christ. The mysteries of the Manichaeans are mentioned in both. The references found in Victorinus and in the anathematisms, for example about the connection of Christ with the παρθένος τοῦ φωτός, are complementary; Mani gives the teaching of the Persians and the Indians, but he is the emissary for Babylon. We probably may place the older part of the anathematisms in the fourth century; Brinkmann (Alexander Lycopolitanus, p. XXIII) is correct in his judgment about the later part. In the anathematisms now there later follows: ἀναθεματίζω τοὺς τὸν Ζαράδην καὶ Βουδδᾶν καὶ τὸν Χριστὸν καὶ τὸν Μανιχαῖον καὶ τὸν Ἥλιον ἕνα καὶ τὸν αὐτὸν εἶναι λέγοντας. It is here that we first have the original *liturgical* formula, which so far as I know has remained unnoticed. We recognize at once the borrowing from very primitive forms of the acclamation or, better, of the confession of faith of the community: εἷς ἐστιν.... The *pentad* which expresses the god of the world and of time seems to me significant. If one considers the fact that the coin inscription deciphered by Lidzbarski appears to characterize Mani as "installed by Mithras", one probably may assume that the four emissaries, diverse in time and place, are here thought of as manifestations of the one "mediator" who dwells in the lightship. Still more significant, of course, is the authentication of a corpus of translated "Zoroastrian" texts in use by the Manichaeans. Of course this says nothing about the age of the texts; adaptations are not only possible, but probable; but they are taken from Zoroastrianism and apply to it as well. We must still leave undecided the question whether this accounts for some peculiar facts which Prof. Schaeder (Reitzenstein-Schaeder II, pp. 275, 282) has noted, and whether we may seize upon a similar explanation with reference to texts that bear a strong Buddhist coloring. Where so many sources are still inaccessible, it is, in my opinion, hardly possible yet to say anything definite about original form and local variations of Mani's system. Meanwhile, it will not be superfluous to state what can be made probably by way of later developments of Zoroastrian teachings before Mani's time.

82. Literally: wake up.

83. That is, of the light-beings.

84. The task of the emissary also with the Mandaeans; Lidzbarski, *Mand. Liturgien*, p. 249, Hymns XXXII and XXXIII.

85. Of course it can also be identified by its light-counterpart as the latter's body; cf. above, p. 54.

86. In this case the Poimandres is somewhat comparable.

87. By way of comparison I add here the mythological antitype from the Manichaean account of the creation of the world, which Prof. Schaeder has reconstructed from the report of Theodore bar Konai. The voice of the living spirit speaks to the primal man who is in chains:

> Blessings on thee, Good in the midst of evils,
> Light in the midst of darkness,
> [God,] who dwellest in the midst of the
> beasts of wrath
> That do not recognize your honor.

And the primal man answers:

> Come to salvation, bringing
> The cargo of peace and of salvation.
> How is it with our fathers,
> The sons of light in their city?

Reitzenstein-Schaeder II 2, p. 263. Anyone who has a feel for religious texts will have no doubt about where the more original force is to be found.

88. In Hippolytus, Elenchos V 26.15 ff.

89. ἐνδέδεται (an altogether Manichaean idea).

90. Cf. *Das Iranische Erlösungsmysterium* 99. A kind of antitype is Enoch, whose purported writings also are based entirely on Iranian foundations.

91. Edited by Griffith, London 1904. Prof. Spiegelberg has revised the translation for my *Hellenistische Wundererzählungen*.

92. Diodorus I 25.

93. *Das Iranische Erlösungsmysterium*, pp. 77, 251, 264.

94. *Ibid.*, p. 101.

95. One may think here, for example, of the Ethiopic book of Enoch.

96. Bardenhewer, *Hermetis Trismegisti qui apud Arabas fertur de castigatione animae liber*, Bonn 1873 (Fleischer's translation, *Hermes Trismegistos an die Seele*, Leipzig 1870, gives only the first part; a Greek prototype is mentioned by Iamblichus, De mysteriis VIII 5), discussed by E. Norden, *Agnostos Theos*, p. 278A. I have analyzed it more in detail in *Die Göttin Psyche*, pp. 50-51.

97. Cf. Appendix XV, p. 398.

98. Examples in Reitzenstein-Schaeder I.

99. Cf. below, Appendix X, p. 311.

100. Philo must have had before him even a writing like the seventh Hermetic book, either in its own final form or in a prototype. I have explained (in the *Gött. Gel. Anz.* 1911, p. 555) the beginning of this book, which was borrowed in its totality from popular Greek philosophy. Cf. VII 1: Ποῖ φέρεσθε, ὦ ἄνθρωποι τὸν τῆς ἀγνωσίας ἄκρατον [λόγον] ἐκπιόντες, ὃν οὐδὲ φέρειν δύνασθε, ἀλλ' ἤδη καὶ ἐμεῖτε with Philo, De ebr. 95: τὸν...ὥσπερ ὑπ' οἴνου φλεγόμενον ἄληκτον καὶ ἐπίσκετον μέθην τοῦ βίου παντὸς καταμεθύοντα καὶ παροινοῦντα διὰ τὸ τοῦ τῆς ἀφροσύνης πόματος ἀκράτου καὶ πολλοῦ σπάσαι. As we shall see, for the mystical language of this time ἀγνωσία is a positive concept; in the hymn of the soul of the Acts of Thomas, the king's son (the divine being) in the world of matter is given a drink of ἀγνωσία (a poisonous or intoxicating draught of matter). Conversely, according to ancient Persian tradition the man Zarathustra receives the divine omniscience (γνῶσις, the capacity for vision) in a cup to drink, and he possesses omniscience as long as the drink remains in his body. Philo is no longer acquainted with the original sense and technical meaning of the words, and here--as remarkably often--by giving them a linguistically elegant paraphrase he transforms them into meaninglessness.

101. Cf. the Greek text in Appendix XV, p. 365.

102. On this cf. Appendix XV.

103. Corpus Hermeticum XII 7.

104. On this cf. the essay "Vorchristliche Erlösungslehren", in the *Kyrkshistorisk Årsskrift*, Uppsala 1922, pp. 94-95.

105. Turfan fragment M 2 (*Die Göttin Psyche*, p. 4): "God Ohrmazd (together) with the final God."

106. *Historia monachorum und Historia Lausiaca*, FRLANT, N. F. 7, Göttingen, 1916.

107. The reader will rather have the impression that it is improbable that a movement so significantly affecting world history arises out of such weak and non-distinctive forces as would appear from this presentation. And if he has some acquaintance with the literature, he will sense a lack of objectivity toward the "liberal theologians", upon whose labors this presentation is much more heavily dependent than the author is aware.

108. A number of prototypes from Iranian and Indian literature, in which the vision of the world-deity provides the basis for the message, may be found in Reitzenstein-Schaeder, Teil I.

109. Corp. Herm. XIII 15: ὁ Ποιμάνδρης, ὁ τῆς αὐθεντίας νοῦς, πλέον μοι τῶν ἐγγεγραμμένων οὐ παρέδωκεν, εἰδὼς ὅτι ἀπ' ἐμαυτοῦ δυνήσομαι πάντα νοεῖν καὶ ἀκούειν ὧν βούλομαι καὶ ὁρᾶν τὰ πάντα.

110. Stobaeus, Ecl. I, p. 275.18 W.: οὐδὲν ἐν σώματι ἀληθές, ἐν ἀσωμάτῳ τὸ πᾶν ἀψευδές. 276.5: οὐδὲν ἐν οὐρανῷ δοῦλον, οὐδὲν ἐπὶ γῆς ἐλεύθερον. 276.6: οὐδὲν ἄγνωστον ἐν οὐρανῷ, οὐδὲν γνώριμον ἐπὶ τῆς γῆς.

111. Cf. below, Appendix XVI.

112. Griffith, *Demotic Magical Papyrus of London and Leiden*, p. 107: "I am this figure of One Drowned (Osiris; see below, p. 275), that testifieth by writing, that rested on the other side (?) here under the great offering-table (?) of Abydos; as to which the blood of Osiris bore witness to her (?) name of Isis; when it (the blood) was poured into this cup, this wine. Give it, blood of Osiris (that?) he (?) gave to Isis to make her feel love in her heart for him night and day at any time, there not being time of deficiency. Give it, the blood of N. born of N. to give it to N. born of N. in this cup, this bowl of wine today, to cause her to feel a

love for him in her heart, the love that Isis felt for Osiris, when she was seeking after him everywhere, let N. the daughter of N. feel it, she seeking after N. the son of N. everywhere; the longing that Isis felt for Horus of Edfu let N. born of N. feel it, she loving him, mad after him, inflamed by him, seeking him everywhere, there being a flame of fire in her heart in her moment of not seeing him." Comparable is the Greek incantation in Wessely, *Denkschr. der Wiener Akademie* 1893, p. 44, line 709, and Kenyon, *Greek Papers* I, p. 105: λόγος λεγόμενος εἰς τὸ ποτήριον· λέγε ἑπτάκις· σὺ εἶ οἶνος <καὶ> οὐκ εἶ οἶνος, ἀλλ' ἡ κεφαλὴ τῆς 'Αθηνᾶς. σὺ εἶ οἶνος <καὶ> οὐκ εἶ οἶνος, ἀλλὰ τὰ σπλάγχνα (i.e, what is innermost, the essence, as in Appendix II, p. 206: οὐρανοῦ σπλάγχνα καὶ γῆς ἔντερα) τοῦ 'Οσίρεως, τὰ σπλάγχνα τοῦ 'Ιαώ...ἐφ' ἧς ὥρας ἐὰν καταβῇ τόδ' εἰς τὰ σπλάγχνα τῆς δεῖνα, φιλησάτω με τὸν δεῖνα τὸν ἅπαντα τῆς ζωῆς αὐτῆς χρόνον. Of course these passages could take on significance only if we could demonstrate something similar in the sacrificial practice. Here, as is usually the case, folklore only provides hints about where we should turn our attention. Who would have ventured, without the abundance of corresponding religious texts, to draw conclusions about the religious view of the awakening of a divine being in us on the basis of the healing magic mentioned above on p. 60? H. Lietzmann's penetrating studies on *Mass and Lord's Supper* recognize alongside the Jewish prototype an early "Hellenistic" expansion. These studies have prompted me once again to take up these indications, which neither purport nor are able to offer an "explanation".

113. Yasht 22. Comparable is the portrayal of the highest heaven, the Garoδman, in the very ancient Damdaδ-Nask; cf. Reitzenstein-Schaeder I, p. 29. On the character of the language cf. Appendix XVII.

114. It is not the perspective of the Mithras liturgy, according to which the initiate in his celestial body and double journeys through the heavens, and yet again it cannot be entirely dissociated from this perspective; this perspective in a certain sense provides the pre-condition for the development of the Pauline conception, and it can do this because it, deeply rooted in the religious views of the Iranians as well as of the Indians, has been widely disseminated, by means of the religious literature, throughout the world of Hellenism.

115. Another series of words and images, not always subject to strict distinction, is offered then by the comparison with the Mandaean and, insofar as it coincides with it, the

Manichaean literature. Here Eastern influences on Palestinian Judaism will come into consideration more strongly than those of actual Hellenism.

APPENDICES AND ELUCIDATIONS

92

I.

Approach to the Material, and Its Definition

What we are concerned with in the present investigations is not the Greek religion or religiosity as it developed in the city-states, nor the individual Oriental folk-religions as such, but a general expression of religious perspectives as it developed on the basis of both the above factors. Certainly the various separate nations and peoples contributed in varying degrees to its formation, but even when the Greeks assumed outward dominion its own specific property could no longer be distilled in its purity. The folk-religions continue to exist, but none of them purports or is able any longer to be limited to its own folk, its own nation. They have to compete in order to stay alive, and membership in the large political entities necessarily gives to this competitive activity its direction, its language, and to a certain degree even its concepts. Their missionary activity can only be directed to the dominant Greek world and to the world of the West that lies beyond it;[1] here also that missionary thrust encounters the least resistance. In this struggle, and with this mixing, there necessarily appear in the very center those sacral actions which give expression to membership and participation in the new religion and to the promise that it offers: those actions are the mysteries. Hence in the investigation of them we shall do best to recognize the essential features or *basic perspectives* of
93 that no longer Hellenic but Hellenistic[2] religiosity with which the greatest of all missionary religions, Christianity, struggled for centuries and by which it also was necessarily influ-

enced in considerable measure. In Christianity we must trace out its *effects* upon world history.

The manner and method of any scientific investigation must be dictated by the state of the materials to be used. For the present study the material available is extraordinarily scanty; we are, after all, dealing with secrets. Individual sacral actions are intimated to us only in outline, and reflections of them can be proven in some circumstances; the religious significance is more frequently given, and the words employed in a technical way in stating this significance permit us to draw inferences about the actions themselves. But we can almost never say which mystery-actions belong to particular religions, and where we assume an adoption by Christianity, we must refrain from what now appears to many a student of the subject as the most important thing, namely a demonstration of the actual origin of a given element. I do not consider this loss to be a crucial one. In the very nature of the case the proof of origin could never provide us with more than an interim result or an apparent conclusion. Even if without that proof the fact of borrowing is assured, still this has only secondary significance. In religio-historical investigations we are not, and never will be, so fortunately situated as to be able to start out from a specific number of well-known primitive religions and then analyze a newly emerging one as the chemist can analyze a mineral spring, whose ingredients he determines according to percentages. Let us take, for example, the two great religions about which we are best informed, the Egyptian, for whose development incomparably abundant material is available to us, and the Persian, which surpasses all others in religio-historical significance: how much of what we can demonstrate in Hellenistic Egypt we now trace back to Persian influence, and how much can we now identify as *Iranian* that

94 only fifteen years ago no one would have ventured to identify thus! We now search everywhere for connecting links and are amazed to discover how much information can be afforded us even by minor and relatively late religious groups such as the Mandaeans. Thus for our investigation only one other procedure is offered, one which I attempted to set forth and to offer theoretical justification for, after the first edition of this book appeared, in the *Zeitschrift für Neutestamentliche Wissenschaft* XIII, 1912, p. 14. In this procedure we do not begin with religions, but with the individual written works and compare as many as possible with each other. The perspectives and the religious language of the individual personality belonging to the Hellenistic stage of development are what is really valuable for us; the question whether we can assign them altogether or even only in the main to a particular religion is only a secondary issue; what we are focusing our attention upon in fact is not this religion, but the religiousness, the piety, of an entire period or stage in the development. Hence the perspectives of the so-called Mithras liturgy are significant for us in spite of the fact that we certainly do not have before us here the liturgy of the official Mithras-mysteries and no one can say how many believers its author attracted. In the "Poimandres" the speaker is one of the demonstrably numerous prophets who in those days felt themselves to be divine beings and desired to redeem mankind by means of their teaching; this fact would be important for us even if we had not recently learned that he used as a basis an ancient Iranian writing, and in spite of the fact that we still do not know how strong was the flock of his followers or how that flock was organized. Piety is a matter of the individual personality and must first be explored in terms of that personality. Then by means of the comparison of a number of such

individual pictures we try to gain an overall picture of the times. This may explain why so many apparently disconnected writings and facts are strung together here. Whether the procedure is correct must be judged according to whether it leads to authentic results.

Anyone who strikes out on a new path must expect that for the most part people will condemn him without a hearing. I have been neither surprised nor discouraged when it has been
95 reported to me that highly regarded colleagues have asserted, "I don't know of any *Hellenistic* mystery-religions", and thus an entirely different meaning has been given to the word "Hellenistic". It has been my hope that the book would offer the reader enough examples in which the religious element obviously is ancient Oriental and the Greek admixture must have entered in long before the beginning of our era;[3] of course I did not attempt to establish a chronological sequence, which indeed could never have been carried through successfully. I am obliged to depart somewhat from this earlier intention because so eminent a historian as Eduard Meyer, in his uncommonly widely disseminated work, *Ursprung und Anfänge des Christentums* (III, p. 393), which is devoted to the religious development of this era, on the basis of a testing of the thesis has rendered his judgment thus: "I cannot regard as established the proof that 'a Hellenistic mystery-religion' or rather several such competing religions had already been developed and disseminated in pre-Christian times; their development--even that of the Mithras-mysteries[4]--rather runs parallel to that of Christianity and in their later elaboration was frequently influenced by the latter." This latter assertion, which in its consequences
96 would have to re-shape completely our view of the relationship of infant Christianity to the surrounding heathen religions,

unfortunately remains without any attempt even to suggest a proof of its validity; I dare not venture to guess at its basis. Nor of course can I say where Meyer has sought that proof and failed to find it. One polemical comment draws exclusively on a passage from Wilhelm Bousset's *Kyrios Christos* (ET, 1970, p. 312), which Meyer in fact has misunderstood. Bousset mentions a statement of Wendland (*Zeitschrift für Neutestamentliche Wissenschaft* V, 1904, p. 353) that the *renascence* of the mystery-cults comes only in the romanticism of the second century of the Christian era. Meyer presents this sentence as authoritative. Unfortunately, however, he forgets that Wendland, who had placed the sentence at the beginning of his religio-historical labors in support of his derivation of the soter-concept from the cult of the emperor, against Wobbermin's derivation of it from the mystery-cult, has associated himself, in his major work, *Die hellenistisch-römische Kultur* (2nd edition, 1912), in essence with my view of the age and the impact of the mystery religions (pp. 184-86 *et passim*) and has stated that Paul cannot be understood apart from an influence exerted by these religions upon him. Meyer, who deals only with the word σωτήρ, then continues: "When Bousset...cites Σαράπιδι καὶ Ἴσιδι σωτῆρσιν, a quotation from the time of Ptolemy IV, as 'proof that the gods of the mysteries also in the earlier times held the title σωτήρ', it is in no way provable that these gods here are addressed as mystery-deities and that the title has a meaning at all different from its meaning with so many other deities who also received it." Bousset has said pretty much the same thing on the next page. Indeed, he likewise neither treated nor intended to treat the question of the age of the mystery religions as such;[5] his subject was exclusively the two derivations, both

of them incorrect in their one-sidedness, of the title of σωτήρ for Christ.[6]

But even though with this limitation of the concept of
97 the mystery-religions my book[7] appears to be just as little regarded as Wendland's major work, Cumont's book on *Oriental Religions in Roman Paganism*, Dieterich's Mithras-liturgies, and others, it will be necessary now at the outset to discuss, using some selected examples, in a summary way the sequential testimonies; I shall begin with the period just before the rise of Christianity.

With the fire of a Zealot Philo of Alexandria (De spec. leg. I 319-325) opposes those Jews who, in order to blend in with the Hellenes, turn to one of the numerous mystery-communities;[8] in that connection he makes an explicit distinction between their secret initiations and the public cultus of the Hellenic city-deities. He goes on to describe apostates who attach themselves to one of the many miracle-working and fortune-telling prophets of these publicly recognized city-deities, and--as is generally overlooked--he portrays these men very much as Lucian later portrays the Alexander of Abonoteichos; like Lucian, he will not call them prophets, but soothsayers. I consider this a "witness" that for me acquires still more significance by virtue of the fact that the same Philo is already familiar with most of the words and concepts of the later language of the mysteries, for example, the so crucially important concept of *rebirth*. It does not matter here that *perhaps* one can infer from Philo's words that he is talking here about smaller communities of a private character. This is the way mystery-religions almost always spread, and I have dealt with precisely such forms; these too, as we shall see shortly, become serious powers even capable of threatening
98 states. Thus I add at once a community that has been much

discussed in the last decade, whose rise we can date with some exactness: I mean the community established by a certain Dionysius in Philadelphia in Lydia, during the second or at the latest the beginning of the first century B.C.; the community's statutes are preserved for us in an inscription.[9] Upon a command of Zeus, this Dionysius combined an earlier cult of the Phrygian mystery-goddess Agdistis, who appears as ruler of the house or of the temple--the temple was private property and housed the old traditional family cult--with the cult of various Hellenic gods (or personifications); cf. line 12: τοῦ[τῳ] δέδωκεν ὁ Ζεὺς παραγγέλ[ματα τοὺς τε ἁ]γνισμοὺς καὶ τοὺς καθαρμοὺς κα[ὶ τὰς θυσίας ἐπι]τελεῖν κατά τε τὰ πάτρια καὶ ὡς νῦν [εἴθισται]; thus both Phrygian and Greek, as Weinreich interprets it. Of course the actual mysteries are not disclosed to us; the ethical obligations laid upon the members could suggest the influence of Orphism, but also that of Judaism, but we cannot say anything certain on this point. In the light of Paul's epistles, anyone likely would think here of the assemblies of the Christian communities, at first in private houses, and of their ethical discipline.[10] There must have been a similar organization among those worshippers of Hypsistos who are often attested in inscriptions in the region of the Bosphorus, though to be sure only in the time after the beginning of the Christian era;[11] in the same city are found various communities of the same deity, separated according to their "fathers" and "priests". Here we also find ἀδελφοὶ εἰσποίητοι united with and yet separated from the γνήσιοι, somewhat like the Gentile Christian and Jewish Christian members of the church in Antioch. The comparison is justified, for Iranian belief that had penetrated that area very early appears to have been assimilated there with Jewish faith. Now a Mysian inscription of the second or first century B.C. (Per-

99

drizet, *Bull. Corresp. hell.* XXIII, 1899, p. 592 and Plate IV) shows us the age of this hybrid cult and at the same time displays a strong similarity with the Dionysos- or Sabazios- mysteries, and in an altar inscription in the Thracian region a certain Sabazios-Thiasos venerates Hypsistos.[12] Such a student of the matter as Cumont has already long ago pointed out that infant Christianity first found its footing and was disseminated in such communities existing between Judaism and paganism.[13] But at this point I shall not go into this matter; instead, I shall select a witness about the great mysteries that tells us--perhaps superfluously--that Philo does not speak of the great and principal, purely Greek mysteries in Alexandria, as for example the Eleusinian, but of actually "Hellenistic" mysteries. From Rome, and indeed from the year A.D. 19, Josephus (Ant. XVIII.3.4) tells of the celebration of a ἱερὸς γάμος of a prominent matron with Anubis, which led to a temporary suppression of the cult of Isis by Tiberius. The priest, bribed by the man who was in love with the matron, reported to her the demand of the deity, which was thus her *call*, and then admitted the man to the bridal chamber where she was. The woman innocently told her husband and her friends about her experience and boasted of the divine favor bestowed upon her; only the impudence of the man who had taken advantage of her subsequently led to the disclosure of all that had taken place. One cannot place Josephus' statements under suspicion on the grounds that one can follow out the motif of such a deception in other, light, entertaining literature. The tone is not that of a bit of fiction or of a prank, but it corresponds in its details to that of a judicial determination that is explicated literarily, much like Livy's account of the unmasking of the Bacchanalia. Josephus could also be very well informed, for

the investigations of Oriental cults were admittedly not limited to the Egyptian ones. Even the Jewish community was affected by them, and more than four thousand Jews, Roman citizens, paid the price of being exiled to Sardinia for a swindle, according to Josephus much more innocent, practiced by four alleged priests. Even the Latin historians mention the matter as a noteworthy step for the Roman government. Now Egyptian belief actually is familiar with the idea of such connections of a deity with a married woman: the sexual union of the god Amon with the queen, who conceives by him the son who is destined to rule, is portrayed in the temple, and inscriptions give us the words exchanged between the two of them, the ἱερὸς λόγος of the sacred account.[14] But wives of high officials also early receive the honorary title identifying them as concubines and lovers of Amon. When theological writings in Greek with which Plutarch is still familiar and which he cites in several places offer a philosophical justification for this idea, their aim certainly is not to vindicate to later Greeks the divine nature of the ancient Pharaohs, but to justify a continuing mystery-practice. Philo now uses these justifications in his allegorical expositions, that is, in the passages where he employs the language of the mysteries: for the

101 mortal father the deity begets the son; he opens the womb, gives the ἀρχαὶ γενέσεως, and while the mortal man makes a virgin a woman, the deity, by his embrace, makes a woman once again a virgin. The survival of these mysteries is attested for Egypt by Rufinus in his Church History, and acquaintance with this view in Judaism is attested by the Midrash of Aseneth, the wife of Joseph. Gnostic mysteries such as the baptism of some of the Valentinians or the prophetic initiation of the gnostic Markos offer us further testimonies--we may not attribute the responsibility for this to Christianity. Fur-

ther, Lucian's report that prominent men in Rome brought their wives to Alexander of Abonoteichos, which itself sets forth such a mystery, becomes somewhat more believable, particularly when we recall similar aberrations in the last days of the czarist regime in Russia. I see no reason after all to deny that the Egyptian mystery whose shameful abuse in the year A.D. 19 led to the suppression of the cult of Isis had already reached Rome with the founding of the Isis-cult and the establishment of the collegium of the *pastophori* under Sulla; in itself it reaches back into an indeterminate early time.

I am led to still another witness by the obvious question of what precedent the imperial government could appeal to. When Livy gives the unusually specific account of the suppression of the bacchanalia in a breadth that is quite disproportionate in spite of considerable abbreviation,[15] I can only presume that it is his intention to offer a pattern for the treatment of such cases for his own and later times. The Augustan government is disinclined toward the incursion of Oriental cults at least since the principate was established. Thus here Tiberius is only continuing the tradition of his

102

predecessor, though to be sure in a more precipitous form. In Greece as in Rome the suspicion of immorality or even of atrocities lies over the secret cults; Philo poses the question, "Why are they secret if they are not criminal?", and the well-known letter of Pliny shows me that already in his time the same suspicion was also raised against Christianity, as it was so often in later times. And when I read further in Livy the speech of the consul, I see that he was explicitly opposing a *foreign* cult.[16] I hardly need to amplify the statement that the identification of the cult's founder as *Graeculus* does not guarantee that he was of genuine Hellenic origin. Livy identifies him as a priest and a prophet; the mystics

too speak in rapture. What we learn of the cult appeared to me, in the first edition of this book, to point more to an Oriental than to a purely Greek origin; such a wild religious mass-movement appeared to me hardly any longer conceivable in the Greece of that time.[17] Of the cult we hear that the rite of initiation was a ἱερὸς γάμος performed by the priest--it was preceded by a *castimonium* of ten days and a baptism, as in Apuleius' case--and we hear of sacred meals with food and wine, in which both sexes participated together. Finally we hear of an evaluation of the immediate revelation of God to the female leader or a priest, for which I know of no examples, at least

103 in the Hellenistic cult;[18] indeed, we hear of alleged ascensions to heaven (13.13). The conjecture was supported, even before the second edition appeared, by the discovery of a decree of Ptolemy Philopator:[19] shortly before that time a similar movement appeared in Egypt, which led to the surveillance of the Dionysos-mysteries ἐν τῇ χώρᾳ, i.e., outside Alexandria. All the priests of the mysteries (*mystai*) had to present themselves in person, demonstrate the source of their teaching through three generations, and submit the wording of their liturgy under seal to a representative of the government.[20] Thus a guard was provided against arbitrary reconstructions on the basis of alleged revelations. The reason for this is obvious. The Greek god had much earlier been equated with Osiris (cf. Wilcken, *Jahrb. des Deutschen Archäol. Instituts* XXXII, 1917, pp. 149-50); other deities from the vicinity soon followed suit;[21] the danger of arbitrarily formed mixed cults was imminent. The decree is aimed at them, and thus it is in and of itself a witness to their existence. Now the history of the spread of religions, for example that of Manichaeism, offers instances enough of the phenomenon that when they are suppressed by force in one place, prominent priests migrate

as missionaries to distant lands. The idea of a connection between the Egyptian and Italian movements, which were so close together in point of time, was an obvious one, and it occurred to me as evidently to a good many others (*Archiv für Religionswiss.* XIX, 1918, p. 191). Already at that time Prof. Cichorius in a letter called my attention to how close the connections between Rome and Egypt were precisely in this period. The impact of these connections is soon thereafter shown by the attempt, by means of the books found in the tomb

104 of Numa (Livy XL 29), to introduce religious innovations into Rome.[22] Cichorius (*Römische Studien*, 1922, pp. 21-22) then was able to supplement my statements by showing that M. Aemilius Lepidus, who as guardian of the children of Philopator had resided in Alexandria from 201 onward and was Pontifex maximus in Rome, had Philopator's decisions which were familiar to him from experience applied to the "Oriental Bacchanalia" (as Cichorius sees them) in Italy. Then in most recent times the discovery in Pompeii of the Casa dei misteri (Casa Item), which in any case belongs to the time of the republic, has provided us with surprising proof of a continuing life for these mysteries; they appear also to have enjoyed a flourishing existence in Campania.[23] If the objection is raised that there is no *compelling* proof here of *Oriental* influence, I could counter by saying that through Livy there is indeed a barbarian and modernizing influence proven; they are *Hellenistic* mysteries, and these as such suffice as proof of the existence also of Orientally influenced mysteries. Yet I do not even need this argument. Livy himself suffices to show what must have been involved in this case.

On the year 139 B.C. the Epitome of Oxyrhynchos (col. VIII 2) remarks: *Chaldaei urbe (e)ti...*, and the first editors of the material made the connection between this and an allu-

sion of Valerius Maximus (I 3.3), which is preserved only in the two excerpts: I (Julius Paris): *Cn. Cornelius Hispalus praetor peregrinus M. Pompilio Laenate L. Calpurnio consulibus edicto Chaldaeos citra decimum diem abire ex urbe atque Italia iussit, levibus et ineptis ingeniis fallaci siderum interpretatione quaestuosam mendaciis suis caliginem inicientes. idem Iudaeos, qui Sabazi Iovis cultu Romanos inficere*[24] *mores conati erant, repetere domos suas coegit.*--II (Nepotianus): *Chaldaeos Cornelius Hispalus urbe expulit et intra decem dies Italia abire iussit, ne peregrinam scientiam venditarent. Iudaeos quoque, qui Romanis tradere sacra sua conati erant, idem Hispalus urbe exterminavit arasque privatas e publicis locis abiecit.* The two excerpts are complementary.[25]

Valerius Maximus, who earlier has mentioned the suppression of the Bacchanalia, evidently utilizes Livy here, as he does extraordinarily often. It appears that Livy has explained the motives for the expulsion in a speech, as he did with regard to the proceedings against the Bacchanalia; in the case of the expulsion of the astrologers, it could be that his concern was to rescue from oblivion an important example for his own times of ancient Roman discipline. The fact that it was feared that the cult of Jupiter Sabazius would undermine public morality[26] and that altars were erected shows that we are dealing here with an orgiastic and certainly *not a genuinely Jewish cult*; even in this case its origin must have been investigated as thoroughly as possible. This time its envoys turned out not to be *Graeculi*, but Hellenized Jews, who had re-discovered their Sabaoth in the Phrygian-Thracian deity Sabazios. This is in harmony with the fact that a bacchic-orgiastic scene is represented on the earliest monument of the cult of Ζεὺς ὕψιστος (Perdrizet, *op. cit.*), and that in the later Sabazios cul-

tus a sexual union of the initiate with the deity is symbolically represented, as also in the later Orphic mysteries (Dieterich, *Mithrasliturgie*, p. 123). Indeed in Asia this deity is also equated with Dionysos. Cumont has already expounded almost all of this in two fine essays (*Acad. des Inscr. Comptes rendus*, 1906, pp. 63-64, and *Musée Belge* XIV, 1910, pp. 55-56), with important supplements offered by Schubart (*op. cit.*) and Kern. Schubart pointed to the references made in III Maccabees 2:28 about the edict of Ptolemy Philopator

106 against the Jews: as a sign of their belonging to the nation, all who persisted in Judaism were to be branded with the ivy-leaf of Dionysos (Sabazios), as was done in various locales with the hierodules of a deity, who in fact in many places even inhabited a particular section of the city and were named along with the citizens; anyone who voluntarily joined a Dionysos-mystery community became a full citizen and was regarded as a Hellene. Kern (*Archiv für Religionswissenschaften* XXII, 1923/24, p. 198) points to a note preserved in Hippolytus (περὶ Χριστοῦ καὶ ἀντιχρίστου, 49) from Jason of Cyrene (?) about Antiochus Epiphanes: τοὺς τότε ἐπαρθεὶς τῇ καρδίᾳ ἔγραφε ψήφισμα βωμοὺς πρὸ τῶν θυρῶν τιθέντας (the Jews) ἐπιθύσειν καὶ κισσοῖς ἐστεφανωμένους πομπεύειν τῷ Διονύσῳ (disregard

107 meant the death penalty).[27] The reference is confirmed on the one hand by Iohannes Lydus (De mens. IV 53, p. 109. 18 W), and on the other hand by I Maccabees 1:55: καὶ ἐπὶ τῶν θυρῶν τῶν οἰκιῶν καὶ ἐν ταῖς πλατείαις ἐθυμίων. Thus here we have, in the seldom practiced sacral usage, which was supposed to attest the solemn consent of all the inhabitants to the cult, full agreement with Valerius Maximus, or Nepotianus: *arasque privatas e publicis locis abiecit.* These Hellenized Jewish communities are to be regarded as followers of (Dionysos)

Sabazios. *Even then they were carrying their missionary activity as far as Rome.* But--it will be objected--here they call their deity Jupiter Sabazius, and this equation, which to be sure was also common elsewhere in the Orient, becomes dominant on Latin soil. Certainly! But on the one hand, no one guarantees that these Hellenized Jews came from the homeland or from Egypt--Valerius Maximus appears to have been very cautious in expressing himself--, and *on the other hand, in Rome they could not call themselves by Dionysos' name, because Dionysos-mysteries were forbidden under penalty of death.* Since the cult of Sabazios also appears closely connected with the cult of the *Magna Mater*--even the surname of Μητρικός occurs--and since Phrygian colonies of Jews were early Hellenized,[28] I see nothing to cast suspicion on Valerius' statements. When Wissowa (*Religion und Kultus der Römer*, second edition, p. 376)[29] nevertheless exclusively emphasizes that the Sabazios cult can be proven to have been in Italy and Rome only from the end of the second century A.D. onward, he fails to note that this is quite understandable; the cult had once been legally forbidden as dangerous to public morals. We would have to assume, and we could prove, that it continued to survive in secret. Even in Trajan's time the Roman Jewish community still was not strictly orthodox,[30] but either altogether or in large part worshiped the Ζεὺς Ὕψιστος Οὐράνιος and the Phrygian Attis together with Yahweh. The proof of this fact, which is extremely important for the primitive history of Christianity, I shall present in Appendix II, since it leads into other connections. For the present I shall only mention that when Attis here evidently appears in place of the Sabazios who had been forbidden by the state--he is in fact likewise connected with the cult of Cybele--a mystery-cult of Attis at that time is a probability. It is true that we are

most inadequately informed about this cult. So far as I know, it still has not been explained to what extent *personal* mysteries (the rite of initiation, the vow of silence, and others) existed in the orgies of Attis in the second century B.C. All the analogies of course argue that the basic features of the cult are to be placed back in the early period, and here also, or rather precisely here, influences from Christianity are less than probable; there is not even the shadow of a basis for the assertion that the cult had existed for a long time while the mysteries only appeared in the Christian era.

109 I prefer to give the study a different direction and to pursue the practice of the Roman government. The treatment of the Bacchanalian cult obviously serves as an example in the procedure followed by the praetor Cornelius Hispalus,[31] while this procedure in turn is imitated by Tiberius: a morally shocking mystery-cult becomes the occasion to fall upon other Oriental teachings that are regarded as injurious also. For we may go still further: the edict of Tiberius, which treats Jews and "mathematicians" in the same way, is after all only a repetition and contemporary expansion of the edict of Cornelius Hispalus; this is shown by Suetonius (Tib. 36), when after mentioning the Jews he says: *expulit et mathematicos, sed deprecantibus ac se artem desituros promittentibus veniam dedit*. Now we may say, on the basis of Tacitus' account (An. II 85), that the adherents to the Jewish as well as the astrological religion were compelled solemnly to renounce the practice of their religion or to leave Italy within a specified time.[32] This is an uncommonly important precedent for later times.

The most detailed report, that of Josephus, shows that the primary cause of offense was not the doctrines but the mysteries. All religions that have an initiatory rite (τελετή)

are intrinsically subject to suspicion, because an oath, or some substitute for an oath, is connected with such a rite.[33] I might go so far as to ask whether the accusations against

.10 the Christians which were repeated on down into the later times and which so strikingly correspond to the suspicions of Christian communities and groups about each other[34] can be understood at all apart from a strongly developed mystery cult, one that first was suspiciously observed by the state and in individual cases suppressed. For my own part, without this presupposition I cannot in any way understand even the account of the first persecution of Christians. Hence the present study cannot bypass a major question that is of significance for world history and that refuses to be settled quickly. That is so much the more impossible since the only account preserved for us has just been characterized by so eminent a historian as

.11 Eduard Meyer as a conscious and deliberate misrepresentation of the facts or of their internal connection. The situation of the philologist who speaks up on Tacitus' behalf against such a charge certainly is not an enviable one, since he appears as a partisan spokesman; that is all the more reason that he has the obligation to bring the demands of his scholarly discipline vigorously into operation, in order to show whether the critic here actually is a judge or rather the attorney for a party.

The well-known state of affairs is this: only Tacitus' account connects the persecution of the Christians with the burning of Rome; in his case this undoubtedly serves the function of making the emperor's responsibility for the burning more probable. For in contrast with all the sources that are preserved--among them the opinion of a contemporary historian who though embittered against Nero is generally conscientious, Pliny--Tacitus leaves some doubt about this guilt, by prefacing his account with the statement that one or some of his prede-

cessors had assumed that the fire started accidentally. He either softens the details related by Dio and Suetonius[35] that most gravely incriminated the emperor or mentions them only as rumors and describes the imperial concern for those deprived of shelter and the other necessities of life.[36] On the other hand he portrays what advantages the emperor gained for himself and for the city in the rebuilding. The accusation and condemnation of the Christians forms the conclusion of the

112 points made *against* him.[37] Tacitus' placing it at this point, in spite of the fact that the proceedings actually took up a considerable amount of time, is in harmony with his custom in dealing with minor issues to neglect the chronological sequence for the sake of the material connection. Besides, he has nothing more by way of dated events to report from the rest of the year. Any reflective author would proceed in the same way.

According to E. Meyer and many historians and philologists[38] the suspicion against the emperor is absurd; Tacitus provides enough points by way of vindication to show this. When most modern presentations nevertheless blame the emperor, according to Meyer this is to be credited solely to the refined skill of Tacitus' presentation, which, while appearing to be entirely objective and non-partisan, imperceptibly convinces the reader with the interpretation that is unfavorable to the emperor. Meyer finds it striking that Tacitus alone connects the persecution of the Christians with the fire (p. 501), but of course once again he explains (p. 506) that Tacitus must have drawn this from one of his sources; according to Meyer, it is not in itself incorrect, but it sets the course of events in a false light. Thus up to this point there is nothing that would argue against the conscientiousness of Tacitus; for the modern historian also must draw on his own

judgment for the light, that is, for the connection of the individual attested facts. Meyer concedes that the accusation
13 against the Christians as those responsible for the fire must actually have been made and eagerly taken up (p. 507)--by Nero? But Tacitus himself says, Meyer notes, that this reason was soon dropped.[39] "He expresses himself, *altogether deliberately, it seems*, very ambiguously: 'Hence those who confessed (*qui fatebantur*) were seized first'--he has *deliberately* [Reitzenstein's italics] left unclear whether he means those who confessed to having committed arson, or to being Christians, and this will continue to be a point of disagreement. His intention in so doing was to provide a transition to the fact that Nero's intended exposure of the arsonists becomes a proceeding against the Christians as such: 'then, upon their information, a great many others were added, not so much for the crime of arson as for the hatred of mankind'." We are not told how that could be; we are only assured, with great emphasis, that the Christians were not condemned as arsonists, and thus as common criminals, but, as Tacitus himself explicitly says in full agreement with all the other reports, because of their religion, as Christians. This is undoubtedly correct, but I do not see how it can be harmonized with the intention attributed to Tacitus to convince the reader of the emperor's guilt in the matter of the fire and with his introductory words. Meyer also appears to sense a contradiction in these two indications and hence to charge Tacitus with having deliberately made unclear statements in order to veil the contradiction. That is to say: Tacitus wanted to cast suspicion on the emperor and to create a false impression, but because he was conscientious he chose his words in such a way that they could also be understood

correctly; indeed, that he also explicitly told the truth, in addition to creating this false impression.

I cannot understand the psychology of such a procedure, and even less can I comprehend the words. According to Meyer

114 Tacitus *intentionally* made an ambiguous choice of the words *qui fatebantur*; the reader was to be able to understand it just as well to mean "who confessed themselves to be arsonists" as to mean "who confessed themselves to be Christians". If he understood it to mean the former, as appears almost necessary after the preceding *non decedebat infamia, quin iussum incendium crederetur; igitur abolendo rumori Nero subdidit reos* (thus *incendii*), he could not understand the "great many others" who were arrested on their information as only Christians, and he is bound to have been amazed that they "were added", not because of arson, but "for the hatred of the human race" (this is the way Meyer translates the reading of the manuscript that he chooses to maintain, *odio humani generis coniuncti*). But added to whom? To the informers, who themselves were released because of their giving this information?[40] Because of their hatred of the human race? How does this fit in with the *eorum indicio* and with the word *vulgus*? If the reader now, frightened off from that interpretation by such contradictions, should attempt to connect *fatebantur* with the confession of Christianity, this expression is at least odd for those who were known as Christians,[41] the rest of the statement is subject to the same difficulties, and indeed those difficulties are even intensified, for if the *fateri* does not refer to the arson, the words *haud proinde in crimine incendii*[42] become utterly devoid of meaning, and the connec-

115 tion between the clauses is completely removed.[43] In that case the author would have been expressing himself, not ambiguously, but meaninglessly. According to Meyer this is

what he did, in order to find the transition that led from Nero's intended exposure of the arsonists to a proceeding against the Christians as such. But according to Tacitus Nero intended from the very outset to hold the Christians as such responsible for the arson. How then can he be seeking here, in intentionally ambiguous words, the *transition* to that stance? Further: Tacitus wants to put the blame on Nero--the latter's blaming others falsely itself shows that he was guilty--and he relieves him of the blame by adding that the general hatred of the human race had forced upon the emperor the condemnation of the Christians as such! I am unable to find here the refined skill in presentation which, though apparently altogether objective and non-partisan, requires the reader to be fully convinced that the unfavorable interpretation is the only proper one (Meyer, p. 502). The fact that it has become the fashion to accuse Tacitus of *intentional* distortion of the truth has led Meyer to make this attempt at interpretation. Hence he has utterly neglected the main question: on what legal grounds were the Christians condemned? He gives a psychological explanation of the universal hatred of the Christians and assures us--evidently in opposition to Mommsen--that even without the burning of Rome the persecution of the Christians would have had to break out within a short time. One may dispute such unprovable assertions or not: the question as to the legal justification for measures whose effect extends over centuries is never superfluous.

Our previous attempts at explanation have not yielded a result that satisfies me. The objections made by Guérin (*Nouvelle Revue historique de droit français et etranger* XIX, 1895, 601) and by Heinze (*Berichte der Sächs. Ges. der Wiss.* LXII, 1910, pp. 292 and 332) against Mommsen's brilliant

essay, "Der Religionsfrevel im römischen Recht" (*Histor.* 116 *Ztschr.* LXIV, p. 389, *Juristische Schriften* III, 389), appear to me entirely compelling, though of course the efforts of these two scholars still are not convincing. Mommsen has stretched the frame too wide for his statements, which juridically speaking certainly are splendid, to secure an adequate foundation for the treatment of Christianity. For that foundation the question may not be simply "What was the attitude of the state toward foreign religion?" but "What was its attitude toward secret religion?" Of course such a secret religion would usually be a foreign one, but not every foreign religion would fall into this category.[44] A certain supervision was required even by the Hellenistic state, in which both Greek and Oriental secret services were traditional (on the latter, cf. the inscription of Philadelpheia, and on the law concerning supervision cf. the edict of Philopator). There too the suspicion was expressed that anything that requires secrecy is criminal, and nocturnal rites of consecration were regarded as immoral and for this reason shunned the light (Philo, De spec. leg. I 320). For Rome the reason for supervision is still more urgent. There are no native Roman mysteries; the woman's festival of the Bona Dea cannot be counted as such, since it was accessible to all. As Cicero expressly affirms (De leg. II 21), the law and the Roman custom were in harmony: *nocturna mulierum sacrificia ne sunto, praeta olla, quae pro populo rite fient, neve quem initianto, nisi, ut adsolet, Cereri Graeco sacro.*[45] All mysteries are forbidden, and, as the continuation shows, all καθαρμοί not commanded by a priest of the Roman state. The rationale for this emphasizes the danger to public morality and appeals explicitly to the *senatus consultum de Bacchanalibus* as the prime precedent. The mystery-oath was regarded as especially dangerous to the state.

This is shown also by the rumors that were circulated about Catiline and his band (Sallust, chapter 22),[46] but it is shown moreover by the mystery community of Philadelpheia, founded under Roman rule, which as a precaution posted in a public place its oath which obligated its members to a strict morality. As Nock has observed,[47] the Bithynian Christians employed a similar precautionary measure, and it did not fail to make an impression on Pliny. Thus Mommsen also must concede (*Strafrecht*, p. 641) that particular sacral forms and particular aims are established, which by law establish the culpability. It is necessary to take these as our point of departure.

Now if we take as a basis Tacitus' account of the first and most serious collision of the authority of the state and Christianity, and compare that of Livy concerning the Bacchanalia, the course of events becomes comprehensible without any artificial constructions. Livy tells (XXXIX 14.10) that immediately after the discovery of the mystery-cult the city was guarded at night by soldiers: *ne qui nocturni coetus fierent utque ab incendiis caveretur*. From these "conspiracies" people expected arson (cf. Catiline) along with all sorts of other (especially sexual) crimes. The plot of a band of criminals appeared to be involved in the fire; it was in the public interest to find those who were guilty; and it is not surprising that people thought of the new secret religion. It was not only the rabble that regarded that religion as a criminal confederacy, but also later on such men as Suetonius and Tacitus. What could easily be ascertained at the outset was well suited to feed the suspicion: the Christians, who were longing for the return of their Lord, anticipated the world-conflagration that was bound up with that looked-for return; the zealots among them assumed a hostile stance toward the pagan

environment and the pagan state, and the moderates adopted a neutral attitude. How this was taken we see further in later pagan utterances as in Minucius (11.1): *quid quod toto orbi et ipsi mundo...minantur incendium, ruinam moliuntur!*[48] Hence one can hardly make an accusation against the Roman government out of one investigation into whether the Christians were responsible for the fire. But in fact in the light of this fact the often discussed question whether the Christians were put to death as arsonists *or* as Christians seems to me to be utterly misleading. Tacitus leaves no doubt on that point: *both* happened. It is not that arsonists had been sought out, who later turned out to be Christians, but "the Christians" had been arrested on suspicion of arson, and "the Christians", or, if one prefers, "Christianity", had been condemned, but--because it bore the blame for the fire. Condemned, and therefore of course forbidden for the future,[49] unless a successor should cancel the decision.

118

Now let us look at Tacitus' wording which we set out to explain: to turn the suspicion of arson away from himself, Nero had accused and condemned to the most frightful death--thus accusation and condemnation must refer to the same crime, or otherwise the whole narrative form becomes meaningless--those *quos per flagitia invisos vulgus Christianos appellabat.* Tacitus himself would not have spoken in this way; in his time the designation *Christianus* undoubtedly was as well established and self-explanatory even in the mouths of the Christians as Pliny, Suetonius, and Ignatius show. The agreement with Acts 11:26[50] convincingly shows that this term stems from Nero's time; they themselves would have used the name ἅγιοι or ἐκλεκτοί as a self-designation; the populace, holding them to be criminals, named them Χριστιανοί after the criminal crucified under Pontius Pilate. If we must trace

the first allusion either directly or indirectly back to the official proceedings, then of course we must do the same with the second also. It is unnecessary to talk about an addition made by Tacitus or even to construct inferences on the basis of the obvious agreement with I Tim. 6:13: ἐνώπιον τοῦ θεοῦ τοῦ ζωογονοῦντος τὰ πάντα καὶ Χριστοῦ Ἰησοῦ τοῦ μαρτυρήσαντος ἐπὶ Ποντίου Πιλάτου τὴν καλὴν ὁμολογίαν. The name of the long-since deceased founder of the religion is stated also in the proceedings against the Bacchanalia; here it is far from unimportant for the judge that the originator[51] had already been put to death as a criminal by a Roman official and that the despised land of the Jews is the homeland of this religion; this too is contained in the records, as of course is the outcome of the hearings. Tacitus' wording offers some difficulties, which to be sure have been exaggerated: *igitur primum correpti qui fatebantur, deinde indicio eorum multitudo ingens haud proinde in crimine incendii quam odio humani generis convicti sunt.* The genuinely Tacitean striving for brevity and imbalance of parts of the sentence that are homogeneous shows us the basic ideas: *primum correpti pauci,*[52] *qui fatebantur, deinde eorum indicio multitudo ingens, quae non fatebatur, sed convicta est,*[53] *non quidem in crimine incendii sed in odio humani generis.* As soon as this sentence is reconstructed, it becomes obvious that the reading *coniuncti* is utterly impossible. There must be a *convicti* to correspond to the *reos* (*incendii accusatos*), *fassi*; Tacitus has assumed a *damnati* following it in the series. The sequence is clear: the former group present no problem, and indeed the basic principle of Roman law is that *confessus pro damnato est*; for such a person no further inquiry is needed; but one who does not confess *must* be convicted. From this it follows that *odio humani generis* corresponds to the words *in crimine incendii.*

These are altogether precise and pointed statements about the outcome of the trials: the full confession of some few is followed by the collapse of the attempt at conviction of the great majority: no punishable act, but only an attitude of hostility toward the world could be proved. Thereupon all of

120 them were condemned to death. These facts of the case would hardly have been misunderstood if the unusual imperfect tense in *qui fatebantur* had not aroused some doubts; thus there arose the remarkable assertion that this *fateri* must precede the arrest,[54] and thus could only mean "those who were accustomed to confess their Christianity". In that assertion no note is taken of the fact that then it would have to be true of the *ingens multitudo* that they did not confess their Christianity, while the bold confessors immediately denounced all Christians. Then it remains utterly incomprehensible how they were convicted of the *odium humani generis* and why they were condemned to a criminal's death; the whole narrative is fragmented and meaningless, while with the other interpretation it progresses clearly and according to a plan. In such a case I would ask first of all: what other tense could Tacitus have used? The form *qui fassi erant* is ruled out; that would mean "those who had already confessed their guilt in the arson". The perfect tense *qui fassi sunt* was subject to misunderstanding and contrary to good style; hardly any other possibility remained but the imperfect of portrayal, or of the accompanying, more subordinate circumstance.[55] The real offense lies in a logical dislocation; everyone expects the simple narrative to read *qui primum corripiebantur, fassi sunt.* The main clause, as everyone feels, had to contain what appears to us to be the main point and is now found in the subordinate clause; otherwise the reader is taken aback. Might Tacitus have intended precisely that? He places the emphasis upon

primum correpti (sunt), and with similar emphasis he places over against that *haud proinde in crimine incendii quam odio humani generis convicti sunt*; a bad attitude could be ascertained, but no specific act, and only such an act is punishable. The objective statements must in fact give pause to any attentive reader. How strange: precisely the very first ones

121 to be arrested confess the arson and name the names of all the Christians; all the others do indeed confess their attitude, but a confession of actual culpable behavior cannot be forced from any of them, and none of them can be convicted. If we are not to assume an accident that was miraculously favorable to the emperor, then the police first seized those of whom they knew that these would confess, because they had been sent into the churches as spies.[56] I think that a reader familiar with the circumstances could hardly form any other opinion, particularly when he immediately thereafter read something that could be restated, as far as its content is concerned, as *qui indicium profitebantur* (cf. An. VI 3). Now the question arises as to which are the exemplary cases and thus the legal norms. In the proceedings against the Bacchanalia it was a matter of a religious practice that demonstrably had led to the gravest offenses, whose oath in fact obligated its adherents to do these things. All the participants were imprisoned, but only those against whom a criminal *action* could be proven were executed. Not even the oath that obligated them to this, and thus clearly set forth their intention, sufficed to incur the death penalty. Here imprisonment was sufficient punishment. Then the *practice of the cult* is forbidden; from now on, everyone who practices it is punished by death; *now it is the crime*. Since Christianity was not yet prohibited, a similar procedure had to be followed. Tacitus obviously regarded a prohibition of Christianity as necessary,

just as Suetonius did; as he explicitly declares, he believed the common rumor that it was a criminal religion whose adherents deserved death. But the crime of which they were accused *at that time* was *not* proven; one would have to search for others, convict them of those, and then place the religion under penalty. The cruelty of the punishment and its transformation into entertainment for the people he thoroughly disapproves; that sort of thing only arouses undesirable sympathy for people who in the interest of the state must be eliminated. The severity of the Roman gives us a contrary impression, but so does the pronounced sense of the tradition of the law, the shameless violation of which shows the judge to be the one actually guilty.

122

In my opinion it is doubtful whether with the available material we actually can prove that the insane emperor, who still craftily strove to cloak his crimes, must have been innocent of setting the fire. What has been adduced--precisely from Tacitus--for this purpose certainly does not suffice. That he had been absent at first is conceivable, particularly if he had the fire set, and his attempt to alleviate the distresses of those affected by the fire then was necessary. We do not know how strongly the contemporary sources followed by Tacitus agreed among themselves; we only learn from him that their agreement was not complete, and only he indicates that only psychological reasons settle the issue for him. Whether one approves of those reasons or not, this does not form the basis for accusing him of intentionally misleading his readers. The connection between the setting of the fire and the proceedings against the Christians, which is found only in his writings,--Dio's account is known only in fragments at this very point, and Suetonius, according to his plan of composition and his judgment, must separate the two[57]--should not

arouse any suspicion at least in the person who regards it as objectively correct. Thus it appears to me that Eduard Meyer's charge against Tacitus is based solely on his interpretation of Tacitus' words and that this interpretation is rendered utterly impossible because of its own internal contradictions.

Now let us see to what extent the next development confirms our construction of the matter. I need only to preface

23

this by noting that, as Guérin has correctly emphasized, as a rule the decision on such general decrees about religion were brought before the Senate and that this also had to be in Nero's interest and best explains the continuing force of the decision. But even if this sanction first came about under Domitian, unfortunately I know too little about his handling of this issue: in any case the crucial precedent had been set by Nero: the underlying issue was the *crimina*, but it was the *nomen* that was made culpable. The results that must issue from this are first shown by Pliny (ep. X 96, 97). A genuine alarm over these results prompts him, who first has strictly followed the general custom, to lay three questions before the emperor. The occasion for this is provided by the fact that he has been obliged to send a number of Christians, as Roman citizens, to the imperial court; it is in his interest to inform the court what has been his procedure and how strong the new sect is in his province. He also wishes to offer counsel according to his knowledge of the situation, but of course he can do this only in the form of stating that he is uncertain and is requesting guidance. The emperor also accepts this counsel in part: full immunity from prosecution is decreed for those who abandon their Christianity, and this immunity remained in effect.[58] For this there was, as we shall see, a precedent. The first question was: is the *nomen ipsum* punished, or the *flagitia*

cohaerentia nomini?[59] It will be seen that the condemnation of the religion ensues from crimes in the civil realm. Even Tacitus believes that the religion evokes such crimes (cf. the words *atrocia aut pudenda*; he must have been thinking of the Lord's Supper). Pliny has sought for such crimes and has not found them. Except for its folly, the cult itself contains nothing offensive. He has been able to prove that there is an oath (*sacramentum*); however, it does not obligate the adherents to commit crimes, as is assumed in the case of the mystery-oaths (the bacchanalian oath), but rather to avoid them; he has also found that they have a sacred meal, but it is morally
124 inoffensive and not actually secret, but open to the entire community. Moreover, many Christians have been neglecting that meal: *post edictum meum, quo secundum mandata tua hetaerias esse vetueram.* Thus in the edict Christianity is not specifically and exclusively prohibited; it is subsumed under the secret societies, by which the religious societies particularly were meant. Therefore Pliny asked the accused Christians three times--apparently at intervals--with specific reference to the penalties involved, whether they were Christians. Only if they persisted did he have them executed, as he was compelled to do, according to his conviction, by law and by duty. Such persistence is open rebellion against the command of the state as well as participation in a bacchanalian observance, according to the decree of the Senate. Pliny asks, secondly: is there a distinction to be made among punishments? In spite of the dreadful harshness of the proceedings against the bacchanalia, a difference was made there, though Nero did not make any distinction in his actions. Finally, as is actually already manifest in the portrayal of what he has done, he asks in the third place: is it possible to show clemency toward those who repent? For political reasons he would

urgently recommend such an exercise of clemency. In fact, he has already been acting accordingly: he has had the person denying his Christianity to offer a sacrifice to the gods--and *maledicere Christo* (thus there is an example for the anathemas later demanded by the church). Here the judicial fiction is that no Christian can do this, and therefore anyone who has done it is *no Christian*, regardless of whatever else may argue against him. The rights of the state are given very strong emphasis. Thus it seems a bit of tragic irony that precisely through this attempt at mildness the inner contradiction between Christianity and the Roman idea of the state and of religion must come to light. Anyone who can read between the lines will sense that Pliny wants more than this. In veiled fashion he poses the question whether the folly of a belief itself is enough to deserve punishment, whether the designation of Christ as God is a capital offense. Any Roman must answer that in the negative. It is Pliny's wish that the *nomen* remain unpunished, but that the *crimina* that might be connected with it be punished. But that would be a yielding on the part of the state and would evoke disgust from such men as Suetonius and Tacitus. Trajan tacitly rejects this, by giving full approval to Pliny's previous procedure; he wants to soften the harshness in a significant measure. The Christians are not to be sought out (*anquirendi non sunt*); denunciations are not to be accepted, but only complaints (?). Herein is the full contrast to Nero's procedure, a noticeable softening as compared with the practice employed in actions against the Bacchanalia. If the Christian comes into conflict with the authority of the state, the *odium* should in no case concern the officials. The principle of *nomen puniendum* is maintained, only it is applied as seldom as possible.[60] In

25

the general establishment of full pardon for the person who officially renounces Christianity it is shown that the state is concerned only with an outward acknowledgment of its rights.

As immense as this concession is for Roman feeling, Trajan has a precedent for it in Tiberius' proceedings against the Jewish propaganda in Rome, and he must have used it in his obvious dilemma, even though the two cases were somewhat different. In the investigation and the prohibition of the Isis-mysteries and of Jewish propaganda among Roman citizens in the year A.D. 19, Tiberius had the Senate accept the decree: *ut quattuor milia libertini generis ea superstitione infecta, quis idonea aetas, in insulam Sardiniam veherentur, coercendis illic latrociniis et, si ob gravitatem caeli interissent, vile damnum; ceteri cederent Italia, nisi certam ante diem profanos ritus exuissent* (Tacitus, An. II 85, on the expansion from Suetonius; cf. above, p. 126). People might seek, on grounds of fairness and justice, for a lightening of the earlier decree. That it had to do essentially with cultic prohibitions one could conclude from Tacitus' words and from Suetonius' statement *coactis qui superstitione ea tenebantur religiosas vestes cum instrumento omni comburere*, and insofar as it had to do with practices from the old Hellenistic-Jewish Sabazios-cult, the Jews could easily yield. Astrology, which with some justice was likewise regarded as a kind of religion, was similarly forbidden only in its practical exercise. The entire regulation, traced back by Philo to Sejanus' influence, had only ephemeral significance. But an example was actually given thereby for no longer punishing one for belonging to a religion earlier declared to be injurious to public morals, if it were abandoned in a definitive way, and Trajan seems to me to have utilized this example with reference to Christianity. This clemency had to be denied the person who relapsed. In

126

the period that followed the state steadily softened its stand; it purports to be satisfied with outward acknowledgment *also* of its own gods; but Christianity cannot grant that recognition, and the fearful and crucial struggle begins. The underlying legal basis for subsuming Christianity under the concept of criminal religions that had been shaped by the Bacchanalia and for the historic consequences issuing from that classification is provided by the one erroneous judgment about the guilt in the burning of Rome. Hence we may also demand from the historian a precise interpretation of the only extant account.

We see the prevailing of a fixed tradition which in fact we can follow also in lesser issues--thus when Neopythagorean wonder-workers are punished by Caesar, Tiberius, and Domitian with the same penalty, banishment from Italy. For the Armenian μαγεία, the religion of magic, the same principle was followed, and, in fact, as I shall show later, here always in the earlier harshness: the state has the right to forbid cultic activities and cultic forms that must or can lead to civil crimes and to impose criminal penalties upon the disobedient. Whether he has participated in crimes makes no difference: he is only asked about participation in the cult. The fact that the presupposition did not hold true for Christianity--at least in its predominant form--was first noted when it appeared too late for reversal and one could only recommend to the official in charge as much restraint as possible. Except for the fateful first mistaken judgment, the matter was not handled differently from individual mystery-religions that were once identified as objectionable. It is conceivable that from about the beginning of the second century A.D. some of the great mysteries had achieved a kind of general official recognition, and for these numerous "wit-

127

nesses" are now available; but this in no way justifies the conclusion that they had not existed earlier, and others besides these as well, nor the conclusion that "the mystery-religions" first arose with Christianity and previously were without significance for the general religious outlook. We have the obligation to look for indications of their existence.

Among these I reckon, first of all, ideas that have the character of the mysteries. As we shall soon show, they are closely related to magical ideas; indeed, the boundaries between cult and magic can never be clearly drawn. They have still closer connections with the so-called secret literature, which to be sure only seldom offers us writings that can be dated. By way of example I cite a recent fascinating discovery of Cumont to which this applies and which certainly is not connected with any actual mystery, but with the basic perspective of everyone.

There is extant a little writing, part of it in Greek and part in medieval Latin translation (Catalogus cod. astrol. graec. VIII 3.134, 4.253), from the physician and astrologer Thessalos of Tralles, who according to the testimonies of Galen and Pliny was held in high regard in Rome under the emperor Nero. In the foreword addressed to the emperor--Nero rather than Claudius[61]--he boasts of having traveled from his place of study, Alexandria, into the interior of Egypt: τῆς ψυχῆς προμαντευομένης θεοῖς ὁμιλῆσαι, συνεχῶς εἰς οὐρανὸν τὰς χεῖρας ἐκτείνων ἐλιτάνευον, δι' ὀνείρου φαντασίας ἤ διὰ πνεύματος θείου χαρίσασθαί μοί τι τοιοῦτο, δι' οὗ γαυριάσας ἱλαρὸς εἰς τὴν 'Αλεξάνδρειαν καὶ τὴν πατρίδα κατελθεῖν δυνηθῶ. Everywhere he inquires εἴ τι τῆς μαγικῆς ἐνεργείας σῴζεται, and finally he finds in Diospolis (Thebes) a venerable old priest of Asklepios[62] who promises to arrange for him to meet a god or the spirit of a deceased person. Both of them wait for

128

three days in strict asceticism;[63] on the fourth day he hastens to the priest, who has already furnished a little temple (οἶκος) that has been purified, and asks to see Asklepios and to talk with him in private (μόνος πρὸς μόνον). The priest reluctantly promises this. He has him sit down opposite the seat where the god customarily sits, goes out, and locks him in. Suddenly the god is there--his beauty and the ornamentation of his garments are beyond description--and, with his right hand raised, greets the hearer by name: "Blessed Thessalos, who are even now honored with God[64] and whom men will venerate as a god in the future, when your successes become known. Ask what you will; I will gladly grant you anything." Thessalos, who has foresightedly smuggled in some writing materials,[65] asks why he has had no success with the directions given by Nechepso about the powers of herbs, and is told that Nechepso had not given them out of divine revelation, but only out of his own knowledge, which to be sure was excellent; but he did not know when and where the herbs should be gathered. Asklepios reveals this, and Thessalos faithfully writes down his statement.

129 The time and the personality of the author make the writing uncommonly interesting; the connections with the magical papyri are conspicuous,[66] but the connections with Apuleius also are inescapable. Even though Thessalos may have secured the experience itself by fraud, he certainly had models to follow, and a miracle of this kind could easily be faked; he splendidly reproduces the religious perspectives and testifies, moreover, to the antiquity of this mystical literature. In fact, we still possess the beginning part of a very ancient alchemistic writing,[67] Βίβλος περιέχουσα τῶν φώτων καὶ οὐσιῶν τὰς ἀποδείξεις διδασκάλου Κομαρίου τοῦ φιλοσόφου [ἀρχιερέως][68] πρὸς Κλεοπάτραν τὴν σοφήν. ἐν ταύτῃ τῇ

βίβλῳ Κομάριος ὁ φιλόσοφος τὴν μυστικὴν φιλοσοφίαν τὴν Κλεοπάτραν διδάσκει ἐπὶ θρόνου καθήμενος καὶ ἐκ τῆς <πολ>λῆς εὐμενείας αὐτοῦ τῆς φιλοσοφίας ἐφαψάμενος. ἐπεὶ οὖν μυστικὴν τὴν γνῶσιν τοῖς νεύμασιν <ἐμυσταγώγ>ησέν τε καὶ τῇ χειρὶ ὑπέδειξιν <εἰς τρεῖς> τόπασας μονὰς καὶ διὰ τεσσάρων στοιχείων γυμνάσας καὶ ἔλεγεν....λαβοῦσα ἡ Κλεοπάτρα τὸ ὑπὸ Κομαρίου γραφὲν ἤρξατο παρεμβολὴν ποιεῖσθαι χρήσεων ἑτέρων φιλοσόφων. Precisely thus does Thessalos presuppose the writing of Nechepso. The names occur again in the list of physicians in the cod. Laur. 71.3: *Escolapius. Podalirius et Machaon eius filii, Asclepius eius nepos Escolapi*,[69] *Hermes Trismegistus, Manetho, Nechepso, Cleopatra regina* (probably the third bearer of the name who was called Isis). The fact that here the *komar* hands over the completed book, while Thessalos copies the statement secretly, makes no more difference than the fact that in the alchemistic writing of Krates[70] the author feels himself caught up into heaven, where he sees Hermes sit-
130 ting upon a κάθεδρα reading in a book, and an angel announces to him the contents of this book. Wellmann is on the right track when he (*Hermes* 35, 1900, 367) attributes those medical forgeries in part to the period of the Ptolemies,[71] as is Cumont when he draws conclusions from this about the religious feeling of the Orientals--though not, of course, of the Egyptians, I would add. In fact this belief in revelation and this type of revelation run through the entire "Hellenistic" magical and religious literature. The literary parallels cited by Boll[72] (*Zeitschr. f. neutest. Wissenschaft* 17, 1916, 129-30) could easily be multiplied; they lead from the Timarchos epigram of Kallimachos all the way down to the medieval story of the alchemist hermit Marianus, who allegedly was the teacher of the Omayyad prince Chalid, and indeed to a legend in the Turkish popular book of the forty viziers.[73] Literary depen-

dence can almost never be demonstrated, because the belief and the practice of magic are so universally manifest. Thus Cumont rightly goes into the psychological presuppositions. The agreement with the belief in the mysteries is often utterly amazing. What Thessalos pictures or Lucian offers in the description of the magician which he himself inserted[74] (Mithrobuzanes: the one redeemed by Mithras?) is the same thing that Apuleius purports to have experienced, only abbreviated and simplified.[75] When in the early or middle Ptolemaic period Petosiris-Nechepso presupposes the mystery-perspectives and in Nero's time Thessalos[76] tries to impose on an educated public, and indeed on the emperor himself, by means of such a bit of fakery, as I see it, we may conclude that the mysteries had already existed earlier in the Orient and were in some measure familiar in their basic outlook and perspectives. How long these perspectives survived in Egypt and what they signified to the pious here I have already attempted to show, more than twenty years ago, through a brief monastic tale which I repeat here (Cotelier, Eccles. graec. mon. I 582): εἶπεν ὁ ἀββᾶς Ὀλύμπιος ὅτι κατέβη ποτὲ ἱερεὺς τῶν Ἑλλήνων (of the heathen) εἰς Σκῆτιν καὶ ἦλθεν εἰς τὸ κελλίον μου καὶ ἐκοιμήθη. καὶ θεασάμενος τὴν διαγωγὴν τῶν μοναχῶν λέγει μοι· οὕτως διάγοντες οὐδὲν θεωρεῖτε παρὰ τῷ θεῷ ὑμῶν; καὶ λέγω αὐτῷ· οὐχί. καὶ λέγει μοι ὁ ἱερεύς· τέως ἡμῶν ἱερουργούντων τῷ θεῷ ἡμῶν οὐδὲν κρύπτει ἀφ' ἡμῶν, ἀλλὰ ἀποκαλύπτει ἡμῖν τὰ μυστήρια αὐτοῦ. καὶ ὑμεῖς τοσούτους κόπους ποιοῦντες, ἀγρυπνίας, ἡσυχίας (restriction to the cells), ἀσκήσεις λέγεις ὅτι οὐδὲν θεωροῦμεν; πάντως οὖν, εἰ οὐδὲν θεωρεῖτε, λογισμοὺς πονηροὺς ἔχετε εἰς τὰς καρδίας ὑμῶν τοὺς χωρίζοντας ὑμᾶς ἀπὸ τοῦ θεοῦ ὑμῶν καὶ διὰ τοῦτο οὐκ ἀποκαλύπτεται ὑμῖν τὰ μυστήρια αὐτοῦ. καὶ ἀπῆλθον καὶ ἀνήγγειλα τοῖς γέρουσι τὰ ῥήματα τοῦ ἱερέως,

καὶ ἐθαύμασαν καὶ εἶπαν ὅτι οὕτως ἔστιν· οἱ γὰρ ἀκάθαρτοι λογισμοὶ χωρίζουσιν τὸν θεὸν ἀπὸ τοῦ ἀνθρώπου. The little story throughout gives the impression of something actually experienced, and for the late period it has a certain significance, because it shows under what opposition the monastic life existed and the story was formed. But even for the early period it seems to me to be not entirely without significance. It splendidly illustrates how self-evidently for the Oriental feeling any kind of ἁγνεία and ἄσκησις provides a basis for claiming revelation. That the dreams of the κάτοχοι in the Sarapieion at Memphis could or must be full of meaning naturally follows from their being of divine nature. But more about this later.

For circumstantial evidence the language actually would have to suffice; here as always the language provides the surest testimony for the philologist.[77] I have posed the question whether one can understand the language of the New Testament at all without the language of the mysteries. The major part of this book was devoted from the outset to answering this question. If it is answered in the negative even for only a small part of the examples that I have taken from Paul, then the priority of paganism is proven and there results for the philologist the obligation to his own discipline to join in the task of explaining this language.[78] The theologian is somewhat limited by the fact that from the very beginning of his studies this world of thought and language is familiar to him and is a part of the given, and therefore he finds little in it that is strange. That should be easier for the philologist, who comes to New Testament Greek from a continuing preoccupation with profane Greek. Thus our collaboration will least repel those very theologians who themselves have become well immersed in profane Greek.

33 As a general norm for my investigation I have earlier established the position that for the period which alone is under consideration here, in procedures and perspectives in which Christianity is in agreement with several different pagan mystery-religions, the priority is probably to be credited to the latter. A borrowing of cultic *terms* from Christianity by paganism is more difficult to conceive; here the burden of proof always falls on the person who would assert the priority of Christianity. Whatever may still be in dispute in individual cases must be judged individually according to the character of the writing and the context of the terms. By way of justification I may add only that most of the Christian authors probably knew something of pagan literature, while only very few of the pagan writers would have known anything of Christian literature, and that in general conversion from paganism to Christianity was more common than conversion from Christianity to paganism. Until this is proved to me to be erroneous, I shall hardly be able to abandon these guidelines, and I must wait for proof that Christianity has influenced the pagan mysteries.[79]

For the purpose of these studies we may omit the question to what extent the cultic terms even of the Hellenistic religions have been influenced by the earlier *Greek* mysteries, which in the main have lost their significance. They do not directly influence Christianity. The earlier literature certainly must have transmitted individual words, but those mysteries that were limited to specific locations will hardly have had any inner impact; they lacked the propagandizing of prophets and missionaries and the support of established communities. It is surprising that Epicurus still makes numerous references to the mysteries and borrows from them, for example,

the use of the word τέλειος as Diels (*Abh. d. Berliner Akad.* 1915, pp. 41 and 93; Philodemus, περὶ θεῶν α', col. 24.12) has shown: οὐδὲ τὸν τε[λείως] τέλειο[ν οἱ θεοὶ π]άντες ἅμα [φοβεῖν] γε[ν]ομίζονται. If one connects this passage with Lucretius I 80-81, one will have to attribute to Epicurus himself or to one of his closest pupils the grand picture that portrays this τέλειος bursting open the gates of the heavenly

134 temple and bringing knowledge back to his disciples as booty (cf. Lucretius III 14, Heinze, p. 52). Of course it is precisely at that point, then, that the question arises in my mind whether Epicurus had not already heard of *Oriental* views of this kind. The agreement with the didactic writings that have their heroes ascend into the heaven of the gods that is guarded by a terrible monster and bring down from there the infallible truth is indeed quite striking.[80]

But even if that is doubtful, I should in any case assume for Poseidonios an acquaintance with the perspectives of Oriental mysteries. I have earlier referred to a passage from Seneca's ninetieth epistle, where he opposes Poseidonios but also makes heavy use of him (§27-30): *non est, inquam,* (*philosophia*) *instrumentorum ad usus necessarios opifex. quid illi tam parvola adsignas? artificem vides vitae; illas* (Codd.: *alias*) *quidem artes sub dominio habet--nam cui vita, illi vitae quoque ornantia serviunt--, ceterum ad beatum statum tendit, illo ducit, illo vias aperit. quae sint mala, quae videantur ostendit, vanitatem exuit mentibus, dat magnitudinem solidam, inflatam vero et ex inani speciosam reprimit, nec ignorari sinit, inter magna quid intersit et tumida. totius naturae notitiam ac suae tradit: quid sint dii qualesque declarat, quid inferi, quid lares et genii, quid in secundam numinum formam animae perpetitae,*[81] *ubi consistant, quid agant, quid possint, quid velint. haec eius initiamenta*

(τέλεται) *sunt, per quae non municipale sacrum,*[82] *sed ingens deorum omnium templum, mundus ipse, reseratur, cuius vera simulacra verasque facies cernendas mentibus protulit. nam ad spectacula tam magna hebes visus est.* §29. *ad initia deinde rerum redit aeternamque rationem toti inditam et vim*
135 *omnium seminum <se in> singula proprie* (ἰδίως) *figurantem.*[83] *tum de animo coepit inquirere, unde esset, ubi, quamdiu, in quot membra divisus. deinde a corporibus se ad incorporalia transtulit veritatemque et argumenta eius excussit. post haec quemadmodum discernerentur vitae aut vocis ambigua; in utraque enim falsa veris immixta sunt. non abduxit, inquam, se, ut Posidonio videtur, ab istis artibus sapiens, sed ad illas omnino non venit.* Seneca himself says in essence that the characterization of the main task of philosophy is taken from Poseidonios, and this is confirmed by its own distinctiveness. For him philosophy is the science of human *and divine matters and of their relation*; he bases religion on the inner experience. From him we have a kind of definition of deity (Stobaeus I, p. 34.26 Wachsm.): πνεῦμα νοερὸν καὶ πυρῶδες, οὐκ ἔχον μὲν μορφήν, μεταβάλλον δὲ εἰς ὃ βούλεται καὶ συνεξομοιούμενον πᾶσιν. That sounds like a formula of Oriental mysticism that repeatedly stresses concerning God: "He becomes what he will, and he remains what he is." It later finds expression in the cult of the Aeon as the παντόμορφος θεός or *omniformis deus*. In the Naassene Preaching it assumes the form of declaring that he is the life-force, in itself ἀχαρακτήριστος, but in the seed of the individual being or thing κεχαρακτηρισμένος. Seneca's words, which in the tradition are hardly comprehensible, seem to me to point to this interpretation. Later we shall also find in Seneca some mystery-terms and images which we must trace back to Poseidonios and in him to Oriental

or, better said, Hellenistic mysteries. Here the order, not altogether understood by Seneca[84] (first the vision of heaven, the deities, and godlike beings, and then of the true ἀρχή), seems to me to point to the same source. It is not unimportant that the image frequently recurs in Plotinus, especially in VI 9.11: οὐδὲ τῶν καλῶν, ἀλλὰ καὶ τὸ καλὸν ἤδη ὑπερθέων, ὑπερβὰς ἤδη καὶ τὸν τῶν ἀρετῶν χορόν, ὥσπερ τις εἰς τὸ εἴσω τοῦ ἀδύτου εἰσδὺς εἰς τοὐπίσω καταλιπὼν τὰ ἐν τῷ ναῷ ἀγάλματα, ἃ ἐξελθόντι τοῦ ἀδύτου πάλιν γίνεται πρῶτα μετὰ τὸ ἔνδον θέαμα καὶ τὴν ἐκεῖ συνουσίαν πρὸς οὐκ ἄγαλμα οὐδ' εἰκόνα, ἀλλ' αὐτό· ἃ δὴ γίνεται δεύτερα θεάματα, τὸ δὲ ἴσως ἦν οὐ θέαμα, ἀλλὰ ἄλλος τρόπος τοῦ ἰδεῖν, ἔκστασις καὶ ἅπλωσις καὶ ἐπίδοσις αὐτοῦ καὶ ἔφεσις πρὸς ἁφὴν καὶ στάσις καὶ περινόησις πρὸς ἐφαρμογήν, εἴπερ τις τὸ ἐν τῷ ἀδύτῳ θεάσεται.[85] Certainly we shall not be able simply to transfer to Poseidonios the extreme mystical feeling of the Neo-Platonist, but we may recognize in him the same picture, the entrance into a temple with the various images of the deities and the emergence from this place into a still more holy place, which allows only the sense of the impersonal, all-permeating divine power. But this itself offers a comparison on the one hand, for example, with Iranian ideas of an ascent to heaven--such as the ἐν θεῷ γίγνεσθαι of Poimandres--, and on the other hand with the powerful picture offered by Lucretius. The latter seems to me to be a re-shaping and an inversion of the conception that we find in Poseidonios.[86] Neither of these corresponds to the Greek arrangement of the temples or the Greek view of deity. Hence I even consider it possible that already in Epicurus' time or shortly thereafter reflections of Oriental mystery-piety had reached Athens, and I cite these passages not to provide still further *proof* of the priority of Hellenistic

mysteries in relation to Christianity--testimonies that are quite otherwise compelling render this absolutely certain, and, I trust, this will be even more clearly set forth in the further course of this book--but to prepare the way for an understanding of the style and manner of perception characteristic of these mysteries. The next appendix is meant also to serve this purpose.

NOTES

1. Even for Paul, other than the Jews only the Ἕλληνες come into consideration; it is a fixed, unitary concept that is attached to the culture. That culture is the instrument of propaganda of the ruling class. There is little question that the propaganda activity of the peoples in various territories represents the religious counter-thrust against a politically oriented and compulsory dissemination of the Greek cult. As a rule, a strong spread of the Greek culture appears to precede that activity, and, since the Greek religion lacks an inner strength, it prepares the way for an Orientalizing of the Greek piety rather than a Hellenizing of the Oriental piety.

2. As I have constantly emphasized, this word has for me the sense of a *designation of essence*. Only thus can one employ it at all in the history of religions, for which the arrival of Roman rule does not signify any kind of break. I also sense it as a deficiency that with this term only one component, and even the less important component, of a mixture is expressed; but I know of no practically usable remedy for that deficiency.

3. If we seek solid witnesses for the dating, we must realize the nature and the limited range of the literary pieces preserved from the time between Alexander and Augustus. Those witnesses cannot have been numerous.

4. Here it seems to be indicated that Meyer gives no credence to the well-known testimony of Plutarch (Pomp. 24) or rather to his ancient source; that source speaks explicitly of the initiatory rites. I can only appeal to the judgment of the best expert, Cumont (see now his *The Mysteries of Mithra*, pp. 36-37). Cumont even regards as entirely possible the associated supposition of Plutarch that the Roman Mithraic community arose at that time (67 B.C.), and he is firmly convinced of the great antiquity of the mysteries. I do not see what can be offered in objection to this view. On the other hand, I cannot share Cumont's confidence in connecting with the actual Mithras-mysteries the report of the elder Pliny (XXX 17) that Tiridates had initiated Nero through *magicae cenae*. A passage from Juvenal will later point us to an Armenian-Iranian cult that fits better into the total context of the passage from Pliny. It too of course was also a mystery cult and was at that time officially recognized for Ar-

menia; hence the king belonged to it. We may also presuppose a certain measure of antiquity for it.

5. His views on this subject are adequately indicated in Chapter VII of his *Hauptprobleme der Gnosis* and in the article on "Gnosis" in the *Realencyclopädie*.

6. Of course even less was he conceding what Eduard Meyer in the next comment has him conceding.

7. I have discussed the Mithras-mysteries not at all, and the Attis-mysteries only incidentally, because I have presupposed the presentations of Cumont and Hepding; in Meyer's work nothing at all appears of what I have cited as demonstrably ancient.

8. The intention here is clear; only these communities can establish an actual commonality of life with the Hellenes. The decree of Ptolemy Philopator, to be discussed later, even recognizes the Jew who has joined such a community as a Hellene and a full citizen. The oath of initiation is regarded as the renunciation of Judaism. In the kingdoms of the Diadochi it was in the state's interest to encourage such sacral associations, so long as they would admit "Hellenes"; this was not the case at first in the Roman empire.

9. Dittenberger, *Sylloge* (Third edition), III, n. 985; cf. Weinreich, *Sitzungsber. der Heidelberger Akademie* 1919, Abh. 16.

10. There are few more absurd assertions than the recent one to the effect that the mystery-religions were intended only for the pure, the righteous, or the holy, and that this constituted their difference from Christianity. The very opposite of this is constantly presupposed by the Hellenistic mysteries--even the passage from Philo under discussion--: it is precisely the sinners, indeed the criminals, that turn to them. Of course before their initiation they are absolved and make their vows to live pure lives henceforth. If they violate their oath, they are excluded from the community until they have been absolved. When Philo pictures the mystery-communities as recruited from robbers, pirates, and throngs of dissolute women, he is not too far from what Paul discloses about the former life of the Corinthian Christians. And yet for Paul the Christians as a community are the ἅγιοι and ἐκλεκτοί.

11. Schürer, *Sitzungsber. der Preuss. Akademie* 1897, pp. 200-201.

12. Oesterr. arch. epigr. Mitteilungen X, 1886, p. 238.

13. *Oriental Religions in Roman Paganism*, 1911, p. xxi. I had at first overlooked Cumont's warning, but later came myself, through the analysis of pagan and Gnostic-Christian writings, to a similar stressing of that part of Judaism that had dissolved in paganism (Reitzenstein-Schaeder, I). The fact that Cumont, in the work cited, explicitly emphasizes that in the Hellenistic Orient, "whose religious development in the last three centuries B.C. is almost wholly unknown to us", lie the closest sources for the West and that he emphasizes, as I do, that the Oriental mystery-religions are determinative for the piety, may be noted in passing. The attempt to set us in opposition to each other is based on selected details from earlier works and on the diversity of the tasks which we have set for ourselves.

14. Norden has recently pointed to the significance of this Egyptian theology in his fine book, *Die Geburt des Kindes*. I shall later come back to this theology and to the passages that are not cited in the text.

15. It is worthy of note that Cicero (De leg. II 37) has precise knowledge of the course of events and presupposes that his readers are similarly informed; for him it is the earliest and the normative example of the penetration and the suppression of a mystery-cult. One might conjecture that in the final analysis it is the *annales maximi* that underlie this information.

16. He would hardly have felt this way about a purely Greek cult of the deity who in fact had long ago been adopted in Rome.

17. Cf. the fine study by K. Latte in *Antike* I, 1915, p. 146.

18. On the other hand, to cite only one example, in the Phrygian inscription published by Ramsay (*Journal of Hellenistic Studies* IV, p. 419), the chief priest and πρῶτος ἀθάνατος of Hecate Epitynchanos receives, on the basis of divine revelations, the right of χρησμοδοτεῖν as well as of νομοθετεῖν, and indeed καὶ ἐν ὅροις καὶ ὑπὲρ ὅρων (this is the correct reading). In this context νομοθετεῖν denotes the

cultic arrangements (cf. in the Mithras-liturgy, ὡς σὺ ἔκτισας, ὡς σὺ ἐνομοθέτησας καὶ ἐποίησας μυστήριον [Dieterich 14. 33]); and the ἀθάνατοι are the initiates (cf. *ibid.*, 2.5: τὰ πρωτοπαράδοτα μυστήρια, μόνῳ δὲ τέκνῳ ἀθανασίαν; 4.7: μεταπαραδῶναί με τῇ ἀθανάτῳ γενέσει; 12.5: ἀπαθανατισθείς. The addition of καὶ ὑπὲρ ὅρων presupposes, as I may mention in anticipation of later studies, that the number of the ἀθάνατοι in their activity as prophets in the area belonging to the temple, their πατρίς, as the inscription says, was limited (cf. the inscription in Bull. de Corr. Hell. XX, p. 393: *Imp. Caesar Augustus fines Dianae restituit*--Αὐτοκράτωρ Καῖσαρ Σεβαστὸς ὅρους Ἀρτέμιδι ἀποκατέστησεν). Propagandizing in the Diaspora requires a special commission and special permission.

19. Cf. Schubart, *Amtliche Berichte aus den Kgl. Kunstsammlungen* XXXVII, Nr. 7.

20. It is assumed that every mystery-cult had liturgies set down in written form, like any somewhat complex magical procedure. Livy's source was familiar with the prayers and the oath pronounced by the priest in the presence of the initiates in the Bacchanalia (18.3), and with the name of the long-since deceased prophet and founder of the religion (8.3).

21. One may think of Dusares and the Ba'alim of various Syrian cities.

22. This too, as I shall emphasize in anticipation of the following, concerned the Senate.

23. I am informed about the paintings only through oral communications by friends, and am not yet able to estimate to what extent they confirm the account given by Livy.

24. This is still used as a formula in Diocletian's edict against the Manichaeans and the mathematicians (Chaldeans).

25. The treatment by Schürer, *Geschichte des jüdischen Volkes* (fourth edition, 1919, III, p. 57), is utterly arbitrary. He tries to attribute to Valerius only the words that the two excerpts have in common.

26. This expression appears later to have acquired the status of a formula (cf. Paulus sent. 5.21: *vaticinatores qui de deo plenos adsimulant, idcirco civitate expelli placuit, ne humana credulitate publici mores ad spem alicuius*--i.e., for the hoped-for advantage of the prophet--*corrumperentur*; cf.

Julius Paris). Philo portrays men of this kind in De spec. leg. I 315. The original meaning is shown in the proceedings against the Bacchanalia.

27. It was not at all the intention of Antiochus thereby to impose upon the Jews a new God, but only the idea and the cultic form which was already familiar to the Hellenized Judaism of the Diaspora. This idea viewed Yahweh as the giver of fertility, just as the Hellenized Syrian in many places viewed his Baal. Prof. Willrich has kindly called my attention to the interesting tetradrachma of Ashkelon, dating from the fourth century B.C. (R. Weil, *Ztschr. für Numismatik* XXVIII, 1910, p. 28; a better reproduction of it in Regling, *Die antike Münze als Kunstwerk*, 1924, Plate XIX, N. 416). This coin represents Jahu (the form of the name attested in Elephantine) as Triptolemos, though of course also in the external form of the Aion or Baaltar, the year-deity. This does not differ from the idea of the law-observing Jew who on a Roman sarcophagus to be discussed later, under the seven-branched lampstand, connects the ἁρβὸς 'Ιαώ of the oracle of Klaros with the winepress. In the edict of Philopator also the equation of Yahweh and Dionysos is presupposed as familiar in wide circles of Judaism; the only additional thing expected of them is to accept the genuinely Hellenic Dionysos-mysteries; then they will be full citizens. When Jews put in Dionysos' place his counterpart, the Thracian Sabazios, this naturally suggests the name of Sabaoth. It is utterly wrong to attribute this equation to the arbitrariness of later philosophers, as Ganschinietz (*Realencyklopädie* IX 715) assumes, or to a foolish misunderstanding of later authors, as Schürer (*op. cit.*) assumes. Whom should we hold responsible for this? Livy would be ruled out; he had a different view of the God of the Jews (Norden, *Agnostos Theos*, pp. 59-60). For Valerius or Julius Paris it would be unusual, to say the least, and altogether improbable; besides, we would then have to assume that Nepotianus invented the reference to the altars. If we reject that idea, this demolishes the entire assumption that the embassy of the Maccabean high priest Simon or, as Schürer expresses it more cautiously, people from their entourage had made proselytes in Rome and therefore were expelled, and thus also the assertion of Eduard Meyer that the Jewish community in Rome arose in the year 139. That community is older than that, and it grows out of the Hellenized Diaspora-Judaism. The coinciding in point of time of the Jewish national embassy and the expulsion of the Hellenistic missionary merchants can at the most suggest the assumption that precisely those law-observing men called attention to the fact that what was in-

volved here was not a genuine national cult, but a reprehensible mixture and innovation. It is not clear to me how E. Meyer (*op. cit.*, II 262, 264; III 460) conceives of the course of events, or to whom he traces the equating of Jupiter Sabazius with Yahweh Sabaoth. It is uncertain whether on this occasion or on that of the conquest of Jerusalem by Pompey Livy spoke of the God of the Jews. [Lydus offers a confirmation even if Willrich, *Archiv* XXIV 171, is correct.]

28. Adolphe Reinach, *Noé Sangariou, Étude sur le déluge en Phrygie et le syncrétisme judéo phrygien*, Paris 1913 (cf. Schürer, *op. cit.*, III, 17-18), offers some material on the influence which they exerted.

29. Cumont's two essays are cited there in note 4, but they are evidently misunderstood. How uncertain are the conclusions drawn from the lack of "witnesses" is shown by the fact emphasized by Wissowa himself (p. 323), that no inscription from the city of Rome before the time of Diocletian attests a taurobolium, while an inscription from Lyons dating from the year A.D. 160 explicitly derives the cult in that city from the Roman cult. I hardly need to recall the accidental discoveries of most recent times such as the proof of a Mithraic temple in Egypt in early Ptolemaic times, the discovery of the tomb of a Mithraic "lioness" in African Tripoli, or others. All this gives just that much greater significance to the indirect attestation.

30. The very tortuous account of Josephus shows that that community was not strictly orthodox in the time of Tiberius. Though the *nomen* and the recognition of Jerusalem are maintained, as is understandable in the Diaspora, the leaders are abandoned.

31. The punishment of the citizens who had been led astray must have been milder, or they all submitted to the decree; the Epitome says nothing on this point.

32. The freedmen (thus Roman citizens) who for religious reasons refused military service appear, according to Josephus, even to have been put to death.

33. It is not Livy alone who calls the Bacchanalia a *clandestina coniuratio*: the well-known *senatus consultum* proposes, using four synonyms, to make every kind of binding commitment subject to punishment. On the basis of thorough knowledge of the official sacral policy Dio also has Maecenas

advise Augustus to punish all religious innovations: the συνωμοσίαι καὶ συστάσεις ἑταιρεῖαί τε that arise from them are dangerous to the state. Pliny (ep. X 96.6) tells us that the latter expression was adopted into official Latin and that *hetaeria* does not signify the religious society in itself--the laws allowed this--but the society that was bound by an oath, one that conducted secret ceremonies (*clandestina coniuratio*). According to Pliny neither of these actually applied to Christianity. The Christians themselves had given some thought to whether their common meal was a mystery in the legal sense; it was in fact open to everyone. Pliny is inclined to recognize this distinction from the individual initiations which were in a certain measure oath-bound. It is judicially significant that even in the time of Pliny the governor's edict did not mention a religion, but only "the societies bound by an oath". It was the regulation of societies, associations, that was involved here.

34. In my *Hellenistische Wundererzählungen* (p. 143, note 2) I have indicated the connection between the two, in my opinion incontestable, and here I shall only add the explanation of the only accusation that was not given an explanation there. Even the "Thyestean banquets" appear to have had some kind of basis in an accusation against certain Gnostics. I have no other explanation for the little story of the monk Daniel (Apophthegmata patrum, in Cotelier, *Eccles. gracae mon.* I 421): a great ascetic is unwilling to believe that the bread in the Lord's Supper actually becomes Christ's body. Two devout brethren fast with him for a week and pray for a revelation. On the next Sunday, when the priest takes the bread, their eyes are opened: they see the bread as a little child. When he lifts his hands to break the bread, they see an angel with a knife come from heaven, pierce the child, and catch its blood in the cup. Then when the priest breaks the bread, they see the angel cut the child's body into small pieces. The ascetic is given one of these bloody pieces and, overcome, he cries out, "Lord, I believe!" Then the vision disappears, and the piece once again is bread. There must be a connection here of the conception attested as Christian and the charge made by the pagans (cf. the wording in Minucius Felix, chapter 9). This assumes no more than that very early in one circle the epiphany of Christ, which it was believed was experienced in the sacrifice of the mass, was connected with the idea of Christ as a child, an idea that was especially cherished in the early period. Dark rumors about this then could cause the suspicion of the *magica sacra* to be transferred

to the Christian mystery (cf. below, p. 185). These were regarded as deserving the death penalty.

35. Gercke ("Seneca-Studien," *Jahrbücher*, Supplement XXII, 1896, pp. 213-14) would like to identify Pliny as the source of both of them. That cannot be proved, and I am convinced that it is impossible. Even for Tacitus it is not possible to limit his sources to just a few, and E. Meyer has rightly rejected this argument.

36. Tacitus certainly did not cite as exoneration the fact that finally on the sixth day, when Nero at long last returned, the fire was halted by the demolition of all the buildings in a belt surrounding the fire. If the emperor was responsible, he would have been achieving his intended result just as well in this way.

37. Here I must also disagree with Leo ("Tacitus", a speech delivered on the Kaiser's birthday in 1896, p. 13): "Tacitus himself treats the fable that Nero had set fire to the city as unbelievable; and yet he does not drop the matter of the suspicion, but refers to it again and again, just as he does not fail to mention every accusation or to express the doubt over whether an enemy of the emperor was at work here." This is refuted by the mention, cited by Leo himself (p. 12) of the "very words" of the brave tribune Subrius Flavus: *"odisse coepi, postquam parricida matris et uxoris, auriga et histrio et incendiarius extitisti"*, and the addition by the author, *"nihil in illa coniuratione gravius auribus Neronis accidisse constitit, qui ut faciendis sceleribus promptus, ita audiendi quae faceret insolens erat"*. Tacitus is inwardly convinced of Nero's guilt, but openly admits that there is no compelling proof of it. The same may be said of other cases cited by Leo. We may refer in passing to Dessau's more sober judgment, which is much more favorable to Tacitus.

38. Among theologians I mention E. Th. Klette (*Die Christenkatastrophe unter Nero*, Tübingen 1907), because Meyer agrees with him on the main points. Only he substitutes for the twofold treatment a single one, citing an "interruption" which is incomprehensible to me. Klette's major mistake, it seems to me, is that he does not take the only account (that of Tacitus) as his point of departure, but rather moves directly to the conclusion, and does not interpret, but rather forcibly adapts it to what he thinks he has gained from wholly inadequate materials.

39. Of course if he had actually said that, he would have utterly destroyed the aim of his presentation as Meyer assumes it, and would have been acting not craftily but foolishly. So then Gercke also assumes not an intention but an act of negligence on Tacitus' part, who has assembled a mosaic from two contradictory accounts without noticing the discrepancies involved.

40. Cf. Juvenal VI 552: *faciet, quae deferat, ipse*; Tacitus, An. VI 3.

41. The passage cited by Andresen from An. XI 1, *fateri gloriamque facinoris ultro petere*, is hardly pertinent here. It has to do with a crime, a *crimen*; at that time in Rome belonging to the Christian community did not yet fit into that category.

42. The translation "because of the crime of arson" somewhat obscures the fact that *in crimine coniuncti* could only mean "included in the accusation", and could not form a contrast to the causal ablative *odio*.

43. This is not improved but worsened if this Roman reader interpreted *quam odio humani generis*, more correctly than Meyer, as *in odio...coniuncti* or here inserted *convicti*. Then it would mean for him that the overwhelming majority renounced their Christianity (!) and were included only as a consequence of their hatred of the human race (or convicted of hatred, but by what means?). Then the condemnation of the Christians would have been sheer madness. It is clear, as I shall note in passing, that *odium humani generis* here must mean more than the separation that the Jew practices; that had never been punished (Zeller, *Ztschr. f. wissensch. Theologie* 1891, pp. 356-57, incorrectly asserts that it could mean only μισανθρωπία); here it is the intent to injure, actual hatred, to which one could attribute arson. But neither the deed nor their belonging to Christianity is proved against them, so they were added to those who confessed Christianity (or declared to be convicted), for whom likewise the deed had not been proven! Who could comprehend that?

44. The real sacrilege, i.e., disruption of the state's cult (Clodius at the festival of the Bona Dea; cf. Heinze), of course has nothing to do with this.

45. An imitation of Greek mysteries (even the priestess must in fact be Greek) is indeed present (Wissowa, *Religion*

und Kult der Römer, second edition, p. 300). But it is as little developed as the sacrifice to the Bona Dea.

46. Meyer rightly points this out; comparable is the passage in Minucius Felix 9.5: *hac foederantur hostia, hac conscientia sceleris ad silentium mutuum pignerantur* (on the expression cf. the *Senatus consultum*).

47. *Classical Review* 1924, p. 58.

48. Stylistic influence exerted by Seneca, Ad Polyb. 1.2, is of course probable. Nevertheless the expression remains characteristic of the feeling of the time with respect to the doctrine of the world conflagration.

49. Suetonius, who does not use Tacitus, confirms the latter's presentation when he counts a suppression of Christianity among the glorious and genuinely Roman actions of Nero.

50. The name arose among their opponents in Antioch; Acts 26:28 also clearly follows this usage: Agrippa says, ἐν ὀλίγῳ με πείθεις Χριστιανὸν εἶναι, and Paul avoids the word (γενέσθαι τοιούτους ὁποῖος κἀγώ εἰμι). The tradition *Chrestianos*, which only apparently is suggested by the contrast with *per flagitia*, would only distract and disturb the reader's attention.

51. In the words *auctor nominis* Tacitus is following the language of his time; *nomen* is also the sect itself, as in Pliny.

52. This must belong in the train of thought, because of the contrasting *ingens multitudo* that follows.

53. Construed following *prehendere in*.

54. We are still seeing the influence of Haase's mistaken view that the imperfect is a purely relative tense, one that has reference to a preterite used elsewhere. It does in fact often occur where the person speaking has no interest in representing the action as still in the process of being executed.

55. Tacitus is rather free about alternating in his usage; cf., for example, XI 19: *sed caede eius motae Chaucorum mentes, et Corbulo semina rebellionis praebabat*; XII 6: *Postquam haec*

favorabili oratione praemisit multaque patrum assentatio sequebatur, and so on.

56. The confession should be given weight similar to that accorded Anicetus' confession that he had committed adultery with Octavia. This is not contradicted, as Gercke seems to assume, by the fact that in the account of the horrible death he says *quamquam adversus sontes et novissima exempla meritos*. Tacitus would render his own account and its position absurd if he connected this with the case of arson. He demands that his reader simply hear him out: they were criminals anyway (cf. above, *per flagitia*) and they were deserving of any punishment that might be meted out. He wants to prevent having his decision taken as a protest against the culpability, still existing in point of law at that time, of the *nomen Christianum*. Pliny's letter to Trajan, to be discussed shortly, probably had already been publicized at that time.

57. Moreover, it would not have been very prudent of the later Christian authors if they had referred back to a guilt with which they were no longer being charged and which had once been established as proven by a judicial judgment, even though prominent historians had subsequently labeled it as an erroneous judgment. It was far more effective when they kept to the accusations actually raised against them, which were never investigated at all, into which indeed the judge did not even venture to inquire, since the *confessio* (the *nomen*) was sufficient. Therein these Christian authors see the shocking and unprecedented occurrences.

58. As *grace*, to be sure. The emperor's words almost entirely rule out any similar mildness in case of a relapse, but he avoids making any absolute rule.

59. One should note this concept, which at the outset must seem strange. As I earlier indicated, following Mommsen, it presupposes a universal norm.

60. Not many accusers would be found who would present to an unwilling judge a complaint (on what grounds?) that the accused person could render illusory simply by denying it. There was no longer any sense of a crime, not a word of *crimina*, nothing of *maiestas* or of the emperor-cult. As Guérin rightly emphasizes, here the character of the judicial process, the *cognitio*, is maintained, even though a question and an answer would suffice to settle the matter: *confessus pro damnato est*.

The *coercitio* is not involved, and yet as much as possible was to be left to the consideration of the official in charge: *neque enim in universum aliquid, quod quasi certam formam habeat, constitui potest*. It is a halfway measure, which exacts a fearful vengeance precisely because it issues from a well-disposed and powerful ruler.

61. Nero's teacher Chairemon had made him especially sensitive to astrology and Egyptian secret literature. He provided a residence in his palace for the magician who boasted that he would visibly fly up to heaven (below, p. 219). In his last period then he adopted Armenian magical arts and methods of manipulating the gods (Pliny, XXX 14-17). He had a lively interest in everything pertaining to magic. [Unfortunately Cumont's essay in the *Revue de Philologie* XLII, 1918, 85-86, is inaccessible to me. In addition to the Catalogus I have used his presentation in "Le culte egyptien et le mysticisme de Plotin," Fondation Eugene Piot, Monuments et memoires XXV 77-78.]

62. Actually the sanctuary here is officially called 'Ασκλεπιεῖον, yet originally Imuthes must have been meant. He also appears in the religious literature as a revelational deity.

63. Apuleius also mentions the ἁγνεύειν. To the impatient Thessalos the waiting-time seems like three years. On the mystery-action cf. below, pp. 310-11.

64. This is the approximate meaning; the textual tradition is corrupt. The vision is the honor (τιμή).

65. ἐγὼ δὲ κατὰ προμήθειαν τῆς ψυχῆς εἶχον ἀγνοοῦντος τοῦ ἀρχιερέως χάρτην καὶ μέλαν.

66. The polemic resembles that in the religious Hermetic writings.

67. My restoration of the text in *Nachr. d. Ges. d. Wissensch.*, Göttingen 1919, p. 24.

68. The word is probably an explanatory gloss on the name (*komar* in Aramaic means "chief priest") which was added in the old edition to the picture as it is described here.

69. The Asklepios who is connected with Hermes Trismegistos is the grandson of the originator of the healing arts also

in Pseudo-Apuleius, Asclepius, c. 37: *Avus enim tuus, Asclepi, medicinae primus inventor, cui templum consecratum est in monte Libyae circa litus crocodillorum.* What is meant must be the 'Ασκληπιεῖον in Thebes, mentioned above (p. 145), which Thessalos had visited. Zielinski thought it was Cyrene, but there are no crocodiles there. *Libyae* only signifies the west bank of the Nile.

70. Berthelot, *La chimie au moyen âge* III 44. Poimandres, p. 361; cf. the "vision" of the monk Saba in Hebbelynck, *Le Museon*, Nouv. Sér. I, p. 20. I have already earlier referred to the vision of Hermas (in the Shepherd I 2.2): βλέπω κατέναντί μου κάθεδραν λευκήν...καὶ ἦλθεν γυνὴ πρεσβῦτις ἐν ἱματισμῷ λαμποτάτῳ, ἔχουσα βιβλίον εἰς τὰς χεῖρας.

71. It had already occurred to the lexicographer Pamphilos to incorporate into his lexicon a mystical plant-name (a code name) from a Hermetic writing which resembled that of Thessalos (Galen, Tom. IX 758K.).

72. Chiefly from the introduction to the Recognitions of Clement and from Lucian's Menippos.

73. *Religionsgeschichtliche Versuche und Vorarbeiten* XIX 2, 1922, pp. 76-77.

74. Cf. my *Hellenistische Wundererzählungen*, p. 20; Boll, *op. cit.*, 146.

75. The οἰκεῖος δαίμων, whom according to Porphyry (Vit. Plotini 10) the Egyptian priest proposes to show to Plotinus in the temple of Isis, is the ἴδιος δαίμων of magic, one's own perfect nature, the heavenly self of the religious texts that bear Iranian influence. It has nothing to do with the personal 'Αγαθὸς δαίμων (Laum, *Stiftungen* II, N. 117).

76. The charlatan is further characterized by the fact that in his burial inscription he is called 'Ιατρονίκης (as well as 'Ολυμπιονίκης).

77. Of course it can only be such a witness on the basis of collations and comparisons; such comparisons and collations are indeed the presupposition for any hypothesis of a borrowing, and the presupposition that such a borrowing is possible is the necessary precondition of any construction of a historical connection. Anyone who with insufficient reasons simply rules out this hypothesis *a priori* then arbitrarily gives the

decisive tendency to his own construction. Of course we can, as a consequence of centuries-long tradition, understand the thought and language of primitive Christian literature purely in terms of Judaism and development within Christianity, for we are familiar with it from our childhood onward, the ideas dogmatically reinterpreted according to the catechism, bent to serve the purposes of edification, and the words faded and lifeless. The question why a particular word or figure is chosen, what it originally meant, and what the contemporary reader had to feel upon encountering it, does not even occur to us any more; for unusual terms like "the body of this death" or "buried by baptism into death" we hear only "the physical frame" or "baptized". Thus the linguistic evidence escapes us. When the whole of modern (i.e., philological) interpretation of Scripture expressly constructs the history of a term, it is--whether the individual intends it or not--oriented to the history of religions, and only if one were to forbid the actual interpretation of the texts could one again ban the history of religions from the history of *our* religion. I hope that on the contrary a stronger involvement of Oriental philologies will rather heighten their influence.

78. Here I leave aside the fact that if he is religiously sensitive, he must feel this also as an obligation to himself; even if he has only a historical interest in the intellectual history of the West, he cannot at all pass over this issue or deny its validity.

79. Of course for me it is no proof when Christian authors speak of imitations perpetrated by Satan.

80. One may compare, for example, those introductory narratives common in the secret literature, which I have discussed in the Festschrift for F. C. Andreas, 1916, pp. 33-34, and in part already in *Poimandres*, pp. 361-64. The agreement seems to me to be compelling.

81. ἀπαθανατισθεῖσαι (*perpetuatae*). Bücheler remarks: *novum vocabulam tum fortasse ex apotheoseon ritibus increbruerat*. Possibly so; but I would say not solely from the one case of apotheosis of the emperor, but from the belief in the ascent of the souls that influenced that apotheosis.

82. Μιᾶς τινος πόλεως ἱερόν.

83. Thus I would prefer to write it. M. Pohlenz has called my attention to Cicero, De nat. d. II 81.

84. In §29 he would have to say *transit* instead of *redit*, but he probably is already thinking of *tum de animo coepit inquirere*; from the vision of the ἀρχή the way leads back to man.

85. The continuation shows even more clearly that a mystery-order is being imitated here. The decree about the Abaton at Philae (H. Junker, Denksch. d. Wiener Akad. 1913) can also make this perceptible.

86. To my surprise, Erich Reitzenstein, in his writing *Theophrast bei Epikur und Lukrez* (Heidelberg, 1924), has shown that we may no longer count Poseidonios as a source of Lucretius. What this distinctive re-shaping of the Stoic idea of God means with respect to Poseidonios I cannot pursue here; I only point out that precisely in him we may at least recognize the combination of Oriental and Greek life of feeling, which in recent times is being sought again in Plotinus. [E. Peterson (*Theolog. Blätter*, edited by K. L. Schmidt, 1926, p. 291) rightly emphasizes that Reinhardt, even in his recent studies of Poseidonios, has not done justice to this testimony, because he ignores the really religious and particularly the Oriental element in Poseidonios. Moreover, the myth in Plutarch's *De facie in orbe lunae* is so closely connected with Oriental ideas that anyone who relates him to Poseidonios must go into those ideas. Similarly the description of the elements in the Κόρη κόσμου, which stems from an earlier Hermetic writing; cf. Reitzenstein-Schaeder I 138.]

II.

Oriental and Hellenistic Cult

In the following I combine some shorter studies of Hellenistic cultic practice which can only be derived from the Orient. What is involved here is first of all a cultic practice that necessarily presupposes closed and closely knit communities, such as the mystery-communities in fact also were. Yet I by no means connect with that the assertion that in all these communities there must necessarily have existed such mysteries. In most cases the question could not be settled, and for our main purpose it would not matter. We must attempt first of all to acquire a feeling for the nature of Oriental piety, making use of as much material as is available.

For our point of departure I choose the institution of confession and penance, which in its original form was indeed proper to most religions, but in Greece as well as in Rome quite early lost its import;[1] the development of civil law restricted it to cultic offenses, and the only loose tie to the national cult weakened its force in this area also.[2] I should like to tie my consideration of the topic to a distinctive Oriental form which Franz Steinleitner has discussed in a splendid dissertation entitled "Die Beichte im Zusammenhang
38 mit der sakralen Rechtspflege in der Antike" (München 1913[3]). He starts out from a number of Lydian and Phrygian inscriptions of the second and third centuries A.D., which contain, in dreadful Greek, confessions of ritual offenses and divine punishments which then are lifted from the penitent by God's miraculous power. Literary witnesses from other regions and

other religions then are presented in a supplement, which itself is in need of enlargement. He does mention Menander's testimony on a quite similar Syrian usage (Porphyry, De abst. IV 15, p. 253 Nauck, Meineke, Fr. com. IV, p. 102), but not the Egyptian, which we shall discuss shortly--Steinleitner could not have known the Babylonian--and he has overlooked two important Latin witnesses which allow us at once to place in Rome what is attested in remote regions of Asia Minor two centuries later. It is an essentially methodological interest that prompts me here to offer an enlargement upon his statements, which in every respect are deserving of our thanks.

Tibullus pictures in Rome the same custom as do those inscriptions, in a passage to which I have frequently called attention because I could not adequately explain the religious presuppositions:

I 2.79 *Num Veneris magnae violavi numina verbo,*
et mea nunc poenas impia lingua luit?
num feror incestus sedes adiisse deorum
sertaque de sanctis deripuisse focis?
non ego, si merui, dubitem procumbere templis
et dare sacratis oscula liminibus,
non ego tellurem genibus perrepere supplex
et miserum sancto tundere poste caput.

139 It is immediately evident that we are dealing here with Oriental penitential ideas, specifically in the fact that all three sins recur among the few that are named in the inscriptions: first the sin of words, in Steinleitner's No. 12: ἐκολάσθη 'Αμμιᾶς ὑπὸ Μητρὸς Φιλείδος εἰς τοὺς μαστοὺς δι' ἁμαρτίαν λόγον λαλήσασα; then Tibullus' first sin by deed, in No. 29: Σώσανδρος 'Ιεραπολείτης ἐπιορκήσας καὶ ἄναγνος εἰςῆλθα εἰς τὸ σύνβωμον.[4] παραγγέλλω μηδένα καταφρονεῖν τῷ Λαιρμηνῷ, ἐπεὶ ἕξει τὴν ἐμὴν στήλην ἐξένπλον (*exemplum*).[5] With the second sin by deed cf. No. 16: Μητρόδωρος Γλύκωνος παι-

δίον ὧν ἀκουσίως κατεάξας στηλλάριον τῆς θεοῦ (a priest must have disclosed to him that his guilt, which apparently lay a long way back, was responsible for his bodily suffering). In all cases we are dealing here with ritual offenses, all the way down to an improper turning around or arriving late for the worship service. I place special value on Tibullus' words *feror* and *si merui*: it could be that he has been accused before the deity of these unintentional sins by deed; if he has actually committed them, he is willing to submit to penance. Such an acknowledgment of guilt to the deity is in fact common in precisely these cults; then the deity decides whether the accusation is just, by imposing, where it is called for, the κόλασις which impels the accused person to undertake sacrifices of cleansing and atonement and, above all, to humble himself by confessing his guilt *before the community*.[6] The divine miracle which is achieved in the cancellation of his κόλασις then restores him to his earlier place in the community; with this acknowledgment of the power of the deity and through the person's confession of belief in the deity the sin is completely cancelled. For the praise and glory of the deity a brief summary of the whole matter is drawn up and published. By way of documentation I cite only the inscription No. 10:

140 [Μη]νὶ 'Αξιοττ(η)νῷ. 'Επ(ε)ὶ 'Ερμογένης Γλύκωνος καὶ Νιτωνὶς Φιλοξένου ἐλοιδόρησαν 'Αρτεμίδωρον περὶ οἴνου, 'Αρτεμίδωρος πιττάκιον ἔδωκεν (a written complaint addressed to the god Men; it evidently has to do with the wine used in the cult, which is delivered or apportioned by Artemidoros). ὁ θεὸς ἐκολάσετο τὸν 'Ερμογένην, καὶ εἱλάσετο τὸν θεόν, καὶ ἀπὸ νῦν εὐδοκεῖ (he stands once again in esteem as before, and has regained his position in the community). Since such a denunciation to the deity is meant to effectuate the κόλασις through him, it naturally can be thought of as magic that produces

injury. Thus the διαβολὴ πρὸς Σελήνην in the great magical papyrus of the national library in Paris is the denunciation of a *sin in words* against the goddess.[7] This is not surprising; the original form of the Lydian and Phrygian inscriptions exhibits striking agreement with the much older Egyptian stone tablet of Nefer-abu (Adolf Erman, *A Handbook of Egyptian Religion*, translated by A. S. Griffith, 1907, pp. 78-79): "I was a man without knowledge, foolish, and knew not what is good and what evil. I committed [spoke?] sin against the mountain summit [the goddess of the necropolis, Merit-seger, the beloved of Osiris]. She chastised me, and I was in her hand by night and by day, and I sat there...like those who are pregnant. I called out for air but it came not to me....Behold, I say to great and small among the workmen: beware of the western summit, who is a lion in the summit. She strikes as a savage lion strikes, and pursues him who sins against her. But when I called to my mistress I found she came to me with sweet breath, and she was gracious to me, when she had let me see her hand, and she turned peacefully to me. She caused me to forget my illness which had befallen me. Verily the western summit is gracious when one calls to her. Hearken, all ye ears upon earth; beware of the western summit." The feeling is universally human. We will not be surprised when we find a similar belief and similar usage in widely scattered places. Only where the religious application and cultic order so precisely corresponds, as in the inscriptions collected by Steinleitner and the libellus (which he rightly compares), which Augustine (Sermo 322) read in the church, will we be obliged to think of a direct imitation and adoption of a pagan usage in the cult of the martyrs which at that time was being cultivated.

141

The people mentioned in the Lydian and Phrygian inscriptions appear to stand in a close relationship with their re-

spective deities; individuals are identified as ἱερός. Corresponding to this term is the Latin title *sacratus*, which can also denote the initiation into the mysteries (Apuleius XI 24) and the Greek ἀθάνατος (above, p. 156, n. 18), which certainly denotes that initiation. As Steinleitner rightly interprets it, that Sosandros in No. 29 has not forfeited his ἁγνεία through perjury; instead, he has sworn chastity for a certain time or a festival, but has not kept his vow. If we may not think of the *mystai* in this connection, we may at least think of circles like that of the *religiosi* or προσήλυτοι of Isis. Actually we also find a similar usage in the ancient (and thus non-personal) mysteries of Isis, or of Osiris at Philae. We see this in the Papyrus Dodgson (discussed by Junker, *op. cit.*, pp. 81-82), which contains an enumeration of cultic sins with ensuing threats. There it is said: "You know what you have done: you have drunk wine in the grove and the garden that are consecrated to the king Osiris Onnophris; you have done what Isis abhors, you have drunk wine in the night when the female deities were wearing garments of mourning." The sinner, who relied on the protection of the goddess Tefnut, appears also to be accused of having engaged in sexual intercourse with his wife during the sacred season, and of having drunk with the Blemmyes, who were aliens excluded from the festival, and in drunkenness slept through the procession to the Abaton. I do not know whether the proclamation of punishment is individually constructed or follows a formula, nor do I know whether the change in name is meant merely to shame the sinner or to exclude him from the community of the servants of Osiris; a close connection with the inscriptions from Asia Minor nevertheless appears to me to be evident.

We are taken a great deal further by the famous passage of Juvenal (VI 511-552) about the superstition of the Roman matrons, from which Steinleitner excerpts only a small part, (142) and which he does not correctly interpret. The poet introduces, in well-considered order, Phrygian, Egyptian, Jewish, and finally Armenian or Commagenian "prophets", and then he passes over to the astrologers. The main point of view is that all this superstition--except the Jewish--is very costly.

(I) *Ecce furentis*
Bellonae matrisque deum chorus[8] *intrat et ingens*
semivir, obscaeno facies reverenda minori,
mollia qui rapta secuit genitalia testa
515 *iam pridem, cui rauca cohors, cui tympana cedunt,*
plebeia et Phrygia vestitur bucca tiara.[9]
grande sonat[10] *metuique iubet Septembris et austri*
adventum, nisi se centum lustraverit ovis--
et xerampelinas veteres donaverit ipsi.[11]
520 *ut quidquid subiti et magni discriminis instat,*
in tunicas eat et totum semel expiet annum,
hibernum fracta glaciae descendet in amnem;
ter matutino Tiberi mergetur et ipsis
verticibus timidum caput abluet, inde superbi
525 *totum regis agrum nuda ac tremebunda cruentis*
erepet genibus. (II) *Si candida iusserit Io,*
ibit ad Aegypti finem calidaque petitas
a Meroe portabit aquas, ut spargat in aedem
Isidis, antiquo quae proxima surgit ovili.
530 *credit enim ipsius dominae se voce moneri:*
en animam et mentem, cum qua di nocte loquantur!
ergo hic praecipuum summumque meretur honorem,
qui grege linigero circumdatus et grege calvo
plangentis populi currit derisor Anubis.
(143) 535 *ille petit veniam, quotiens non abstinet uxor*
concubitu sacris observandisque diebus
magnaque debetur violato poena cadurco.
ut (mss.: *et*) *movisse caput visa est argentea serpens,*
illius lacrimae meditataque murmura praestant,
540 *ut veniam culpae non abnuat ansere magno*
scilicet et tenui popano corruptus Osiris.
(III) *Cum dedit ille locum, cophino faenoque relicto*[12]
arcanam Iudeaea tremens mendicat in aurem,
interpres legum Solymarum et magna sacerdos

545 *arboris ac Summi fida internuntia Caeli.*
implet et illa manum, sed parcius; aere minuto
qualiacumque voles Iudaei somnia vendunt.
(IV) *Spondet amatorem tenerum vel divitis orbi*
testamentum ingens calidae pulmone columbae
550 *tractato Armenius vel Commagenus haruspex;*
pectora pullorum rimabitur, exta catelli,
interdum et pueri; faciet quod deferat ipse.

Acts of penance are mentioned here only in I and II, but I must interpret the entire passage in context. At the beginning of the year--the poet exaggeratedly speaks of the Tiber being frozen over--the Archigallus demands an expiatory offering for the year just ended. Otherwise the κόλασις, which in fact is seen in the inscriptions usually as the fever, is threatened for the season when fever is prevalent. The expiatory offering itself is small and of little value--a hundred eggs; but the prominent woman must give the fine clothes which she has worn in the past year (*veteres*). One wonders whether these do not signify here the figure of her earlier body. Should the action that follows cause the κόλασις to attach itself to these gifts, then it has itself become a different κόλασις. We immediately recognize in this action the mystery-baptism, an ἀνακαίνισις: plunging into the Tiber over one's head three times, then crawling on one's knees, clad only in undergarments, around the sacred grounds.[13] This leads to the Egyptian initiations. What Isis demands is no less severe. She is to bring genuine water from the imaginary source of the Nile.[14] This means a pilgrimage to Egypt. The command to do this is believed to have been received from the goddess herself; here one may think of the dream of Apuleius (XI 3). The ὁμιλεῖν θεοῖς is indeed especially emphasized in the Egyptian cult. In Juvenal also it is understood as a τιμή (*dignatio*); for the words *en animam et mentem, cum qua di nocte loquantur* are meant to have an admiring tone--not a

44

scornful one, for which the preceding portrayal would provide no occasion; Philo also boasts of this very thing (De Cherubim 27: ἤκουσα...παρὰ ψυχῆς ἐμῆς εἰωθυίας τὰ πολλὰ θεοληπτεῖσθαι). The ridicule only comes later: when the matron has thus been won for the community, here (*hic*) is another priest, who demands special honors and rewards; he is the *Anubophorus* or *Anubiacus*, who represents his god, the servant of Osiris. For this cult, which adopts a generous attitude toward prominent proselytes, indeed demands confession and penance also, but it permits a priest to assume *both* of these tasks vicariously;[15] on behalf of the woman he utters, in studied contri- 145 tion, the humble prayer of penitence, when the silver serpent, in which Agathos Daimon, Sarapis, or Osiris is represented, is turned away from the sinful servant, and he offers the expiatory sacrifice (not, as Steinleitner thinks, the payment of penance), which is modest in this case also: a goose and a cake. Inscription No. 32 also clearly distinguishes καθαρμοῖς καὶ θυσίαις εἱλασάμην τὸν κύριον.

Especially important for our purposes is the portrayal of the Jewish woman, who appears never yet to have been understood by the interpreters. Of course both the orthodox and the Hellenistic Jew taught the "law"; even of that swindler about whom Josephus (Ant. XVIII 81) wrote it is said that προσεποιεῖτο μὲν ἐξηγεῖσθαι σοφίαν νόμων Μωυσέος. But is a *magna sacerdos arboris* conceivable in Judaism at all? It will not do to cite, in support of this idea, the ancient Semitic tree-cult, and nothing is explained by the fact that trees also are sometimes mentioned in connection with the synagogues. We must first of all begin with the remarkable expression: *arboris* appears like the name of a deity. There is only one cult, that of Attis, that offers an explanation for this. The

festival identified with the words *arbor intrat* is interpreted by Ovid (Met. X 105) to mean the bringing in of Attis, and therefore the theory is that *Attis has been changed into the tree*, and Attis actually has--here one may recall the inscriptions about the Attis-orgies--high priestesses. In numerous places Juvenal presupposes that the contents and the language of the Metamorphoses are well known; it is only with this interpretation that the expression fully shows the imprint of his style. In this way also the ensuing designation προφῆτις τοῦ Οὐρανοῦ τοῦ Ὑψίστου appears in a new light. This time Friedländer has been able to explain the designation of God by referring to Hecataeus and Strabo (Poseidonios) as well as to Juvenal XIV 96, but not the designation as προφῆτις nor the identifying adjective *summi*. Both are at once explained by that syncretistic Phrygian cult of Ζεύς or θεὸς ὕψιστος, who is also called Ζεὺς Ὕψιστος Οὐράνιος (Cumont, Pauly-Wissowa IX 444) and who has προφῆται in his cult. He could be connected with Attis, who as "shepherd of the white stars" and moon-god holds sway over becoming and passing away on earth (Damascius περὶ ἀρχῶν II 214.4 Ruelle). This prophetess announces some dreams that are given by God, and she does this for a small sum.[16] In his scorn for the Jews Juvenal probably at the same time meant to remind the reader of the Roman proverb, *anus quod vult somniat*. It is important to note how much was known by the general public in Trajan's time about these secret cults. For Juvenal's statements in fact are confirmed in all respects by what I, following Cumont's lead in part, have concluded from the reports of the historians about the development of the Roman Jewish community; in the two and one-half centuries intervening the traces of that community's origins have not been obliterated. Indeed, those traces linger even longer.

46

This is proved by the fragment of a late Roman sarcophagus, to which Cumont has devoted an extraordinarily fine discussion in the *Revue Archéologique* (Ser. V, Tom. IV, 1916, p. 1). He correctly labels it "Jewish-pagan". It is presently in the Thermen Museum, though it was earlier in the Kircherianum and thus is probably of Roman origin (Garrucci, *Storia dell' arte cristiana* I 12; VI, Plate 491, n. 19). On the medallion on the front side, where we would expect the portrait of the deceased, which in fact is forbidden to the Jew, we see the seven-branched lampstand; but this medallion is supported by the same two winged goddesses of victory whom we often encounter on pagan sarcophagi, and beneath it a bacchic scene is portrayed: satyrs, identified by the *lagobolon*, are pressing out the wine. To the right and the left stand the winged genies of the four seasons. Next to the winepressers, of course, stands autumn, an effeminate Bacchus-lad, turned to the right, in his right arm a basket with fruit, with the left hand holding up two dead fowl (geese?), and at his feet a small figure, which Cumont interprets as a child, riding on a horse. Behind him winter hastens on, lifting up a hunting trophy with his right hand; but only the right hand, a piece 147 of the arm loosely draped with a cloak, and the outstretched left foot are to be seen; the rest has been broken off, as are spring and summer on the other side of the sarcophagus. The story of the development of this picture is a remarkable one, but unfortunately it has escaped Cumont, because he has overlooked the works of P. Savignac and E. Michon in the *Revue biblique* (1913, pp. 106 and 111) and of H. Thiersch in the *Zeitschrift des Deutschen Palästina-Vereins* (1914). These scholars have given a detailed report on a probably Jewish sarcophagus in the museum at Jerusalem, which exhibits the model used by the Roman stonecutter and which is dated by

Thiersch in the height of the Antonine period. It was found in the plundering of a tomb in an Arcosolian burial-place at the village *turmus 'aija* (old Shiloh). I give the description provided by Thiersch: "The youthful Bacchus is represented in the center,[17] flanked by Eros-like winged genies of the four seasons, in pairs, with their characteristic attributes. In the lower half of the frieze, moving among these loosely arranged chief figures, are satyrs, Silenus on the donkey (Cumont's riding boy), geese, and, at the extreme left and right, the symbolic figures of the earth (with animal herds) and the seas (with a fisherman in a boat). The narrow sides show geese amidst the fruit and grape harvest." If the reader compares the illustrations in the plate included in this book, he will recognize how fully the two coincide in their composition, in the combination of large and small figures, even down to the very gestures. It is only the middle part that the creator of the Cumont type has arbitrarily altered, evidently because for him it went against the grain to portray God; the medallion that is supported by the goddesses of victory repre-

48 sents the Jewish religion.[18] The perspective which underlies the entire portrayal we can best recognize in the famous oracle of Apollo of Klaros (Macrobius I 18.20), discussed by Cornelius Labeo. This oracle then in turn must be compared with the well-known Sarapis-oracle to King Nikokreon (*ibid.*, I 20.17):[19] the inquirer has been unable to learn anything from "mystai" of the Ὕψιστος θεός about the latter's nature; they were not permitted to speak, so he turns to Apollo, who instructs him:

> ὄργια μὲν δεδαῶτας ἐχρῆν νηπεύθεα κεύθειν·
> εἰ δ' ἄπα τοι παύρη σύνεσις καὶ νοῦς ἀλαπαδνός,
> φράζεο τὸν πάντων ὕπατον θεὸν ἔμμεν 'Ιαώ,
> χείματι μεντ' 'Αίδην, Δία δ' εἴαρος ἀρχομένοιο,
> 'Ηέλιον δὲ θέρευς, μετοπώρου δ' ἁβρὸν 'Ιαώ.

The God of the Jews is the god of the year, thus the Aion, the god of the world and of eternity, who rules in the autumn in his true manifestation as ἁβρὸς 'Ιαώ ("Ιακχος and 'Αιών); he is the ὕψιστος θεός. This is understandable. Volz, in his work *Das Neujahrsfest Iahves*, 1912, has interpreted the Feast of Tabernacles, that is, the autumnal festival, as the ancient new year's festival; and this interpretation has been carried further by Mohwinckel and, more recently, by A. v. Gall (Βασιλεία θεοῦ, Heidelberg, 1926, pp. 19-20), While there is much here that remains beyond my powers to judge, because of a lack of knowledge of the language or of the subject, still, on the basis of the prayers, I can with some certainty demonstrate that the basic outlook belongs to the Hellenistic period. The ancient prayer at the feast of the new moon, which P. Fiebig (*Die Mischna, Text, Übersetzung und ausführliche Erklärung 8. Traktat Rosch ha-schana*, 1914) puts as late as the time of Jesus, begins (Fiebig, p. 27): "Praised be thou, Yahweh our God, King of the world (βασιλεὺς τοῦ αἰῶνος), who dost create the fruit of the vine; praised be thou, Yahweh our God, King of the world, who in the circles of the learned scholars hast instructed them and taught them the times of the months" (the

149 following text praises Yahweh as God of the times, Aion, and explicitly mentions the στιγμὴ ἀμέριστος, to which the Naassene Preaching--see Reitzenstein-Schaeder I 172--traces the development of the Aion). In the modern German prayer-book, the ritual for the ceremony of the "ushering in of the Sabbath", which I cite from Lietzmann's splendid book, *Mass and Lord's Supper*, p. 165, the explication of the Aion-idea has disappeared, but the introduction still reads: "Blessed art Thou, Yahweh our God, King of eternity, Who has created the fruit of the vine. Blessed art Thou, Yahweh our God, King of eternity." We see how the god Abrasax or Abraxas is connected

with Yahweh, and the latter with Dionysos or Iakchos. We encounter a revised Syrian interpretation of the Aion, which was probably originally Iranian,[20] in this oracle, which corresponds to a Hellenistic-Jewish cult.[21]

The same understanding of Yahweh is exhibited on the tetradrachma of Ashkelon mentioned above (p. 158, n. 27), which represents him as Aion (Baaltar, Zeus); it is exhibited also by the sarcophagus of Jerusalem or *turmus 'aija*, in the equation of Aion with Dionysos, though to be sure in a somewhat different version, namely with the whole added to the four parts and pictured in the middle of them. We also find this type in Rome. Prof. Thiersch, who has kindly advised me on these matters, refers to a Roman sarcophagus, formerly in the Villa Carpegna but now unfortunately no longer accessible, whose description in Matz and Duhn (No. 2355; II, p. 94) corresponds point by point to the Jerusalem sarcophagus; the variations, which are only quite insignificant, show a need for demonstrating his independence on the part of the stone-
50 cutter,[22] who nevertheless was working from an established model. Here we have the inscription handed down to us: *Aur. Agapetilla / ancilla dei que / dormit in pace vixit annis XXI / menses III dies III / pater fecit.* The idea that here we have to do with a Christian woman is supported by the presence on the lid, which bears the inscription, of two women in relief, whom Matz and Duhn identify as *orantes*. Yet I do not venture to decide this question;[23] *dormit in pace* is also a Jewish formula (Garrucci, *Dissertationi archeologique* II 154), and according to the passage from Juvenal, an *ancilla dei* was conceivable also in Roman Judaism; at any rate the sarcophagus-type is borrowed from that source. Here I leave aside other monuments which E. Michon and H. Thiersch relate to the passages cited, because their connection with Judaism is uncer-

tain. I should only raise an explicit objection to the assertion of Kohl-Watzinger (p. 200) that the Dionysian elements in the Jewish ornamentation of synagogues and coffins are without
151 significance[24] and that they acquire a reference to the continuation of life in the hereafter only in Christianity.[25] They give too little attention to that Hellenizing process in Judaism which leads in extreme instances to a complete dissolution into paganism and the mystery religions, but also does not leave the homeland untouched. For the Roman community the evidence is now sufficient, I think, that one must reconsider the question whether even after the later withdrawal of the Sabazios community there were not still some connections with Judaism.[26] In any case, Cumont's observations about the worshipers of Hypsistos and Sabazios have found strong confirmation. His interpretation of Livy's statement, preserved by Valerius Maximus, about the cult of Jupiter Sabazios in Rome that was suppressed in the year 139 has become indisputable. Thus in conclusion we may cite a "witness" that he has overlooked. As I mentioned earlier, his prohibition of all the mysteries is attested by Cicero (De leg. II 37) as Roman tradition, by his reference to the generally known suppression of the Bacchanalia, and he *justifies* it by saying that a wise lawgiver "in the middle of Greece" has issued a similar prohibition; then he continues: *novos vero deos et in his colendis nocturnas pervigilationes sic Aristophanes, facetissumus poeta veteris comoediae, vexat, ut aput eum Sabazius et quidam alii dei peregrini iudicati e civitate eiciantur.* This had meaning and point for his readers if they knew that there were still servants of this Sabazios in Rome and Italy, and by means of the assertion of the Greek poet it *justified* the deity's of-
152 ficial expulsion from Rome, which had once followed the suppression of the Bacchanalia and which Cicero knew of and approved.

The oracle to which Labeo appeals deserves still another word. That oracle purports to explain the nature of the Ὕψιστος θεός and identifies him with the four seasons of the year. The fact that therein Zeus signifies the spring is remarkable enough and from the very outset suggests the conjecture that that tetrad of divinity is meant also to represent the four major religions which basically proclaim only the one God: Zeus the Hellenic, the sun-god the Syrian (Persian?), the god of the underworld Sarapis the Egyptian,[27] and Iao (the name that combines in itself the middle, first, and last of the vowels) the Jewish religion. Such a system borrows its form from primitive tetradic formulas which we can trace from Orphism down to Manichaeism and even beyond, and which are constantly assuming new shapes; but they always have to do with the world-deity, who in fact is indicated on the sarcophagi by earth and ocean.[28] This is in harmony with the tendency, to be treated later in more detail, of all the Hellenistic mystery religions, but it also corresponds to a tendency that very early made itself effective in Judaism. A person is not willing to surrender his own god, but on the contrary wishes to make him the true lord of the world by discovering him again in the gods of the other nations. We find a classic example of this effort in a religious document that comes from the East and that is contemporary with that satire of Juvenal from which we started out and to which we now return: I refer to a homily from an altogether Hellenized Phrygian mystery-community that worships the mother of the gods and Attis, but at the same time appeals to the Jewish prophets and writers of the psalms and recognizes the Septuagint as sacred text. We could hardly expect to find a better confirmation of the connections. To be sure, we now know this

153 homily, the so-called Naassene Preaching,[29] only in a Christian revision, but all the Christian additions betray themselves, sometimes by their awkward position, sometimes by their misinterpretation of the meaning; no philologist who has worked with the material regards them as genuine. Here we cannot avoid assuming that the relatively original mingling continued to be maintained in those communities; but the weaving together of diverse elements became more and more prevalent. There is the belief that one possesses the *one great* religion which is found obscured among all the great nations; Egyptians, Assyrians, Greeks, Thracians, all share it, and it provides the dominant force molding Persian speculation; the Jewish element also is heavily influenced by it, and that element preserves the Persian-Jewish hope in God's emissary, obscured in its homeland, in a purer form than it exhibits in that homeland. Of course that emissary is identified with Attis. These people gave up nothing when they added Christ to the other names of this emissary and appropriated Christian writings as well. How then am I to assume that as E. Meyer asserts without offering any proof, Christianity actually developed syncretism? By its very origin and nature it is exclusive, it proclaims only one Lord, and it opposes *all* pagan religions. And how is it supposed to have created the mysteries when, as we have seen, at that time it was itself a mystery religion only in a very limited sense? Did Christianity on its own initiative and without any basis form the words, and then paganism create cultic actions out of those words? One needs only to test this assumption on specific examples, such as the idea of the bride of the deity, or the ascent of the soul, to sense how unnatural and self-contradictory it would be; moreover, if one traces out the *idea* in paganism that underlies the cultic action wherever it can be

demonstrated to be earlier, one can readily be convinced that the assumption would be unhistorical as well. Of course, such a study would also provide compelling evidence that a judgment can be pronounced concerning the mystery cults only by a person who actually knows the basic perspectives and the nature of gnosticism.

54

In this connection the comparison with the Naassene Preaching has still another significance for the passage from Juvenal. That Preaching acknowledges the mysteries of all peoples; its author wants to create the impression of having been initiated into a large number of them. We are to assume the same of the prominent matron whom Juvenal portrays: the emissaries of the various religions appear in her boudoir one after another. Thus Juvenal becomes a witness to an interpretation and a usage which with respect to prominent men we can demonstrate in the inscriptions only at a much later date. Earlier one did not venture publicly to manifest such a belief.

In Juvenal this portrayal is closely connected with that of the most dangerous and most costly procedure for probing into the future; the last two portrayals are meant to form a contrast, as in a sense the first two had done. The word *haruspex* of course is intended only to identify the kind of prophecy; it obviously has to do with *magica sacra*, an actual ἀπόρρητον, the practice of which was punishable by death. Juvenal himself indicates this, and hence he would not have dared to make more specific statements, even if he had been able to do so. He appears also to be speaking here of a *cult*, and he has a certain idea of its origin: *Armenius vel Commagenus*. This is in striking agreement with the description which Pliny provides (XXX 14-17) of the magical arts of Nero; his teachers are Armenian "magicians" whom King Tiridates brought with him to Rome;[30] Pliny also knows that what is

involved is a specific religion, and he speaks of the rite of initiation, the *magicae cenae*. The fact that a historian lets Tiridates, in his homage to Nero, describe Mithras as his god and that in Cappadocia Mithras is venerated by magicians is 155 no longer justification for our seeing in these *cenae* the iniatory rite of the actual Mithras-mysteries. Almost all the Oriental mysteries can be shown to have had sacred meals. Pliny seems to be pointing to specific atrocities which were much discussed in his time, and he emphasizes as characteristic the idea of divine compulsion, which is familiar to us through the magical papyri, and he makes no mention of the Mithras cult; for him the word *magus* signifies primarily the magician, but at the same time the priest as well.

In itself the Zoroastrian religion is hostile to the art of magic, as is Manichaeism later on; only the deity or the priest of the adversaries is called "the magician" (cf. the Zoroastrian legend in A. v. Le Coq, *Sitzungsber. d. Preuss. Akad.*, 1908, p. 398);[31] but the pre-Zoroastrian magical cult never died out completely, and in isolated communities it apparently continued for a long time.[32] As is shown by the use of the term, the Greeks must have become acquainted very early with such μάγοι; the word, which Zimmern regards as originally Babylonian, is generalized into the designation for a trade or profession, like *Chaldaeus* (or *Babylonius*). When they gained some measure of acquaintance with the Zoroastrian religion, they discovered with some amazement that its magicians did not practice "magic" (Deinon, Pseudo-Aristotle in the Μαγικός, and before them evidently Plato, Alcibiad. 122a, who by means of the explanation θρησκεία θεῶν wants to rule out the misunderstanding; and finally Aristotle himself). The history of philosophers preserves this correct perspective; it is from such that Philo (*Quod omnis probus liber* §74, Cohn-Reiter) draws

the statement ἐν Πέρσαις μὲν τὸ μάγων (στίφος) οἳ τὰ φύσεως ἔργα διερευνώμενοι πρὸς ἐπίγνωσιν τῆς ἀληθείας καθ' ἡσυχίαν τὰς θείας ἀρετὰς τρανοτέραις ἐμφάσεσιν ἱεροφαντοῦνταί τε καὶ ἱεροφαντοῦσιν, ἐν 'Ινδοῖς δὲ τὸ γυμνοσοφιστῶν, οἳ πρὸς τῇ φυσικῇ καὶ τὴν ἠθικὴν φιλοσοφίαν διαπονοῦντες ὅλον ἐπίδειξιν ἀρετῆς πεποίηνται τὸν βίον. He also uses the same source in De spec. legibus III 100 (Cohn): τὴν μὲν οὖν ἀληθῆ μαγικήν, ὀπτικὴν ἐπιστήμην οὖσαν, ᾗ τὰ τῆς φύσεως ἔργα τρανοτέραις φαντασίαις αὐγάζεται (cf. Apuleius, De mag. 26).[33] But here he sets over against it, as a παράκομμα, the sorcery-like magical practice. The latter also is later practiced in Persia itself; Strabo (762) is acquainted there not only with the Μάγοι but also with νεκρομάντεις, λεκανομάντεις and ὑδρομάντεις, whose arts are evidently considered by the later (i.e., the alleged) Ostanes, in his Περὶ μαγείας; indeed, later there was an effort also to find magical books from Zarathustra as well. This priestly magical art is a theme among Roman authors; in their works it appears in combination with an Oriental, though not a Zoroastrian, form of religion. I find the proof of this in Tacitus. The charge against Libo (An. II 27) cites *magorum sacra* along with *Chaldaeorum responsa* and *somniorum interpretes*, indeed separated from the conjuring-up of the dead, which of course a Roman would do. In Statilius Taurus' case (An. XII 59) the charge refers to *magicae superstitiones*, and thus implies his belonging to a faith. Clearest of all is the case of Servilia, the daughter of Soranus (An. XVI 31): she had sacrificed all her possessions to the leaders of this cult, but in so doing had never practiced the cultic magic; to the members of the cult with whom she was confronted, she replied: *viderint isti, antehac mihi ignoti, quo nomine sint, quas artes exerceant; nulla mihi principis mentio nisi inter numina fuit.* She acknowledged that she had

participated in the cult, but swore: *nullos impios deos, nullas devotiones* (Libo was accused of these) *nec aliud infelicibus precibus invocavi, quam ut hunc optimum patrem tu, Caesar, vos, patres, servaretis incolumem.*[34] Nevertheless her participation in the cult was sufficient to incur the death penalty. Because these offenses were supposed to have occurred in the cult, she was condemned; it did not matter how many of them could be proved against the individual who was accused

157 (see above, p. 137). Juvenal also thinks that such a *magus* predicts and effects desired fatalities; he mentions the sacrifice of a child--an accusation that is always made against all *magi*--and the sacrifice of a dog.

Fornari (*Notizie delle Scavi* 1918, p. 51) offers the brilliant conjecture that the subterranean basilica discovered in 1917 at the Porta Maggiore in Rome stood in the gardens of that Statilius Taurus mentioned by Tacitus. It would be splendid if this conjecture could be proved; then we would even have the cultic location of one of these magical-mystery communities. However, this very assertion seems to me to have been severely shaken by Lanciani (*Bulletino della Commiss. arch. comunale di Roma*, 1920, pp. 70-71). To be sure, Fornari may have correctly identified the purpose and the age of the basilica.[35] In support of his identification, one can cite the fact that bones of a dog (and of a pig) were found under the apse, and that one of the wall decorations shows the *magician* Medea as she is making it possible for Jason to seize the golden fleece.[36] But these two points are not compelling; as Lanciani rightly emphasizes, the variegation of representations on the walls mocks any coherent and unitary explanation. Nevertheless the main stress must be placed upon the picture in the apse, and this has not yet been given a certain interpretation. It could represent Sappho's leap from the "Leucadian" rock only if the artist

took as his basis a divergent type, the voyage of Aphrodite portrayed in the marriage songs.[37] Hence I prefer to refrain from assigning a name and a type to this mystery community. The most recent finds, to which Lanciani also refers, themselves show how little our knowledge suffices for such identification; the most widely divergent cults could come into consideration. The fact that we now know so many such buildings seems to me not exactly favorable to the assertions of E. Meyer. To a lesser or greater degree they all exhibit, 58 along with the pressure to conform to a type that always dominates an art that is practiced in handwork, a distinctive feeling for two conceptual worlds and religions which had already begun in the Orient and naturally was further intensified in the Occident. It is only in the old traditional perspectives that people can, between two religions, make the ideas of the new one inwardly comprehensible and hence appropriate the pictorial form of representation that is familiar to them, because this form continues to hold for them some value for feeling, even in cases where the individual features are in conflict.[38]

One may well ask whether there is not already discernible even in Tibullus such a combined, or better, a mixed sensitivity. Juvenal's detailed portrayals give us a certain right to relate the penitential practices which he describes either to a Phrygian or to an Egyptian cult; indeed, Tibullus also mentions both in his poems. And yet he does not intend to represent himself as a *mystes* of Isis or of any form of the *Magna Mater*, and when he wishes to portray the δεισιδαιμονία that seized him in his despair, he mentions only Venus as a deity. One is immediately reminded that in another passage, anticipating death, he says:

I 3.51 *parce, pater. timidum non me periuria terrent,*
non dicta in sanctos impia verba deos......
57 *sed me, quod facilis tenero sum semper Amori,*
ipsa Venus campos ducet in Elysios.

It is the hope that in the Isis-mysteries this goddess gives to her servants (Apuleius XI 6: *me...campos Elysios incolens ipse tibi propitiam frequens adorabis*). But it is no longer exclusively related to Isis.[39] This is shown by the inscription--stemming, as it appears, from about the
159 Flavian era, and influenced by the Tibullus corpus--C. I. VI 21521 = Bücheler Carm. ep. II 1109 (v. 27: *nam me sancta Venus sedes non nosse silentum iussit et in caeli lucida templa tulit*), and the much later C. I. III 686 = Bücheler II 1233 (v. 5: *te sortita Paphon pulchro minus ore notabat diva, set in toto corde plicata inerat*--v. 12: *et reparatus item vivis in Elysiis*). But it seems clear to me that only the Oriental rites revived these mystery-hopes and transferred them to Venus. Tibullus is speaking out of a general acquaintance with these rites.[40] He too attests in a general way the age and the impact of a Hellenistic mystery-religion.

One wonders whether we may attempt to press still further back. I am well aware of the danger involved in such an attempt, and I have no intrinsic objection to a presentation that proposes to be satisfied with setting forth facts that are certainly handed down--thus here something like the fact that in a couple of small cultic communities in western Asia the same custom prevailed which Augustine pictures for us in the Christian cultus. Such a presentation is of service to science, and indeed is indispensable to it, as for example the exemplary presentation of the facts in Wissowa's splendid work *Religion und Kultus der Römer*. Only I would no more acknowledge it as the ultimate goal of our research than Usener

on his part could acknowledge Wissowa's book. The person who, fully conscious of the dangers, attempts through constant comparison to discover the context and the original meaning of those facts also is working scientifically.[41] The more we enlarge our field of vision in so doing, and the more carefully we observe even minutiae, the more readily will we avoid the mistakes to which a Usener not infrequently is demonstrably subject. Of course they can never be entirely avoided; but the principle stoutly advocated by the wittiest Greek esthetist, that to be free of error does not mean the highest praise, holds true for scientific work even more than for art, and we see again and again that anyone who wishes merely to recognize "certainly attested facts" himself falls into the most arbitrary constructions. How easy it is, using the example cited, to assert: at the time when those inscriptions were placed in Lydia and Phrygia, Christianity was already rather widespread there; we can demonstrate the underlying perspective in the Psalms, and indeed in the gospel; thus Augustine has revived an ancient Christian custom that has also exerted an extensive influence upon paganism!

Thus I turn our attention once again to the cult and the feeling out of which those inscriptions arose. I need not explain the age-old and widespread feeling that every misfortune and especially every illness is sent from God, a sign of his wrath and punishment for an offense. What is distinctive about these penitential inscriptions lies in their composition as a kind of sermon; they are specifically called εὐλογίαι (cf. 13: ἀνέθηκα εὐλογίαν; 14: εὐχαριστήριον ἀνέστησα; 3: καὶ ἀπὸ τοῦ νῦν εὐλογοῦμεν, εὐλογῶν [εὐχαριστῶν] ἀνέθηκα; or 18.9: εὐλογῶν σου τὰς δυνάμεις, i.e., the miracles; cf. 31: εὐχαριστῶ Μητρὶ Λητῷ ὅτι ἐξ ἀδυνάτων δυνατὰ πυεῖ). Thus they, like the general prayers of thanksgiving for deliverance, be-

long to the classification of aretalogy. They attest *what was once in fuller form declaimed in the cult at the appropriate shrine.* In this setting the confession of sin itself is intended as a warning to the believers; hence it is said repeatedly, "I warn everyone not to underestimate the power of this god or that one", or "not to commit this or that sin". One's own discipline, and indeed even the stele that perpetuates its memory, is described as an ἐξένπλον or an ἐξενπλάριον for all the members of the community.

To emphasize this religious character of the actions that lay back of these inscriptions, I cite only one, unfortunately a mutilated one (No. 32): καθαρμοῖς κὲ θυσίαις ε[ἱλασάμην τὸν Κ]ύριον, ἵνα μυ τὸ ἐμὸν σῶ[μα σώ]σι, κε ΜΟΠC (probably αὖθις) μὲ ἀποκαθέστησε [τῷ ἐμ]ῷ σώματι. διὸ παραγγέλλω μηθένα ἄθυτον

161 αἰγοτόμιον (flesh of a goat not sacrificed) ἔσθειν, ἐπεὶ παθῖτε (παθεῖται) τὰς ἐμὰς κολάσεις.[42]

With this inscription I compare an actual literary monument of a much earlier time, namely the hymn of thanksgiving of an ancient Babylonian king which we can date at the latest around 1000 B.C. Now, thanks to the information kindly provided by Prof. Zimmern, I can present it somewhat more fully than previously[43] was possible. Only the middle portion is extant; the superscription and motto is "I will pay homage to the lord of wisdom". The one offering the prayer relates his earlier misery in grave illness; his tomb was already opened, the lamentations were already being voiced, and those hostile to him were rejoicing. Then, while in a sleep-like twilight state he experienced three visions: a youth sent from God drives away the worst of his woes; a second messenger sent by Lal-ur-Alimma brings the bundle of tamarisk twigs necessary for prayer,[44] and the water of life; and a third emissary

comforts him. Then appears Marduk's messenger, "the servant of the lady of the revival of the dead", and the demons of sickness disappear. The slave's mark is erased from his brow, and his chains are loosed. Marduk has smitten the fist of his adversary and shattered his weapons; Marduk has put bit and bridle in the mouth of the lion that would eat him. The one who has been delivered goes to Babylon and to the temple Esagila:

"To prostrate myself and to pray, / I entered into Esagila,
[I who had des]cended into the grave, / I returned to Babylon:
[In the gate] of the fulness of life (joy) / with the fulness of life I was bles[sed],[45]
[In the g]ate of the great guardian spirit / my guardian spirit came near [to me] again,
In the gate of salvation / I beheld salvation (*salus*),
In the gate of life / life was imparted to me,
In the gate of the sunrise / I was (again) counted among the living,
In the gate of the bright omens (explanation of the omens) / my omens became bright,
In the gate of the dissolving of sins / my ban was dissolved,
In the gate of inquiry / my mouth made inquiry,
In the gate of the banishing of sighs / my sighing was banished,
In the gate of the purification with water / I was sprinkled with the water of purification,
In the gate of atonement / I was seen at the side of Marduk,[46]
In the gate of the pouring out of the fulness / I was laid down at the feet of Sarpanitu,
In prayer and supplication / I groaned before them,
Fine incense / I laid down before them."

An enumeration of the sacrifices follows; then it is said that the people of Babylon, who had already prepared for the burial, sat at the festive banquet:

"The people of Babel saw / how (or: that) he makes [him] alive,

All mouths / praise the loftiness (of Marduk):
'Who was it who commanded / that he should behold the sun (?),
In whose mind was it / that he should take up his journey again?
Who but Marduk / has brought him (back) from death to life?
What kind of goddess other than Erua (Sarpanitu; thus Landsberger) / has given him [back] his breath?
Marduk was able / to awaken (him) from the tomb (to make him alive),
Sarpanitu was minded / to rescue (him) from annihilation.
Wherever the earth is placed, / the heavens are extended,
The sun shines, / fire blazes,
All those whom Aruru / has created (has molded their bits of clay),
Who are filled with the breath of life / go thither (the limbs are extended),
All lands (?people?) together / praise Marduk!'"

Only fragments are extant of the conclusion of the hymn, which hardly was much longer.

It is not the hymn intended for the ceremony of thanksgiving itself, but probably a literary reflection of such a ceremony. Thus in form it diverges from the actual cultic hymn. According to Zimmern, elsewhere in the Babylonian hymns of redemption the portrayal of suffering and the petition for deliverance occupy a very large amount of space, but the deliverance itself and the thanks to the deity are usually dismissed with a few typical phrases. Now in this hymn of course the one speaking is not conscious of any particular sin: he has not neglected the cultus of the gods, has not abused their names in taking an oath, and has always striven to act in a pious manner. But by his adding that man does not know what is good in God's sight and what is sinful, he does betray the same view of illness and trouble as punishment; where we can-

.64 not identify the reason, we must believe in the wisdom of the gods. It is a religious development that almost necessarily emerges and is reflected in the gospel narratives: the simple admonition to the one healed, "Go and sin no more, lest something worse befall you", becomes the didactic-theological miracle narrative (John 9): "Illness and healing can only have the aim of revealing God's miraculous power and praising him." Aretalogy is always the aim, the essential; it determines the cultic usage; but the latter has grown up out of the sense of sin and the compulsion for penance, and few ancient peoples exhibit these more vigorously than do the Babylonians.[47]

As is well known, this cultic usage existed among the Israelites also; this is attested by the psalms of thanksgiving. Indeed, we have a hymn which, precisely like the Babylonian one just cited, was not composed for the festival itself, but contains a dramatic description of the festival. It is Psalm 21: ὁ θεός, ὁ θεός μου, πρόσχες μοι, ἵνα τί με κατέλιπες; first the portrayal of the misery and of the nevertheless rock-firm faith, then the promise διηγήσομαι τὸ ὄνομά σου τοῖς ἀδελφοῖς μου· ἐν μέσῳ ἐκκλησίας ὑμνήσω σε,...τὰς εὐχάς μου ἀποδώσω ἐνώπιον τῶν φοβουμένων αὐτόν,[48] and finally the reference to the festal meal and to the praise uttered by all the people. On the basis of a similar cultic usage, I am convinced of a direct impact of Babylonian sacral poetry. The fact that here also there is no mention of any sin can no longer cause any surprise. Here too the consciousness of the connection between sin and punishment continues to live among the people, but the festival practice no longer makes any reference to it.

.65 However, it is not because of those penitential inscriptions that I have so extensively treated the Babylonian text

in a book on Hellenistic mysteries. That text also offers a great deal with respect to those mysteries, even though it does not offer an account of a mystery in the strict sense of the term.[49] It seems to me that here a connection of the mysteries with the earlier general cultus appears. It cannot be accidental that a number of actual mysteries, particularly the Isis-mystery portrayed by Apuleius, but also the Egyptian consecration of the king, exhibit precisely the same sequence--for example, the καθαρμοί and the θυσίαι--, the same structure of sacred actions: baptism, transformation of the temple, which signifies the heavens or the world, and festal banquet. The number of gates (stations?), in each of which the divine gift for which it is named is imparted to the one offering the prayer, shows still more clearly that there is an underlying specific theology which perhaps had even played a role in the construction of the temple; one may think of the seven gates of the underworld, in each of which Ishtar loses a part of her ornamentation during the descent and receives it again during the ascent. The fact that the names of the twelve gates are Sumerian makes possible the assumption that the sacred action which is connected with them already existed among the Sumerians; only according to Zimmern it appears hardly to be expected that here the action already had an even deeper significance. It would be conceivable that the action, transposed into other contexts, passes over to other peoples also. As little as we can say with certainty here,[50] still this 166 example seems to me valuable to show how ancient general cultus can become, in another setting, a mystery and can influence the Hellenistic period.

Anyone who wishes to discern the essence of Hellenistic mystery religions must pay particular attention to the similarities of their cultic practices and perspectives to the

ancient Oriental popular cults and general perspectives. If these are demonstrable, then proofs of the age of the mysteries are almost superfluous. Hence I shall discuss as briefly as possible a couple of other examples, and I choose for my point of departure a complicated cultic action for which we have ancient explanations handed down through the priestly caste. In the *Archiv für Religionswissenschaft* XXII, 1924, pp. 87-88, Frau Luise Troje has explained an ancient Indian sacrificial ritual for the erection of the fire-altar (Agnicayana)[51] which in its origins reaches back into the earliest, perhaps even pre-Vedic, times and whose priestly interpretation in the Satapatha-Brahmana is repeatedly given in the presence of Buddha. Numerous expansions and elaborations are attached to the original leading idea, of building the altar in five strata as an image of the world and of placing on it, as a symbol of the vital force that prevails in the cosmos, the world-creating principle, the sacred torch (Agni); various cultic actions that originally have the same meaning are ranged alongside each other. We can also demonstrate something similar in other cults; most mysteries that develop into organizations are inclined in this direction by their very nature. This process is permeated with cosmic and soteriological significance: the lord of the sacrifice re-creates the aged god of the times and the world, or begets him in himself anew: for an entire year he carries, as a symbol of the macrocosmos, its vital force (fire) in his bosom, the fire-container bound to the body, and then allows it to become manifest, but at the same time he himself thereby becomes this god, or rather his inner Self becomes the deity's inner Self, its vital force, Agni. Some day it will transport him to heaven. The cultic action has

become a mystery in the full sense of the term and exerts an influence on cultic mysteries of the Hellenistic world. But even where the cultic features have altogether disappeared, the religious conception is maintained, and in a tractate that shows Iranian influence we hear the prescription (Corp. herm. XI 20): τοῦτον οὖν τὸν τρόπον νόησον τὸν θεὸν ὥσπερ νοήματα πάντα ἐν ἑαυτῷ ἔχειν τὸν κόσμον ἑαυτόν <τε> ὅλον. συναύξησον σεαυτὸν τῷ ἀμετρήτῳ μεγέθει· παντὸς σώματος ἐκπηδήσας καὶ πάντα χρόνον ὑπεράρας Αἰὼν γενοῦ, καὶ νοήσεις τὸν θεόν. μηδὲν ἀδύνατον σεαυτῷ ὑποστησάμενος σεαυτὸν ἥγησαι ἀθάνατον καὶ πάντα δυνάμενον νοῆσαι, πᾶσαν μὲν τέχνην, πᾶσαν δὲ ἐπιστήμην, παντὸς ζῴου ἦθος. παντὸς δὲ ὕψους ὑψηλότερος γενοῦ καὶ παντὸς βάθους ταπεινότερος. πάσας δὲ αἰσθήσεις τῶν ποιητῶν σύλλαβε ἐν σεαυτῷ, πυρός, ὕδατος, ξηροῦ καὶ ὑγροῦ· καὶ ὁμοῦ πανταχῇ εἶναι, ἐν γῇ, ἐν θαλάττῃ, ἐν οὐρανῷ· μηδέπω γεγενῆσθαι, ἐν τῇ γαστρὶ εἶναι, νέος, γέρων, τεθνηκέναι, τὰ μετὰ τὸν θάνατον. κἂν ταῦτα πάντα ὁμοῦ νοήσῃς, χρόνους, τόπους, πράγματα, ποιότητας, ποσότητας, δύνασαι νοῆσαι τὸν θεόν. That certainly is no longer any sort of mystery, but the same Oriental conception of the world as man or as God that I earlier[52] have traced from India all the way into Orphism is underlying here also, and here also there shines through the soteriological idea that man, when he realizes it, is or becomes in his own conscious self the Self of the world-deity.[53]

168 Among the many very ancient cultic actions and cultic conceptions of this ritual there appears one that is especially helpful for explaining later ones: in the center of the altar there is fitted, as a symbol of the world-self, a golden figure of a man, and it is interpreted as the "heavenly (divine) body" of the lord of the sacrifice, "his immortal, his

divine form". Beside it is placed a tile that is supposed to represent his earthly body and to safeguard the lord of the sacrifice against prematurely going the way of his heavenly body. As old as it is, this interpretation is hardly original. In its original meaning the gold again is probably the representation of Agni, thus of the fire and the vital force; I recall that in the Iranian cosmogony the powers of the primal man who is sent to earth and who vanishes there flow into the earth as metals; in that process, the real life-force, the seed, is gold. A cruder form, in which one can better speak of a building-sacrifice, stands alongside this in the Indian ritual: five different living beings--in fact they are divided into five classes--are sacrificed and fitted into this building, the world-structure, so that it has life and the common soul in itself. But that priestly interpretation of the golden man, even if it is later, deserves still closer examination. Unfortunately I cannot pursue the speculative development of the conception of a second, immaterial body in the Indian ritual. But everyone is familiar with the belief, expressed in the Iranian liturgy (Yasht 22), that after death the soul of the devout person meets its own self in the form of a beautiful maiden, which has become so beautiful through his good thoughts, words, and works (a basic distinction that is Persian as well as Indian). United with this maiden then the soul ascends to heaven and is venerated as Ohrmazd (the ancient world-deity that is transformed into the ethical). I have earlier[54] given sufficient discussion to the designation (here *daena*) which appears sometimes to mean religion (religious knowledge) and sometimes a personality, and from the almost complete similarity of the Mandaean and the Manichaean teaching about heaven I have drawn the conclusion that the Mani-

chaean expression *grev* (the Self) in some way corresponds to 169 the Zoroastrian *daena*. Now I am able to offer full proof of this. The primal man Gayomard (mortal life) is not only the soul (the life) of the world, but also true religion, correct knowledge of God. The beginning of "religion" is reckoned from him even chronologically.[55] In harmony with this is the fact that only the followers of the true religion have "life"; life and knowledge are indissolubly connected. The soteriological significance of the conception naturally had to follow from that view. It would take us too far afield to trace out the altogether similar development in the Indian context; only I should like to emphasize with special gratitude, precisely because on details I often must take issue with her, how greatly Frau Luise Troje has advanced our studies through her constant comparison of Indian teachings and cults.

The soul achieves full deification in death, but it also achieves it in the revelation, which accordingly is sometimes understood as a dying, and sometimes as a preliminary stage to dying. Here the mysteries whose typical forms we are investigating enter in. When in the brief selections I prefer Aryan forms, this is because they have been least noticed; indeed, their very existence has been disputed.

The opening part of a magical text which has been made known by Dieterich under the name of the Mithras-liturgy mentions that heavenly body; therefore I shall give it in full here. On the whole text I remark only that it presents the ἱερὸς λόγος for a secret cultic action and that there were also such ἱεροὶ λόγοι for all true mysteries (cf. the decree of Ptolemy Philopator published by Schubart; above, p. 121). Yet this ἱερὸς λόγος bears strong literary features; in the introduction, as he begins his work, the author in a certain sense introduces himself. It is not intended to be merely a

preface, but a very general preparation for the person who is being initiated, and it pictures for him therefore what he will experience and *feel*. The language is ceremonial--after the brief foreword of the author one may compare the stately sentences of the first prayer with the prayer in the first prooemium of Lucretius--and the conclusion is finely drawn.
70 It is presupposed that the deity has *actually* formed the intention to cause the person being initiated to be reborn. Thus it must in some way have made this intention known to him; in other words, it must have "called" him. However, no external goal is indicated as the object of this will, but deification. This in itself distinguishes this text from all other magical texts, in which the will of the man is always emphasized and a particular external aim is indicated, and occasionally an elevation of the religious position of the one performing the magic as a *result* of the sacred action may also be mentioned. Here the magical action is God's will and worship, and in the first prayer as well as in the conclusion of the "action" it ends with the declaration of the person performing the action that he submits to this will. We have no option but to understand the word μυστήριον in the introduction and conclusion in a purely religious sense. The fact that Dieterich sensed this is here his first great philological achievement.[56] The text in its entirety now offers the instruction before the mystery, as Apuleius pictures it for us. This instruction is necessary in every mystery in which the person being initiated himself is supposed to act and experience, not simply to be a spectator; to this extent of course it resembles the directions to the magician. In the Isis-mysteries in Apuleius' account it is also imparted by the mystagogue from a *book* written in hieroglyphics; hence

one could be tempted also to interpret the introduction in these terms. But, as Dieterich sensed, it is not suited for that purpose. For by its very nature that preparation of the initiate can be accomplished only in oral instruction. There is no introduction into the actual mysteries in the form of a book or an epistle; the presence of the teacher, who indeed imparts the initiatory rites or leads the initiate, is essential. Thus an enigma is posed by the words ἵλαθί μοι, Πρόνοια καὶ Ψυχή, τάδε γράφοντι τὰ πρωτοπαράδοτα μυστήρια μόνῳ δὲ τέκνῳ ἀθανασίαν. The enigma is solved, of course, when we

171 consider the fact that in Hellenistic edifying literature, for example in Philo, it is quite customary to designate a portion of a book as intended only for those who have been initiated.[57] I shall return to this point later. Here perhaps a modern comparison will help us to evaluate this properly, though of course it presupposes our altogether different circumstances. A father can begin his notes by saying, "This confession is intended only for my son." If a generally accessible novel begins in this way, I immediately recognize the literary form that is chosen for a particular purpose. Here I believe that I can recognize it from still other signs.

The priests of Dionysos mentioned in the decree of Ptolemy Philopator must demonstrate a lineage of three generations from whom they have received their consecration and the ἱεροὶ λόγοι connected with it; this is in keeping with the characterization in the introduction of τάδε τὰ πρωτοπαράδοτα μυστήρια, which is explained by the remark that Mithras himself delivered them and the power connected with them to the writer through his supreme

172 emissary (*tarkumen*),[58] so that the writer could make the heavenly pilgrimage *alone* (ἀλήτης οὐρανὸν βαίνω; cf. Diet. p. 8.5:

173 ἐγώ εἰμι σύμπλανος ὑμῖν ἀστὴρ καὶ ἐκ βάθους ἀναλάμπων). When

the writer now hands them on to his son--only to his son may he give them--they are πρωτοπαράδοτα.[59] Thus the following mystery is new; it is constituted by him. Of course it is not said therewith whether it is new in all parts. Livy indeed shows us that the individual leaders of the Dionysos-mysteries could make alterations "on the basis of divine revelation". As is well-known, we can now demonstrate the presence of the Mithras cult in Egypt as early as the third century B.C.; this is not surprising subsequent to the Persian overlordship and with the continuing existence of the Πέρσαι τῆς ἐπιγονῆς, but in itself it proves nothing about the later official Mithras-mysteries, which of course are also demonstrably present in Egypt in the time of the Caesars. Dieterich's idea that here we have actually the official ἱερὸς λόγος of the highest of the classes of initiates appears to me at least incapable of proof. Cumont has already rightly emphasized the fact that in them the heavenly journey is described differently. The variants, which here as in most of the magical texts are introduced with ἐν ἄλλῳ or οἱ δὲ, further show that the text circulated in various magical books: such a breach of the obligation of silence would be unexampled and hardly conceivable. I must also acknowledge that Cumont is correct in saying that chapter XIII of the Hermetic corpus (see above, pp. 47ff.) exhibits a certain similarity. There also--of course in the form of a narrative--a regeneration-mystery is described; and there of course it is a purely conceptual one, without any external apparatus. But one wonders whether this external apparatus in the Mithraic text ever actually existed at any point, and thus whether the description was any more than a form intended to stimulate the imagination. It appears to me that this would place too great de-

mands even on our technique of stage and cinema, and the way in which the feelings of the person being initiated are described seems designed rather to hinder the illusion than to 174 evoke it. Even though this may remain undecided and incapable of determination, the significance of the find and of Dieterich's book is not affected by how many or how few believers this religious writing gained. Dieterich has shown with admirable clarity--and this is his second, even greater philological achievement--how the religious imagination of the author worked and how mystery-images developed; he has also done justice throughout to the recognition of Iranian elements, but has likewise conceded the influences of alien elements. Anyone who adds details here is not denying but is only fulfilling the obligation of actually and consciously expressing gratitude for Dieterich's work.

Let us now examine in detail the first prayer together with the introduction. In printing the text I place mystical combinations of letters in square brackets, the other additions and variants that are necessary or customary in the magical tradition in parentheses, and restorations in angled brackets. The structure of the main part of the prayer, which I have marked off by dashes, is this: after the invocation (lines 7-16) there follows the presupposition of the entire prayer: "if it is your will" (16-29); then, connected with the conclusion, a twofold justification for the request: "since I am to be counted worthy of the revelation that is to follow" (29-39) and "since I as a man cannot achieve it" (39-42); then the main clause, "so for the present remain behind, my human nature" (42-44). Then a new, brief sentence is offered as further justification: he can make such a demand because he is not only a man, but also the son (of the deity).

Ἵλαθί μοι, Πρόνοια καὶ Ψυχή,[60] τάδε γράφοντι[61]
τὰ πρωτοπαράδοτα μυστήρια, μόνῳ δὲ τέκνῳ ἀθανασίαν,
ἀξίῳ μύστῃ τῆς ἡμετέρας δυνάμεως, ἥν ὁ μέγας θεὸς
Ἥλιος Μίθρας ἐκέλευσέν μοι μεταδοθῆναι ὑπὸ τοῦ
5 ἀρχαγγέλου αὐτοῦ, ὅπως ἐγὼ μόνος ἀλήτης[62] οὐρανὸν,
βαίνω καὶ κατοπτεύω πάντα.--Γένεσις πρώτη τῆς ἐμῆς
5 γενέσεως [αεηιουω], Ἀρχὴ τῆς ἐμῆς ἀρχῆς[63] πρώτη
[πππσσσφρ], πνεῦμα πνεύματος τοῦ ἐν ἐμοὶ πνεύματος
πρῶτον [μμμ], πῦρ τὸ εἰς ἐμὴν κρᾶσιν (τῶν ἐν ἐμοὶ
10 κράσεων) θεοδώρητον τοῦ ἐν ἐμοὶ πυρὸς πρῶτον[ηυ-
ηιαεη], ὕδωρ ὕδατος τοῦ ἐν ἐμοὶ ὕδατος πρῶτον [ωωω-
αααεεε], οὐσία γεώδης τῆς ἐν ἐμοὶ οὐσίας γεώδους
πρώτη [υηυωη], σῶμα τέλειον (ἐμοῦ τοῦ δεῖνα τῆς
δεῖνα) διαπεπλασμένον ὑπὸ βραχίονος ἐντίμου καὶ
15 δεξιᾶς χειρὸς ἀφθάρτου ἐν ἀφωτίστῳ καὶ διαυγεῖ κόσμῳ ἔν τε ἀψύχῳ καὶ ἐψυχωμένῳ [υηιαυιευωιε]--ἐὰν δη[64]
ὑμῖν δόξῃ [μετερταφωθ μεθαρθαφηριν· ἐν ἄλλῳ· ιερεζαθ]
μεταπαραδῶναί με τῇ ἀθανάτῳ γενέσει ἐχόμενος[65] τῇ
ὑποκειμένῃ μου φύσει, ἵνα μετὰ τὴν ἐνεστῶσαν καὶ
20 σφόδρα κατεπείγουσάν με χρείαν ἐποπτεύσω τὴν ἀθάνατον Ἀρχὴν τῷ ἀθανάτῳ πνεύματι [ανχρε φρενες ουφι-
ριγχ] (τῷ ἀθανάτῳ ὕδατι) [ερονουιπαρακουνηθ] (τῷ
στερεοτάτῳ ἀέρι)[66] [ειοαηψεναβωθ], ἵνα νοήματι μεταγεννηθῶ [κραοχραξροιμ][67] ἐναρχόμενος καὶ πνεύσῃ ἐν
25 ἐμοὶ τὸ ἱερὸν πνεῦμα [νεχθεν απο του νεχθιναρπιηθ],
ἵνα θαυμάσω τὸ ἱερὸν πῦρ [κυφε], ἵνα θεάσωμαι τὸ
ἄβυσσον τῆς ἀνατολῆς φρικτὸν ὕδωρ [νυω θεγω εχω ου-
χιεχωα] καὶ ἀκούσῃ μου ὁ ζῳογόνος καὶ περιχεχυμένος
αἰθήρ [αρνομηθφ],--ἐπεὶ μέλλω κατοπτεύειν σήμερον
30 τοῖς ἀθανάτοις ὄμμασι, θνητὸς γεννηθεὶς ἐκ θνητῆς
ὑστέρας,[68] βεβελτιωμένος ὑπὸ κράτους μεγαλοδυνάμου
καὶ δεξιᾶς χειρὸς ἀφθάρτου, ἀθανάτῳ πνεύματι τὸν
6 ἀθάνατον Αἰῶνα καὶ δεσπότην τῶν πυρίνων διαδημάτων,
ἁγίοις ἁγιασθεὶς ἁγιάσμασι, ἀρτίας[69] ὑπεστώσης μου
35 πρὸς ὀλίγον τῆς ἀνθρωπίνης μου ψυχικῆς δυνάμεως, ἥν
ἐγὼ πάλιν μεταπαραλήμψομαι μετὰ τὴν ἐνεστῶσαν καὶ
κατεπείγουσάν με πικρὰν ἀνάγκην ἀχρεοκόπητον[70] (ἐγὼ
ὁ δεῖνα ὃν ἡ δεῖνα) κατὰ δόγμα θεοῦ ἀμετάθετον[71]
[ευηυϊαεηια ωειανιυαιεω],--ἐπεὶ οὐκ ἔστιν μοι ἐφικ-
40 τὸν θνητὸν γεγῶτα συνανιέναι ταῖς χρυσοειδέσιν μαρμαρυγαῖς τῆς ἀθανάτου λαμπηδόνος [ωηυ αεω ηυα εωη
υαε ωιαε], ἔσταθι, φθαρτὴ[72] βροτῶν φύσι, καὶ αὐτίκα
<ἀποδέχου> με ὑγιῆ[73] μετὰ τὴν ἀπαραίτητον καὶ κατε-
πείγουσαν χρείαν. ἐγὼ γάρ εἰμι ὁ υἱός[ψυχω δε μου
45 προχω πρωα ἐγὼ εἰμι μαχαρφν μου πρω ψυχων[74] πρωε].

The brief introductory prayer of the author is explained on the one hand by the initiate's obligation to remain silent and the consciousness on the part of these religious authors that they are able to write only under the inspiration of their God,[75] and on the other hand by prototypes of form in the magical literature. Here I emphasize only one piece, important in its contents also, from Pap. Lond. 121 (Kenyon, *Greek Papyri in the British Museum* I, p. 100, line 505), which bears the superscription σύστασις ἰδίου δαίμονος: Χαίρετε, Τύχη καὶ δαῖμον τοῦ τόπου τούτου καὶ <ἡ> ἐνεστῶσα ὥρα καὶ ἡ ἐνεστῶσα ἡμέρα καὶ πᾶσα ἡμέρα, χαῖρε τὸ περιέχον, ὅ ἐστιν γῆ καὶ οὐρανός. The introductory prayer appears to extend to this point. The deification of the particular place and the

177 particular time leads, in its generalization, to the prayer to earth and heaven. Now begins the actual magical invocation: Χαῖρε, Ἥλιε, σὺ γὰρ εἶ ὁ ἐπὶ τοῦ ἁγίου στηρίγματος σεαυτὸν ἱδρύσας ἀοράτῳ φάει. σὺ εἶ ὁ πατὴρ τοῦ παλινγενοῦς Αἰῶνος, σὺ εἶ ὁ πατὴρ τῆς ἀπλάτου Φύσεως· σὺ εἶ ὁ ἔχων ἐν σεαυτῷ τὴν τῆς κοσμικῆς φύσεως σύγκρασιν καὶ γεννήσας τοὺς ε΄ πλάνετας ἀστέρας, οἵ εἰσιν οὐρανοῦ σπλάγχνα καὶ γῆς ἔντερα καὶ ὕδατος χύσις καὶ πυρὸς θράσας.[76] Above Aion and Φύσις, which are often connected with each other and are identified as the sun and the moon, there appears here as a higher unity a God of invisible, immaterial light, who contains within himself the Kosmos.[77] Corresponding to the four (originally five) elements of that Kosmos that rests in God are the five planets, actually of course not those elements in their material manifestation, but their innermost being, their very essence, what the author of the Mithras liturgy calls πῦρ πυρός, πνεῦμα πνεύματος. Our inner man, our character, indeed is determined by the planets, and the Damdad-Nask, which belongs to the fifth century B.C.,

expressed this view thus: that at the demise of the divine primal man, who bore within himself the very essence of the planets, this essence then flowed as metal and seed into the earth, from which then seven human pairs, corresponding to the essence of the planets (there, following the later reckoning, seven in number), arose.[78] Thus every country, every people, and every person actually has his ἴδιος δαίμων. A Hermetic writing which uses this Nask but unfortunately is preserved only in lengthy excerpts in an Arabic magical writing describes this δαίμων as "perfect nature", φύσις τελεία, or as the "perfect I". It is basically a unitary divine being, but still different for each person, and to be addressed differently, according to the planet whose essence predominates in the person (or people, or country). From the δαίμων the man of action receives success, the power to win, and the scholar receives the revelation of truth (cf. Reitzenstein-Schaeder I, chapters 3 and 4). If we look now at the London papyrus, we discern a certain connection between the introductory prayer and the main prayer: from the invocation, which would have been understood by every person in antiquity, of the demon of this place and this hour the introductory prayer passes over to the invocation of the God of space and time, and this conception is the point of connection for the beginning of the main prayer. Is it perhaps similar in the Mithras liturgy? In the Πρόνοια, it is true, we recognize the προὼν (νοῦς) of the Naassene Preaching, for which I can only refer to that book; but in the Ψυχή[79] we recognize the God who gives life to the world, who indeed is identified with that first "man" who descended into the world, and who is the world-soul but at the same time resides in each one of us. But then in the Mithras liturgy also the introductory prayer is connected with

the main prayer. For the moment I leave aside the explanation of 'Αρχή and Γένεσις. There follows the enumeration of the four elements, or rather of their essential being, which lies back of the element utilized to form the body of the person praying, and of their combination in the σῶμα τέλειον. Formed by God himself, it sojourns in the light-world and at the same time in the darkness of the material world; the counterpart is the corporeal body, the φθαρτὴ βροτῶν φύσις (or ἀνθρωπίνη ψυχικὴ δύναμις). Thus the σῶμα τέλειον can only be the heavenly double, the φύσις τελεία of the magician. We may now recall that in the twenty-second Yasht in fact this heavenly double guides the soul upward to God. There it is identified as the (religious) self of the soul; and among the Mandaeans we hear the same thing in almost all the funeral liturgies, i.e., the ascension liturgies (e.g., Lidzbarski, Genza l. III 31, p. 559.29):

> I go to meet my likeness,
> and my likeness comes to meet me;
> He caresses me and embraces me
> When I return *from imprisonment*.

179 We can immediately add a third portrayal. In the hymn of the soul in the Acts of Thomas, certainly originally Iranian (above, pp. 58ff.), the king's son (the soul) on his return from the realm of the dead (the material world) is met by his celestial garments, which have been preserved there and ornamented with his deeds in the world. Clothed in these garments he ascends to the heavens. The use of the garments as a figure for the *body* is so universally customary in all the mystery cults and in almost every religious language that I need not go into that subject in more detail. Quite in the same way according to the belief of the Manichaeans (Flügel, *Mani*, p. 100) the soul of the pious is met by the maiden who is similar

to this soul;[80] the robe is brought to the soul by its divine escort. As the Mandaeans also teach, the robe is preserved in heaven for the soul. Now we can understand at once that Apuleius, if he would remain in Corinth, would have to pray there on festival days to his heavenly robe which after the mystery he had deposited in the temple--according to the Egyptian understanding the symbol of heaven. Precisely so, indeed, the Mithraic initiate prays to his σῶμα τέλειον. When Apuleius was commanded after a specified time had elapsed to repeat the initiation which he had already had, as is customary with the Phrygian baptism of blood and the old Egyptian consecration of kings, this could be accomplished only in this garment of light. Since he was now sojourning in Rome, he preferred to undergo an entirely new initiation.[81]

It is extremely important that the Manichaean hymns also are acquainted with the concept of the "Self" or the "Personality" and employ adjectives to distinguish their meaning. The soul in the body is the captive self, and the writing preserved in Chinese translation speaks in detail of this captivity of the self or of the (divinely given) soul in matter or in the body.[82] In the hymns the "living self" or the light-self or the original self is contrasted with this captive part as an independently acting person--we may think of the Zarathustra song (above, p. 56)--and is also called our original light-nature, which is our father and our mother.[83] That is also the standard predication of the God Aion, the world-deity who is male and female and is represented by the sun and the moon; according to the Indo-Persian equation of the macrocosm and the microcosm, the primal man or the soul, i.e., the world-soul, the world-self. Thus the most widely diverse possibilities are offered for describing his essence in formulae: in the Indo-Persian lists of elements[84] by the divine names and sun,

moon, and the five material elements, astrologically utilized by the divine names and the five (with sun and moon, seven) planets, which are connected with those material elements (above, pp. 206-7), conceptually perceived ψυχή (as a divine name), νοῦς, ἔννοια, φρόνησις, ἐνθύμησις, λογισμός (Acta Archelai 10). If the final series is to be expanded from the old number of five to the number of seven, 'Αρχή and Γένεσις are inserted, as are sun and moon in the penultimate series. Now the diverse systems are related, as the Mithras liturgy shows: Ψυχή (as a divine name) and 'Αρχή and Γένεσις take as their continuation, instead of the conceptual parts (νοῦς, ἔννοια, etc.) the spiritual-material elements, or the latter are simply omitted and it is only said that the primal man, i.e., the world-soul combines in himself 'Αρχή and Γένεσις, as in the instructive passage in the Martyrium Petri, chapter 9 (Bonnet, *Act. Apost. apocr.* I 94.4): "Ανδρες, οἷς ἐστιν ἴδιον τὸ ἀκούειν (cf. the ἄνδρες ὁρατικοί of Philo, the persons gifted with the powers of vision) ἐνωτίσασθε ἃ νῦν μάλιστα ὑμῖν ἀναγγελῶ ἀποκρεμάμενος· γινώσκετε τῆς ἁπάσης φύσεως τὸ μυστήριον καὶ τὴν τῶν πάντων ἀρχὴν ἥτις γέγονεν. ὁ γὰρ πρῶτος ἄνθρωπος, οὗ γένος ἐν εἴδει ἔχω ἐγώ, κατὰ κεφαλὴν

181 ἐνεχθεὶς (from above; he is the κορύβας, i.e., ἀπὸ κορυφῆς βάς of the Naassene Preaching,[85] which here offers the Judaized and Hellenized Persian Gayomard-doctrine) ἔδειξιν Γένεσιν τὴν οὐκ οὖσαν <ἐν τῇ φύσει> πάλαι· νεκρὰ γὰρ ἦν αὕτη μὴ κίνησιν ἔχουσα. κατασυρεὶς οὖν ἐκεῖνος ὁ καὶ τὴν 'Αρχὴν τὴν ἑαυτοῦ εἰς γῆν ῥίψας τὸ πᾶν τοῦτο τῆς διακοσμήσεως συνεστήσατο. Here we recognize quite clearly the Jewish-Christian gnosis, for which Christ is almost always the world-soul, because he is equated with the πρῶτος 'Αδάμ, who as the divine world-self was already a fixed concept for that gnosis even before the adoption of the belief in Christ, and thus with the divine

πνεῦμα in matter. Thus we understand the thought of the author of the Mithras liturgy and recognize that the entire first prayer pertains to this Ψυχή or this Self, which had already been invoked in the prefatory part.

Corresponding to the introductory prayer is the concluding prayer after the vision of this divine being: κύριε, χαῖρε, δέσποτα ὕδατος, χαῖρε, κατάρχα γῆς, χαῖρε, δυνάστα πνεύματος (magical words have replaced the enumeration of the four elements). κύριε, πάλιν γινόμενος (Pap. γενόμενος) ἀπογίγνομαι αὐξόμενος, καὶ αὐξηθεὶς τελευτῶ, ἀπὸ γενέσεως ζωογόνου γενόμενος εἰς ἀπογενεσίαν ἀναλυθεὶς πορεύομαι,[86] ὡς σὺ ἔκτισας, ὡς σὺ ἐνομοθέτησας καὶ ἐποίησας μυστήριον.[87] A dissolution, a passing away, is described here. The reference here cannot be to the earthly body--indeed, a considerable time earlier the initiate had already left that body and will once again immediately assume it whole and intact--but must be to his "Self". *The man in him* must pass away when the deity is born or he is born as the deity. Comparable of course is the Indian idea of a total disengagement from the imaginary I; only here it is positive, turned into an ethical entity, and it moves toward the attainment of a new self, the divine I. It is of great significance that we can demonstrate such a conception already in paganism. Even though the one thus reformed returns to his own body, still he is a different person, inwardly altogether disengaged from this body. As we saw in the analysis of the thirteenth Hermetic chapter, he has also incorporated into himself the inward components of his double, or of God, which consist of ethical or intellectual gifts. Mani has attempted, in his system, to vindicate this same idea, which in any case is earlier than Mani: five virtues are the gifts of νοῦς, ἔννοια, φρόνησις, ἐνθύμησις, λογισμός, thus the

82

parts or members or elements of God; I shall have to treat this more explicitly in Appendix XIII on virtues and vices as members; here I should like only to refer to a Manichaean fragment, M 133, extant only in bits and pieces in the Soghdian language. I have become acquainted with this fragment through the kindness of Prof. Andreas, and Prof. Bang's discovery of a concept of "original light-nature" has enabled me to understand it. The powers of the soul, such as knowing, meditating, understanding, etc., are enumerated and characterized as issuing from one's "own" knowing, meditating, and so on. In this connection the word "own" always refers to the ἴδιος δαίμων, that heavenly Self, our original nature or perfect nature, from whose elements indeed the Mithras liturgy also derives the elements in us.

The initiate prays to his divine prototype, which lives in the suprasensual world (thus for Iranian thought the god-filled light-world: ἐψυχωμένος), and he commands his own mortal nature: while he travels through the heavens, it is to remain behind for the present and to rest; at God's direction he will put it on again, undamaged and undiminished, μετὰ τὴν ἀπαραίτητον καὶ κατεπείγουσαν χρείαν (34; cf. 29: μετὰ τὴν ἐνεστῶσαν καὶ κατεπείγουσάν με πικρὰν ἀνάγκην, cf. also line 17). This can only mean the distress of death, which this self-determined separation from the body, the *voluntaria mors*, always brings with it. The best explanation is afforded by

183 the Persian apocalypse of Arda Viraf, the second chapter of which I would have to place in this very same setting. When Viraf is destined for the heavenly journey, he places great value upon his going *voluntarily*; the sisters bewail his certain destruction; the priests comfort them with the assurance that after *seven* days they will return Viraf to his sisters safe and sound, and for seven days and nights they conduct

religious services around the lifeless body. The connection between narrative and mystery-prescription is marvelously clear here; the mystery-perspective is the soil out of which the religious narrative, the prophecy, grows; we may actually draw conclusions from the one to the other. The very same schema is followed by the Mandaean book Dinanukht[88] (Lidzbarski, Genza r. VI, p. 205), only the details are imaginatively expanded. Here too the prophet is lifted up to heaven in order to bring back the pure truth in opposition to the false teachings that have seized a place; here also upon his return he finds himself being lamented as dead. He burns the false books, gathers disciples, and for a number of years previously made known to him continues to teach the true religion. One wonders whether the ascension of John was not originally thought of in the same way.[89] In that connection, the particulars of the portrayal, in spite of the fantastic embellishment, are closely related to what we know about conceptions of the Mithras initiate from tombstones or from literary witnesses: storms bear him upward, and he climbs a ladder from the gate of one sphere to the next. Somewhat different is the idea in the liturgical prayer interpreted above: ἐπεὶ οὐκ ἔστιν ἐφικτὸν θνητὸν γεγῶτα (i.e., as man, only on the basis of his birth into mortality) συνανιέναι ταῖς χρυσοειδέσιν μαρμαρυγαῖς τῆς ἀθανάτου λαμηδόνος. One can recall the Egyptian idea of a wandering through the twelve hours of the night and the rising of the soul of the dead king with the rising of the sun; and one can also compare the fact that the Isis-initiate, after his wandering is completed, is represented and

184 venerated as sun-god. But that idea also recurs in different versions among other peoples. Hardly Egyptian, although certainly Oriental, is the view expressed in a Giessen papyrus that the deified ruler ascends to heaven with the sun-*chariot*

(Clio VII 278; cf. *Neue Jahrbücher f. d. klass. Altertum* XXI 365). It is clear only that the idea of the ecstatic absorption into God is formed entirely in keeping with the idea of the resurrection,[90] and the mystery is borrowed from the cult of the dead.--Finally, one purely linguistic comment before I leave this document, made available to us by Dieterich, which is so important in the history of religions. The prayer is sensed to be a unity throughout; not so the language. I have already pointed out that the divine world of light and the material world are contrasted as διαυγὴς καὶ ἐψυχωμένος and as ἀφώτιστος καὶ ἄψυχος κόσμος; here soul and light are what is divine. When the words ἔσταθι, φθαρτὴ βροτῶν φύσι (line 39) correspond to the ἀρτίας ὑπεστώσης μου πρὸς ὀλίγον τῆς ἀνθρωπίνης μου ψυχικῆς δυνάμεως (line 27), the ψυχικός apparently is "human"; the divine power within us is characterized in line 19 as πνεύσῃ ἐν ἐμοὶ τὸ ἱερὸν πνεῦμα,[91] and when in line 21 it is said νοήματι μεταγεννηθῶ, we really expect πνεύματι. Paul also uses νοῦς and πνεῦμα quite similarly in I Cor. 2:11 and 15:16. In other passages in the liturgy πνεῦμα is only the breath or even just the air. This is quite comprehensible to one who is familiar with the indefiniteness of the corresponding labels in Oriental languages; what the word ψυχή came to mean for the Greeks does not altogether coincide with any Oriental word; on the other hand, such a concept as "the Self, the I", cannot be expressed in Greek at all, and requires a substitute of a different sort.[92] We could expect a fixed terminology only if this mysticism grew out of the Greek intellectual and spiritual life; the fact that any such terminology is utterly lacking, and that Greek and apparently non-Greek usage are interwoven vindicates my feeling that Oriental thought has been appropriated by Greek-

185

speaking men without any special philosophical revision.[93] We shall have to go into this matter more fully later on.

I should like now to compare with the Mithras liturgy a magical practice that stems from an entirely different belief and populace, in order to see whether a cultic source also underlies the latter. In the great Paris magical papyrus (Wessely, *Denkschr. d. Wiener Akademie* 1888, p. 48, lines 154-55) we find the alleged writing of a priest Nephotes to the last king of free Egypt, the wise (i.e., knowledgeable in magic) Psammetichos, who, like his mirror-image Nektanebos in the Alexander fiction, practices lecanomancy. The magician, who has a guide (μυσταγωγός) with him, is to lie down naked, though provisioned as for burial, with his eyes both tightly closed and bound. Then he is to address the following prayer to Seth or Typhon (lines 179-80): Κραταιὲ Τύφων, τῆς ἄνω σκηπτουχίας σκηπτοῦχε καὶ δυνάστα, θεὲ θεῶν, ἄναξ, ἐγὼ [εἰμὶ] ὁ σὺν σοὶ τὴν ὅλην οἰκουμένην ἀνασκαλεύσας [καὶ] ἐξευρών <τε> τὸν μέγαν Ὄσιριν, ὅν σοι δέσμιον <προσ>ήνεγκα, ἐγὼ [εἰμὶ] ὁ σὺν σοὶ συμμαχήσας τοῖς θεοῖς--οἱ δὲ (i.e., other copies): πρὸς τοὺς θεούς--, ἐγὼ [εἰμὶ] ὁ κλείσας (ῥαίσας?) οὐρανοῦ δισσὰς πτύχας καὶ κοιμίσας δράκοντα τὸν ἀθεώρητον, στήσας θαλάσσης (Pap. θάλασσαν) ῥεῖθρα, ποταμῶν νάματα, ἄχρις οὗ κυριεύσῃς τῆσδε τῆς σκηπτουχίας, ὁ σὸς στρατιώτης ὑπὸ θεῶν νενίκημαι (νικώμενος?), πρηνὴς ῥέριμμαι μήνιδος ἕνεκεν (Pap. εἵνεκεν) κενῆς· ἐγείρου, ἱκετῶ, τὸν σόν, ἱκνοῦμαι, φίλον καὶ μή με ῥίψῃς χθονοριφῆ, ἄναξ θεῶν. δυνάμωσον, ἱκετῶ, δὸς δέ μοι ταύτην [τὴν] χάριν, ἵν' ὅταν τινα αὐτῶν τῶν θεῶν φράσω μολεῖν ἐμαῖς ἀοιδαῖς, θᾶττον ὀφθῇ μοι μολών. The conception is clear: as Seth's warrior the initiate has fought for his god against the other gods, in order that Seth might rule over Egypt, or the earth. Now he lies wounded or rather dead; his God will awaken him. Certainly underlying this are the ancient

186 mysteries of Osiris, in which the battle of the gods is actually enacted (Plutarch's source, in De Is. et Os. 19, still knows of this; cf. Wiedemann, *Mélanges Nicole*, p. 574, and now H. Schaefer, *Die Mysterien des Osiris in Abydos*; Sethe's *Untersuchungen zur Geschichte und Altertumskunde Ägyptens* IV 2, 1904). As is known, Herodotus pictures the battle (II 63): ἐνταῦθα μάχη ξύλοισι καρτερὴ γίνεται, κεφαλάς τε συναράσσονται καί, ὡς ἐγὼ δοκέω, πολλοὶ καὶ ἀποθνήσκουσι ἐκ τῶν τρωμάτων· οὐ μέντοι οἱ Αἰγύπτιοι ἔφασαν ἀποθνήσκειν οὐδένα. Now this is explained for us: the Egyptians believe that the deity vivifies the dead; most of those who are stunned with the blow of the charcoal indeed will actually be awakened again. The name of the priest, who himself must also have received this initiation, takes us a bit further. Professor Spiegelberg has pointed out (*Zeitschr. für äg. Sprache u. Altert.* 1926, p. 35) that according to Epiphanius' testimony (de vita prophetarum 8), νεφωθ means the crocodile, and that this reference is confirmed by the Greek-Coptic glossary published by Bell and Crum, p. 197, No. 405. Thus Nephotes is also attested as the name of a deity. But we can press on still further. This deity Nephotes plays a role in the Osiris mystery, indeed in his form as a crocodile. Proof of this is given by the great mystery-inscription of Philae (H. Junker, "Das Götterdekret über das Abaton," *Denkschr. d. Wiener Akademie* 1913, p. 43), in which it is remarked on the festival of the sixteenth of Choiak: Horus came and brought the members of Osiris to the water on this day in his (Horus') form of a crocodile, in order to assemble them (or something approximating this) in the house of Osiris. Junker refers to the black granite figure of the crocodile which bears on its back an Osiris-mummy, in the Berlin Museum 11486, and to other documentation which would take us too far afield here. Since we have before us here the mys-

teries in their re-formulation and adaptation to Seth-Typhon, the crocodile-deity has become a servant of Seth, whose sacred animal the crocodile is, in fact, in other traditions; but by the statement that he brought thither (προσήνεγκα, not προσήγαγον) it betrays the re-structuring of the same mystery. That would fit in splendidly with Professor Spiegelberg's already well-founded conjecture that the initiates are called by the name of the sacred animal of their god; indeed, one could be tempted to interpret in this sense the word in the glossary written in Greek as βαινεφωθ. Yet I prefer not to venture further into this area that is strange to me, and I would be happy if I can pay my thanks to the Egyptologist for his abundant instruction, by making a small contribution on my own part. Nor do I venture to guess how the myth was re-shaped among the worshipers of Seth. I only hope to have shown that magic is connected with this myth and is related to the public cultus and the popular belief.

I return to the magical procedure. Like the prefatory part, the aftermath of the prayer is written in prose: ταῦτά σου εἰπόντος τρὶς σημεῖον ἔσται τῆς συστάσεως τόδε--σὺ δὲ μαγικὴν ψυχὴν ἔχων ὁπλισθεὶς μὴ θαμβηθῆς--ἱέραξ γὰρ πελάγιος καταπτὰς τύπτει σε ταῖς πτέρυξιν εἰς τὸ πλάσμα σου, ταῦτα αὐτὰ δηλῶν, ἐξαναστῆναί σε. σὺ δὲ ἀναστὰς ἀμφιέσθητι λευκοῖς εἵμασιν καὶ ἐπίθυε ἐπὶ θυσιαστηρίου γεΐνοῦ ἄτμιστον λίβανον σταγονιαῖον λέγων τάδε· συνεστάθην σου (Pap. σοι) τῇ ἱερᾷ μορφῇ, ἐνδυναμώθην τῷ ἱερῷ σου ὀνόματι, ἐπέτυχόν σου τῆς ἀπορροίας τῶν ἀγαθῶν, κύριε, θεὲ θεῶν, ἄναξ, δαῖμον. ταῦτα ποιήσας κάτελθε (return to the world) ἰσοθέου φύσεως κυριεύσας [τὴν] διὰ ταύτης τῆς συστάσεως (union with God) ἐπιτελουμένης. Manetho says of Amenophis, who is venerated as deity (fr. 52; Josephus, Contra Apionem I 26): θείας δοκοῦντι μετεσχηκέναι φύσεως κατά τε σοφίαν καὶ πρόγνωσιν τῶν ἐσομένων. By virtue of his

deification then the initiate can make correct predictions from the basin of water or can conjure up the dead. This also explains how the Ἀπαθανατισμός of the Mithras liturgy can be used for magical purposes; it provides the necessary preparation for the actual magic. A comparison of the two sets of religious documents of course also shows a great difference. How easily Nephotes manages the mystery-like part of the instructions, compared with the immense apparatus that the Mithras liturgy had to set in motion! The entire manifestation of the deity and the union with him is placed in the inner experience of the person lying there with bound eyes; indeed, the 188 three strokes with the bird's wing signifying this experience can be given by the mystagogue without any preparation.

We must assume here that the initiate upon his bier has actually invoked a deity, and that the latter has appeared and responded. Now we find precisely this in a Christian monastic practice which is attested for us in Egypt in the *Apophthegmata patrum* (Cotelier, *Ecclesiae graecae monumenta* I 703). The devout monk Jacobus wishes to explore for himself and his companions the question whether the church of Christ is represented by the Nestorians or by the Catholic church to which he belongs. He puts on his shroud--the garment in which he took his vows as a monk--, goes into a solitary cell in the desert, and lies there for forty days without food or drink, being tormented by demons. After this period has elapsed, there appears to him a youth with radiant countenance--Christ himself--and asks what he desires; he presents his doubts and receives the information: "You are right, where you are." The body of the unconscious monk then is found at once before the door of the orthodox church. In the same way he wrests from God total ἀπάθεια, and thus an ἰσόθεος φύσις. In the secret Egyptian alchemist literature we find (Berthelot, *La chimie au moyen*

âge II 320) a text, unfortunately sadly mutilated: the initiate who wishes to attain revelation in the innermost heavens must, at the very first gate, exchange soul for soul and body for body (that is, his earthly self for the heavenly), and at each of the following gates in a forty-day fast must die again (compare this with the view in Philo, Quaest. in Exodum II 49-52). The iambic prayer in the Nephotes magic appears to point to something similar in the words καὶ μή με ῥίψῃς χθονορίφῇ. It assumes that the purportedly deceased one is lying up in the air and has made the attempt at the celestial journey. It is often said that in this attempt the deity casts down to the earth the person who is not fully worthy or not fully protected (Wessely, *op. cit.*, p. 107, line 2507; cf. my Poimandres, p. 227), and this corresponds to the general view. Thus Nero heard of the pronouncements of a Greek prophet or magician who claimed that he could fly up to heaven and commanded him to make the attempt (Dio Chrysostom, or. 21.9 [Arn. II, p. 288. 18]; Juvenal III 77). There was much talk about the anticipated and repeatedly postponed attempt, later, when Rome's first actual "aviator", who proposed to portray Icarus' flight in the circus,[94] suffered a fatal fall directly in front of the emperor's box (Suetonius, Nero 12), the popular recollection, under the influence of the belief in magic, connected the two, and somewhat later under the same influence the Christians transferred the story to Simon Magus, Peter's adversary. Hence on the basis of the story about the monk I should assume that there actually existed in later Egypt a corresponding personal mystery which had borrowed its ideas from such public portrayals. Ancient popular custom can have had a similar impact in other places. On this point, however, it remains beyond our powers to determine whether alien influences also had an effect outside that national point of beginning; nothing

else migrates so easily as magical practices and magic-like cultic practices that are not comprehended. The best parallels for such mystery-like securing of revelation through the imitation of death is again offered by the Persian book of Arda Viraf, especially chapter 2. But is it really likely that a prayer--and a prayer in verse form at that--has been taken over from the ἱερὸς λόγος of that so clearly Egyptian-Hellenistic mystery? From the metrical form I should infer from the very outset another kind of mystery literature from which this prayer has been appropriated as a bit of embellishment.

In the secret astrological literature we encounter the metrical form as early as the writings of Petosiris and Nechepso,[95] and indeed in a heavenly journey which we can discern to some extent from the prooemium to the sixth book of Vettius Valens (Kroll, p. 240) and the allusions in Manilius (I 40) and Ovid (Fast. I 297), as well as from a reference in Proclus (In rem p. II 344 Kroll). Nechepso, when he had turned away from the vices and lusts of this world and directed his thoughts exclusively to the celestial world, offers this picture:

190

> ἔδοξε δή μοι πάννυχον πρὸς ἀέρα
> . . . .
> καί μοί τις ἐξήχησεν οὐρανοῦ βοή,
> τῇ σάρκας ἀμφέκειτο πέπλος κυανόχρους
> κνέφας προτείνων.

Under the guidance of this divine being he travels through heaven,[96] enjoys the blessed vision of which Vettius also boasts (σεμνυνόμενος ἐπὶ τῇ περιχυθείσῃ μοι ὑπὸ τοῦ δαίμονος οὐρανίᾳ θεωρίᾳ), and converses with the gods themselves (Vettius: τὰ θεῖά μοι προσομιλεῖν ἐδόκει; cf. Proclus: τὴν μὲν οὖν 'Ανάγκην τίνα δεῖ νομίζειν καὶ πρότερον εἴπομεν καὶ μαρ-

τουροῦσαν ἔχομεν τὴν ἱερατικὴν παραδοῦσαν καὶ αὐτοπτικὴν κλῆσιν τῆς μεγίστης θεοῦ ταύτης καὶ διδάξασαν πῶς ὀφθείσῃ προσιέναι δεῖ. <δεῖ> γὰρ ἄλλον τρόπον καὶ παραδοξότερον ἢ τοῖς ἄλλοις θεοῖς, εἴ τῳ ταύτα γράφων Πετόσειρίς ἐστιν ἀξιόχρεως ἀνήρ, παντοίαις τάξεσιν θεῶν τε καὶ ἀγγέλων συναλισθείς). He is also sanctified and made immortal by this celestial journey (cf. the imitation, reduced as always to human terms, in Vettius 242.14: θείᾳ καὶ σεβασμίᾳ θεωρίᾳ τῶν οὐρανίων ἐντυχὼν ἠβουλήθην καὶ τὸν τρόπον μου ἐκκαθᾶραι πάσης κακίας καὶ πάντος μολυσμοῦ καὶ τὴν ψυχὴν ἀθάνατον προλεῖψαι). He also wishes to proclaim secrets through this account of his vision; Vettius indeed still speaks (242.22) of μυστικαὶ καὶ ἀπόρρητοι ἀγωγαί; but these are not μυστηρία in the cultic sense. It is the reflection of the mystery in doctrinal or rather edificatory writing, which appears early alongside the actual mysteries, just as prophecy appears alongside the priestly cultic actions. It is Oriental, not Greek religion that is involved here. I cannot here go into the broad prospects that open up from this point--the beginning of Parmenides' didactic poetry undoubtedly is influenced by an Oriental prototype--but must confine myself to the Hellenistic forms. The first and for us now the oldest Hermetic writing, the so-called Poimandres, in which we discern the re-working of an old Persian writing,[97] gives the great "mystery" of creation in the form of a vision, thus detached from any action; the thirteenth gives its counterpart that stems from the same circle of ideas, the 'Απαθανατισμός in a form that stands immeasurably nearer to the mystery-form, but also as a didactic writing which in its ideas bears a certain similarity to Nechepso-Petosiris. Here we cannot make any scrupulous distinctions, at least in a presentation not of

the individual official mysteries, but of the *basic conceptions of the mystery religions*.

In any case the representation of the vision of Nechepso is most closely and strikingly related to the Mithras liturgy. Of course in the latter the goddess Ἀνάγκη plays no role at all--as we have seen, in it ἀνάγκη is only the crisis of death[98]--and what underlies the portrayals is not the astronomical picture of the heavens, but a wholly fantastic, imaginative picture. But through Proclus himself (*op. cit.*, II 345.6) we know that in the official rites Ἀνάγκη stood at the center, as with Nechepso, and for the initiate there are prescribed a number of invocations--of course in prose form--which in the beginning, middle, and end always give the name as Θέμις καὶ Ἀνάγκη; it is the paraphrase of the Iranian concept *asa*. Thus Dieterich's major finding, that we are dealing with the writing of a believer in Mithras, rightly stands. Only we may no more identify it with the ἱερὸς λόγος of a particular mystery than we may identify the poetic prayer in the Nephotes-magic or in Petosiris-Nechepso with the ἱερὸς λόγος of an Egyptian mystery. It is hoped that this brief survey of a couple of "mysteries" has shown that a strict separation of the two types of religion that were discussed (above, pp. 7ff.) perhaps never can be made, or at least no longer in their Hellenistic re-formulations. Other mysteries will be treated later in the course of our presentation.

NOTES

1. In the Samothracian mysteries, which to be sure appear to exhibit Phrygian influences, we still find traces in the closing years of the fifth century (Plutarch, Apophth. Lac. 217D, 229D), and in Rome as late as Cicero's time.

2. It has to be a different story, of course, where in closed communities like the mystery community in Philadelpheia (above, p. 117) ethical commandments also were sworn to under oath; here the church discipline of the Christians will have its model (cf. Pliny, ep. X 96).

3. This dissertation has also appeared as a book, published in Leipzig. Though I ordered the book repeatedly, accidental circumstances prevented my receiving it, and hence I was unable to use it in my work on *Iranisches Erlösungsmysterium*, pp. 251-52. [Here I can only mention the statements of E. Peterson in his uncommonly comprehensive and useful book Εἷς θεός, pp. 200-1. His fine exposition of Augustine's "Confessions" has in the meantime been given an interesting continuation and expansion by M. Zepf, *Augustins Confessiones* (Heidelberger Abh. zur Philosophie u. ihrer Geschichte, Heft 9).]

4. One may think of the Agdistis shrine with its many altars in Philadelpheia.

5. Two additional items of documentation for ἄναγνος are offered by Nos. 24 and 26, and the same offense is found in Nos. 22 and 23.

6. Tibullus' penitential exercises also are thought of as being performed publicly; cf. Seneca, de vit. beata 26.8: *cum aliquis genibus per viam repens ululat...concurritis.*

7. In sacral language, διαβάλλειν means "to announce, to disseminate"; cf. Corp. herm. XIII 22 (Poimandres 348): μηδενί, τέκνον, ἐκφαίνων τῆς παλιγγενεσίας τὴν παράδοσιν, ἵνα μὴ ὡς διάβολοι λογισθῶμεν.

8. They seem to appear already united.

9. Cf. the relief of an Archigallus in Wendland, *Die hellenistisch-römische Kultur*, second edition, Plate VII. It is almost an illustration of Juvenal.

10. As we learn from the papyrus, he is holding her sins up before her.

11. That bequest of πορφύρα (purple cloth) καὶ χρυσός to the temple at Jerusalem, which according to Josephus (Ant. XVIII 81) was exacted by a Jewish swindler from the matron Fulvia, could rest upon a similar belief. It is difficult to punctuate this passage after line 519. The woman does penance through baptism for the sins of the entire year.

12. The scholia on IV 14 (cf. Friedländer) show that the oven was already known in antiquity.

13. The poet says, exaggeratedly, the entire Campus Martius. Originally it probably was only the temple.

14. At Aswan, where the Nile enters Egypt (cf. the description of the baptism of the dead in the Pap. Rhind I, below, p. 274. This alleged source was represented accordingly on Hadrian's gate at Philae; W. Spiegelberg, "Die Glaubwürdigkeit von Herodots Bericht über Ägypten," *Orient und Antike*, Heft 3, 1926, p. 19); again Meroe is an exaggerated form of expression. The water was used for baptism, and I consider it likely that what is meant is this cultic act that is pictured by Apuleius, and *spargat* means *spargi faciat*; of course it is conceivable also that Juvenal has heard of the washings of the temple, for which water purportedly from the Nile (actually from the Tiber) was used.

15. What is involved here again is a *ritual* sin which is also mentioned in the inscriptions (No. 22 in Steinleitner): Ἀτθὶς ἡ Ἀγαθημέρου ἱερὰ βιασθεῖσα ὑπὸ αὐτοῦ (by the spouse). Juvenal also makes reference to this point briefly by his use of the word *uxor*. The inevitable punishment (*poena*, κόλασις) would be a grave illness. The sin-offering is small, and naturally so much the greater is the recompense for the priest who takes upon himself the painful penitential ceremony. The Phrygian-Lydian cult also is familiar with the principle of vicarious substitution in these matters (Inscription 17). Accordingly, one may interpret the portrayal of a "simulated" confession and self-castigation in Apuleius, Met. VIII 28, as such a substitution. It is important to note that it constitutes, and indeed replaces, a part of the service of worship. Thus in the Christian imitation, it is not the recipient of grace himself who presents his *libellus*, but the priest, and during a span of two years the worship service in Augustine's church some seventy times consisted of the reading and dis-

cussion of such *libelli* (De civ. dei XXII 8), even though Augustine devoted only one sermon to each (in special cases it was evidently more).

16. In Lucretius (I 103-4), the *vates* of Memmius also proclaim to him their *somnia*. This passage, highly important for cultural history, has hitherto been badly misinterpreted.

17. As his symbol, above him the *mystica vitis* (Lygdamus 6.1; cf. Josephus, Ant. XV 295).

18. It is also conceivable that it is meant to identify the deceased person as a Jew; the seven-branched lampstand, like the Christian cross, is also used to identify the dwelling of the Jew or the Christian; cf. Kohl-Watzinger, *Antike Synagogen in Galilaea*, 1916, p. 191. We recognize the stonemason's model from the sarcophagus of the Palazzo Barberini (pictured by Cumont), where the bearers of the medallion themselves probably are to be interpreted as the four seasons. E. Michon gives an abundance of other examples in his footnotes. I find the lampstand within the circle also in P. Gaudence Orfali, *Capharnaum*, 1922, p. 93, as a bit of ornamentation of the synagogue (?) in Tiberias.

19. The oracles cited by Augustine (De civ. dei XIX 23) from Porphyry belong to the same series. They probably stem from Asia Minor (Hecate is the goddess of oracles there), and are likewise favorable toward Judaism, which there had partially merged with paganism; their date cannot be determined.

20. On this point I must refer to the second part of my book, *Das iranische Erlösungsmysterium*.

21. It was a mistake for Ganschinietz (*Realenzyklopädie* IX 708) to seek to trace it back to Labeo's "theology that reduced everything to a Neoplatonic scheme". The assumption that Labeo invented the oracle is utterly unlikely; the conjecture is only an attempt to avoid a particular interpretation.

22. In the center stands Dionysos wrapped in a himation which leaves the torso free; he has placed his left arm around a large vine that grows up from the ground, and in his right hand he is holding a kantharos, so that the wine is flowing from it; the wine is being caught by a small satyr, who in his right hand is holding up a cup, while in his left arm he is

holding a lagobolon. On the other side, in an equally small figure, Silenus is represented on a plunging ass, supported by a satyr. On the left and the right are the figures of boys as the four seasons of the year: on the left, winter, nude except for the chlamys that is knotted at the breast, holding in his right arm a reed-staff, and in the left hand some geese; then spring, likewise nude except for the chlamys, with a twig in his right arm, and in the left a basket with flowers. On the right side is summer, clad in the chlamys, holding a sickle in his right hand, and in the left a basket overflowing with ears of grain; then autumn, with his right hand holding up a hare, and in his left a thyrsos. Below on the right side sits a panther (the panther next to autumn also appears on the sarcophagus of the Palazzo Barberini). Between winter and spring Tellus is situated, wearing a crown of ears of grain, and holding a twig; situated between summer and autumn is Oceanus, also wearing a crown. In the rounded corners are lions which are rending stags, and hunters blowing horns.

23. Even Kohl and Watzinger (*op. cit.*, p. 187) judge that Christian art is connected with the Jewish art of the Orient. That the latter is itself dependent upon Hellenistic-Syrian art is evident in the very nature of the case and is confirmed by the decoration of the Galilean synagogues. Of course Hellenistic-Syrian art also had an influence, independent of the relationship just cited, on the pagans of the West.

24. The treading-out of the wine, which is represented on Cumont's sarcophagus beneath the seven-branched lampstand, recurs in the decoration of the Galilean synagogue in Chorazin (Kohl-Watzinger, p. 50, illustration 99b). [The picture (discussed by Peterson, *op. cit.*, p. 37) in a tomb at Jerusalem, in which two sirens (angels? *orantes*?) in relief are holding the crown of victory for a man named Baruch, might just as easily have belonged to a Jewish Christian as to a Gentile Christian.]

25. Of course this is not intended to say that in the innumerable places in Rome where one or more genies or erotic figures appear with the symbols of the seasons of the year, a belief in immortality or even only a confession of the god of the year or of the world lies consciously in the background. What originally had religious significance in the East often enough retained a purely ornamental value, but the religious application does not issue from that value.

26. The circumstances of the well-known tomb of Vincentius, the priest of Sabazios, at least suggest this conjecture.

27. It would be conceivable also that Attis represents the Phrygian religion, since on the sarcophagus of the Palazzo Barberini winter appears personified as Attis. Yet the other seasons of the year lack any such characterization.

28. Cf. Reitzenstein-Schaeder I, chapters II and III; for Mani, see above, p. 101, n. 81. The confessions of εἷς ἐστιν Ζεύς, Ἥλιος, Ἅιδησ, Σάραπις, and the like are in fact also universally known.

29. On this unique document, which in my *Poimandres* I treated only halfway correctly, cf. now Reitzenstein-Schaeder, Part I, chapter IV, and the appendices.

30. According to Iranian custom he himself must have been initiated into their knowledge (Philo, De spec. leg. III 100). For the injurious kind of magic of course Philo also mentions love-magic. The fact that in his treatment the people practicing it are from the dregs of society does not argue against the fact that priests of a barbarian nation do the same thing.

31. Only in the remarkably preserved opposing tradition is Zarathustra the magician, who is conquered by Ninos.

32. We are unable to say to what extent it has been mixed with the Babylonian magical cult.

33. Since we have some measure of acquaintance with the Damdaδ-Nask, we sense the appropriateness of this characterization. The possession of a doctrine of the creation of the world and an explanation of the world revealed through a vision must have appeared to the Greeks as the most distinctive thing about this religion.

34. In fact, according to Philo (De spec. leg. III 101) these "magicians" promise μισοῦντας εἰς ὑπερβάλλουσαν εὔνοιαν ἄξειν. Hence Servilia admits the prayers. Exact reports of these very proceedings are available (Pliny, ep. 5.5); Tacitus only selects the most impressive points. Tibullus (I 2.62) describes a sacrifice.

35. On this, cf. von Duhn, *Archäolog. Anz.* 1921, p. 106.

36. In the hymn of the soul in the Acts of Thomas, the king's son seizes the pearl from a giant serpent; he has previously put the beast to sleep by enchantment.

37. Cf. now Kerényi, *Archiv für Religionsw.* XXIV 61.

38. In my "Weltuntergangsvorstellungen" I have explained a number of examples of this psychologically interesting process from the Nordic art of approximately the tenth century A.D., and have pointed out misunderstandings that now seem amusing to us. There the task of interpretation was an easy one, since the new religion is known to us even in detail. Where this is not the case, our art almost necessarily fails us.

39. Isis too is indeed a goddess of love, but everyone senses that the mention of her here must have been destructive of a sense of Pathos for all Romans. Only Delia may be a believer in Isis (v. 23: *tua...Isis*).

40. In *Hermes* 57, pp. 357-58, I have attempted to explain the poetic feeling that the beloved lives a life that is pure and free from sin. We have it in its purest form in the much mishandled ode *Integer vitae*.

41. Only because he did this could Steinleitner at all recognize the significance of those inscriptions. Where such a procedure is entirely lacking, we do not advance beyond a mere collection of curiosities. There is no shortage of examples of this result.

42. Cf. the passage, already cited by Steinleitner, from Menander's Δεισιδαίμων (fr. 4 Mein.):

παράδειγμα τοὺς Σύρους λαβέ·
ὅταν φάγωσ' ἰχθῦν ἐκεῖνοι διά τινα
αὐτῶν ἀκρασίαν, τοὺς πόδας καὶ γαστέρα
οἰδοῦσιν· ἔλαβον σάκιον, εἶτ' εἰς τὴν ὁδὸν
ἐκάθισαν αὐτοὺς ἐπὶ κόπρου, καὶ τὴν θεόν
ἐξιλάσαντο τῷ τεταπεινῶσθαι σφόδρα.

43. *Das iranische Erlösungsmysterium*, pp. 157 and 253; cf. now B. Landsberger in the *Textbuch zur Religionsgeschichte* by E. v. Lehmann and H. Haas, p. 311.

44. If the translation is correct, we could see here the prototype of the barsom twigs in the Persian cultus. According to Anquetil's testimony (Windischmann, *Zoroastrische Studien*, p. 276) they are from the wood of the tamarisk tree, and Strabo (XV 733) mentions these (Greek μυρίκη) as the material

of this bundle among the magicians. I can document the same miraculous bundle of twigs two thousand years later among the Manichaeans (below, p. 270).

45. The names of the gates are all Sumerian and are interpreted by the corresponding action; on the name of the eleventh cf. Zimmern in my book *Das iranische Erlösungsmysterium*, p. 254, note 3, and now *Zeitschrift der Deutschen Morgenländischen Gesellschaft* LXXVI, 1922, p. 49.

46. According to the myth, Marduk also was gravely wounded and taken captive, but was set free and healed (Zimmern).

47. I point incidentally in this connection to the significance of penance among the Mandaeans, where it appears combined with the mystery of baptism (right Ginza II 2, in Lidzbarski, p. 54) and where we find a structured church discipline which can lead even to exclusion from the community (right Genza I 161, in Lidzbarski, p. 24.9). I may point also to the penitential discipline of the Manichaeans, the internal structure and religious significance of which W. Bang (*Muséon* XXXVI, 1923, pp. 137-38) has explained through a comparison with Christian penitential manuals (Bang combines in an especially exemplary fashion the insights of philology and religious scholarship). Unfortunately I know too little about penitential practice in Buddhism.

48. Even the exhortation to fear the Lord and the treatment of the individual case as *exemplum* are not lacking.

49. The fact that it does not deal with the soul's salvation, σωτηρία in the sense of a survival hereafter, is less decisive in this regard--as Apuleius shows, a Hellenistic mystery also can be understood in this way--than the fact that the sense of a secret (= mystery) is lacking.

50. At the present time we have not yet begun a scientific study of the migrations of cultic practices; of course it is already a certainty that such migrations occurred extensively. The process of exchange continues down to relatively late times; indeed, we see an action like the taurobolium or baptism pass from one mystery religion into another. In my judgment it follows from this that for our consideration and for religio-historical labors with respect to Christianity the determination at least of the meaning attributed to a cultic action at a particular time, if not of the original meaning,

has an intrinsically higher importance than the determination of its ultimate point of departure among a particular people (cf. above, p. 112).

51. Anyone who wishes to get an idea of how much further the religio-historical study has taken us in these matters should compare the statements of A. Weber, *Indische Studien* XIII, which were almost wholly unaffected by this kind of study.

52. Reitzenstein-Schaeder, I 3.

53. One should avoid dismissing such a religious feeling with the catchword pantheism. Its rise lies beyond all philosophy. This is shown by such non-philosophical religions as, for example, the Egyptian, and the magical conceptions of many peoples elsewhere also preserve traces of such a feeling for nature or for God. One may compare with the Hermetic text the description of a magical text in Griffith, *Stories of the High Priest of Memphis* I 3.13, p. 92: "reading the first formula, thou wilt charm the heaven, the earth, the underworld, the mountains, the seas. Thou wilt discern what the birds of heaven, and the creeping things shall say, all. Thou shall see the fish of the deep, there being power of god resting upon water over them. Reading the second formula if it be that thou art in Amenti, thou art again on earth in thy (usual) form; thou wilt see the Sun rising in heaven with his cycle of deities, and the Moon in his form of shining." One senses how in the original conception the vision (γνῶσις) is connected with the sense of power over creation; thus ἐξουσία has both meanings.

54. *Das iranische Erlösungsmysterium*, pp. 30-31. Reitzenstein-Schaeder, Teil I.

55. Denkard IX 53.18; cf. Reitzenstein-Schaeder I, pp. 4-5.

56. One can best realize this when one sees how Gruppe (Bursian's *Jahresber.* 137, 1908, 229-30) utterly fails to understand this achievement. I regret that so discerning a scholar as Cumont even in his most recent publications ignores Dieterich's accomplishment.

57. In the astrological, alchemist, and other secret literature as intended for the son only.

58. Perhaps it is not superfluous to remark that the word ἀρχάγγελος in no way justifies our thinking of Jewish or Christian influence. In Greek renderings of Persian views ἄγγελος is a fixed term, and Cumont (*The Oriental Religions in Roman Paganism*, 1911, p. 266, n. 38) has altogether rightly claimed a dedicatory inscription *Diis angelis* for the Mithraic faith. To the numerous passages which he cites I add one that is especially instructive for philologists and specialists in Iranian studies: in the *Theologumena arithmetica* (p. 41 Ast) the epic surname of Athena (the number seven) Ἀγελεία is explained from Nikomachos of Gerasa: ἢ μᾶλλον--ὃ καὶ Πυθαγορικώτερον (in fact the Pythagoreans regard their master as a pupil of Zoroaster)--ἐπειδὴ καὶ Βαβυλωνίων (Zoroaster is supposed to have taught Pythagoras in Babylon) οἱ δοκιμώτατοι καὶ Ὀστάνης καὶ Ζωροάστρης (i.e., Zoroaster with Ostanes) ἀγέλας κυρίως καλοῦσι τὰς ἀστρικὰς σφαίρας...ἀπὸ τοῦ σύνδεσμοί πως καὶ συναγωγαὶ χρηματίζειν δογματίζεσθαι παρ' αὐτῶν τῶν φυσικῶν λόγων, ἃς ἀγέλους κατὰ τὰ αὐτὰ καλοῦσι ἐν τοῖς ἱεροῖς λόγοις, κατὰ παρέμπτωσιν δὲ τοῦ γάμμα ἐφθαρμένως ἀγγέλους διὸ καὶ τοὺς καθ' ἑκάστην τούτων τῶν ἀγελῶν ἐξάρχοντας ἀστέρας καὶ δαίμονας ὁμοίως ἀγγέλους καὶ ἀρχαγγέλλους προσαγορεύεσθαι, οἵπερ εἰσὶν ἑπτὰ τὸν ἀριθμόν, ὥστε Ἀγελεία (ἀγγελία Ast) κατὰ τοῦτο ἐτυμότατα ἡ ἑβδομάς. The ἱεροὶ λόγοι can only be theological (not magical) writings; the citing of Ὀστάνης καὶ Ζωροάστρης (elsewhere usually only Ὀστάνης) is explained by Pliny XXX 8: *primus...commentatus est de ea* (about the teaching of Zoroaster) *Ostanes Xerxen regem Persarum bello...comitatus* (the teaching of the magicians who accompanied Xerxes, cited by Cicero, De Leg. II 26, could go back through some intermediate source to Ostanes). What is meant here are the seven Amesha-Spentas, as Minucius Felix 26 shows: *Magorum et eloquio et negotio primus Hostanes angelos, id est ministros et nuntios dei, eius venerationi novit assistere.* Thus the astrological references, like the etymological comments that are inseparable from them, are a later Greek addition, probably from a "Pythagorean" source; it is highly possible that this addition goes back to Aristoxenos, who in fact is the first to tell us that Pythagoras was a pupil of Zarathustra and who tells us more particulars about the latter's teaching. What remains is important enough, only it is unclear whether Ostanes has Ohrmazd and *six* angels constitute the sacred number, as do the fifth century Damdaδ-Nask and Theopompus' source, or whether he knows of *seven* angels in addition to the deity. Perhaps it is still more interesting to the philologists that we now are able more clearly to recognize the tradition of the old academy concerning the chief teachers of the Persian religion. As is known, Diogenes Laertius

(prooem. §2) testifies: ἀπὸ δὲ τῶν Μάγων, ὧν ἄρξαι Ζωροάστρην τὸν Πέρσην, Ἑρμόδωρος μὲν ὁ Πλατωνικὸς ἐν τῷ περὶ μαθημάτων φησὶν εἰς τὴν Τροίας ἅλωσιν ἔτη πεντακισχίλια--Ξάνθος δὲ ὁ Λυδὸς εἰς τὴν Ξέρξου διάβασιν ἀπὸ τοῦ Ζωροάστρου ἑξακισχίλιά φησι--καὶ μετ' αὐτὸν πολλούς τινας μάγους κατὰ διαδοχήν, Ὀστάνας καὶ Ἀστραμψύχους καὶ Γωβρύας καὶ Παζάτας, μέχρι τῆς τῶν Περσῶν ὑπ' Ἀλεξάνδρου καταλύσεως. What is of primary interest to us is the διαδοχή, of which we otherwise in fact know nothing at all (the comparison with the philosophical διαδοχαί must have been obvious, since Eudoxos described Zoroastrianism as a philosophy). The "magician" Gobryas appears as a contemporary of Socrates in the Axiochos composed in the old academy (on the dating cf. Immisch, *Philologische Studien zu Platon*, I); his grandfather had participated in Xerxes' war against Greece, and thus was a contemporary of Ostanes. This means that the author based his invention on Hermodorus' references to the διαδοχή; thus they are also the source for determining the date of Ostanes in Pliny XXX 8. He, and not the later mentioned magician from the time of Alexander, is the historical personality. The same thing must also hold true for Astrampsuchos, whose name likewise has passed over into the magical literature; I do not recall Pazates in that literature. Hermodorus fills the gap between the subsequently pre-dated Zoroaster and Ostanes with the general words πολλοί τινες μάγοι; this justifies Pliny, who reads of a διαδοχή and cites only its first member, in saying of the teaching of Zoroaster: *nec claris nec continuis successionibus custoditam primus...Ostanes* (in addition he attempts to fill in the gap from his own learning); he does some re-structuring, but by the very word *successio* he betrays his dependence on the major text of Hermodorus which he has taken from Hermippus (cf. Reitzenstein-Schaeder I, p. 4). Herewith we seem to gain an entirely new bit of knowledge of Zoroastrian school-leaders (and authors?) before Alexander, but also a more exact insight into the sources of Diogenes Laertius and Pliny, ultimately the Greek characterization of the Avesta which exactly corresponds to the Persian.

59. Thus Wendland; Usener's conjecture πατροπαράδοτα conflicts with the context, according to which the writer must be the only one who has received these initiations and this power from the emissary of Mithras.

60. Dieterich reads Τύχη; cf. Preisendanz, *Deutsche Literaturzeitung* 1917, col. 1433 (I cannot accept his further conclusions; for Psyche I refer to the unusual passage of Martianus Capella II 142; Hiller v. Gärtringen has kindly

reminded me of the representation on a still uninterpreted tombstone relief of earlier times, Hermes 37.121). The two deities form a unity.

61. Pap. γραφεντι; Dieterich's emendation; Pap. πραταπαραδοτα; Wendland's emendation.

62. Pap. αιητης; Dieterich reads αἰητὸς (for ἀετὸς), but βαίνω does not fit in with this.

63. Pap. αρχη; ἀρχῆς is Wendland's emendation.

64. Pap. δε; δὴ is Usener's emendation.

65. Dieterich reads ἐχόμενον; but the participle is put in the absolute form; it belongs to the preceding με "me--I who have held fast"; cf. Blass-Debrunner, p. 75; Rademacher, p. 86; Crönert, *Nachrichten der Gött. Gesellschaft der Wissenschaften*, 1922, p. 42.

66. τῷ στερεῷ καὶ τῷ ἀέρι is Dieterich's reading, who (p. 56) recalls Poseidonios and therefore proposes to introduce a new enumeration of the elements. Correct is only πνεύματι (cf. line 26); but the interpolator misunderstood it and in fact sought to introduce what Dieterich correctly explains from Orphic formulae.

67. Pap. κραοχραξροιμεναρχομαι; Dieterich reads ἵνα ἐνάρχωμαι. Decisive for me is a comparison of Plato's use (Sympos. 210a and 211c) of ἄρχεσθαι in the mystery (in contrast to τελευτᾶν) with Paul's word (Gal. 3:3): οὕτως ἀνόητοί ἐστε; ἐναρξάμενοι πνεύματι νῦν σαρκὶ ἐπιτελεῖσθε. The words νόημα and πνεῦμα correspond, as do νοῦς and πνεῦμα in Paul.

68. Cf. the repetition in the prayer 12.2 Dieterich: ἄνθρωπος ἐγώ, γενόμενος ἐκ θνητῆς ὑστέρας καὶ ἰχῶρος σπερματικοῦ καὶ σήμερον τούτου ὑπό σου μεταγεννηθέντος, ἐκ τοσούτων μυριάδων ἀπαθανατισθεὶς ἐν ταύτῃ τῇ ὥρᾳ κατὰ δόκησιν θεοῦ ὑπερβαλλόντως ἀγαθοῦ.

69. Pap. αγιασμασι αγιας. The slip of the pen is understandable in the light of the three words of the same stem; I have made the emendation following Wessely, Denkschr. 1888, p. 94, line 1975: ἀλλὰ φύλαξον ἅπαν μου δέμας ἄρτιον εἰς φάος ἐλθεῖν (the meaning is "undamaged"). On the non-aspirated form ὑπεστώσης cf. Dieterich.

70. Here as frequently ἀχρεοκόπητον means "unabridged" and hence "undamaged".

71. Pap. αμεταθετου; Dieterich's emendation.

72. Pap. φθρατη, in the familiar metathesis.

73. For ὑγιῆ Dieterich writes ὑρίει (= ὑφίει), which is incomprehensible to me. The meaning must correspond to the ἀχρεοκόπητον. In the practice of magic one wears φυλακτήρια bearing the formula διαφύλαξόν με ὑγιῆ, ἀσινῆ, ἀνειδωλόπληκτον (Wessely, Denkschr. 1888, p. 71, line 1079; cf. 1062).

74. Dieterich still considers the words ψύχω δὲ, ἐγώ εἰμι and ψύχων to be the original text. According to established style the magician must mystically characterize the deity who he claims to be. That this was not necessary for the original text is shown by the Hermetic regeneration-mystery: ἐγῶ γάρ εἰμι ὁ υἱὸς θεοῦ or, in brief, ὁ υἱός is entirely sufficient; for this title cf. also Zosimus (*Poimandres*, p. 105).

75. It now becomes especially evident to us in the Pap. Oxyrh. 1381.

76. One part appears to have been excised or intentionally omitted. The continuation takes an entirely different turn and shows signs of significant Egyptian revision.

77. Thus Helios certainly is not original; furthermore, in the conclusion οὐρανός evidently stands for the Indian *akasa*, the space that is only filled with air.

78. It is altogether understandable, and indeed perhaps it is already prefigured in the Orient, that from this, Greek medicine makes a determination of character by means of the four actual elements that are combined in the human body.

79. This cannot at all mean an individual soul, but only the Indian *atman*, originally the breath, then what is spiritual and at the same time the essential, the Self. Thus νοῦς and ψυχή can be thought of as separate, but also as united. In the system of Poimandres, God is both, because he is φῶς καὶ ζωή.

80. The similarity of the portrayal in the Turfan fragments--of course the same is true also in the Mandaean hymns--

with that of the Yasht 22 (and of the Vendidad) is uncommonly strong.

81. Metam. XI 29: *si tecum nunc saltem reputaveris exuvias deae, quas in provincia sumpsisti, in eodem fano depositas perseverare nec te Romae diebus sollemnibus vel supplicare iis vel, cum praeceptum fuerit, felici illo amictu illustrari posse.*

82. Cf. L. Troje, "Die Zwölf und die Dreizehn im Traktat Pelliot," pp. 134-35.

83. Bang, "Manichäische Hymnen," *Muséon* XXXVIII, 1925, p. 14.

84. Cf. Reitzenstein-Schaeder, p. 75; below, p. 278.

85. Cf. Reitzenstein-Schaeder, pp. 168.1, 111, and 192-93.

86. "Having come to be from life-giving (thus earthly) birth, now dissolved into no-more-being-born (Being itself), I return into the world." Cf. the thirteenth Hermetic tractate. Significant also for the view of Indian Nirvana is the newly constructed term ἀπογενεσία.

87. I sense a clear reference to the prefatory part: the writer has received this mystery from Mithras himself through the highest emissary, and he passes it on only to his son; he is still the only one out of many millions (above, p. 232, n. 68). The entire piece of writing is a unity; nowhere is it possible to sense or demonstrate any sort of influences of Christianity.

88. The Persian name, "The one who speaks in accordance with religion" (Andreas), can be reproduced in the Greek language of formulae as ὁ λέγων τὴν ἀλήθειαν.

89. According to Mandaean tradition he also brings a renewal of religion. Important also is the burning of the earlier books, in Genza r. VI.

90. In fact the words εἰς θεὸν χωρεῖν have both meanings.

91. Cf. later, 10.22 Dieterich, where πνεῦμα is used for the soul wandering through heaven: ὥστε ἀπὸ τῆς τοῦ θεάματος

ἡδονῆς καὶ τῆς χαρᾶς τοῦ πνεῦμά σου συντρέχειν καὶ συναναβαίνειν.

92. It is an exceptional case when Porphyry ventures, in De abst. I.29, to say: εἰς τὸν ὄντως ἑαυτὸν ἡ ἀναδρομή and πρὸς τὸν ὄντως ἑαυτὸν ἡ σύμφυσις. The entire passage shows heavy use of eastern religious concepts.

93. For that reason itself I cannot explain a concept like πνεῦμα from the language of an author like Philo.

94. Herein also modern technology has its prototype in antiquity.

95. According to Boll both names pertain to the same personality. The writing itself falls in the early Ptolemaic period.

96. The οὐρανὸν βαίνειν or οὐρανοβατεῖν is explicitly attested.

97. Reitzenstein-Schaeder I 1; above, p. 11.

98. Here I must entirely disagree with Dieterich.

III.

Mystai, Divine Warriors, and Divine Captives

192 Now in these introductory considerations and investigations let us turn once more to the cultic form and its Hellenistic portrayals. The story of Apuleius' conversion, which though fictionalized was written out of full acquaintance with a mystery religion, a document which is of unique significance for us, must be most carefully compared with our other scanty references and explained from them. He appeals to Isis for deliverance, receives in a dream the promise of her help and the demand that he consecrate his life to her, experiences the miracle, and now is admonished by the priest of Isis (XI 15): *quo tamen tutior sis atque munitior, da nomen sanctae huic militiae, cuius non olim sacramento etiam rogabaris.* Thus Helm's reading; and he has produced the standard manuscript out of *rogaueris*, perhaps because the writer, like Helm, was thinking of the demand made in the dream (XI 6). Only the voluntary application (*nomen dare*) must necessarily precede the oath of loyalty (*sacramentum*). Hence the reading must remain *rogaberis*. Only the initiation serves as the oath of loyalty. We must compare Apuleius' words with Livy (XXXIX 15. 13), who offers in opposition to the Bacchus initiates: *hoc sacramento initiatos iuvenes milites faciendos censetis, Quirites? iis ex obsceno sacrario eductis arma committenda?* This device makes sense only if Livy knew that the oath was generally customary in the mystery cult of his time, and if the first initiation was connected with taking the oath of fidelity, in-

deed if the word *sacramentum* had already assumed almost the significance of *initiation*, as was true later in Christianity. In it the initiate pledges lifelong obedience and service; cf. the declaration (Apuleius XI 6) *plane memineris et penita mente conditum semper tenebis reliqua vitae tuae curricula ad usque terminos ultimi spiritus vadata* and the repetition (XI 15) *nam in eos, quorum sibi vitas <in> servitium deae nostrae maiestas vindicavit, non habet locum casus infestus* (it is also said in XI 6 that in a certain sense they are exempted from εἱμαρμένη). Thus Apuleius becomes a δοῦλος θεᾶς. As is to be

193 expected, the change is expressed in a twofold way, in religious as well as in national terms. The goddess opens the realm of the dead and the world of salvation (σωτηρία); entrance into her service puts an end to the old life through a kind of momentary death (cf. the Mithras liturgy, above, p. 211) and through a kind of rebirth transplants one into a new life. The gnostic conception, also appropriated by Hermetic thought, that this new life is fulfilled in another world and precisely thereby is delivered from εἱμαρμένη is not yet made explicit, but it clearly underlies the entire perspective; cf. XI 21: *numen deae soleat...sua providentia quodam modo renatos ad novae reponere rursus salutis curricula.* I hardly need need to stress the agreement with the views common to Christianity. The fact that on the other hand there was the thought of belonging to a new people (and nation) is shown by the designation προσήλυτος or ἐπηλύτης, *advena.* In Apuleius the latter term alternates with *religiosus* (θεραπευτής; the connections with Jewish usage are obvious); cf. XI 26: *eram cultos*[1] *denique adsiduus, fani quidem advena, religionis autem indigena.* The word *indigena* is not Apuleius' own formulation, but a fixed term of the Hellenistic mystery religions, which, in spite of having become international, still pre-

served in their sacral language the conceptions of national religions. This is shown in Quintilian XII 10.25 by the description of the struggle of the Atticists against Cicero: *haec manus quasi quibusdam sacris initiata* (the military image should be noted; cf. Apuleius XI 14: *e cohorte religionis unus*) *ut alienigenam et parum superstitiosum* (the reading should be left this way; Quintilian is saying that he does not recognize their *religio*; they themselves would have said *religiosum*) *devinctumque illis legibus insequebatur*. The word *alienigena* as a contrast to *indigena* is modeled after the Hellenistic ἀλλογενής in contrast to οἰκογενής (LXX, Gen. 17:27).[2] But the later priestly forgery of the *carmen Marci vatis* places it in contrast to *Troiugena*. Thus the inscription placed by the Roman authorities on the marble fence surrounding the inner court of the temple at Jerusalem (Dittenberger, *Orient. gr. inscr.* 598) uses it for ἀλλοεθνής or *advena*, and Luke also uses it in this sense (Luke 17:18: not Jewish in race and religion). Especially instructive about the perspective of the mysteries is the class of the ἀδελφοὶ εἰσποίητοι in the Jewish-Iranian mystery-communities of the Ὕψιστος cult (Schürer, *Sitzungsber. d. Preuss. Akad.*, 1897, pp. 200-201). They are accepted into "the tribe of souls". Now the passage from Quintilian becomes comprehensible. The fanaticism of the adherents to the mystical cults and their hatred for those who did not strictly observe their ritual laws[3] apparently was noted frequently. The concept of the *sancta militia* explains the designation of the third level of the Mithras initiates as *milites*; the concept of the *indigena* accounts for the designation of the fifth level as *Persae*; and the composition of the Parthian army with its mercenary soldiers (part of them prisoners whose lives the king had spared) and native-born warriors explains

the succession of ranks. Even when this distinction is obliterated, in Mani's company the catechumens who are not yet obligated to a lifelong commitment are called soldiers or warriors (for the monks who stood above them he borrowed from Indian and Greek usage the title of "the perfect"). The basic feeling of this religious contest has deep roots in the Iranian religious feeling and is not attached to any single organization. But in addition, we are not even certain that it is only Iranian religion that produces this feeling, and we shall not be able to draw firm conclusions about time or national origin from such linguistic observations. We can only determine the *religious* origin. I have emphasized this, and I maintain it, against Cumont's earlier references to the use among later philosophers or the self-consciousness of officials in the kingdoms of the Diadochi.

195 But back to Livy. We have seen that even before his time the concept of initiation was connected with the word *sacramentum*. As I said then, this presupposes that not only was the service of the initiate generally regarded as military service for his deity, but also the first initiation was regularly connected with an oath. It really should not be necessary to stress that; indeed, it is clear that without the oath the mystery simply is no μυστήριον. But in modern literature about "Hellenistic mysteries" that fact is not seldom ignored,[4] and in the philological-historical studies of the relationship of the state to the religions it is not always given sufficient weight. Dramatic presentations and cultic actions that are open to the public appear in most of the mystery religions, but these are not mysteries in the full sense of the term. They are distinguished from what I called, above, "personal mysteries". It is only these latter that incorporate one into a new people, a new class of men; their

inner connection with the Diaspora rests upon that fact. Moreover, only they offer a specific claim, the assurance of a religious benefit. Because this latter kind of mystery may not be open to the public and generally accessible, and because it consists in a kind of knowing (i.e., according to the Oriental perspective a vision), it is bound up with an oath.[5] It is significant that we now in recent times are able to demonstrate for Orphism the age of such an oath.[6] Hence it is the general view that where there is a rite of initiation, an oath also is administered. Therefore Christianity is regarded as a mystery religion.[7] For the oath that is employed at the initiation in the actual mystery religions we have a testimony in Hippolytus, Elench. p. 2.9 Wendland: τὰ ἀπόρρητα μυστήρια, ἅ τοῖς μυουμένοις μετὰ μεγάλης ἀξιοπιστίας παραδιδόασιν οὐ πρότερον ὁμολογήσαντες, εἰ μὴ τὸν τοιοῦτον δουλώσωνται χρόνῳ ἀνακρεμάσαντες καὶ βλάσφημον πρὸς τὸν ὄντως θεὸν κατασκευάσαντες καὶ περιεργίᾳ γλιχόμενον τῆς ἐπαγγελίας ἴδωσι. καὶ τότε δοκιμάσαντες δέσμιον εἶναι τῆς ἁμαρτίας[8] μυοῦσι, τὸ τέλειον τῶν κακῶν[9] παραδιδόντες, ὅρκοις δήσαντες μήτε ἐξειπεῖν μήτε τῷ τυχόντι μεταδοῦναι, εἰ μὴ ὁμοίως δουλωθείη.[10] Corresponding to this is the oath, modeled after a mystery oath, of the Baruch apocalypse of Hippolytus (*ibid.*, 133.2): τηρῆσαι τὰ μυστήρια ταῦτα καὶ ἐξειπεῖν μηδενὶ μηδὲ ἀνακάμψαι ἀπὸ τοῦ ἀγαθοῦ ἐπὶ τὴν κτίσιν. The period of probation, the yearning for the initiation, the lifelong commitment, the pledge of silence, all these recur in Apuleius. For the probationary period, whose end cannot be determined by himself but only by the goddess, he must take up residence in the temple area. It appears that he is not permitted to leave the area; anything that he may need from the city he must secure through the assistance of others. Thus he is represented as a prisoner

(δέσμιος) of the goddess, and since we also hear that he is favored with continual revelations, a comparison with the κάτοχοι of Sarapis is at least suggested.[11] The service is described in chapter 22: *sedulum quot dies obibam culturae sacrorum ministerium* (cf. chapter 6: *sedulis obsequiis et religiosis ministeriis et tenacibus castimoniis*). He is obligated to practice asceticism--it is a taking upon oneself the yoke; he is not thereby a priest; cf. XI 30: *inanimae protinus castimoniae iugum subeo* and XI 19: *deae ministeriis adhuc privatis adpositus*. As he himself says, he takes the yoke upon himself willingly. Does not Jesus ben Sirach indicate acquaintance with something similar when in Ecclesiasticus 51:23ff. he has wisdom say: ἐγγίσατε πρὸς μέ, ἀπαίδευτοι, καὶ αὐλίσθητε ἐν οἴκῳ παιδείας...τὸν τράχηλον ὑμῶν ὑπόθετε ὑπὸ ζυγόν, καὶ ἐπιδεξάσθω ἡ ψυχὴ ὑμῶν παιδείαν? In the logion in Matt. 11:25, whose unity and Hellenistic origin Norden has demonstrated in his brilliant book *Agnostos Theos* (pp. 277ff.), ἄρατε τὸν ζυγόν μου καὶ μάθετε ἀπ' ἐμοῦ indeed also denotes full surrender to the divine master. Such private participants in the cult who reside in the temple are familiar in the worship of Sarapis in later times in Alexandria; cf. the portrayal by Rufinus, Hist. eccl. XI 23, p. 1026.29f.: the sanctuary embraces various *adyta* for the mystery cult, and *exedrae et pastoforia domusque in excelsum porrectae, in quibus vel aeditui vel hi quos appellabant* ἁγνεύοντας, *id est qui se castificant* (= *purificant*), *commanere soliti erant*. Here the word ἁγνεύοντας is not, as it is occasionally elsewhere, a designation for the priests, but for these volunteers. The name κάτοχοι is not directly attested here, but the idea is here in kindred formulations; on a later inscription (Dittenberger, *Or. gr. inscr.* 262) in Baitokaike near Apameia it occurs, apparently for a priestly or semi-

priestly collegium. Their God likewise appears to be an oracular deity; so he himself chooses his high priest. Finally, at least a similar custom appears transferred to Greek temples and Greek deities; Philodemus, Περὶ θεῶν α′, col. 17.6, has been restored quite confidently by Diels (*Abh. d. Preuss. Akad.*, 1915, pp. 29 and 76.2) to read: [τῶν δ]ιὰ τοῦ ζῆν λελ[αχ]ότων κατακλεισθ[ῆνα]ι ἐν 'Απόλλωνος ἢ 'Αθηνᾶς. Of course what is said here need not involve a lifelong legal bond, and κατάκλειστοι (or ἔγκλειστοι) and κάτοχοι are synonyms, as we shall see.

98 It is not certain whether the ἁγνεύοντες at Alexandria mentioned by Rufinus are in any way to be connected with those men whom we give the pejorative label of κάτοχοι, who are attested by so many documents for the beginning of the second century B.C. in the Sarapeion at Memphis; but this question is of no significance for the complete and clear portrayal of Apuleius, and it has only slight significance for our knowledge of the mysteries, since there is no witness of any sort for a connection between the κατοχή there and the actual mysteries. Besides that, the "Serapeum papyri" have lost much of their significance for the general history of religions since Weingarten's derivation of Christian monasticism from the Sarapis-κατοχή has generally been abandoned. And yet I should affirm that they continue to hold an importance for the knowledge of the religious views and especially of the mystery conceptions of their time, and that they have increased in methodological interest, through the long and changeful dispute between two eminent scholars, Sethe and Wilcken. It is my hope that the question of how much we really know about this phenomenon, for the evaluation of which such an overwhelming abundance of material appears to be available,[12] may also provide some enlightenment

about the scope of what is attainable for those readers who gain from my book specific information about individual mysteries, while we still are able only to discern in some measure the basic perspectives and effects.

Some will deny any immediate connection with Christian monasticism. But even those people, if they believe that they must ascribe a religious character to that individual phenomenon in the Sarapis cult of Memphis, will not be able to dispute its connection with the tendency, ultimately expressed in monasticism, of Oriental piety toward total withdrawal from the world and from active life--toward asceticism, to take the word in its broadest sense. A unitary tradition, favored by the attitude of the times, makes its way from India by way of Persia--one may think of Mani, who need not have been the first borrower--and among the various peoples is combined with local forms of the worship of God. By its
199 main tendency pressing toward a certain organization, it is combined almost everywhere with an understandable striving of individuals to place themselves wholly at the service of a deity, to spend as long a time as possible in his temple or its environs.[13] The endeavor to make the submission to the deity outwardly manifest also and to restrict the needs of the body as much as possible, the aspiration for ecstasy and vision, the feeling of attaining a higher rank thereby, all this is humanly so understandable that I hardly need even to mention it. Philo also shows the development of generally recognized fixed forms and perspectives; but I hasten on to the Christian re-shaping of them, especially on Egyptian soil.[14] The ἀπόταξις, the renunciation of the worldly life, is a free decision, evoked as a rule by a revelation, an inner call. It signifies a vow of service that binds the individual, but the nature of this service

he freely determines; it is quite diverse. If he joins an existing fellowship, of course he must meet its minimum standards, but he can add his own stricter rules; more rigorous service bestows a higher dignity. The goal is to become a pneumatic, non-corporeal--a concept that will engage our attention later. As soon as it is reached, the vow of service is dissolved. According to the older gnostic view of asceticism, the ascetic may once again do everything that was earlier forbidden him, and even return into the world; according to the later view, which was first ecclesiastically recognized, he thereby becomes wholly independent; he becomes a priest. The ascetic becomes conscious of his entrance upon this state of perfection through some marvelous achievement in which he is successful--like finding a lost needle in the dark. Or a particular vision is required: Christ on a chariot of light or a throne, surrounded by all the angels.[15] We can understand the church's promptly taking steps against these visions: they are the devil's delusions; anyone who claims to have had them is placed in chains as a possessed person. Attainment of perfection no longer brings with it release from service, but only the orderly calling to a higher office in the church.

Let us turn now to the dispute over the κατοχή in Memphis. E. Preuschen, who in the second edition of his book *Mönchtum und Sarapiskult* (1903) interpreted those men as "possessed ones", was first followed by U. Wilcken and his pupil W. Otto (*Priester und Tempel im hellenistischen Ägypten*; Bd. I 1905; Bd. II 1908). Sethe interpreted them as convicts and at first denied any religious significance of the κατοχή. The lexical analysis which A. Dieterich (*Berl. philolog. Wochenschr.* 1905, column 15) has set forth in exemplary fashion following Bouché-Leclerq (*Mélanges Perrot*), offers us a free

choice between two interpretations: attested in profane usage and linguistically understandable without difficulty is the word κατοχή as confinement, imprisonment, κατέχειν as placing in bonds, confining, and thus also κάτοχος as a prisoner; but the same attestation and comprehensibility pertains also to κατέχεσθαι (ἐκ θεοῦ) in the sense of ecstatic rapture (thus

201 bound up with θεοφορεῖσθαι or κορυβαντιᾶν, as already in Plato, Symp. 215), κάτοχος as one possessed by a god, and κατοχή for the condition of being possessed.[16] Only the linguistic connection in which the respective words appear in the letters and petitions of men living in Memphis at that time can determine the meaning; they actually do this quite

202 unequivocally. As has already been rightly emphasized by Bouché-Leclerq, their official designation is always ἐν κατοχῇ ὤν (or τῶν ἐν κατοχῇ ὄντων, perhaps also ἐνκατεχόμενος) ἐν τῷ μεγάλῳ Σαραπιείῳ to which may be added, by way of more specific definition, ἐν Μέμφει and the indication of the years that the κατοχή lasts. The expression stressing the place is comprehensible only if κατοχή means confinement, not if it means ecstasy. In the latter case, people expected in official usage the addition of the divine name, but the place would not matter. An indication of the duration of the rapture in that connection would be nonsensical.[17] This consideration is intensified by the not entirely uncommon further identification of a building, not one in which these men are possessed, but one in which they reside; cf. Wilcken, N. 6, line 3: παρὰ [Πτολ]εμαί[ου τοῦ Γ]λαυκίου Μακ[εδῶν ἐγκατεχομέ]νου ἐν τῷ Σαραπ[ι]είῳ [᾽Ασταρτιείῳ ἔτ]η δέκα, οὐκ [ἐξεληλυθότος] τὸ παστοφ[όριον], ἐν ᾧ ἐνκέκ[λ]ε[ιμαι ἕως τ]ῆς σήμερον ἡμέρας, and further line 8: εἰσελθόντων εἰς τὸ ἐν τῷ μεγάλῳ Σαραπιείῳ ᾽Ασταρτιεῖον, οὗ καὶ ἐγκατέχομαι ὡς καὶ ἔφην,[18] and finally line 18: καὶ τὰς τῶν ἄλλων ἐγκατό[χ]ων παρα[θ]ήκ[α]ς

προσ[εσ]ύλησαν. On a similar occasion the same Ptolemaeus writes two years later (Wilcken, N. 8, line 8): παραγενομένων ἐπὶ τὸ ἐν τῷ ἱερῷ Ἀσταρτιεῖον, ἐν ᾧ τυγχάνω ἐν τῇ κατοχῇ γεγονὼς τὰ προκείμενα ἔτη...; line 18: Δίφιλον δέ τινα τῶν παρακατεχομένων ὑπὸ τοῦ Σαράπιος θεραπευτῶν. The formation of ἐγκάτοχος or ἐγκατοχεῖν θεῷ makes the interpretation of "possessed ones" linguistically impossible;[19] the same is true to an even greater degree with the designation of the neighbors as παρακατεχόμενοι (in N. 7, line 16, he uses ὁ παρ' ἐμοῦ for these). Anyone can understand "fellow prisoner"; the term "fellow possessed" is a contradiction in language, because it is illogical. Thus the deity performs the binding or fettering to the particular place; cf. the inscription of Priene (N. 195, around 200 B.C.): οἱ κατεχόμενοι ὑπὸ τοῦ θεοῦ. Those who are bound serve him and honor him; cf. the inscription from Smyrna (C. I. Gr. 3163): ἐγκατοχήσας τῷ κυρίῳ Σαράπιδι (for his honor, for his service; cf. the inscription from Farasha: ἐμάγευσε Μίθρῃ[20]) παρὰ ταῖς Νεμέσεσιν. Finally, full confirmation is provided by the publication by Revillout, rediscovered by W. Spiegelberg, of a Demotic epistle, which Sethe (Papyrus-Institut Heidelberg, Schrift 2, 1921) has edited (now in Wilcken 6 a). An ἐγκατοχῶν named Harmais says that he has given himself to the deity (Sarapis) and his shrine, that he worships the goddess (Astarte), and that for eighteen years he has guarded her temple. "I do not come out of the wall surrounding the shrine, because I am with the goddess in the inner part of my place (living quarters)[21] with Ptolemaeus." It is the same man whom Ptolemaeus (N. 7, line 16) has described as ὁ παρ' ἐμοῦ (for παρ' ἐμοί). In light of this the cultic meaning of κατοχή appears fully assured, as does the voluntary commitment to the deity who binds one on the basis of

the vow. As Wilcken now also emphasizes, only the deity can release one from that bond. The duration and stringency of the service provide the basis of a claim to consideration, and even veneration; in fact, they are the occasion for boasting. In all this we are dealing with a form of asceticism--in the broad sense of the term mentioned above.

204 Of course I still find it necessary to defend even this modest gain in assured material. First of all, I must defend my interpretation of the passage from N. 8 cited above: Δίφιλον δέ τινα τῶν παρακατεχομένων ὑπὸ τοῦ Σαράπιος θεραπευτῶν. It is true that Kenyon, Sethe, and other scholars interpret these words as being spoken by a servant who is quite distinct from the ἐν κατοχῇ ὄντες. In that case the expression would be as awkward and unnatural as one can imagine. One would expect an indication of the priestly or servant status of Diphilos, but not a distinction "a servant, indeed, but a servant who is held by the will of the deity". And with such an interpretation, what are we to make of the composite <u>παρα</u>κατεχόμενος? Someone who is confined in the same vicinity? If Ptolemaeus is trying to distinguish Diphilos' position from his own, why then the utterly superfluous equation that resides in his choice of the term κατέχεσθαι? Can I entirely separate παρακατέχεσθαι in the construction from ἐγκατέχεσθαι? Now the θεραπευταί of a deity are hardly different from the σεβόμενοι, as Plutarch (De Is. et Os. 44) alludes to σεβόμενοι τὸν Ἄνυβιν, people who revere him above all else, take him as their patron deity, and when they are able to do so, serve him cultically also. If they live at a temple, then as a body they can assume specific functions; if they live some distance away, they can go to it for festivals and then temporarily live there, as did that Nicanor whom Wilcken (p. 52) cites for us.

Wilcken correctly comments (p. 55): θεραπευταί is the general concept, which also includes within itself ἐγκάτοχοι as a special and elevated class. All the more do I regret having to disagree with him entirely on the interpretation of still another passage already cited: in N. 6, lines 3ff. (see above, p. 246) Wilcken proposes completely to separate ἐγκατέχεσθαι from ἐγκεκλεῖσθαι and would make the former signify divine confinement, and the latter a punitive imprisonment or siege of some kind.[22] Wilcken himself concedes that that goes against a natural interpretation of the words ἐγκατεχομένου ἐν τῷ Σαραπιείῳ [Ἀσταρτιείῳ][23] ἔτη δέκα, οὐκ ἐξεληλυθότος τὸ παστοφόριον, ἐν ᾧ ἐγκέκλειμαι ἕως τῆς σήμερον ἡμέρας. But it also contradicts Ptolemaeus' own use of language. The word ἐγκέκλειμαι, which here refers to the Astartieion, or to its Pastophorion, is replaced in line 8 by ἐγκατέχομαι, ὡς καὶ ἔφην; cf. in N. 5, line 9: τὸ...Ἀσταρτιεῖον, οὗ καὶ ἐν κατοχῇ εἰμι μέχρι τῆς σήμερον, and 7.10: ἐπὶ τὸ Ἀσταρτιδεῖον, ἐν ᾧ κατέχομαι ἱερῷ.[24] *The two words are used entirely without distinction.* How then was the recipient of the petition to understand that altogether in the introduction, thus in the *personal statement*, with the word ἐγκέκλειμαι Ptolemaeus was complaining about a criminal deprivation of his freedom? I consider this simply impossible. Thus the passage to which Wilcken appeals (N. 5, line 46) is incorrect: ἀξιῶ οὖν, ἐὰν φαίνηται, μὴ ὑπεριδεῖν με ἠνομημένον καὶ ἐγκεκλειμένον; it should read ἐγκεκλημένον (an injustice has been done to him, and this prompts the complaint). In the corresponding text in N. 6, line 33: μὴ ὑπεριδεῖν με...ἀγνωμόνως πολιορκούμενον καὶ ὑβριζόμενον καὶ ἀνομούμενον, πολιορκεῖν could even mean "accuse", as it occasionally does in Greek and as *oppugnare* does in Latin; yet the similar complaints in N. 15 and 16 suggest that we should rather interpret it in the general sense as

"oppress". Intrusion by force or throwing stones through a window can be characterized as πολιορκεῖν, but never as ἐγκλείειν.

Now it is possible to agree with Wilcken's objection: *Harmais* (N. 6 a) in fact only says that he is not permitted to leave the walled area enclosing the Sarapieion, and according to Ptolemaeus' words (7.16) he had been found in the Dromos, and thus outside his house. Thus *Ptolemaeus* cannot have been restricted to the temple of Astarte and the Pastophorion.[25] I would respond by saying that it is entirely possible, and in the later cult was even generally customary, that the individual ascetic would intensify for himself the general demands,[26] and that Ptolemaeus finally boasts[27] that in the style of later hermits he has a young servant who provides him with everything necessary for life. Equally unconvincing to me is an auxiliary argument of Wilcken that Ptolemaeus had once left the Astartieion and talked with Sarapion in the temple of Sarapis; for this high official, who had come to offer a sacrifice, is reminded in 53.6 (cf. Wilcken, p. 272) that he has spoken ἐνόπι τοῦ Σαρᾶπι. That could not have happened in the Astartieion, according to Wilcken, because the goddess held sway there. I am willing to concede that the simplest interpretation would be that it happened in the temple of Sarapis, but not that this interpretation is so compelling that on the basis of it we may overturn a fact so expressly and so frequently attested as οὐκ ἐξεληλυθὼς τὸ παστοθόριον, ἐν ᾧ ἐν κατοχῇ εἰμι (ἐγκέκλειμαι) ἔτη.... The person thus separated from his god could have in his room some portrayal of Sarapis; many another possibility is conceivable--one may recall Paul's ἐνώπιον θεοῦ (Gal. 1:20) and παραγγέλλω σοι ἐνώπιον τοῦ θεοῦ (in the epistle; I Tim. 6:13)--but none of them provable. Earlier, going against the reserve that we

206

must always maintain in guessing at the events that are only alluded to in these epistles, I myself was in error in thinking that we could draw conclusions from N. 70, a letter written by Apollonios in unrestrained passion and stammering language to his brother Ptolemaeus. I was allured into guessing at riddles by the fact that here he calls his brother πατήρ (instead of ἀδελφός) and uses the words σῴζεσθαι and βαπτίζεσθαι, which stem from sacral language.[28] Wilcken translates thus: "for they cast us into a great morass, and when you saw (in a dream) that we would be saved (from it), then we were baptized", and he remarks (p. 334) that "the concept of βαπτίζεσθαι fits in so splendidly with the picture portrayed by the ἐνβέβληκαν <ἡ>μᾶς[29] εἰς ὕλην that it would destroy this picture if one tried herein to find a figurative meaning like Reitzenstein's 'baptism'. That is in fact utterly excluded." It is my opinion that certainty cannot be gained here at all, for ὕλη is not the word that necessarily produces this picture, ἴδῃς refers to something that is to be done in the future, and βαπτιζόμεθα and ἡμᾶς are only conjectural; the subjunctive is also possible. Such passages are better left aside. The only thing that is proved is--and for the later statements this is important enough--that Ptolemaeus prophesies on the basis of dreams and declares that certain deities are speaking through him.

Both of us agree--and this is the main thing--that the description of the novitiate in Apuleius, to which I had first called attention, offers striking and instructive agreements. Apuleius characterizes himself (XI 19) as *deae ministeriis adhuc privatis adpositus contuberniisque sacerdotum individuus et numinis magni cultor inseparabilis*. He does not leave the temple area at all; whatever is to be done outside must be attended to for him by others. When Harmais describes

his situation by saying, "I am with the goddess", the words in Apuleius correspond to this: *me...ad deae gratissimum mihi refero conspectum.* He emphasizes above all that every night brings him significant dreams. This is also especially emphasized with the ἐγκάτοχοι. When they note down their dreams, perhaps Apuleius shows the reason for this: when both the novice and the priest or *mystes* dream the same thing in the same night, the divine command (e.g., for the initiation) is irrefutably determined.[30] In Apuleius the miracle is also repeated at the second initiation, for which in fact he is once again a novice (chapter 27). The *perspective* is much more ancient; we see this in the fact that in the book of Acts the baptism of Cornelius, like that of Paul, must be justified by the same double dream. Indeed, we can demonstrate in still later Christian perspective that in a religiously significant imprisonment revelatory dreams are expected and therefore are noted down. Thus the first part of the *Passio Montani*, in a slight revision, contains dreams which the imprisoned Christians wrote down and shared with the community, and the second part, written considerably later, contains the supplementary narrative of an educated author. These dreams, which understandably refer predominantly to the "release from imprisonment", the martyr's death, and thus the baptism of death, insure veneration for the person whom God has honored with a revelatory dream and thus has attested as inspired. As bishop, Cyprian may not consider his dreams as valid for others; when in the first trial he is sentenced to exile, to being interned in the city of Curubis, and here a dream informs him about his forthcoming execution, his biographer takes pains to prove that this was a genuine revelatory dream and that therewith God had honored and attested his servant. On the other hand, Perpetua, not yet

even baptized, is told, as soon as she is actually in prison, that she has a claim to a revelatory dream, and such a dream of her likewise unbaptized brother appears still later even to have been circulated in the community independently and to have been regarded as a revelatory writing. Thus general perspectives of the later period provide us with an understanding of the religious perspectives in the Hellenistic cult.

Wilcken correctly emphasizes that only the deity can release the person whom he has bound, and it appears to me an essential requirement that a sacral action also give outward expression to that release. It is understandable that we know nothing more of that action, because with it the prisoner leaves the Sarapieion, and thus the tradition is interrupted for us. We can even say something more and thus can fill in a gap in Wilcken's presentation. Otto had already stressed the point that the κατοχή must have had an aim.[31] Such an aim in fact underlies all those expressions of "asceticism", wherever we find them in Hellenism. To put it in paradoxical terms, there is nothing that is so little "for God's sake" as these various forms of extraordinary service: it is supposed to provide for the one who renders the service the perfection of knowledge, protection in the world beyond, an inner dignity or power, or something of the sort. Above all, the κατοχή must have a *purpose* precisely because, in the very nature of the idea, it has a definite goal and is not a lifelong calling. With this of course we have reached the limits of our knowledge; we have come very close to the *mystery-perspective*, an actual mystery is not attested for us, and therefore we may not--on this point I now agree with Wilcken--claim such.

But we may, indeed we must, more closely focus upon the nature of the release, regardless of the scantiness of the allusions afforded us by the account of Ptolemaeus' dream (Wilcken, N. 78). In the dream he prayed for release (ἄφεσις). In the next dream he sees himself on a high tower in a kind of transfiguration (his face is so splendid that he cannot show it to anyone);[32] an old woman promises to guide him to the god (δαίμων) Knephis, in order that he may worship him. He actually sees the god and, abandoning the account of the dream, now exhorts the recipients of the letter and his friends: εὐφράνεσθαι, οἱ παρ' ἐμοῦ πάντες· ἄφεσίς μοι γίνεται ταχύ. Later the god commissions him: exhort the twin sisters to come (to me from Memphis): εἰπέ τε (Papyrus ἰπή τε) ὅτι ἐκπορεύομαι. ὁ 'Αμ[ῶσις] ἥκει ἐπ' ἐμέ, ἔδωκέ μοι τὴν ὁδὸν καὶ διέσ[τη τὸ π]αστοφόριον ἔμπροσθέν μου. I have set forth here the restorations made by Wilcken, which in the latter part are altogether certain. In the case of the former part, I am doubtful. Wilcken sees in this epistle the confirmation of his interpretation of the ἐγκλεισμός as a case of non-religious confinement to the Pastophorion which has nothing to do with the religious confinement, the κατοχή. Thus he restores the name of Amosis, who is named in N. 5 and 6 as the representative of the high priest. This high official has, through his intervention, assured him of the possibility of once again leaving his house.[33] The words, with all their figurative splendor, are not very appropriate for this, and any connection with the vision of Knephis is lacking. It appears to me that the working of a deity is being portrayed: he created a path for me, and the Pastophorion opened up before me (thus in the description of the vision in Corp. Hermet. I 4: εὐθέως πάντα μοι ἤνοικτο ῥοπῇ; Lucretius III 16: *moenia*

mundi discedunt). The deity liberates, just as Wilcken insists he must do. So I venture to ask whether it should not be restored to read ὁ Ἄμ[μων][34] ἥκει ἐπ' ἐμέ. Ptolemaeus himself mentions (N. 77) a vision of this deity, and as Sethe states in various places, Knephis is connected with this deity.[35] It cannot be determined whether Ptolemaeus thought of him as a servant of Ammon, or saw the two as identical. Now at last we understand the connection: out of concern for the twin sisters, Ptolemaeus has besought Isis for ἄφεσις, that is, from the promised restriction to the Astartieion. The appearance of Ammon has brought him the fulfillment of this plea and dissolved his confinement.[36] Of course the 211 general obligation of the κατοχή in the Sarapieion remains in effect; he is still a κάτοχος in the following year, but then N. 12 explicitly tells us that he can go about freely: he goes to the seller of rushes who is in the Sarapieion. For the dissolution even of the general κατοχή we may assume that there are similar conceptions or forms, and therewith we acquire a new comparison with Apuleius, whose release in the initiation also is introduced by a dream which brings him together with the gods.[37] This seems to me to eliminate the essential distinction that Wilcken wanted to make between ἐγκέκλεισμαι and ἐν κατοχῇ εἰμι. It appears also, in light of the Philodemus passage, that free imitations of the Sarapis-κατοχή also occurred in the cult of other deities.

So in conclusion I turn our attention to the other accounts of the κάτοχοι, not for the purpose of learning details about the service in the Sarapieion at Memphis or of characterizing the later cult of Sarapis, but in order to fit a generally Hellenistic phenomenon into the overall picture of the piety of that time.[38] Here again I can only offer some supplements to Wilcken's carefully made collections. Anyone

who is familiar with the practice among Christian ascetics of
212 wearing chains--even the tombs have offered us confirmation for the numerous testimonies in literature--and who recalls Jerome's description (Ep. 22.28): *quibus feminei contra apostolum crines* (thus "unshorn"), *hircorum barba, nigrum pallium et nudi in patientia frigoris pedes*, will immediately understand the portrayal of Manetho (Apot. I 237): φοιβητὰς ἢ μάντιας οἵ θ' ἱεροῖσιν Ἑζόμενοι ζώουσιν ὀνείρατα μυθίζοντες. Οἱ δὲ καὶ ἐν κατοχῇσι θεῶν πεπεδημένοι αἰεὶ[39] Δεσμοῖσιν μὲν ἔδησαν ἑὸν δέμας ἀρρήκτοισιν. Εἵματα μὲν ῥυπόωντα, τρίχες δ' οὐρῇσιν ὅμοιαι Ἵππων κηροπαγεῖς ὀλοὸν τηροῦσι κάρηνον. Οἱ δὲ καὶ ἀμφιτόμοισι σιδηρείοις πελέκεσσιν Ἔνθεα λυσσώοντες ἑὸν δέμας αἱμάσσουσιν. All that the Roman of that time sums up under the concept of *fanaticus* (one who is not a priest and yet belongs to a particular *fanum*) is comprehended in a single group.[40] Thus the *fanatici* of Bellona are included; they too prophesy (cf. Tibullus I 6.83-84, and Juvenal IV 123). In the glossaries the word κάτοχος also is explained by the word *fanaticus*[41]--with special emphasis upon their prophesying activity--and connected in our glossaries with the explanations of *fanaticus*, e.g., *qui in templo divinat vel templi minister* (apparently for θεραπευτής), is also an explanation that directly describes the nature of the κατοχή, but has not yet been correctly set forth: *qui templum diu* <*non*> *deserit* (οὐκ ἐξεληλυθὼς...ἔτη δώδεκα ἕως τῆς σήμερον ἡμέρας). It is only all too understandable that the astrological authors usually speak ill of these people. They are in fact their rivals, who moreover are more sought after by the common folk. In contrast to them the astrologer is proud of his *science*; he can actually utter *the truth*, while they only pretend to do so
213 (like the ἐγκάτοχος Ptolemaeus, who scornfully writes to his brother [Wilcken, N. 70]: πρὸς τοὺς τὴν ἀλήθειαν λέγοντας

and ψεύδη πάντα). In fact, we have an entire declamation of this sort which splendidly shows the professional jealousy of the astrologers, in the second part of Propertius IV 1: the opponents are the temple oracles and the μάντεις, *augures, haruspices*. The *Babylonius* (this is an identification of status; only the following word can bring the name, and it must be Egyptian) Horus adduces as an example of his art: *idem ego, cum Cinarae traheret Lucina dolores. Et facerent uteri pondera lenta moram, 'Iunonis votum facite: impetrabile' dixi: illa parit, libris est data palma meis.* In the Alexander fiction Nectanebus practices the same activity, and later on the ascetic also practices it as well. In the Historia Lausiaca (chapter 36) the author tells us from his own experience, and thus it is well attested: there was a pregnant woman in Bethlehem who was unable to give birth; the holy Poseidonios was called, he came with his pupils, recognized what was wrong, knelt down twice, praying for expulsion of the demon, and then called on those present to εὔξασθε· ἄρτι γὰρ ἐξελαύνει τὸ πνεῦμα τὸ ἀκάθαρτον. It happened, and the woman gave birth. This makes Propertius understandable. The stories of the monks tell us that the Christian ascetics and hermits were constantly being approached by Christians and pagans alike for advice in times of illness and for prophecies. We may apply this also to their pagan rivals. Public esteem for asceticism steadily rose, and in the case of the individual ascetic, it increased in proportion to the achievements (πόνοι) which he undertook or affected. For their opponents were constantly making this accusation; anyone who is familiar with the accusations of Christian authors against the *catenati* will not be surprised when Claudius Ptolemaeus (Tetrab. 42.16) puts the κάτοχοι between woman-chasers and procurers, and of course also in the vicinity

of the μυστηριακοί, or when Vettius Valens (63:29) says: ἣ ἐγκάτοχοι ἐν ἱεροῖς γίνονται παθῶν ἣ ἡδονῶν ἕνεκα (for the sake of the passions or the lusts of the ascetics). Such individual statements can be interpreted only in their respective contexts and in terms of their tendency. But then they provide here a unitary picture.

214 Finally, if we inquire about the linguistic influences of the phenomena discussed here upon *early* Christianity, we must not set our expectations too high at the outset. The passage in Hippolytus (above, p. 241) can be compared with the previously unexplained terms δεσμοὶ τοῦ εὐαγγελίου and δέσμιος 'Ιησοῦ Χριστοῦ in Paul, especially in the epistle to Philemon. In Hippolytus I could not fully explain the sacral counterpart to δέσμιος τῆς ἁμαρτίας; neither the Greek nor the Latin language has a word for the almost personally understood concept of religion or of faith which, for example, the word *den* (*daena*) has for the Persian; but for Paul τὸ εὐαγγέλιον is a similar concept; he feels himself to be its servant (δοῦλος) and can now, in prison (ἐν δεσμοῖς), say, in exaggeration and with a kind of play on words, δέσμιος τοῦ εὐαγγελίου and δέσμιος 'Ιησοῦ Χριστοῦ. He is even more firmly bound to both, even outwardly, and thereby he has received still higher status (the πόνοι bestow status upon the Christian also). The feeling is understandable: the expression, especially the harsh and affected genitival combination, becomes more understandable if there was already present in general language a concept of the δέσμιος θεοῦ. All of us can readily understand his feeling as a στρατιώτης of his Lord and the idea of the ὅπλα τοῦ φωτός--I need not refer to Harnack's well known writing on *Militia Christi*--but, as the passage from Livy cited above shows, the figure is generally Hellenistic. Did Paul, who of course wanted to write in a

way understandable to his readers, get it from this source? For the imitation of this idea in Ephesians 6:10-18 we shall have to assume so, since H. Junker (*Bibliothek Warburg, Vorträge* I, p. 140) has shown us, in the same area in which the figure appears to have developed, a similarly extensive statement in the *Menug i xrad* 43.4: there the individual virtues are described as protection for the back, protection for the body, armor, defense, shield, thigh protectors, bow, arrow, and spear; indeed, even the gauntlet appears not to have been overlooked. Precisely in the Ephesian epistle Hellenistic mystery-formulas with Iranian coloring are heaped up.[42] But what would Paul be losing in true originality if indeed he 215 had borrowed the figure from the general religions of his time? I simply do not understand the passion of the attacks directed against such an assumption, and therefore I do not here enter into the basic issue in a case which, like this one, cannot be decided with certainty. It will depend in considerable measure on the number of words and figures that Paul has in common with the mystery religions. It is easy, but utterly pointless, constantly to refer back to one single individual case and to speak of the possibility of "spontaneous parallel developments". Of course we must recognize such, when, for example, in Babylonian and Egyptian magic of the earliest period kindred primitive perspectives are exhibited which can readily be explained psychologically. But anyone who wants to use the same explanation with a number of striking figures and expressions among people of the same time who were in constant contact with each other and spoke the same language is demanding that we renounce the assistance of philological and historical labors in favor of an arbitrarily formed opinion. The philologist, even in studying the language of a Paul, must employ the same standards as, for

example, the specialist in the German language employs in studying the language of the young Goethe. Only a person who extends the concept of inspiration to include even the external form of the language could deny him this right and this obligation. In that case of course we would have to label the Greek of the New Testament as exclusively correct and original.

NOTES

1. θεραπευτής; cf. above, p. 248.

2. In Latin the usage was quickly broadened, but the contrast to *indigena* or *domesticus* still is often discernible. Corresponding to the affected word-play in Pseudo-Callisthenes III 26 is the poetic use of *alienigenus* for *alius generis*.

3. Cf. the penance required for the slightest shortcoming; above, pp. 169ff.

4. Thus in the richly suggestive book by R. Kittel, *Die hellenistischen Mysterienreligionen und das Alte Testament*, 1924.

5. Thus, as Augustine shows us, in Manichaeism the *auditor* still is not permitted knowledge of certain religious writings.

6. Cf. p. 279.

7. Not entirely without justification, though also not entirely correctly. An oath was actually taken early, and Pliny (Ep. X 96.6) correctly places high value upon it; he understands it to be an oath of initiation, since in large measure it corresponds to the oath of a soldier: *ne furta facerent, ne latrocinia, ne adulteria committerent, ne fidem fallerent, ne depositum abnegarent*. A. D. Nock (*Classical Review* 1924) properly compares this oath that is taken every Sunday with the mystery oath of the Agdistis community of Philadelpheia (above, p. 117), and similar ethical obligations were also imposed in other mystery cults. The necessity arose for something similar in Christianity as soon as it was no longer demanded that one belong to Judaism and to observe the entire "law"; this is shown by the statements concerning the apostolic council, about which I shall not allow myself any further judgment. The acceptance of the Old Testament did not replace, but much more demanded a definite restriction. I emphasize explicitly that in Philadelpheia also this obligation in an oath is distinguished from the actual oath of initiation.

8. In the proclamation of the mystery δέσμιον τῆς θεοσεβείας or τοῦ θεου.

9. In the proclamation of the mystery τὸ τέλειον τῶν ἀγαθῶν.

10. In the proclamation of the mystery μήτε ἐξαγορεύειν μήτε τελεῖν.

11. We find such in Smyrna only a little later (C. I. G. 3163: ἐγκατοχήσας τῷ κυρίῳ Σαράπιδι). This still would not say that the Isis temple at Corinth also appropriated the designation of κάτοχοι.

12. Wilcken has recently collected this material in three large fascicles of his first volume of *Urkunden der Ptolemäerzeit* and has interpreted it with great care. Of course I cite the documents following him, and I am happy to be able to associate myself with his present judgment on the main points, without having to modify my earlier assertions in more than a single point.

13. For this attitude I refer to the Ion of Euripides or the account of the youth of Apollonius of Tyana. For Judaism R. Kittel (*Die hellenistischen Mysterienreligionen und das Alte Testament*, 1924) has recently pointed to similar and still more strongly spiritualized feelings (I single out especially Psalm 27:4 and Kittel's explanation, p. 90). They were also given expression in cultic form. The Lord's brother James spends as much time daily as possible in the temple. I consider entirely believable the report of the Greek historians (Josephus, Contra Ap. II 89; cf. *Das iranische Erlösungsmysterium*, p. 180) that there was in the temple a κατάκλειστος; that he was being kept for the Kronos sacrifice that was customary among the wild mountain tribes I regard of course as understandable fictionalizing. Prof. E. Peterson has called my attention in a letter to a note of Al-Ghazali stating that John the Baptist as a child had seen people in the temple who had been chained there, and this impression later caused him to become an ascetic. This would not be entirely unbelievable if only the source were somewhat more reliable. I acknowledge that we do not have any solid information with regard to the κατοχή in Memphis about the nature of the asceticism and that the observation that some of those locked up lived on the alms of the pilgrims cannot take the place of such solid information; but is not the confinement itself an "asceticism"?

14. For details I refer to my book, *Historia monachorum und Historia Lausiaca* (FRLANT, N. F. 7, Göttingen 1916).

15. In the old Cyprian legend (cf. *Nachr. d. Göttinger Ges. d. Wissenschaften* 1917, p. 45) Christ indicates that, since he has thus appeared to a pagan, the latter must after his baptism immediately be chosen to be a presbyter.

16. Ganschinietz (Pauly-Wissowa X 2526ff.) has completely ignored this linguistic usage which has been explained by many scholars, the formation of the composite ἐγκατοχεῖν, the meanings of κατέχω, and other points, just as he has almost totally ignored the distinction between the active and the passive use of the substantive. In his view κάτοχος is a primal concept, meaning one possessed, and all the phenomena, convulsion, frenzy, ecstasy, inspiration, enthusiasm, excitement, fall under that concept. "Thus it happens that later all the gods have their κάτοχοι." In the attached list we read for ὕπνος: οὐ μὴ ἐξεγερεῖς τὸν ὕπνῳ κάτοχον (Sophocles Trach. 970), and along with it for (a god?) ὀργιασμός: μαντική τε καὶ κάτοχος τοῖς περὶ Διόνυσον ὀργιασμοῖς; then for οἱ κατάσχητοι (!) ὑπὸ φόβου (Etym. M.; see βαμβαίνει, *explanatory* words of a Cyril glossary); then for πόθος: κάτοχος τῷ πόθῳ γεγενημένη (Suidas, s. v. κεκρατημένος; I do not find this interpretation; Ganschinietz offers the *explanation* as a lemma); and finally for γῆ: τἄμπαλιν δὲ τῶνδε γαίᾳ κάτοχα μαυροῦσθαι σκότῳ (Aesch. Pers. 223). It is the old prayer to the dead to send blessing and to restrain evil (cf. Choeph. 141, Phrynichos Kom. in Photius 141.19 Reitz.); but is evil itself possessed? Then Homer would have offered a better example (πρὶν καὶ τινα γαῖα καθέξει) and at the same time would have shown that it does not have to do with a state of being possessed. Belonging to the κάτοχος Ἑρμῆς, the god who binds by magical means, of course is the κάτοχος Μοῦσα, who is supposed to bind the youth (in "Aspasia" Athen. V 219 d), and one can say κάτοχος λίθος: "the gravestone holds"; but those who belong to Hermes do not thereby become gravestones. Further, when Hesychius also explains κάτοχοι by ἱερεῖς Ἑρμοῦ, he means people who practice the binding magic, but he does not testify that the priests originally bore the *name* of their god. Pollux says that one can also say of the place ἔνθεος καὶ ἐπίπνους, but it does not thereby become possessed, and the Latin illustration *possessus numine* (*deserit averso possessam numine sedem*; Lukan VI 314) is not an altogether happy choice; in fact, the continuation reads *Caesar et Emathiae lacero petit agmine terras*: Caesar leaves Epirus, which he had chosen as *sedes belli* against the will of Mars (cf. *aversis Musis carmina tangere, averso Apolline*; Propertius IV 1.74), and goes to Thessaly. That an offended deity would make a

place possessed is a strange idea. Finally, when I even read *mente commotus* as a testimony for the primal conception of κάτοχος, I wonder why ἐκπλήττεσθαι, ταράσσεσθαι, φοβεῖσθαι and others are lacking. At the very end we hear only a very little about the ἐγκατοχοῦντες in the Sarapieion--not even the literature that was already available then in the main. Everywhere we find superficiality, arbitrariness, obscurity, and deprecatory judgments.

17. Religious ecstasy is never understood as a continuing condition, nor is it understood, as gnosis is, as a realm; finally, it would be the poorest recommendation for the petitions, which have been very thoughtfully constructed, in part utilizing sustained conceptions, to say that they had been written in a state of ecstasy or rapture that lasted so-and-so many years.

18. In the parallel version the two passages read (Wilcken N. 5, line 3): πα[ρὰ Πτολεμαίου] τοῦ Γλαυκίου Μακεδόνος ὄντος ἐν τῷ [με]γάλῳ Σαραπιείῳ ἐν κατοχῇ ὢν ἔτη δ[έκα] οὐκ ἐξεληλυθὼς τὸ παστοφόριον ἐν ᾧ [ἐ]νκέκλειμ[αι] ἕως τῆς σήμερον and (line 8) εἰσῆλθον εἰς τὸ ἐν τῷ [μεγάλ]ῳ Σαραπ[ιε]ίῳ Ἀσταρτιεῖον, οὗ καὶ ἐν κατοχῇ εἰμι μ[έ]χρι τῆς σήμερον. From a third version (Wilcken 7) I note παρὰ Πτολεμαίου... τῶν ὄντων ἐν κατοχῇ ἐν τῷ μεγάλῳ Σαραπιείῳ ἔτος ἤδη δέκατον and παραγενόμενοι ἐπὶ τὸ Ἀσταρτιδεῖον, ἐν ᾧ κατέχομαι ἱερῷ, εἰσεβιάζοντο βουλόμενοι ἐκσπάσαι με καὶ ἀγαγῆσαι. The three expressions ἐν κατοχῇ εἶναι, ἐγκεκλεῖσθαι, and (ἐγ)κατέχεσθαι alternate quite freely.

19. The spatial connection implied in ἐν is tolerable only if it is also found in the second part of the composition, but not if spiritual condition is being expressed. "Confined in" the Sarapieion only expresses in an especially strong way the limitation of freedom; "possessed in" the Sarapieion is in conflict with the train of thought. Of course the same is true for ἐγκατεχόμενος, and indeed to a greater degree.

20. Cf. Cumont, *The Oriental Religions in Roman Paganism*, 1911, p. 263; H. Grégoire, *Comptes rendus Acad. des Inscr.* 1908, pp. 434-35.

21. Cf. 5.10 = 6.9, τόπος, and Wilcken on this passage.

22. Just what kind remains entirely unclear. Ptolemaeus' being bothered by house-searches does not constitute an ἐγκλεισμός.

23. This restoration is uncertain.

24. Cf. also No. 13, lines 7-12; N. 15, line 11. Thus Wilcken in no way utilizes an appeal to the fact that N. 6 is only a concept.

25. Wilcken himself in this connection has portrayed the situation with exemplary clarity: the intrinsically altogether unequivocal statements about the limitation on movement for both Ptolemaeus and Harmais are in sharp contradiction with each other, although *both* men are ἐν κατοχῇ. Wilcken holds this to be absolutely inconceivable and attempts--without success--to reinterpret the tradition, the religio-historical method which explains it by demonstrating the same contrast in kindred and better known religious structures and showing that the presupposition is false. But thereby at the same time the explanation offered by Wilcken's opponent, Sethe, itself, in its extrapolations loses its real basis; and Wilcken's more recent interpretation, relieved of that apparently insoluble difficulty, suffices to explain everything.

26. The other ascetics then do not take kindly to this; for this reason Makarios must leave a cloister.

27. I compare the comical story of the monk Serapion (Hist. Laus. c. 37, p. 115 Butler). He inquires as to who in Rome has taken asceticism farthest, and learns that it is a devout maiden who has not left her chamber for many years. He immediately goes to her, finds her on her bed, and asks her, "What are you doing?" "I am wandering." "What are you?" "Dead." Then he commands her: ἔξελθε καὶ πρόελθε. She objects: εἰκοστὸν πέμπτον ἔτος ἔχω καὶ οὐ προῆλθον. People would consider her a lunatic. He counters by saying that that would not matter to a person really dead. So she acquiesces, and the two of them go to the church. Here he commands her: Do as I do, and undress completely. She cannot do this, and he exults: ἐγώ σου νεκρότερός εἰμι... ἀπαθῶς γὰρ καὶ ἀνεπαισχύντως τοῦτο ποιῶ. Thus he broke her pride and left her deeply humiliated.

28. The words are: ψεύδη πάντα καὶ οἱ παρὰ σὲ θεοὶ (the gods with him! Are these images, or do they only function as πάρεδροι δαίμονες?) ὁμοίως, ὅτι ἐνβέβληκαν ὑμᾶς εἰς ὕλην μεγάλην καὶ οὗ (οὐ?) δυνάμεθα ἀποθανεῖν, κἄν (not certain) ἴδῃς ὅτι μέλλομεν σωθῆναι, τότε βαπτιζώμεθα, and later ἰ καὶ αὐτοὺς δεδώκαμεν καὶ ἀποπεπτώκαμεν πλανόμενοι ὑπὸ τῶν θεῶν καὶ πιστεύοντες τὰ ἐνύπνια. The scornful address, πρὸς τοὺς

τὴν ἀλήθειαν λέγοντες, uses a cultic expression; cf. the Phrygian inscription in the *Journal of Hellenic Studies* IV 1883, p. 420: δῶρον ἔλαβον χρησμοδοτεῖν ἀληθείας.

29. Papyrus ὑμᾶς.

30. In IX 6 the goddess has already referred to this coinciding of dreams also in connection with breaking a magical spell.

31. I 123. Following Preuschen, Otto conjectures that it is healing of an illness. In light of the preceding statements this appears to me impossible. Incarceration in the temple of Sarapis and confinement in the Astartieion do not go together.

32. In the Acts of Thomas (chapter 8, p. 111 Bonwetsch) the apostle has a similar experience when his God enters into him; likewise Stephen, in Acts 6:15.

33. According to Wilcken, the deity had freed him from πολιορκία.

34. I choose this form of the name because Ptolemaeus uses it in N. 77. If in spite of the width of the letters it does not fill up the space, one could also think of Ἀμμοῦν.

35. First of all, *Berliner philol. Wochenschrift* 1896, column 1528; Pauly-Wissowa III 2352.

36. This is the still more splendid dream which Ptolemaeus earlier mentions. With a certain natural rhetoric he places the reference to this experience at the conclusion and precedes it with the admonitions: the epistle is meant to resonate with exultation and gratitude.

37. The dream is even more closely connected with the so-called Mithras liturgy, which itself appears like an artistically elaborated dream and which first brings the *mystes* together with the Aion, and then with Mithras. But the closest resemblance is found in the dreams of the alchemist Zosimus (Poimandres, pp. 9-10; indeed, the alchemist also is familiar with asceticism and confinement): in a dream he experiences the fearful mystery of the dismemberment of the body which makes one into a πνεῦμα, and now feels himself actually to be initiated. The Historia Lausiaca (chapter 29) tells that a monk, after praying for a long time to be delivered from the

lust of the flesh, dreamed that he met three angels who at his request emasculated him; after this dream he never again was afflicted by this temptation. When Evagrius and Jerome in a dream make a vow to God, they feel themselves bound by this vow (though of course not permanently in Jerome's case), and the people of their environment agreed with their feeling. In all these cases the background of these dream experiences is a religious idea; the fact that this idea is akin to the mysteries is important for our purposes, but the question whether it also was ever really enacted is of less importance.

38. Of course I omit the passages which can simply be connected with incarceration.

39. The κατοχή lasts so long that it can be scornfully described as never-ending. It is demonstrated by the more rigorous persons by chains. Hence even in Philodemus we may not put any weight on the phrase διὰ τοῦ ζῆν as though it were a sacral-legal definition. Apuleius also says something similar.

40. The extension of the usage in Latin is conditioned by the fact that the *fanatici* of Bellona were for a long time the only representatives of this kind of προφῆται or *vates* known in Rome.

41. Hence Vettius Valens (Kroll 73.24) calls them ἀποφθεγγόμενοι ἢ καὶ διανοίᾳ παραπίπτοντες (prophets or demented persons). The Roman Festus says (Acts 26:24): Μαίνῃ, Παῦλε.

42. Cf. *Das iranische Erlösungsmyst.*, pp. 235-36 (there also at least a proof of non-Pauline manner of expression and concept); cf. *ibid.*, pp. 6, 135-36.

IV.

The Religious Impact of Persian Rule

Eduard Meyer's reflections[1] were first taken up and carried forward in the pioneering work of H. Gunkel, *Zum religionsgeschichtlichen Verständnis des Neuen Testaments* (Göttingen, 1903); he himself also returned to them in the work *Ursprung und Anfänge des Christentums*. For southern Russia and the kingdom of the Bosporus, and thus for the areas in which Jewish and Persian belief came into close contact, archaeological finds and linguistic observations prove par- 216 ticularly early Iranian influences;[2] for the later period I need only to point to Dio of Prusa (XXXVI 39 Arnim). In one part of Cappadocia the marriage of the local deity, here called Bel,[3] was still celebrated quite late in conjunction with the Zoroastrian religion; Bel chose her because she was very wise and more beautiful than any of the goddesses. This can only mean that the festival serves as the official adoption of this religion (Lidzbarski, *Ephemeris f. semitische Epigraphik* I 66); Strabo's well-known statement about the magicians in Cappadocia (733) offers us an enlargement upon this. For Commagene I may only refer to the no less well-known inscription of Antiochus IV. For the small tribe of the Mandaeans, as we mentioned earlier, the depreciation of the old Semitic divine name *ilah* and the adoption of varying Persian divine names also attest a change in religion, which of course did not lead to the full appropriation of a unified new religion.

Let me add a pure "Hellenistic" example of such a blending of religions. In my treatment of the goddess *Psyche* (1917, pp. 23ff.) I have dealt in more detail with the cosmogony set forth by Dieterich in the *Abraxas*. Combined with an altogether differently oriented prayer, it is handed down in two sharply divergent versions as a kind of amulet in a papyrus of the fourth century, but in its origin it goes back certainly to a time significantly earlier than the appearance of Mani. At that time, we could not fully prove that the content in essence had been affected by Iranian influences, but now, since the Hermetic Poimandres and the basic doctrine of the Naassene Preaching have been established as Iranian, it can hardly be disputed.[4] Because of the length of the piece and the very difficult, highly varied tradition, I can cite only the basic features here: a primal deity produces, by

17 means of his sevenfold laughter, the first *created* deities. At the first laughter there appears the all-illuminating brilliance, the god of fire and of the (light-)world; at the second, the all-filling water and the ruler of the abyss; at the third, Νοῦς or Hermes, and at the fourth, Genna (Γένεσις), the goddess of all procreation; at the fifth, Moira as the goddess of justice (*asa*) with the balances, for which Hermes contends with her until a divine utterance grants them to both of these deities. At the sixth laughter there appears the Aion--it is not clear whether he is characterized in Greek as Κρόνος or Καιρός. He carries a scepter as the sign of his rule, but he surrenders this to the first created deity, Ohrmazd. In exchange for it the latter gives him the glory (τῆν δόξαν τοῦ φωτός) and dominion over time and all that happens in it. A brilliance flows from the glory; the "queen", who is thought of as the moon-deity, receives this brilliance--the sun and the moon symbolize and together form

the Aion. At the seventh laughter of the primal deity, Psyche arose, and with her, motion. The deity said, "You are to set in motion all things and, when Hermes leads you, gladden all things." Then everything was set in motion and was filled with the breath of life. After this begins the second act of the drama of creation, unfortunately extant only in the opening part. The deity (of the abyss?) saw Psyche and was amazed, he bowed down to the earth (matter) and blew, and the earth gave birth to an omniscient dragon; but the (good) deity gestured, and an armed being appeared (it is the primal man, who here is separate from Psyche). Then we hear that the earth (matter) rises up and wishes to touch the fixed heavens; then the god Iao calls out, and out of the cry there comes a strong deity who stills the uproar; he contends with the armed man over who is stronger, but God decrees that the two of them together shall hold sway over ἀνάγκη--καὶ οὐκέτι οὐδὲν ἠτάκτησεν τῶν ἀερίων, and the order of the universe is assured. I have earlier overlooked the fact that the most distinctive feature of this doctrine of creation, the exchange of the insignia of rule between Ohrmazd and Zarvan--that is, between the deity introduced by Zarathustra and the old Iranian supreme deity--is even represented on the Mithraic monuments (e.g., Osterburken and Neuenheim; Cumont-Latte, p. 99). Originally this had to do with the wonder-working barsom

218 twigs; cf. the Armenian Eznik II 5: "The barsom twigs which Zarvan had in his hand he gave to his son Ohrmazd and said, 'Up till now I have offered sacrifices for you, but now you shall offer them for me'" (H. Junker, "Über iranische Quellen der hellenistischen Aionvorstellung," *Bibliothek Warburg*, Vorträge I, p. 172). The age and reliability of the Eznik tradition and its survival on the one hand in the Mithras faith, and on the other hand in Manichaeism,[5] are herewith

documented. We will not be surprised when in the Byzantine era among the Bulgars and the Serbs God the Father begets the Son thus: he lies down with a twig of basil under his arm, and then sends this twig to Mary.[6] With our attention hereby drawn to the Iranian tradition, we immediately recognize in the deity of water and the abyss, who stands in second place in the Abraxas cosmogony, Ahriman--in the Poimandres also the ὑγρὰ φύσις is the opposite of the light[7]--while Hermes appears to correspond to Vohu Mano. Then the two accounts widely diverge. In the conclusion we are surprised once again to see the primal man, this time altogether conforming to Mani's view of him as the armed man (ἔνοπλος), as the adversary of the dragon, and of course alongside him a god Iao, who has been borrowed from elsewhere. We have--in a twofold version, in fact--a liturgical piece from a Greek-speaking syncretistic community; a cosmogony, which in its basic features is Iranian-Hellenistic, is introduced by a prayer which seems on the surface to be Egyptian, though it is not.[8] The Iranian part has truly historical value because

19 it proves how heavily Mani himself was influenced by earlier constructions in the very features that give the most appearance of being his own, and how strongly the Persian deities were grecized in that time. We may regret that we cannot determine the name and locus of this community, or, better said, of this Gnostic sect; the nature of the syncretism of that time nevertheless teaches us to recognize it more clearly than would many a much-discussed construction. Dieterich could not fully explain this unique document, but the fact that he recognized its importance signifies a tremendous philological achievement, for which of course he was ill repaid by his times.

A similar puzzle is offered to us by the fragments of a Manichaean apocalypse which has been published by A. v. Le Coq ("Türkische Manichaica aus Chotscho II," *Abh. d. Preuss. Ak.* 1919, p. 5). Mithras conquers the magically powered war-god of a neighboring people, who has represented himself as the longed-for redeemer of the believers and has demanded worship of himself. Further, in the original version of the Persian Bahman-Yasht, which reaches back into early times,[9] Mithras is, at the end of the world, the adversary of Ahriman and the real redeemer. All this points to a religious position of this deity such as we must assume for the Mithras mysteries and as he appears to have in the early monuments from southern Russia. Since the Manichaean literature has preserved for us various old Persian legends,[10] as for example that Zarathustra comes to Babylon and here conquers and slays the magically powered god of the city--here also the portrayal corresponds to the struggle between the redeemer-god and Ahriman--I do not believe that Manichaeism borrows that portrayal of the anti-messiah from Judaism or Christianity, where in essence it has neither a preparatory background nor a point of contact and thus remains utterly enigmatic. I believe instead that Judaism took, along with the idea of the Messiah, the idea also of his adversary indirectly from Iran. Until further discoveries are made, the intermediate source remains entirely hidden from our view.

In earlier passages I have dealt with the Persian features in the late Egyptian cult or theology, and I shall have to deal with these again later. It was my intention here only to bring together a few individual features which are characteristic of Hellenistic syncretism.

220

NOTES

1. Above, p. 17.

2. Prof. Jacobsohn has shown me that the Scythian names and the unusual Greek designation of the Black Sea as Πόντος Ἄξεινος (North Sea) necessarily point in this direction.

3. From this I conclude that Babylonian influence had already earlier been at work upon the local cult.

4. Of course I am abandoning the attempt to find in the prefixed abbreviation the name of Asonakes, the alleged teacher of Zarathustra.

5. The queen of the Abraxas cosmogony appears here (in the Soghdian version even by name, Ramratukh); cf. F. W. K. Müller, *Handschriftenreste aus Turfan* II, p. 102.

6. *Ztschr. Rad*, Band X, 1870, pp. 252-53; cf. Reitzenstein, *Weltuntergangsvorstellungen*, Uppsala 1924, p. 66.

7. We find this perspective attributed to the Egyptians in Hippolytus, Elench. IV 43.8 (Wendland p. 66.7); it may even be late Egyptian, but it also occurs in Gnostic doctrines that unquestionably exhibit Iranian influence. The fact that, in the Poimandres, alongside this, evil is characterized as ὁ ἐπὶ τοῦ πυρός shows the inconsistency of the author.

8. For all this I must refer to my treatment, cited above.

9. Reitzenstein-Schaeder I, chapter II.

10. Cf. Le Coq, *Sitzungsber. d. Preuss. Ak.* 1908, pp. 398-99.

V.

The Report of Apuleius

Heretofore (*Archiv f. Religionswiss.* VII 1904, pp. 393-94, and *Berl. philol. Wochenschrift* 1919, column 942), I have not sharply enough distinguished the various applications and interpretations of the initiatory actions portrayed by Apuleius. In spite of the fact that it involves a Greek community, for the Isis-initiation we shall first of all adduce, for purposes of comparison, Egyptian rites, preferably of course those of more recent times. In the Book of the Dead a baptism of the dead is often represented. Prof. Spiegelberg has referred me to an especially instructive example in Papyrus Rhind I, dating from the second half of the first century B.C. Here, in column 6, the deceased person is pictured, precisely as in the early representations of the king, standing between two gods, who are letting a sacred liquid, whose drops are described in those representations as life and strength (?), trickle over his head. The gods also are the same; for even though the writer pictured two Anubises, still the captions show that Horus and Thoth are meant, as in the case of the king's baptism. The text says: "You are cleansed with the water that comes from Elephantine,[1] and with the natron from El-Kab, and with the milk from Gim." The effect is described in the Demotic text (col. 5.2): "You worship the sun of the morning and the moon (and) the air and the water (and) the fire; you venerate those who have gone to their rest, after your years have passed." The hieratically written parallel

text says: "You venerate [or something like this] the one who inhabits the horizon, who shines with gold, and the one
21 who enlarges his form [the moon] (and) the air (and) the restorer of life [the Nile, or the water] (and) the eye of Horus [thus here the fire]; you see those who have gone to their rest, after your years have passed." In Apuleius, after a general bath of purification, which of course must already possess religious significance, since all the *religiosi* accompany him to it,[2] there follows a ceremonial prayer and the περιρραντισμός (*praefatus deum veniam purissime circumrorans abluit*); then in the temple the instruction and a ten-day period of ascetic discipline; then the mystery, about the content and meaning of which it is stated: *accessi confinium mortis et calcato Propersinae limine per omnia vectus elementa remeavi; nocte media vidi solem candido coruscantem lumine; deos inferos et deos superos accessi coram et adoravi de proximo*. Of all this, the papyrus attests to us the visit to the underworld and the veneration of the dead, and further a veneration paid to [thus also a pilgrimage through] three elements, fire, water, and air, to which are added two higher deities, the sun and the moon. The sun in fact is also mentioned in Apuleius. The agreement is so extensive that we can say with certainty that the same religious perspective governs both passages. The περιρραντισμός brings the revival of the deceased which is represented in the mystery. Hence it will not be too bold to see in the first bath of purification the *voluntaria mors* of which Apuleius speaks. According to Egyptian belief the person who drowned in the Nile becomes immortal. Here I can only briefly refer to the significant essay by Griffith (*Zeitschr. f. ägypt. Sprache* XLVI, p. 132), "Herodotus II 90, Apotheosis by Drowning".[3] The official term for deification, ἐκθεοῦν or ἀποθεοῦν (cf., e.g., the

decree of Kanopos, lines 54, 56), therefore is used for the drowning of a sacrificial animal in a sacred liquid (Pap. Berol. I 5, Londin. CXXI 629, Paris. Bibl. Nat. 2456, 2457). The first one thus deified is Osiris, who according to the belief of later times was *three days and three nights* in the 222 flood of the river before he was revived (Pap. Londin. XLVI 256; cf. Pap. Bibl. Nat. 875). The language usage is explained in Strabo (XV 720) by the burial inscription of that Indian who with good fortune surmounted the heaps of ruins: Ζαρμανοχηγᾶς 'Ινδὸς ἀπὸ Βαργόσης κατὰ τὰ πάτρια 'Ινδῶν ἔθη ἑαυτὸν ἀπαθανατίσας κεῖται. Thus as ἀποθεοῦν can also be used to speak of the ending of the old life in the initiation, so apparently can ἀπαθανατίζειν as well. Therefore in a Phrygian inscription (see below, p. 320), the *mystai* are called ἀθάνατοι. Once again, this explains the notion of the Gnostics that martyrdom or death does not concern them, since they have already received ἀθανασία. Connected with this also is the characterization of those about to be initiated as *morituri* or the assignment of a burial place in the sacred plot to living *mystai* as καθιεροῦν (below, p. 320). The Egyptian belief appears to be native to Syria also, or to have been appropriated there; cf. the inscription from Hauran discussed by Clermont-Ganneau (*Recueil d'archéologie orientale* II 63): ὑπὲρ σωτηρίας αὐτοκράτορος Τραϊανοῦ....Μεννέας Βελιάβου τοῦ Βελιάβου πατρὸς Νετείρου τοῦ ἀποθεωθέντος ἐν τῷ λέβητι, δι' οὗ αἱ ορταὶ ἄγωνται. Large water-basins are found in front of temples in Syria, as for example in Baalbek (cf. H. Thiersch, "Zu den Tempeln und zur Basilika von Baalbek," *Nachrichten d. Ges. d. Wissensch.*, Göttingen 1925, p. 10; Cumont, in Pauly-Wissowa IV 2240-41), and, as we shall see, in the region of Hauran the Jordan acquires the same religious significance as the Nile has in Egypt.[4] Thus here the dispute attested among the Man-

daeans, as to whether one should baptize with living (i.e., flowing) water or with still water, is understandable.

But more about this later. First we must concern ourselves with the elements which the Papyrus Rhind lists: air, water, and fire. They are often represented on tombstones, as for example on a tombstone from Walbersdorf near Oedenburg, which dates from the early days of the empire (Harald Hofmann, *Jahreshefte d. österr. Instituts* XII, 1909, p. 224; and likewise Cumont, *ibid.*, Beiblatt 213), and on the tombstone from Carnuntum (certainly before the year A.D. 71) pictured by Cumont (*Études syriennes* 1917, p. 70; cf. 104.1). Here, besides the elements, the sun--or, less probably, the moon--is pictured in the highest position. Cumont properly refers to the representation of the ascent of the soul in the Hermetic Λόγος τέλειος, or Apuleius' Asclepius (chapter 28): *cum fuerit animae e corpore facta discessio, tunc arbitrium examenque meriti eius transiet in summi daemonis potestatem, isque eam cum piam iustamque perviderit, in sibi conpetentibus locis manere permittit. sin autem delictorum inlitam maculis vitiisque oblitam viderit, desuper ad ima deturbans procellis turbinibusque aeris, ignis et aquae saepe discordantibus tradit ut inter caelum et terram mundanis fluctibus in diversa semper aeternis poenis agitata rapiatur.* According to a widely held Oriental belief--one may think, for example, of the Mandaeans--the place of torment lies between earth and the heaven of the gods from which the soul comes; in the ascent even the pious soul must pass through it (cf. Eunapios fr. 29, in Cumont, *op. cit.*, 104.1). Hofmann and Cumont have already noted echoes of this in the Mithras-faith and in Mithraic art; others can be demonstrated in Mandaeism and Manichaeism.[5] Yet in the dissemination and manifold reshaping of the Iranian belief about the soul a definite point

of beginning cannot be proved. Only one thing can be said with certainty: this idea of a list of the elements, climaxing in the sun and the moon, is not Egyptian. To be sure, the Papyrus Rhind attests that it also became Egyptian, and those who directed the Isis mystery in Corinth must have appropriated it from Egypt. The total agreement of the papyrus and the tombstones in the selection of precisely these elements from a

224 list that was, as we shall see, longer, can in no way have been accidental. Only up to this time we know too little about the age and the source of the Syrian belief in immortality, of which one thinks immediately. That it is influenced by magic, and thus is connected with mysteries, appears, in light of the total character of the Semitic religions, almost certain. Nöldeke notes ("Syrische Inschriften," *Zeitschr. f. Assyriologie* XXI, 1908, p. 155) that a tombstone of a deceased person whom apparently celestial powers have called to themselves says that now he sees all "height and depth, distance and nearness, hiddenness and clarity". From this Nöldeke infers a mystery, and to this extent he is correct. Here the idea of being transported upward by an eagle appears widespread, but other ideas also appear to be intermingled. Of course there is nothing to point to a Christian origin or influence. These ideas are much earlier.

To a large extent we can trace the fuller list from India and Persia.[6] For the latter the earliest witness is offered by Herodotus I 131, who according to the instruction of a non-Zoroastrian Iranian cites the following as the earliest deities of the Persians: heaven, sun, moon, earth, fire, water, wind.

225 The apologist Aristides (chapters 4-7) lists them for the Persian-Chaldean teaching: heaven, earth, water, fire, breath of wind, sun, moon, and (primal) man--the last-named as the totality, the Self of the seven elements. Three similar ogdoads

are named by Didymos in his explanation of the proverb Πάντα ὀκτώ, an explanation which we must construct from Theon of Smyrna (104.20 Hiller) and Zenobios (V 78). The first of these three, essentially Iranian, but probably coming from the lands bordering on the Black Sea: fire, water, earth, heaven, moon, sun, Mithras,[7] night; the second, closely agreeing with the first, from an *Orphic* oath: the primal deities are fire, water, earth, heaven, moon, Phanes, night; the third, following a late Egyptian theology under Orphic influence: breath of wind, heaven, earth, water, night, day, Eros, and Osiris. Didymos' immediate authority, a certain Euandros who is unknown to us, names as his authority Timotheus, and this latter appears to be that Attic exegete and Eumolpide, who together with Manetho helped to hellenize the Sarapis cult for the first Ptolemy. This is shown by the utterly non-Egyptian "Egyptian" theology of Hecataeus and Manetho: sun and moon create five deities, air and fire, earth and water, and Psyche (or the πνεῦμα); together they form an eighth divine being, the Aion. Corresponding to this, the Sarapis theology (Macrobius, Sat. I 20.17) names: heaven, water, earth, the atmosphere, and as the whole, Sarapis; in the magical papyri they are: sun, moon, heaven, the atmosphere, earth, water, (Aion). Added to this is the fr. 168 of the Orphika (Kern) which I have discussed on page 94 of the work cited: it lists earth, heaven, breath of wind, fire, water, sun, moon, and then Zeus as the whole. Added to this list, moreover, are numerous later revisions which take us onto Syrian soil and are found predominantly in the lists of deities in the Gnostic sects. As we saw in Appendix II, the ascent of the soul in the material identified by Dieterich as the Mithras liturgy is also to be understood in terms of this Iranian system which was early taken over in Egypt:

226 the initiate first calls on Γένεσις and 'Αρχή, then on πνεῦμα, πῦρ, ὕδωρ, οὐσία γεώδης, and finally on the σῶμα τέλειον, all these not as the elements that are in him but as their divine prototypes, actual deities; they are supposed to make possible the journey heavenward, for he must make his way through them. The idea becomes more comprehensible to us, as I repeat here,[8] when we compare the strictly corresponding prayer in the papyrus from London CXXI 505-6: a god who dwells in invisible light, here called Helios, is called upon as the father of the Aion and of Physis: he bears within himself the entire κοσμικὴ σύγκρασις and is the one who begets the *five* planets, which constitute the innermost essence of the four elements of heaven, earth, water, and fire. Here the sun and the moon still have, as Aion and Physis (as in the Mithras liturgy, as Γένεσις and 'Αρχή), the exceptional position granted them in Manetho and Hecataeus; the five planets also identify the four (in Iranian, five) elements, whose celestial primal materials thus overlap in spheres.[9] According to the very ancient Avestan Damdad-Nask the divine primal man receives from the planetary spheres this celestial primal material, *which resides as metal in those individual planetary spheres*, and brings it into matter that can be perceived by the senses. The counterpart is offered by the well-known heavenly journeys through five or seven realms of torment (planetary spheres), for which the Mandaean texts of the dead provide abundant documentation and which also pass over into the general astrological conceptions.

Up to this point no explanation has been given of a later statement of Apuleius to the effect that during this wandering, which lasts the entire night, he was initiated by means of twelve sacred garments (24: *mane factum est, et perfectis sollemnibus processi duodecim sacratus stolis*; the Greek prob-

ably ἁγιασθείς). In this mystery-language, as I hardly need to document with examples, a new garment signifies a new form. The best parallel is offered by a late Manichaean text, which
27 to be sure perhaps does not any longer presuppose an actual mystery, but only preserves an image from one; it is the tractate, preserved in Chinese, which Chavannes and Pelliot have published in the *Journal Asiatique* N. S. X 18 (1911). In the portrayal and interpretation of the three days which in their twelve hours bring perfect divinity to the soul, it is said (p. 566): "Le second jour c'est la semence pure de l'Homme nouveau. Les douze heures, ce sont les douze rois lumineux des transformations successives,[10] ce sont aussi les merveilleux vêtements de la forme victorieuse de Yichou (Iésus) qu'il donne a la nature lumineuse; au moyen de ces vêtements merveilleux il pare la nature intérieure et fait que rien ne lui manque; la tirant en haut, il la fait monter et avancer et se séparer pour toujours de la terre souillée." An enumeration of the individual hours is given by the Turkish counterpart (Le Coq, *Türkische Manichaica aus Chotscho* III 16-17): they are specific virtues, the last of which is light-being. Undoubtedly we have here once again the description of an ascent, but I am unable to say how it was connected in the mystery with the ascent through the elements, nor can I say whence it originates. Of course one could think of Iranian origins; but the Babylonian quasi-mystery (above, p. 193) also contains an ascent which is connected in some way with the twelve hours, and in Egypt the sun-god has twelve different forms; the soul of the deceased wanders in various forms through the twelve hours of the night and at sunrise is born as god. The ritual of the baptism of the dead indeed assures us of connections with Egypt, and I have earlier thought of the transformation of the temple, i.e., of the world, which

the king has to undertake upon his ascending the throne--in fact, a new life begins for him too, and therefore like the deceased person he must undergo a baptism of revivification.[11]

228 Finally, L. Troje (*Die Dreizehn und die Zwölf im Traktat Pelliot*, 1925, p. 111.2) calls attention to Indian parallels. In the ancient hymn Rigveda I 164. 12: "They call him in the farther half of heaven the Sire five-footed (i.e., with five stations), of twelve forms (this refers to the number of months in the year), wealthy in watery store"; and Prajapati, who as the world-deity is himself both time and space, accordingly has the sacred number seventeen as his symbol.

Since Apuleius himself says (XI 23) that he does indeed intend to arouse a pious yearning for knowledge but intends to communicate of the δρώμενον only so much that the reader in no case will get a clear conception (*ecce tibi retuli, quae quamvis audita ignores necesse est*), I shall refrain from offering a definite solution. The fact that we are dealing with a syncretistic cult is shown even by the name of the initiating and thus leading priest, Mithras[12]--in the Phrygian cult also the divine name Attis is transferred to the priest--, and still better by the description of the following community festival, about which Apuleius is under no constraint to keep silence. When he emerges from the Adyton he is placed on a pedestal as a statue and embodiment of the world-deity in the presence of the goddess, upon his head a crown, from which radiate bleached palm leaves, in his right hand the blazing torch, around his body a byssus garment with rich, colorful embroidery, and a cloak falling from his shoulders to his ankles. This is not Osiris, into whom the divinized deceased person in Egypt was obliged to turn. The ornamentation of the head appears again in the Syrian Baalsamim (cf. H. Cr. Butler, *Publications of the Princetown Uni-*

versity, Archaeological Expeditions to Syria 1904 and 1909, Divis. II, Sect. A, Part 6, p. 304; and in a slightly different form in Baalbek, in Dussaud, *Revue archéologique*, Ser. IV, tom. I 139). He describes the garment: *quaqua tamen*
229 *viseres, colore vario circumnotatis insignibar animalibus: hinc dracones Indici, inde gripes Hyperborei* (griffins?), *quos in speciem pinnatos* (Cod. *pinnatae*) *alitis generat mundus alter: hanc Olympiacam stolam* (celestial garment) *nuncupant*. The serpents of India and all sorts of legendary or real animals are actually represented in India on the body of the world-deity,[13] and in the Christian era such garments are exported from India to Egypt and certainly to other countries as well (Philostratos, Vit. Apoll. II 20). The use of a representation of the *mystes* as a statue of the deity could point to the Syrian cultural sphere. The alchemistic writing of the alleged Cleopatra comes from there, as is shown by, among other things, the designation of the priest who gives the revelation as *komar* (κομάριος); it presupposes a similar resurrection- and deification-mystery, the conclusion of which is formed by the representation of the deified one as a statue of the light-deity: ἐτελειώθη τὸ μυστήριον καὶ ἐσφραγίσθη ὁ οἶκος (the *shekinah*, which is understood as a building, or as the temple of the deity) καὶ ἐστάθη ἀνδριὰς πλήρης φωτὸς καὶ θεότητος.[14] In the Mandaean celestial journeys also the conclusion is almost always the "outfitting" in his *shekinah* of the perfected one who is clothed with the celestial garment.

Perhaps still more important for religio-historical purposes are the references to the twofold baptismal action. I must go back somewhat further. It was not long ago that a prominent representative of New Testament exegesis published, in a dispute with Wellhausen and Ed. Schwartz, the interpretation of Jesus' question to the sons of Zebedee (Mark 10:38),

δύνασθε...τὸ βάπτισμα, ὃ ἐγὼ βαπτίζομαι, βαπτισθῆναι, to mean "Can you bear to see your work submerged under water as I do?" That time appears to us to have died away, and I think that there is no theologian who would lament its passing. It dealt with the words in worse fashion than did the old rationalism with the narratives. We feel that we cannot take the comparison of baptism and death at all seriously enough because early

230 Christianity took it thus. Everyone will think at once of Rom. 6:2ff.: οἵτινες ἀπεθάνομεν τῇ ἁμαρτίᾳ, πῶς ἔτι ζήσομεν ἐν αὐτῇ; ἢ ἀγνοεῖτε ὅτι ὅσοι ἐβαπτίσθημεν εἰς Χριστὸν Ἰησοῦν, εἰς τὸν θάνατον αὐτοῦ ἐβαπτίσθημεν; συνετάφημεν οὖν αὐτῷ διὰ τοῦ βαπτίσματος εἰς τὸν θάνατον, ἵνα ὥσπερ ἠγέρθη Χριστὸς ἐκ νεκρῶν διὰ τῆς δόξης τοῦ πατρός, οὕτως καὶ ἡμεῖς ἐν καινότητι ζωῆς περιπατήσωμεν. One will also think of the not entirely happy imitation in Col. 2:12, written, as I believe, by a later imitator of Paul: συνταφέντες αὐτῷ ἐν τῷ βαπτίσματι, ἐν ᾧ καὶ συνηγέρθητε διὰ τῆς πίστεως τῆς ἐνεργείας τοῦ θεοῦ τοῦ ἐγείραντος αὐτὸν ἐκ τῶν νεκρῶν.[15] I shall come back to these passages later; for the present it will suffice to point out that the church also later views martyrdom as a substitute for baptism and, conversely, sees in Jesus' baptism the whole contest with death and the devil which according to the church's view then is fulfilled in the passion.[16] This entire perspective cannot have arisen out of the concept of the bath of purification, whether the washing of the priest before he enters the sanctuary or that of the proselytes, even though in later Jewish sources weak reminiscences of this mystery-conception could be demonstrated. What is at work here is a mystery-like feeling.

That Egyptian idea of an *Apotheosis by drowning* (above, pp. 275-276) would afford us a point of contact here, and the

231 description of Osiris, "who was three days and three nights

in the flood of the river", certainly calls for comparison. But in any case it is more obvious to think of the familiar baptist sect of the Mandaeans, whose connection with John the Baptist now is incontestable, since its tradition about him has points of contact with the Christian tradition, though it cannot stem from that source. The end of John's life is related in Genza r. I 2.153 (Lidzbarski p. 53.18): "On the day when Johana's measure is full, I myself (Hibil) come to him, appear to Johana as a small boy three years and one day old, talk with him about baptism, and instruct his friends. Then I take him out of his body, lead him victoriously upward to the world that is pure brilliance, baptize him in the white Jordan of living, surging water, clothe him in radiant garments and crown him with turbans of light, establish praise in his pure heart with the praise of the light-angel, with which they praise their Lord without ceasing for all eternity." It is the baptism in the celestial Jordan, which corresponds to the Egyptian celestial ocean (the Nile); the deities that return to heaven from exile, such as Ptahil, Abathur, and Joshamin, must first be baptized in this celestial Jordan (Genza r. XV 3), approximately the same as in the book of Baruch by the Gnostic Justin (Hippolytus, Elench. V 26.2, Wendland p. 133.5), for the ascending God Elohim as well as for the πνευματικοὶ ζῶντες ἄνθρωποι. The considerably later piece in Genza r. V 4 pictures baptism somewhat differently: Manda d'Haije comes to Johana as a small boy and asks for baptism; John first tells him to wait, and then from the miracles (according to the familiar word in the psalms the Jordan flows backwards) he recognizes that the god in whose name he baptizes is himself asking for baptism. So now he, Johana, asks to be baptized. The god answers (Lidzb., p. 193.15): "When I place my hand upon you, you will leave

your body." Then it is said: "In the Jordan he removed his clothing from him, he removed from him his clothing of flesh and blood, he clothed him with a robe of radiance and crowned him with a pure, good turban of light."[17] Then together they

232 take the celestial pilgrimage which is often portrayed in the hymns of the dead; at the conclusion Johana requests that all who are true believers (the Mandaeans) may likewise ascend.-- It is inconceivable to me that this invention could have developed out of the gospel account, but I do recognize an influence in the other direction, back upon early Christian tradition, when I read in the *Opus imperfectum in Matthaeum* (Migne, P. G. 56.658): *"Modo interim sine"* (Matt. 3:15) *ostendit, quia postea Christus baptizavit Iohannem, quamvis in secretioribus libris manifeste hoc scriptum sit "et Johannes quidem baptizavit illum in aqua, ille autem Iohannem in spiritu"*. Thus there was a tradition that Jesus also baptized John in the Jordan, and this tradition actually survives in pictorial representations and in full form in the Mandaean version. The *secretiores libri* meant this second baptism to mean only a baptism in the Spirit; apparently it is Gnostics who are meant here, as Irenaeus (I 21.4) pictures them; they say that the mystery is performed without any symbol through the recognition of the ineffable Greatness. John recognized Christ (Manda d'Haije); thereupon he was baptized by him.

Consequently we would have to assume that the baptism of

233 the dying or of the departed was customary among the Mandaeans also, even if it were not attested by Siouffi (*Études sur la religion des Soubbas*, p. 120). As among the Egyptians, it simply follows from the religious significance which the river has for them. It is a divine being, the divine life-force. It is highly noteworthy that in the same context (I 21.5) Irenaeus tells of a Gnostic baptism of the dying, at

which the magical formulas are uttered that the ascending soul is to pronounce to the hostile powers between earth and heaven in order to secure free passage through them. The idea entirely corresponds to the Mandaeans' hymns of the dead; moreover, as Nöldeke saw,[18] the self-understanding of the soul σκεῦός εἰμι ἔντιμον corresponds to the Mandaeans' formula. The liturgical meaning is this: as with Apuleius the baptism is followed by the instruction about the celestial pilgrimage, the actual δρώμενον, here they are simultaneous; indeed, the δρώμενον is missing. The Mandaean hymns of the dead replace the δρώμενον with the account of the experiences of the first one to ascend. I cannot regard the so-called proxy-baptism, which appears in the Corinthian community in the apostolic age and is widespread in Gnosticism,[19] as a new Christian creation, but only as an adaptation of a pagan mystery-usage to Christian conceptions and prescriptions.

We must make a strict distinction: cultic ablutions and baths of purification, as they appear in numerous religions, have nothing to do with baptism as we encounter it here; here it has to do with ζωοποιεῖν, the imparting of another life to something dead, or to something that has voluntarily died. The best explanation here is offered by that alchemistic writing of Cleopatra to be discussed later, which rests entirely upon mystery conceptions; cf. my edition in *Nachr. d. Gesellsch. d. Wissensch.*, Göttingen 1915, p. 15.42: πῶς κατέρχονται τὰ ὕδατα τὰ εὐλογημένα τοῦ ἐπισκέψασθαι τοὺς νεκροὺς παρειμένους καὶ πεπεδημένους καὶ τεθλιμμένους ἐν σκότῳ καὶ γνόφῳ ἐντὸς τοῦ Ἅιδου, καὶ πῶς εἰσέρχεται τὸ φάρμακον τῆς ζωῆς καὶ ἀφυπνίζει αὐτοὺς ὡς ἐξ ὕπνου ἐγερθῆναι. The Mandaean baptism still exhibits this basic mystery-like feature so fully that it cannot possibly stem from Christian baptism or even just from the Jewish proselyte ablutions. The same

holds true for Paul in the passages cited; but Paul also is familiar with baptism as a bath for purposes of purification. One need only compare I Cor. 6:9-11: ἢ οὐκ οἴδατε ὅτι ἄδικοι θεοῦ βασιλείαν οὐ κληρονομήσουσιν; μὴ πλανᾶσθε. οὔτε πόρνοι οὔτε εἰδωλολάτραι οὔτε μοιχοὶ οὔτε μαλακοὶ οὔτε ἀρσενοκοῖται οὔτε κλέπται οὔτε πλεονέκτοι, οὐ μέθυσαι, οὐ λοίδοροι, οὐχ ἅρπαγες βασιλείαν θεοῦ οὐ κληρονομήσουσιν. καὶ ταῦτα, τινές, ἦτε. ἀλλὰ ἀπελούσασθε, ἀλλὰ ἡγιάσθητε, ἀλλὰ ἐδικαιώθητε ἐν τῷ ὀνόματι τοῦ κυρίου 'Ιησοῦ καὶ ἐν τῷ πνεύματι τοῦ θεοῦ ἡμῶν. Certainly, but the aim here is clear: the contrast to πόρνοι, κλέπται, ἅρπαγες ἦτε is supposed to be formed by καθαροί, ἅγιοι, δίκαιοι ἐγένεσθε. All the emphasis is placed on the last term, for ἄδικοι θεοῦ βασιλείαν οὐ κληρονομήσουσιν. Paul is also familiar with the more Jewish-Christian interpretation; no one disputes that. The point is that along with it he knows and employs the Hellenistic and mystery-like interpretation as well.

NOTES

1. The point where the Nile enters Egypt is regarded as its origin. Juvenal (VI 527: *ibit ad Aegyptii finem*) is familiar with the fact that people secured water from that point (see above, pp. 174, 175).

2. Hence it must have taken place in the temple area in a basin of water designed for this purpose.

3. Griffith offers an exemplary demonstration of how the statements of the magical papyri, which are so much scorned, are to be made useful.

4. The Euphrates has at least a similar significance for Mesopotamia. The lustration-baptism which Lucian describes in his Menippos 6 (perhaps following Menippos) is later imitated in Rome in the Tiber (see Juvenal VI 523); there a complete immersion is required.

5. I mention one especially striking detail from the book Dinanukht (Genza r. Book VI). When the death-angel has taken him from the body, it is said: "Winds, winds, take him hence, storms, storms, drive him forth, ladders, ladders, convey him into the heights" (the formula is repeated at each new sphere; two different perspectives, the one pictured above and the one known from the Mithras mysteries, are combined in it).

6. Cf. for India, Oldenberg, *Vorwissenschaftliche Wissenschaft, Weltanschauung der Brahmana-Texte*, pp. 58-59, and for Persia, Reitzenstein-Schaeder, *op. cit.* I, pp. 72-73. Here I shall not give any further exposition of the fact that in the adoption of the five divine elements--light-earth, light-water, illuminating fire, illuminating wind, gentle breeze (πνεῦμα, originally ancestral spirits?)--Mani connects with the old Persian list of elements (fire, water, metal, earth, plants; cf. the Chinese list: fire, water, earth, gold, wood). Since we have learned to trace the ancient series of five of the Iranian religions and since De Saussure has demonstrated its inner rationale, this appears to me beyond refutation. Zarathustra reinterpreted them, and Mani also, following him, connected with each of them a spiritual power. How the number then was increased to seven can be traced in the representations of man as microcosm. In that connection, as Prof. Andreas has kindly shown me, traces of

the early interpretation emerge especially in the Soghdian, for example in Fragment M.14: as images (image?) of the new man (the divine self in us, the Adakas of the Mandaeans) there are enumerated with the old forms of the names, in part even in the older script, as the present-day Persian tradition shows, the following: the devout wind-spirit, the wind, the best truth (in the Gathas like fire, here like light), water, and fire. The Iranian tendency toward systematic arrangement and the comparison with Indian thought allows us here in some measure to trace out the development.

7. The name is correctly given in the tradition; cf. Reitzenstein-Schaeder I 194; cf. also Schol. Plat. Alc. 122e: ὡς τῷ Μίθρᾳ οἰκεῖον τὸν ἑπτὰ ἀριθμόν, ὅν διαφερόντως οἱ Πέρσαι σέβουσιν.

8. Cf. above, Appendix II, p. 206.

9. I recall also having seen in the Cod. Vindobonensis 2337, among the sketches which represent the cosmos as a man, one that actually pictures this.

10. Or: *de transformation secondaire*. In any case the twelve light-aeons, the last of whom is in fact the full light (Müller, *Handschriftenreste* II, p. 44).

11. A different attempt at solution is only indicated by Cumont (*Acadêm. des Inscr. Comptes rendus* 1920, p. 282) rather than explained, even though he even provides a drawing in support of it. According to this, the astrological speculations of Petosiris are supposed to have passed over into the Alexandrian mysteries. I concede that the journey through all the elements can be understood in this way, but I do not see how the other statements of Apuleius can be reconciled with this. Of course Cumont will have proved his thesis for the Pseudo-Platonic dialogue of Axiochos and thereby have offered an important contribution to the recognition of the influences of Oriental mystery-like ideas upon Hellenism. But is the thesis not subject to dispute at all?

12. Mithras is represented as the guide of the soul on the monument of King Antiochus IV of Commagene.

13. Cf. Reitzenstein-Schaeder I, pp. 86, 91, 83.

14. *Nachr. d. Ges. d. Wissenschaften*, Göttingen 1919, p. 18, line 141; on this writing cf. below, pp. 398ff.

15. The Apostolic Constitutions still take this quite seriously.--One will do best to leave I Peter 3:21 out of consideration here; like 4:1, it provides only a judaizing and weakening echo of the idea.

16. In my *Weltuntergangsvorstellungen*, pp. 37ff., I have discussed a number of witnesses to this idea, which so far as I know had not previously received consideration, and explained Ode of Solomon 24 in these terms. From it we see that the Manichaean interpretation of Jesus' baptism stems from earlier Gnostic teachings; cf. Cotelier's (above, p. 101 n. 81) anathemas: ἀναθεματίζω οὖν, ὡς εἴρηται, τοὺς παρὰ ταῦτα φρονοῦντας καὶ ἄλλον μὲν λέγοντας εἶναι τὸν γεννηθέντα ἐκ Μαρίας καὶ βαπτισθέντα, μᾶλλον δέ, ὡς αὐτοὶ λαροῦσι, βυθιστέντα, ἄλλον δὲ τὸν ἐκ τοῦ ὕδατος ἀνελθόντα καὶ μαρτυρηθέντα (by the heavenly voice), ὅν καὶ ἀγέννητον Ἰησοῦν καὶ Φέγγος ὀνομάζουσιν ἐν σχήματι ἀνθρώπου φανέντα· καὶ τὸν μὲν εἶναι τῆς κακῆς ἀρχῆς, τὸν δὲ τῆς ἀγαθῆς μυθολογοῦσιν. The point of contact is afforded by the myth of the descent of the god Ohrmazd, who at his ascent in fact becomes a different god. Closely akin is the Mandaean myth of the baptism of John, presently to be discussed, but it cannot have been the model for Mani, nor can it be an imitation of a Manichaean version. Underlying both of them is an earlier Oriental myth, a trace of which I hope I have demonstrated in the passage cited.

17. The view is widely held that the vision of God in his majesty results in the death of the person. By means of the highest vision of the world-deity (in the oracle given below, p. 409, the deity of time), not only is the inner self totally separated from the body, but the latter also disintegrates. Thus we are taught by the Hermetic writing X 4, in a reference to writings no longer extant: ἐπλήρωσας ἡμᾶς, ὦ πάτερ, τῆς ἀγαθῆς καὶ καλλίστης θέας, καὶ ὀλίγου δεῖν ἐπετάσθη (Codd. ἐσεβάσθη; cf. §5 ἀναπετάσαι) μου ὁ τοῦ νοῦ ὀφθαλμὸς ὑπὸ τοιαύτης θέας.--Οὐ γὰρ ὥσπερ ἡ τοῦ ἡλίου ἀκτις πυρώδης οὖσα καταυγάζει καὶ μύειν ποιεῖ τοὺς ὀφθαλμοὺς, οὕτω καὶ ἡ τοῦ ἀγαθοῦ θέα, τοὐναντίον δὲ ἐκλάμπει (like ἀναλάμπει in §6, active) καὶ ἐπὶ τοσοῦτον....ἐφ' ὅσον δύναται ὁ θεώμενος (Scott; Codd. δυνάμενος) δέξασθαι τὴν ἐπεισροὴν τῆς νοητῆς λαμπηδόνος. ὀξυτέρα μὲν γάρ ἐστιν εἰς τὸ καθικνεῖσθαι. ἀβλαβὴς δὲ καὶ πάσης (Codd. πάσης καὶ) ἀθανασίας ἀνάπλεως. ἧς (Codd. ἣν) οἱ δυνάμενοι πλέον τι ἀρύσασθαι [(τῆς θέας)] κατακοιμίζονται πολλάκις [(δὲ)] ἀπὸ τοῦ σώματος εἰς τὴν καλλίστην ὄψιν, ᾧπερ (MC ὅπερ; A ὥσπερ) Οὐρανὸς καὶ Κρόνος οἱ ἡμέτεροι πρόγονοι ἐντετυχήκασιν. The voluntary death which is assumed by the Isis-initiate, the

recipient of the Phrygian baptism of blood, the one who prays in the Mithras liturgy, but also the initiate of the bacchanalia pictured by Livy, is actually a bitter oppressive peril. The same perspective explains how it is that the seer is attested when in his proclamation he falls dead (cf., in Egypt, pottery oracles and prophecy of the lamb), or how Lucan's Pythia barely escapes alive.

18. *Ztschr. f. Assyriologie* XXX, 1916, p. 160; cf. my treatment, "Das mandäische Buch des Herrn der Grösse und die Evangelienüberlieferung," *Sitzungsber. d. Heidelberger Akad.* 1919, Abh. 12, pp. 86ff.

19. Cf. Lietzmann's commentary, second edition, p. 83.

VI.

The Hellenistic Concept of Pistis

Up until recently it was still regarded as an attack upon Christianity to assert that a religious force or feeling similar to faith could even earlier have existed in paganism. I have never been able to understand how we could conceive of one of the better known Oriental religions, such as the Persian, without such a force, and it is even less clear to me how we could think of the acceptance of Hellenistic mysteries without it. Of course it is true that the use of the Greek word πίστις in this sense is not exactly common in pagan literature. But it is not totally absent, as has been asserted; a couple of hastily collected examples will suffice to show this. It appears in Egyptian magic, understood in a personal sense; cf. Dieterich, *Jahrb. f. Philologie*, Supplem. XVI, p. 807, line 17: ἐγὼ ἡ Πίστις ἡ εἰς ἀνθρώπους εὑρεθεῖσα καὶ προθήτης τῶν ἁγίων ὀνομάτων εἰμί, ὁ ἅγιος ὁ ἐκπεφυκὼς ἐκ τοῦ
35 βυθοῦ. For a form of the "emissary of God" an abstract term such as Σοφία or Achamoth is inserted. Likewise, in the Abercius inscription (v. 7), which along with Dieterich I take to be Phrygian, there appears Πίστις πάντη δὲ προῆγε καὶ παρέθηκε τροφὴν πάντη (on this reading cf. Hepding, *Attis*, p. 188.4) as the guiding deity. Not greatly different is the personification of the Zoroastrian "religion" in the Cappadocian inscription mentioned above (p. 268); the god Bel chooses this personified religion as his spouse. The characterization of the believers as πιστοί appears to be presupposed in the Isis hymn found in Pap. Oxyrh. 1380, line 152:

ὁρῶσί σε οἱ κατὰ τὸ πιστὸν ἐπικαλούμενοι. The substantive in Apuleius XI 28 appears to attest to the usage in the language of the Isis mysteries: *plena iam fiducia germanae religionis obsequium divinum frequentabam.* In any case, the best documentation is offered by Corp. Herm. IX 10 (Parthey, p. 66.11): ταῦτά σοι, ὦ Ἀσκληπιέ, ἐννοοῦντι ἀληθῆ δόξειεν <ἄν>, ἀγνοοῦντι δὲ ἄπιστα. τὸ γὰρ νοῆσαί ἐστι τὸ πιστεῦσαι, ἀπιστῆσαι δὲ τὸ μὴ νοῆσαι. ὁ γὰρ λόγος οὐ (A μου; MC μοι; brilliantly emended by Scott) φθάνει μέχρι τῆς ἀληθείας· ὁ δὲ νοῦς μέγας ἐστὶ καὶ ὑπὸ τοῦ λόγου μέχρι τινὸς ὁδηγηθεὶς φθάνει μέχρι (Mss. φθάνειν ἔχει) τῆς ἀληθείας καὶ περινοήσας τὰ πάντα καὶ εὑρὼν σύμφωνα τοῖς ὑπὸ τοῦ λόγου ἑρμηνευθεῖσιν ἐπίστευσε καὶ τῇ καλῇ πίστει ἐνανεπαύσατο (Mss. ἐπανεπαύσατο). τοῖς οὖν τὰ προειρημένα ὑπὸ τοῦ θεοῦ νοήσασι μὲν πιστά, μὴ νοήσασι δὲ ἄπιστα ταῦτα καὶ τοσαῦτα περὶ νοήσεως καὶ αἰσθήσεως λεγέσθω (to be punctuated thus). Here ἐννοεῖν in the beginning has almost the meaning of ἔννουν εἶναι or νοῦν ἔχειν (as in I 18: ἀναγνωρισάτο ὁ ἔννους ἑαυτὸν ὄντα ἀθάνατον), and it denotes the divine gift of correct religious knowledge, the higher soul, the πνεῦμα, though of course at the same time it also has the meaning of that inner comprehension that it carries in the closing section of our quotation; the latter indeed is possible only for the ἔννους. Similarly, λόγος is first the *ratio*, but then also the word. In the conclusion I have restored ἐνανεπαύσατο because this mysticism is familiar with a κύκλος τῆς ἀληθείας καὶ πίστεως as the place where God is enthroned in the highest heaven (Wessely, *Denkschr. d. Wiener Akad.* 1888, p. 70, lines 1012ff.), and it appeared to me to be better connected with the idea of the περινοεῖν. This rare word also has a mystery-like sound; cf. Plotinus, Ennead VI 9.11: τὸ δὲ (that loftiest, purely spiritual vision) ἴσως ἦν οὐ θέαμα, ἀλλὰ ἄλλος τρόπος τοῦ ἰδεῖν, ἔκστασις καὶ

236

ἄπλωσις καὶ ἐπίδοσις αὐτοῦ καὶ ἔφεσις πρὸς ἀφὴν καὶ στάσις καὶ περινόησις πρὸς ἐφαρμογήν,[1] εἴπερ τις τὸ ἐν τῷ ἀδύτῳ θεάσεται; cf. also Clement of Alexandria, Strom. V 71:1: ἐποπτεύειν δὲ καὶ περινοεῖν τήν τε φύσιν καὶ τὰ πράγματα. Finally, the words τὰ προειρημένα ὑπὸ τοῦ θεοῦ are explained by the fact that the Hermetic piece is a postscript and appendix to the λόγος τέλειος πρὸς 'Ασκλεπιόν.

We see that the concept πίστις was already present in the Persian sphere; the Oriental words that could allow us to delineate the concept more precisely would have to be traced out in the enumeration of the seals and the spiritual-ethical members of God among the Manichaeans; the designations for faith are available to us in Arabic, Turkish, Soghdian, and Chinese. We find the Greek again in the so-called Chaldaic Oracles, where πίστις, ἀλήθεια and ἔρως form a πηγαία τριάς; but I shall later deal with this and with the allusion in Porphyry, Ad Marcellam 24, in more detail.

In light of all this, it is altogether understandable that Philo of Alexandria, who is heavily influenced by this hellenistic piety, first elaborates for Judaism this concept of πίστις (cf. Bousset, *Die Religion des Judentums im neutestamentlichen Zeitalter*, second edition, p. 514).

NOTES

1. Porphyry (De abst. I 29) calls this σύμφυσις τοῦ θεωροῦντας καὶ θεωρουμένου and πρὸς τὸν ὄντως ἑαυτὸν σύμφυσις.

VII.

Philosopher and Prophet

The most famous miracle of Nigidius Figulus, the finding of a sum of money that had been stolen, is mentioned by Pomponius in the Atellane Philosophia (Ribbick, third edition, v. 109): *ergo, mi Dossenne, cum istaec memore meministi, indica, qui illud aurum abstulerit.--non didici ariolari gratiis.* Even if the attack is not directly aimed at Nigidius, the assumption still would be that the prophets and soothsayers who were wandering about through the cities and who are often ridiculed in Roman comedy, promised similar things in return for payment; the magical papyri give indications of this, as is well known. Pomponius' title by no means
37 requires us to think of one particular "philosopher". In the magical papyri (Wessely, *Gr. Zauberpapyri* I, *Denkschr. d. Wiener Akad.* 1888, p. 48, line 157, and elsewhere) σοφιστής denotes one who possesses secret knowledge and secret power, the magician.[1] This goes back to a general Oriental feeling: in late Persian, as E. Littmann has shown me, *failasuf* denotes both the wise man and the swindler and deceiver; in Hindustani the latter meaning predominates; in the present the word is especially commonly used for a quack (*Religionsgesch. Versuche u. Vorarbeiten* XIX 2, p. 86).[2] Now Pomponius shows us how ancient the usage is.

Still another *religious* title of honor, ἄνθρωπος θεῖος, had already been devalued in Greece in Plato's time and was used in an ironic sense (Ion. 542; cf. 533, 536), but in the

more humble circles it still retained its old meaning; cf. Philodemus, Περὶ θεῶν α΄, (Diels, *Abh. d. Preuss. Akad.* 1915, pp. 17 and 57.7: διόπερ ο[ὐχ ἣν ἔδοχ' ὁ] σοφὸς [β]ουλ[ή]ν, ἀλλ' ἅ[περ ἂν παραι]νῶσ[ι]ν οἱ θ[ε]ῖοι καλού[μενοι ἡγεῖται δεκτ]έ[ον]. In the restoration of the text Diels apparently had in mind the famous passage from Lucretius (I 102): *tutemet a nobis iam quovis tempore vatum terriloquis victus dictis desciscere quaeres; quippe etenim quam multa tibi iam fingere possunt somnia, quae vitae rationes vertere possint fortunasque tuas omnis turbare timore.* Thus he explains the θεῖοι as *vates*, and in substance he certainly is correct in this, if one only interprets the Latin usage correctly. When Livy, in his description of the bacchanalia (XXXIX 13.11), says: *viros velut mente capta* (μαινομένους) *cum iactatione fanatica corporis vaticinari*, he means all speaking in ecstasy; the Greek translation would be προφήτης, not μάντις, the mind *deo plenus.*[3] Thus is the much discussed passage in 238 Irenaeus (I 13.3 St.) to be understood: when the Gnostic Marcus says to the woman to whom God has descended, ἄνοιξον τὸ στόμα σου, λάλησον ὁτιδήποτε, καὶ προφητεύσεις, he only means, "Whatever you say will be God's word" (ἐν πνεύματι ῥηθήσεται). That Arellius Fuscus who in Seneca (Suas. IV) prompts Alexander to doubt astrological prophecy presents Oriental ideas which we can demonstrate in the religions of the East, point by point: *novae oportet sortis is sit, qui iubente deo canat, non eodem contentus utero, quo inprudentes* (οἱ ἐν ἀγνοίᾳ) *nascimur. quandam imaginem dei praeferat, qui iussa exhibeat dei*[4]*...ponat iste suos inter sidera patres et originem caelo trahat. agnoscat suum vatem deus non eodem vitae fine, aetate* <*plus quam*> *humana* (Mss. *magna*) *extra omnem fatorum necessitatem caput sit, quod gentibus futura praecipiat.*

As a rule, we place the appearance of such prophets too late, because we only have portrayals of them in detail from a later time. And yet Philo, in the passage mentioned earlier (De spec. leg. I 315), draws a picture for us which rather closely corresponds to that of Alexander of Abonoteichos: κἂν μέντοι τις ὄνομα καὶ σχῆμα προφητείας ὑποδύς, ἐνθουσιᾶν καὶ κατέχεσθαι δοκῶν, ἄγῃ πρὸς τὴν τῶν νενομισμένων κατὰ πόλεις θρησκείαν θεῶν, οὐκ ἄξιον προσέχειν ἀπατωμένους ὀνόματι προφήτου· γόης γάρ, ἀλλ' οὐ προφήτης ἐστὶν ὁ τοιοῦτος, ἐπειδὴ ψευδόμενος λόγια καὶ χρησμοὺς ἐπλάσατο. I shall select one single feature in order to make this kind of prophecy somewhat more vivid. Akin to the passage from Livy is the description in Apuleius XI 16: *ad istum modum vaticinatus sacerdos egregius fatigatos anhelitus trahens conticuit.* He has discerned in the spirit the experiences and thoughts of Apuleius, whom he meets, precisely as does the astrologer Horus with Propertius, whom he meets (IV 1).[5] In the papyri a

239 magician pleads for such a miraculous power (Wessely, *Denkschr. d. Wiener Akad.*, 1888, pp. 133, 134, lines 249, 279; Kenyon, *Greek Papyri* I 79): ἐὰν μὴ γνῶ τὰ ἐν ταῖς ψυχαῖς ἁπάντων Αἰγυπτίων, Ἑλλήνων, Σύρων, Αἰθιόπων παντός τε γένους καὶ παντὸς ἔθνους· ἐὰν μὴ γνῶ τὰ γεγονότα καὶ τὰ μέλλοντα ἔσεσθαι· ἐὰν μὴ γνῶ τὰς τέχνας αὐτῶν καὶ τὰ ἐπιτηδεύματα καὶ τὰς ἐργασίας καὶ τοὺς βίους καὶ τὰ ὀνόματα αὐτῶν καὶ πατέρων αὐτῶν καὶ μητέρων καὶ ἀδελφῶν καὶ φίλων καὶ τῶν τετελευτηκότων; and later on, ἕως ὅτε διαγνῶ τὰ ἐν ταῖς ψυχαῖς ἁπάντων ἀνθρώπων, Αἰγυπτίων, Σύρων, Ἑλλήνων, Αἰθιόπων, πάντος γένους καὶ ἔθνους τῶν ἐπερωτώντων με καὶ κατ' ὄψιν μοι ἐρχομένων καὶ λαλούντων καὶ σιωπώντων, ὅπως αὐτοῖς ἐξαγγείλω τὰ προγεγονότα αὐτοῖς καὶ ἐνεστῶτα καὶ τὰ μέλλοντα αὐτοῖς ἔσεσθαι, καὶ γνῶ τὰς τέχνας αὐτῶν καὶ τοὺς βίους καὶ τὰ ἐπιτηδεύματα καὶ τὰ ἔργα καὶ τὰ ὀνόματα αὐτῶν καὶ τῶν τεθνεώντων καὶ πάντων, καὶ

ἀναγνῶ ἐπιστολὴν ἐσφραγισμένην[6] καὶ ἀπαγγείλω αὐτοῖς πάντα ἐξ ἀληθείας.[7] No doubt every philologist has thought, while reading these lines, of Apollonius of Tyana, the prototype of a Hellenistic θεῖος for Philostratus, and it is to be hoped that many a theologian also has thought of Paul. In his communities προφητεύειν is an established part of the cultus; he says in I Cor. 14:24 what he expects of it: ἐὰν δὲ πάντες προφητεύωσιν, εἰσέλθῃ δέ τις ἄπιστος ἢ ἰδιώτης, ἐλέγχεται ὑπὸ πάντων, ἀνακρίνεται ὑπὸ πάντων, τὰ κρύπτα τῆς καρδίας αὐτοῦ φανερὰ γίνεται, καὶ οὕτως πεσὼν ἐπὶ πρόσωπον προσκυνήσει τῷ θεῷ, ἀπαγγέλλων ὅτι ὄντως ὁ θεὸς ἐν ὑμῖν ἐστιν. For explanation it actually is not sufficient to point to the story of Peter and Ananias; what is involved there is not deception or guilt, but the point is the activity of the "prophet" in proof of divine power, in reading the heart of the non-pneumatic person or the pagan. Ignatius still practices this, when through his confession he becomes a pneumatic, just as still later it is a quite universal practice of the monk who has become "perfect". But the phenomenon itself was already present long before the rise of Christianity, and Propertius describes it in IV 1 precisely as it is represented among the Christians of the earliest period. I need not detail the fact that the
240 same holds true for glossolalia; for Lukian's descriptions I refer to my book *Hellenistische Wundererzählungen*.

The fact is important enough. No one claims that the content of the early Christian ἐνθουσιασμός was borrowed from paganism; but it should no longer be disputed that its form and conception are actually appropriated, as well as the expectation of miracles. It is what is time-bound, external, which we should recognize and acknowledge with equanimity.

NOTES

1. Hence the Egyptian priests also can be thus named; cf. Philostratus, Vit. Apollonii V 27 (cf. Walther Otto, *Ägyptische Priestersynoden in hellenisticher Zeit, Sitzungsber. d. Bayr. Akad.* 1926, Abh. 2, p. 23).

2. From such passages we can form an idea of the Greek mercenaries who traveled through the Orient. There is striking agreement with the picture given in Juvenal III 75-78.

3. The Greeks retained the old religious idea only in transferring it to art; hence in Latin then even *vates* acquires the meaning of "poet". Conversely, *deo plenus* migrates from poetic language into juridical language and becomes a fixed concept like θεῖος (above, p. 157, n. 26).

4. When the apostle Thomas, at the marriage of the king's daughter, announces the commission of his God, his form is transfigured.

5. Cf. *Gött. Gel. Anz.* 1911, p. 556; above, p. 257.

6. Like Alexander of Abonoteichos.

7. Cf. the references in Pap. Berol. I 174; Parthey, *Abh. d. Preuss. Akad.* 1865, p. 125.

VIII.

Mystery and Primitive Religion

The self-proclamation of Isis in Apuleius (XI 5) runs thus: *cuius numen unicum multiformi specie, ritu vario, nomine multiiugo totus veneratur orbis. inde primigenii Phryges Pessinuntiam deum matrem, hinc autochthones Attici Cecropeiam Minervam, illinc fluctuantes Cyprii Paphiam Venerem, Cretes sagittiferi Dictynnam Dianam, Siculi trilingues Stygiam Proserpinam, Eleusinii vetustam deam Cererem, Iunonem alii, Bellonam alii, Hecatam isti, Phamnusiam illi, et qui nascentis dei Solis inchoantibus inlustrantur radiis Aethiopes Ariique priscaque doctrina pollentes Aegyptii caeremoniis me propriis percolentes appellant vero nomine reginam Isidem.*

What we have here is a literary restructuring and abbreviation of a cultic prayer. I conclude this on the one hand from similar invocations in the magical papyri, which pronounce the name of a deity in various languages and among various peoples, and on the other hand from a monument of the *national* Isis cult, the so-called Isis litany (Pap. Oxyrh. 1380). Naturally it shows in essence only the cultic place of the *Egyptian* goddess; consideration of other peoples and cults is peculiar to the Diaspora and its mystery-worship. As in Apuleius the Phrygians are called the first men, but the Egyptians are called the teachers of true religion, in the Phrygian Naassene Preaching the latter are praised (Hippolytus V 7.22; Wendland p. 83.22): Αἰγύπτιοι, πάντων ἀνθρώπων μετὰ τοὺς Φρύγας ἀρχαιότεροι καθεστῶτες καὶ πᾶσι τοῖς ἄλλοις ἀνθρώποις ὁμολογουμένως τελετὰς καὶ ὄργια θεῶν πάντων ὁμοῦ μετ'

·1 αὐτοὺς πρῶτον καταγγελκότες <καὶ> ἰδέας καὶ ἐνεργείας <θεῶν>, ἱερὰ καὶ σεβάσμια καὶ ἀνεξαγόρευτα τοῖς μὴ τετελεσμένοις τὰ Ἴσιδος ἔχουσι μυστήρια. A balancing of the claims of the two countries apparently has taken place in the sacral tradition, for which the way was prepared as early as the second century B.C. in the so-called Φρύγια γράμματα: an Egyptian deity has recorded the Phrygian and Egyptian history of the gods (cf. *Poimandres*, 164ff.). Then the Naassene Preaching in its development enumerates the peoples who have "mysteries", in order to find Attis, whom it seeks to extol, in the Assyrian Adonis, the Egyptian Osiris, the Arcadian Hermes, in Geryones and Men, in the Adamna of the Samothracians, in the Korybas of the Thracians and the Phrygians, and finally in the Papas of the latter people. This immediately becomes understandable when we read in Pseudo-Lukian (De dea Syria 15) as one of the sacred traditions that Attes the Lydian had founded the mysteries among the Phrygians, Lydians, Samothracians, and Syrians (Assyrians), and again when we see in the same author that even in the shrines themselves it was no longer really known whether the dying and rising god was Adonis or Attis or Osiris (or Dionysos). A gradual development leads from the first, still quite natural identifications to a conscious theology that seeks to preserve the national claim and yet take due account of what is universally felt; to that end it sometimes employs the formulas of euhemerism and sometimes those of reserving judgment, in both cases naturally strongly influenced by Greek thought, but not shaped by that thought alone. In some places there is explicit mention that the individual nations enumerated in the Naassene Preaching also claimed to be the earliest men, and elsewhere it is otherwise attested (for the Samothracians, for example, by Origen, Against Celsus I 16). Thus corresponding to this part at the outset is

the enumeration of those places where the human race is supposed to have originated; once again the places where mysteries exist are especially emphasized (just as in Apuleius). Clement of Alexandria (Protr. I 6; Stählin p. 7.7) splendidly exhibits the formula-like nature of these enumerations in their entirety, in his imitation of such a proclamation: εἴτ᾽ οὖν ἀρχαίους τοὺς Φρύγας διδάσκουσιν αἶγες μυθικαί, εἴτε αὖ τοὺς Ἀρκάδας οἱ προσελήνους ἀναγράφοντες ποιηταί, εἴτε μὴν αὖ τοὺς Αἰγυπτίους οἱ καὶ πρώτην ταύτην ἀναφῆναι τὴν γῆν θεούς τε καὶ ἀνθρώπους ὀνειρώσσοντες· ἀλλ᾽ οὐ πρό γε τοῦ κόσμου τοῦδε τούτων οὐδὲ εἷς, πρὸ δὲ τῆς τοῦ κόσμου καταβολῆς ἡμεῖς. The various euhemeristic and Stoic attempts to identify a place of origin for humanity and religion (cf. Diodorus I 10, 11 with III 2 and Justin II 1.5 or Diodorus III 67 and Philo of Byblos; cf. also Schol. on Apollonios Rhodios IV 262) gain for this later period a heightened religious significance. If the Ethiopians are the first men, then one will find among them the original form of religion; but if they are only the degenerate descendants of the Indians, they must go to the latter in order to learn true religion (the Pythagoras saga and Apollonius of Tyana). I have already indicated in the first part of this work that the practice of magic corresponds to this enumeration of the various peoples and divine names in the mysteries.

242

IX.

The Internalizing of the Mysteries

Neither μυστήριον nor τελετή is an established concept for Hellenistic religious language. Both terms first of all denote the cultic action which consists of the δρώμενον and the λόγος, but they also appear for the λόγος or the teaching alone, and ultimately they denote all for which γνῶσις is required and for what imparts γνῶσις; cf. Pap. Lugd. V (Dieterich, *Jahrb. f. kl. Phil.*, Suppl. XVI, p. 806, line 5): ἐπικαλοῦμαι καὶ εὔχομαι τὴν τελετήν; Abraxas 180.18: ἄρξαι δὲ λέγειν τὴν στήλην (the formula) καὶ τὸ μυστήριον τοῦ θεοῦ, ὅ ἐστι Κάνθαρος (book titles like Μονάς, Κλείς, Κρατήρ). The usual word here would be simply ὁ λόγος, and therefore λόγος appears for τελετή or μυστήριον; the λόγος τῆς παλιγγενεσίας (Corp. Herm. XIII 13, 22) effects the rebirth, is its παράδοσις, and thus the μυστήριον. The ἐποπτίδες βίβλοι of the Roman Valerius Soranus effect τὰ τέλεα καὶ ἐποπτικὰ μυστήρια (cf. Plato, Symp. 210 a). Thus out of the concept τελεία τελετή is developed the further τέλειος λόγος. The effect of both is the τελείωσις. Thus the conclusion of the λόγος τέλειος πρὸς 'Ασκληπιόν, extant in Latin, presupposes that during the instructional discourse the hearers actually have beheld God.[1] The same is at least suggested by the introduction to Apuleius' Ascl. 1, also extant only in Latin: *deus, deus te nobis, o Asclepi, ut divino sermoni interesses adduxit, eoque tali, qui merito omnium antea a nobis factorum vel nobis divino numine inspiratorum videatur esse religiosa pietate divinior, quem si intellegens videris, eris omnium*

43

bonorum tota mente plenissimus (then it is immediately added that the *omnia bona* are only the *unum bonum*, namely God). It is the customary announcement of the initiation into the mysteries, as is shown by Hippolytus' jeering word cited above (p. 241): τὸ τέλειον τῶν κακῶν παραδιδόντες. The λόγος given letter for letter is the mystery.

For an evaluation of the Hermetic writings it is important that the Christian-Gnostic writings, whose date is easier to determine, bear precisely the same character; in them also the sacred action is supposed to be achieved, and can be achieved, within the reader during the reading of the document. In them also the experience of the first divine founder is readily related, in order to operate upon the reader by the magic of analogy. In Justin's Baruch-apocalypse (Hippolytus, Wendland p. 132.24-25) the first book contains the oath: ὀμνύω τὸν ἐπάνω πάντων, τὸν 'Αγαθόν, τηρῆσαι τὰ μυστήρια ταῦτα καὶ ἐξειπεῖν μηδενί, μηδὲ ἀνακάμψαι ἀπὸ τοῦ 'Αγαθοῦ ἐπὶ τὴν κτίσιν. Here the first part naturally pertains to the reader alone, and the second, a Judaizing imitation of the oath of loyalty in the mysteries (the *sacramentum*), pertains to the ascending divine being and to the reader. After he, as a novice, has taken this oath, i.e., has read it, the book has him entering into the actual heavens, to behold the 'Αγαθός face to face (p. 125.25-26). He moistens his mouth with the "living water" that separates the world of the senses from the super-sensual world, and lets himself be baptized in it, ἐν ᾧ λούονται οἱ πνευματικοί, <οἱ> ζῶντες ἄνθρωποι. The best parallel is at once offered by the Hermetic regeneration-mystery. As Hermes tells of his own rebirth, so Baruch appears also to

244 have related the ascent of his 'Ελωείμ (129.6). The latter, upon reaching the gate of heaven, hears a voice sounding forth from the light: αὕτη ἡ πύλη τοῦ κυρίου, δίκαιοι εἰσέρχονται

δι' αὐτῆς. After the blessed vision that he has enjoyed there within, he wants to return in order to fetch his Pneuma, which has remained behind among men "bound", that is, united with their ψυχαί, and is being tormented by the ruler of matter, Edem; but the 'Αγαθός does not allow him to go. Therefore he sends Baruch, who now is guiding and instructing the *mystai*. I hardly need to emphasize the fact that this captive Pneuma here corresponds to a captive Self in the Manichaean hymns--in fact, the Greek could hardly find a fully adequate translation for the concept of the Self. When we hear how the divine emissary who is to retrieve the Pneuma is chosen in heaven, we recall the Mandaean and particularly the Manichaean liturgy, in which the same thing is recounted at length. In fact, it is essentially Mani's entire doctrine of redemption that we encounter here a century before Mani's time, 'Ελωείμ as the god Ohrmazd, who has left behind in matter his equipment, the world-soul, which the emissary, the call, now must retrieve. I am reminded of the Zarathustra hymn that was employed among the Manichaeans because in fact in Jewish circles Baruch is equated with Zarathustra. One can now pose the question whether it is at all conceivable that this form of the literary mystery and this thought-content arose within Christianity and then passed from there into paganism. Moreover, it cannot have arisen within Judaism, but was indeed appropriated into Judaism. The idea of a heavenly ocean which separates the world of becoming and passing away from the eternal world is found again among the Peratae, who believe that they pass through the waters of that ocean into immortality, just as Israel once passed through the Red Sea; and we find among the Mandaeans an idea that is similar, though with less Jewish coloration. Finally, in Philo's time we find the same idea combined with a cultic celebration in the major festival of

the Therapeutae (Philo, De vit. cont. 83 Cohn; p. 485 M.). Their nocturnal celebration ends with the veneration of the rising sun with the prayer for εὐημερία, ἀλήθεια and ὀξυωπία λογισμοῦ. It is hoped that the later discussion of the word

245 γνῶσις, which Philo avoids (below, p. 402), will make it evident to the reader that the religious term γνῶσις which has passed over into the philosophical sphere is concealed among the latter two of those three terms.[2] Indeed, the Gnostic always prays in conclusion that he may be preserved in γνῶσις and may not forfeit this kind of life (below, p. 367; Corp. Herm. I 32). Philo's concluding sentence also points this out: θεραπευτῶν μὲν δὴ περὶ τοσαῦτα, θεωρίαν ἀσπασαμένων φύσεως καὶ τῶν ἐν αὐτῇ,[3] καὶ ψυχῇ μόνῃ βιωσάντων,[4] οὐρανοῦ μὲν καὶ κόσμου πολιτῶν,[5] τῷ δὲ πατρὶ καὶ ποιητῇ τῶν ὅλων γνησίως συσταθέντων[6] ὑπ' ἀρετῆς. Here we can clearly discern the use of pagan mysteries in a Jewish Gnosticism and its influence upon Christian Gnosticism as well.

As to form, this apocalypse of Baruch is--apart from the conclusion--closely akin to the so-called Mithras-liturgy; the magical text is a direct reflection of the religious text, and the latter provides the best explanation of the former. Herein we recognize how one could expect a religious effect, a heightening of the divine in the reader, even from the reading of such a magical text; and this fact confirms me in my interpretation of the much-disputed little writing.

NOTES

1. Cf. the Greek text preserved in the Papyrus Mimaut, below, in Appendix XV, pp. 365ff. In addition, of course λόγος τέλειος can also denote simply the especially lofty discourse.

2. For him the γνωστικοί are the ὁρατικοὶ ἄνδρες.

3. Cf. Corp. Herm. I 3: μαθεῖν θέλω τὰ ὄντα καὶ νοῆσαι τὴν τούτων φύσιν καὶ γνῶναι τὸν θεόν (it is the knowledge of the world in the vision of God).

4. As pneumatics; cf. below, p. 405.

5. Later on the monk (as a pneumatic) is called οὐρανοπολίτης.

6. United with him; cf. p. 97, n. 47; 316. This occurs through the rite of initiation, the passing through the sea and the entrance into heaven.

X.

Love-Union with God

The idea of the ἱερὸς γάμος, which in itself can be demonstrated almost everywhere, can be traced especially well in Egypt, where the pictorial representations of the begetting of the Pharaoh by the deity are explained in detail by inscriptions. Here I may pass over at once to the theological representation and rationale in the Hellenistic period. Plutarch offers it in two passages. The first of these is Quaest. conv. VIII 1.3: καὶ ὅλως ἄρρενι θεῷ πρὸς γυναῖκα θνητὴν ἀπολείπουσιν
246 (οἱ Αἰγύπτιοι) ὁμιλίαν· ἀνάπαλιν δ' οὐκ οἴονται θνητὸν ἄνδρα θηλείᾳ θεῷ τόκου καὶ κυήσεως ἀρχὴν παρασχεῖν, διὰ τὸ τὰς οὐσίας τῶν θεῶν ἐν ἀέρι καὶ πνεύμασι καί τισι θερμότησι καὶ ὑγρότησι τίθεσθαι. The second, still clearer, is in Vit. Numae 4: καίτοι δοκοῦσιν οὐκ ἀπιθάνως Αἰγύπτιοι διαιρεῖν, ὡς γυναικὶ μὲν οὐκ ἀδύνατον πνεῦμα πλησιάσαι θεοῦ καί τινας ἐντεκεῖν ἀρχὰς γενέσεως, ἀνδρὶ δὲ οὐκ ἔστι σύμμιξις πρὸς θεὸν οὐδὲ ὁμιλία σώματος. It is clear that here we have the Hellenistic justification of a cultic practice and a cultic conception that is detached from the deification of the king. The cultic action with which it is connected actually still was in existence in the time of the empire; this is shown by the account related by Josephus (above, p. 118) and by Rufinus, Hist. eccl. XI 25: *Sacerdos erat apud eos Saturni* (Agathos Daimon?) *Tyrannus nomine. hic quasi ex responso numinis adorantibus in templo nobilibus quibusque et primariis viris, quorum sibi matronae ad libidinem placuissent, dicebat Saturnum sibi praecepisse,*

ut uxor sua pernoctaret in templo. tum is qui audierat gaudens, quod uxor sua dignatione numinis vocaretur,[1] *exornatam comptius, insuper et donariis onustam, ne vacua scilicet repudiaretur, coniugem mittebat ad templum. in conspectu omnium conclusa intrinsecus matrona Tyrannus clausis ianuis et traditis clavibus discedebat, deinde facto silentio per occultos et subterraneos aditus intra ipsum Saturni simulacrum patulis erepebat cavernis*[2]*--erat autem simulacrum illud a tergo exesum et parieti diligenter adnexum--ardentibusque intra aedem luminibus intentae supplicantique mulieri vocem subito per simulacrum aeris concavi proferebat, ita ut pavore et gaudio infelix mulier trepidaret, quod dignam se tanti numinis putaret adloquio.*[3] *posteaquam quae libitum fuerat vel ad consternationem maiorem vel ad libidinis incitamentum disseruisset numen inpurum, arte quadam lineolis obductis repente lumina extinguebantur universa. tum descendens obstupefactae et costernatae mulierculae adulterii fucum profanis commentationibus inferebat. haec cum per omnes miserorum matronas multo iam tempore gererentur, accidit quandam pudicae mentis feminam horruisse facinus et adtentius designantem cognovisse vocem Tyranni ac domum regressam viro de fraude sceleris indicasse.* 7
We certainly may attribute details to the imagination of Rufinus, but the mystery practice is well attested. By means of it the women become mistresses or concubines of the deity. Philo[4] is familiar with the theological justification of this practice, and he employs it without any strain at all in an allegorical exposition in De Cherubim 42: ἵνα δὲ τῶν ἀρετῶν[5] χύσιν καὶ ὠδῖνα εἴπωμεν, ἀκοὰς ἐπιφραξάτωσαν οἱ δεισιδαίμονες τὰς ἑαυτῶν ἢ μεταστήτωσαν· τελετὰς γὰρ ἀναδιδάσκομεν θείας τοὺς τελετῶν ἀξίους[6] τῶν ἱερωτάτων μύστας, οὗτοι δ' εἰσὶν οἱ τὴν ἀληθῆ καὶ οὖσαν ὄντως ἀκαλλώπιστον εὐσέβειαν μετὰ ἀτυφίας ἀσκοῦντες· ἐκείνοις δ' οὐχ ἱεροφαντήσομεν κατεσχημένοις ἀνιά-

τῳ κακῷ, τύφῳ ῥημάτων καὶ ὀνομάτων γλισχρότητι καὶ τερθρείαις ἐθῶν, ἄλλῳ δὲ οὐδενὶ τὸ εὐαγὲς καὶ ὅσιον μετροῦσιν. ἀρκτέον οὖν τῆς τελετῆς ὧδε.[7] ἀνὴρ μὲν γυναικί, ἄνθρωπος δ' ἄρρην ἀνθρώπῳ θηλείᾳ τὰς ἐπὶ γενέσει παίδων ὁμιλίας ἐπακολουθῶν τῇ φύσει συνέρχεται ποιησόμενος· ἀρεταῖς δὲ πολλὰ καὶ τέλεια τικτούσαις θέμις οὐκ ἔστιν ἀνδρὸς ἐπιλαχεῖν θνητοῦ· μὴ δεξάμεναι δὲ παρά τινος ἑτέρου γονήν, ἐξ ἑαυτῶν μόνον οὐδέποτε κυήσουσι. τίς οὖν ὁ σπείρων ἐν αὐταῖς τὰ καλὰ πλὴν ὁ τῶν ὄντων πατήρ, ὁ ἀγέννητος θεὸς καὶ τὰ σύμπαντα γεννῶν; σπείρει μὲν οὖν οὗτος, τὸ δὲ γέννημα τὸ ἴδιον, ὃ ἔσπειρε, δωρεῖται. γεννᾷ γὰρ ὁ θεὸς οὐδὲν αὑτῷ, χρεῖος ἅτε ὢν οὐδενός, πάντα δὲ τῷ λαβεῖν δεομένῳ. παρέξω δὲ τῶν λεγομένων ἐγγυητὴν ἀξιόχρεων τὸν ἱερώτατον Μωυσῆν· τὴν γὰρ Σάρραν εἰσάγει τότε κύουσαν, ὅτε ὁ θεὸς αὐτὴν μονωθεῖσαν ἐπισκοπεῖ (Gen. 21:1), τίκτουσαν δ' οὐκέτι τῷ τὴν ἐπίσκεψιν πεποιημένῳ, ἀλλὰ τῷ σοφίας τυχεῖν γλιχομένῳ, οὗτος δὲ 'Αβραὰμ ὀνομάζεται. γνωριμώτερον δ' ἐπὶ τῆς Λείας ἐκδιδάσκει λέγων, ὅτι τὴν μὲν μήτραν ἀνέῳξεν αὐτῆς ὁ θεὸς (Gen. 29:23)-- 248 ἀνοιγνύναι δὲ μήτραν ἀνδρὸς ἴδιον--ἡ δὲ συλλαβοῦσα ἔτεκεν οὐ θεῷ--ἱκανὸς γὰρ μόνος καὶ αὐταρκέστατος ἑαυτῷ--, ἀλλὰ τῷ κάματον ἀναδεχομένῳ ὑπὲρ τοῦ καλοῦ 'Ιακώβ, ὥστε τὴν ἀρετὴν δέχεσθαι μὲν παρὰ τοῦ αἰτίου τὰ θεῖα σπέρματα, τίκτειν δέ τινι τῶν ἑαυτῆς ἐραστῶν, ὃς ἂν τῶν μνηστήρων ἁπάντων προκριθῇ. Philo then warns that one should speak of this mystery only to those who have been initiated (§48)[8] and he himself passes over to a still loftier mystery, the exposition of Jer. 3:4: οὐχ ὡς οἶκόν με ἐκάλεσας καὶ πατέρα καὶ ἄνδρα τῆς παρθενίας σου. Now the *soul* is the recipient of the divine seed; through intercourse with the soul God makes it into a virgin: ἀνθρώπων μὲν γὰρ ἡ ἐπὶ γενέσει τέκνων σύνοδος τὰς παρθένους γυναῖκας ἀποφαίνει· ὅταν δὲ ὁμιλεῖν ἄρξηται ψυχῇ θεός, πρότερον αὐτὴν οὖσαν γυναῖκα παρθένον αὖθις ἀποδείκνυσιν. The governing idea here apparently is the *sursum vocatio* or rebirth, the birth

of the divine being within us, which in fact is bound up with the "virgin" number seven (cf. below, p. 343). The connection with the Hellenistic mysteries here is clear, but even in the first part Usener has sensed, probably correctly, the influence of a mystery perspective, which indeed alone explains the choice of the external form: for a human father God creates the ἀρχαὶ γενέσεως for a divine child.

The influence of Egyptian-Hellenistic mystery ideas upon Judaism, which is especially important for us here, is also exhibited in the narrative literature. As an example I cite the midrash of Aseneth, the wife of Joseph, which admittedly is available only in a form that has undergone successive revisions, the last one Christian (P. Battifol, *Studia Patristica*, Paris 1889). Joseph, who appears as a representative of Pharaoh, and indeed finally becomes Pharaoh, on a tour stops at the home of the Egyptian priest Pentephres and is supposed to be greeted there by the latter's beautiful daughter, a pure virgin; but the devout Israelite turns away from the servant of false gods. Aseneth, who, moved at the sight of him, has recognized the vanity and sinfulness of her father's faith, does penance in sackcloth and ashes for *seven days* in her solitary tower and pleads with God for mercy for her sins. When on the eighth morning she is praying, facing toward the east, she sees the heavens parted in the vicinity of the morning star, a beam of light break forth, and a man's figure, issuing from the beam, coming toward her. According to the features preserved from the original narration it is unmistakably the sun-deity himself in the form of Joseph. After she has adorned herself, at his command, in wedding garments, he tells her that Joseph will return this very morning and will make her his wife; she will also be re-created for immortality. Thereupon the emissary, having fulfilled his mission, could depart;

but Aseneth urges him to come to her couch, which no one else has ever touched; she intends to bring him bread and wine, but he asks only for a bit of honey, the food of immortality in the initiation for the Persian also, that is, of the person who is fully adopted into the nationality, in the Mithras mysteries. The divine envoy creates this food through his word and has Aseneth eat of it, then returns to heaven in a chariot of fire, and Joseph is immediately present again. We need only to recall the first magical papyrus of Berlin (*Poimandres*, 226; only one detail has been changed by Eitrem's collation, *Forhandlinger i Videnskapsselskapet i Kristiania* 1923, pp. 1-2) to recognize how mystery features can also intrude into a Jewish midrash: the union with the δαίμων πάρεδρος who makes one immortal is achieved by setting before him wine and food and drawing him to the couch. The almost total agreement with the old Egyptian idea of the begetting of the Pharaoh by the sun-god hardly needs to be emphasized here.[9] Here as in no other case we can recognize the transition of ancient Oriental belief into sacral action and the Hellenistic transformation of the action into narrative.

The separation here of a proclamation from the actual ἱερὸς γάμος is repeated also in a narrative of the Acts of Thomas (chapters 4ff.). The apostle has come into a city

250

whose king at that very time intends to betroth his only daughter. He goes to the feast, to which everyone is invited, but he does not eat or drink; instead, smearing all his sense-organs with ointment and thus deadening them, he sits in ecstasy. His form is changed, he radiates with beauty, and a miracle attests that a deity has entered into him. Then he begins, in the Hebrew language, which no one but the flute-player understands, a hymn to "his bride",[10] the daughter of light; only the conclusion of the hymn betrays the fact that

he means the celestial marriage at which all participants will receive the food of immortality and will drink of the wine which prevents one's ever thirsting again. The king commands the divine envoy to come into the bridal chamber and to voice a prayer for (or over) his daughter.[11] At first he refuses, for he does not yet feel his God with him; but then he acquiesces, prays over the newly wedded couple to Jesus, imparts to them his blessing, laying his hand on them, and then in company with the entire bridal entourage leaves the bridal chamber. But when the young husband is about to lead his bride to the couch, Jesus is suddenly beside her *in the form of Thomas.* He seats himself upon the couch and proceeds to instruct them both in a frightfully solemn discourse about the vanity of the lust of the senses and of earthly marital relations. When the parents visit the young couple the next morning, they find them firmly determined to maintain their chastity. During the night they both have consummated the only true marriage with the Lord; the bride speaks of the ἀγάπη, ἧς ᾐσθόμην ταύτῃ τῇ νυκτί...τὸν ἄνδρα, οὗ ᾐσθόμην σήμερον, and the bridegroom praises the Lord: ὁ μακράν με τῆς φθορᾶς ποιήσας καὶ σπείρας ἐν ἐμοὶ τὴν ζωήν...ὁ σεαυτὸν κατευτελίσας ἕως ἐμοῦ καὶ τῆς ἐμῆς σμικρότητος, ἵνα ἐμὲ τῇ μεγαλοσύνῃ παραστήσας ἑνώσῃς σεαυτῷ...οὗ ᾐσθόμην, καὶ νῦν οὐ δύναμαι ἀμνημονεῖν τούτου, οὗ ἡ ἀγάπη ἐν ἐμοὶ βράσσει.[12] The meaning will be recognized: they have anticipated the celestial marriage of the great Psyche (Achamoth, Wisdom) and of the individual souls that are inseparable from her with the redeemer and his angels, and the apostle's hymn has proclaimed this marriage in advance, and has called people to it.

251

Now let us return from the narrative to the cultic action. Irenaeus tells (I 13.3) of the prophetic initiation of the Gnostic Marcos: he chooses for himself wives of promi-

nence and promises them μεταδοῦναί σοι θέλω τῆς ἐμῆς χάριτος ...ὁ δὲ τόπος τοῦ μεγέθους ἐν ἡμῖν ἐστι, δι' ἡμᾶς ἐγκαταστῆσαι. λάμβανε πρῶτον ἀπ' ἐμοῦ καὶ δι' ἐμοῦ τὴν χάριν. εὐτρέπισον σεαυτὴν ὡς νύμφη ἐκδεχομένη τὸν νυμφίον ἑαυτῆς, ἵνα ἔσῃ ὃ ἐγὼ καὶ ἐγὼ ὃ σύ. καθίδρυσον ἐν τῷ νυμφῶνί σου τὸ σπέρμα τοῦ φωτός. λάβε παρ' ἐμοῦ τὸν νυμφίον καὶ χώρησον αὐτὸν καὶ χωρήθητι ἐν αὐτῷ.--ἰδοὺ ἡ χάρις κατῆλθεν ἐπὶ σέ. ἄνοιξον τὸ στόμα σου καὶ προφήτευσον. After prayers and formulae the exhortation is repeated even more insistently: ἄνοιξον τὸ στόμα σου, λάλησον ὁτιδήποτε, καὶ προφητεύσεις.[13] The continuation corresponds in some degree with the individual portrayal of Rufinus; this is not surprising, for Marcos is in fact an Egyptian. Since what is involved here is the reception of the πνεῦμα, it is understandable that according to the same Irenaeus (I 21.3) some of the Marcosians combined baptism with the ἱερὸς γάμος: νυμφῶνα κατασκευάζουσι καὶ μυσταγωγίας ἐπιτελοῦσι μετ' ἐπιρρήσεών τινων τοῖς τελειουμένοις, καὶ πνευματικὸν γάμον φάσκουσιν εἶναι τὸ ὑπ' αὐτῶν γινόμενον κατὰ τὴν ὁμοιότητα τῶν ἄνω συζυγιῶν. How tenaciously primitive belief holds on may finally be shown by a little story from our own time that offers a counterpart to the narrative from the Acts of Thomas. In Egypt even today it is common to call a demented woman "the bride of the *zar*" (demon), usually, of course, without much thought being given to the expression. But in Cairo a Mohammedan student from the town of Minyeh told my friend Prof. E. Littmann in good faith that in his home town a *zar* had recently announced, *through the mouth of a woman magician*, that he wanted a girl from a particular family for his wife; hence a marriage feast was actually prepared, guests were invited to it, and finally the bride was conducted into the chamber and the chamber was locked. The student was firmly convinced that then, invisible to all human eyes, the *zar*

252

had actually come and had become the spouse of the maiden. Thus we have still an ancient Oriental initiatory action; for as is well known, demented and mentally ill persons are regarded in a certain sense as holy.

In many places the prostitution of the male or female servants of a temple apparently is connected with similar perspectives. Maximos of Aigai (Philostratus, Vit. Apoll. I 12) tells us that a Cilician ruler comes to the youthful Apollonios, who is residing in the temple of Asklepios as "friend and servant" of the latter, with the request: σύσστησόν με τῷ θεῷ; cf., in the Acts of Thomas, ἵνα ἐμὲ τῇ μεγαλωσύνῃ παραστήσας ἑνώσῃς σεαυτῷ. This serves to explain what Epiphanius relates about the sect of the Phibionites: they see in sexual union with a member of the same community the means of passing again through the 365 successive concentric spheres of the Aions and thus of presenting themselves to a new god: they say μίγηθι μετ' ἐμοῦ, ἵνα σε ἐνέγκω πρὸς τὸν ἄρχοντα, or προσφέρω σε τῷ δεῖνι, ἵνα με προσενέγκῃς τῷ δεῖνι. These are age-old and crude folk-ideas which of course have nothing to do with Christianity, but could have an influence on the mysteries. If I am not mistaken, we have herewith explained the initiatory rite of the bacchanalia described by Livy, and thus of a Hellenistic mystery. And here now the series is concluded.

NOTES

1. These words, *dignatione numinis vocaretur*, are mystery-words; cf. below, pp. 320ff.

2. Cf. the narrative of Thessalos, above, pp. 144-45.

3. The expression ὁμιλεῖν θεῷ is ambiguous.

4. Norden, in his *Die Geburt des Kindes*, pp. 76-77, explains the divergence from Plutarch with extraordinary sensitivity. My offering the passages here once again is done to allow the mystery-like character of the presentation to emerge in bold relief.

5. He has equated Sarah, Rebekah, and Leah with the ἀρεταί.

6. Cf. the Mithras liturgy, above, p. 204.

7. In a certain sense here begins the instruction that precedes the initiation. To be compared with the following is *Quod Deus sit immutabilis* §4-5, where reference is made to Hannah and Samuel as is done in Luke.

8. It is the oath taken before the rite of initiation begins.

9. Cf. E. Norden, *Die Geburt des Kindes*, p. 83. Norden has detailed the implications for the infancy narrative about Jesus that are important for the theologian. I could only weaken what he says, and therefore I prefer to refer to his work.

10. Thus the Syrian tradition of the often-discussed hymn (cf. my *Hellenistische Wundererzählungen*, p. 136).

11. In the Hellenistic view the ἱερὸς γάμος with the deity does not exclude the human γάμος, but only consecrates it. The view is especially clear here.

12. The Egyptian queen says, "Thy dew saturates all my members."

13. That is to say, the words are divine revelation: the woman has received the πνεῦμα; cf. Livy 39.13.11: *viros velut mente capta cum iactatione fanatica corporis vaticinari.* It is the same idea as is found in the famous term *plena deo.*

XI.

Election, Call, Justification, Glorification

Pausanias (X 32.13) tells of the shrine of Isis at Tithorea: οὔτε ἔσοδος ἐς τὸ ἄδυτον ἄλλοις γε ἢ ἐκείνοις ἐστίν, οὓς ἂν αὐτὴ προτιμήσασα ἡ Ἶσις καλέσῃ σφᾶς δι' ἐνυπνίων. They alone, as is said further, have ἄδεια. Pausanias himself also testifies elsewhere that a similar belief is found also in other cults, and that the stories of the sudden death of intruders connect the punishment of the deity with divulging the secrets, not with the mere intrusion. But since Pausanias here employs mystery-terms, this does not prevent me from comparing Apuleius, who (XI 21) speaks of dreams and propounds

253 the principle that one may *neque vocatus morari nec non iussus festinare*; intrusion without being called is a capital offense. Along with *vocatus* Apuleius also uses *nuncupatus*, and he is especially fond of using *destinatus*, for example in the passage cited: *praecipua evidentique magni numinis dignatione iam dudum felici ministerio nuncupatum destinatumque*, and in XI 19: *me iam dudum destinatum*. Here it appears we have to do with specific concepts of the mystery cults. First of all I compare with Pausanias a couple of witnesses for the τιμᾶσθαι ὑπὸ θεοῦ, which apparently is rare on inscriptions (cf. Nock, *Journal of Hellenic Studies* XLV, 1925, p. 100). The person who is *singled out* by the deity, i.e., is chosen to be a *mystes*, in Phrygian cults of the Ἑκάτη Σώτειρα, which must have corresponded somewhat to the Ἶσις Σώτειρα, may be given a tomb within the temple precincts; he is himself indeed ἀθάν-

ατος. This follows from Le Bas-Waddington, *Voyage* V 805: τιμηθέντα ὑπὸ Σωτείρης Ἑκάτης κατιέρωσαν; from I. Keil-Premerstein, *Denkschr. d. Akademie Wien* LIV 2, p. 241: τὸν πατέρα Τρόφιμον καὶ τὴν μητέρα Ἄμμιον ἔτι ζῶσαν ἀπειέρωσαν τιμηθέντας ὑπὸ Σωτείρης Ἑκάτης; and above all from the inscription published by Ramsay, *Journal of Hellenic Studies* IV, 1883, pp. 419-20: ἀθάνατος Ἐπιτύνχανος τιμηθ(ε)ὶς ὑπὸ Ἑκὰτης πρώτης, δεύτε[ρ]ον ὑπὸ Μάνου Δάου [Ἡ]λιοδρόμου Διός, τρίτον <ὑπὸ> Φοίβου Ἀρχηγέτου Χρησμοδότου ἀληθῶς δῶρον ἔλαβ[ο]ν χρησ[μ]οδοτ[ε]ῖν ἀλη[θε]ίας[1]...τοῦτο ἔχω τὸ δῶρον ἐξ ἀθανάτων ἁπάντων. He characterizes himself as μυηθ[ε]ὶς ὑπὸ Καλῆς, ἀρχιερ(ε)ίας δημοτικῆς, and is himself ἀρχιερεύς and ἀθάνατος.[2] Thus we have to do with a *mystes* who is "graced" by three different gods. Indeed, Apuleius also through the favor of three different gods, Isis, Osiris, and Agathos Daimon, similarly attained the highest priesthood, and he says concerning this (XI 29): *adsidua ista numinum dignatione laetus...ter futurus quod alii vel semel vix conceditur*. Corresponding to the expression *dignatio* is the Greek τιμή. This is shown by the words of Pausanias, compared with those of Rufinus (Hist. eccles. XI 25; above, p. 310), *gaudens quod uxor sua dignatione numinis vocaretur* (cf. also Apuleius XI 22: *o, inquit, Luci, te felicem, quem propitia voluntate numen augustum tantopere dignatur*). Now we see even more clearly that the ἐν κατοχῇ ὄντες of Sarapis have an ἀξίωμα, since their dreams are significant; thus they have the ὁμιλία πρὸς τὸν θεόν. When the Christians ecclesiastically developed the promise that the Spirit would come upon the person imprisoned because of his faith, these perspectives contributed their part; rules were devised; already on his journey the prisoner Ignatius has the πνεῦμα and is, in a certain sense, a μύστης; in the case of Cyprian, who has a dream not in

prison but in internment in Curubis, it can be disputed whether this was a divine revelation, a τιμή. His biographer takes the position that it was (cf. my treatment, "Die Nachrichten über den Tod Cyprians," *Sitzungsber. d. Heidelberger Akad.* 1913, Abh. 14, p. 50; and *Nach. d. Ges. d. Wiss.* Göttingen 1916, pp. 417-18). Even in the language itself the adaptation to pagan feeling is exhibited. One may think of the address of the brother to the martyr Perpetua during her imprisonment (chap. 4): *domina soror, iam in magna dignatione es: tanta es, ut postules visionem et ostendatur tibi an passio sit an commeatus. et ego quae me sciebam fabulari cum domino*[3]... *fidens repromisi ei dicens: Crastina die tibi renuntiabo.*[4] The Greek text here also offers us an important term from the Greek mystery-language: Κυρία ἀδελφή, ἤδη ἐν μεγάλῳ ἀξιώματι ὑπάρχεις, τοσαύτη οὖσα ὡς, εἰ αἰτήσειας ὀπτασίαν, λάβοις ἄν, εἰς τὸ δειχθῆναί σοι, εἴπερ ἀναβολὴν ἔχεις ἢ παθεῖν μέλλεις. κἀγώ, ἥτις ᾔδειν με ὁμιλοῦσαν θεῷ...πίστεως πλήρης οὖσα ἐπηγγειλάμην αὐτῷ εἰποῦσα· Αὔριόν σοι ἀπαγγελῶ.[4] This is reminiscent of the wish of Thessalos of Tralles (above, p. 145). It appears to me that the words quoted from Apuleius are to be interpreted accordingly; now perhaps they will allow us to penetrate somewhat more deeply into the perspectives of the *mystai*.

255 His entire presentation is dominated by the idea that the goddess has chosen her servant from earliest times (XI 21: *eligit*); her πρόνοια leads him gradually to σωτηρία, and this πρόνοια stands in opposition to the rule of εἱμαρμένη or τύχη (*casus infestus*; as *Fortuna videns* it stands over against the *Fortuna nefaria*: XI 15); cf. XI 5: *iam tibi providentia mea inlucescit dies salutaris*; cf. XI 6, XI 25. In the appendix devoted to the word γνῶσις I shall have to go into still greater detail to show how in religious circles the pressure

of the idea of a planetary compulsion, εἱμαρμένη, leads to a yearning for liberation and how this is connected with a stronger development of the concept of πρόνοια. The concept is not a purely philosophical one, since the πρόνοια is related only to those who belong to the deity and does not take the place of εἱμαρμένη, but appears alongside it as its counterpart; in it, as in εἱμαρμένη, everything is determined from the very beginning.

Now I certainly would not go so far as simply to derive Paul's doctrine of predestination from this. That doctrine is rooted in the experience of his own conversion and call, which he is able to account for and to render comprehensible only thus. The same can also be said for Augustine. The fact that he finds the doctrine of predestination in Paul is far from sufficing to explain the fact that a considerable time after his conversion he adopts it and in such a way sets it at the very center of his religious thought: he can only comprehend the miracle that has happened to him by saying that it is God alone who has acted in it.[5] And yet we can say with certainty here that without Paul's doctrine Augustine would never have arrived at his own; it supplies the necessary precondition. Thus, in spite of the much more limited material that is available to us, we may attempt also in Paul's case to try to discern the preconditions or presuppositions that made possible for him the formation of this religious conviction, and in so doing we shall have to give especially careful consideration to the help that the language affords us.

256 With Paul also--in utter contrast to Judaism and to Greek thought--it is God alone who acts. This is inward experience, but it is also the necessary presupposition for his activity among the Gentiles, the presupposition for his pneuma-faith. The idea that there are two *essentially* different classes of

men, an idea that underlies all gnosis and which I shall later pursue further, had been firmly maintained not only in Zoroastrianism, and indeed first of all in most of the religions that were bound up with nationalism, but in Judaism also, even in Philo. Now--since the crucifixion of Jesus--Israel is no longer the "people of his possession", but God needs a people, a "tribe of souls" in whom correct knowledge about him, and the inner relationship to him, exists; he must *choose* that people for himself.[6] The gift to the individual that makes him different *in essence* and sets him in a position different from that of all other men, that imparts to him that correct knowledge and that inner relationship, the Pneuma, is freely given. It comes without merit on the part of the recipient, and yet it is a τιμή; it elevates one into a filial relationship with God. These are trains of thought that recur in all mystery religions, though certainly not in equal strength; indeed, they must recur, whenever these religions undertake missionary work. Even the distinction as to whether particular ones, like the religion of Mithras, maintain the fiction of a national connection or, like the religion of Isis, require fulfillment of certain prescriptions of folk religion at least of the *mystai* may not be regarded as essential. The message of John the Baptist proclaims even at the boundaries of Judaism that God can create a new people and that he is creating such through the sacrament. However, it is not in the sacraments in themselves that the inner affinity of Christianity with the mystery religions consists, but in the basic perspective and in the fact that from the very beginning it is sent on mission. If one senses how this implies the requirement of an initiatory rite, then the adoption of baptism, which in fact Jesus did not perform, in the constituting of the first community appears obvious.

57 If one examines in this perspective the Pauline terminology and recalls at the same time that Philo, without ever having been himself initiated into Hellenistic mysteries, is familiar with their terminology and assumes that they are generally known among his readers, the agreements with the mystery terminology will no longer seem strange. The investigation becomes difficult in the case of words that appear also in the Septuagint,[7] and thus belong to two entirely different circles of language. Of course it is precisely there that the investigation also becomes especially rewarding. We must then focus as sharply as possible on the context of the passage and determine the original meaning of the word in each of the two language circles.

As an example, to which the passage from Pausanias cited above led me--at first quite accidentally--I take Rom. 8:30: οὓς δὲ προώρισεν, τούτους καὶ ἐκάλεσεν, καὶ οὓς ἐκάλεσεν, τούτους καὶ ἐδικαίωσεν, οὓς δὲ ἐδικαίωσεν, τούτους καὶ ἐδόξασεν. The strictly rhetorically constructed climax (cf. the examples from Scipio: *vi atque ingratis coactus cum illo sponsionem feci, facta sponsione ad iudicem adduxi, adductum primo coetu damnavi, damnatum ex voluntate dimisi;* or: *ex innocentia nascitur dignitas, ex dignitate honor, ex honore imperium, ex imperio libertas*) has God making a person into σύμμορφος τῆς εἰκόνος τοῦ υἱοῦ αὐτοῦ in four successive actions. This is, as I hope to show more precisely in the excursus on Paul, a Hellenistic conception. Of these four actions, the first two are mentioned in Apuleius in the same sequence and juxtaposition as coming before the mystery (*destinatus - vocatus*). The Hermetic mystery mentions and distinguishes the other two in the sacred proceeding itself; in §9, in speaking of the destruction of the evil inclinations that stem from the body, and thus of the death of the old man, it uses the term ἐδικαι-

ὤθημεν, and for the birth of the new, divine man it uses the word ἐθεώθημεν; and these are used in deliberate antiphony. Paul's avoidance of this latter word is understandable; it 258 will be shown that in his writings δοξάζομαι can also mean a μεταβολή within man, the emergence of Christ in the person still living. It appears to me not too bold to assume an influence of Hellenistic language here.

It was not only the devout Jew who hoped to be found righteous before God or to be "acquitted" by him; the Egyptian also anticipated a "justification" in the judgment of the departed, and it certainly is connected with this general conception that in the Middle Kingdom it was customary never to mention a deceased person without appending to his name the formula, "who is found righteous (or: true) with his voice". Erman (*Ägypt. Religion*, second edition, p. 117) suggests that the best translation of the meaning is with the term "the justified one"; the usage appears similar to that of ὁ μακαρίτης. Quite similarly the Persian anticipates a judgment of the dead at the Cinvad bridge; the later ideas of the Mandaeans correspond entirely; of course a divine emissary also brings to the soul of the elect person in advance the crown of righteousness, the crown of light or crown of victory (the glory) of the Zoroastrian hymn (above, p. 57). For that soul a judgment is no longer necessary. The Hermetic literary mystery (chapter XIII, above, p. 47), which in essence shows Iranian influence, apparently follows this view. At the mystical dissolution of the body, which here is the bearer of the twelve sinful tendencies or attributes, the δικαιοσύνη descends upon us--or, rather, the soul has been elevated into the sphere of δικαιοσύνη and receives it here; two different views are mingled in the text. The effect is described thus: χωρὶς γὰρ κρίσεως[8] ἰδὲ πῶς τὴν ἀδικίαν ἐξήλασεν. ἐδικαιώθη-

μεν, ὦ τέκνον, ἀδικίας ἀπούσης. The author wages a polemic directly against the idea of a judgment and a pronouncement of vindication; he wants to rule out this idea for his readers: without any judgment we have been relieved of the attribute of ἄδικοι and have attained the attribute of δίκαιοι; we have become sinless. Now this must also be the meaning of Paul; of course the fact that in the Hermetic text nine more

59 evil attributes are named, while in Paul this one embraces them all, makes no difference as far as the definition of the term is concerned: with Paul also, δικαιωθῆναι means to become free of sin. In his language the positive completion of this idea is δοξασθῆναι, evidently in the sense of σύμμορφον γίνεσθαι τῆς εἰκόνος τοῦ υἱοῦ αὐτοῦ,[9] while for the Hermetic author it is θεωθῆναι.[10] The subject here is not at all the earlier sins or their remission. The complete parallelism of the ideas and words is evident here.

Now no one will for this reason derive the doctrine of justification in Paul from the mystery belief; its origin in Judaism is too clear for that and is discernible precisely in the polemic. And yet in my opinion the impact of Hellenistic ideas also is not even contestable. I compare a passage like Rom. 6:1-14, which corresponds fully to Hellenistic mystery conceptions (συνετάφημεν οὖν αὐτῷ διὰ τοῦ βαπτίσματος εἰς τὸν θάνατον; cf. Lietzmann's splendid commentary or the statements above, pp. 284ff.): we have voluntarily let ourselves be buried in Christ's death through baptism, in order to lead a new, sinless life in him: τοῦτο γινώσκοντες, ὅτι ὁ πάλαιος ἡμῶν ἄνθρωπος συνεσταυρώθη, ἵνα καταργηθῇ τὸ σῶμα τῆς ἁμαρτίας, τοῦ μηκέτι δουλεύειν ἡμᾶς τῇ ἁμαρτίᾳ. <u>ὁ γὰρ ἀποθανὼν δεδικαίωται ἀπὸ τῆς ἁμαρτίας</u>. εἰ δὲ ἀπεθάνομεν σὺν Χριστῷ, πιστεύομεν ὅτι καὶ συνζήσομεν αὐτῷ.[11] For me, no explanation formed on the basis of the Jewish concept of δικαιοῦν (God

pronounces vindication) can do justice to the words underlined above. If one takes the word ἀποθανών in an "ethical" sense (i.e., "died to sin"), the thesis that the person who is sinless is righteous in God's sight is indeed illuminating, clear, 260 and self-evident, but it lacks any connection with its setting; if one thinks of actual, physical death and translates this to read, "The person who has died is absolved because he has paid the penalty with his death", something is introduced that is not contained in the words, and the logical structure of the clauses is not made any clearer thereby. Now some interpreters concede that understanding the entire sentence would be made easier by the interpretation, "is made free from sin", but at the same time regard this interpretation as linguistically impermissible; others attempt to introduce it in an over-refined way, such as: "through death in baptism satisfaction is achieved for the demands of law *for sin*"--but therewith the basic meaning of δικαιοῦν is abandoned, and the thesis becomes so much subject to dispute that Paul could hardly have used it as proof. A fourth interpretation, still different and yet bearing some resemblance to the others, has the apostle proposing only the "very simple and undisputed observation" that the deceased person, because he is no longer active, also is no longer sinning; but this interpretation would put this triviality into the curiously complicated form of saying that the death of man is an actual judgment of God, who thereby pronounces him free from the power of sin.

It appears to me that the context requires first of all that the subject be seen not as a purely physical act of dying, nor a merely figurative one, but above all a *voluntary* dying and surrendering oneself to death.[12] Everything becomes simple and clear as soon as we set the mystery conceptions in the background: we may no longer sin; for in the mystery

we have assumed Christ's person and his lot and have let our natural man be crucified in order that the σῶμα τῆς ἁμαρτίας may pass away--in the mystery conception the expression is of marvelous import--and we may no longer serve sin. For anyone who has died--that "dissolution" of the natural man is for this conception something altogether real and essential--no longer has the attribute of ἀδικία, no longer stands under its spell, has lost his old nature. Again, the emphasis is placed only on the negative aspect of that transformation that is wrought by the mystery. It is only with the words, "But if we have died with Christ, we shall also live with him", that the apostle passes over to the positive aspect, the anticipation of a divine life (pagan: a life as God). The impact of the Hellenistic usage appears to me to be certain in this passage, and in others, like I Cor. 6:11, for example, at least probable: ἀλλὰ ἀπελούσασθε, ἀλλὰ ἡγιάσθητε, ἀλλὰ ἐδικαιώθητε ἐν τῷ ὀνόματι τοῦ κυρίου Ἰησοῦ καὶ τῷ πνεύματι τοῦ θεοῦ ἡμῶν. To be sure, the view of baptism here is not one that is characteristic of the mysteries, but one that is explainable in terms of the action itself, and that recurs in the Jewish proselyte baptism. We do not have a delineation of three successive stages, but three synonyms interconnected: καθαροί, ἅγιοι, δίκαιοι ἐγένεσθε. On the other hand, Gal. 2:19, 20 is wholly dependent upon the mystery-like interpretation of baptism, though of course without actually identifying it: ἐγὼ γὰρ διὰ νόμου νόμῳ ἀπέθανον, ἵνα θεῷ ζήσω. Χριστῷ συνεσταύρωμαι, ζῶ δὲ οὐκέτι ἐγώ, ζῇ δὲ ἐν ἐμοὶ Χριστός· ὃ δὲ νῦν ζῶ ἐν σαρκί, ἐν πίστει ζῶ τῇ τοῦ υἱοῦ τοῦ θεοῦ τοῦ ἀγαπήσαντός με καὶ παραδόντος ἑαυτὸν ὑπὲρ ἐμοῦ. As the death of the old man, baptism, which in fact bestows the πνεῦμα or the Χριστὸς ἐν ἡμῖν, also lifts the later earthly life out of the realm of νόμος into that of πίστις, which in fact it begets

and bestows. When even here Paul calls this a δικαιωθῆναι (οὐκ ἐξ ἔργων, ἀλλὰ διὰ πίστεως), we sense how for him the two series of ideas that are connected with the word have merged in an utterly distinctive fashion. Whether we, who approach this issue with entirely different linguistic and conceptual presuppositions, can altogether accept this or even have a feeling for it is not the question; the question is only what Paul felt and said.

But let me return to the beginning point. There is nothing to forbid our assuming the Hellenistic usage in Rom. 8:30 also and thus translating ἐδικαίωσε as "made sinless (by nature)". This is in harmony with the addition here also of a positive declaration as completing the statement: ἐδόξασεν. Of course the final decision about the entire passage can be made only if the word δόξα--which Deissmann (*Jahrb. f. d. klass. Altertum* 1903, p. 165) indeed conjectures for profane Greek with the meaning of "brilliance, glorification" but can- 262 not prove--has been demonstrated to belong to the language of the mysteries, and when if at all possible still another case of this thought-context in a Hellenistic version is found. For--to emphasize this once more--in such investigations everything hinges on the contexts of the passages involved.

NOTES

1. Cf., in Apollonius' letter to Ptolemaeus, the latter ἐν κατοχῇ ὤν (Wilcken, *Urkunden der Ptolemäerzeit*, N. 70 = Paris 47): Πρὸς τοὺς τὴν ἀλήθειαν λέγοντες and πλανόμενοι ὑπὸ τῶν θεῶν καὶ πιστεύοντες τὰ ἐνύπνια (cf. above, p. 265, n. 28). The expressions have the character of formulae.

2. He has become immortal. There appear to be different ranks among the ἀθάνατοι; the highest rank is formed by the ἀθάνατοι πρῶτοι.

3. The Latin expression is less fitting here than the Greek.

4. The ascetics in the Apophthegmata patrum speak in similar fashion.

5. Cf. my presentation in *Vorträge der Bibliothek Warburg*, Bd. II. The sense of God, totally different from that of antiquity, brings about the radical change. I acknowledge that it too bears the marks of the mysteries; however, Augustine does not borrow it from the mystery-belief, but gets it from Paul.

6. I may only recall a profound but purely pagan saying in the Poimandres (§31): ἅγιος ὁ θεός, ὅς γνωσθῆναι βούλεται καὶ γινώσκεται τοῖς ἰδίοις.

7. I do not take into account individual parts, as for example the book of Ecclesiasticus. Comparisons can be undertaken at first only with the main part.

8. The mss. read κτίσεως; this is Parthey's emendation. Scott's placing χωρὶς γὰρ κρίσεως just before ἐδικαιώθημεν is unnecessary. The words that are emphasized are almost always placed first.

9. Comparable is Rom. 6:5: εἰ γὰρ σύμφυτοι γεγόναμεν τῷ ὁμοιώματι τοῦ θανάτου αὐτοῦ, ἀλλὰ καὶ τῆς ἀναστάσεως ἐσόμεθα (since the ὁμοίωμα τῆς ἀναστάσεως is an ἐγερθῆναι διὰ τῆς δόξης τοῦ πατρός, σύμμορφον γίνεσθαι τῆς εἰκόνος τοῦ υἱοῦ is a δοξάζεσθαι.

10. Later even explained: θεὸς πέφυκας καὶ τοῦ ἑνὸς παῖς ὅ κἀγώ.

11. I Peter 4:1 offers a paraphrase: Χριστοῦ οὖν παθόντος σαρκὶ καὶ ὑμεῖς τὴν αὐτὴν ἔννοιαν ὁπλίσασθε. ὅτι ὁ παθὼν σαρκὶ πέπαυται ἁμαρτίας εἰς τὸ μηκέτι ἀνθρώπων ἐπιθυμίαις, ἀλλὰ θελήματι θεοῦ τὸν ἐπιλοίπον ἐν σαρκὶ βιῶναι χρόνον. Here, as with Ignatius and in the Latin accounts of martyrdoms, παθεῖν and *pati* mean "to die". The usage appears to be late Jewish.

12. As Christ surrendered voluntarily to death, so we also are to surrender voluntarily to death (of the old man). Then we are free from sin.

XII.

Designations for Transformation

I shall summarize very briefly the customary designations for transformations, so that the reader may here be confronted with what is compelling in a proof that is based purely upon the language employed. The title of Apuleius' work attests a general designation μεταμόρφωσις; he can append the last book only because what we have in the mysteries also is such a transformation. In the text he usually employs the word *reformari*; cf. XI 16: *hunc omnipotentis hodie deae numen augustum reformavit ad homines. felix hercules et ter beatus, qui vitae scilicet praecedentis innocentia fideque meruerit tam praeclarum de caelo patrocinium, ut renatus quodammodo statim sacrorum servitio desponderetur*; XI 27: *Asinium Marcellum... reformationis meae non alienum nomen*; XI 30: *Osiris non <in> alienam quampiam personam reformatus.* Here the connection of *reformari* and *renasci* issues from sacral language. Plutarch (De Is. et Os. 72, p. 379 E) knows of a teaching of the Egyptians: ταῖς ψυχαῖς τῶν θανόντων, ὅσαι διαμένουσιν, εἰς ταῦτα μόνα (namely ζῷα) γίγνεσθαι τὴν παλιγγενεσίαν, and Nemesius (De nat. hominis, chapter 2: Migne XL 581) cites Κρόνιος μὲν γὰρ ἐν τῷ περὶ παλιγγενεσίας· οὕτω δὲ καλεῖ τὴν μετενσωμάτισιν. From these we see that the two expressions alternate in religious language, as is the case with the synonym of παλιγγενεσία, ἀναγέννησις, in the Mithras liturgy, where the verbal forms ἀναγεννᾶσθαι and μεταγεννᾶσθαι alternate. When the alchemist Zosimos describes, in his visions that are to be more

fully discussed later, how he is "renewed" (καινουργεῖται), he says (Berthelot, *Les alchemistes grecs* 108.17): ἕως ἂν ἔμαθον μετασωματούμενος πνεῦμα γενέσθαι. Seneca (Ep. 6.1) teaches us the Latin word for this: *intellego, Lucili, non emendari me tantum* (cf. βελτιοῦσθαι in the Mithras liturgy), *sed transfigurari. nec hoc promitto iam aut spero, nihil in me superesse, quod mutandum sit. quidni multa habeam, quae debeant colligi, quae extenuari, quae attolli? et hoc ipsum argumentum est in melius translati animi,*[1] *quod vitia sua, quae adhuc ignorabat, videt....cuperem itaque tecum communicare tam subitam mutationem mei.* Even if Seneca had not gone on clearly to contrast the teachings of philosophy, which one may repeat, with those of the mysteries, which one must keep secret, we could not fail to recognize both words and ideas from the mysteries. His spirit is *suddenly* transposed into a better being, even though it is not yet entirely pure and spotless, as the mystery-belief would have it. It is only from the idea of the mysteries that we can comprehend that Seneca therewith feels himself to have been transposed into a new body, which of course is not an earthly body; the words of Zosimos provide the explanation: μετασωματούμενος πνεῦμα ἐγενόμην. In the Mithras liturgy also the heavenly body in which the *mystes* encounters the gods is the πνεῦμα, and for the connection of these conceptions we may compare what Paul says in Rom. 12:2: μεταμορφοῦσθε τῇ ἀνακαινώσει τοῦ νοῦ. One can hardly think here of ancient Greek mysteries. I should like to venture the conjecture that this figure from the mysteries is mediated to Seneca through Poseidonios (cf. above, p. 150).

The outward symbol of this *transfiguratio* in every cult is the garment; it provides the indication of the μορφὴ θεοῦ. Thus Plutarch describes for us (De Is. et Os. 77) the Osiris robe (ἓν ἁπλοῦν τὸ φωτοειδές), and in chapter 3 the black and

white robe of the 'Ισιακοί (they are the λόγος, and this λόγος is ἐνδιάθετος and προφορικός); and Porphyry (De abst. IV 16) describes the robe, embroidered with pictures of animals, of the lion-rank of the Mithras *mystai*: like their god, the sun-deity, they have made the pilgrimage through the twelve signs of the zodiac.[2] Just as the *mystes* of the Mithras liturgy prays to his heavenly body (or self), so Apuleius, at the recurrence of the festival day, is to pray to his celestial robe and, if the goddess commands it, to put it on again; it is kept in the temple where he had received his initiation; cf. XI 29: *exuvias deae, quas in provincia sumpsisti, in eodem fano depositas perseverare nec te Romae diebus sollemnibus vel supplicare iis vel, cum praeceptim fuerit, felici illo amictu illustrari posse.* The word *illustrari*, here quite rarely used, obviously corresponds to the Greek φωτίζεσθαι. It is used for any initiation; cf. XI 28: *principalis dei nocturnis orgiis inlustratus*; XI 27: *magni dei deumque summi parentis, invicti Osiris, necdum sacris inlustratum* (contrasted with *deae quidem me tantum sacris inbutum*, previously *initiatus*).[3] When I compare the mystery-prayer of the thirteenth Hermetic writing (§20), τὸ πᾶν τὸ ἐν ἡμῖν σῷζε (make alive; in Syriac σωτήρ is the one who makes alive, the πνεῦμα ζωοποιοῦν of Paul) ζωή, φώτιζε φῶς, πνευμά<τιζε> θεέ, I should interpret φωτίζειν here to mean "make into light". Indeed, according to Iranian belief light is the divine part of our souls; according to late monastic belief the perfect man is inwardly light; when he lifts his hands in prayer, the rays of light radiate from his fingertips and the words from his mouth (the πνεῦμα λεκτικόν) ascend like a chain of sparks or a stream of fire. For the monks later, as for the *mystai*, the shroud is the initiation robe (and the robe in which he pleads for revelation, and thus ascends to God). When the

perfected one is wearing it, it glows and displays marvelous figures and symbols (Damascius in Photius, Bibl. cod. 242, p. 343, 29 Bek.; cf. the portrayal of the celestial garment in the hymn of the soul in the Acts of Thomas). I find a similar conception of the robe of light and crown of light in the ideas of the Manichaeans and the Mandaeans, only with the difference that among the latter the baptism in the stream of light (the light-Jordan) is added. This is important, because the Mandaean baptismal practice undoubtedly is connected with the baptism of John, from which alone Christian baptism can stem. This would best account for the Christian designation for this rite of initiation, φωτισμός. Indeed, there must be

265 a connection with the pagan designation, attested by Apuleius, of φωτίζεσθαι for τελεῖσθαι, and Justin's explanation (Apol. I 61), καλεῖται δὲ τοῦτο τὸ λουτρὸν φωτισμός, ὡς φωτιζομένων τὴν διάνοιαν τῶν ταῦτα μανθανόντων, too obviously bears the stamp of a rationalizing reinterpretation to be believable. If it were correct, the κατηχούμενοι could rather have been called φωτιζόμενοι. But φῶς and πνεῦμα can only be attained together, because the two together constitute the essence of the deity or the divine soul.

NOTES

1. Cf. βεβελτιωμένος in the Mithras liturgy.

2. This is the common belief; the scholarly interpretation that makes it refer to metempsychosis is connected with it, but hardly indicates the original idea.

3. Apuleius uses another word with a different meaning in XI 17: *(dea) quae suae lucis splendore etiam deos inluminat* (Asclepius, chapter 23, otherwise: *homo fictor est deorum...et non solum inluminatur, verum etiam inluminat nec solum ad deum proficit verum etiam conformat deos*).

XIII.

Virtues and Vices as Members

The basic perspective of the Hermetic writing, which is foreign to us, that a specific number of vices form the natural man, and a like number of virtues form the god or the new man, is proved by the epistle to the Colossians to be relatively ancient. The presuppositions are there ever since Zarathustra reshaped the originally material elements of the world, of man and of God into spiritual forces, though he did not follow through with this. Of course the increasing ethicizing of the religions of the Near East also shared in making the idea current, and Yasht 22 already exhibits the idea that the heavenly self of man is formed by his good thoughts, words and deeds, just as the devilish self is formed by the evil ones. The systematizing[1] is accomplished under the impact of the theological-speculative cosmology, which in fact is at the same time an anthropology, and is heavily influenced by astrology. Two systems appear to have developed side by side. A system with five components and which, as the Damdad-Nask shows, very early developed into the seven-part system, was originally connected with the list of elements; later it was connected with the expanded list of divine powers, which is assimilated to the expanded list of the planets (the sun and the moon are added to the five planets; cf. above, p. 278). Another system arises out of the divisions of time--or from the signs of the zodiac, in astrological terms; in fact, the physical body of man is divided up and assigned to those signs

266

also--: twelve parts go together to form the totality of the universe, of God, and of man. This system appears most clearly in Mani's teachings, which are set forth in the Turfan fragments, in the account given by Theodore bar Konai, and above all according to Mani's own presentation in the Θησαυρός found in Augustine's De natura boni, c. 44.[2] Twelve children of the primal deity (Zarvan) or of the emissary, the light-aeons, form the god himself; they are virtues, or, better, "powers", the last of them the light itself. This system is presupposed when the transformation of the man into a divine being is achieved by means of putting on twelve divine and deifying garments.[3] The antiquity of the idea is attested on the one hand by Apuleius, and on the other hand by the Christian reconstruction of it in the Shepherd of Hermas, Sim. IX 15. More difficult to grasp is the idea of the series of five. We must start out from the report of the Fihrist (*Flügel*, p. 95). The Manichaeans require belief in God, his light, his power, and his wisdom; his light is the sun and the moon, his power is the gentle breeze, wind, light (earth), water, fire. This is the old list of elements whose Greek origin we saw above (p. 279): sun, moon, breeze, wind, earth, water, fire. Now the Manichaean adds as a fourth main part his wisdom, that is, meekness, knowledge, reason, mystery, insight.[4] These are the parts which Mani assigns to the God of the rational world, and thus to the world-soul or the soul of the primal man. With a certain amount of surprise we discover here also, alongside those seven elements as a totality, the world-god, above whom of course the primal deity stands.[5] The system certainly was not invented by Mani, and of course it may not have been the original system in his teaching. The Fihrist itself offers two additional descriptions on pp. 93 and 86. In the former passage it is said that the *light-earth* has five members--

;7

gentle breeze, wind, light, water, and fire--and the *light-ether* likewise has five members; these are those five intellectual powers that constitute the soul of the primal man. When it now is added that these ten members of the ether and the earth in their totality form the great splendor, it is clear that this great splendor is simply the primal man in body and soul. Just as according to the Turfan fragments the elements lie superimposed like successive layers or shells, according to the portrayal of the Fihrist (p. 87) so also do the intellectual powers (the light-earth makes the observation, the αἴσθησις, receives from it the outermost and weakest of the intellectual elements--cf. the equation with ranks in the church, p. 95--and then repeats it to the next, until it penetrates to the innermost). The strictly systematic arrangement shows that the sun and the moon could have no place here; underlying this is the list of elements corresponding to the Chinese list. The third enumeration (p. 86) brings a real difficulty: the material members (breeze, etc.) are attributed to the *light-earth*, and the intellectual ones to the *light-ether*, but the latter also form the material members of the primal deity, and in this deity these members are set in contrast to five spiritual members, love, faith, loyalty, generosity, and wisdom, thus five virtues. Augustine attests for Mani himself the placing of the *light-earth* and the *light-ether* alongside and yet at the same time within the primal deity; unattested is the position of the five ethical elements as spiritual members of this primal deity. In the Chinese (*Journal Asiatique* X 18, 1911, pp. 499-500) they appear as gifts of those intellectual elements that appear for them in the "new man", and thus constitute the soul of the true believer. I do not yet venture to draw a conclusion.[6]

268 A connection of the lists of five with the twelve-part system

is artificially created in the Chinese text; it appears to me to be secondary here also. The lists of five are in themselves age-old in the canon of the elements, while in the later imitations of that canon they are in part arbitrary, and in their combinations very free.[7] The Persian Damdad-Nask, which appears before the middle of the fifth century, now shows how these pentads, because the whole can always be added to them, become hexads, alongside which then again a whole can stand.[8] It is from that source that the Great Bundahisn (chap. 28.6, Goetze, p. 63) has the comparison: "the soul is like Ohrmazd; reason, understanding, memory, insight, knowledge, and the gift of interpretation[9] <are> like those six Amahrspand that stand before Ohrmazd". Here we have attested in Zoroastrianism the intermediate stage, at which it moved from the five divine elements to the six; later we find them increased to seven, and we understand how in Gnosticism, for example with Simon of Gitta, the series of the intellectual powers (νοῦς, etc.) becomes a six-part series instead of a five-part series. But from the one poor fragment we gain still much more. In the Yasht 22 the individual soul was venerated as Ohrmazd, and thus was equated with him. In later Gnosticism it becomes the primal man, the divine soul that slumbers within us. Manichaeism's equating the soul with Ohrmazd[10] is only the consistent continuation of the ancient Persian feeling. Finally, the fragment shows how the Zoroastrian spiritualizing of the originally sensual elements in the assimilation of Ohrmazd and the soul necessarily leads to that distinguishing, which cannot be done conceptually, of five (later six) intellectual powers. The formation of Mani's system is thereby explained and is confirmed as to its antiquity.

So now, equipped with altogether different instruments, we approach the third chapter of Colossians. As I mentioned

above (p. 284), the author takes his basic idea from the epistle to the Romans (chapter 6), but gives it a new turn, which in its unusual character is too little noted. The Christians have died with Christ and are raised with him, but their life still is hidden with Christ in God; only when their Lord is revealed (at his return) will they also be revealed ἐν δόξῃ (in glory, and in the heavenly body). Appended to this is the exhortation: νεκρώσατε οὖν τὰ μέλη ὑμῶν τὰ ἐπὶ τῆς γῆς, πορνείαν, ἀκαθαρσίαν, πάθος, ἐπιθυμίαν κακήν (Persian *az*) καὶ τὴν πλεονεξίαν, ἥτις ἐστὶν εἰδωλολατρεία (as service to Mammon); it concludes with ἀπεκδυσάμενοι τὸν παλαιὸν ἄνθρωπον σὺν ταῖς πράξεσιν αὐτοῦ. The positive part begins: καὶ ἐνδυσάμενοι τὸν νέον, τὸν ἀνακαινούμενον εἰς ἐπίγνωσιν, κατ' εἰκόνα τοῦ κτίσαντος αὐτόν (all these words are also Iranian terms), and explains it thus: ἐνδύσασθε οὖν ὡς ἐκλεκτοὶ θεοῦ ἅγιοι καὶ ἠγαπημένοι σπλάγχνα οἰκτιρμοῦ, χρηστότητα, ταπεινοφροσύνην, πραΰτητα, μακροθυμίαν. If those vices were members of the old man, these virtues must be members of the new man. This helps also in the explanation of the Hermetic writing. For the New Testament passage I must at once assume a literary prototype in Iranian-Hellenistic mysticism. The Christian author, who does not rightly understand the system and makes numerous additions to it,[11] as does the author of the Hermetic writing also, owes very little to the system as far as content is concerned, nor the strict moral seriousness, nor the worse-than-awkward enumeration and distinction of vices and virtues, none of the added details, but only the structure of the whole and the mystical figurative idea. For this reason the case is typical; one can say, with equal right, "very little", or "a great deal", at least if one thinks of the psychological presuppositions and of the impact of this appropriation. Because of the stylistic defects and the intensity of the mys-

ticism, I have never attributed this epistle to Paul himself. The consideration of this relationship to a literary source strengthens me in my conviction; Paul is never so lacking in independence; even where he borrows, he remains original. Connected with the prototype of the Hermetic writing which offered a list of seven divine powers is the extraordinarily important description of ἀναγέννησις or παλιγγενεσία (both words are used by Philo without distinction for the "renewing" of the κόσμος also) in the Quaestiones in Exodum II 46: *sursum autem vocatio prophetae secunda est nativitas (sive regeneratio) priore melior: illa* (that soul) *enim commixta per carnem etiam corruptibiles habet parentes, ista vero incommixta simplexque anima principalis (vel spiritus principis) mutata a genita ad ingenitam, cuius non est mater, sed pater solus, qui est universorum. quam ob rem et sursum vocatio, sive, ut diximus, divina nativitas, contigit ei fieri secundum naturam septenarii semper virginis.*[12] When I read this passage for the first time I had some question whether one must not regard it as a Christian interpolation, and it was only when I compared it with the Hermetic writing, which provides us with all the preconditions for it, that I became convinced of its genuineness. Now, by means of a comparison with De vita Moys. (II 288 Cohn) I can demonstrate that genuineness even more convincingly; the heavenly pilgrimage at death indeed must correspond to the heavenly pilgrimage experienced in ecstasy: χρόνοις δ' ὕστερον, ἐπειδὴ τὴν ἐνθένδε ἀποικίαν ἔμελλεν εἰς οὐρανὸν στέλλεσθαι καὶ τὸν θνητὸν ἀπολιπὼν βίον ἀπαθανατίζεσθαι μετακληθεὶς ὑπὸ τοῦ πατρός, ὅς αὐτὸν δυάδα ὄντα, σῶμα καὶ ψυχήν, εἰς μονάδος ἀνεστοιχείου φύσιν ὅλον δι' ὅλων μεθαρμοζόμενος εἰς νοῦν ἡλιοειδέστατον. To translate ἀναστοιχειοῦν here as "to dissolve" is to deprive the passage of its vividness (cf. μεθαρμοζόμενος); it is inserted from the mystical

idea of στοιχεῖα as members (hence ὅλον δι' ὅλων) for ἀναγεννᾶν or ἀνακαινοῦν. The call which here transplants (μετακαλεῖ) leads upward (ἀνακαλεῖ); μετακαλεῖν and ἀνακαλεῖν alternate just as freely as do μεταγεννᾶν (cf. here μεθαρμόζεσθαι) and ἀναγεννᾶν in the Mithras liturgy. Philo also can use the word employed there, ἀπαθανατισμός. The concept νοῦς ἡλιοειδέστατος[13] also is altogether Iranian, and the following portrayal, ἤδη γὰρ ἀναλαμβανόμενος καὶ ἐπ' αὐτῆς βαλβῖδος ἑστώς, ἵνα τὸν εἰς οὐρανὸν δρόμον διϊπτάμενος εὐθύνῃ, entirely corresponds, perhaps not accidentally, to the Mandaean descriptions of how the soul, equipped for the heavenly flight (or the walk, or being carried), mounts "the battlements" and takes one last look before "the escort" arrives.

It appears to me that therewith we have demonstrated the genuineness of the passage from the Quaestiones in Exodum, the dissemination of the Iranian belief in immortality, and the antiquity of the gnostic idea that bound up with the reception, or better with the awakening, of the πνεῦμα in man is the ἀνάστασις, the rapture into the beyond, and with the latter the cessation of the earthly life.

But we can press still further. It is unfortunate that we philologists always treat Philo only as a Greek and trace back to Greek philosophy everything that is not manifestly from the Old Testament. In so doing we not only obscure what is really vital in him, his religiousness, but we ourselves create utterly mistaken ideas out of his basic concepts, because we seize upon the Greek words. This could easily be demonstrated in the case of concepts such as λόγος and πνεῦμα, but that would lead us too far afield.[14] So I shall take only one often discussed passage, to place it in its original context and then to see what follows from it.

272

In De fuga et inventione §§108-112, Philo proposes to explain according to the physical (i.e., the cosmic) allegory the prescriptions in Lev. 21:10, 11, concerning the high priest: καὶ ὁ ἱερεὺς ὁ μέγας ἀπὸ τῶν ἀδελφῶν αὐτοῦ, [τοῦ] ἐπικεχυμένου ἐπὶ τὴν κεφαλὴν τοῦ ἐλαίου τοῦ χριστοῦ καὶ τετελειωμένου ἐνδύσασθαι τὰ ἱμάτια, τὴν κεφαλὴν οὐκ ἀποκιδαρώσει καὶ τὰ ἱμάτια οὐ διαρρήξει, καὶ ἐπὶ πάσῃ ψυχῇ τετελευτηκυίᾳ οὐκ εἰσελεύσεται, ἐπὶ πατρὶ αὐτοῦ οὐδὲ ἐπὶ μητρὶ αὐτοῦ οὐ μιανθήσεται. According to his method (that is, apparently according to an already established method of his rabbinical predecessors), he does not take the context as a foundation, or even consider it,[15] but proceeds exclusively by attaching to individual words edifying pictures which in no way fit in with the text and which are constantly changing: λέγομεν γὰρ τὸν ἀρχιερέα οὐκ ἄνθρωπον ἀλλὰ λόγον θεῖον εἶναι, πάντων οὐχ ἑκουσίων μόνον ἀλλὰ καὶ ἀκουσίων ἁμαρτημάτων ἀμέτοχον. οὔτε γὰρ 'ἐπὶ πατρί', τῷ νῷ, οὔτε 'ἐπὶ μητρί', τῇ αἰσθήσει, φησὶν αὐτὸν Μωυσῆς δύνασθαι μιαίνεσθαι, διότι, οἶμαι, γονέων ἀφθάρτων καὶ καθαρωτάτων ἔλαχεν, πατρὸς μὲν θεοῦ, ὅς καὶ τῶν συμπάντων ἐστὶ πατήρ, μητρὸς δὲ σοφίας, δι' ἧς τὰ ὅλα ἦλθεν εἰς γένεσιν· καὶ διότι 'τὴν κεφαλὴν κέχρισται ἐλαίῳ', λέγω δὲ τὸ ἡγεμονικὸν φωτὶ αὐγοειδεῖ περιλάμπεται, ὡς ἀξιόχρεως 'ἐνδύσασθαι τὰ ἱμάτια' νομισθῆναι--ἐνδύεται δὲ ὁ μὲν πρεσβύτατος τοῦ ὄντος λόγος ὡς ἐσθῆτα τὸν κόσμον (γῆν γὰρ καὶ ὕδωρ καὶ ἀέρα καὶ πῦρ καὶ τὰ ἐκ τούτων ἐπαμπίσχεται), ἡ δ' ἐπὶ μέρους ψυχὴ τὸ σῶμα, ἡ δὲ τοῦ σοφοῦ διάνοια τὰς ἀρετάς--καὶ ὅτι 'τὴν κεφαλὴν οὐδέποτε ἀπομιτρώσει', τὸ βασίλειον οὐκ ἀποθήσεται διάδημα, τὸ σύμβολον τῆς οὐκ αὐτοκράτορος μέν, ὑπάρχου δὲ καὶ θαυμαστῆς ἡγεμονίας. 'οὐδ' αὖ τὰ ἱμάτια διαρρήξει'. ὅ τε γὰρ τοῦ ὄντος λόγος δεσμὸς ὢν τῶν ἁπάντων, ὡς εἴρηται, καὶ συνέχει τὰ μέρη πάντα καὶ σφίγγει κωλύων αὐτὰ διαλύεσθαι καὶ διαρτᾶσθαι, ἥ τ' ἐπὶ μέρους ψυχή, καθ' ὅσον δυνάμεως μεμοίραται, τῶν τοῦ

σώματος οὐδὲν ἀποσχίζεσθαι καὶ ἀποτέμνεσθαι μερῶν παρὰ φύσιν
273 ἐᾷ, τὸ δ' ἐπ' αὐτῇ πάντα ὁλόκληρα ὄντα ἁρμονίαν καὶ ἕνωσιν ἀδιάλυτον ἄγει τὴν πρὸς ἄλληλα. ὅ τε κεκαθαρμένος τοῦ σοφοῦ νοῦς ἀρρήκτους καὶ ἀπήμονας διαφυλάττει τὰς ἀρετάς, τὴν φυσικὴν αὐτῶν συγγένειάν τε καὶ κοινωνίαν ἁρμοσάμενος εὐνοίᾳ παγιωτέρᾳ.

Let us consider first the sentence beginning ἐνδύεται δὲ ὁ μὲν πρεσβύτατος. What corresponds to the individual soul (ἐπὶ μέρους ψυχή) cannot have been an earliest Logos,[16] but only the total soul or world-soul, expressed in Iranian terms as the primal man, or Gayomard. In the Manichaean religious documents we have frequently recurring descriptions of how at his descent he puts on the five elements--it is natural that in place of the five Philo puts the Greek number four--one over another, and this process is presupposed in the astrological reshaping (because of the seven planets and spheres the number of elements is increased to seven) in the Damdad-Nask and in the Hermetic writing Poimandres that is derived from it. Philo is still under the influence of the old idea of the macrocosm and microcosm, and thus of the world-deity as the gigantic human figure that bears on his robes the representation of all things visible; this is shown particularly by the words καὶ τὰ ἐκ τούτων. The clearest antitype is offered by the Hellenistic-Jewish Naassene Preaching, which places this primal man as the great soul over against the individual souls. It is becoming increasingly clear that preceding those Jewish-Christian sects that viewed the anointed one (Christ) as the world-soul there were Jewish-Gnostic sects that were more strongly affected by the particulars of Iranian theology than by the Judaism of their homeland. Philo avoids speaking about the parts of this primal soul just as he does about the parts of the individual

soul; in the Iranian prototype their number must have corresponded to the number of the elements. Mani's ten-part "great glory" is borrowed from an Iranian theology that is *earlier than Philo*. But Philo offers us still more. If we examine the phrase ἡ δὲ τοῦ σοφοῦ διάνοια τὰς ἀρετάς, we see that according to the total context, here also διάνοια (later νοῦς) is only inserted for ψυχή.[17] Thus in the same system he also found the old Persian idea that the soul of the perfected one, his heavenly counterpart, consists of his moral character (or is clothed in that character), by which he has become like the god Ohrmazd; moreover, he found it in the same form, as it is exhibited in the Manichaean lists mentioned above, as five φυσικῇ τινι συγγενείᾳ τε καὶ κοινωνίᾳ organically connected virtues. When in the conclusion of the passage reproduced above this heavenly counterpart is also called ὁ κεκαθαρμένος τοῦ σοφοῦ νοῦς, one could conjecture that the Chinese writing, which treats the theme of the qualities of the "purified" man, most purely preserves the original context.[18] In any case, there is very ancient attestation of the connection of the three lists of five. When in Philo moreover the whole is distinguished from the five individual members--the whole holds them together εὐνοίᾳ παγιωτέρᾳ--the similarity to the Colossian epistle is so striking[19] that inferences are justified. About the anointing, Philo emphasizes only the radiance which in consequence of that anointing surrounds the head, in order then to speak, following the text, of the diadem, the symbol of rulership and lordship; every reader will recognize the "glory" of the Persians, which in fact the primal man wears.[20]

Let me summarize: it is not an exposition of the Jewish text that is given; it will be recalled that from the words of that text, καὶ ἐπὶ πάσῃ ψυχῇ τετελευτηκυίᾳ οὐκ εἰσελεύσεται,

ἐπὶ πατρὶ αὐτοῦ οὐδὲ ἐπὶ μητρὶ οὐ μιανθήσεται, there comes the explanation that from his parents sinlessness is attributed to him, since his father is God and his mother is Sophia (immediately before this she is called αἴσθησις). Reminiscences of the Stoa can easily be demonstrated, but the ideas do not stem from there. Underlying is Iranian speculation, but its strict systematizing and internal validation is not adopted along with it. The religious feeling of the circles for which such a presentation is intended does not require any clear development of thought; a completely syncretistic religiosity demands only the stimulation of feeling by means of a skillful stirring of the diverse conceptual material that slumbers in it. Our most important task is to reanimate that conceptual material and to date it with Philo's help, not to sketch a system of Philo's "philosophy".[21] Even if I actually analyze only one such passage or attempt to evaluate only one document like the Isis hymn of Oxyrhynchos (Pap. 1380), I can only regard as completely at odds with the facts the undocumented assertion of Ed. Meyer that it was Christianity that first brought syncretism to its full flowering.

NOTES

1. This process begins extremely early, at first in very primitive form. The Indian statement, "The Perusha is twenty-one-fold, for it has ten fingers, ten toes, and the I", which I have traced into the Iranian sphere (Reitzenstein-Schaeder I 120), is explained, as Prof. Jacobsohn has showed me, by the fact that a considerable number of "primitive" peoples identify man with the number twenty. Fingers and toes appear at first to be the most important members. When one derives the pentadic system from such original thinking, one will understand what prompted the addition of the "I" (the body) as the whole. But in the following I shall not go into these earliest forms.

2. Presented in exemplary fashion in Cumont, *Recherches sur le Manichéisme* I, p. 35; cf. Schaeder, in Reitzenstein-Schaeder II, p. 80.

3. Cf. above, p. 280.

4. More correctly, five designations for the religious intellect; cf. Schaeder, *op. cit.* The Greek translation is νοῦς, ἔννοια, φρόνησις, ἐνθύμησις, λογισμός.

5. An assimilation to the list of twelve appears to be intended by means of the insertion of the number five, but it is a secondary stage; in this list the sun and the moon can have no place, because the parts must be of the same kind. That is the basic psychological law of this construction of series.

6. The entire pentad corresponds to the original five seals and could have been inserted subsequently.

7. Thus it seems to me methodologically dubious to take as a starting-point such a combination--and a particularly artificial one at that--in order to explain this entire development, as L. Troje does in the book *Die Dreizehn und die Zwölf im Traktat Pelliot.* The Samkhya system (five crude elements--these are the old Indian ones, in agreement with Mani--, five fine elements, five senses of touch, five senses of perception, the internal organ of perception, the organ of subjectivation, and the organ of judgment) agrees with Mani's system only in the first pentad, and is so totally differently oriented that I would be unwilling to assume any direct connec-

tions. Of course only the specialist in Indian studies will be able to form a conclusive judgment, but every reader will be grateful to Frau Troje for the abundance of sensitive individual observations and explanations. It will be shown that we can fully explain Mani without resorting to the Samkhya system. The book which I published in association with Prof. Schaeder will show how far it is from my intention to deny all connections between Iran and India; it is precisely through L. Troje that I have learned to pay attention to these connections.

8. Cf. A. Goetze, "Persische Weisheit im griechischen Gewande," *Zeitschrift f. Indologie und Iranistik* II, 1923, pp. 60-61; and Reitzenstein-Schaeder I, chapter 4.

9. The translation of the concepts cannot be given with perfect sharpness of focus; it is clear that only intellectual powers, which of course are at the same time religious forces, are meant.

10. In addition, of course, there is the equation with the deity of the series of twelve (the god of time as the world-deity). Again and again we find the two systems side by side.

11. It is utterly impossible to look to him as the inventor of the system or even as the model for Mani.

12. Pythagorean. The number seven denotes Athena; cf. above, p. 231, n. 58.

13. In Mani's view the twelfth aion is the full light.

14. Cf. *Das iranische Erlösungsmysterium*, MS 106, note 1, for a critique of Leisegang's method. A seminar project of Dr. Hans Drexler, who at that time was my cherished student, then led me further along the way that had already been indicated in the work cited above, so that in this area I myself have become his pupil.

15. In passages like this one we can discern particularly clearly the essential distinction between the pneumatic and the scientific explanation--one of the finest achievements of the Greek mind.

16. Philo has inserted the word here because it serves him elsewhere as a designation for the primal man (or the

world-soul). He has no more a fixed conception of the Logos than he has an allegedly Platonic idea of man.

17. To be sure, for the heavenly part of the soul, the soul or the pneuma of the regenerated person; here he is called ὁ σόφος, since he possesses intellectual powers.

18. That document offers a detailed description of this καθαίρειν and regards it as a basic concept. Similarly Corp. herm. XIII (cf. §§15, 7, 8). Even here there begins the fusion with the system of twelve parts.

19. Col. 3:14: ἐπὶ πᾶσι δὲ τούτοις τὴν ἀγάπην, ὅ ἐστιν σύνδεσμος τῆς τελειότητος. For similar Indian ideas cf. Reitzenstein-Schaeder I, p. 134.

20. Cf. the description of it in the Abraxas cosmogony, below, p. 456.

21. It is important for the history of religion as well as of later philosophy to observe how many different religious ideas were generally familiar and operative in a large commercial city in that time. Of course, far more important, it seems to me, is the task posed by Philo for the specialist in Iranian matters in that he presupposes a number of ideas which are attested only centuries later on Iranian soil, or in areas under Iranian influence. We suspect how misleading is the popular saying, "Only what is found in the Avesta is Iranian", and yet only in a few cases can we press through to clear information. In fact, all the preliminary labors in this area still are lacking; among the most urgently needed of these I would count a reliable translation of the Armenian Philo tradition. The demand made to theologians that they search for the basic Oriental ideas in Gnostic systems behind the more or less accidentally chosen Greek words can no longer be put off. To be sure, that demand can be met only if the principle of order and the cosmological or anthropological foundations of the systems are duly observed.

XIV.

The New Manichaean Fragments

In the lecture with which this work began I paraphrased (pp. 53ff.) the context of the superscriptions of the hymns as that context was presented to me in the version of M. 4 offered by F. W. K. Müller; the texts are given in my book, *Das Iranische Erlösungsmysterium*, pp. 13-14. It was only when the above presentation was in the press that I received, through the kindness of the authors, the treatise *Die Stellung Jesu im Manichäismus*, by E. Waldschmidt and W. Lentz (*Abh. d. Preuss. Akad.* 1926). This treatise confirms me in the belief that I was correct in connecting the detailed member-hymns with the excerpt in M. 4,[1] in my arrangement of the sequence of pages, and in my interpretation (p. 15.1) of the twelve members, whose number I determined, as the twelve part-aions of the one Aion, the twelve hours of the one light-day.[2] Out of new material the authors add (p. 68) that in another, sharply different version (T II K 178) the whole is characterized as "the Twelve-Member Exposition of the Living I",[3] and I may take pleasure in the fact that I myself have conjectured the existence of such another version (*Das Iranische Erlösungsmysterium*, p. 27), even though I regarded a connection between the two versions as possible. Now I must concede that as in error. But it appears to me that the authors fall victim to the same error. They propose, as it appears, conversely to judge the first version by the second, which they have published: according to them, these are penitential prayers, the collapse of the world is not the theme, and the

276

designation of "redemption mystery" is incorrect in every respect. All this appears to me too hasty a judgment. The version that I have labeled as the main version begins: "And the gods for your sake have gone forth and appeared, And have destroyed death and slain the darkness." In Manichaeism as in Christianity and in Zoroastrianism this happens only at the collapse of the world, at the full redemption. The title in M. 4 points to this redemption, where it also speaks of the time of which the redeemer spoke. The promised translation by Prof. Andreas no doubt will provide still further signs of this; I shall not go further into the matter, since even at this point I cannot relate any more than is in my book mentioned above. Unfortunately, it appears that the authors have not read the comprehensive presentation of my views (*op. cit.*, pp. 95-96). There I have explicitly pointed out that this liturgical corpus of twelve hymns or groups of hymns sung *in antiphonal arrangement* no longer represented for the

77 Manichaeans an actual mystery (p. 96), but only served, like Corp. herm. XIII, for purposes of edification (even then my evidence was the large number of manuscripts; the pictorial character of the hymns; the lack of a δρώμενον; and the occurrence of the individual hymns in another context as well; the Mandaean liturgical book served me only for purposes of clarification). Of course behind them lies the mystery idea. When a similar liturgical form recurs in a penitential usage or when on a folio sheet one half presents a gospel-hymn whose content still is not determined and the other, separated from the first half by we do not know how many other folios, offers a member-hymn, in my opinion this says nothing. The authors deny that the Manichaeans had mysteries--incidentally, without mentioning the testimonies of Victorinus and of the Anathematisms--, because Mani wished everyone, even the *auditores*,

to be saved and to this end attributed crucial significance to penance. But all the mystery religions do the same, as they can be shown. Augustine testifies that the *auditores* were not permitted acquaintance with certain writings and teachings of Mani; that in itself suffices to prove the mystery-character of his religion.

I do not need to offer any reassurance that no one can more happily and more gratefully welcome the rich treasures that the two authors have opened up to us and will continue to open up than do I, who for ten years have sought for and concerned myself with small fragments of those treasures. I fully understand why they themselves first emphasize what is now most surprising to us of that tremendous discovery, although it had to be most strongly noted before the unlocking of the Oriental sources, the impact of Christianity upon Mani. I would only deplore it if thereby that prevailing indifference of the theologians and historians of religion were once again evoked, which for so long has been a burden to these studies. This danger arises by virtue of the fact that on the one hand the authors draw, and indeed were obliged to draw, a topical boundary, and a very restrictive one at that--it was their intention only to treat Mani's teaching about Jesus--, but at the same time they pronounce a judgment about Mani's religion 278 as a whole. They concede that they transfer to Jesus much from earlier redeemer-figures; he is adapted to them or is combined with them, and yet if no divine name is named, a designation that is once used for Jesus--perhaps only by transference--is for them sufficient justification to make an entire text refer to him. The non-Christian figures or concepts which come into consideration alongside him as "redeemed redeemer" or messenger or judge are at most fleetingly mentioned, but are not treated; and the question to which re-

ligion the basic thought and tone of the individual passage belonged is not even posed. Any connection with the New Testament, even if it is only in a universally disseminated figure such as that of the clothing of the soul, suffices to posit Christianity as the source; indeed, this way of viewing the matter is *demanded as a matter of principle* and is justified with the statement that "In Mani's time, Christianity was a solidly formulated entity."[4] The fact that the late Jewish, and with it also the Christian, hope of immortality itself grows out of the Iranian, which even according to the view of the authors likewise had a direct influence upon Mani, makes this methodological demand completely unacceptable to me; here too we are talking about a solidly formulated entity. Hence we must investigate which of the two forms Mani more closely approximates, whether in individual features or in basic thinking. If he stands closer to the Iranian, then I can only use it--indeed, I must use it--in explanation of the New Testament form. I am choosing examples because it would be idle to discuss the theoretical question which after all can only be determined in terms of the individual case.

The Pauline conception of a Pneuma in us, which is at the same time the Lord, the Christ, in us exhibits undeniable similarity to a Manichaean conception which I once had to ascertain quite painstakingly (*Das Iranische Erlösungsmysterium*, p. 31) from the Persian and Manichaean tradition without the help of specialists in the field. It now lies before us in

9 overwhelmingly abundant documentation; I refer to the conception that the devout person has a second, non-material "Self",[5] and this Self is the counterpart to his light-soul and at the same time the divine emissary who one day will lead this light-soul upward to heaven. In the recently discovered texts this light-self, which apparently is connected with

the light-soul, is often called Jesus. He is the light-self of the individual soul, but also of all souls.[6] In the Mithras liturgy, which we can cautiously place earlier than all ex- [280] pressions of Manichaeism, this light-self is a body that is formed by the primal deity in the light-world, consisting of the four (or five) light-elements, from which the material elements that form our bodies have issued;[7] it is a divine being whom the *mystes* must petition when he wishes to ascend into the light-world. I cannot at all dissociate that view from a statement of the Denkard (VII 2.15, 16) to the effect that the spiritual body of Zarathustra was formed in the light-realm many thousands of years before the birth of the prophet and had remained with the archangels; it is this σῶμα τέλειον or light-self that dwells in God's presence while Gayomard (the primal man) in the meantime represents religious knowledge in the material world. Moreover, in the much-discussed Yasht 22 this light-self of the soul comes as a beautiful virgin to meet the ascending soul of the devout; it has become so beautiful through the good thoughts, words, and deeds of the soul, and thus is its reflection.[8] United with the soul, it is venerated in heaven as Ohrmazd, who in fact also appears in Manichaeism as primal man. Consequently I really cannot understand it when Wendland and Lentz are so greatly put off by the Zarathustra hymn reported above (p. 56) that they declare that they will be able to discuss (and to consider) it only after Mani's relation to Zarathustra is fully clear. Is it not already made clear by Mani's solemn recognition of the three emissaries who were sent before him, Zarathustra, Buddha, and Jesus? And by the coins of Peroz, to which v. Wesendonk has just called our attention once again in [281] the *Ephemerides Orientales* of the Harrassowitz firm (September 1926)?[9] Later Zoroastrianism also believed in a light-self:

why should not a Zoroastrian have his prophet awakened by his light-self (instead of by the "Good Mind"), and why should Mani or one of his followers insert Jesus as the light-self-- of Zarathustra? The only question here is whether the idea of awakening arises out of the belief in Jesus or out of the belief in a light-self. But I would go on: can Mani's main utterances about Jesus' activity,[10] even when we eliminate all the Iranian additions such as the association of Jesus with the "Good Mind", the moon, the light-virgin, and so on, arise out of Christianity at all? Where then in Christianity is a really clear conception of the light-self? Where is the teaching that Jesus himself comes to awaken that light-self or to lead it upward? Where, finally, is the entire basic conception of that divine, immaterial material that is called Light and Life?

When I nevertheless emphasize a similarity with Paul, I must say at once that in my opinion, it is utterly impossible that he has "borrowed" from the Iranian sphere the belief about Christ in us and in the ἐκκλησία. I am able to search for its *origin* only in the apostle's personal experience and feeling; but the thought-form in which he proposes to make it comprehensible to others is influenced by the environment. Even here it is not purely Persian, for this environment and particularly Paul himself think in the Greek language; for them, *grev* is not a concept capable of being expressed; the word πνεῦμα must be employed and must bring with it the thought-connections that appertain to it in Greek. However-- and this is strange, but it still must be traced out by the historian of religions in its most diverse developments--the original perspective still continues to have its impact: this πνεῦμα or this Christ is a figure, consists of definite members,[11] and must be perfected in the individual and in the

282

community. These are not merely figurative expressions, but inward perspectives which from time to time are slumbering in the consciousness or break forth, just as, on the other hand, does the feeling that we have within us the νοῦς Χριστοῦ, or that he brings ζωή (or, is the πνεῦμα ζωοποιόν). Paul himself says in two passages that he is acquainted with the belief in a divine Anthropos and presupposes that belief; it has its counterpart--not its immediate source--in a late Jewish belief in the *bar-nasha*, the "Son of Man". In these two religious perspectives that spring from the same root we find the inner connection of the Pauline sense of Christ--I deliberately refrain from saying "Christology", for we are not talking about a system, such as we are constantly trying to construct with modern concepts. From the component elements of that sense, that feeling, about Christ it is understandable that Mani felt the inner affinity and could appropriate so much. But anyone who only lifts from Mani the statements that refer to "Jesus" and proposes to explain the spirit and the emergence of his religion accordingly is proceeding unhistorically and is essentially predetermining what he proposes to prove.

Herewith I have answered, in essence, the methodological demand of the editors that for the exposition and interpretation of Christianity nothing should be adduced from Manichae-

283

ism that can somehow be compared with it. They explicitly include among these items (p. 33; cf. p. 28) the mention of the twelve garments by which Jesus remakes the soul, purifies it, and lifts it up from the earth. It prompts some reservations in my mind that in Apuleius these twelve garments are bestowed upon the *mystes* of Isis in a δρώμενον, and that Christianity knows nothing similar. On the other hand, we find the basic idea,--indeed, still more, the entire systematic structure of

a part of the Manichaean tractate on which the authors rely transferred in Philo to the πρεσβύτατος θεοῦ λόγος, for him the primal man (above, p. 345). The religious system, which Philo did not invent but presupposed as familiar, is older than Christianity and even in Mani does not stem from Christianity. Before we form a judgment as to the nature and source of the Manichaean system, we will do well to determine how much of that system is attested as earlier. This now has already been done in a number of cases, but as a whole it still calls for much painstaking labor.

The case is altogether similar with Mandaeism, which the authors wish to exclude from their presentations. Since its documents are all undated, and I have acknowledged and still acknowledge the possibility that *in specific items* it has been influenced by Manichaeism, the authors demand that all of those documents should be excluded from investigations of Manichaeism and its relation to Iranian religion. I consider this demand unjustified. We should look at the very closely related doctrine of the ascent of the soul in both religions--it is precisely in Mandaeism that we can treat separately a coherent and cohesive set of ideas--: here Mani kept the four Persian stages, while as a rule the Mandaeans, like the author of the Poimandres, insert in their place the astrological stages, and some of them wage a vigorous polemic against the Persian teaching as idolatry; but they preserve more strictly than does Mani--at least according to the view of the authors whose work we are discussing--the entire character of analogy-magic, and indeed individual Iranian ideas, like that of the soul as Nitufta (discussed above, p. 16); important Manichaean ideas are totally lacking, and in its basic ethical ideas
34
Mandaeism agrees more closely with Zoroastrianism than with Manichaeism.[12] It would be arbitrary to deny that it was

also directly influenced by Zoroastrianism; thus we may adduce the latter for the sake of comparison.

Since my "Studien" have appeared, it is unnecessary for me to state what a prominent position I assign to philology, and even to detailed philology, in the work of the history of religions. The person investigating religion must constantly learn from philology and allow himself to be corrected by it. But the representative of detailed philological work may also find it useful, when he moves into this area, to become familiar with the observations and methods of research in the field of religion. When Erwin Rohde, instead of fighting against research in folklore, made use of it and placed it at the service of philology, he did his permanently valuable work. I should like to conclude the discussion with the specialist in Iranian matters with the wish that he will soon open up to us the rest of his treasures; only then will we be able in some measure to form a judgment.

NOTES

1. Of course the authors then proceed to explain M. 4 as only a brief collection of community hymns, which hardly fits in here.

2. This is attested by the tractate published by Chavannes and Pelliot.

3. The "Living I" is a body, and thus according to Chaldean-Iranian perspective has twelve members. Thus the interpretation is somewhat different.

4. Here the authors obviously get into the religio-historical issues which they explicitly avoid with respect to the Iranian sphere. It is in this lack of clarity that the danger lies.

5. I have preferred this expression because it corresponds to original kindred Indian views; the authors insert "I" for it. The Persian word (*grev*), which also can mean "body" and "nature" (φύσις), offers the possibility of a doctrine of the soul which is difficult for western thought to comprehend, to which I have devoted the most detailed attempt to expound its meaning for Christianity in a lecture originally delivered in Basel on "Vorchristliche Erlösungslehren" (*Kyrkohistorisk Arsskrift*, Uppsala 1922, pp. 94ff.). [In any case, related in its import is the Aramaic word *qnuma*, which indeed is also used to translate the Greek word αὐτός, which seems to me to be important for the history of the idea. A. W. Wigram's book, *History of the Assyrian Church* (London 1910), to which Prof. Bang called my attention, shows how this word, drawn into the dispute over the two natures in Christ, allows us more precisely to define its relation to the Greek words ὑπόστασις, οὐσία, φύσις and πρόσωπον (*persona*). To be sure, in such investigations of two words from totally different languages we must keep in mind Wigram's appropriate analogy: their relation to each other cannot be other than that of two circles that partially overlap, covering a part of their surface in common, but having different centers. No translation is simply correct and suitable for all cases. If *monuhmed* in one instance can signify γνῶσις, there is nothing to prevent its having, in other passages, the value of νόησις or νοῦς, or its appearing in still other connections for the "Self". While in Turkish the word *oz* signifies this "Self", in another connection it can (in spite of Lentz's word to the contrary,

pp. 37 and 74) also denote "life", as Bang has compellingly demonstrated (*Muséon* 36.187 and 38.10, 11). The main thing is that we attempt here to feel our way into the basic idea and to arrive approximately at the center of the circle that is to be defined.]

6. The fact that the soul indeed is thought of as immaterial, but yet again as material also, like God himself--we may think of the definition of divine nature as φῶς καὶ ζωή--, compels the view, strange to us, that the totality of this material is a divine being, or, in another version, *the* divine being. The relation of the particular to the universal (or of the part to the whole) is fluid, as in the case of the god of time and of the world (the Aion). The view is so universally disseminated that it passes over into Christianity also: the Pneuma lives in the individual and in the totality (the ἐκκλησία). It can also be conceived of and characterized in corporeal and personal terms, and then it is the primal man, and yet again for the totality it is religion, the knowledge of God. The parallels from India teach us that we cannot at all seek in Judaism or in Christianity for the emergence of this Oriental thought-form.

7. This itself contains the idea that this σῶμα τέλειον is the primal man. If we consider the fact that with respect to a deity the νοῦς can also be identified as πρόνοια, we will also connect the introductory epiclesis ἵλαθί μοι Πρόνοια καὶ Ψυχή with this god-man, who is νοῦς καὶ ψυχή, as is said in the Poimandres (now we find the pair of terms recurring frequently in the Manichaean documents).

8. One may think of the garment in the hymn of the soul in the Acts of Thomas, which took form with the deeds of the king's son.

9. The Anathematisms will correctly exhibit the belief of the next generation: the four "emissaries", Zarathustra, Buddha, Jesus, and Mani, are only four manifestations of the "emissary" or of the "third emissary", the sun-god (Mithras). Hence what is said about Jesus can, in other passages, also be transferred to Mani. The authors' failure to make much distinction between Mani's self-designations and the beliefs of his church seems to me an error. One may think of Christianity and Buddhism in this regard.

10. The authors proceed only from the *name* of Jesus, and its frequent occurrence in the Chinese roll which contains the new texts certainly bears witness that Mani took more account

of Christianity than we had previously had to assume, and that not only in writings intended for the West. But it by no means follows from that that the basic ideas of his system stem from Christianity. In his combination of the three great religions Mani consistently and imaginatively carries forward the striving for universality which the mystery religions before him had developed; but it is not the names, but the religious ideas that are connected with the names that provide an insight into his inner feelings and thus into the origin of his system. Note what is said above, p. 92, n. 17.

11. Of course he is also viewed as a structure. This has its counterpart in Mandaean texts, but certainly not only in them.

12. Especially characteristic is the Mandaeans' passionate rejection of asceticism; and it is precisely in asceticism that Mani appears to have been strongly influenced by India.

XV.

The Concepts of Gnosis and Pneuma

The words γνῶσις and γνωστικός, πνεῦμα and πνευματικός must be studied from the same perspective, but they nevertheless are best treated separately. To my regret, I was earlier unable to find preliminary studies, and was myself able to offer only provisional attempts because of inaccessible materials. The fact that in all essentials they have been fully confirmed in Norden's grandly conceived book *Agnostos Theos* allows me to repeat them here with only slight alterations.[1]

285 If the context does not immediately make clear the connection, the word γνῶσις requires a genitive. Hence it is necessary for us to ask what genitive has been suppressed as self-evident and thus unnecessary when the word acquired its technical meaning. For the Hermetic literature (and the magical papyri which are always in agreement with that literature) the answer is immediately evident; there the γνῶσις θεοῦ is an almost personally conceived δύναμις, somewhat like πίστις (cf. p. 293). The fact that in the Corp. herm. XIII 8, a γνῶσις χαρᾶς stands alongside the γνῶσις θεοῦ is to be explained by the compulsion evident there to enumerate ten different δυνάμεις. The goal is everywhere γνῶναι θεόν, and God is extolled: ὃς γνωσθῆναι βούλεται καὶ γινώσκεται τοῖς ἰδίοις (Corp. herm. I 31). This meaning emerges most clearly in the concluding prayer of the Λόγος τέλειος, the Asclepius of Pseudo-Apuleius. I once found it in the Papyrus Mimaut (Pap. Par. I 2391 fr. 1) and after a hurried collation published it in the *Archiv f.*

Religionsw. VII 393. More recently, Eitrem has published (*Skrifter utgit av Videnskapsselskapet i Kristiania* 1923 II, p. 1) a new and fruitful collation, and W. Scott still later has happily provided some emendations in his edition of the Hermetica. The textual tradition in the papyrus is extraordinarily poor, and that of the very free Latin translation is not good; only on the major questions is it possible to arrive at full certainty. In the following, I place the letters that have faded out in the papyrus in square brackets, and words that have been restored in angled brackets; if they are attested by the Latin version, they are in parentheses.

[Χ]άριν σοι οἴδαμεν <καὶ> ψυχῆ<ν> πᾶσα<ν> καὶ καρ-
δίαν πρός [σε] ἀνατεταμένην, ἄφραστον ὄνομα, τετιμημένον
86 [τῇ] τοῦ θεοῦ προσηγορίᾳ, (ὅτι σὺ μόνος εἶ κύριος), καὶ
εὐλογούμενον τῇ τοῦ (πατρὸς εὐλογίᾳ), ὅτ[ι] πρ[ὸς] πάντας
5 καὶ πρὸς πάσας πατρικὴν εὔνοιαν καὶ στοργὴν καὶ φιλίαν

1-2 καὶ ψυχ.--ἀναταμένην only Pap. Apuleius has for this: *summe, exsuperantissime; tua enim gratia tantum sumus cognitionis lumen consecuti.* The magician omits the reference to what precedes; what he inserts comes from the prayer of Poimandres §13: δέξαι λογικὰς θυσίας ἁγνὰς ἀπὸ ψυχῆς καὶ καρδίας πρός σε ἀνατεταμένης.

1 Pap. ψυχὴ πᾶσα. Omission of the final ν is very common in the papyrus, and the zeugma is an easy one.

3-4 Scott's restoration from Ap. *et honorandum nomine* (my reading; codd. have *nomen*) *divino quod* (thus Scott; codd. *unum quo*) *solus dominus es* (Scott; codd. *deus est*).

4 Pap. [θε]οῦ for πατρός (such incorrect repetitions are frequent); for εὐλογίᾳ perhaps θεολογίᾳ also would be conceivable; cf. Ap. *et benedicendum religione paterna* (thus Scott; codd. *benedicendus*).

4 Instead of ὅτ[ι], Pap. οσ. For πάσας, Pap. πάντας.

καὶ ἔτι γλυκυτέ[ρα]ν ἐνέργ[εια]ν ἐν<ε>δείξω χαρισάμενος
ἡμῖν νοῦν, [λόγ]ον, γνῶσιν· νοῦν μὲ<ν>, ἵνα σε νοήσωμεν,
λόγον <δέ>, [ἵν]α σε (ὑπολογήσωμεν), γνῶσιν, ἵνα ἐπιγν-
(όντες σε χαρ)ῶ μεν. §2. (φωτὶ οὖν σου σωθέντες) χ[αί-
10 ρομε]ν ὅτι σεαυτὸν ἡμῖν ἔδειξας (ὅλον), χαίρομεν ὅ[τι ἐν
π]λάσμασιν ἡμᾶς ὄντας ἀπεθέω[σ]ας τῇ σεαυτο[ῦ χάριτ]ι.
χάρις ἀνθρώπου πρός σε μ[ία] τὸ (σὸν μέγεθος) [γ]νωρίσαι.
ἐγν[ωρίσαμ]έν (σε), ὦ (ζωὴ) τῆς ἀνθρωπίνης ζωῆς, [ἐ]γνω-
ρίσαμέ[ν (σε), ὦ φῶς] ἁπάσης γνώσεως, ἐγνωρίσαμέν σε, ὦ
15 μήτρα [παντοφ]όρε ἐ<ν> πατρὸς φυτείᾳ, ἐγνω<ρί>σαμέν <σε>,

5-7 Pap. επιγλυκυτα[τη]ν. Ap. *et quaecumque est dulcior efficacia* (cf. Scott).

7 Pap. υμιν.

8 For ὑπολογήσωμεν Pap. ἐπικαλέσωμεν. Ap. *ut te suspicionibus indagemus* (spiritual perception is the theme).

8-9 Pap. ινα επιγνωσωμεν. Ap.: *ut te cognoscentes* [*gaudeamus*] *ac lumine* (thus Scott; codd. *numine*) *salvati tuo* <*gaudeamus*> Scott. A γνῶσις χαρᾶς is treated in Corp. Herm. XIII.

11 πλάσμα of bodies; cf. Wessely, *Denkschr. d. Wiener Akad.* 1888, p. 50, line 211: τύπτει σε πτέρυξιν εἰς τὸ πλάσμα σου; Eitrem, *op. cit.*, line 259: γεννηθὲν ἐν παντὶ πλάσματι ἀνθρωπίνῳ. The literary document probably had ἐν σώμασιν; cf. Corp. herm. X 6 (below, p. 369): τὴν ψυχὴν ἀποθεωθῆναι ἐν σώματι ἀνθρώπου κειμένην.

13 Ap. *intellegimus te, o vitae nostrae* (to be written thus; codd. *vere* or *vera*). Apuleius more correctly places this clause after the next one: God is φῶς καὶ ζωή (always in this order); then τὸ ἀγαθόν is often added as a third member (sometimes with the interpretation as τὸ σπέρμα).

14 Pap. εγνωρισαμενων μητρα. Scott παντοφόρε, Pap. εμητροσφυτια (an error from repetition). Ap. *o naturarum omnium fecunda praegnatio*.

ὦ (τοῦ) [πάντα κυο]φοροῦν[τ]ος αἰώνιος διαμονή. §3. οὕτως οὖ[ν (σὴν) χάριν] προσκυ[ν]ήσαντες μ[η]δεμίαν ᾐτήσα-
μεν [χάριν, πλὴν θ]έλησον ἡμᾶς δια[τ]ηρηθῆναι ἐν τῇ σῇ
γν[ώ]σ[ει καὶ...ῃ [πρὸς] τὸ μὴ σφαλῆνα τοῦ τοιούτου
20 [βίου].

The γνῶσις appears first as χάρισμα, and it is in fact distinguished from νοῦς or νόησις and λόγος (cf. Corp. herm. XII 12: δύο ταῦτα τῷ ἀνθρώπῳ ὁ θεός...ἐχαρίσατο τόν τε νοῦν καὶ τὸν λόγον). In the transition from §1 to §2 we see that it imparts σωτηρία and consists in God's being revealed wholly to man and making him into a god through this glimpse (θέα) in the mortal body. Of course γνῶσις or γνωρίζειν is also the thanks that man can render; God wants to be recognized; hence there follows the fourfold praise of God (according to Corp. Herm. I, φῶς and ζωή belong together as the first pair; then as the second, μήτρα παντοφόρε and τοῦ πάντα κυοφοροῦντος αἰώνιος διαμονή;[2] on the structure of the prayer compare the prayer of Urbicus, below, p. 394). All petitions for external gifts evidently are excluded; the devout person may pray only

---

16 Pap. στα...φορου . τος. God is ἀρρενόθηλυς, Father and Mother, and he is the Aion. Instead of διαμονή Eitrem reads αιαμονη, but the letters are very similar; αἰώνιος διαμονή is a formula-like construction, and it is assured by Ap., *cognovimus te totius naturae tuo conceptu plenissimae* (to be written thus; codd. *plenissime*) *aeterna perseveratio.*

17 Restoration following Ap., *bonum bonitatis tuae hoc tantum deprecamur, ut nos velis servari* (Scott; codd. *servare*) *perseverantes in amore cognitionis tuae et numquam ab hoc vitae genere separari*; cf. the Poimandres prayer (Corp. herm. I 32): αἰτουμένῳ τὸ μὴ σφαλῆναι τῆς γνώσεως τῆς κατ' οὐσίαν ἡμῶν, ἐπίνευσόν μοι καὶ ἐνδυνάμωσόν με καὶ τῆς χάριτος ταύτης φωτίσω τοὺς ἐν ἀγνοίᾳ.

for abiding in γνῶσις; through the unique process it becomes an abiding *condition*, a new *life* that is different from the earlier life (precisely the life of σωτηρία). The context compellingly shows that in this connection the γνῶσις is the γνῶσις θεοῦ.

I shall pursue the ideas a little further through the

288 Hermetic writings without regard to whether the mystical language is more or less strongly transposed into philosophical language. It is in fact clear that philosophy does not create these ideas, but takes them over from religion, at first as mere figures, in order to offer assurance that it can vouchsafe the same gifts as can religion (cf. Poseidonios, above, p. 150), and later of course as its own ideas, but always without significantly influencing their essence. Corp. herm. IX 4 contrasts the children of the world with the ἐν γνώσει ὄντες; since our earth is the locus of wickedness, the latter are derided, hated, and even slain by the children of the world; but the devout person (θεοσεβής) endures everything αἰσθόμενος τῆς γνώσεως (it is apparently a spiritual vision, and indeed a vision of God). πάντα γὰρ τῷ τοιούτῳ, κἂν τοῖς ἄλλοις ᾗ (Codd. τὰ) κακά, ἀγαθά ἐστιν, καὶ ἐπιβουλευόμενος πάντα ἀναφέρει εἰς τὴν γνῶσιν (reference to God) καὶ τὰ κακὰ μόνος ἀγαθοποιεῖ. I may remark in passing that Paul in Rom. 8:28 is in agreement with this: οἴδαμεν δὲ ὅτι τοῖς ἀγαπῶσιν τὸν θεὸν πάντα συνεργεῖ εἰς ἀγαθόν, τοῖς κατὰ πρόθεσιν κλητοῖς οὖσιν. ὅτι οὓς προέγνω, καὶ προώρισεν συμμόρφους τῆς εἰκόνος τοῦ υἱοῦ αὐτοῦ...οὓς δὲ προώρισεν, τούτους καὶ ἐκάλεσεν, καὶ οὓς ἐκάλεσεν, τούτους καὶ ἐδικαίωσεν, οὓς δὲ ἐδικαίωσεν, τούτους καὶ ἐδόξασεν. The first idea certainly can be explained at once in light of Paul's own feelings; it is noteworthy only that it appears in a context which exhibits a number of words and concepts of Hellenistic mystery-religions (cf. above, pp. 327ff., and for προγινώσκειν, p. 381). Hardly less clear

is the concept of γνῶσις in the strongly philosophically flavored passage in Corp. herm. X 4: ἐπλήρωσας ἡμᾶς, ὦ πάτερ, τῆς ἀγαθῆς καὶ καλλίστης θέας, καὶ ὀλίγου δεῖν ἐπετάσθη (Codd. ἐσεβάσθη) μου ὁ τοῦ νοῦ ὀφθαλμὸς ὑπὸ τῆς τοιαύτης θέας. The vision of the good does not dazzle or deceive, and the supersensual light is not injurious; indeed, it is full of immortality: ἧς οἱ δυνάμενοι πλέον τι ἀρύσασθαι [τῆς θέας] κατακοιμίζονται πολλάκις ἀπὸ τοῦ σώματος εἰς τὴν καλλίστην ὄψιν, ᾗπερ (Codd. ὥσπερ or ὅπερ) Οὐρανὸς καὶ Κρόνος οἱ ἡμέτεροι πρόγονοι ἐντετυχήκασιν (reference to a lost mystery-document similar to chapter XIII, in which two "gods" of the corporeal life fall asleep 289 to the blessed vision). The Father confirms this; (§5) the pre-condition is that the earthly man is utterly quiescent: τότε γὰρ αὐτὸ ὄψει, ὅταν μηδὲν περὶ αὐτοῦ ἔχῃς εἰπεῖν. ἡ γὰρ γνῶσις αὐτοῦ καὶ θέα (thus Plasberg; Scott βαθεῖα, Codd. θεία) σιωπή ἐστι καὶ καταργία πασῶν τῶν αἰσθησεων. οὔτε γὰρ ἄλλο τι δύναται νοῆσαι ὁ τοῦτο νοήσας οὔτε ἄλλο τι θεάσασθαι ὁ τοῦτο θεασάμενος, οὔτε περὶ ἄλλου τινὸς ἀκοῦσαι οὔτε τὸ σύνολον τὸ (CA lacks) σῶμα κινῆσαι. πασῶν γὰρ τῶν σωματικῶν αἰσθήσεών τε καὶ κινήσεων ἐπιλαθόμενος (MAC ἐπιλαβόμενος) ἀτρεμεῖ. περιλάμψαν δὲ πάντα τὸν νοῦν καὶ τὴν ὅλην ψυχὴν ἀναλάμπει καὶ ἀνέλκει διὰ τοῦ σώματος καὶ ὅλον αὐτὸν εἰς οὐσίαν (into the divine or supersensual) μεταβάλλει. ἀδύνατον γάρ, ὦ τέκνον, τὴν ψυχὴν ἀποθεωθῆναι ἐν σώματι ἀνθρώπου κειμένην, θεασαμένην τοῦ ἀγαθοῦ <τὸ> κάλλος, <ἀλλὰ χωρίζεσθαι αὐτοῦ καὶ μεταβάλλεσθαι ἐν> τῷ ἀποθεωθῆναι (Philo, Quaest. in Genes. IV 1 and 4, is comparable). I have restored the text with the words μεταβάλλεσθαι ἐν, with some certainty, I believe, for the following reasons: the word ἀδύνατον, attested in the manuscripts and necessary in the context, cannot be challenged, and the τῷ ἀποθεωθῆναι in the

conclusion, which is without connection, necessarily indicates a gap; the son goes on to ask, πῶς λέγεις, ὦ πάτερ, and receives the answer πάσης ψυχῆς, ὦ τέκνον, διαιρετῆς μεταβολαί; and the entire continuation hinges on the concept of μεταβολή. Described first is the ἑαυτὸν διεξελθεῖν of the thirteenth chapter, then the transformation into a divine being which is there broadly portrayed; it remains uncertain whether μεταβάλλεσθαι is to be completed with a new designation for being, something like εἰς πνεῦμα; cf. Origen, περὶ εὐχῆς 9.2, p. 319.4 K.: καὶ ἡ ψυχὴ δὲ ἐπαιρομένη καὶ τῷ πνεύματι ἑπομένη τοῦ τε σώματος χωριζομένη, καὶ οὐ μόνον ἑπομένη τῷ πνεύματι, ἀλλὰ καὶ ἐν αὐτῷ γινομένη--ὅπερ δηλοῦται ἐκ τοῦ 'πρὸς σε ἦρα τὴν ψυχήν μου'--πῶς οὐχὶ ἤδη ἀποτιθεμένη τὸ εἶναι ψυχὴ πνευματικὴ (originally probably πνεῦμα) γίνεται; it is in harmony with this that in the Hermetic writing it is further said of the human soul (§7): ἀρχὴν ἀθανασίας ἴσχουσιν εἰς δαίμονας (πνεύματα) μεταβάλλουσαι, εἶθ' οὕτως εἰς τὸν θεῶν χορὸν χορεύουσι (Scott χωροῦσι). χοροὶ δὲ δύο θεῶν, ὁ μὲν τῶν πλανωμένων, ὁ δὲ τῶν ἀπλανῶν· καὶ αὕτη ψυχῆς ἡ τελειοτάτη δοξα.[3] I hope that I have proved that the idea of a deification and transfiguration of the living man arises out of the mystery faith; it is achieved by means of γνῶσις or the θέα θεοῦ. The *full* γνῶσις or θέα, because one incorporates into oneself much of the ἀπόρροιαι θεοῦ, produces a κατακοιμέζεσθαι ἀπὸ τοῦ σώματος εἰς τὴν καλλίστην ὄψιν. I compare with this the first chapter, the actual Poimandres: here too it is said (§26), τοῦτό ἐστι τὸ ἀγαθὸν τέλος τοῖς γνῶσιν ἐσχηκόσι θεωθῆναι. I know no better way to explain the word τέλος, borrowed from the language of the mysteries, than to refer to Plato's portrayal of the mysteries in his Symposion 210e: ὃς γὰρ ἂν μέχρι ἐνταῦθα πρὸς τὰ 'Ερωτικὰ (Eros-initiation) παιδαγωγηθῇ, θεώμενος ἐφεξῆς τε καὶ ὀρθῶς τὰ καλά, πρὸς τέλος ἤδη ἰὼν τῶν 'Ερωτικῶν

ἐξαίφνης κατόψεταί τι θαυμαστὸν τὴν φύσιν καλόν; 211b: ὅταν δή τις ἀπὸ τῶνδε διὰ τὸ ὀρθῶς παιδεραστεῖν ἐπανιὼν ἐκεῖνο τὸ καλὸν ἄρχηται καθορᾶν, σχεδὸν ἄν τι ἅπτοιτο τοῦ τέλους.[4] As Plato himself contrasts, at the last stage of his ascent, the τέλος with an ἄρχεσθαι καθορᾶν, so does the Poimandres set it over against the reception of γνῶσις. To become God is the consummation, the goal; but one only fully attains this goal with the actual abandonment of the body in death, while γνῶσις is already attained through the vision of the Νοῦς and of the process of creation. What is demanded (§3) is: μαθεῖν θέλω τὰ ὄντα καὶ νοῆσαι τὴν τούτων φύσιν καὶ γνῶναι τὸν θεόν; the fulfillment is indicated (§27) by the words: διδαχθεὶς τοῦ παντὸς τὴν φύσιν καὶ τὴν μεγίστην θέαν (thus reference is made to the mystery of rebirth in chapter XIII in the beginning of the following chapter with the words: ἐπεὶ ὁ υἱος μου Τὰτ ἀπόντος σου τὴν τῶν ὄντων ἠθέλησε φύσιν μαθεῖν-- it is almost a formula for beholding God). Of course the Poimandres speaks of an ἑαυτὸν ἀναγνωρίζειν ἀθάνατον ὄντα along with a γνῶσις θεοῦ; connected with the former is the definition ὁ νοήσας ἑαυτὸν εἰς θεὸν χωρεῖ. This corresponds exactly to the teaching of the Naassenes (Hippolytus, p. 96.7 W.): ἀρχὴ γάρ, φησίν, τελειώσεως γνῶσις ἀνθρώπου, θεοῦ δὲ γνῶσις ἀπηρτισμένη τελείωσις (as the preceding words show, this refers to the γνῶσις of the τέλειος ἄνθρωπος, the perfect man, who according to the teaching of the Poimandres has become immortal through the reception of the νοῦς). The same division of the mystery apparently is connected with the doctrine of the Anthropos which is common to both systems. Thus in I 32 (cf. below, p. 422, n. 2) the full γνῶσις apparently is distinguished from the γνῶσις that is κατ' οὐσίαν ἡμῶν and corresponds to our nature on earth. Yet elsewhere there is also some uncertainty as to whether a full γνῶσις and θέα

θεοῦ is at all possible during one's lifetime; the idea of the dying of the old man is not always so pronounced as in chapter XIII; it is true that the message θεὸς πέφυκας (XIII 14) is combined with it, but as a rule it applies only to the person who has actually died.[5] On this point, Christian and pagan have the same feeling. With one as with the other it is less a matter of a change of idea than a change in the level of the momentary feeling, as we find it also in Paul. His having died to the world sometimes has greater, sometimes lesser force of reality; the nature of the πνευματικός sometimes remains human, and sometimes it is heightened, both ethically and intellectually, into the divine; and even the γνῶσις is sometimes an absolute γνῶσις, and sometimes a γνῶσις κατ' οὐσίαν ἡμῶν and only fragmentary. But back to the lexical study.

292 The figure for the γνῶσις is always light, and no expression occurs more frequently than τὸ τῆς γνώσεως φῶς. It is only a further development when φωτίζει, which is originally said of the revelation itself, is transferred to the message of salvation that issues from the revelation (cf. Corp. herm. I 32; Clement, Strom. V 10.64, II 369 Stählin; Usener, *Weihnachtsfest*, p. 169). In Apuleius, as is only natural in the portrayal of the mysteries, the metaphysical meaning also appears: the vision of God, who indeed by his very nature is φῶς, makes a person also φῶς, as in other mysteries occurs with the entrance of the deity or of the πνεῦμα; this also is called φωτίζειν. Both effects, the bestowal of γνῶσις and the transformation of nature, lie in the very essence of the mystery; the two necessarily belong together, because both are joined in the nature of the deity; cf. the mystery-prayer in Corp. herm. XIII 19: τὸ πᾶν τὸ ἐν ἡμῖν σῷζε, ζωή,[6] φώτιζε, φῶς, πνευμά<τιζε>, θεέ. God, who is himself πνεῦμα, makes a person πνεῦμα by bestowing ἀθανασία and γνῶσις; indeed, he is

himself also ζωὴ καὶ φῶς (cf. X 5: the νοητὴ λαμπηδών is πάσης ἀθανασίας ἀνάπλεως). Once again, in my opinion, the usage is shown to be non-Jewish. The light-theology itself, at least in its later, fully stated form, appears first to have entered into Judaism from the Iranian sphere.

The counterpart concept ἀγνωσία best shows that originally the topic was only the γνῶσις θεοῦ. Corp. herm. I 27, ὦ λαοί, ἄνδρες γηγενεῖς, οἱ μέθῃ καὶ ὕπνῳ ἑαυτοὺς ἐκδεδωκότες καὶ τῇ ἀγνωσίᾳ τοῦ θεοῦ, νήψατε· παύσασθε δὲ κραιπαλῶντες θελγόμενοι ὕπνῳ ἀλόγῳ, may be compared with VII 1: ποῖ φέρεσθε, ὦ ἄνθρωποι, μεθύοντες, τὸν τῆς ἀγνωσίας ἄκρατον [λόγον] ἐκπιόντες, ὅν οὐδὲ φέρειν δύνασθε, ἀλλ' ἤδη αὐτὸν καὶ ἐμεῖτε; στῆτε νήψαντες, ἀναβλέψατε τοῖς τῆς καρδίας ὀφθαλμοῖς, καὶ εἰ μὴ πάντες δύνασθε, οἵ γε καὶ δυνάμενοι. ἡ γὰρ τῆς ἀγνωσίας κακία ἐπικλύζει πᾶσαν τὴν γῆν καὶ συμφθείρει τὴν ἐν τῷ σώματι κατακεκλεισμένην ψυχήν, μὴ ἐῶσα ἐνορμίζεσθαι τοῖς τῆς σωτηρίας λιμέσιν. The combination of the two figures of drunkenness and sleep is already found in the Zarathustra fragment (above, p. 56). The figure provides the presupposition for the entire mysticism of awakening among the Mandaeans and Manichaeans. The thirty-third Ode of Solomon is to be compared with Corp. herm. VII, as is the κήρυγμα of the Baptist in the Q-source of the gospels (in addition, the preaching of the prophets portrayed by Celsus: Origen, Contra Celsum VII 8). The figure of the flood (of ἀγνωσία) recurs in the Mandaean book of John, chapter 11. In the midst of the discussion of the resurrection in Paul's treatment in I Cor. 15:34 there is inserted a warning against the children of the world who doubt that there is any such resurrection at all and who therefore are servants of the body: ἐκνήψατε δικαίως καὶ μὴ ἁμαρτάνετε, ἀγνωσίαν γὰρ θεοῦ τινες ἔχουσιν. The entire context shows that for him ἀγνωσία θεοῦ is not a negative but a positive concept, in which love

for the world and sinful inclination are combined with the lack of higher knowledge. In the Septuagint, ἀγνωσία does not occur in this way (in a different way in Wisd. Sol. 13:1). The fact that the figure of drunkenness is combined with this concept, even though this figure also appears in the Septuagint, makes me think here of a direct dependence on Hellenistic mysticism. There--in the Κόρη κόσμου, for example (Stobaeus, Ekl. 402.27 Wachsm.)--the word ἀγνωσία also has the same meaning: it is the source of rebellion against God and of sin. It is precisely the κακία ψυχῆς (Corp. herm. X 8). We are brought still closer to Paul by Corp. herm. XI 20ff.: ἐὰν οὖν μὴ σεαυτὸν ἐξισάσῃς τῷ θεῷ, τὸν θεὸν νοῆσαι οὐ δύνασαι· τὸ γὰρ ὅμοιον τῷ ὁμοίῳ νοητόν. συναύξησον σεαυτὸν τῷ ἀμετρήτῳ μεγέθει, παντὸς σώματος ἐκπηδήσας καὶ πάντα χρόνον ὑπεράρας Αἰὼν[7] γενοῦ, καὶ νοήσεις τὸν θεόν. The description that follows, which should be compared with the rebirth mystery and the account of Apuleius, portrays the essence of γνῶσις still more clearly: μηδὲν ἀδύνατον ἐν σεαυτῷ ὑποστησάμενος σεαυτὸν ἥγησαι ἀθάνατον καὶ πάντα δυνάμενον νοῆσαι, πᾶσαν μὲν τέχνην, πᾶσαν δὲ ἐπιστήμην, παντὸς ζώου ἦθος (cf. p. 198, above). 294 παντὸς δὲ ὕψους ὑψηλότερος γενοῦ καὶ παντὸς βάθους ταπεινότερος. πάσας δὲ τὰς αἰσθήσεις τῶν ποιητῶν[8] σύλλαβε ἐν σεαυτῷ, πυρός, ὕδατος, ξηροῦ καὶ ὑγροῦ, καὶ ὁμοῦ πανταχῇ εἶναι, ἐν γῇ, ἐν θαλάττῃ, ἐν οὐρανῷ, μηδέπω γεγενῆσθαι, ἐν τῇ γαστρὶ εἶναι, νέος, γέρων, τεθνηκέναι, τὰ μετὰ τὸν θάνατον. κἂν ταῦτα πάντα ὁμοῦ νοήσῃς, χρόνους, τόπους, πράγματα, ποιότητας, ποσότητας, δύνασαι νοῆσαι τὸν θεόν. Then there follows the contrast, which seems to me to explain the context of Paul's thought: ἐὰν δὲ κατακλείσῃς σου τὴν ψυχὴν ἐν τῷ σώματι καὶ ταπεινώσῃς αὐτὴν καὶ εἴπῃς 'οὐδὲν νοῶ, οὐδὲν δύναμαι, φοβοῦμαι τὴν θάλασσαν, εἰς τὸν οὐρανὸν ἀναβῆναι οὐ δύναμαι.[9] οὐκ οἶδα τίς ἤμην, οὐκ οἶδα τίς ἔσομαι', τί σοι καὶ τῷ θεῷ; οὐδὲν γὰρ δύνασαι τῶν

καλῶν καὶ ἀγαθῶν, φιλοσώματος καὶ κακὸς ὤν, νοῆσαι. ἡ γὰρ τελεία κακία τὸ ἀγνοεῖν τὸ θεῖον, τὸ δὲ δύνασθαι γνῶναι καὶ θελῆσαι καὶ ἐλπίσαι ὁδός ἐστιν εὐθεῖα, διὰ (Codd. ἰδία) τοῦ ἀγαθοῦ φέρουσα καὶ ῥᾳδία. ὁδεύοντί σοι πανταχοῦ συναντήσει, πανταχοῦ ὀφθήσεται κτλ. (Cf. Norden, *Agnostos Theos*, pp. 102ff. One can also refer to I Clem. 38.3.) Even in this most heavily philosophically re-shaped description the mystery-idea shines through everywhere;[10] the γνῶσις θεοῦ is acquired on that pilgrimage through the twelve hours and figures and through the elements. Because it transforms the nature, it is also the τελεία ἀρετή, just as ἀγνωσία frequently is the τελεία κακία (it is concerned only about the body, not the origin of man or the life after death, and it says, "Let us eat and drink, for tomorrow we die"). From this conception of the γνῶσις θεοῦ it also follows that at first it is something absolute, like the πνεῦμα; one either has it or does not have it; a gradation is first introduced later, because of practical necessity and the notion of a gradually dawning vision and a gradual ascent to God, or the idea of various heavens and gods; but the designation Γνωστικός, like Πνευματικός, shows that in feeling the old interpretation repeatedly breaks through.

95 The idea that the γνῶσις is a way is explained out of the mystery-idea (cf. Plato); of course it recurs frequently, as in Corp. herm. X 15: οὐ γὰρ ἀγνοεῖ τὸν ἄνθρωπον ὁ θεός, ἀλλὰ καὶ πάνυ γνωρίζει καὶ θέλει γνωρίζεσθαι. τοῦτο μόνον σωτήριον ἀνθρώπῳ ἐστίν, ἡ γνῶσις τοῦ θεοῦ. αὕτη εἰς τὸν Ὄλυμπόν ἐστιν ἀνάβασις. τούτῳ (Codd. οὕτω or οὕτως) μόνῳ ἀγαθὴ ψυχή. Corp. herm. VI 5: μία γάρ ἐστιν εἰς αὐτὸ (the beholding of the καλὸν καὶ ἀγαθόν) ἀποφέρουσα ὁδός, ἡ μετὰ γνώσεως εὐσέβεια (in X 19, γνῶσις itself is called the ἀγὼν τῆς εὐσεβείας, and in X 9, the ἀρετὴ ψυχῆς, though of course along with this it is also called

τέλος ἐπιστήμης; in the same passage it is said of the γνοῦς ἑαυτόν that he is καὶ ἀγαθὸς καὶ εὐσεβὴς καὶ ἤδη θεῖος). This is reminiscent of that hymn of the Naassenes in Hippolytus 103.18 W., where Jesus says: σφραγῖδας ἔχων καταβήσομαι, αἰῶνας ὅλους διοδεύσω, μυστήρια πάντα δ' ἀνοίξω, μορφὰς δὲ θεῶν ἐπιδείξω, τὰ κεκρυμμένα τῆς ἁγίας ὁδοῦ, γνῶσιν καλέσας, παραδώσω. But one may not take this one passage as a point of departure for the entire question of the concept of γνῶσις, as Bousset attempted in his foundational work, *Hauptprobleme der Gnosis*, p. 277. Of course the concepts μυστήρια θεοῦ (secrets of God) and γνῶσις θεοῦ belong together, and the cultic action in which God discloses those secrets, the μυστήριον or the τελετή, also imparts this γνῶσις (for the connection between the two concepts, cf. also Wessely, *Denkschr. d. K. K. Akad.* 1888, p. 106, line 2476: διέβαλεν γὰρ σοῦ τὰ ἱερὰ μυστήρια ἀνθρώποις εἰς γνῶσιν, a passage in which διέβαλεν is used precisely as in Corp. herm. XIII 22: ἵνα μὴ ὡς διάβολοι λογισθῶμεν). But the significance of this cultic action must be comprehended in terms as broad and deep as possible; otherwise it will remain incomprehensible how πνευματικός can be used in place of γνωστικός.

Of course in the further development other objective genitives in connection with γνῶσις can also appear; yet the original concept usually shows through. An example from the magical literature is offered by the formula of conjuration (Pap. Lugd. V; Dieterich, *Jahrb. f. klass. Phil.*, Supplem. XVI, p. 799, line 19) in which a magician proposes to constrain the deity who has allegedly appeared to him once to come again: ἐγώ εἰμι, ᾧ συνήντησας ὑπὸ τὸ ἱερὸν ὄρος καὶ ἐδωρήσω τὴν τοῦ μεγίστου ὀνόματός σου γνῶσιν, ἣν καὶ τηρήσω μηδενὶ μεταδιδούς, εἰ μὴ τοῖς σοῖς συνμύσταις εἰς τὰς σὰς ἱερὰς τελετάς. The perspective is especially well exhibited

296

by the idea that the initiated person himself can in turn initiate novices, and by the imitation of the mystery-oath (cf. above, p. 241). Pap. Berol. II 128 is similar: ἐγώ εἰμι ὁ δεῖνα, ὅστις σοι ἀπήντησα καὶ δῶρόν μοι ἐδωρήσω τὴν τοῦ μεγίστου σου ὀνόματος γνῶσιν. It would be a mistake here to think only of Moses; Zarathustra also comes into consideration; and in the myth of Julian also, for example (Discourse VII.230 B = 298.18 H.), Hermes as the μυσταγωγός finds the *mystes* at the foot of the holy mountain; a "vision or ecstasy" shows him the Helios (299.26 H.), and is connected with it in the Convivium (336 C = 432.1 H.): σοὶ δέ, πρὸς ἡμᾶς λέγων ὁ 'Ερμῆς, δέδωκα τὸν πατέρα Μίθραν ἐπιγνῶναι. But the ὑπαντᾶν θεῷ is a generally common idea in mystical literature, and the "mountain" is the place of revelation (Corp. herm. XIII 1). What the knowledge of the name signifies for the magician I need not discuss, or at least can content myself with a formula in which a magician boasts of his γνῶσις and describes its effects (Poimandres, p. 20): οἶδα τὸ ὄνομά σου τὸ ἐν οὐρανῷ λαμφθέν, οἶδά σου καὶ τὰς μορφάς,...οἶδά σε, 'Ερμῆ, καὶ σὺ ἐμέ· ἐγώ εἰμι συ καὶ σὺ ἐγώ. I only add that I know no passage in these papyri in which γνῶσις does not signify a knowledge that is acquired in supernatural fashion.

The use of language in the papyri can be compared at once with the usage in that didactic writing of the Peratae that begins in Hippolytus 108.14 W. with: ἐγὼ φωνὴ ἐξυπνισμοῦ ἐν τῷ αἰῶνι τῆς νυκτός (thus the one calling, or the call itself, of the Iranian texts). It is the time of ἀγωνσία, of which the Hermetic writings also frequently speak. The revelational writing first adds to that authentic name of a deity that only the γνωστικός knows the presumed name, in formulas like this one: ὅν ἡ ἀγνωσία ἐκάλεσε Κρόνον, or ταύτην δὲ ἡ ἀγνωσία ἐκάλεσε Ποσειδῶνα; and just as the magician gives assurance

that he knows the name that God has caused to shine in the heavens in writing of flame, so the Peratae give assurance (113.18 W.) that the person who has the eyes of those who are celestial (μακάριοι ὀφθαλμοί; cf. in the mystery of Mithras

297 ἀθάνατα ὄμματα), the ἰδεῖν δυνάμενος, sees the forms of their gods in the heavens, while the οὐκ εἰδώς notes nothing of this.[11] Here ἡ ἀγνωσία (τοῦ θεοῦ) only signifies οἱ ψυχικοί.

The mystery of the celestial pilgrimage explains a further use of the word in the Hermetic writings. In the visions, as a rule, it is a god who leads, and in the cultic actions, as a rule, it is a deified *mystes*; so occasionally in those writings a guiding into the kingdom of γνῶσις is spoken of, and γνῶσις is conceived of in spatial terms; cf., e.g., Corp. herm. VII 2: ζητήσατε χειραγωγὸν τὸν ὁδηγήσοντα ὑμᾶς ἐπὶ τὰς τῆς γνώσεως θύρας, ὅπου ἐστὶ τὸ λαμπρὸν φῶς τὸ καθαρὸν σκότους, ὅπου οὐδὲ εἷς μεθύει, ἀλλὰ πάντες νήφουσιν ἀφορῶντες τῇ καρδίᾳ εἰς τὸν ὁραθῆναι θέλοντα. It is true that here, following Oriental ideas, what is discussed is a palace of γνῶσις, as indeed in the apocalypses heaven often appears as a king's palace with various halls; nevertheless the figure is illumined from Apuleius XI 22: *adest tibi dies votis adsiduis exoptatus, quo deae multinominis divinis imperiis per istas meas manus pissimis sacrorum arcanis insinueris.* Conversely, it explains the obscure expression of Apuleius (it had already been said, in XI 21, that the priest accompanied him into the ἄδυτον). In Corp. herm. I also, which is closely connected with VII, §§26 and 29 deal with the ὁδηγός; here too the intrinsically quite understandable and widely used figure is borrowed from the language of the mysteries in which it already appears in Plato. I hardly need to emphasize that in the Hermetic passage cited, τὸν ὁραθῆναι θέλοντα is a paraphrase of the formula that in I 31 reads ἅγιος ὁ θεός, ὅς

γνωσθῆναι βούλεται καὶ γινώσκεται τοῖς ἰδίοις, and in X 15, ἀλλὰ γνωρίζει καὶ θέλει γνωρίζεσθαι. The ἀφορᾶν τῇ καρδίᾳ εἰς θεόν, which in the continuation is described as νῷ καὶ καρδίᾳ ὁρᾶν, corresponds to the γνῶναι θεόν. The forfeiture of the body as the ὕφασμα τῆς ἀγνωσίας and the σκοτεινὸς περίβολος is named as the necessary condition for that γνῶναι θεόν, as it is elsewhere for the full γνῶσις. The usage does not occur only here; scattered throughout all these writ-

98 ings as synonyms for γνῶσις the following are inserted: νοῆσαι θεόν (as νόησις, as immediate perception of the suprasensual, stands in contrast to αἴσθησις, so in other passages does γνῶσις), ὁρᾶν θεόν, θεᾶσθαι, θεωρεῖν, and in magical usage εἰδέναι as well (cf., e.g., V 2: νόησις μόνη ὁρᾷ τὸ ἀφανές, ὡς καὶ αὐτὴ ἀφανὴς οὖσα. εἰ δύνασαι, τοῖς τοῦ νοῦ ὀφθαλμοῖς φανήσεται...ἄφθονος γὰρ ὁ κύριος, θαίνεται διὰ παντὸς τοῦ κόσμου. νόησον [Codd. νόησιν], ἰδεῖν καὶ λαβέσθαι αὐταῖς ταῖς χερσὶ δύνασαι καὶ τὴν εἰκόνα τοῦ θεοῦ θεάσασθαι. Stobaeus, Ekl. I 21.9, p. 194.11 Wachsm.: ὁ ταῦτα μὴ ἀγνοήσας ἀκριβῶς δύναται νοῆσαι τὸν θεόν, εἰ δὲ καὶ τολμήσαντα δεῖ εἰπεῖν, καὶ αὐτόπτης γενόμενος θεάσασθαι καὶ θεασάμενος μακάριος γενέσθαι.--μακάριος ἀληθῶς, ὦ πάτερ, ὁ τοῦτον θεασάμενος.--ἀλλ' ἀδύνατον, ὦ τέκνον, ἐν σώματι τούτου εὐτυχῆσαι. Stobaeus, I 3.52, p. 63.2 Wachsm.: θεοπτικὴ δύναμις). The individual writings can be distinguished according to whether the technically employed word γνῶσις is entirely avoided, appears rarely, or occurs frequently.[12] Even Philo appears to avoid it, as we shall see, and perhaps it is not accidental that Plutarch, who elsewhere uses γνῶσις only rarely, in the writing De Iside et Osiride, chapter 2, precisely in the interpretation of the mysteries uses it so entirely in the mystical sense: ὧν τέλος ἐστὶν ἡ τοῦ πρώτου καὶ κυρίου καὶ νοητοῦ γνῶσις, ἣν ἡ θεὸς παρακαλεῖ ζητεῖν παρ' αὐτῇ καὶ μετ'

αὐτῆς ὄντα καὶ συνόντα. Yet he appears in this connection to speak of a θείωσις--indeed of a making into an ἀνὴρ θεῖος; cf. Corp. herm. X 9: ὁ γνοὺς...ἤδη θεῖος (quite different is the use of γνῶσις for example in chapter 11, p. 355 B.). I should conjecture that, like the idea, so also the word itself is appropriated from Oriental, though of course hardly from Jewish, usage. I should also conjecture that from the very beginning there is combined with it the sense of an immediate connection, a συναφή, just as, according to the general view, the latter is adduced by the cult and especially by its loftiest formation in the mystery (cf. the very instructive statements of Sallust, περὶ θεῶν καὶ κόσμου, chapter 16). Be that as it may, it is only the expressions that change; the concept itself is fixed.

299 Did Paul also have this concept at hand? According to Preuschen's lexicon of the New Testament and early Christian literature, which as a rule faithfully reflects the interpretation which until recently was dominant, of course γνῶσις in Paul is supposed to signify "rational knowledge", and as documentation he cites I Cor. 12:8: ᾧ μὲν γὰρ διὰ τοῦ πνεύματος δίδοται λόγος σοφίας, ἄλλῳ δὲ λόγος γνώσεως κατὰ τὸ αὐτὸ πνεῦμα (even with the addition of "teaching that is according to knowledge"), and 14:6: γλώσσαις λαλῶν...ἢ ἐν ἀποκαλύψει ἢ ἐν γνώσει ἢ ἐν προφητείᾳ ἢ ἐν διδαχῇ. I need not speak any more about 13:1, 2, than I did about the passages discussed above: ἐὰν ταῖς γλώσσαις τῶν ἀνθρώπων λαλῶ καὶ τῶν ἀγγέλων...καὶ ἐὰν ἔχω προφητείαν καὶ εἰδῶ τὰ μυστήρια πάντα καὶ πᾶσαν γνῶσιν. In light of this connection of the concepts, how is that interpretation at all possible? It is well known that ἀγάπη is set in contrast with them. In 13:8 the apostle takes up the theme of this contrast: ἡ ἀγάπη οὐδέποτε ἐκπίπτει· εἴτε δὲ προφητεῖαι, καταργηθήσονται· εἴτε γλῶσσαι, παύσονται· εἴτε

γνῶσις, καταργηθήσεται. ἐκ μέρους δὲ γινώσκομεν καὶ ἐκ μέρους προφητεύομεν (the two are related, and hence are both pneumatic activities). ὅταν δὲ ἔλθῃ τὸ τέλειον, τὸ ἐκ μέρους καταργηθήσεται...βλέπομεν γὰρ ἄρτι δι' ἐσόπτρου ἐν αἰνίγματι, τότε δὲ πρόσωπον πρὸς πρόσωπον· ἄρτι γινώσκω ἐκ μέρους, τότε δὲ ἐπιγνώσομαι, καθὼς ἐπεγνώσθην. The conclusion shows, first of all, that what is meant is the γνῶσις θεοῦ (Gal. 4:9: νῦν δὲ γνόντες θεόν, μᾶλλον δὲ γνωσθέντες ὑπὸ θεοῦ; I Cor. 8:3: εἰ δέ τις ἀγαπᾷ τὸν θεόν, οὗτος ἔγνωσται ὑπ' αὐτοῦ). Attribution of man's γνῶσις to God occurs also in Hermetic writings; cf. X 15: οὐ γὰρ ἀγνοεῖ τὸν ἄνθρωπον ὁ θεός, ἀλλὰ καὶ πάνυ γνωρίζει καὶ θέλει γνωρίζεσθαι. τοῦτο γὰρ μόνον σωτήριον ἀνθρώπῳ ἐστίν, ἡ γνῶσις τοῦ θεοῦ. Corresponding to this is the mystery idea of a προορίζειν, *destinare* (cf. above, p. 320), and in Paul's writings, προγινώσκειν also appears for προορίζειν (Rom. 8:29). Someday Paul will behold God as clearly as God beheld him when he "saw" him and chose him; now we call γνῶσις the κατ' οὐσίαν ἡμῶν γνῶσις, that *beholding* δι' ἐσόπτρου ἐν αἰνίγματι. Once again in the use of the technical term Paul is in full agreement with Hellenistic mysticism, and it is only modern arbitrariness that forces upon him a meaning that neither the language usage of that time nor the context of the passages will allow. The concept of γνῶσις appears to become still lowlier where Paul speaks of the γνῶσις of which the Corinthians are boasting and which he at first does not deny. In I Cor. 8:1 he says with gentle irony: περὶ δὲ τῶν εἰδωλοθύτων οἴδαμεν ὅτι πάντες γνῶσιν ἔχομεν. ἡ γνῶσις φυσιοῖ, ἡ δὲ ἀγάπη οἰκοδομεῖ. εἴ τις δοκεῖ ἐγνωκέναι τι (i.e., to have attained a degree of γνῶσις; the idea of the graduated vision in the mysteries shows through here), οὐδέπω οὐδὲν ἔγνωκεν, καθὼς δεῖ γνῶναι. εἰ δέ τις ἀγαπᾷ θεόν, οὗτος ἔγνωσται ὑπ' αὐτοῦ. The same

contrast with ἀγάπη would itself have to show that here we are moving in the same thought-circles; true γνῶσις is attained only when one arrives at that full γνῶναι, καθὼς ἐγνώσθημεν. Of course even that still human γνῶσις θεοῦ liberates one and lifts one above the νόμος (we shall shortly encounter the idea again in pagan mysticism; the γνωστικός is indeed the πνευματικός); but not all have it. It is explicitly said that the γνῶσις bestows ἐξουσία (8:9), as does the πνεῦμα. It probably is unnecessary to say, finally, that passages like Rom. 2:20 do not use the combination of γνῶσις and ἀλήθεια to refer to a "rational knowledge"; I very much doubt whether Paul, who so often speaks of γνῶναι θεόν, would allow such at all.

In the Hermetic writings the realm of γνῶσις is heaven (cf. above, p. 105, n. 109; Stobaeus, I 61.1, p. 276.6 Wachsm.), the world of the suprasensual, into which the vision of God lifts us. Hence it necessarily removes one from the realm of εἱμαρμένη; cf. Corp. herm. XII 9: πάντων ἐπικρατεῖ ὁ νοῦς, ἡ τοῦ θεοῦ ψυχή,[13] καὶ εἱμαρμένης καὶ νόμου καὶ τῶν ἄλλων πάντων, καὶ οὐδὲν αὐτῷ ἀδύνατον, οὔτε εἱμαρμένης ὑπεράνω θεῖναι ψυχὴν ἀνθρωπίνην οὔτε ἀμελήσασαν, ὅπερ συμβαίνει, ὑπὸ εἱμαρμένην θεῖναι. The explanation is offered by the transformation of the entire being which is portrayed in detail in the rebirth-mystery; and a parallel, which to be sure is drawn out into externals, is offered by the promise of the priest of Isis to Apuleius (XI 15): *nam in eos, quorum sibi vitas <in> servitium deae nostrae maiestas vindicavit, non habet locum casus infestus* (Isis governs even *fatum*; cf. XI 6, and even more XI 25; on the entire view cf. above, p. 322). Zosimos found the same view in lost Hermetic writings (*Poimandres*, pp. 102ff.), and he states that Hermes calls the natural men, who are unable to perceive with their sense anything suprasensual in themselves, ἄνοες and playthings of εἱμαρμένη;

301

according to him, however, the "philosophers" (on this designation of the Gnostic cf., for example, Asclepius, chapter 12: *philosophiae, quae sola est in cognoscenda divinitate frequens obtutus et sancta religio*) stand *above* εἱμαρμένη. So then he teaches: ὅτι οὐ δεῖ τὸν πνευματικὸν ἄνθρωπον τὸν ἐπιγνόντα ἑαυτὸν οὔτε διὰ μαγείας κατορθοῦν τι, ἐὰν καὶ καλὸν νομίζηται, μήτε βιάζεσθαι τὴν Ἀνάγκην, ἀλλ' ἐᾶν ὡς ἔχει φύσεως καὶ κρίσεως. πορεύεσθαι δὲ διὰ μόνου τοῦ ζητεῖν ἑαυτὸν καὶ θεὸν ἐπιγνόντα κρατεῖν ἀκατονόμαστον τριάδα, καὶ ἐᾶν τὴν εἱμαρμένην ὃ θέλει ποιεῖν τῷ ἑαυτῆς πηλῷ, τουτέστι τῷ σώματι. καὶ οὕτως, φησί, νοήσας καὶ πολιτευσάμενος θεάσῃ τὸν θεοῦ υἱὸν πάντα γινόμενον τῶν ὁσίων ψυχῶν ἕνεκεν, ἵνα αὐτὴν ἐκσπάσῃ ἐκ τοῦ χώρου τῆς εἱμαρμένης ἐπὶ τὸν ἀσώματον. Of this υἱὸς θεοῦ it is said that φωτίζει τὸν ἑκάστης νοῦν; he draws the νοῦς upward ὑπ' αὐτοῦ ὁδηγούμενον εἰς ἐκεῖνο τὸ φῶς. The idea, which likewise occurs in Iamblichus, περὶ μυστηρίων VIII 4-7 and X 5, 7, is attributed to an Egyptian prophet who had already earlier been mentioned by the elder Pliny (*Poimandres*, p. 107). In Zosimos of course the details are freely reworked, yet one feature in particular appears to correspond to the old idea, namely that the γνῶναι (or ἐπιγνῶναι) bestows a certain power. Thus Apuleius (Apol. 26) mentions, as the popular conception of the *magus*, who actually is the true priest (with others, such as Apollonius of Tyana, Ep. 16, 17, the ἀνὴρ θεῖος): *qui communione loquendi cum deis immortalibus ad omnia quae velit incredibili quadam vi cantaminum polleat.* He can inflict ruin upon whomever he will, and there is no protection at all against this *occulta et divina potentia.* Here this view is turned into a religious one. Similarly, in Corp. herm. I 32, the person who is blessed with γνῶσις acquires ἐξουσία. Further, in chapter XIII, the reborn person similarly acquires power over nature and in his prayer com-

02

mands the heavens, the earth, and the elements. It is evidently the same power that the magician gains through his assimilation to his god, and the rationale for it is naturally the same: the γνῶσις has made him a god: the τέλειος γνωστικός lives in the higher world as a god or as a part of the deity.

It is also the basic perspective of Christian Gnosticism, and it is so widely and generally disseminated that it is hardly possible to lift out specific details. Those πύλαι or θύραι τῆς γνώσεως we find again among the Naassenes, who assert of themselves as the τέλειοι γνωστικοί or πνευματικοί (Hippolytus 102. ις, 14 W.): καὶ ἐσμὲν ἐξ ἁπάντων ἀνθρώπων ἡμεῖς Χριστιανοὶ μόνοι ἐν τῇ τρίτῃ πύλῃ ἀπαρτίζοντες τὸ μυστήριον καὶ χριόμενοι ἐκεῖ ἀλάλῳ χρίσματι (it is Paul's third heaven, the πεδίον τῆς ἀληθείας of the Hermetic writings; the explanation is provided by the pagan celestial pilgrimages that I have collected in the appendices to the book on Poimandres). Then the Valentinians teach that Christ elevates those who are his out of the realm of εἱμαρμένη into the realm of his πρόνοια; they believe that even the prophesyings of the astrologers are applicable only until baptism (Exc. ex Theodoto 78), and regard the γνῶσις of what we were and what we have become to be effective along with baptism (*ibid.*; cf. above, p. 375; Corp. herm. XI 21); a transformation of nature, a μεταβολὴ ψυχῆς takes place (*ibid.*, 77); henceforth the soul is free of the ἀκάθαρτα πνεύματα, and indeed it has power over them. Then the Peratae teach (Hippolytus, p. 111.9 W.): ἡμεῖς οἱ τὴν ἀνάγκην τὴν γενέσεως ἐγνωκότες καὶ τὰς ὁδούς, δι' ὧν εἰσελήυθεν ὁ Ἄνθρωπος εἰς τὸν κόσμον ἀκριβῶς δεδιδαγμένοι, διελθεῖν καὶ περᾶσαι τὴν φθορὰν μόνοι δυνάμεθα (cf. above, p. 374). Then the Sethians teach (Hippolytus 124.2 W.): ἡμεῖς οἱ ἀναγεννώμενοι πνευματικοί, οὐ σαρκικοί, ὧν

ἐστι τὸ πολίτευμα ἐν οὐρανοῖς ἄνω (cf. Philo's reinterpretation, above, p. 308, and the strongly Hellenistically flavored passage Phil. 3:20). Whether in this connection it is γνῶσις alone that provides total detachment from the body (Iren. I 21.4), whether the ἐπιρρήματα of the mysteries must be combined with the γνῶσις (Epiphanius, haer. XXXI 7), or whether the liturgical action also is involved, are questions that do not affect the basic perspective. They are as inconsequential as whether a mystery itself brings one to perfection, or whether several--indeed, even 365 or 730--sacred actions serve to bring one together with an equal number of deities or archons, as with the Gnostics whom Epiphanius (haer. XXVI 9) describes:: every συνουσία with a *mystes* lifts them into a new Aion; they demand μίγηθι μετ' ἐμοῦ, ἵνα σε ἐνέγκω πρὸς τὸν ἄρχοντα; the συνίστασθαι θεῷ bestows the γνῶσις of God and along with it the μεταβολή of one's own being and the power of God (cf. *Hellenistische Wundererzählungen*, p. 53). The γνῶσις makes one a πνεῦμα, and the *mystes* becomes φύσει πνευματικός; cf. the teaching of the Valentinians in Irenaeus I 6.1: τὴν δὲ συντέλειαν ἔσεσθαι, ὅταν μορφωθῇ καὶ τελειωθῇ γνώσει πᾶν τὸ πνευματικόν, τουτέστιν οἱ πνευματικοὶ ἄνθρωποι οἱ τὴν τελείαν γνῶσιν ἔχοντες περὶ θεοῦ καὶ τῆς 'Αχαμώθ. μεμυημένους δὲ μυστήρια εἶναι τούτους ὑποτίθενται (Latin: *qui perfectam agnitionem habent de deo et hi qui ab Achamoth initiati sunt mysteria: esse autem hos semet ipsos dicunt*)... αὐτοὺς δὲ μὴ διὰ πράξεως, ἀλλὰ διὰ τὸ φύσει πνευματικοὺς εἶναι πάντη τε καὶ πάντως σωθήσεσθαι δογματίζουσιν. ὡς γὰρ τὸ χοϊκὸν ἀδύνατον σωτηρίας μετασχεῖν...οὕτως πάλιν τὸ πνευματικὸν ...ἀδύνατον φθορὰν καταδέξασθαι.[14] Thus the famous proclamation of Valentinus in Clement, Strom. IV 13.89 (p. 603 P = 287.9 Stählin) how the Gnostic has taken death upon himself, and in and through himself has destroyed it: ὅταν γὰρ τὸν

μὲν κόσμον λύητε (for the Gnostic it passes away with the σῶμα), ὑμεῖς[15] δὲ μὴ καταλύησθε, κυριεύετε τῆς κτίσεως καὶ τῆς φθορᾶς ἁπάσης (in the thought of Marcos also the γνῶσις θεοῦ makes one immortal; cf. Irenaeus I 15.2). This is to be understood directly in terms of the mystery of rebirth of the Hermetic writings.[16] It also immediately offers the explanation

304 of teachings like the doctrine of the Marcosians which Irenaeus relates with irony (I 13.6): τελείους ἑαυτοὺς ἀναγορεύοντες, ὡς μηδενὸς δυναμένου ἐξισωθῆναι τῷ μεγέθει τῆς γνώσεως αὐτῶν...ἀλλὰ πλείω πάντων ἐγνωκέναι καὶ τὸ μέγεθος τῆς γνώσεως τῆς ἀρρήτου δθνάμεως μόνους καταπεπωκέναι.[17] εἶναί τε αὐτοὺς ἐν ὕψει ὑπὲρ πᾶσαν δύναμιν· διὸ καὶ ἐλευθέρως πάντα πράσσειν μηδένα ἐν μηδενὶ φόβον ἔχοντας. διὰ γὰρ τὴν ἀπολύτρωσιν ἀκρατήτους καὶ ἀοράτους γίνεσθαι τῷ κριτῇ. Wherever the latter formula appears, which is closely connected with magical practice, the idea of the pneumatic substance underlies it, and everywhere we find the mystery-belief connected with it (e.g., Irenaeus, I 24.6).

But even when we leave the actually gnostic systems and turn to the ideas that are formed in the wider circles of Hellenistic communities, we find similar perspectives. I have earlier compared the passage on the Hermetic rebirth-mystery (XIII 3), ὁρᾷς με, ὦ τέκνον, ὀφθαλμοῖς, ὅτι δέ <εἰμι οὐ> κατανοεῖς ἀτενίζων σώματι καὶ ὁράσει, with the words of the portrayal of the mystery in the Acts of John (chapter 11) which Jesus speaks to his disciples: τίς εἰμι ἐγώ, γνώσῃ ὅταν ἀπέλθω. ὃ νῦν ὁρῶμαι, τοῦτο οὐκ εἰμί· <ὃ δέ εἰμι> ὄψει, ὅταν σὺ ἔλθῃς, that is, when you enter into the suprasensual world. The view that one enters into that world when one has lost all sexual feeling and with it also the sense of shame provides the explanation for the fragment of an apocryphal gospel (Oxyrhynchus Pap. 655; Preuschen, *Antilegomena*, second

edition, p. 26): λέγουσιν αὐτῷ οἱ μαθηταὶ αὐτοῦ· πότε ἡμῖν ἐμφανὴς ἔσῃ καὶ πότε σε ὀψόμεθα; λέγει· ὅταν ἐκδύσησθε καὶ μὴ αἰσχυνθῆτε. That fragment then in turn sheds light on the fragment of the Gospel of the Egyptians (Clement, Strom. III 13.92) in which Salome asks: πότε γνωσθήσεται τὰ περὶ ὧν ἤρετο, and receives the answer: ὅταν τὸ τῆς αἰσχύνης ἔνδυμα πατήσητε. I hope that I have demonstrated (*Hellenistische Wundererzählungen*, p. 68) that a mystery-conception (of the marriage of souls) underlies this view that strikes us as so strange. The theme is always a twofold vision, in a being that by its very nature is itself twofold, and the higher vision, wrought by the transformation of the nature of the person who has the vision, is called γνῶσις. It was very wrong to call in question precisely the crucial word in the Gospel of the Egyptians. It is true that philosophy since the time of Poseidonius appropriated these mystery-perspectives as *figures*, in order to offer itself to the educated Greek as a loftier substitute for the "religion of the barbarians", but it is impossible to derive Christian Gnosticism in its essence from that philosophy and to picture it as incidentally borrowing the usage of the mysteries and magic from the popular belief. Christian Gnosticism does not arise out of the *figures*, but out of the *essential* idea which is connected with magic; otherwise neither the language usage of γνῶσις and γνωστικός nor the identification of the latter term with πνευματικός would be comprehensible. The basic idea is that the γνῶσις θεοῦ renders one πνεῦμα, and it is an Oriental religious idea. Lexical research of course only confirms what Weingarten has already taught us, by way of allusion, in Sybel's *Histor. Zeitschrift* (N. F. IX, 1881, p. 460), about the "pagan mystery-character" of Gnosticism: nothing is more thoroughly wrong than to consider Gnosticism

as a first attempt at Christian philosophy or philosophy of religion, and indeed to view it at all in terms that are related to its theoretical elements.

R. Liechtenhan (*Die Offenbarung im Gnostizismus*, Göttingen 1901, pp. 98ff.) has offered the most thoroughgoing attempt to set forth what γνῶσις actually means. Of course he does this without any regard for the development of the usage, without any utilization of pagan and religio-historical material, and above all without any distinction between the concepts of old traditional and continuing revelation. The question of individualism in the total development is not even raised; though the vision is considered, the mystery as source of γνῶσις is not *adequately* noted. Nevertheless his painstaking collections can in many respects serve to confirm and to complement the previously gained knowledge. One may compare that major doctrinal writing of Marcos in Irenaeus I 14

306 with Corp. herm. I (the so-called Poimandres):[18] αὐτὴν τὴν πανυπερτάτην ἀπὸ τῶν ἀοράτων καὶ ακατονομάστων τόπων Τετράδα κατεληλυθέναι σχήματι γυναικείῳ πρὸς αὐτόν...καὶ μηνῦσαι, αὐτὴ τίς ἦν, καὶ τὴν τῶν πάντων γένεσιν, ἣν οὐδενὶ πώποτε οὔτε θεῶν οὔτε ἀνθρώπων ἀπεκάλυψεν. Even the revelation that follows agrees at first with the beginning of the Poimandres. We recognize the γνωστικός in the continuation (§3): ταῦτα δὲ σαφηνίσασαν αὐτῷ τὴν Τετρακτὺν εἰπεῖν· θέαν δή σοι καὶ αὐτὴν ἐπιδείξω τὴν 'Αλήθειαν. κατήγαγον γὰρ αὐτὴν ἐκ τῶν ὕπερθεν δωμάτων, ἵν' ἐσίδῃς αὐτὴν γυμνὴν καὶ καταμάθῃς τὸ κάλλος αὐτῆς καὶ ἀκούσῃς αὐτῆς λαλούσης κτλ. One may compare individual descriptions like that in §4: ταῦτα δὲ ταύτης εἰπούσης προσβλέψασαν αὐτῷ τὴν 'Αλήθειαν καὶ ἀνοίξασαν τὸ στόμα λαλῆσαι λόγον. Hippolytus (123.22 W.) testifies that Valentinus was preceded by an appearance of the Λόγος who suddenly appears before him as a newborn infant, is asked

who he is, replies that he is the Logos, and then relates a cosmogony (which is the τραγικὸς μῦθος; cf. Epiphanius XXXI 3: μυθοποιουμένη τραγῳδία). Unfortunately, we do not have either of the introductions, but we see that for these messages of the prophets to their communities in Christianity and paganism there was a common fixed form, which the Shepherd of Hermas also imitates, and we can now follow through Iran and India the basic idea, the elevation of one to the status of prophet through the vision of the world-deity and of the world's coming into being.[19] We may compare with the same writing of Marcos another writing of the Valentinians (Epiphanius XXXI 5.1), which began: Νοῦς ἀκατάργητος τοῖς ἀκαταργήτοις χαίρειν. ἀνονομάστων ἐγὼ καὶ ἀρρήτων καὶ ὑπερουρανίων μνείαν ποιοῦμαι μυστηρίων πρὸς ὑμᾶς, οὔτε ἀρχαῖς οὔτε ἐξουσίαις οὔτε ὑποταγαῖς οὔτε πάσῃ συγχύσει περινοηθῆναι δυναμένων, μόνῃ δὲ τῇ τοῦ 'Ατρέπτου 'Εννοίᾳ πεφανερομένων. In the introductory narrative as well as in the dry recitation of the names, the continuation of this writing corresponds to the writing of Marcos. The speaker here is not a human recipient of a revelation, but the πνεῦμα ἀθάνατον, who speaks to πνεύματα ἀθάνατα and labels men (6.1), in contrast to itself, the ἐπίγειοι.

307 It would be superfluous to heap up additional examples. Anyone who in spite of the pagan parallels chooses to see here nothing but figures and forms of speech without content will never be convinced; and anyone who fully senses the unusual character of the perspectives will conclude, even from Paul's declaration in I Cor. 15:51, ἰδοὺ μυστήριον ὑμῖν λέγω (cf. Rom. 11:25) and from his identifying himself as πνευματικός, what γνῶσις can be for him uniquely. As we saw earlier, he connected προφητεύειν and ἐν γνώσει λέγειν as fixed parts of the cult of the community (p. 380), and in-

terpreted προφητεύειν precisely as did the Hellenistic mystery communities (p. 300) among whom it was customary in worship. Was ἐν γνώσει λέγειν customary there also? One slight hint seems to suggest that. The apostle calls the member of the community who is not blessed with a χάρισμα an ἰδιώτης (I Cor. 14:23, 24), and in II Cor. 11:6 he speaks of himself as an ἰδιώτης τῷ λόγῳ, ἀλλ' οὐ τῇ γνώσει. The unusual usage would be explained immediately in Hellenistic communities, because in them every *mystes* is in principle a priest (on ἰδιώτης in contrast to the priest, e.g. the decree of Canopus, line 52). But I acknowledge that here other attempts at explanation also are possible.

Anyone who wants to try really to understand the peculiar strengthening and deepening of the belief in God in paganism from the time of Poseidonios down to Neo-Platonism, in its peculiarities and its sublimity, will especially delight in tracing out the development and the frequency of individual concepts and words. In that process Paul's store of language and imagery must necessarily acquire a special significance when it must be decided whether a conception arises out of philosophical or religious ideas. Plato, though perhaps influenced by Iranian feeling, still speaks as a philosopher (Theaet. 176 B) of a ὁμοίωσις with God. When Hierokles (Commentary on the χρυσᾶ ἔπη, Mullach, Fr. phil. graec. I 462, 467, and 463) speaks of it and thinks of it as being wrought by the vision of God or the γνῶσις τῶν ὄντων, mystery-conceptions underlie this, as Paul proves in II Cor. 3:18. Moreover, when in this very passage Paul speaks of a μεταμορφοῦσθαι in this connection, or when in Rom. 12:2 he offers the
308 admonition, μεταμορφοῦσθε τῇ ἀνακαινώσει τοῦ νοός, that proves, if our major thesis is correct, that Seneca, Ep. 6.1, is using a figure from the language of the mysteries, perhaps

appropriated from Poseidonios: *intellego, Lucili, non emendari me tantum, sed transfigurari. nec hoc promitto iam aut spero, nihil in me superesse, quod mutandum sit....hoc ipsum argumentum est in melius translati animi...cuperem itaque tecum communicare tam subitam mutationem mei.*[20] The original meaning of the figure is preserved here; in other passages (e.g., 94.48) it is weakened. The Greek words would be μεταμορφοῦσθαι, μεταβάλλεσθαι, and μετατίθεσθαι. A good bit more could be cited now, but for me the main concern at present is not the question of what the philologist can gain from an analysis of the Pauline store of language for the explanation of profane literature.

A detailed exploration of the word πνεῦμα would have to lead us much farther than the investigation of the concept γνῶσις. If we take paganism as our point of departure again, as is the only correct methodology, it is advisable to begin this time with the magical papyri, which repeatedly offer the word in the most widely diverse expressions.

It is said of *man*, in contrast to σῶμα, σκῆνος, σάρξ: Pap. Berol. I 177 (of the Parhedros): τελευτήσαντός σου τὸ σῶμα περιστελεῖ, ὡς πρέπον θεῷ, σοῦ δὲ τὸ πνεῦμα βαστάξας εἰς ἀέρα ἄξει σὺν ἑαυτῷ. εἰς γὰρ Ἅιδην οὐ χωρήσει ἀέριον πνεῦμα συσταθὲν κραταιῷ παρέδρῳ (while πνεῦμα ἀέριον here is the soul, immediately preceding this it is the Parhedros itself; cf. line 96: γινώσκεται ὅτι οὗτός ἐστιν ὁ θεός· πνεῦμά ἐστιν ἀέριον, ὃ εἶδες; line 49: ἀερίων πνευμάτων; cf. line 284: καὶ εὐθέως εἰσέρχεται τὸ θεῖον πνεῦμα; line 312: ὅπως ἂν πέμψωσί μοι τὸ θεῖον πνεῦμα). Wessely, Denkschr. d. K. K. Akad. 1888, p. 93, line 1948: δέομαι, δέσποτα ἥλιε, ἐπάκουσόν μου καὶ δός μοι...τὴν κατεξουσίαν (the magical power) τούτου τοῦ βιοθανάτου πνεύματος (the spirit, the ghost of the murdered one), οὗπερ ἀπὸ σκήνους κατέχω τὸ (Pap. τοῦ)

δεῖνα, ἵν' ἔχω αὐτὸν μετ' ἐμοῦ βοηθόν. *Ibid.*, p. 139, line 309 473, Kenyon, *Greek Papyri* I, p. 80: ἐπικαλοῦμαί σε τὸν κτίσαντα γῆν καὶ ὀστᾶ καὶ πᾶσαν σάρκα καὶ πᾶν πνεῦμα (soul). Cf. Wessely, *ibid.*, p. 83, line 1528: καῦσον αὐτῆς τὰ σπλάγχνα, τὸ στῆθος, τὸ ἧπαρ, τὸ πνεῦμα, τὰ ὀστᾶ, τοὺς μυελούς. When an offering is sacrificed to the deity, it is said of him that λαμβάνει πνεῦμα (Dieterich, *Abraxas* 170.16; 171.13).

The same usage, which evidently stems from an Oriental source, is transferred to the deity; cf. Wessely, *ibid.*, p. 120, line 2987: σὺ εἶ ἡ ψυχὴ τοῦ δαιμόνος τοῦ 'Οσίρεως[21] ἡ κωμάζουσα ἐν παντὶ τόπῳ, σὺ εἶ τὸ πνεῦμα τοῦ Ἄμμωνος (earlier, in 2983: σὺ εἶ ἡ καρδία τοῦ Ἑρμοῦ); cf. *ibid.*, p. 72, line 1133: χαίρετε πάντα ἀερίων εἰδώλων πνεύματα.

Related, but yet to be separated from this, is the use of πνεῦμα as a designation for deity in the case of indefinite and minor deities (like πνεῦμα δαιμόνιον), or in combinations like δαίμων ἢ πνεῦμα, and then in the address of specific deities as well: Pap. Lugd. V, Dieterich, *Jahrb. Supplem.* XVI, p. 803, line 34: εὐχαριστῶ σοι, ὅτι μοι [ἐφάνη] τὸ ἅγιον πνεῦμα, τὸ μονογενές, τὸ ζῶν; Wessely, *Denkschr.* 1888, p. 140, line 8: ἐπικαλοῦμαί σε, ἱερὸν πνεῦμα; *Denkschr.* 1893, p. 54, line 1029, Kenyon, p. 114: δεῦρό μοι, πυριλαμπὲς πνεῦμα; p. 39, line 568, Kenyon, p. 102: τὸ πνεῦμα τὸ ἀεροπετές; Dieterich, *Abraxas* 190.5, in the magic for raising the dead, for which in fact there are fixed directions: ὁρκίζω σε, πνεῦμα ἐν ἀέρι φοιτώμενον, εἴσελθε, ἐνπνευμάτωσον, δυνάμωσον, διαέγειρον τῇ δυνάμει τοῦ αἰωνίου θεοῦ τόδε σῶμα (cf. above, p. 391, Pap. Berol. I 177). As in the raising of the dead the deity enters into the corpse, so in the light-magic he enters into the fire; Wessely, *Denkschr.* 1888, p. 68, line 965: εἴσελθε ἐν τῷ πυρὶ τούτῳ καὶ ἐνπνευμάτωσον αὐτὸν (*sic*)

θείου πνεύματος καὶ δεῖξόν μοι σου τὴν ἀλκήν. God likewise comes as πνεῦμα into the living man; *ibid.*, p. 72, line 1115: χαῖρε, τὸ πᾶν σύστημα τοῦ ἀερίου πνεύματος, χαῖρε τὸ πνεῦμα τὸ διῆκον ἀπὸ οὐρανοῦ ἐπὶ γῆν καὶ ἀπὸ γῆς τῆς ἐν μέσῳ κύτει τοῦ κόσμου ἄχρι τῶν περάτων τῆς ἀβύσσου, χαῖρε, τὸ εἰσερχόμενόν με καὶ ἀντισπώμενόν μου καὶ χωριζόμενόν μου κατὰ θεοῦ βούλησιν ἐν χρηστότητι πνεῦμα. As the πνεῦμα within the world, although itself God, is distinguished from God, so it also appears as his instrument or his veil or his throne; Wessely 1888, p. 146, line 243: δεῦρό μοι ἐν τῇ ἁγίᾳ σου περιστροφῇ τοῦ ἁγίου πνεύματος, παντὸς κτίστα, θεῶν θεέ, τύραννε πανόσιε,· ὁ διαστήσας τὸν κόσμον τῷ σεαυτοῦ πνεύματι (cf. 1893, p. 64, line 10: τὸ περὶ σε ἔχον πνεῦμα, and Dieterich, *Jahrb. f. Phil.*, Supplem. XVI, p. 814.18 and 817. 21, as well as Kenyon, *Greek Pap.* I, p. 119, line 962, the designation for God ὁ ἐπὶ κενῷ πνεύματι, "who sits enthroned upon the 'empty air'", or Wessely, 1893, p. 54, line 1026, Kenyon, p. 114: ὁ ἐν τῷ στερεῷ πνεύματι, "who sits enthroned upon the 'solid air'", the wall around the κόσμος). The deity is for men πνευματοδώτης (Wessely, *Denkschr.* 1888, p. 79, line 1371), and one addresses him: ὄνομα σου καὶ πνεῦμά σου ἐπ' ἀγαθοῖς (Dieterich, *Abraxas* 196.19). It may be mentioned in passing also that the idea that the man thus blessed is a temple or house of the deity or the spirit and must therefore be pure both in body and in spirit already appears in magical practice; evidence of this is offered by Apuleius, Apoll. 43: *ut in eo...divina potestas quasi bonis aedibus digne diversetur*, with which we may compare the declamation of Arellius Fuscus on Kalchas (Seneca, suas. III 5): *"cur iste in[ter] eius ministerium placuit? cur hoc os deus elegit? cur hoc sortitur potissumum pectus, quod tanto numine impleat?"*

Especially characteristic of the entire idea is the prayer of the prophet Urbicus (Pap. Lugd. V, Dieterich, *Jahrb.*, Supplement XVI, p. 812, lines 12ff.), whose Oriental origin is exhibited in the still discernible psalm-like structure of the sentences and in the division of the formulas into four parts, an arrangement common in Egypt: ἠνοίγησαν αἱ πύλαι τοῦ οὐρανοῦ, ἠνοίγησαν αἱ πύλαι τῆς γῆς, ἠνοίγη ἡ ὅδευσις τῆς θαλάσσης, ἠνοίγη ἡ ὅδευσις τῶν ποταμῶν, ἠκούσθη μου τὸ πνεῦμα ὑπὸ πάντων θεῶν καὶ δαιμόνων. The universe is unlocked to the prayer of the *mystes* (cf. Corp. herm. XIII 17: πᾶσα φύσις κόσμου προσδεχέσθω τοῦ ὕμνου τὴν ἀκοήν. ἀνοίγηθι γῆ κτλ.). Here the word πνεῦμα denotes prayer, the (magically powerful) word, as with Eitrem, *Videnskapsselskapet Skrifter* II 1923, p. 34, line 276: τήνδε ἀξίωσιν <τὴν> λιτανίαν, τὴν προσύφωσιν (?), τὴν ἀναφορὰν τοῦ πνεύματος τοῦ λεκτικοῦ. The deity, who is πνεῦμα, has heard his πνεῦμα. This is stated in strictly corre-

311 sponding phrases: ἠκούσθη μου τὸ πνεῦμα ὑπὸ πνεύματος οὐρανίου, ἠκούσθη μου τὸ πνεῦμα ὑπὸ πνεύματος ἐπιγείου, ἠκόυσθη μου τὸ πνεῦμα ὑπὸ πνεύματος θαλασσίου, ἠκούσθη μου τὸ πνεῦμα ὑπὸ πνεύματος ποταμίου (the genitive πνεύματος each time denotes the totality of the divine beings who reside in this part of the world). Since they have heard his word, they now are to bestow on him their power: δότε οὖν πνεῦμα τῷ ὑπ' ἐμοῦ κατεσχευασμένῳ μυστηρίῳ, θεοί, οὓς (Pap. θεοὺς) ὠνόμασα καὶ ἐπικέκλημαι, δότε πνοὴν τῷ ὑπ' ἐμοῦ κατασχευασμένῳ μυστηρίῳ (the instrument of magic). In similar passages, we find δὸς δύναμιν used in place of δότε πνεῦμα, and πνεῦμα and δύναμις appear as completely synonymous, even where they denote divine beings. The sensory meaning of πνεῦμα becomes particularly clear here in its being appropriated through πνοή; the deity bestows life and power by means of breathing upon one.

The adjectival form πνευματικός is also found, of course as is the corresponding form ψυχικός in only one passage, in the technical meaning of suprasensual (as only the πνεῦμα can be), and thus essentially in a purely "gnostic" usage; Eros (Harpocrates) is addressed (Wessely, *Denkschr.* 1888, p. 89, line 1778) as πάσης πνευματικῆς αἰσθήσεως κρυφίων πάντων ἄναξ (one can perceive the mysteries of God only with the πνευματικὴ αἴσθησις; the counterpart to this is found in Corp. herm. XIII 6, where it speaks of an αἰσθητῶς νοεῖν of the suprasensual).

Underlying here is a language usage that labels the invisible life-force within us the πνεῦμα (air in motion); its likeness to the invisible power above us (God) is strongly felt; as the Pneuma in us appears in contrast to the σῶμα, so the πνεῦμα in general appears as the suprasensual in contrast to the sensual.

The underlying idea recurs among many peoples (one may think of the *animus* or *anima*, or the development of the concept of *atman* in Indian thought), and of course it is not foreign to Greek thought; here also in ancient times πνεῦμα is found for "soul" (cf. Rohde, *Psyche*, third edition, II 258.3); but the ἄνω τὸ πνεῦμα διαμένει κατ' οὐρανόν (Epicharm fr. 265 Kaibel, cf. Euripides Suppl. 533) quickly becomes the αἰθὴρ μὲν ψυχὰς ὑπεδέξατο, σώματα δὲ χθών. It is well known
2 that the Stoa regarded the πνεῦμα as the *substance of the soul*; strictly speaking, it is the preliminary stage of the ψυχή, and birth is a μεταβολὴ τοῦ πνεύματος εἰς ψυχήν, yet the usage also is quite flexible; an Epictetus may ask (II 1.17): θάνατος τί ἐστι;...τὸ σωμάτιον δεῖ χωρισθῆναι τοῦ πνευματίου, ὡς πρότερον ἐκεχώριστο (cf. Epicharm fr. 245 Kaibel). But that would hardly suffice to account for the Hellenistic language usage which I have traced out above.

Philosophy does not exert any significant influence, but rather an Oriental usage. Nevertheless it is noteworthy that all the passages in Paul can be explained in terms of the Hellenistic usage (and particularly those in which it cannot at all be determined whether he is speaking of the πνεῦμα of man or of a divine πνεῦμα, as for example in I Cor. 5:4, 5). The theologian will have to decide whether *all* of them can just as easily be understood from the Hebrew usage of *ruach* and *nephesh* or from the usage of πνεῦμα in the Septuagint. If I see it correctly, the observation of Paul's relative independence of any influence from the Septuagint (Deissmann, *Die neutestamentliche Formel "in Christo Jesu"*, pp. 66-67) applies not only in a syntactical respect, but also quite often in a lexical respect as well; only one must, in order to render this discernible, keep in view the pagan literary circles whose language can be similar.

Magic and mystery have still preserved in its simplicity the ancient and in part universally human conception. When the Mithras-*mystes* wishes to behold God by means of the πνεῦμα and is supposed to breathe, in him, the ἱερὸν πνεῦμα, the first prescription is: ἕλκε ἀπὸ τῶν ἀκτίνων πνεῦμα τρὶς ἀνασπῶν, ὃ δύνασαι, καὶ ὄψει σεαυτὸν ἀνακουφιζόμενον καὶ ὑπερβαίνοντα εἰς ὕψος, ὥστε σε δοκεῖν μέσον τοῦ ἀέρος εἶναι; the θεία θέα follows, as in mantic practice it regularly follows the breathing-in of the flames of the altar (cf., e.g., Statius Achilleis I 520ff.). The further idea that every deceased person becomes πνεῦμα and every πνεῦμα has miraculous knowledge and power is also well known from mantic practice. From folk theology I cite the imitation of an originally edifying vision of Hades in the alchemist Zosimos (Berthelot, *Les alchimistes grecs*, pp. 107ff.). In a dream he sees a high altar, with a flight of steps leading up to it and an-

3 other flight leading down from it (similar is the idea of heaven in the Mandaean book Dinanukht: man must ascend a number of steps, as in the Mithraic initiation in the familiar portrayal by Celsus, Origen, VI 22). A man who stands at the upper border, Ion, as Zosimos later learns, (Bernh. Karle conjectures Αἰών) ὁ ἱερεὺς τῶν ἀδύτων, proclaims (p. 108.5): πεπλήρωκα τὸ κατιέναι με ταύτας τὰς δεκαπέντε σκοτοφεγγεῖς κλίμακας καὶ ἀνείναι με τὰς φωτολαμπεῖς κλίμακας (similarly in the Isis mysteries *et passim*), καὶ ἔστιν ὁ ἱερουργῶν καὶ καινουργῶν με· ἀποβαλλόμενος τὴν τοῦ σώματος παχύτητα καὶ ἐξ ἀνάγκης ἱερατευόμενος πνεῦμα τελοῦμαι. In a later vision Zosimos himself has ascended the steps and beholds in the cavity of the altar boiling water, and men in it; he is instructed by a guide (p. 109.9): αὕτη ἡ θέα, ἣν ὁρᾷς, εἴσοδός ἐστι καὶ ἔξοδος καὶ μεταβολή. It is, as he learns in response to further questions (p. 109.12), the τόπος τῆς ἀσκήσεως: οἱ γὰρ θέλοντες ἄνθρωποι ἀρετῆς τυχεῖν ὧδε εἰσέρχονται καὶ γίνονται πνεύματα φυγόντες τὸ σῶμα. One becomes this only through a painful transformation (cf. 108.17): ἕως ἄν ἔμαθον μετασωματούμενος πνεῦμα γενέσθαι. He asks his guide: καὶ σὺ πνεῦμα εἶ; and receives the answer, καὶ πνεῦμα καὶ φύλαξ πνευμάτων. Zosimos also experiences this detachment from his body and then hears that therewith he has achieved the descent on the steps (to Hades, and necessarily also the ascent), and thereby has become τέλειος; a divine voice sounds forth: ἡ τέχνη πεπλήρωται.

The indication in the detailed statement of the chemical processes in images drawn from the language of the mysteries has its counterpart in many other writings; again and again the πνεῦμα or ψυχή is separated from the σῶμα of a material, or σῶμα, ψυχή, and πνεῦμα are mentioned side by side, and of course we also encounter the σῶμα πνευματικόν and other con-

cepts of Hellenistic mysticism, as for example δόξα. Especially clear is the origin in the purported instruction of a queen Cleopatra[22] to the philosophers (alchemists), a writing which once introduced the earliest anthology of alchemistic literature and was translated *from the Aramaic* by an Egyptian-Greek editor. I have published it in the *Nachrichten der Gesellschaft der Wissenschaften*, Göttingen, 1919, pp. 1ff. (in Berthelot, *op. cit.*, 293.3-298.9). Presupposed everywhere are the mysteries of rebirth or resurrection (awakening), in part with a very close resemblance to Iranian formulas which are preserved in Mandaean or Manichaean texts. One should compare questions like p. 292.18: πῶς κατέρχονται τὰ ὕδατα τὰ εὐλογημένα τοῦ ἐπισκέψασθαι τοὺς νεκροὺς παρειμένους καὶ πεπεδημένους καὶ τεθλιμμένους ἐν σκότῳ καὶ γνόφῳ ἐντὸς τοῦ Ἅιδου, καὶ πῶς εἰσέρχεται τὸ φάρμακον τῆς ζωῆς καὶ ἀφυπνίζει αὐτοὺς ὡς ἐξ ὕπνου ἐγερθῆναι, and portrayals like that in 293.16: ὅταν δὲ ἐνδύσωνται τὴν δόξαν ἐκ τοῦ πυρὸς καὶ τὴν χροιὰν τὴν περιφανῆ, ἐκεῖ ὁράσεις μείζονες, ἐκεῖ δόξα κεκρυμμένη, τὸ σπουδαζόμενον κάλλος καὶ χοότης μεταβληθεῖσα εἰς θεότητα; 296.14: τότε φωτίζεται τὸ σῶμα καὶ χαίρεται ἡ ψυχὴ καὶ τὸ πνεῦμα ὅτι (Ms. ὅτε) ἀπέδρα τὸ σκότος ἀπὸ τοῦ σώματος καὶ καλεῖ ἡ ψυχὴ τὸ σῶμα τὸ πεφωτισμένον· Ἔγειραι ἐξ Ἅιδου καὶ ἀνάστηθι ἐκ τοῦ τάφου καὶ ἐξεργήθητι ἐκ τοῦ σκότους· ἐνδέδυσαι γὰρ πνευμάτωσιν καὶ θείωσιν, ἐπειδὴ ἔφθακεν καὶ ἡ φωνὴ τῆς ἀναστάσεως καὶ τὸ φάρμακον τῆς ζωῆς εἰσῆλθεν πρὸς σέ. τὸ γὰρ πνεῦμα πάλιν εὐφραίνεται ἐν τῷ σώματι [καὶ ἡ ψυχὴ ἐν ᾧ ἐστιν] καὶ τρέχει κατεπεῖγον ἐν χαρᾷ εἰς τὸν ἀσπασμὸν αὐτοῦ καὶ ἀσπάζεται αὐτό. καὶ οὐ κατακυριεύει αὐτοῦ σκότος, ἐπειδὴ ὑπέστη <πλῆρες> φωτός, καὶ οὐκ ἀνέχεται αὐτοῦ χωρισθῆναι ἔτι εἰς τὸν αἰῶνα. καὶ <ἡ ψυχὴ> χαίρεται ἐν τῷ οἴκῳ αὐτῆς, <ἐν ᾧ ἐστιν>, ὅτι καταλιποῦσα (Ms. καλύπτουσα) αὐτὸ ἐν σκότει εὗρεν αὐτὸ πεπλησμένον φωτός, καὶ ἡνώθη αὐτῷ, ἐπειδὴ θεῖον γέγονεν κατ' αὐτήν, καὶ οἰκεῖ ἐν

314

αὐτῷ (Ms. αὐτῇ)· ἐνδύσατο γὰρ θεότητος φῶς [καὶ ἡνώθησαν] καὶ ἀπέδρα ἀπ' αὐτοῦ τὸ σκότος. καὶ ἡνώθησαν πάντες ἐν ἀγάπῃ, τὸ σῶμα καὶ ἡ ψυχὴ καὶ τὸ πνεῦμα καὶ γεγόνασιν ἕν. It should be noted how in this pagan portrayal of a mystery a division of man into three parts, into body, soul, and spirit, is an underlying assumption, which recurs in the Mandaean religion as well as in many passages in Paul. Philo (De vita Moys. II 288; see above, p. 343) has the same view of deification. Comparable also is 297.8: τὸ γὰρ πῦρ αὐτοὺς ἥνωσεν καὶ μετέβαλεν, καὶ ἐκ τοῦ κόλπου τῆς γαστρὸς αὐτοῦ
15 ἐξῆλθον--ὁμοίως (Ms. ὅμως) καὶ ἐκ τῆς γαστρὸς τῶν ὑδάτων καὶ ἐκ τοῦ ἀέρος τοῦ διακονοῦντος αὐτοῖς--[23] καὶ αὐτὸ ἐξήνεγκεν αὐτοὺς ἐκ τοῦ σκότους εἰς φῶς καὶ ἐκ πένθους εἰς φαιδρότητα καὶ ἐξ ἀσθενείας εἰς ὑγείαν καὶ ἐκ θανάτου εἰς ζωήν, καὶ ἐνέδυσεν αὐτοὺς θείαν δόξαν πνευματικήν, ἣν οὐκ ἐνδιδύσκοντο τὸ πρίν (cf. I Cor. 15:42, 43), ὅτι ἐν αὐτοῖς (the three elements) κέκρυπται ὅλον τὸ μυστήριον καὶ <το> θεῖον ἀναλλοίωτον ὑπάρχει. διὰ γὰρ τῆς ἀνδρείας αὐτῶν συνεισέρχονται ἀλλήλοις τὰ σώματα <καὶ> ἐξερχόμενα ἐκ τῆς γῆς ἐνδύονται φῶς καὶ δόξαν θείαν, ἐπειδὴ ηὐξήθησαν κατὰ φύσιν καὶ ἠλλοιώθησαν τοῖς σχήμασι καὶ ἐξ ὕπνου ἀνέστησαν καὶ ἐκ τοῦ ῞Αιδου ἐξῆλθον. ἡ γαστὴρ γὰρ ἡ τοῦ πυρὸς ἔτεκεν αὐτοὺς (for αὐτὰ) καὶ ἐξ αὐτῆς ἐνεδύσαντο δόξαν καὶ αὕτη ἤνεγκεν εἰς ἑνότητα μίαν καὶ ἐτελειώθη ἡ εἰκὼν σώματι καὶ ψυχῇ καὶ πνεύματι καὶ ἐγένοντο ἕν. The resurrection is a rebirth from God. The concept of the image (namely of the divine primal man) plays a major role among the Mandaeans and Manichaeans. I shall return later to the distinctive usage of the word δόξα, which Paul therefore does not at all merely borrow from the Septuagint and which therefore he himself must have developed. I know of no text that would have a closer lexical affinity with the mystical passages in

Paul than these parabolic discourses of a text of which I have given a few examples here, a text which unfortunately is in substance incomprehensible to me, but which certainly is purely pagan.

The task would be both attractive and rewarding for a chemist who is schooled in the history of religions, but for me the task of explaining the figurative language of the alchemistic tradition in terms of the mysteries is too difficult; therefore I shall limit myself to the basic perspectives of the vision of Zosimos and to the introduction. In any case the prototype was a popular theological narrative of the τόπος κολάσεως, where men will be detached from their bodies and thus become πνεύματα, i.e., at first only souls; transplanted into this narrative is the idea from the mysteries that through a kind of voluntary death or of ἄσκησις the τέλειος will become πνεῦμα (here in the higher sense, a kind of θεῖον πνεῦμα). This idea is not foreign to us. When Apollonius even after his death wishes to remain among the "Hellenes" and to participate in their sacrifices and assemblies (*Hellenistische Wundererzählungen*, pp. 49, 50), a certain point of contact for this idea is offered in very early Greek perspectives, but in any case an even stronger influence is exerted by the newer mystical perspective that the θεῖος ἄνθρωπος or πνευματικός remains as πνεῦμα with those who belong to him. The question perhaps may be posed as to whether there is any sort of connection between these ideas of Pneuma and that mystical literature that in late Judaism is connected with the names of earlier prophets and θεῖοι ἄνδρες. Yet I prefer at first not to pursue it into the area of great literature, but for the present to stay in the area of popular discourse and perspective. As my last example I choose the portrayal of Phoenician and Palestinian prophets which Celsus claims (in Origen, VII 9)

316

to give from his own personal knowledge: each one says, ἐγὼ ὁ θεός εἰμι, ἢ θεοῦ παῖς, ἢ πνεῦμα θεῖον. These words certainly are a lively reminder of the words of the Montanist prophetess Maximilla (Eusebius, HE V 16.17; p. 466.20 Schwartz): "ῥῆμά εἰμι καὶ πνεῦμα καὶ δύναμις", but there is nothing to justify the assumption that Celsus intends to be describing Montanists (cf. also *Poimandres*, p. 222). Mandaean and other purely pagan texts also speak in similar ways. The instructive statements offered by G. P. Wetter in his book *Der Sohn Gottes* (FRLANT, NF IX, Göttingen 1916) may be significantly expanded. Basic perspective and use of language are alike with the Christian and the pagan. We must break the habit of seeking and observing the "effects of the Spirit" exclusively among Christians and of thinking of Christian or Jewish sources at every mention of a θεῖον, ἱερόν or ἅγιον πνεῦμα. There must be few assertions that in spite of their far-reaching consequences are so thoughtlessly or so groundlessly made as the thesis, still championed by Cremer in 1899, that the concepts πνεῦμα θεοῦ or πνεῦμα ἀνθρώπου are exclusively biblical (Hauck, *Realenzyklop.*, third edition, VI, pp. 444, 454, 457; cf. now H. Leisegang, *Der heilige Geist*).

The construction in language and concept, comprehensible in and of itself, now passes, by way of the mystery religions,
7 into a thought-circle in which an entirely different conception of the human ψυχή was gradually developed and became securely fixed thanks to philosophy. It is obvious that thoroughgoing lexical investigations here would be bound to let us trace out to some degree the struggle between two intellectual worlds and to discern the ascendancy of the one or the other, but all the preliminary labors for such study are yet lacking; I too am able only to offer a couple of isolated comments. It will be clear from the outset that the new ter-

minology is able at least to prevail in philosophical language.

Perhaps Philo provides the evidence. It is true that he is familiar with the concept πνεῦμα also as referring to the divine spirit that descends upon man,--that was to be expected, following the basic view of Judaism and Philo's relationship to the Septuagint, and in fact the word is found now and then, as for example in De somniis II 38 (p. 692 M. = 252 Wendland): ὑπηχεῖ δέ μοι πάλιν τὸ εἰωθὸς ἀφανῶς ἐνομιλεῖν πνεῦμα ἀόρατον. However, where it applies, he avoids it and replaces it with purely Greek expressions. He also is familiar with the two classes of men, the γνωστικοί or πνευματικοί and the ψυχικοί, as is to be expected in the light of his relationship to the mystery-perspectives; but he avoids those technical terms; cf., e.g., Quod deus sit immutabilis 11 (p. 218 M. = 55 Wendland): οἱ μὲν ψυχῆς, οἱ δὲ σώματος γεγόνασι φίλοι. οἱ μὲν οὖν ψυχῆς ἑταῖροι νοηταῖς καὶ ἀσωμάτοις φύσεσιν ἐνομιλεῖν δυνάμενοι...οἱ δὲ συμβάσεις καὶ σπονδὰς πρὸς σῶμα θέμενοι ἀδυνατοῦντες ἀπαμφιάσασθαι τὸ σαρκῶν περίβλημα. For him those are the ὁρατικοὶ ἄνδρες, and thus a class of men closely corresponding to the γνωστικοί; for the γνῶσις θεοῦ is for him also essentially θέα, and the φιλοθεάμονες ἄνδρες, as it is said in another passage (De somniis II 41, p. 694 M. = 271 Wendl.), are the true priests; the τέλειος--he even uses the technical term--is the μέγας ἱερεύς who enters the ἄδυτον, and as long as he remains there, he is no longer a man, though of course for the devout Jew also not entirely God (De somniis II 34, 35, 28; p. 689, 690, 684 M. = 230-34, 189 Wendl.). I need only to recall the ἱερεὺς τῶν ἀδύτων in the vision of Zosimos. Finally, the "true magic", which Philo as well as Apuleius, Apol. 25 (probably following Poseidonios) appears to regard as a kind of priesthood, is for him an ὀπτικὴ ἐπι-

318

στήμη (De spec. leg. III 18; p. 316 M. = III 100 Cohn). The word is characteristic; Plato had spoken of a γνωστικὴ ἐπιστήμη in the Sophists, and γνῶσις and ἀγνωσία had already begun, with him, to assume a technical connotation, but that connotation arises out of the contrast with πρᾶξις and embraces only conceptual knowledge; this probably was the reason that Philo avoided the words offered to him with a different meaning by the mystery-language and substituted expressions of a sacral character that were less subject to misunderstanding. Now it is the ὁρατικοί--this cannot be stressed emphatically enough--who in Philo's thought practice allegorical exposition, and they are to be the only ones practicing it; cf. De plant. 9 (p. 335 M. = 36 Wendl.): ἰτέον οὖν ἐπ' ἀλληγορίαν τὴν ὁρατικοῖς φίλην ἀνδράσιν or De Abrah. 36 (p. 29 M. = 200 Cohn): ἀλλὰ γὰρ οὐκ ἐπὶ τῆς ῥητῆς καὶ φανερᾶς ἀποδόσεως ἵσταται τὰ λεχθέντα, φύσιν δὲ τοῖς πολλοῖς ἀδηλοτέραν ἔοικε παρεμφαίνειν, ἣν οἱ τὰ νοητὰ πρὸ τῶν αἰσθητῶν ἀποδεχόμενοι καὶ ὁρᾶν δυνάμενοι γνωρίζουσιν. Cf. *ibid.*, 41 (p. 34 M. = 236 Cohn): ἀσώματα δὲ ὅσοι καὶ γυμνὰ θεωρεῖν τὰ πράγματα δύνανται, οἱ ψυχῇ μᾶλλον ἢ σώματι ζῶντες. It seems to me particularly clear here that the γνωστικοί are meant here; he calls them ὁρατικοί because the figure, common also in the Hermetic writings, of the eye of the heart or of the spirit is a special favorite of his; cf., e.g., De Abrah. 12 (p. 9 M. = 57 Cohn): ὅρασις ἡ μὲν δι' ὀφθαλμῶν...ἡ δὲ διὰ τοῦ τῆς ψυχῆς ἡγεμονικοῦ; 15 (p. 12 M. = 70 Cohn): διοίξας τὸ τῆς ψυχῆς ὄμμα; 17 (p. 13 M. = 78 Cohn): ἡ διάνοια τότε πρῶτον ἀναβλέψασα εἶδε; 18 (p. 13 M. = 84 Cohn): ὁ σοφὸς ἀκριβεστέροις ὄμμασιν ἰδών τι τελεώτερον νοητόν; 24 (p. 19 M. = 122 Cohn): ἡ ὁρατικὴ διάνοια; 31 (p. 24 M. = 162 Cohn): the διάνοια takes ὄψις as its starting-point for σκέψις, ὅρασις becomes the beginning of σοφία and is elevated to the θέα of the imperishable, τὸν

σύμπαντα οὐρανὸν καὶ κόσμον γλιχομένη θεάσασθαι (cf. the Poimandres). The expressions are philosophically colored, and indeed often the ideas themselves, but basically what is involved is always γνῶσις, not philosophy. Thus for him the 319 literal sense is the σῶμα, and the secret meaning is the ψυχή of the Scripture; cf. De vita contempl. 10 (p. 483 M. = 78 Cohn): ἅπασα γὰρ ἡ νομοθεσία δοκεῖ τοῖς ἀνδράσι τούτοις (the Therapeutae) ἐοικέναι ζῴῳ, καὶ σῶμα μὲν ἔχειν τὰς ῥητὰς διατάξεις, ψυχὴν δὲ τὸν ἐναποκείμενον ταῖς λέξεσιν ἀορατὸν νοῦν, ἐν ᾧ ἤρξατο ἡ λογικὴ ψυχὴ διαφερόντως τὰ οἰκεῖα θεωρεῖν ὥσπερ διὰ κατόπτρου τῶν ὀνομάτων, ἐξαίσια κάλλη νοημάτων ἐμφερόμενα κατιδοῦσα καὶ τὰ μὲν σύμβολα διαπρύξασα καὶ διακαλύψασα, γυμνὰ δὲ εἰς φῶς προαγαγοῦσα τὰ ἐνθύμια τοῖς δυναμένοις ἐκ μικρᾶς ὑπομνήσεως τὰ ἀφανῆ διὰ τῶν φανερῶν θεωρεῖν. The comparison of the text with the image in a mirror appears earlier and may already have exerted an influence on Paul (I Cor. 13:12: δι' ἐσόπτρου ἐν αἰνίγματι) through another intermediary. In fact, he too speaks of γνωσις.

The Gnostic Ptolemaeus--to mention this only in passing--in his letter to Flora also labels the literal sense τὸ σωματικόν or τὸ φαινόμενον, and the secret meaning τὸ πνευματικόν. With him there still is no mention of "pneumatic exposition", but that general designation τὸ πνευματικόν arises out of expressions like ἡ κατὰ τὸ φαινόμενον νηστεία or ἡ σωματικὴ νηστεία with which ἡ πνευματικὴ νηστεία (among the Mandaeans the "major" fast), ἡ πνευματικὴ καρδία, and the like are contrasted. This is essentially nothing more than an extension of Paul's πνευματικὸν βρῶμα, πνευματικὸν πόμα (I Cor. 10:3, 4). In the same passage, under the impetus provided by these words, Paul describes Christ as πνευματικὴ πέτρα. This leads then to further expansions such as Ignatius offers in πνευματικὸς στέφανος, πνευματικαὶ μαργαρῖται (somewhat differently the

Epistle of Barnabas, πνευματικὸς ναός, and II Clement, πνευματικὴ ἐκκλησία). Rev. 11:8, τῆς πόλεως τῆς μεγάλης, ἥτις καλεῖται πνευματικῶς Σόδομα καὶ Αἴγυπτος, is to be altogether distinguished from these, since here πνευματικῶς apparently means "in the language of the πνευματικοί and of the πνεῦμα", that is, prophecy. If we add the fact that Ptolemaeus also speaks of an ὄμμα ψυχῆς, it is clear that he is entirely in agreement with Philo, only he has preserved the concept πνεῦμα for ψυχή. For him also the justification of allegory lies in the fact that it is discovered by the ὁρατικός or τέλειος; otherwise it would be a bit of arbitrary interpretation.

Perhaps most instructive in a lexical regard is the familiar passage in Philo's De migr. Abrah. 16 (p. 450 M. = 89 Wendl.): εἰσὶ γάρ τινες οἳ τοὺς ῥητοὺς νόμους σύμβολα νοητῶν πραγμάτων ὑπολαμβάνοντες τὰ μὲν ἄγαν ἠκρίβωσαν, τῶν δὲ ῥᾳθύμως ὠλιγώρησαν...νυνὶ δ' ὥσπερ ἐν ἐρημίᾳ καθ' ἑαυτοὺς μόνοι ζῶντες ἢ ἀσώματοι ψυχαὶ γεγονότες (cf. Ignatius Smyrn. 2: οὖσιν ἀσωμάτοις καὶ δαιμονικοῖς; the ones being attacked themselves would have said πνεύμασιν or πνευματικοῖς) καὶ μήτε πόλιν μήτε κώμην μήτ' οἰκίαν μήτε συνόλως θίασον ἀνθρώπων εἰδότες, τὰ δοκοῦντα τοῖς πολλοῖς ὑπερκύψαντες, τὴν ἀλήθειαν γυμνὴν αὐτὴν ἐφ' ἑαυτῆς ἐρευνῶσιν (cf. Marcos, above, p. 388) ...μηδ' ὅτι ἡ ἑορτὴ σύμβολον ψυχικῆς εὐφροσύνης ἐστὶ καὶ τῆς πρὸς θεὸν εὐχαριστίας, ἀποταξώμεθα ταῖς κατὰ τὰς ἐτησίους ὥρας πανηγύρεσι· μηδ' ὅτι τὸ περιτέμνεσθαι ἡδονῆς καὶ παθῶν πάντων ἐκτομὴν καὶ δόξης ἀναίρεσιν ἀσεβοῦς ἐμφαίνει, καθ' ἣν ὑπέλαβεν ὁ νοῦς ἱκανὸς εἶναι γεννᾶν δι' ἑαυτοῦ, ἀνέλωμεν τὸν ἐπὶ τῇ περιτομῇ τεθέντα νόμον. ἐπεὶ καὶ τῆς περὶ τὸ ἱερὸν ἁγιστείας καὶ μυρίων ἄλλων ἀμελήσομεν, εἰ μόνοις προσέξομεν τοῖς δι' ὑπονοιῶν δηλουμένοις· ἀλλὰ χρὴ ταῦτα μὲν σώματι ἐοικέναι νομίζειν, ψυχῇ δὲ ἐκεῖνα· ὥσπερ οὖν σώματος, ἐπειδὴ ψυχῆς ἐστιν οἶκος, προνοητέον, οὕτω καὶ τῶν ῥητῶν νόμων ἐπιμελητέον. The

separation of σῶμα and ψυχή is so surprisingly inserted into the ideas of a *naturalis* and a *civilis theologia*, following Poseidonios (cf. Agahd, M. Terenti Varronis antiqu. rer. div. libri, in *Jahrb. f. Phil.* Suppl. XXIV, pp. 143ff., and Philo's conclusion, c. 17, §95: ἐκεῖνα μὲν οὖν ἔοικε τοῖς φύσει, ταῦτα δὲ τοῖς θέσει νομίμοις), and the portrayal of the utterly individualistic tendency of the Pneumatics is so fitting, that I do not doubt that Philo was familiar with the expression (for them it would be πνεύματα γεγονότες; cf. also p. 308, above, on the Therapeutae). But the concept of the ψυχή as the spiritual and divine element in man had become too well established and dominant for him to have been able to adopt that terminology. While Paul moreover speaks of πνευματικὰ σώματα and compares the most mature to the sun, we have already seen (above, p. 343) that Philo has his Moses transformed out of the duality of body and soul into a unitary νοῦς ἡλιοειδέστατος. Here also it appears to me that the concept πνεῦμα has been

321 transferred into the philosophical language. Yet when Hierocles (Mullach, Frgm. philos. graec. I 479) speaks of ψυχικὸν σῶμα, he does not at all mean what Paul means by πνευματικὸν σῶμα; it is rather the ethereal body, the πνευματικόν or αὐγοειδὲς ὄχημα of the Neo-Platonists (cf., e.g., Zeller III 2^4, p. 714); but the context in Hierocles, who regards the mysteries as a cleansing and purification of the ψυχικὸν σῶμα, shows that the concept has been transferred from the language of the mysteries into philosophical language; of course the Stoic assimilation of πνεῦμα and ψυχή also functioned here.

Under the influence of Plato, poets and orators quite early began to imitate the religious language; apart from that language, Horace (Od. IV 6.29) would be incomprehensible: *spiritum Phoebus mihi, Phoebus artem carminis nomenque dedit poetae*; here τὸ πνεῦμα is the *ingenium* alongside the *ars*, the

πνεῦμα θεοῦ; in II 16.38, *mihi parva rura et spiritum Graiae tenuem camenae Parca non mendax dedit*, the πνεῦμα λεπτόν is is already a paled concept, "the pale spirit of Greek poetry". In II 20.1, 2, *non usitata nec tenui ferar penna biformis per liquidum aethera vates*, the concept of the προφήτης (ὁ ἔχων τὸ πνεῦμα) is connected with the hope even of a personal survival and life hereafter that is denied to all others; because Horace is *vates*, he is δίζωος and has two σώματα (cf. *Neue Jahrb. f. d. Altertumswissenschaft* 21. 99). The expression changes in its value according to the level of the mood, and sometimes it assumes a profoundly religious tone, while at other times it sinks to the level of a conventional formula.

From the territory of the Greek language I select Pseudo-Longinos, to whom my colleague Bruno Keil has called my attention. It is characteristic that, of the four examples, two have been contested by eminent specialists in the Greek language. Of the two that are not disputed, one is 13.2 (p. 30. 20 Vahlen, third edition): πολλοὶ γὰρ ἀλλοτρίῳ θεοφοροῦνται πνεύματι τὸν αὐτὸν τρόπον, ὅν καὶ τὴν Πυθίαν λόγος ἔχει τρίποδι πλησιάζουσαν, ἔνθα ῥῆγμά ἐστι γῆς ἀναπνεῖν ὥς (ὅ) φασιν ἀτμὸν ἔνθεον, αὐτόθεν ἐγκύμονα τῆς δαιμονίου καθισταμένην δυνάμεως παραυτίκα χρησμῳδεῖν κατ' ἐπίπνοιαν, οὕτως ἀπὸ τῆς τῶν ἀρχαίων μεγαλοφυίας εἰς τὰς τῶν ζηλούντων ἐκείνους ψυχὰς ὡς ἀπὸ ἱερῶν στομίων ἀπορροιαί τινες φέρονται (cf. Philo, De vita Moys. II 7, p. 140 M. = II 40 Cohn: συνδραμεῖν λογισμοῖς εἰλικρινέσι τῷ Μωυσέως καθαρωτάτῳ πνεύματι). The other is 33.5, p. 61.17: τί δὲ 'Ερατοσθένης ἐν τῇ 'Ηριγόνῃ; διὰ πάντων γὰρ ἀμώμητον τὸ ποιημάτιον 'Αρχιλόχου πολλὰ καὶ ἀνοικονόμητα παρασύροντος...κἀκείνης τῆς ἐκβολῆς τοῦ δαιμονίου πνεύματος, ἣν ὑπὸ νόμον τάξαι δύσκολον, ἆρα δὴ μείζων ποιητής. In fact the idea of a πνεῦμα or of πνεύματα θεοφορίας

(cf. Dioskurides, Anthol. Pal. VI 220.4) was longest preserved or earliest revived in aesthetics. Two other passages that were disputed, though defended by Vahlen, are c. 8.3 (p. 14.6): τὸ γενναῖον πάθος...ὥσπερ ὑπὸ μανίας τινὸς καὶ πνεύματος ἐνθουσιαστικῶς ἐκπνέον καὶ οἱονεὶ φοιβάζον τοὺς λόγους, and 9.13 (p. 21.3): τῆς μὲν Ἰλιάδος γραφομένης ἐν ἀκμῇ πνεύματος (the fact that here πνεῦμα has become almost equivalent to "the spirit" is shown by the contrasting γῆρας; it is the divine spirit, but as an abiding gift).

Certainly the starting point, as a rule, is only the Platonic idea of the divine inspiration of the poet, the θεία μανία, the equating of προφητεύειν and poetic composition in ancient lyric poetry, and images, drawn from ancient perspectives, of an ἐμπνέειν or προσπνέειν (cf. Hesiod, Theog. 31; especially peculiar, Tibullus II 1.35: *huc ades adspiraque mihi*; the πνεῦμα of the absent Messalla is addressed). But the very history of a word like *vates* or of a phrase like *plena deo* (cf. Norden, *Hermes* 28.506; commentary on Aeneid VI, p. 143) would serve to demonstrate the revival of the religious sense, and any of these conventional expressions can now be elevated repeatedly to the originally religious meaning. Always underlying is a feeling that places the human νοῦς in contrast to the divine πνεῦμα. The fact that since Vergil's famous description of the Sibyl the portrayals of religious inspiration by the deity have become increasingly common confirms the observation (cf. Aen. VI 46: *deus, ecce deus*; 50: *adflata est numine quando iam propiore dei*; 78: *magnum si pectore possit excussisse deum*). Perhaps I may here offer in somewhat broader context the passage from Lucan (Phars. V 161ff.) cited in the lecture that forms the first part of this book (above, p. 71):

23

tandem conterrita
virgo confugit ad tripodes vastisque ad-
ducta cavernis haesit et invito concepit
pectore numen, quod non exhaustae per tot
iam saecula rupis spiritus ingessit vati,
tandemque potitus pectore Cirrhaeo non
unquam plenior artus Phoebados inrupit
Paean mentemque priorem expulit atque
hominem toto sibi cedere iussit pectore.

The connection itself shows that here *mens* does not denote mind or intelligence, but only what is specifically human, the ψυχή. For this time there emerges a dual being which derives only its σῶμα from man. The θέα μεγίστη or θεία θέα, the vision which the deity enjoys and which makes one a deity, is described in v. 177:

venit aetas omnis in
unam congeriem miserumque premunt tot saecu-
la pectus--

the *mystes* of the rebirth-mystery indeed also beholds within himself the ἄπλαστος θέα that lifts him out of time and space--

tanta patet rerum series, atque omne fu-
turum nititur in lucem, vocemque petentia
fata luctantur, non prima dies, non ultima
mundi, non modus oceani, numerus non derat
harenae.

This passage (its conclusion stems from Herodotus I 77) shows especially well how in the feeling of this time mantic practice and religious prophecy (a kind of cosmogonic and eschatological revelation) are connected. Philo also speaks (Quis rer. div. heres. 263) of prophecy: to discern the future is not an attribute of man, and yet Moses is everywhere called, with respect, a prophet: he has seen God face to face. παγκάλως οὖν τὸν ἐνθουσιῶντα μηνύει φάσκων 'περὶ

ἡλίου δυσμὰς ἔκστασις ἐπέπεσεν' (Gen. 15:12) ἥλιον διὰ συμβόλου τὸν ἡμέτερον καλῶν νοῦν· ὅπερ γὰρ ἐν ἡμῖν λογισμός, τοῦτο ἐν κόσμῳ ἥλιος, ἐπειδὴ φωσφορεῖ ἑκάτερος...ἕως μὲν οὖν ἔτι περιλάμπει καὶ περιπολεῖ ἡμῶν ὁ νοῦς μεσημβρινὸν

324 οἷα φέγγος εἰς πᾶσαν τὴν ψυχὴν ἀναχέων, ἐν ἑαυτοῖς ὄντες οὐ κατεχόμεθα· ἐπειδὰν δὲ πρὸς δυσμὰς γένηται, κατὰ τὸ εἰκὸς ἔκστασις καὶ ἡ ἔνθεος ἐπιπίπτει κατοκωχή τε καὶ μανία. ὅταν μὲν γὰρ φῶς τὸ θεῖον ἐπιλάμψῃ, δύεται τὸ ἀνθρώπινον, ὅταν δ' ἐκεῖνο δύηται, τοῦτ' ἀνίσχει καὶ ἀνατέλλει. τῷ δὲ προφητικῷ γένει φιλεῖ τοῦτο συμβαίνειν. ἐξοικίζεται μὲν γὰρ ἐν ἡμῖν ὁ νοῦς κατὰ τὴν τοῦ θείου πνεύματος ἄφιξιν, κατὰ δὲ τὴν μετανάστασιν αὐτοῦ πάλιν ἐξοικίζεται· θέμις γὰρ οὐκ ἔστι θνητὸν ἀθανάτῳ συνοικῆσαι.[24] The explanation is more ancient, as is shown by De somniis I 118: ἔνιοι δὲ ἥλιον μὲν ὑποτοπήσαντες εἰρῆσθαι νυνὶ συμβολικῶς αἴσθησίν τε καὶ νοῦν, τὰ νενομισμένα καθ' ἡμᾶς εἶναι κριτήρια, τόπον δὲ τὸν θεῖον λόγον (meant to be an interpretation of the words in Gen. 28:11, ἀπήντησε τόπω· ἔδυ γὰρ ὁ ἥλιος) οὕτως ἐξεδέξαντο· ἀπήντησεν ὁ ἀσκητὴς λόγῳ θείῳ δύντος τοῦ θνητοῦ καὶ ἀνθρωπίνου φέγγους. ἄχρι μὲν γὰρ ὁ νοῦς τὰ νοητὰ καὶ τὰ αἰσθητὰ αἴσθησις οἴεται παγίως καταλαμβάνειν καὶ ἄνω περιπολεῖν, μακρὰν ὁ θεῖος λόγος ἀφέστηκεν. The terms θεῖον πνεῦμα and θεῖος λόγος can be used interchangeably by Philo, but he cannot substitute ψυχή for ἀνθρώπινος νοῦς. The pagan perspective also is acquainted with a continuing indwelling of the "holy spirit" that no longer needs to be induced by ecstasy; besides the passage from Horace already cited, one may compare, for example, Quintilian's longer Declamations IV 3 (p. 70.4 Lehnert): *homo qui, quod certum habeo, plurimis meruerat experimentis, ut ad illum velut ad oracula deorum plenumque sacro spiritu pectus hominum sollicitudines metusque confugerent.* When Christian authors later objected to the insistence on the

external signs of ecstasy as attestation of the ἐν πνεύματι λαλεῖν or προφητεύειν (e.g., Miltiades, περὶ τοῦ μὴ δεῖν προφήτην ἐν ἐκστάσει λαλεῖν), even this is nothing peculiar to the Christian development. We need only to think of the portrayal of θεῖοι ἄνδρες like Apollonius. The first appearance of Alexander of Abonoteichos forms the contrast to this attitude.

Lucan's portrayal best leads us to the two passages in the catholic epistles which I have omitted considering in the lecture that forms the first part of this book. The first of

325

these is Jude 18-19: "In the last times there will be scoffers, who will live according to the lusts of their godlessness; these are the ones who foster divisions, ψυχικοί, πνεῦμα μὴ ἔχοντες." The other is James 3:13-15: "Whoever is wise and understanding among you should show the fruits of upright conduct and the meekness of his wisdom; if you have jealous bitterness and strife in your hearts, do not boast of your wisdom; οὐκ ἔστιν αὕτη ἡ σοφία ἄνωθεν κατερχομένη, ἀλλ' ἐπίγειος, ψυχική, δαιμονιώδης." In the gospel of John the contrast to the true divine inspiration is formed by δαιμόνιον ἔχειν (cf. *Poimandres*, 223.2), which is imputed to the Samaritans; in Hermas, Mand. XI, a similar feeling informs the contrast between πνεῦμα ἐπίγειον (cf. below, p. 461) and πνεῦμα θεῖον. Of course Hermas ignores the concept ψυχικός and prefers to call the prophets πνευματοφόρος. His portrayal of the ψευδοπροφῆται shows that he equates them with the pagans, and that in fact the Hellenistic prophetic phenomenon in Christian and pagan communities exhibited similar features; cf. Mand. XI 2: οἱ δίψυχοι ὡς ἐπὶ μάντιν ἔρχονται καὶ ἐπερωτῶσιν αὐτόν, τί ἄρα ἔσται αὐτοῖς· κἀκεῖνος ὁ ψευδοπροφήτης, μηδεμίαν ἔχων ἐν ἑαυτῷ δύναμιν πνεύματος θείου, λαλεῖ αὐτοῖς κατὰ τὰ ἐπερωτήματα αὐτῶν καὶ κατὰ τὰς ἐπιθυμίας τῆς

πονηρίας αὐτῶν...τινὰ δὲ καὶ ῥήματα ἀληθῆ λαλεῖ· ὁ γὰρ διάβολος πληροῖ αὐτὸν τῷ αὐτοῦ πνεύματα, with Pap. Berol. I 174: ἐὰν δέ τίς σε ἐρωτήσῃ, τί κατὰ ψυχὴν ἔχω, ἢ τί μοι ἐγένετο ἢ γε μέλλει γενέσθαι, ἐπερώτα τὸν ἄγγελον (the πάρεδρος δαίμων), καὶ ἐρεῖ σοι σιωπῇ· σὺ δὲ ὡς ἀπὸ σεαυτοῦ λέγε τῷ ἐπερωτῶντί σε (cf. above, p. 299). In the two passages from the epistles cited above, those men who boast of their "wisdom" and claim the name of πνευματικοί are equated with the pagans: they are serving the demons and are immoral. Hence of course they are only ψυχικοί; the possession of the πνεῦμα is conceivable only within the full community. The term is used in both passages in the technical sense, in the same sense as in Paul's usage, only here ψυχικός has further fallen in value, since here it is hurled back, from the position of a more judaizing, that is, an ecclesiastical and works-righteousness tendency, against the individualistic and hellenistic gnosis; even here its original meaning is only "human". Moreover, it
326 certainly is shown that there is no distinction of a third category of σαρκικοί. Ignatius also is unacquainted with such a category; for him πνεῦμα and σάρξ, in adjectival form πνευματικός and σαρκικός (= ἀνθρώπινος), are the two complementary opposites (cf., e.g., Smyrn. 13:2: ἀγάπη σαρκική τε καὶ πνευματική, with Eph. 5:1: συνήθεια οὐκ ἀνθρωπίνη, ἀλλὰ πνευματική); for him Christ is σαρκικός τε καὶ πνευματικός, γεννητὸς καὶ ἀγέννητος (Eph. 7:2). How did mature Gnosticism in its major systems come to combine the two pairs of opposites and to distinguish three categories, σαρκικοί, ψυχικοί, and πνευματικοί? The explanation that they are only elicited from the one Pauline passage (I Cor. 3:1) will satisfy few; after all, this passage would have to be turned upside down in order to draw from it the inference of the σαρκικοί as the lowest class of men. A certain point of beginning probably

is offered first of all by the three fold Oriental division of man, mentioned earlier, into body, soul, and spirit. In connection with the familiar basic tendency of Gnosticism we may also point out that the Hellenistic mystery religions likewise distinguish three classes of men and between the unbelievers and the τέλειοι place the proselytes or *religiosi*. The need for making a distinction between the two lower classes then necessarily had to intensify in a religion that sought to stand in contrast to all others and therefore had to find a quite different way to set the two higher classes in sharp opposition to that lowest class. In particular, the concept of the church now was fully developed and was effective, even where it was not acknowledged in its full scope; the Gnostic did not want to leave it (cf. above, p. 96, n. 44, and for the Valentinians, especially E. Schwartz, *Nachr. d. Kgl. Ges.* Göttingen 1908, pp. 130ff., and n. 1 on p. 131). But now in language there was a return to the concept of the ψυχικός, and it was now significantly elevated in contrast to the earlier devaluation. This also can certainly be explained by the fact that in the Hellenistic area the idea of the divinity of the ψυχή was so firmly rooted and the contrast of ψυχή and σῶμα (σάρξ) was so strongly felt. The substantive ψυχή, which the depreciation that pertains to ψυχικός never succeeded altogether in covering, is again and again connected
327 with the deity (cf., e.g., the prayer of the Mithras liturgy), or it appears alongside πνεῦμα almost as synonymous. A weakening of the contrast between ψυχικός and πνευματικός inevitably had to appear. Nevertheless the original idea is maintained. The Valentinians whom Irenaeus pictures (I 7.1), for example, describe the ἱερὸς γάμος of Achamoth and the Soter with the addendum: τοὺς δὲ πνευματικοὺς ἀποδυσαμένους τὰς ψυχὰς καὶ πνεύματα νοερὰ γενομένους, ἀκρατήτως καὶ ἀοράτως ἐντὸς πληρώ-

ματος εἰσελθόντας, νύμφας ἀποδοθήσεσθαι τοῖς περὶ τὸν Σωτῆρα ἀγγέλοις, and the Marcosians (*ibid.*, I 21.5) picture the ἀπολύτρωσις similarly: αὐτὸν δὲ πορευθῆναι εἰς τὰ ἴδια (cf. Wessely, *Denkschr. d. K. K. Akad.* 1888, p. 71, line 1060: χώρει, κύριε, εἰς ἰδίους οὐρανούς, εἰς τὰ ἴδια βασιλεῖα, εἰς ἴδιον δρόμημα, at the dismissal of the deity), ῥίψαντα τὸν δεσμὸν αὐτοῦ, τουτέστι τὴν ψυχήν. Here the ψυχή is an ἐπίγειον ἔνδυμα τοῦ πνεύματος, and what is elsewhere said of the σῶμα is here transferred to the ψυχή; it is only the surrender of the ψυχή that renders one a full πνεῦμα. In the passages cited above (p. 369, and n. 3 on p. 422) Origen and Philo, in a different way and yet with some similarities, come to terms with the difficulty of defining the relationship of the ψυχή to the πνεῦμα (or νοῦς); they assume a transformation of the ψυχή into the πνεῦμα (or νοῦς); but according to this view also the ψυχή must pass away.

Then of course the much discussed question of whether Christ on earth had a ψυχή must also be connected with that basic outlook. In a splendid book (*Vom Zorne Gottes*, Göttingen, 1909), M. Pohlenz has set forth how totally the answer to this question is dependent upon the Greek philosophical view of the ψυχή and on the dogma, self-evident to the Greeks, that God must be free of πάθη. Harnack's thesis that it is Greek philosophy, not Oriental belief, that is decisive for the first formation of dogmas could hardly be more effectively defended than by these fine and lucid expositions. It appears to me, however, that perhaps too little attention is given to the basic issue of the source of the new element that enters, the πνεῦμα. Its introduction by Gnosticism first renders the inquiry intelligible and makes sense of the attempted solution that states that since Christ is God,

28 in him the πνεῦμα must have appeared in place of the ψυχή. But the thesis of the Great Church that was formed in accordance with this view, namely that if Christ was a man, he must have had a ψυχή, only fully comes to life in the awareness of the underlying perspective of the πνευματικός, who is *no longer* a man. It is true that the arguments are brought out of the arsenal of Greek philosophy, and the reminiscence of the basic perspective of the mystery religions is only faint; Gnosticism is overcome, but the legacy that is brought out of the Orient, the concept of the πνευματικός, continues to exert an influence, as it does in the Greek church even down to modern times.

It would be worthwhile to trace out somewhat further how the philosophy that was more and more becoming religious struggled to manage the new concept of the πνεῦμα and to fit it into its terminology or to translate it. The impact upon religious literature is shown when in the Hermetic writings there is a general substitution of νοῦς for πνεῦμα, ἔννους for πνευματικός, and ἄνους for ψυχικός (on Paul's usage cf. p. 431); more rarely we find λόγος, yet Corp. Herm. I 6 offers us τὸ ἐν σοὶ βλέπον καὶ ἀκοῦον λόγος κυρίου (here distinguished from the νοῦς, his Father) ἐστίν. Moreover, XII 6, 7, offers the initially surprising designation of ἐλλόγιμος (elsewhere ἔννους) for the Pneumatic who, completely sinless because he is delivered from the compulsion of εἱμαρμένη, can appear to sin only in the body (cf. p. 65); it is characteristic that by way of explanation it is added: ὧν ἔφαμεν τὸν νοῦν ἡγεμονεύειν. The opposite is ἄλογοι (equivalent to ψυχικοί), and of course these ἄλογοι are compared with the ἄλογα ζῷα (thus frequently in this literature, but also in Jude 10). It is from this context that Rom. 12:1 is to be explained: παραστῆσαι τὰ σώματα ὑμῶν θυσίαν ζῶσαν, ἁγίαν, εὐάρεστον τῷ

θεῷ, τὴν λογικὴν λατρείαν ὑμῶν. Neither Greek usage nor the context nor Paul's circle of thought will allow the interpretation that "rational worship" is meant here. Lietzmann is entirely correct in emphasizing that the Hermetic *terminus technicus* λογικὴ θυσία lies in the background here (I 31: δέξαι λογικὰς θυσίας ἁγνὰς ἀπὸ ψυχῆς καὶ καρδίας πρὸς σὲ ἀνατεταμένης. XIII 18: ὁ σὸς λόγος δι' ἐμοῦ ὑμνεῖ σε, δι' ἐμοῦ δέξαι τὸ πᾶν λόγῳ λογικὴν θυσίαν. 21: Τὰτ θεῷ πέμπω λογικὰς θυσίας· θεὲ καὶ πάτερ, σὺ ὁ κύριος, σὺ ὁ νοῦς· δέξαι λογικὰς θυσίας, ἃς θέλεις ἀπ' ἐμοῦ...διὰ τοῦ Λόγου). We do still discern in the Hermetic thought how the formula arose. It was coined when in the mystical cult the prayer of thanksgiving, the sacrifice in words, appears in place of the thank-offering, the ἔργον, that is common in the mystery cult (cf. the conclusion of Asclepius). It was intensified by the idea that the initiated person himself is the Λόγος θεοῦ conceived of in personal terms; he can offer only such sacrifices (Corp. herm. XIII; cf. Plutarch, De Is. et Os. 3). For Paul the consciousness of the contrast of λόγος and ἔργον has already disappeared; for him λογικός simply means "spiritual, spiritualized". In fact, Zahn has the meaning exactly right when he says that it is the λατρεία that is appropriate to the πνευματικός and is peculiar to him; but the language itself cannot be explained without the development of the *terminus technicus* in Hellenistic mysticism. This dependence upon that mysticism is shown by I Pet. 2:5: ἀνενέγκαι πνευματικὰς θυσίας εὐπροσδέκτους θεῷ διὰ 'Ιησοῦ Χριστοῦ (cf. Corp. herm. XIII 21: θεῷ πέμπω λογικὰς θυσίας--σύ, ὦ τέκνον, πέμψον δεκτὴν θυσίαν τῷ πάντων πατρὶ θεῷ. ἀλλὰ καὶ πρόσθες, ὦ τέκνον, "διὰ τοῦ Λόγου"). The two terms completely blend into each other; while Paul (I Cor. 10:3, 4), in an obvious transfer of Old Testament ideas into the perspective of the mysteries, speaks

329

of a πνευματικὸν βρῶμα καὶ πόμα, in the later epistle of I Peter (2:2) there stands the following in contrast: ὡς ἀρτιγέννητα βρέφη τὸ λογικὸν ἄδολον γάλα ἐπιποθήσατε, ἵνα ἐν αὐτῷ αὐξηθῆτε εἰς σωτηρίαν, εἴπερ ἐγεύσασθε ὅτι χρηστὸς ὁ κύριος. The context shows that here λογικός means "rendering sinless, sanctifying", in short πνευματικός in the sense of θεῖος, a sense which this word also carries immediately following this in the formula οἶκος πνευματικός, ἱεράτευμα ἅγιον. It is to be hoped that in the present time it is no longer possible to take I Pet. 2:2 as a reminiscence of the altogether differently structured passage in I Cor. 3:2: γάλα ὑμᾶς ἐπότισα, οὐ βρῶμα· οὔπω γὰρ ἐδύνασθε. That passage of the Phrygian *mystes* in Sallust, Περὶ θεῶν 4, is too well known to allow that interpretation: ἑορτὴν ἄγομεν διὰ ταῦτα· καὶ πρῶτον μὲν ὡς καὶ αὐτοὶ πεσόντες ἐξ οὐρανοῦ καὶ τῇ Νύμφῃ συνόντες ἐν κατηφείᾳ ἐσμέν, σίτου τε καὶ τῆς ἄλλης παχείας
30 καὶ ῥυπαρᾶς τροφῆς ἀπεχόμεθα· ἑκάτερα γὰρ ἐναντία ψυχῇ (philosophical language for πνεύματι; on the ῥυπαρὰ τροφή cf. Porphyry, De abstin. I 41, 42). εἶτα δένδρου τομαὶ καὶ νηστεία, ὥσπερ καὶ ἡμῶν ἀποκοπτομένων τὴν περαιτέρω τῆς γενέσεως πρόοδον. ἐπὶ τούτοις γάλακτος τροφή, ὡς ἀναγεννωμένων. ἐφ' οἷς ἱλαρεῖαι καὶ στέφανοι καὶ πρὸς τοὺς θεοὺς οἷον ἐπάνοδος. In the *Archiv für Religionswissenschaft* VII 403 and in *Poimandres*, p. 228, I have traced similar ideas in the Egyptian materials (the king drinks the milk of Isis and thereby acquires divine attributes; the magician drinks milk from a black cow, and something divine is immediately stirred within him); Griffith (*Demotic Magical Papyrus*, p. 137) and Dieterich (*Abraxas*, 172.12 and 181.2) would take us still further; the two latter passages show that here the drinking of milk denotes the beginning, and the drinking of wine the completion of divinity in us; the challenge to receive the drink is worded τὴν ἀπό-

γευσιν δέξαι. It seems to me obvious and not unimportant that the two "deutero-Pauline" passages, which I was compelled to treat so broadly, are more closely connected with the Hellenistic formulas and the usage in the mysteries, and thus go back directly to both; what was in Paul only a subsidiary idea becomes in them the main thing. Something of this sort can be demonstrated in various places; the perspectives of the mysteries, which in Paul still are in the background, press strongly to the fore in the so-called deutero-Paulinism, and Paul by no means provides the occasion for this to occur everywhere. Therewith it is also proven that the concept λογικὴ θυσία or πνευματικὴ θυσία is Hellenistic. Thus we may also mention in passing an attempt to give a mystical meaning to justify animal sacrifice, which created the most offense in mystical circles and yet could not be banned from the cultus of the mysteries: the same Sallust (16) offers that attempt: αἱ μὲν χωρὶς θυσιῶν εὐχαὶ λόγοι μόνον εἰσίν, αἱ δὲ μετὰ θυσιῶν ἔμψυχοι λόγοι, τοῦ μὲν λόγου τὴν ζωὴν δυναμοῦντος, τῆς δὲ ζωῆς τὸν λόγον ψυχούσης (cf. the designation πνεῦμα λαμβάνειν for the acceptance of the bloody sacrifice, above, p. 392; once again with the philosopher the word ψυχή is substituted for πνεῦμα, but the demand that in the ἀναφορά, the ψυχή or πνεῦμα should be combined with the λόγος does not come from philosophy, and this demand is generally familiar; one who regards 331 the sacrifice of the word as alone pleasing to God prays προσδέξαι μου τὴν...ἀξίωσιν <την> λιτανίαν, τὴν προσύφωσιν, τὴν ἀναφορὰν τοῦ πνεύματος τοῦ λεκτικοῦ and emphasizes with this last word that the deity expects no other πνεῦμα; cf. above, p. 394, and *Poimandres*, p. 151).

That use of λογικός for πνευματικός went back to an attempt to reproduce the concept πνεῦμα in philosophical terminology. That is shown by the same Hermetic writing from which

I took my point of departure, still more clearly in the continuation in XII 13: δοκεῖς δέ μοι, ὦ τέκνον, ἀγνοεῖν ἀρετὴν καὶ μέγεθος λόγου· ὁ γὰρ μακάριος θεὸς Ἀγαθὸς δαίμων ψυχὴν μὲν ἐν σώματι ἔφη εἶναι, νοῦν δὲ ἐν ψυχῇ, λόγον δὲ ἐν τῷ νῷ. τὸν οὖν θεὸν τούτων (in §12, λόγος and νοῦς are identified as the two gifts of God that render one immortal) <νόμιζε> πατέρα. ὁ οὖν λόγος ἐστὶν εἰκὼν καὶ νοῦς τοῦ θεοῦ (the words that follow, καὶ τὸ σῶμα δὲ τῆς ἰδέας, ἡ δὲ ἰδέα τῆς ψυχῆς, lead into another train of thought). Here λόγος (or, as in I 6, λόγος and νοῦς) is the special divine gift of the elect, the πνεῦμα; the concept is familiar, but the word is avoided. Here the theme is throughout that special χάρισμα; this is shown by the fact that only the word and not the idea is borrowed from philosophy; what we have here are attempts at translation of an Oriental concept, attempts that at any rate considerably pre-date the times of Paul and Philo and have passed over into common usage. Where they are adopted, of course at the same time the Greek idea which was originally combined with them extends its influence and hinders the achievement of any clarity. Where the word πνεῦμα is itself accepted into the *philosophical* terminology, it once again undergoes a partial devaluation, in the sense of the Stoic designation for the material of the soul, and in Corp. herm. X 13, for example, we hear: ὁ νοῦς ἐν τῷ λόγῳ, ὁ λόγος ἐν τῇ ψυχῇ, ἡ ψυχὴ ἐν τῷ πνεύματι, τὸ πνεῦμα ἐν τῷ σώματι. τὸ δὲ πνεῦμα διῆκον διὰ φλεβῶν καὶ ἀρτηριῶν καὶ αἵματος κινεῖ τὸ ζῷον καὶ ὥσπερ τρόπον τινὰ βαστάζει. Thus the πνεῦμα becomes the shell, the ἔνδυμα τῆς ψυχῆς, and the latter becomes the ἔνδυμα τοῦ νοῦ (*ibid.*, §17; cf. p. 454). This is reminiscent of Platonic teachings, but it is unlikely that it first arose in that school; the entire perspective is only the inversion, necessary in philosophy, of the Gnostic doctrine according to

332

which the ψυχή is the ἔνδυμα τοῦ πνεύματος (above, p. 414).

These inadequate attempts to render possible the impossible and to relate an Oriental-religious concept to the sophisticated doctrine of the soul in Greek philosophy may be less than satisfactory to the philosopher, but they should be important to the historian, and perhaps still more to the theologian. They offer recurrent points for comparison and connections with New Testament theology and the history of dogma. I do not altogether understand how one can detach the development of Christology from the development of the common conceptions of the θεῖος ἄνθρωπος and the relationship of man and God, or how one can posit Greek philosophy and not Oriental piety as the decisive element in Christian γνῶσις without also making the attempt to explain the concept of the πνεῦμα and πνευματικός, or even considering it. It is most clearly shown by the language of asceticism, which indeed is closely connected with Gnosticism. Hence I have attempted to trace out that language (in the book *Historia Monachorum und Historia Lausiaca*, FRLANT 24, Göttingen 1916, pp. 210ff.), in order to be able to evaluate that interpretation of Gnosticism in terms of that language. The pneumatic person is ἐκσπασθεὶς ἐκ τοῦ χώρου τῆς εἱμαρμένης ἐπὶ τὸν ἀσώματον; he is himself ἄσαρκος, or ἄυλος. He consists entirely of light-substance which breaks forth in fiery rays when he lifts up his hands in prayer or opens his mouth (as the Mandaeans say, he actually becomes the pearl that illumines the dark house). It is through him and for his sake that the world continues to exist.[25] He does not need earthly food or sleep. What γνῶσις is is shown by the narrative of how the monk decides whether Melchizedek was human or divine, or whether a transsubstantiation actually is achieved in the Supper: he asks God to open his eyes and to show him the patriarchs or the process in the sacrament.--Vision ren-

333

ders one perfect, and the perfect one is subject to no law and to no authority; he is a priest by an inward law. Since here we have abundant literature available, we can recognize the origin of individual ideas more clearly than in other areas. The ascension that is related first in Athanasius of Amun, but then later of every prominent monk, corresponds in many features to portrayals of the Manichaean fragments and is reminiscent of the stories about Buddha. On the other hand, similar perspectives are found in the Parsee as well as in the Mandaean religion (on the former, cf. Yasht 22); it may have penetrated late Judaism from there. A large and attractive task is opened up for the researcher, to demonstrate on the one hand the Oriental origin, and on the other hand the stages of the occidentalizing of this thought-world by the Jewish, the Greek, and finally the general Western feeling. It is not Christian by birth, but it has become Christian through powerful religious personalities.

NOTES

1. I have not cited Leisegang's well-known book, *Der heilige Geist*, for the Pneuma concept, since Philo, upon whom the most widely diverse influences were exerted, seems to me not to be the appropriate starting-point for this study. (Cf. *Das iranische Erlösungsmysterium*, p. 106, n.1.) So far as I know, there are no preliminary studies on the Oriental sources. In the Manichaean Turfan fragments we find two designations for the soul that can be distinguished etymologically somewhat as "life-soul" and "consciousness-soul", but in actual usage are hardly strictly distinguished; in addition there is a concept "the Self" (*grev*, earlier usually translated, incorrectly, as "spirit"). In the Mandaean funerary texts, the spirit is sometimes named as a third component alongside body and soul; yet this "spirit" appears to be conceived of indeed as incorporeal, but lower than the soul. Apparently the division of the immaterial element in man into two parts has various prototypes, but we are unable to say anything more specific about this at the present time.

2. Cf. Corp. herm. V 9: εἰ δέ τί με καὶ τολμηρότερον ἀναγκάζεις εἰπεῖν, τούτου ἐστὶν οὐσία τὸ κύειν πάντα καὶ ποιεῖν (Bräuninger, "Zu den Schriften des Hermes Trism.," p. 26.1, rightly rejects Scott's mistaken emendation κινεῖν; cf. Usener, *Archiv f. Religionswissensch.* VII 295, "Jacobusbrief 1, 18," βουληθεὶς ἀπεκύησεν ἡμᾶς λόγῳ ἀληθείας). The androgynous creator-deity is an ancient idea in the Orient (cf. Reitzenstein-Schaeder I, chapters 3 and 4), which is always preserved in the Aion, and hence is not first introduced by the author of the Poimandres in connection with the primal man. Moreover, the βουλὴ θεοῦ (or the θέλημα which Bräuninger treats in the same place; cf. Reitzenstein-Schaeder I, p. 190) certainly does not first belong to late Persian speculation; it is the σοφία. The words of Clement's Paedagogus I 6 S (114 P), τὸ θέλημα αὐτοῦ ἔργον ἐστὶν καὶ τοῦτο κόσμος ὀνομάζεται, explain Corp. herm. XIII 89: σὴ βουλὴ ἀπὸ σοῦ, ἐπὶ σὲ τὸ πᾶν.

3. Glorification; cf. Paul, in I Cor. 15:41, in the same context of ideas: ἄλλη δόξα ἡλίου καὶ ἄλλη δόξα σελήνης; further, Philo, De vita Moys. III 39, p. 179 M = I 288 Cohn: ἔμελλεν εἰς οὐρανὸν στέλλεσθαι καὶ τὸν θνητὸν ἀπολιπὼν βίον ἀπαθανατίζεσθαι μετακληθεὶς ὑπὸ τοῦ πατρός, ὅς αὐτὸν δυάδα ὄντα, σῶμα καὶ ψυχήν, εἰς μονάδος ἀνεστοι-

χείου φύσιν, ὅλον δι' ὅλων μεθαρμοζόμενος εἰς νοῦν ἡλιοειδέστατον. Even here the Septuagint as source of the usage is unlikely.

4. The continuation in the Poimandres reads: λοιπὸν τί μέλλεις; οὐχ ὡς πάντα παραλαβὼν καθοδηγὸς γίνῃ τοῖς ἀξίοις, ὅπως τὸ γένος τῆς ἀνθρωπότητος διὰ σοῦ ὑπὸ θεοῦ σωθῇ; this exhibits consideration for the mysteries, in the idea that the *mystes* can immediately initiate others, and in the words πάντα παραλαβών, καθοδηγός, ἄξιος, and σωθῆναι.

5. Cf., for example, from the myth of Julian, πρὸς Ἡράκλειον, the proclamation of Helios, p. 304.4 Hertl.: μέμνησο οὖν ὅτι τὴν ψυχὴν ἀθάνατον ἔχεις καὶ ἔκγονον ἡμετέραν ἑπόμενός τε ἡμῖν ὅτι θεὸς ἔσῃ καὶ τὸν ἡμέτερον ὄψει σὺν ἡμῖν πατέρα, with the proud and fully gnostically meant words of Hippolytus (292.20 W.): ἕξεις δὲ ἀθάνατον τὸ σῶμα καὶ ἄφθαρτον ἅμα ψυχῇ...ὁ ἐν γῇ βιοὺς καὶ ἐπουράνιον βασιλέα ἐπιγνούς, ἔσῃ δὲ ὁμιλητὴς θεοῦ...γέγονας γὰρ θεός...ὅσα δὲ παρακολουθεῖ θεῷ, ταῦτα παρέχειν ἐπήγγελται θεός, ὅταν θεοποιηθῇς, ἀθάνατος γεννηθείς--τουτέστι τὸ Γνῶθι σεαυτόν--ἐπιγνοὺς τὸν πεποιηκότα θεόν--cf. Corp. herm. 18; cf. Pythagoras, Carmen aurcum 71.

6. The σωτήρ is the "one who makes alive".

7. Scott reads αἰώνιος, contrary to linguistic argument and with a mistaken explanation. For the concept I refer to the Naassene Preaching, where the primal man or the world-soul is the Aion.

8. The elements are ποιητοὶ θεοί.

9. Among the Mandaeans, in order to gain heaven the soul must pass over the *suf*-sea, the θάλασσα τῆς φθορᾶς; for a similar idea see above, p. 307.

10. Cf. the magical idea above, p. 230, n. 53.

11. Similarly, in Indian mysticism (Bhagavad Gita XI 8, 9) the deity himself gives man his eye, so that he may behold his celestial form.

12. Bräuninger, in the dissertation cited above (p. 100), offers a description. The same distinction can be demonstrated in the monastic narratives.

13. It is the πνεῦμα as the divine soul. Scott excises these words because he fails to recognize that they correspond to the following ἀνθρωπίνη ψυχή. The latter term signifies the human soul in the actual sense, that which even the ψυχικός has. The separation of the God-given and the human parts of the soul is the foundation of all gnostic religion; for the former, the designations νοῦς and πνεῦμα alternate at will among pagans and Christians (Paul) alike, yet ψυχή is also found among some individual Gnostics.

14. It is, indeed, Life (God) in its very substance.

15. Your "Self" in contrast to the body; the latter corresponds to the κόσμος, and the former is God.

16. Corp. herm. XIII 14: εἰπέ μοι, ὦ πάτερ, τὸ σῶμα τοῦτο τὸ ἐκ δυνάμεων (divine powers) συνεστὸς λύσιν ἴσχει ποτέ. The Father answers: that is impossible; you indeed are God.

17. Zarathustra drinks (Bahman-Yasht 2) omniscience (γνῶσις) from a cup. By means of the same draught Arda Viraf is insured against the demons that lie in wait for him on his celestial pilgrimage.

18. Thus in the last analysis the Damdad-Nask of the Avesta.

19. Reitzenstein-Schaeder, Part I.

20. Cf. above, p. 333.

21. Thus the Ba of the god Osiris; cf. H. Junker, *Denkschr. d. Wiener Akad.* 1903, pp. 26 and 58.

22. She is also mentioned in the medicinal literature; cf. above, p. 146.

23. Addition: through these three elements the soul ascends to God (above, p. 277).

24. The continuation of this passage, which portrays the prophet as nothing but an instrument without a will of its own, upon which God plays, bears a close affinity to the last of the Hermetic chapters (cf. my *Poimandres*, pp. 355-56).

25. The monks asserted this of themselves. Originally it is said of "Man" as the world-soul, and thus it dominates the Mandaeans' doctrine of redemption.

XVI.

Paul as a Pneumatic

I can offer the attempt at a justification for my interpretation of Paul only by setting forth how I understand the connections of the individual passages. In the lecture that forms the first part of this book (p. 73) I have already indicated that in so doing I am following only *one* train of thought and can neither sketch a system of "Pauline theology" nor give a picture of the apostle. A picture of the πνευματικός such as he had in view in his last period should of course be provided by the detailed interpretation for the few philologists who still read Paul in the original language; hence my presentation was made in broad terms; it was my judgment that even here it was permissible to avoid polemics insofar as possible.

The basically decisive passage is found in I Cor. 2:14; but it, in order to be made comprehensible, must be traced out in terms of how it developed. The apostle starts out from the fact that the believers in Corinth have separated into individual θίασοι and in true Hellenistic fashion have named themselves for their teachers. They are saying, ἐγῶ μέν εἰμι Παύλου, ἐγῶ δὲ 'Απολλῶ, ἐγῶ δὲ Κηφᾶ, ἐγῶ δὲ Χριστοῦ. The interpretation requires few words. It will better be shown later

334 that Pfleiderer is correct in rejecting the assumption of an actual Christ-party, of which nothing at all is known and whose label, in relation to the others, would be meaningless (*Paulinismus*, second edition, p. 316 n.). The words ἐγω δὲ

Χριστοῦ, essentially only the utterance always made by the individuals *alongside* the earlier ones, are added, under the demands of rhetoric, as a fourth member, in order to show by this contrast how inappropriate are those declarations of belonging to men, because they make these men equal with God. The expression Χριστοῦ εἶναι (cf. θεοῦ εἶναι in Ignatius) in fact signifies for Paul a mystical connection with Christ and is fully equivalent to ἐν Χριστῷ εἶναι or Χριστὸν ἐν ἑαυτῷ ἔχειν; in fact, it can even be stated as τὸ πνεῦμα ἔχειν; cf. Rom. 8:9: ὑμεῖς δὲ οὐκ ἐστὲ ἐν σαρκί, ἀλλὰ ἐν πνεύματι, εἴπερ πνεῦμα θεοῦ οἰκεῖ ἐν ὑμῖν. εἰ δέ τις πνεῦμα Χριστοῦ οὐκ ἔχει, οὗτος οὐκ ἔστιν αὐτοῦ. εἰ δὲ Χριστὸς ἐν ὑμῖν, τὸ μὲν σῶμα νεκρὸν κτλ. Like a good pedagogue, then, the apostle appears first to chide only his own party: "Was Paul crucified for you, or were you baptized in his name (as is the case with the Χριστοῦ εἶναι)?" He himself did not even baptize; if he had, that could have provided at least external occasion for such a misuse of his name, by making him the ἱερεύς for whom Hellenistic communities named themselves. He was only the bearer of the proclamation. In Paul's now giving a more specific description of this proclamation (verse 17: οὐκ ἐν σοφίᾳ λόγου) the train of thought appears to digress. In fact the portrayal of the divine wisdom in contrast to human wisdom is intended to impress upon the rival parties that they must not judge his preaching by their own wisdom. Thus in 2:1-5 he comes back to this proclamation; it did not consist ἐν πειθοῖ,[1] σοφίας λόγοις, ἀλλ' ἐν ἀποδείξει πνεύματος καὶ δυνάμεως, and thus it had that legitimation from God that is compelling for any Hellenistic mind, to which a still stronger claim is laid in the second epistle. With the following verse (2:6), Paul comes back to his own party: the true wisdom, the σοφία θεοῦ, he can proclaim only ἐν τελείοις. He has been unable to reveal it

even to his own followers in Corinth, and cannot do so even now; they too are incapable of judging what he has taught, and they still do not know what his final word will be in their disputes (3:1: οὐκ ἠδυνήθην λαλῆσαι ὑμῖν ὡς πνευματικοῖς). Between two verses that belong together there is inserted, as a new digression, the praise of that deep, hidden σοφία, unfathomable even to the ἄρχοντες τοῦ αἰῶνος τούτου, which God has revealed to the apostle διὰ τοῦ πνεύματος (2:7, along with its background in 1:13, shows how strongly Paul sensed the injurious effect of this boasting and how he wanted that boasting to be understood). For the πνεῦμα fathoms everything, even the deep things (thoughts) of God. This is first explained in 2:11: τίς γὰρ οἶδεν ἀνθρώπων τὰ τοῦ ἀνθρώπου, εἰ μὴ τὸ πνεῦμα τοῦ ἀνθρώπου τὸ ἐν αὐτῷ; οὕτως καὶ τὰ τοῦ θεοῦ οὐδεὶς ἔγνωκεν, εἰ μὴ τὸ πνεῦμα τοῦ θεοῦ. In this there is presupposed the usage, common in the magical papyri, of πνεῦμα for the spiritual part, the soul, of man, and another usage that corresponds to that one and is likewise attested in the same papyri, according to which πνεῦμα also denotes the spirit or the soul of a god (cf. p. 392); of course it was easier for the Hellenists, to whom the concept of emanation is familiar, to connect with this the πνεῦμα θεοῦ as the gift that is bestowed upon us, the ἀπόρροια of God; Paul's argument presupposes a fixed Hellenistic language of formula (τὰ τοῦ ἀνθρώπου and τὰ τοῦ θεοῦ receive their specific coloration from the preceding words, τὰ βάθη τοῦ θεοῦ, what is inward and innermost; hence τὸ ἐν αὐτῷ is not an idle addition, but it explains and clarifies the entire assertion). While it is said here first of all only that a person who has the πνεῦμα has full knowledge of the μυστήριον of the deity and of his σοφία, now Paul very emphatically adds that he has received this πνεῦμα ἐκ τοῦ θεοῦ. With an obvious reference

back to verse 6 (σοφίαν δὲ λαλοῦμεν ἐν τοῖς τελείοις, σοφίαν δὲ οὐ τοῦ αἰῶνος τούτου), he declares: ἡμεῖς δὲ οὐ τὸ πνεῦμα τοῦ κόσμου ἐλάβομεν, ἀλλὰ τὸ πνεῦμα τὸ ἐκ τοῦ θεοῦ, ἵνα εἰδῶμεν τὰ ὑπὸ τοῦ θεοῦ χαρισθέντα ἡμῖν (that is, God's plan of salvation; cf. verse 8; from the knowledge, of course, a proclaiming is supposed to follow; the train of thought changes direction slightly, so that the following ἃ καὶ λαλοῦμεν can have reference to the entire proclamation, not solely to the discourse ἐν τελείοις) ἃ καὶ λαλοῦμεν, οὐκ ἐν διδακτοῖς ἀνθρωπίνης σοφίας λόγοις, ἀλλ' ἐν διδακτοῖς πνεύματος (ἀνθρωπίνης σοφίας of course belongs first of all to λόγοις; διδακτοῖς standing alone carries the derogatory meaning of "that which can be learned", or "that which is taught". It is only in the contrast--these things are taught to us because they are the words of the πνεῦμα--under the constraint of rhetoric in parallelism that πνεύματος is joined with διδακτοῖς). Therewith at first we have only a repetition of what has already been said in verse 4, namely that his preaching was done ἐν πνεύματι; then, in keeping with Paul's style, it is the next three much-disputed words that add what is new, providing the point of connection with what is to follow. He describes how one learns from the πνεῦμα; πνευματικοῖς (ancient variant reading πνευματικῶς) πνευματικὰ συγκρίνοντες. The interpretation, "interpreting spiritual things to men of the spirit", that has recently been proposed again, appears doubtful to me, because of the change in gender and the assumption of an extraordinary meaning for the verb; still more dubious, of course, is the interpretation, "giving expression to heavenly things in heavenly language", which also disrupts the context. I refer to II Cor. 10:12: (οὐ γὰρ τολμῶμεν ἐγκρῖναι ἢ συγκρῖναι ἑαυτούς τισι τῶν ἑαυτοὺς συνιστανόντων· ἀλλὰ αὐτοὶ ἐν ἑαυτοῖς ἑαυτοὺς μετροῦντες καὶ συγκρίνοντες ἑαυτοὺς

ἑαυτοῖς οὐ συνιοῦσιν--συγκρίνειν is a precondition for any judgment): thus 2:13 would mean, "by our comparing spiritual gifts and revelations (which we already possess) with spiritual gifts and revelations (which we receive: cf. the following τὰ τοῦ πνεύματος and I Cor. 12:1ff., περὶ δὲ τῶν πνευματικῶν and their enumeration), and judge and understand them accordingly". In this interpretation of the passage, the ἐν πνεύματι λέγειν, which Paul of course claims for his missionary preaching also, does not entirely rule out human activity; the two work together. Of course the person not yet thus endowed cannot learn thus at all: ψυχικὸς δὲ ἄνθρωπος οὐ δέχεται τὰ τοῦ πνεύματος τοῦ θεοῦ (the genitive τοῦ θεοῦ, which makes the contrast even sharper--at first, man and God belong to two different worlds, before the miraculous transformation of the former--is intended still more strongly to evoke a recollec-

337 tion of 1:17ff.). μωρία γὰρ αὐτῷ ἐστιν, καὶ οὐ δύναται γνῶναι, ὅτι πνευματικῶς ἀνακρίνεται (i.e., as only the πνευματικός can do; cf. Rev. 11:8). The construction is changed, in a rhetorical play that is a favorite device of Paul's; πνευματικοῖς πνευματικὰ συγκρίνειν is the same as πνευματικῶς ἀνακρίνειν (to test and judge, ἐλέγχειν; cf. I Cor. 14:24). In this context the entire sentence only sets the stage for the counterpart: ὁ δὲ πνευματικὸς ἀνακρίνει τὰ πάντα, αὐτὸς δὲ ὑπ' οὐδενὸς ἀνακρίνεται. This is a proud claim, that not only attributes to this one marvelous being an absolute knowledge and infallibility, but also denies to all others (of course what is meant are only the non-pneumatic persons) any right to pass judgment on him, and denies them any hope even of understanding him. It is the basic attitude of the church, which is based upon the preaching of the pneumatic person; hence in Hermas (Mand. XI) the community can pass judgment on the pneumatic person only in light of his moral conduct and

not in terms of his teaching. The Didache (chapter 11) explicitly intensifies the same rule (cf. Harnack, *Texte und Untersuchungen* II, pp. 120ff.). Both of these early Christian writings expressly identify the demand for pay as the mark of the false pneumatic. This could account for the special emphasis constantly made by Paul on the fact that he does not make use of Jesus' permission for the apostle to live by the gospel. Of course he must have found this view already present in Hellenistic circles, a fact that should not be so surprising, since προφητεύειν or *vaticinari* occupied a fixed place in the cultus of the mystery communities (cf. above, pp. 299ff.). That utter autonomy is a basic idea of all the prophetic enterprise (cf., e.g., Wellhausen, *Das Evangelium Marci*, p. 28). But back to the passage in I Corinthians.

The focal point in verse 15 lies in the second half of the verse: αὐτὸς δὲ ὑπ' οὐδενὸς ἀνακρίνεται. This is shown by the context and by the aim of the entire presentation. Therefore the continuation is connected only with this part of the verse; it is the proof from Scripture by the saying, τίς γὰρ ἔγνω νοῦν κυρίου, ὅς συμβιβάσει αὐτόν, which is concluded with the clause, ἡμεῖς δὲ νοῦν Χριστοῦ ἔχομεν. As difficult as it is for me here to contradict scholars whom I most sincerely respect, this clause can conclude the proof only if for *Paul and his hearers* νοῦς and πνεῦμα are or at least can be fully identical. Only in that case can the apostle thus reconstruct and reshape the quotation from the Septuagint (Is. 40:13). Any interpretation of the word νοῦς as "mind" or "intention" robs the entire passage, in my judgment, of its sense; νοῦς here must be that divine *fluidum* which is bestowed only on the favored person and renders him a πνευματικός. Now according to ordinary Greek the word cannot have that meaning. But we are acquainted now with this alternation of the two

words and concepts in Hellenism; indeed, we are acquainted with an entire tendency in Hellenistic mysticism that venerates a god called Νοῦς who bestows the νοῦς as a heavenly gift upon his chosen ones; this gift immediately produces an absolute knowledge of the universe (πάντα γνωρίζειν) and immortality; the person thus favored is called ἔννους and becomes the divine teacher of his brethren. As is known, the system is given in detail in the Poimandres, which one would have to copy out in full to show how here νοῦς everywhere means what is identified in other remains of pagan mysticism as πνεῦμα. Thus some lost Hermetic writings cited by the pagan Zosimos (cf. *Poimandres*, pp. 102, 103) contrast the πνευματικὸς ἄνθρωπος with the ἄνοες. Still clearer is a passage from the Κρατὴρ ἢ Μονάς (§4): ὅσοι μὲν οὖν ἐβαπτίσαντο τοῦ νοός (God has sent down the νοῦς in a large κρατήρ; a κρατήρ is always used in the Greek mysteries for purification or baptism), οὗτοι μετέσχον τῆς γνώσεως καὶ τέλειοι ἐγένοντο ἄνθρωποι τὸν νοῦν δεξάμενοι. The *baptism with the spirit* makes one a τέλειος ἄνθρωπος; the unbaptized are, as it is said later, without νοῦς and without γνῶσις, consigned to the αἰσθήσεις alone, like the ἄλογα ζῷα (cf. Jude 10). If τέλειος here means, on the one hand, "perfect" ("full men"), on the other hand, it apparently also means "having become complete *in baptism*". "Perfect", i.e., initiated, is a fixed concept in most of the Oriental religions and throughout Gnosticism. The formation of the concept arises out of the fixed sacral formula τέλεια μυστήρια (in Athens the major, and hence the second, initiatory rite; Plato, Sympos. 210 a and elsewhere), and of

339 course it is connected with the conception that there is a fixed, established route and hence also an ἄρχεσθαι and a τελευτᾶν in the mysteries, and that the climax, the consummation (τέλος), is the vision of God (*ibid.*, p. 210-212 a). In

the Hellenistic period the formula is generally used for the μυστήριον or τελετή that is correct and thus leads to full vision (cf., e.g., Pap. Lugd. V, Dieterich, *Jahrb. f. kl. Phil.* Supplem. XVI, p. 811, line 26: τέλει τελείαν τελετήν; Hippolytus, Elenchus, p. 2.17 W.; Apuleius XI 26: *plenissime videbar iam dudum initiatus,* and XI 29: *quid subsicivum quamvis iteratae iam traditioni remansisset. nimirum perperam vel minus plene consuluerunt in me sacerdos uterque*). Since τελετή and μυστήριον can also denote the secret prayer (the λόγος ἀπόκρυφος) or the revelatory writing (cf. p. 305), there also appears in this literature a λόγος τέλειος, and we saw earlier (pp. 370-72) that it leads to the vision of God and thus to full γνῶσις and corresponds to what we call mystery. Its object is νόησις, according to the usage of this literature the perception (αἰσθάνεσθαι) of the suprasensory, in contrast to actual αἴσθησις, the perception of the sensory; this connection is so fully sensed that Corp. herm. IX 1 can begin: χθές, ὦ 'Ασκληπιέ, τὸν τέλειον ἀποδέδωκα λόγον, νῦν δὲ ἀναγκαῖον ἡγοῦμαι ἀκόλουθον ἐκείνῳ καὶ τὸν περὶ αἰσθήσεως λόγον διεξελθεῖν. αἴσθησις γὰρ καὶ νόησις διαφορὰν μὲν δοκοῦσιν ἔχειν, ὅτι ἡ μὲν ὑλική ἐστιν, ἡ δὲ οὐσιώδης. Every reader must know that the τέλειος λόγος can only pertain to the νόησις. Thus in the language of the mysteries and in Philo, τέλειος (of course primarily in the sense of "the one who lacks nothing") becomes the designation for the person who has the capacity for νοεῖν in this sense and therewith has full γνῶσις. It is an obvious subsidiary idea that he thereby becomes τέλειος ἄνθρωπος, *man* in his highest and fullest development; but it nevertheless remains only a subsidiary idea. In the saying of Paul cited above, σοφίαν δὲ λαλοῦμεν ἐν τοῖς τελείοις, I find only the main idea (a reference to age there is not at all possible, but because of what precedes it a refer-

ence to the γνῶσις θεοῦ is necessary; it is only because of
340 that γνῶσις that in 3:1 the word can be assimilated by the designation πνευματικός; but, characteristic of the apostle's style, precisely in this assimilation he becomes conscious of the subsidiary idea of the "full man" which is connected with the word in the passage from the Κρατήρ cited above; one can explain the language of Paul from that passage, but not conversely that passage from Paul). It is important to me to state at the very outset that like the entire train of argument in I Cor. 2:15, 16, so also the development of thought from chapter 2 to chapter 3 is based upon the Hellenistic language of formula and is incomprehensible without it--at least for the philologist who would first understand the individual words ψυχικῶς.

As I have already indicated, Paul turns back from that lengthy digression and appends to 2:6, σοφίαν δὲ λαλοῦμεν ἐν τοῖς τελείοις, the postscript, ἐν ὑμῖν δὲ οὐκ ἠδυνήθην, or rather, as it is now said in 3:1: κἀγώ, ἀδελφοί, οὐκ ἠδυνήθην λαλῆσαι ὑμῖν ὡς πνευματικοῖς. He is searching for a contrast to this term; he cannot very well use ψυχικός, for the Corinthians are after all baptized, they are ἐν Χριστῷ and thus are already partakers in the πνεῦμα; but they are not yet τέλειοι; a new figure that is at least foreshadowed in the Phrygian mysteries (cf. above, p. 417) symbolizes this: they are still νήπιοι ἐν Χριστῷ; even in the child the νοῦς, which was equated with the πνεῦμα, is still undeveloped; the child leads a more vegetative life. Hence we can understand Paul's choice of the word σάρκινοι, which by no means is intended to place the person involved among the ψυχικοί; it obviously does not fully exclude the πνεῦμα, because, unlike the term ψυχικός, it is not borrowed from an established terminology that is calculated to express *an exclusive contrast*, and it is only saying

that in the conflict between flesh and spirit, which Paul assumes to be present even in the converted, the former still has the upper hand. Of course the expression would be impossible without the conviction that in the τέλειος or πνευματικός the σάρξ is annihilated, at least in its effects. Thus now the very existence of that conflict can provide him with the proof that the Corinthians up to the present are not yet πνευματικοί: ὅπου γὰρ ἐν ὑμῖν ζῆλος καὶ ἔρις, οὐχὶ σαρ-

341 κικοί ἐστε καὶ κατὰ ἄνθρωπον περιπατεῖτε; once again it is the addendum that provides the point of connection for the further--one could say the metaphysical--statement: ὅταν γὰρ λέγῃ τις "ἐγὼ μέν εἰμι Παύλου", ἕτερος δὲ "ἐγὼ Ἀπολλῶ", οὐκ ἄνθρωποί ἐστε. It is the conclusion of the entire presentation from 1:12 down to this point, the solution from the perspective of which all that lies between there and here is meant to be understood, and it cannot be interpreted sharply enough. The ψυχικός is simply man, and the πνευματικός is *no longer man at all*. What the latter is is not said, and it is wrong and unjustifiable when modern interpreters purport to detect behind this a contrast, ἀλλὰ υἱοὶ θεοῦ or something of the sort. The fixed concept of a supraterrestrial and supernatural being must exist in that community, or otherwise the entire statement is untenable. I need not say that in this connection ἐγώ εἰμι Παύλου has the same mystical secondary sense as in 1:12ff. Nor is it necessary to argue, against other interpreters, that our passage does not stand in contrast to 3:13, where the subject is only the ἐκκλησία as a temple in which the πνεῦμα τοῦ θεοῦ resides. Another mystical train of thought is operative here, which cannot be sharply enough distinguished from the first one; here, as most probably in the view of the Jerusalem congregation, the community is the bearer of the πνεῦμα (which originally is

the form in which the resurrected one abides in the circle of those who belong to him). In the train of thought first discussed, the πνευματικὸς κατ' ἐξοχήν stands as absolutely complete in and of himself. To that claim, ἐγὼ μέν εἰμι Παύλου, Paul offers in the following passage (3:22) the contrast: εἴτε Παῦλος εἴτε 'Απολλῶς εἴτε Κηφᾶς...πάντα ὑμῶν, ὑμεῖς δὲ Χριστοῦ, Χριστὸς δὲ θεοῦ, and places all that the pneumatic person does as only service to the community (later on he will return to this very point); but all this should not obscure the bluntness with which in the first part of his exposition he rejects any and all judgments passed upon his teaching by friend or foe and claims a position which we can comprehend only with difficulty. Only from this perspective does the polemic to which the second epistle in turn responds become understandable.

In this context the technically used term πνευματικός corresponds to the concept πνεῦμα ἔχειν; in the second passage, 342 where it is set in contrast to the word ψυχικός, it corresponds to the concept πνεῦμα εἶναι. The question will be asked as to how far this second passage confirms the view previously arrived at, and to what extent it presupposes that the community is familiar with established concepts for these two terms. The same view is found, as is well known, in the same epistle in the discussion of the resurrection (15:35ff.). Let us first survey that fifteenth chapter, which forms a closely knit unity. At the outset the apostle sums up the content of his κήρυγμα, which is also the κήρυγμα of all true apostles and which, if it actually is true, brings σωτηρία to the believers (the parenthesis in verse 2, ἐκτὸς εἰ μὴ εἰκῇ ἐπιστεύσατε, prepares the way for the discussion in verse 12; cf. verse 14, κενὴ δὲ καὶ ἡ πίστις ὑμῶν); it has four main points:

Χριστὸς ἀπέθανεν, ἐτάφη, ἠγέρθη, ὤφθη. From this it follows that for the community there can be no question whether a resurrection of the dead is possible; otherwise the κήρυγμα would be in vain, in vain Paul's exertions, in vain the faith of the community; σωτηρία would be impossible (in verse 18, ἀπώλοντο refers back to verse 6, and back still further to verse 2, δι' οὗ καὶ σώζεσθε, τίνι λόγῳ εὐηγγελισάμην ὑμῖν εἰ κατέχετε). The resurrection is the kernel and content of all εὐαγγελίζειν (cf. verses 1 and 2 with verse 19), and Paul as an eyewitness can once more affirm that it actually has taken place, in order then immediately to draw the decisive conclusions (to support these conclusions he has earlier shown what would have to follow from the opposite assumption): hence the spell is broken, Christ *must* become the firstfruits of a multitude; Ἄνθρωπος has brought death, Ἄνθρωπος also brings the resurrection. It is incorrect in verse 21, ἐπειδὴ γὰρ δι' ἀνθρώπου ὁ θάνατος, καὶ δι' ἀνθρώπου ἀνάστασις νεκρῶν, to try to detect an added ἑνός to the genitive ἀνθρώπου, following the pattern of Rom. 5:12ff. There the number "one" is required by the contrast (verse 12, πάντας ἀνθρώπους; verse 15, εἰς τοὺς πολλούς), and it is affected by the fact that ἄνθρωπος is an appellative; a category is being discussed. On the other hand, here it stands, without the article, as a proper name, and we shall see that it also continues to be used thus and must be understood thus; here two individuals are intended. The next verse teaches us that the first Anthropos was Adam (ὁ 'Αδάμ), and the second was the Messiah (ὁ Χριστός); the latter brings universal restoration of life; but there is a sequence (τάγματα): the Messiah himself the ἀπαρχή (and ἀρχή), next those who already belong to him at his return, and finally τὸ τέλος. This last word has a dual meaning here: on the one hand it denotes those who are last (balancing the ἀρχή) and on the

343

other hand it means the end of the world, when these last ones will rise (ὅταν). It is the annihilation of all power that opposes God, and the last enemy is death (thought of in entirely personal terms). It too must be destroyed; indeed, God's word says (Ps. 8:7), πάντα ὑπέταξας ὑποκάτω τῶν ποδῶν αὐτοῦ. If every enemy is to be destroyed, then that includes death (thus it is thought of as an ἐξουσία or ἀρχή, as in Iranian thought). As if to counter a misunderstanding, the apostle further emphasizes that of course the ὑποτάξας himself cannot be among the ὑποτεταγμένα, but receives the dominion back from the one whom he had commissioned, and then God is all in all. For this theology, the concept "God" and the concept "life" are necessarily identical, just as death is the ultimate content of everything that is in opposition to God; of course this is not stated, nor is the distinctive concept Ἄνθρωπος explained; these are the presuppositions of Pauline theology that are familiar to the community. Moreover, it is not said that with the annihilation of death *those who had died earlier will arise.* But for the community this idea apparently is bound up with that of the τέλος, the end of the world, and the arguments that follow, which are drawn from the twofold conviction, are directly connected with this idea: if death ends everything, why do many among you let yourselves be baptized (by proxy) for the dead, and why do I daily place myself in danger and hope for reward? Have nothing to do with anyone who teaches that; he is corrupt and will corrupt you (in verse 34, as in Hermetic thought, ἀγνωσία θεοῦ, also an ethical concept, meaning almost the same as "godless", "estranged from God"; γνῶσις in fact is the immediate, direct connection with God). Now the apostle passes over to the contest with this godless person, by calling him a fool. The person in question may be attempting to achieve a specific

portrayal and then to use it to prove the impossibility of this idea of resurrection; so he asks πῶς ἐγείρονται οἱ νεκροί, ποίῳ δὲ σώματι ἔρχονται.[2] The apostle's immediate response is that the body, the σῶμα--he is not speaking of the body devoid of its soul, but alive, vital--is only the seed, which perishes and from which something entirely different comes. And just as the purely material part of the earthly σῶμα, the σάρξ that is excluded from the resurrection, is different in the different creatures, so also in a higher sense there are different σώματα, primarily σώματα ἐπίγεια and σώματα ἐπουράνια, and just as both have a different share in the δόξα θεοῦ, so also even among the σώματα ἐπουράνια there are once again great differences: ἄλλη δόξα ἡλίου καὶ ἄλλη δόξα σελήνης (verse 41). The unusual use of the term δόξα, going beyond the usage of the Septuagint in combining the concepts of honor, praise, power, and brilliance, recurs in quite similar fashion in the papyri (cf. above, pp. 370, 398); as among the Mandaeans and Manichaeans, δόξα must be an essential attribute and indeed the very substance of God and of all that is divine (the sentence is parallel to ἄλλη μὲν ἀνθρώπων, ἄλλη δὲ σάρξ κτηνῶν). Paul only lightly suggests that he assumes the diversity of the δόξα of those who are glorified; his main intention is to prevent the Corinthians from too closely connecting the οὐράνιον σῶμα with the idea of man according to his form or material (in short, according to the ἐπίγειον σῶμα), and he wants to emphasize God's power by his own free will to give to the various beings a share in his δόξα and his nature. Verse 42 emphasizes the difference between the two kinds of σῶμα and refers back to the picture that was begun in verse 37, as though it had been preceded by ὡς τὸν κόκκον ἄλλον φαμὲν τοῦ φυτοῦ: οὕτως καὶ ἡ ἀνάστασις τῶν νεκρῶν· σπείρεται ἐν φθορᾷ (also a spatial concept, as

in Iranian thought: in matter), ἐγείρεται ἐν ἀφθαρσίᾳ (in the kingdom of God), σπείρεται ἐν ἀτιμίᾳ, ἐγείρεται ἐν δόξῃ (definitions of nature), σπείρεται ἐν ἀσθενείᾳ (above, p. 399), ἐγείρεται ἐν δυνάμει. The summation is: σπείρεται σῶμα ψυχικόν, ἐγείρεται σῶμα πνευματικόν. The word σάρκινον had to be avoided, because it could evoke the image of the lifeless body
345 that is placed in the tomb; Paul, however, wishes to identify the entire "natural man" as to his essence and outward form as the seed from which the new, utterly different formation grows, but which itself must first die. When in precisely this connection he chooses the word ψυχικόν, he assumes that the recipients of his epistle are familiar with this concept, for which no groundwork had been laid here, that they will immediately identify it with φυσικόν and ἐπίγειον, and that they know that the word is used only as a contrast to πνευματικόν. Because one of these concepts necessarily calls for the other, he can append the observation, εἴ ἔστιν σῶμα ψυχικόν, ἔστιν καὶ πνευματικόν. Thus the contrast here is not, as has been claimed, between σάρξ and πνεῦμα, but exclusively between ψυχή and πνεῦμα, only the σάρξ belongs to the former, and the δόξα to the latter. Perhaps I may say at this point that the Iranian idea of resurrection, according to which the bits of light contained in the decaying body are later released from that body and are reunited in a kind of new, indefinable body with a spiritual part that disappeared at death, is more clearly evident here than, for example, in the Syriac Apocalypse of Baruch, with which it has been compared (49ff.: Surely the earth then will give back the dead whom it receives to preserve them, by changing nothing in their appearance....And after the appointed day has passed, then the appearance of those who are guilty will change, and the splendid appearance of those who act uprightly as well...whose brilliance then

will radiate in diverse forms, etc.). This Iranian idea is adopted by Judaism in various reformulations, and we may interpret Paul only in his own terms and within his own framework, particularly in the passage which purports to expound his perspective in context. The late Jewish perspective that serves as a basis for him he now proposes to vindicate out of the ancient tradition of his people and to bring it into harmony with that tradition. Hence he does not continue along the line required by the first declaration, "There are, as we believe, also two Adams; the first one was ψυχικός, and hence the second one must be πνευματικός." Not stating the actual connection between the ideas, as he so often fails to do, he inserts for the first part the divine word that supports and documents it: οὕτως καὶ γέγραπται· Ἐγένετο ὁ πρῶτος Ἄνθρωπος εἰς ψυχὴν ζῶσαν. For him the main thing is the word ψυχή; that word in itself shows the deficiency of this being. So he adds: ὁ ἔσχατος εἰς πνεῦμα ζωοποιοῦν. ἀλλ' οὐ πρῶτον τὸ πνευματικόν, ἀλλὰ τὸ ψυχικόν, ἔπειτα τὸ πνευματικόν.[3] It is not surprising that he has inserted the word πρῶτος into the quotation from Gen. 2:7 in order to provide a point of connection for his own addendum, since it does not alter the meaning; he is striving for conciseness. Again, as in verse 44 in the sentence, εἰ ἔστιν σῶμα ψυχικόν, ἔστιν καὶ πνευματικόν, the presupposition is evident that the pair of words ψυχή and πνεῦμα form a set of opposites which exert a reciprocal influence. If there is an Ἄνθρωπος who had or was only ψυχή, there must also be one who has or is only πνεῦμα; but the latter is the second, not, as has been asserted, the first. An established theology that is familiar to the community is presupposed and will be shown to have been foundational for Paul; but we must first follow his line of proof still further in order rightly to comprehend this presupposition. The statement in Genesis,

46

which Paul's readers must be familiar with, reads thus: καὶ ἔπλασεν ὁ θεὸς τὸν ἄνθρωπον χοῦν ἀπὸ τῆς γῆς καὶ ἐνεφύσησεν εἰς τὸ πρόσωπον αὐτοῦ πνοὴν (Philo: πνεῦμα) ζωῆς, καὶ ἐγένετο ὁ ἄνθρωπος εἰς ψυχὴν ζῶσαν. From this Paul infers ὁ πρῶτος Ἄνθρωπος ἐκ γῆς χοϊκός, ὁ δεύτερος Ἄνθρωπος ἐξ οὐρανοῦ. οἷος ὁ χοϊκός, τοιοῦτοι καὶ οἱ χοϊκοί, καὶ οἷος ὁ ἐπουράνιος, τοιοῦτοι καὶ οἱ ἐπουράνιοι. καὶ (this is the inference, the conclusion of a strictly constructed syllogism) καθὼς ἐφορέσαμεν τὴν εἰκόνα τοῦ χοϊκοῦ, φορέσομεν καὶ τὴν εἰκόνα τοῦ ἐπουρανίου (i.e., the σῶμα ἐπουράνιον). With this the proof of the resurrection is fully concluded. Now let us look for the presuppositions.

In his discussion of the passage in Genesis, Philo (Leg. alleg. I 31; cf. II 4) starts out from a distinction between two classes of men who are different in nature and in origin, 347 a distinction that is found again almost verbatim in the early Gnostic Satornilus (Hippolytus, Elench. VII 28.6; Irenaeus I 24.2; Epiphanius XXIII 2,.3).[4] It is basic for all of Gnosticism, and it has nothing to do with a Platonic idea of man;[5] instead, it goes back to an extension of the Zoroastrian idea that men in the full sense are only those who confess the true religion and that the primal man is the embodiment of the true religion, of the knowledge about God, or as it is expressed in the Poimandres, of the νοῦς. Only one who belongs to him, that is, who in a mystical fashion comes from him, returns to God. It is understandable that Judaism appropriated this doctrine from this source, along with the belief in immortality: the chosen people of Yahweh must occupy this special position; their religion bestows it on them. For Philo (De conf. ling. 41 and 146, 147), all Jews are as υἱοὶ ἑνὸς ἀνθρώπου (Gen. 42:11): ἕνα καὶ τὸν αὐτὸν ἐπιγεγραμμένοι πατέρα οὐ θνητὸν ἀλλ' ἀθάνατον ἄνθρωπον θεοῦ, ὅς τοῦ ἀϊδίου λόγος ὢν ἐξ ἀνάγκης καὶ

αὐτός ἐστιν ἄφθαρτος (cf. 146: κατὰ τὸν πρωτόγονον αὐτοῦ λόγον, τῶν ἀγγέλων πρεσβύτατον ὡς ἀρχάγγελον, πολυώνυμον ὑπάρχοντα· καὶ γὰρ ἀρχὴ καὶ ὄνομα θεοῦ καὶ λόγος καὶ ὁ κατ' εἰκόνα ἄνθρωπος καὶ ὁ ὁρῶν, 'Ισραὴλ προσαγορεύεται, 147 καὶ γὰρ εἰ μήπω ἱκανοὶ θεοῦ παῖδες νομίζεσθαι γεγόναμεν, ἀλλά τοι τῆς ἀειδοῦς εἰκόνος αὐτοῦ Λόγου τοῦ ἱερωτάτου. θεοῦ γὰρ εἰκὼν λόγος ὁ πρεσβύτατος, 148 καὶ πολλαχοῦ μέντοι τῆς νομοθεσίας υἱοὶ πάλιν 'Ισραὴλ καλοῦνται). We can see how this πρεσβύτατος λόγος later becomes the Torah, or how later the devout Jew takes comfort in the view that all the Gentiles are under *heimarmene*, but not the nation of Israel.[6] It is the basic idea of gnosis, not a philosophical Logos doctrine, that is at work here. Paul appropriates the same basic idea, not in the philosophical form, but in the still unphilosophical form which it must have taken among the rabbis, but he completely reshapes it. It is not Judaism and its law, but the knowledge of God brought by Christ from heaven, the Pneuma, that creates the true tribe of souls that is immortal. He breaks decisively with the reliance on the double account of creation which the rabbis had already been seeking in an inappropriate fashion: that heavenly Anthropos is in fact the second, not the first. The true religion and the new "humanity" begins only with Christ.

48

In this connection, now, of course a question arises: how could he, when he surrenders that support from the double account in Genesis, nevertheless hold to the certainty of a second Anthropos in such a way that he builds this entire conclusion, on which so very much depends for him, solely upon it? The answer can only be that the gnostic thesis of the difference in nature of the two classes of man is for him and his community a fact of faith and experience that is beyond all doubt. Paul is a gnostic; for him as for all gnostics

the bearer of the πνεῦμα is φύσει different from the Psychic, and this concept φύσει demands a different species connection, into which one is placed by the new birth. Here one idea follows from another, but we must not conceive of the apostle as a philosopher who has devised a system. The system is already present in the beliefs of the environment. I have already referred to the slightly later pagan form of the Naassene Preaching,[7] where two Anthropoi are distinguished: the heavenly Anthropos, thought of in altogether non-individual terms, essentially a collective concept, who also is called Logos, and the same being individually in the specific man. There that heavenly Anthropos awakens and guides the earthly one; in fact, individual men are the fruit, the offspring of the heavenly man; through them the ἄκαρπος Ἄττις is the πολύκαρπος. Some will object that the idea of the two Anthropoi or Adams is employed here differently from the use in Paul. Hence I shall cite another counterpart that will bring
349 us still closer to Paul, both in time and in location, namely the teaching of the Mandaeans. According to that teaching, the heavenly man (Adam) resides in every believer, and it only needs to be awakened and to remain awake in order to be assured of the resurrection. But the emissary who awakens him and leads him upward is himself again that heavenly man, even though the names are changed; what resides in the individual is his image, his very self, just as he, conversely, can be described as the self and image of the individual. But still more: one among the varying names that are now brought into a system is Enosh or Anosh, i.e., Ἄνθρωπος. It is the *bar nascha* of Jewish eschatology, the Son of Man, i.e., Man. A very definite religious expectation is connected with this idea in wide circles of Judaism, and Jesus shared that expectation; he felt himself to be the *bar nascha*. If I have cor-

rectly interpreted verse 21 in a purely logical way, then Paul was acquainted with the title "Son of Man" and, at least here, acknowledged it, though of course he translated it into proper and understandable Greek.[8] Of course I concede that with him the conception assumes a different shape. In the Pauline definition, πνεῦμα ζωοποιοῦν, that basic Iranian perspective which survived and developed in Israel's environment emerges much more strongly. Now we can understand it even better: that inner Self, what is innermost within us, indeed cannot be rendered in Greek except by use of the word πνεῦμα, and the concept of life is indissolubly connected with the divine, but so also is the concept of redemption; in Syriac the σωτήρ is the one who makes alive. It is only from the definition, ὁ δὲ κύριος τὸ πνεῦμά ἐστιν, which Bousset has rightly identified as the foundation of Pauline Christology,[9] that we can fully understand that marvelously profound saying, "I live, yet not I, but Christ lives in me", and indeed the entire conception of Χριστὸς ἐν ἡμῖν. The most instructive counterpart is offered by the prologue to the gospel of John, in which Prof. H. H. Schaeder[10] has recently identified and sought to demonstrate philologically an Aramaic hymn to Enosh in a slightly revised Christian version. But those two apocalypses which in the same book[11] I have distilled from the Ascension of Isaiah and a fragment of the Naassene Preaching that exhibits Jewish though not Christian coloration, can give us a profound impression of the tendency of messianic hopes in Judaism, a tendency connected with the Son-of-Man concept, and perhaps from this side the attempt can be made to understand Paul. Precisely when he as a Jew shared those hopes or at least desired to be able to believe in them and yet was persecuting the Christians as followers of a false Messiah, the appearance of the resurrected one,

i.e., the inner certainty of having seen him, must lead him to transfer that theological system to him. But these are conjectures that overstep the boundaries of the philological task. To fill them out, I have only a couple of small points to add. In verses 45-47, one should not look for anything special behind the fact that the πρῶτος ἄνθρωπος first is contrasted with an ἔσχατος, and then with a δεύτερος. If the sequence is stressed, and all the emphasis is placed upon it, then, even if only two elements are under consideration, the second can be thus identified with the superlative; cf. Euripides, Androm. 390: ἐκοιμήθην βίᾳ σὺν δεσπόταισι· κᾆτ' ἔμ', οὐ κεῖνον κτενεῖς, τὸν αἴτιον τῶνδ' ἀλλὰ τὴν ἀρχὴν ἀφεὶς πρὸς τὴν τελευτὴν ὑστέραν οὖσαν φέρει; or Propertius II 10.7: *aetas prima canat Veneres, extrema tumultus* (for *prior* and *posterior*). This is psychologically comprehensible. Further, unique is the use in verse 49 of the figure, καθὼς ἐφορέσαμεν τὴν εἰκόνα τοῦ χοϊκοῦ, φορέσομεν καὶ τὴν εἰκόνα τοῦ ἐπουρανίου. Of course the figure of the garment for the body is everywhere understandable and can be documented; but the appearance of εἰκών here for the garment is in striking harmony with the late Iranian funeral texts, where garment and image are completely interchangeable; in the Hymn of the Soul in the Acts of Thomas, the garment grows with the deeds of the hero for whom it is preserved; he sees himself in it as in a mirror, 351 because it is like him, and it hastens toward him. The Mandaean funeral texts offer an abundance of other examples.

In verse 50, then, Paul changes to a didactic form, and we can detect the difference. He first cites the presupposition for all that has preceded as well as for what follows, the fundamental dogma of later Iranian eschatology: matter itself (σὰρξ καὶ αἷμα), that which is merely perishable (the φθορά, as in Iranian thought, a concrete concept), is ex-

cluded from the divine world (ἀφθαρσία). What then will become of those who experience the day of the return in the material body? Must they first put off the body, that is, die, even though death has been overcome, or, as it is said among the Mandaeans and Manichaeans, has been slain? Paul teaches that for them, in place of death and resurrection, which indeed are only a transformation, there is another kind of transformation. It resembles a clothing of matter with the immaterial, in which the former disappears in the latter: δεῖ γὰρ τὸ φθαρτὸν τοῦτο ἐνδύσασθαι ἀφθαρσίαν (thus τὸ ἄφθαρτον) καὶ τὸ θνητὸν τοῦτο ἐνδύσασθαι ἀθανασίαν (τὸ ἀθάνατον). The apostle solemnly repeats this statement, by declaring that when this happens, the saying of Isaiah (25:8) will be fulfilled: κατεπόθη ὁ θάνατος εἰς νῖκος. This prompts me to conjecture in the word ὁ θάνατος here a concrete concept τὸ θνητόν (just as φθορά appears for τὸ φθαρτόν). Arguing for this is the expression in II Cor. 5:4 which evidently was framed in recollection of this statement: ἵνα καταποθῇ τὸ θνητὸν ὑπὸ τῆς ζωῆς. Once the reverse was true; then matter had overcome (swallowed up) the divine and apparently conquered it. This thought lets him make a free rendering of Hosea 13:14 (he avoids the word ᾅδης) and at the same time explain: ποῦ σου, θάνατε, τὸ κέντρον; ποῦ σου, θάνατε, τὸ νῖκος; τὸ δὲ κέντρον τοῦ θανάτου ἡ ἁμαρτία, ἡ δὲ δύναμις τῆς ἁμαρτίας ὁ νόμος. Here too θάνατος still appears to be used for matter, for τὸ θηντόν, and indeed for what is mortal in the individual person. For, as the conclusion shows, Paul conceives of the process as though the individual Christian conquers death (that in himself that is perishable), and sin along with death, through Christ's intervention. Christ's victory (verse 26) results in the victory of the Christian, who indeed bears Christ within himself.

Paul certainly does not draw this directly from Iranian 352 thought; only in order to characterize the ideas of his time I point out that in later Iranian thought a first struggle of Ohrmazd ("Man") with matter, in which he is defeated and swallowed up, is balanced by a second struggle at the end of all things, in which Ohrmazd conquers and destroys matter or perishability (destruction, death, but also greed, sin).

I am aware that the interpretation that I have given to the word θάνατος in verse 45 will evoke strong opposition, even though it is strongly supported by the fact that only thereby is the victory of the individual Christian clearly set over against Christ's victory (verse 26; the deceased individual also receives, in the late Iranian ritual for the dead, the crown of victory, or the crown of righteousness). Hence I shall trace out first of all the peculiar use of language. Anyone who is in any measure familiar with Mandaean and Manichaean texts will sense in the entire passage an Oriental coloring (e.g., in the use of φθορά and ἀφθαρσία, τὸ θνητόν and ἀθανασία). It is clearest in the use of the word θάνατος. I shall first compare a passage from Corp. herm. VII, a peculiar writing already used by Philo, in which there is a remarkable intertwining of basic Oriental perspectives and formulas from Platonic philosophy, as I have already demonstrated in the *Göttinger Gelehrte Anzeige* 1911, pp. 555ff. Here, in §2, we read: ζητήσατε χειραγωγὸν τὸν ὁδηγήσοντα ὑμᾶς ἐπὶ τὰς τῆς γνώσεως θύρας, ὅπου ἐστὶ τὸ λαμπρὸν φῶς τὸ καθαρὸν σκότους (Iranian term), ὅπου οὐδὲ εἷς μεθύει, ἀλλὰ πάντες νήφουσιν (Iranian figure) ἀφορῶντες τῇ καρδίᾳ εἰς τὸν ὁραθῆναι θέλοντα. οὐ γάρ ἐστιν ἀκουστὸς οὐδὲ λεκτὸς οὐδὲ ὁρατὸς ὀφθαλμοῖς, ἀλλὰ νῷ καὶ καρδίᾳ. πρῶτον δὲ δεῖ σε περιρρήξασθαι ὃν φορεῖς χιτῶνα, τὸ τῆς ἀγνωσίας ὕφασμα, τὸ τῆς κακίας στήριγμα, τὸν τῆς φθορᾶς δεσμόν, τὸν σκοτεινὸν περίβολον, τὸν

ζῶντα θάνατον, τὸν αἰσθητ<ικ>ὸν νεκρόν, τὸν περιφόρητον τάφον, τὸν ἔνοικον λῄστην, τὸν δι' ὧν φιλεῖ μισοῦντα καὶ δι' ὧν μισεῖ φιλοῦντα (mss. φθονοῦντα).[12] τοιοῦτός ἐστιν ὃν

53 ἐνεδύσω ἐχθρὸν χιτῶνα, ἄγχων σε κάτω πρὸς αὐτόν, ἵνα μὴ ἀναβλέψας καὶ θεασάμενος τὸ κάλλος τῆς ἀληθείας καὶ τὸ ἐγκείμενον ἀγαθὸν μισήσῃς τὴν τούτου κακίαν, νοήσας αὐτοῦ τὴν ἐπιβουλήν, ἣν ἐπεβούλευσέ σοι τὰ δοκοῦντα καὶ μὴ <ὄντα αἰσθητήρια χαρισάμενος, τὰ δὲ> νομιζόμενα αἰσθητήρια ἀναίσθητα ποιῶν τῇ πολλῇ ὕλῃ αὐτὰ ἀποφράξας (cf. I 22: πυλωρὸς ὢν ἀποκλείσω τὰς εἰσόδους) καὶ μυσαρᾶς ἡδονῆς ἐμπλήσας, ἵνα μήτε ἀκούῃς περὶ ὧν ἀκούειν σε δεῖ, μήτε βλέπῃς περὶ ὧν βλέπειν σε δεῖ. In connection with the figures used for the body, one certainly can recall Plato's equating of σῶμα and σῆμα; but the individual expressions (e.g., λῄστης, a designation for the body as well as for matter that is common among the Mandaeans) are far more closely reminiscent of Iranian formulas, and it is precisely among these that one encounters among the Manichaeans "the dead one who is born"; indeed, the formula "the body of death" is still more a fixed expression among Mandaeans and Manichaeans, and thus is protected against the suspicion of having been borrowed from Christianity. When this utterly peculiar expression recurs in Paul's writings in Rom. 7:24, without compelling reason (the context would have allowed him to say τίς με ῥύσεται ἐκ τοῦ σώματος τούτου, or, following verse 10, even ἐκ τοῦ θανάτου; the combination is strange), I regard this in itself as convincing proof that Iranian formulas and figures have reached him by way of Jewish eschatology. Since the train of thought of Rom. 7 undoubtedly forms part of the background of the passage from which I started out, I Cor. 15:55, 56, and Iranian eschatological ideas also exert some influence, I consider the interpretation of θάνατος given there to be linguistically utterly

unassailable. I should like to go even further.

The figure of the garment for the body is so obvious that it must be demonstrable in most literatures, like the figure of the house. Its application will have been most common where in the cult of the dead the white robe (or a robe of the gods) is put on the deceased person as a symbol of the heavenly body, as this must also have been customary in part in Iranian territory (even among the Parsees it is at least a white wrapping). Here the figurative expression frequently appears in place of the original designation; or 354 two figures are intermingled: the righteous one puts on the luminous habitation, and the soul dwells here in the garment of consuming fire; the body is the cloak of clay, or the descending deity dwells in the garment of tears (in the world as the house of tears). Such distinctive features can also gain further evidentiary force in connection with other characteristics. Hence I shall briefly analyze still another passage from Paul that is related to I Cor. 15, namely II Cor. 4:16ff. Paul feels his outward man being consumed and perishing day by day (διαφθείρεσθαι), and in necessary connection with that experience, the inward man being renewed day by day (ἀνακαινοῦσθαι). The fact that he often spoke of dying daily and contrasted the ἀνακαίνωσις, the miracle of the new creation, with death explains his choice of words here. The expression ἔσωθεν ἄνθρωπος in this connection is in itself just as ambiguous as the term πνεῦμα (above, pp. 391ff.), and could mean, in a purely natural sense, that inner man with whom we speak in the process of thinking and conversing with ourselves (cf. Philo, Quod det. pot. insid. §23 Cohn; Tertullian, Adv. Prax. 5, L. Rosenmeyer, Quaest. Tertullianae [Strassburg 1909], p. 1; it would be absurd to go back to Plato's distinction of an outward and an inward Socrates for such a conception); it

is by no means necessary for the source in this case to be philosophical; the word λόγος or συνείδησις, and indeed everyday experience itself would easily lead to that usage. On the other hand, it *can* denote that divine nature in us which, as we have seen, is bestowed in the mystery. Thus the late pagan author Zosimos (*Poimandres*, p. 104) distinguishes from the first man an ἔσω αὐτοῦ ἄνθρωπος πνευματικός and teaches that every one of us bears within himself a φωτεινὸς καὶ πνευματικὸς ἄνθρωπος, who is also called in brief τὸ φωτεινὸν ἡμῶν πνεῦμα; the essential designation for this being is Φῶς; he is the Adakas of the Mandaeans; it is he who was originally in "Paradise" and was persuaded by the evil one to enter into the corporeal Adam. The same idea also is found here and there among the Mandaeans. Among the Manichaeans he is called ὁ καινὸς ἄνθρωπος; according to them he consists of five elements, like the natural man, but these elements are also divine powers (cf. the similar idea in Col.
55 3; above, p. 342). The context must determine which interpretation we should give to the expression here. It seems to me that there is no room for doubt: Paul is satisfied; the easily bearable oppression of the moment is creating for him for eternity a splendid abundance and weight (βάρος) of δόξα. I shall no longer attempt to derive this curious expression from the Hebrew word *kabod*, since I have read in the Mandaean literature that the ascending soul bears a burden (βάρος) in the presence of which the worlds tremble; it is the fullness of splendor. Paul justifies this hope of his (5:1) thus: οἴδαμεν γὰρ ὅτι ἐὰν ἡ ἐπίγειον ἡμῶν οἰκία τοῦ σκήνους καταλυθῇ (cf. Corp. herm. XIII 15: καλῶς σπεύδεις λῦσαι τὸ σκῆνος; what is meant here is the σῶμα ἐπίγειον of the first epistle), οἰκοδομὴν ἐκ θεοῦ ἔχομεν, οἰκίαν ἀχειροποίητον αἰώνιον ἐν τοῖς οὐρανοῖς (also a Mandaean idea; to be compared

also is the body made by God himself in heaven which the *mystes* of the Mithras liturgy knows is his). καὶ γὰρ ἐν τούτῳ στενάζομεν, τὸ οἰκητήριον ἡμῶν τὸ ἐξ οὐρανοῦ ἐπενδύσασθαι ἐπιποθοῦντες, εἴ γε καὶ ἐκδυσάμενοι οὐ γυμνοὶ εὑρεθησόμεθα. Here there is exhibited that intermingling of the two figures which is familiar to us from Iranian thought. Of course there will be disagreement as to the interpretation. Anyone who wishes to explain the εἴ γε (like εἴ περ) simply can only follow the interpretation that for the ἐπενδύσασθαι, the putting on of an outer garment over an already present cloak, the *indispensable pre-condition* is that, even if we must put off the earthly garment, we must have beneath it another cloak over which the heavenly garment is placed; anyone not having it could not receive the σῶμα ἐξ οὐρανοῦ or οὐράνιον. Again Paul assumes that his readers know what this second, absolutely necessary cloak is, and he repeats only by way of emphasis (verse 4): καὶ γὰρ οἱ ὄντες ἐν τῷ σκήνει στενάζομεν βαρούμενοι, ἐφ' ᾧ οὐ θέλομεν ἐκδύσασθαι, ἀλλ' ἐπενδύσασθαι, ἵνα καταποθῇ τὸ θνητὸν ἡμῶν ὑπὸ τῆς ζωῆς. Certainly we sense this garment of the earthly body as an oppressive burden, but we do not long simply to put it off (to die, and to be dead), but to receive in place of it or on top of it that *other* outer garment that gives us a new *life*. The lack of clarity of expression lies in the fact that here Paul counts himself among those who themselves will live to see the day of the Lord and will put on the heavenly garment over the earthly one, but that he also takes into account those who have previously died, and thus have put off the earthly garment; for *both* the possession of an ἔσωθεν ἄνθρωπος was a necessary presupposition for the acquisition of the σῶμα ἐπουράνιον. Hence in verse 3 I may not connect εἴ γε καί, but must relate the last word to the ἐκδυσάμενοι (εἰ καὶ

356

ἐξεδυσάμεθα): if, even though we had earlier been obliged to put off the earthly body, we otherwise would not be found unclothed. In order to declare that he is firmly convinced of this for all cases, Paul uses the positive expression in spite of the case in mind (*irrealis*). A similar example of grammatical liberty or subtlety will later engage our attention. Paul continues: ὁ δὲ κατεργασάμενος ἡμᾶς εἰς αὐτὸ τοῦτο θεός (cf. I Cor. 15:57: τῷ διδόντι ἡμῖν τὸ νῖκος), ὁ καὶ δοὺς ἡμῖν τὸν ἀρραβῶνα τοῦ πνεύματος (cf. Suidas: ἀρραβών· ἡ ἐν ταῖς ὠναῖς παρὰ τῶν ὠνουμένων διδομένη πρώτη καταβολὴ ὑπὲρ ἀσφαλείας). It is only the new image that brings the thought fully to its conclusion: the ἔσωθεν ἄνθρωπος, which we bear concealed beneath the ἐπίγειον σῶμα as a kind of ἔνδυμα, is also the earnest. For Paul as for Zosimos it is the πνεῦμα. The commentaries rightly point to the parallelism with Rom. 8:23: καὶ αὐτοὶ τὴν ἀπαρχὴν τοῦ πνεύματος ἔχοντες καὶ αὐτοὶ ἐν ἑαυτοῖς στενάζομεν υἱοθεσίαν ἀπεκδεχόμενοι, τὴν ἀπολύτρωσιν τοῦ σώματος ἡμῶν· τῇ γὰρ ἐλπίδι ἐσώθημεν. Even the last clause finds its counterpart in II Cor. 5:7: διὰ πίστεως γὰρ περιπατοῦμεν, οὐ δι' εἴδους. The ἀπαρχή is the πρώτη καταβολή; the πνεῦμα ἔχειν is the beginning, the initial stage of the πνεῦμα εἶναι. To me it is not insignificant that in Apuleius also (XI 23) the day of initiation into the mystery is described as *dies divino vadimonio destinatus*; it gives the divine *guarantee* for the promised full σωτηρία, a guarantee that is repeated from time to time, as is well known. It provides the basis for the *fiducia germanae religionis*, which Apuleius also (XI 28) grounds in the reception of the πνεῦμα (cf. *spiritu faventis Eventus*, i.e., of the 'Αγαθὸς δαίμων). How closely Paul's usage is related to the language of the mysteries is shown also by the Hermetic mystery of rebirth (Corp. herm. XIII): there too the υἱοθεσία only occurs after

the total dissolution of the earthly body and the detachment from the world, which there of course comes before the earthly death; only after that is it said (§14) θεὸς πέφυκας καὶ τοῦ ἑνὸς παῖς. The usage τῇ γὰρ ἐλπίδι ἐσώθημεν is explained by §1: μηδένα δύνασθαι σωθῆναι πρὸ τῆς παλιγγενεσίας; the σωτηρία is the new life which at present we have only in hope, i.e., as a hoped-for life. Hence in conclusion we may mention that in the Hermetic literature also, of course in passages that have been influenced in part by Greek philosophy, the πνεῦμα is identified as a garment (e.g., in X 17).

357

As is known, in II Cor. 3:18 Paul describes that material transformation which must already here on earth have occurred with the Christian, so that he might be able to receive the σῶμα οὐράνιον: ἡμεῖς δὲ πάντες ἀνακεκαλυμμένῳ προσώπῳ τὴν δόξαν κυρίου κατοπτριζόμενοι (beholding and reflecting) τὴν αὐτὴν εἰκόνα μεταμορφούμεθα ἀπὸ δόξης εἰς δόξαν, καθάπερ ἀπὸ κυρίου πνεύματος (cf. I Clem. 36:2). The expression μεταμορφούμεθα, which is common in the language of the mysteries (cf. above, p. 333; Apuleius XI 30: *non in alienam quampiam personam reformatus*) seems a bit strange here, since it does not altogether fit in with δόξα (glory); the μεταμόρφωσις does not consist in a transformation of the *form*, but of the nature or the degree of glory, and indeed Paul is conscious of the peculiarity of the usage, since he deliberately makes the artificial combination τὴν αὐτὴν εἰκόνα μεταμορφοῦσθαι, and in Rom. 8:29 he interprets the σύμμορφον εἶναι τῆς εἰκόνος τοῦ θεοῦ υἱοῦ as an effect of the δοξάζεσθαι. One might almost surmise that he found these expressions already at hand, and that for him the μορφὴ θεοῦ is something *essential* in connection with the divine σῶμα ἀσώματον. Passages like Phil. 3:21 (ὃς μετασχηματίσει τὸ σῶμα τῆς ταπεινώσεως ἡμῶν σύμμορφον τῷ σώματι τῆς δόξης αὐτοῦ) and Phil. 2:6 (ἐν μορφῇ θεοῦ ὑπάρχων,

in contrast to μορφὴν δούλου ἔλαβεν) fit in with such a conjecture. Now the μορφὴ θεοῦ is a concept familiar to the Hellenistic mysteries, a concept which at first of course is interpreted in a purely external sense; the magician must know the ὀνόματα and the μορφαί of his god, and then he knows his *essence*; in this way, the μορφή, as well as the ὄνομα, becomes significant and almost possesses an independent existence of its own; the ὄνομα or the μορφή acts; both then are combined with πνεῦμα (cf. above, p. 393): ὄνομά σου καὶ πνεῦμά σου ἐπ' ἀγαθοῖς, and Wessely (*Denkschr. d. K. K. Akad.* 1888, p. 73, line 1174): πρόσεχε, μορφὴ καὶ πνεῦμα (God is both); cf. in Paul: καθάπερ ἀπὸ κυρίου πνεύματος. Mysterious influences issue from the μορφὴ θεοῦ (cf. above, p. 217): συνεστάθην σου τῇ ἱερᾷ μορφῇ, ἐδυναμώθην τῷ ἱερῷ σου ὀνόματι, ἐπέτυχόν σου τῆς ἀπορροίας τῶν ἀγαθῶν. Thus the soul itself must assume the μορφὴ θεοῦ, and God brings this about, by entering into the soul (cf. above, p. 98, n. 59): ἔμβηθι αὐτοῦ εἰς τὴν ψυχήν, ἵνα τυπώσηται τὴν ἀθάνατον μορφὴν ἐν φωτὶ κραταιῷ καὶ ἀφθάρτῳ (it is the φωτίζεσθαι or *illustrari* in the metaphysical sense; cf. Apuleius XI 29). We saw earlier that the vision of God has the same effect. Hence it is immediately understandable that an abiding vision of God produces in us a μεταμόρφωσις, a transformation in nature in an ever increasing glory to one and the same image. I have several times discussed the Hellenistic idea of ὁμοίωσις through the vision, and the most I can do here is to add a reference to Corp. herm. XVII (*Poimandres*, p. 354): ἔστιν, ὦ βασιλεῦ, καὶ σωμάτων (to be completed with εἴδη or something of the sort) ἀσώματα. ποῖα; ἔφη ὁ βασιλεύς. τὰ ἐν τοῖς ἐσόπτροις φαινόμενα σώματα ἀσώματα οὐ δοκεῖ σοι εἶναι;...οὕτως ἀντανακλάσεις εἰσὶ τῶν ἀσωμάτων πρὸς τὰ σώματα καὶ τῶν σωμάτων πρὸς τὰ ἀσώματα, τουτέστι τοῦ αἰσθητοῦ πρὸς τὸν νοητὸν κόσμον καὶ τοῦ νοητοῦ πρὸς

τὸν αἰσθητόν. This certainly is a late rationale, influenced by Platonic philosophy, supporting the assumption of a σῶμα ἀσώματον, but this concept itself is evident in the rebirth-mystery; indeed, the σῶμα πνευματικόν or οὐράνιον is the basic concept of this entire mystery perspective; thus it is possible that the comparison is already an ancient one, particularly since the idea of man as a counterpart of his God is also very primitive.

Once again we have a thought-context that is essentially Hellenistic, and it appears to me that in that context the peculiar combination of the concepts δόξα and πνεῦμα (cf. the words καθάπερ ἀπὸ κυρίου πνεύματος) convincingly points to a mystery-conception which is most clearly evident in the alchemistic writing, (above, p. 398); similarly in Corp. herm. X 6, 7 (above, p. 370). If the interpretation of light as the essence of the deity could have arisen in various places inde-

359

pendently, the peculiar usage of the word δόξα surely could not have done so. The interpretations which I have felt obliged to infer from the context for Paul's words, ἄλλη δόξα ἡλίου καὶ ἄλλη δόξα σελήνης (above, p. 443), all recur in the magical papyri. There we read (Dieterich, *Abraxas*, 176.5): σὺ γὰρ ἔδωκας ἡλίῳ τὴν δόξαν καὶ τὴν δύναμιν, or (*ibid.*, in the fire-magic, 191.3) ἄκουε, πῦρ, ἔργον εὑρήματος θεοῦ, δόξα τοῦ ἐντίμου φωστῆρος. This embraces the idea of honor (cf. ἐντίμου) as well as of power. I take this as a starting point for interpreting the prayer of the magician to Isis (Kenyon, *Greek Pap. Brit. Mus.* I 100 = Wessely, *Denkschrift d. K. K. Akad.* 1893, line 512): δόξασόν με, ὡς ἐδόξασα τὸ ὄνομα τοῦ υἱοῦ σου Ὥρου: the utterance of the magical formula glorifies the speaker himself (gives him divine power) and glorifies (praises) the deity. Another magician (Wessely, *Denkschr. d. K. K. Akad.* 1888, pp. 73, 74, lines 1171-1200) says,

following the address, δεῦρό μοι ὁ ἐνφυσήσας τὸν σύμπαντα κόσμον, ὁ τὸ πῦρ κρεμάσας ἐκ τοῦ ὕδατος καὶ τὴν γῆν χωρίσας ἀπὸ τοῦ ὕδατος...κόσμου κτίστα, τὰ πάντα κτίστα, θεὲ θεῶν, following with ἐφώνησά σου τὴν ἀνυπέρβλητον δόξαν, ὁ κτίσας θεοὺς καὶ ἀρχαγγέλους καὶ δεκανούς. αἱ μυριάδες τῶν ἀγγέλων παρεστήκασι καὶ ὕψωσαν τὸν Οὐρανόν, καὶ ὁ κύριος ἐπεμαρτύρησέ σου τῇ Σοφίᾳ, ὅ ἐστιν Αἰῶν<ι>, καὶ εἶπεν σὲ σθένειν, ὅσα καὶ αὐτὸς σθένει. It will be seen here that quite recent Jewish magical literature exerts an influence, though the basis is ancient. In the creation account of Abraxas, which I have demonstrated (in the essay "Die Göttin Psyche in der hellenistischen und frühchristlichen Literatur," *Sitzungsber. d. Heidelberger Akademie* 1917, Abh. 10, pp. 23ff.) to be part of an ancient Iranian sacred writing, a passage of the fuller version, which I now would restore somewhat differently (see *ibid.*, p. 31; Dieterich, *Abraxas*, 183.64), reads thus: καὶ ἐφάνη Κρόνος (thus Dieterich; Preisendanz Καιρός; pap. κρος) κατέχων σκῆπτρον μηνύον βασιλείαν καὶ ἐπέδωκεν τῷ θεῷ τῷ πρώτῳ κτιστῷ. καὶ λαβὼν ἔφη· Σὺ τὴν δόξαν τοῦ φωτὸς περιθέμενος ἔσῃ μετ' ἐμὲ ὡς πρῶτος ἐπιδούς μοι σκῆπτρον, πάντα δὲ ὑπὸ σὲ ἔσται. τοῦ δὲ περιθεμένου (pap. περιθεμένω) τοῦ φωτὸς τὴν δόξαν ὁ [δὲ] τρόπος τοῦ φωτὸς ἔδειξέν τινα αὖραν. ἔφη ὁ θεὸς τῇ Βασιλίσσῃ· Σὺ περιθεμένη τὴν αὖραν τοῦ φωτὸς ἔσῃ μετ' αὐτὸν περιέχουσα τὰ πάντα· αὐξήσεις τῷ φωτὶ ἀπ' αὐτοῦ λαμβάνουσα καὶ πά<λι>ν ἀπολήξεις δι' αὐτοῦ· σὺν σοὶ πάντα αὐξήσει καὶ μειωθήσεται. The passage is an important one for the history of religions; it provides a certain testimony that the ancient deity Zurvan was supplanted through the substitution of Ahura Mazda; later on people invented a transferral of dominion or of its insignia which was even portrayed in Mithraic art; in some particular tribes, of course, he remained, along with his queen, in first place. The position of the queen as the

moon goddess here could be a result of Greek revision (in the Iranian version the moon is male; in Mani's thought it is guided by the male-female παρθένος τοῦ φωτός). Important also is the precise description of the *x^{v}areno*, the δόξα τοῦ φωτός. It is the διάδημα (τροπός in fact is the round twisted loop made of leather) and like the crown of victory (or of righteousness) among the Mandaeans and Manichaeans, its weaker copy is the αὖρα τοῦ φωτός (the halo or aureole). Even here it contains both the essence and the power of the light (of God). The word occurs innumerable times in the Manichaean texts and passes over into other languages, e.g., the Armenian (there the Greek always paraphrases it with δόξα). The concept apparently oscillates between brilliance, renown, power, and divinity; we even hear of a δόξα of religion or of belief, and its elements are enumerated. It is the basic concept of Iranian religion.[13] I was mistaken when I earlier attempted, because of the Septuagint, to derive the corresponding usage of δόξα from the Egyptian; G. P. Wetter (*Phos*, p. 76.2) more correctly saw that the concept, formed in Iran, came into Judaism and to Egypt quite early along with light-mysticism. In the saying of Paul from which I set out and to which I finally come back (II Cor. 3:18), in the combination of the two words δόξα and πνεῦμα the idea of a total *transformation of nature* by means of the γνῶσις θεοῦ finds its expression, and this idea itself, like the use of the two words, is itself *non-Jewish*. Other passages then may be judged accordingly, as for example I Cor. 2:7: ἀλλὰ λαλοῦμεν θεοῦ σοφίαν ἐν μυστηρίῳ τὴν ἀποκεκρυμμένην, ἥν προώρισεν ὁ θεὸς πρὸ τῶν αἰώνων εἰς δόξαν ἡμῶν. Thus what is meant here is not an elevation of dignity or even of praise, but a kind of ἀποθέωσις, a μεταμόρφωσις through the γνῶσις θεοῦ and the reception of the πνεῦμα (cf. verses 9 and 10). Only now, it appears to me,

361

do we have adequate validation of my earlier assertion that in the words of Rom. 8:30, οὓς δὲ προώρισεν, τούτους καὶ ἐκάλεσεν, καὶ οὓς ἐκάλεσεν, τούτους καὶ ἐδικαίωσεν, οὓς δὲ ἐδικαίωσεν, τούτους καὶ ἐδόξασεν, the δοξάζειν corresponds to the θεοῦν or ἀποθεοῦν of the literature of the Hellenistic mysteries (above, pp. 329ff.).

The last four chapters of the second epistle correspond to the first three chapters of the first epistle, whatever the intervening events may have been, and they show how the sense of being πνευματικός must have intensified during the struggle. Paul's claim to be such must in fact have been disputed by the two parties of followers of Peter and Apollos; what was at stake was the justification for their very existence. They turned upon Paul his own proof that they were only νήπιοι ἐν Χριστῷ: ὅπου γὰρ ἐν ὑμῖν ζῆλος καὶ ἔρις, οὐχὶ σαρκικοί ἐστε καὶ κατὰ ἄνθρωπον περιπατεῖτε. He himself is bringing in ἔρις and ζῆλος, and so it may also be said of him that κατὰ ἄνθρωπον περιπατεῖ (cf. 10:2, in the introduction to this whole section: τοὺς λογιζομένους ἡμᾶς ὡς κατὰ σάρκα περιπατοῦντας). Thus he too is only ἄνθρωπος, and thus σαρκικός; his boasting is untrustworthy, a παραφρονεῖν; worst of all, his attestation by virtue of the fact that his preaching among them was done ἐν ἀποδείξει πνεύματος καὶ δυνάμεως is insufficient; all Christians have autonomy, because they all stand in direct connection with the Master.

His first response to that first mentioned accusation (κατὰ σάρκα περιπατεῖ) is his reference to the *military service of his office* (cf. Harnack, *Militia Christi*, p. 14); he fulfills that office οὐ κατὰ σάρκα and is constrained by it to engage in a kind of battle (verse 5): λογισμοὺς καθαιροῦντες καὶ πᾶν ὕψωμα ἐπαιρόμενον κατὰ τῆς γνώσεως τοῦ θεοῦ (i.e., against the unerring and sure knowledge that is given to *him*)

καὶ αἰχμαλωτίζοντες πᾶν νόημα εἰς τὴν ὑπακοὴν τοῦ Χριστοῦ. The declaration, which concludes with a reference to his coming and to punishment of disobedience, is taken up in the conclusion (13:1) with the affirmation that this Christ speaks in him and through his mouth (ἐπεὶ δοκιμὴν ζητεῖτε τοῦ ἐν ἐμοὶ λαλοῦντος Χριστοῦ). This feeling provides the transition to the first part of the exposition: εἴ τις πέποιθεν ἑαυτῷ Χριστοῦ εἶναι. His opponents have not called themselves πνευματικοί, but have only acknowledged what he has even demanded of them, the confession Χριστοῦ εἰμι, and have based their claim upon that (the fact that we are not dealing with a Christ-party but with that mystical connection is especially clear here; they have stated what Χριστοῦ εἶναι signifies for them, and according to the apostle's view thereby have been sounding their own trumpet). In contrast to this, Paul still does not wish to boast of his broader ἐξουσία, although his coming will show that he could do so without fear of disgrace (the note is sounded again in 13:10); but he does not want to issue *threats* in letters. Indeed, his opponents are already saying: αἱ μὲν ἐπιστολαὶ βαρεῖαι καὶ ἰσχυραί, ἡ δὲ παρουσία τοῦ σώματος ἀσθενὴς καὶ ὁ λόγος ἐξουθενημένος. The accusation has great significance for him, much greater than one could expect for a reproach concerning a physical weakness, an illness; and the explanation that Jewish Christians could interpret this illness as a punishment for sins is not adequate to account for the fact that everything that follows is dominated by the ideas "I will glory in my ἀσθένεια" and "when I am weak, then *I am strong*".[14] This becomes comprehensible only when we consider the fact that Paul has said of his oral proclamation that it was done ἐν ἀποδείξει πνεύματος καὶ δυνάμεως, and that this imparting of a δύναμις to the preacher is already an essential demand in the Hellenistic belief (cf. Corp. herm. I 32: αἰ-

τουμένῳ τὸ μὴ σφαλῆναι τῆς γνώσεως...ἐπίνευσόν μοι καὶ ἐνδυνάμωσόν με, καὶ τῆς χάριτος ταύτης φωτίσω τοὺς ἐν ἀγνοίᾳ); indeed, light is shed upon the connection itself from this angle. Even in that imitation of religious ἐνθουσιασμός in the poetical and rhetorical literature that is so familiar to the philologist (cf. Seneca, Suas. III), free and improvised discourse is proof of the possession of the πνεῦμα. Suspicion is also cast upon the bearer of the πνεῦμα in the religious sense when he exhibits δύναμις only in epistles that have been labored over, not in direct proclamation. That would not be a genuine πνευματικός. Perhaps one may go even further. Hermas (Mand. XI) contrasts two interpretations of the function of prophecy; according to one, which he himself shares, "the angel of the prophetic spirit" fills the favored person with the πνεῦμα only in the assembly of the community and after the prayer of the congregation, while this is the very place where the false prophet loses his power and falls silent; the latter "prophesies" in solitude or before only a few. It appears to me quite possible that a similar idea already existed in the Corinthian community. In verse 11 Paul adds, with a severe threat, that he will show his opponents that he has δύναμις in personal discourse also; this makes it impossible for me to see in verse 8, in the words καυχήσομαι περὶ τῆς ἐξουσίας ἡμῶν, ἧς ἔδωκεν ὁ κύριος εἰς οἰκοδομὴν καὶ οὐκ εἰς καθαίρεσιν ὑμῶν, in the relative clause, an interpolation from 13:10. Its recurrence there in an altogether different and conciliatory sense appears to me intentional. It is true that here the apostle declares that he does not wish to threaten, in order not to give further stimulus to that accusation, but he does indicate that he possesses a distinctive and mysterious power. In magical usage the word ἐξουσία denotes any supernatural

and mysterious power that is grounded in a special relationship with God and a special γνῶσις. The Hermetic literature internalizes the conception, but preserves it, and there the πᾶσα ἐξουσία is also full power over nature and the πνεύματα, as for example the divine power to be holy and sinless (cf. above, p. 383; Corp. herm. XIII 17; I 32). Even in our present passage we may not speak of a right of the apostolate simply to exclude from the community. Any specific idea would disrupt the ethos of the passage. Paul has already spoken in the first epistle (5:3ff.) of a mysterious power, and in fact has in essence made use of it: ἐγὼ μὲν γὰρ ὡς ἀπὼν τῷ σώματι, παρὼν δὲ τῷ πνεύματι ἤδη κέκρικα ὡς παρὼν τὸν οὕτως τοῦτο κατεργασάμενον, ἐν τῷ ὀνόματι τοῦ κυρίου ἡμῶν 'Ιησοῦ συναχθέντων ὑμῶν καὶ τοῦ ἐμοῦ πνεύματος σὺν τῇ δυνάμει τοῦ κυρίου ἡμῶν 'Ιησοῦ παραδοῦναι τὸν τοιοῦτον τῷ σατανᾷ εἰς ὄλεθρον τῆς σαρκός, ἵνα τὸ πνεῦμα σωθῇ ἐν τῇ ἡμέρᾳ τοῦ κυρίου. It is fruitless to attempt to decide whether in this "exclusion from the community" the community itself is to participate or not. It is hardly unintentional that the apostle allows the interpretation that he alone has decided the next time he is present to hand over the sinner to Satan in the presence of the community. The passage can just as well, and perhaps with even stronger justification, be read as a threat that the next time the community is assembled, his spirit, invisibly present, will do this handing-over through the power of God. In any case, we must connect the words τοῦ ἐμοῦ πνεύματος σὺν τῇ δυνάμει τοῦ κυρίου ἡμῶν 'Ιησοῦ Χριστοῦ (cf. II Cor. 13:4); of the community all that is said is συναχθέντων ὑμῶν ἐν τῷ ὀνόματι τοῦ κυρίου ἡμῶν 'Ιησοῦ; the natural word-order is changed in order to heighten the rhetorical effect of the solemn sentence; the community is to be present--as Hermas also requires--but the apostle alone

364

is the bearer of the power. According to the words an exclusion from the community itself is not the main object of *his* judgment, but corporal punishment or even destruction by Satan; it is later said that *the community* is to expel the guilty person: ἐξάρατε τὸν πονηρὸν ἐξ ὑμῶν αὐτῶν (verse 13; cf. verse 7: ἐκκαθάρατε τὴν παλαιὰν ζύμην, and verse 12: οὐχὶ τοὺς ἔσω ὑμεῖς κρίνετε)--it is the discontinuance of any association, which the apostle can indeed advise but in which he himself does not participate. *His* action is altogether differently characterized; his imitator in I Tim. 1:20 regards it simply as a kind of magical action (τινὲς...περὶ τὴν πίστιν ἐναυάγησαν· ὧν ἐστὶν Ὑμέναιος καὶ Ἀλέξανδρος, οὓς παρέδωκα τῷ σατανᾷ, ἵνα παιδευθῶσιν μὴ βλασφημεῖν; cf. the ideas of the power of the magician who has commerce with God, in Apuleius, above, p. 382; the conceptions of penance, pp. 169ff.; and Philo, De spec. leg. III 100 Cohn). In any case, in our passage, as Bachmann puts it, there is speaking a spirit that believes itself authorized to maintain judicial powers of a higher kind. We see also that the recipients of the epistle expect that he can maintain these powers only when he is *present in person.* Only thus does that threat in the second epistle become comprehensible, the threat of that ἐξουσία which Paul could demonstrate upon his coming. But it is utterly unjustified and arbitrary to reduce this "judicial power" to an authority *in canon law*, so to speak, to exclude persons from the community and to strip it of its mystical powers insofar as possible. In the second epistle Paul apparently makes a concession on one point; the miraculous power remains bound up with his personal presence. But he heightens his claim; he claims for himself that miraculous power even without the community, and indeed even in opposition to it, but he deliberately leaves the threat undefined.

He has the power and could use it εἰς καθαίρεσιν; and it is his intention to use it, and he has received it from God, εἰς οἰκοδομήν. With the transitional statement that he does not intend now to boast in his epistle of this ἐξουσία, for he does not venture to equate himself with those men who are commending themselves, he now returns to those adversaries who assert concerning themselves: Χριστοῦ ἐσμεν. They cannot deny what is obvious, namely that Paul too can say the same concerning himself. Hence there must be a μέτρον, a gradation in the degree of the mystical connection with Christ and of the knowledge that is grounded in this connection. Those men base their claim to autonomy upon the fact of the Χριστοῦ εἶναι (while he claims to have an ἐξουσία even over them); and this in turn is based upon the fact that they do not measure themselves in comparison with others, but only with themselves. God provides the measure, by showing his δύναμις in the success of the preaching; hence the community itself is his measure; he does not need to use alien measures and alien work for boasting, as do his opponents (in verse 17 I Cor. 1:31 is intentionally repeated; he has once justified his boasting by means of this quotation; "that boasting is not based on παραφρονεῖν; but even if it were based thereupon, bear with me"; it is the transitional formula which appears frequently from this point onward).

In the introduction to chapter 11, Paul returns to the charge that there is ζῆλος in him too and that it proves that he too is "only a man". In him is rather the ζῆλος θεοῦ. He has brought the community as a pure bride to Christ, and now he fears that she is violating this marriage (a Jewish idea). If the conclusion of the next sentence is correct, I can understand

366 it only by taking it, as Schwartz does, as a question: "for if someone should come and preach another Jesus and you receive another πνεῦμα (which presupposes a different God) and accept a

different message (teaching), would it be right for you to tolerate this?" In this case, we have an imaginary case set forth in the form of a condition assumed to be fact, such as we also encounter in Paul's usage later on. The problem is that the verb ἀνέχεσθαι (*pati*) alongside λαμβάνειν and δέχεσθαι, expressions of their own activity, seems suspicious to me; I would prefer to read, following the hints of a parallel tradition, καλῶς ἂν εἴχετε;--"would it then be well with you?" This means: would that not be disloyalty to Christ, calamity for you? must I not therefore be zealous for God's sake and yours? It is a psychologically subtle touch for him to pose the apodosis as impossible, while the protasis appears to him as possible. The question posed in whatever case would, of course, be correct only if Paul has brought the genuine Jesus, the full πνεῦμα, and the true message and doctrine. So now he necessarily adds: *for* I believe that in no respect did I myself then (the perfect is used for the aorist; cf. 12:11) fall behind the super-apostles (τῶν ὑπερλίαν ἀποστόλων); εἰ δὲ καὶ ἰδιώτης τῷ λόγῳ, ἀλλ' οὐ τῇ γνώσει. This clearly corresponds to the portrayal of his missionary preaching in I Cor. 2:4: οὐκ ἐν πειθοῖ (cf. below, p. 497, n. 1), σοφίας λόγοις, ἀλλ' ἐν ἀποδείξει πνεύματος καὶ δυνάμεως, and at the same time is directed against the charge found in II Cor. 10:10: ἡ παρουσία ἀσθενὴς καὶ ὁ λόγος ἐξουθενημένος: in the art of discourse I may have nothing special (ἰδιώτης, to be εἷς τῶν πολλῶν), but in γνῶσις, on which alone it depends whether I have brought the genuine Jesus, the full πνεῦμα, and the true message, I am not inferior to any τῶν ὑπερλίαν ἀποστόλων (cf. also I Cor. 9:2-5). If with this term Paul means some nameless opponents in Corinth or even the hitherto only suspected proclaimers of a different Jesus, this boast is worse than

petty, but worst of all, the basis given for it is false; how ever, it becomes clear and understandable if he means the original apostles; if he is not inferior to them in γνῶσις, then anyone who proclaims a different Jesus is enticing the community to be unfaithful to the genuine Jesus. We must return to this when Paul repeats this same point. First of all, 367 by appending a contrast, he returns once more to the charge of κατὰ σάρκα περιπατεῖν or σαρκικὸν εἶναι. Of course the conclusion of verse 6 cannot be correct in any of the various versions that have been handed down, since in every one of them there is lacking any continuity of thought with the following verse 7; the longest version, which in itself is linguistically impossible, appears to be the place to begin. ἐν παντί requires the addition of an adjective, something like the following: ἀλλ' οὐ τῇ γνώσει, ἀλλ' ἐν παντὶ <ἀμέμπτους ἡμᾶς> φανερώσαντες ἐν πᾶσιν εἰς ὑμᾶς. ἢ ἁμαρτίαν ἐποίησα κτλ. He says φανερώσαντες ἐν πᾶσιν, because he intends at once to add that this boast of his will not be silenced in all Achaia, and he asks with some bitterness whether his selflessness was a sin (cf. later 12:13, ἀδικία), because κατὰ σάρκα περιπατεῖν contains within it the idea of sin (cf. later 12:18: τῷ αὐτῷ πνεύματι περιπατήσαμεν), and because his conduct did not correspond to a specific authorization from Jesus. It appears that the question in 12:16 as to whether he has dealt with them as πανοῦργος has reference to that missing adjective which I have supplied, ἀμέμπτους, or whatever it may have been. On his next visit also Paul intends to conduct himself in the same way, to deprive those who have been wishing that he would act as they do of any occasion for strife and suspicion; they are unfaithful servants, false apostles, ministers of Satan, who only pretend to be servants of Christ and whom God will give the reward that is due them. There is nothing

to indicate that they are in Corinth; everything points to opponents such as Paul frequently encountered in his missionary activity, and as are portrayed in Phil. 3:18. Verse 4 has expressed the concern that such opponents, who necessarily preach another Jesus, will come to Corinth also; Paul gives us no reason to connect them with the ὑπερλίαν ἀπόστολοι in verse 5 (on the contrary: such a connection would destroy the sense of verse 5); he deliberately leaves obscure whether he is thinking at all of specific men.

On the other hand, after a new, still more biting apology for his boasting, he comes back to the first idea of his polemical exposition: εἴ τις πέποιθεν ἑαυτῷ Χριστοῦ εἶναι... καὶ ἡμεῖς Χριστοῦ. But the little sentence, which nevertheless is impressive because of the loftiness of its claim, still functions: λογίζομαι γὰρ μηδὲν ὑστερηκέναι τῶν ὑπερλίαν ἀποστόλων; and it identifies the new theme and the new μέτρον by which he measures himself. What is involved here is an argument with a Petrine community: ἐν ᾧ ἄν τις τολμᾷ (intensification of πέποιθεν), τολμῶ κἀγώ. Ἑβραῖοί εἰσιν; κἀγώ. Ἰσραηλεῖταί εἰσιν; κἀγώ. σπέρμα Ἀβραάμ εἰσιν; κἀγώ. διάκονοι Χριστοῦ εἰσιν; παραφρονῶν λαλῶ· ὑπὲρ ἐγώ (verses 13-15 show that the διάκονοι Χριστοῦ are apostles; of course the same verses show with equal certainty that they are not false apostles and envoys of Satan).[15] Otherwise, what would be special about this last boast, for which Paul offers such a lengthy apology? It must be observed that in the polemic of this chapter Paul does not take back a single assertion of the first epistle, but in fact intensifies all of them (even the warning against ζῆλος and ἔρις is repeated in 12:20 in intensified form). There he had referred to his apostolate, justified it with the miracle of his conversion (15:3ff.), and at the same time explicitly placed himself beneath Peter

and the other original apostles as the last and least of all, indeed as actually not even worthy of the name; just as he has received the title only by God's grace, so also it is only by God's grace that he has "labored more than any of them". Now even in II Cor. 10:12ff. the measure of labor for him was the standard by which God measures those who are his. In the new comparison with the ὑπερλίαν ἀπόστολοι it is at first the same standard again, only this time in the κόποι more emphasis is placed upon the θλῖψις which in Paul's view gives δόξα. As a second and new measure now there are added the ὀπτασίαι καὶ ἀποκαλύψεις, which likewise bestow δόξα. In both he has reached the highest level possible. Now in 12:11 he returns to the idea of 11:16: boasting of myself may be foolish, but you have compelled me to do it; for you should have been my boast: οὐδὲν γὰρ ὑστέρησα τῶν ὑπερλίαν ἀποστόλων, εἰ καὶ οὐδέν εἰμι. The pointed expression cannot refer to unknown Corinthians nor to some emissaries of the Jerusalem community; this is proven by the rationale that is offered: τὰ μὲν σημεῖα τοῦ ἀποστόλου κατηργάσθη ἐν ὑμῖν ἐν πάσῃ ὑπομονῇ, σημείοις καὶ τέρασιν καὶ δυνάμεσιν. τί γάρ ἐστιν, ὃ ἡττήθητε ὑπὲρ τὰς λοιπὰς ἐκκλησίας, εἰ μὴ ὅτι αὐτὸς ἐγὼ οὐ κατενάρκησα ὑμῶν. The assurance that no Christian community has experienced more of the δύναμις θεοῦ and that in the Corinthian community Paul has proven himself to be the ἀπόστολος in the highest sense necessarily requires that, as all the church fathers interpreted it, the ὑπερλίαν ἀπόστολοι in comparison with whom Paul utters his ὑπὲρ ἐγώ actually are the Twelve, or, in our particular case, Peter. He no longer claims in his "foolishness" merely to be the πνευματικός, but in δόξα the chief of the apostles. Of course, precisely for that reason he is obliged to distinguish the "man" for whom he demands this from his own weak "I". The fullest

369

answer then is given also to those adversaries who based their claims on a mere Χριστοῦ εἰμι. "God's standard of measurement" has raised Paul himself to a level above that of the original apostles. It will have to be shown in chapter 13 whether this interpretation is correct.

Hence this is also the context of that mysterious and solemn account of his vision which is intended to surpass the miracle of conversion that was related in the first epistle, and to prove that ἐν γνώσει he was not and is not inferior to the original apostles: οἶδα ἄνθρωπον ἐν Χριστῷ (of course "man in Christ" is a *single* concept that is chosen primarily because Χριστοῦ εἰμι presupposes both ἐν Χριστῷ εἰμί and that doctrine, which we are constantly encountering, of the almost divine ἄνθρωπος) πρὸ ἐτῶν δεκατεσσάρων, εἴτε ἐν σώματι οὐκ οἶδα, εἴτε ἐκτὸς τοῦ σώματος οὐκ οἶδα, ὁ θεὸς οἶδεν (following the prayer in the Mithras liturgy, I interpret this to mean "whether in a kind of body or altogether outside my body", but it matters little, even if one ascribes no importance to the absence of the article in the first phrase; what is more important is the fact that Paul raises this question at all and thereby shows that there are diverse conceptions of the "rapture"), ἁρπαγέντα τὸν τοιοῦτον ἕως τρίτου οὐρανοῦ (on this expression cf. Philo, De vit. cont. Rei. §12). καὶ οἶδα τὸν τοιοῦτον ἄνθρωπον, εἴτε ἐν σώματι, εἴτε χωρὶς (ἐκτὸς?) τοῦ σώματος οὐκ οἶδα, ὁ θεὸς οἶδεν, ὅτι ἡρπάγη εἰς τὸν παράδεισον καὶ ἤκουσεν ἄρρητα ῥήματα (*quae voce meliora sunt*, says Apuleius XI 23 of the proclamation of the celestial journey), ἃ οὐκ ἐξὸν ἀνθρώπῳ λαλῆσαι (Apuleius XI 23: *dicerem, si dicere liceret*; but here ἀνθρώπῳ probably means more than τινί; the ἄνθρωπος οὐκέτι τέλειος, i.e., one who as yet is only man, like the Corinthians according to his earlier assertion, may not hear it;

once again Paul is maintaining his claim to be more). ὑπὲρ
370 τοῦ τοιούτου καυχήσομαι, ὑπὲρ δὲ ἐμαυτοῦ οὐ καυχήσομαι, εἰ μὴ ἐν ταῖς ἀσθενείαις μου (ὑπὲρ τοῦ τοιούτου here cannot be neuter, because then the contrast with ὑπὲρ ἐμαυτοῦ would disappear, and because the twice chosen τὸν τοιοῦτον apparently is used in rhetorical anaphora). It is the εἰ καυχᾶσθαι δεῖ, τὰ τῆς ἀσθενείας μου καυχήσομαι of the first proof (from the κόποι, in 11:30) in a new expression and with a new explanation; just as according to his interpretation the κόποι that afflict the body--he refers to them in 12:10--precisely in a necessary reciprocal operation heightened the δόξα and δύναμις of that ἄνθρωπος ἐν Χριστῷ in him, so also did that suffering that God had prescribed for him as a counterbalance to the ἀποκαλύψεις, so that he cannot consider himself as a unitary being, as himself glorified by them. What is glorified is only that divine being in him that becomes stronger, the weaker he himself becomes: ὅταν γὰρ ἀσθενῶ τότε δυνατός εἰμι. Closely connected with this idea is the appeal to the apostle's δύναμις which he has already demonstrated to the Corinthians, as is the conclusion also, after the brief digression in 12:14-21. He senses in himself an ἐξουσία, a divine power, based on full knowledge, to judge and hence to destroy or to save, and he will not spare them a second time. His opponents wish to put to the test the spirit in him (δοκιμή here in the same sense as δοκιμάζειν and πειράζειν); indeed, they have said: ἡ δὲ παρουσία τοῦ σώματος ἀσθενής--but it will be shown in their punishment. Thus the thought runs; only here, after the appeal to the highest revelation and the loftiest apostolic power, Paul chooses, for the concept πνευματικὸν εἶναι, which he earlier has defined as νοῦν Χριστοῦ εἰληφέναι, the strongest expression: ὁ ἐν ἐμοὶ λαλῶν Χριστός, in order then to be able to add, in a mysterious

threat, that Christ is not ἀσθενής but has power over those who indeed have been baptized into him and are Χριστοῦ. In what follows this threat with a Christ living personally in him emerges even more strongly: it is true that Christ was weak and died, but he lives through the power of God; so also Paul, even though he is weak, will live with him in the *power of God over the community*. Thus their δοκιμή will 371 rather be turned against themselves; they will themselves be tested. Paul hopes that even before his arrival they will recognize that he is δόκιμος; if they should fail to do so, that will be a sin, and he will have to reveal in their punishment his δόκιμον εἶναι, the possession of the Spirit and of power. Thus he stoutly maintains the proud saying that the Pneumatic αὐτὸς ὑπ' οὐδενὸς ἀνακρίνεται; he submits to their judgment only his conduct, not his teaching. He has already given examples of his power to work wonders, and now he can give evidence of it in a new way, can demonstrate his ἐξουσία over the community, for *Christ lives in him*. Certainly there is much here that can remind us of the prophetic consciousness in ancient Israel--the individualism that underlies that consciousness had been revived in lay circles and in the Diaspora through syncretism and Hellenism and naturally related to ancient native elements--but the tendency of this new prophetic phenomenon toward an almost dogmatic speculation and its persuasion of a miracle of transformation in one's own person is not Jewish; the Hellenistic mystery-faith has reshaped the ancient Israelite prophetic phenomenon and produced something entirely new.

Paul has demonstrated, by means of the all-surpassing vision, that he is not inferior to any of the original apostles ἐν γνώσει. He has already employed this idea once in another version.

Paul concludes the earlier discussed explanations concerning the heavenly and earthly bodies (II Cor. 5:6) by saying ἐνδημοῦντες ἐν τῷ σώματι ἐκδημοῦμεν ἀπὸ τοῦ κυρίου, and he declares he would prefer ἐκδημῆσαι ἐκ τοῦ σώματος καὶ ἐνδημῆσαι πρὸς τὸν κύριον. Hence even now his whole desire and striving is (verse 9) εἴτε ἐνδημοῦντες εἴτε ἐκδημοῦντες εὐάρεστοι αὐτῷ εἶναι. This--and, as is shown by what follows, especially the words εὐάρεστοι αὐτῷ εἶναι--provides the point of connection for verse 13: εἴτε γὰρ ἐξέστημεν, θεῷ, εἴτε σωφρονοῦμεν, ὑμῖν. Between these two verses there is inserted, as is often done in Paul's writings, a subsidiary idea, which ultimately leads to the same goal and which along with the εὐάρεστοι εἶναι also considers the word φιλοτιμούμεθα, and in fact also explains his choice of words. We seek to be well-pleasing to God, for we must one day be "made manifest" before him for reward or punishment. Thus in fear of this judgment 372 we seek to win men and in so doing are manifest before God (rhetorically reconstructed out of the simple idea "as God knows"; the rhetorical contrast of ἀνθρώπους and θεός then leads to the addition, "and men know it also", συνοίδασιν, that is, that it is done in the fear of God; their consciences must bear him witness) and, it is hoped, in your consciences as well. For I do not intend now to praise myself again and to boast (his φιλοτιμεῖσθαι is not concerned with human praise), but rather to give you occasion for boasting of me before those who boast of themselves before people, but in their very hearts and consciences cannot properly do so. A bridge naturally leads from this idea to verse 13; the fact that he is manifest to God and to the Corinthians' consciences is indeed given its justification with the sentence beginning εἴτε...εἴτε. However, as far as the main idea is concerned, verses 10-12 could be dropped; verse 9 would connect with

verse 13 without a break: ...εἴτε ἐκδημοῦντες εἴτε ἐνδημοῦντες εὐάρεστοι αὐτῷ εἶναι. εἴτε γὰρ ἐξέστημεν, θεῷ, εἴτε σωφρονοῦμεν, ὑμῖν. "Our experiences of ecstasy happened and happen for God's sake. They are a service to him, a worship which quite self-evidently makes one εὐάρεστος θεῷ." It is the usual Hellenistic interpretation, which hardly requires any further explanation. The complete equating of the ἐκστῆναι in the vision with the ἐκδημῆσαι in death likewise corresponds to the general Hellenistic perspective and language (cf., e.g., εἰς θεὸν χωρεῖν in the Hermetic writings). This double meaning is assumed to be so self-evident that because of it the word σωφρονεῖν, which denotes the very opposite of ecstasy, also takes on the meaning of "to live on earth" (ἐνδημεῖν ἐν σώματι). The ἐνδημεῖν ἐν σώματι will likewise be pleasing to God and will be in keeping with his will, because it is only for your sake. This is meant to be proved, and could be proved, solely by the principle: "for Christ's love *for all men* (and thus for you also) constrains us to this; he intends *all* to share in his death and his resurrection". But therewith only one half of the idea is fully given. It is also the will of God that Paul also no longer lives for himself; indeed, he himself has died, in

73

that he died with Christ. The εἰ δὲ σωφρονοῦμεν ὑμῖν is taken up: ὑπὲρ πάντων ἀπέθανεν, ἵνα οἱ ζῶντες μηκέτι ἑαυτοῖς ζῶσιν. The two ideas intermingle in the genuinely Pauline statement: "for the love of Christ constrains us, we who have recognized that if one died for *all, all* are dead, and one died for all so that anyone who truly lives (lives in him) no longer lives to himself but for the one who for him died and has risen." The *consequence* of this is to be (verse 16): ὥστε ἡμεῖς ἀπὸ τοῦ νῦν οὐδένα οἴδαμεν κατὰ σάρκα, and in this connection οὐδένα apparently is intended to be set

in contrast with the thrice strongly emphasized ὑπερ πάντων and οἱ πάντες; on the other hand, there must be some effect felt of the idea that he himself and, as he sees it, all men are dead. "Thus for me there is now no longer any man according to the flesh, I know no one and I have inward and intimate connection with no one." What is meant here must be not an intellectual perception, but a feeling, a relationship that exists between the γνώριμοι. Once again two ideas are intermingled: "Christ has died for all men, and hence for me there is no longer anyone who is more closely or more distantly related", and "I have died and have been raised to a new life; for me the natural man no longer exists, it is nothing to me." Verse 17 is closely connected with this second idea, though not entirely smoothly: ὥστε εἴ τις ἐν Χριστῷ, καινὴ κτίσις. τὰ ἀρχαῖα παρῆλθεν, ἰδοὺ γέγονεν καινὰ τὰ πάντα: being transplanted into Christ is like a new act of creation (the expression is deliberately chosen so that there is a reminiscence of the creation of the world that culminated in Adam; the opposites Χριστός and 'Αδάμ have been brought to the apostle's mind by verse 15); the entire earlier world has collapsed, and everything has become new (the neuter forms τὰ παλαιά and τὰ πάντα, like the immediately following τὰ δὲ πάντα, deliberately leave it unclear whether what is meant is the nature of man or the world into which he is transposed). How can an individual man as man and part of the earlier world mean anything special to him there? Nationality, family, friendship and acquaintance, all that could make distinctions and provide special relationships has passed away with the old world.

374 This is easily understood; yet the saying is incomplete; it aims at something that is not yet said, and in fact there is inserted between the two sentences already discussed an intermediate link that must necessarily be interpreted from them,

a brief sentence that was the reason it has been necessary for me to go into the entire passage: εἰ δὲ καὶ ἐγνώκαμεν κατὰ σάρκα Χριστόν, ἀλλὰ νῦν οὐκέτι γινώσκομεν. For me, it is altogether out of the question to take this as stating a real condition and to have the apostle say that he once upon a time occasionally *saw* Jesus; and I no longer need to refute such assumptions as that Paul exaggeratedly described such occasional observation as ἐγνωκέναι in order to claim an equal status with the μαθηταί, or to contrive to make ἐγνωκέναι artificially bear the meaning of a "discursive knowledge of the specific dignity of Christ". But there can be no talk of an actual inner connection of Paul with Jesus. Of course that has been passionately disputed by the splendid exegete Johannes Weiss, and against Wrede's well known statements he has asserted that on the contrary Paul must have gained an impression of Jesus' person and teaching that was strong, immediate, and definitive for Paul's own life; but I need not go into more detail on the niceties of argument and proof, because for me and certainly for many readers this assumption would directly charge the writer of the Galatian epistle with falsehood. I must deal with only one assertion which challenges the philologist all the more since it is represented as generally conceded; I refer to the assertion that if Paul actually had *not* known Jesus, in our passage he would have had to write, with a clear emphasis upon condition contrary to fact, εἰ δὲ καὶ ἔγνωμεν κατὰ σάρκα Χριστόν. Such an insistence means to apply the strict rules of copybook grammar mechanically to an author who uses a lively, vivid language, rich in nuances and allusions, to express a unique, complicated, and at the same time often volatile feeling. I am pleased that linguistic experts like E. Schwartz and B. Keil have confirmed and expanded my judgment about this passage.

Paul has sharply contrasted two times and two ways of thinking, and of the second, the present, he has said with all definiteness: ἀπὸ τοῦ νῦν οὐδένα οἴδαμεν κατὰ σάρκα. He wishes to carry this forward with intensification and, if this is to be done in a proper sentence, he must necessarily use the present tense again: Χριστὸν νῦν οὐκέτι γινώσκομεν. Then it is only the perfect tense that can form the contrast to that, as εἰ ἐγνώκαμεν ἄλλους, νῦν οὐκ οἴδαμεν, εἰ ἐγνώκαμεν Χριστόν, νῦν οὐκέτι γινώσκομεν. A fully completed past is in fact set in contrast to the present. Accordingly, I myself would not take offense at the choice of tenses in an explicit statement of condition contrary to fact, particularly since we have a kind of anacolouthon here. But the relationship of the two clauses in fact is not actually conditional (as though the two actions stood in a causal relationship to each other and from the certainly incorrect main clause οὐκ ἄν ἀγίνωσκον--γινώσκω δὲ--the incorrectness of the assumption also followed εἰ ἔγνων κατὰ σάρκα). We are dealing instead with that really purely adversative use of the conditional particle which directly contests the causal connection: even though the one fact or assumption may be in itself correct, the other is *not* therefore also correct. Here, in the very nature of the case, the *potentialis* can enter, but the *irrealis* only in a certain expansion of its function. We could restate the meaning thus: θές (ποίησόν) με κατὰ σάρκα ἐγνωκέναι Χριστόν, or: καίτοι καὶ εἰ ἐγνωκῶς εἴην, or: εἰ ὅτι μάλιστα ἔγνωκα. In each case the contrast would be: νῦν οὐκέτι γινώσκω. In these suggestions, I have emphasized in the expressions that we are dealing with an assumption, not a fact; but this distinction is by no means always made by living and actually lively language, especially in concessive conditional clauses--the term is somewhat too narrow. From

the abundance of examples collected by Stahl (*Kritisch-historische Syntax des griechischen Verbums*, pp. 414ff.), one may compare, for example, Plato, Laches 182c; Thucydides VI 89.3; Herodotus VII 10; Isocrates XIV 58, XVI 48; Homer, Iliad 13.58. The intention is often enough evident, as in the words in Iliad 20.371, 372, which are especially emphasized by repetition: τοῦ δ' ἐγὼ ἀντίος εἶμι, καὶ εἰ πυρὶ χεῖρε ἔοικεν, εἰ πυρὶ χεῖρε ἔοικε, μένος δ' αἴθωνι σιδήρῳ (even if he resembles or should resemble). Of course this is also transferred into the past; cf. Xenophon, Memorab. II 2.7: ἀλλά τοι εἰ καὶ ταῦτα πάντα πεποίηκε καὶ ἄλλα τούτων πολλαπλάσια (even assuming that she has actually done what you say), οὐδεὶς ἂν δύναιτο αὐτῆς ἀνασχέσθαι τὴν χαλεπότητα. Euripides, Suppl. 528, takes us still closer to Paul: εἰ γάρ τι καὶ πεπόνθατ' 'Αργείων ὕπο--τεθνᾶσιν (assuming that you have suffered). In all three of these cases the speaker does not intend to decide whether the assumption actually is true, or at least he places no emphasis at all upon it; it is only the fact set over against the assumption that is intended to appear as certain. It is entirely from this perspective that Paul is to be understood; his use of the indicative in the assumption only heightens the definiteness of the main affirmation, and the slight irregularity of form, which he has chosen with remarkable delicacy, further draws the attention particularly to the sentence: εἰ δὲ καὶ ἐγνώκαμεν κατὰ σάρκα Χριστόν--ἀλλὰ νῦν οὐκέτι γινώσκομεν: "even assuming that I was close to Christ in his human time (or: as man)--now I no longer know him." Here the thought certainly refers to the original apostles and their personal relations with the common Lord, but I should not look for an actual polemical intention therein. That personal love and attachment is only represented as irrelevant; it does not elevate the μαθητής

above the apostle; the bond that unites the *new man* with his *God* is quite different. For Paul, a *human* attachment, even if it should be to the person of an incarnate God, is not religious; between human love and acquaintance, on the one hand, and the knowledge and love mediated by one's entering into Christ (or Christ's entering into him), on the other hand, there is a wide separation that renders the former utterly worthless and superfluous for the latter. It is a curiously modern and yet in essence genuinely Pauline feeling. Love for a historical person and acceptance of a teaching, even if he had been close to this person and had himself heard this teaching, could not have become for him the religion that fills one's entire life and challenges one to self-evident sacrifice. Now and then, perhaps, in the consideration of the most recent development of religious feel-

377 ing in wide circles, we may have some doubts as to whether a bare knowledge about an infinitely exalted man and teacher can produce, or indeed even merely maintain, a vital religion, and whether the bond of personal devotion and veneration that unites the individual or a community with a teacher has such religious force to continue working. But even though these doubts may arise, we are entirely justified in attempting to understand Paul in terms of such modern ideas and doubts. I should prefer to use them as the avenue for approaching the introduction to the Galatian epistle which a man like Lagarde (*Deutsche Schriften*, Göttingen 1886, pp. 71ff.) found so offensive. Certainly they must at first appear strange to anyone who does not misrepresent and dilute Paul by the arbitrary introduction of statements from the book of Acts. Even in his earliest missionary preaching he had pronounced an anathema against anyone who would bring any different message, and had legitimized his own message by the fact that at his conversion

he had seen Christ; now he intensifies both of these elements where Jewish Christian missionaries want to teach his community something different. As he extends the anathema to any and all, even if it should be an angel from heaven, so also he forthrightly emphasizes for his message the absence of *all* human tradition and teaching (verse 12: the Hellenistic mystery words). Precisely what one could have expected of him, namely that after his vision he had sought counsel and instruction, is what he had *not* done, and he rejects the idea with an expression that minimizes the value of such (προσανατίθεσθαι σαρκὶ καὶ αἵματι). He had not, for example, gone to Jerusalem, and later on, when he did go there, he did not apply to as many eyewitnesses as possible with questions about Jesus' life and teaching. In the most solemn fashion he declares that he did not do what in our view would have legitimized his εὐαγγέλιον but according to his view would have reduced it to an εὐαγγέλιον κατὰ ἄνθρωπον, while he builds the unconditional necessity and correctness of his own teaching upon that *one* vision. It is of no primary consequence that these words were born out of conflict and that they portray the apostle's conduct at the time of his conversion as he subsequently wanted to interpret it and to have it interpreted. On the main points 378 his conduct after his conversion corresponds to the portrayal: after the tremendous experience he did not concern himself with forming an acquaintance with as much as possible about the Jesus whom he had persecuted from trustworthy witnesses, such as Peter (ἱστορῆσαι Κηφᾶν) and thereby to acquire a full picture of the historical Jesus. He would have had the opportunity to do so, and he senses that it could have been expected of him. The fact that even later he did this only briefly, and that first he went into solitude "to Arabia" can be comprehended only in terms of a frame of mind, perhaps not yet

clear, for which from the very outset the real world and historical phenomena do not at all provide certain knowledge and only inward experience has an unassailable certainty. Paul had already been a mystic before his conversion; this in fact is also confirmed by that allegorical interpretation of Scripture which sets aside the facts in the sacred tradition of his people in favor of a construction that is based solely on his own inner conviction. But he is also a dominating person by nature, whose zeal for the tradition is not crippled even in that time by this individualistic reshaping of the tradition, as was the case with others of his countrymen (cf. Philo, above, p. 406), but who wishes with utmost strength to impose upon others his own feelings as the norm.

Once again we can sense as modern much of what at first appears strange. The reluctance of that deep and independent nature to make its entire inward life dependent on the trustworthiness and the purity of the recollections of any other man, the vague sense that such a faith does not offer true strength but rather a veiling of one's own weakness, we can also well understand. Even in his first stay in Jerusalem the condition of the tradition, which precisely because of its richness was confusing and incomprehensible, and the uncertainty and contradictions that must have attached to the recollections of Jesus' words are bound to have strengthened this feeling. If in the decisions with which he soon thereafter was confronted a saying of the Lord was to be decisive for Paul, how easily could an opponent bring forward a new saying, or a φευδαπόστολος invent one! And how utterly impossible then was the investigation of authentic and inauthentic, of correct and incorrect interpretation, of contradiction and agreement! The only possible way then would have been to attach oneself to one particular witness, to become that per-

379

son's μαθητής, and to proclaim τὸ κατὰ Πέτρον καὶ 'Ιάκωβον εὐαγγέλιον. But above the diversity of tradition there stands in the community the one brief common confession, "Jesus died for our sins and was raised by God; he is the Χριστός", and the community also believed in the πνεῦμα, the *continuing* revelation in Christ and through him which alone legitimizes the community over against Judaism. This afforded the man to whom his own experience, the inward vision, was a necessity and therefore a reality, the right to consider *all* tradition as less worthy in comparison. The πνεῦμα θεοῦ, who after all can only be one, guarantees the unity of all true proclamation and at the same time insures for Paul himself full liberty: II Cor. 3:17: ὁ δὲ κύριος τὸ πνεῦμά ἐστιν· οὗ δὲ τὸ πνεῦμα κυρίου, ἐλευθερία; I Cor. 9:1: οὐκ εἰμὶ ἐλεύθερος, οὐκ εἰμὶ ἀπόστολος, οὐχὶ 'Ιησοῦν τὸν κύριον ἑώρακα. It is curious that the inner connection of the three questions themselves is so little regarded by careful interpreters. The affirmation here cannot have reference to freedom from the law.

But even if we can comprehend this development as a necessary and inevitable one, still there remains an element that must appear somewhat strange. I include in that category above all the total equation of the vision of the glorified Christ with the knowledge of the entire content of "his gospel". If we interpret the introduction to Galatians and the conclusion of II Corinthians precisely, the two are bound together. It does not suffice to say, "Paul was a visionary", or "He believed that in his conversion-vision he had received the commission to be missionary to the Gentiles". For him and his communities there must be bound up with the unique vision of God a continuing authorization and enablement to discern everything out of their own resources, and hence the

possession of the πνεῦμα in the highest sense. Here a fixed sacral concept of the πνευματικός holds sway, which I, at least, can derive only from the mystery religions.[16] It is related to the idea of the reception of the πνεῦμα in baptism which was formed in the community at Jerusalem and still more 380 strongly in the first Hellenistic communities--in my opinion this idea also is of Hellenistic origin--but they do not entirely coincide. While there the πνεῦμα appears rather as a spirit of purity, the possession of which determines one's membership in the community, the bearer of the πνεῦμα, here there is added, as a new, individualistic element, γνῶσις, knowledge. The πνευματικός must be not only sinless, but also in possession of a knowledge that is infallible, perfect, and independent of all instruction. The inevitable combination of the two ideas leads to the contradiction which Paul's opponents at Corinth vaguely and yet correctly sensed. One gets the feeling that one of the ideas was formed in the community's life, and the other in a solitary soul. A community of saints is conceivable, but not a community of πνευματικοί (even Philo senses this; above, p. 405). Of course the attempt at solution (by means of the concept of the νήπιοι ἐν Χριστῷ or of Χριστὸς οὔπω τέλειος ἐν ἡμῖν and by the assumption of a μέτρον) was already given in Hellenism; even for the ethical effect of the πνεῦμα it was necessary to assume in actuality a gradual unfolding; here too there were contradictions which Paul sensed profoundly.

Moreover, since I earlier attempted to discover why for Paul any connection with the living Jesus could appear as religiously worthless, and indeed as something that he would renounce if he had had it, perhaps here I need not give so much emphasis to this strange attitude. We are too clearly confronted by the enigma that the complete separation of two

worlds--which for Paul is not a figure and a manner of speaking, but a most profound feeling that dominates his entire inner being--here separates not only a Paul who has died (and continues to live only in worthless appearance) and a risen Paul, but also a Jesus who has died and a resurrected Christ. The former belongs to the world that is past, and the latter to the new world, and the religious connection of the one who is truly resurrected belongs only to this latter; it is the connection of the πνεῦμα with "*the* πνεῦμα". Once again perhaps there can be demonstrated a certain inconsistency be-
31 tween this kind of feeling and Paul's confession, taken in all its profundity, of the Jesus who died for our sins; and once again that separation of a twofold world and a twofold personality is foreshadowed in Hellenistic mysticism. Under syncretistic influence the devout Jew had already made a separation between two worlds, the present and the coming one, the former worthless and vain, already practically only an illusion, and the latter full of glory and of eternal duration. That that second world and the βασιλεία θεοῦ have already dawned must also temporarily have been the feeling of the first Jewish Christian community. But the way in which the two worlds for Paul are interwoven is Hellenistic. In order to recognize this one needs only to compare the idea of the σῶμα οὐράνιον and the δόξα that are already in us now and to pose the question whether this idea fully comports with the intensity of the eschatological hopes found in Paul, which, certainly already under syncretistic influence also, still are more strongly Jewish and are also peculiar to the Jerusalem community.

In this connection I should like once more expressly to emphasize a lexical peculiarity. For the union of man and God, ancient thought knew two basic patterns, which Rohde in

his master work perhaps should have distinguished from each other more sharply: the elevation of man to God (heavenly journey, ecstasy in the specific sense), and the descent of God into man. Of course in Oriental religions, for example in the Egyptian and Iranian, we naturally find the two ideas obviously separated, as a rule. Hellenism adopts both ideas or revives them; one may trace out how even in the conceptions of mantic practice, which are most closely connected with the second, forms of the first penetrate. When Cicero had the bad taste to insert into the poetic glorification of his consulate an ascension to heaven, quite in keeping with the patterns of Hellenistic religious narratives, examples for this may have been provided for him by Poseidonios or, better, the author of De republica VI, who in fact attributes to the good leader of

382 the state a special relationship to the gods; the idea still is clear. It is another matter when, for example, in Statius Kalchas there is the admonition (Achilleis I 508): *heia, inrumpe deos et fata latentia vexa laurigerosque ignes, si quando, avidissimus hauri*[17] (cf. Theb. III 550). Here the two ideas are combined as they are in all of Hellenistic mysticism and particularly in the Hellenistic mysteries. When the same mingling of the two ideas is found in Paul (cf., e.g., the passage from Rom. 8:9, 10, already cited above: ἐστὲ... ἐν πνεύματι, εἴπερ πνεῦμα θεοῦ οἰκεῖ ἐν ὑμῖν· εἰ δέ τις πνεῦμα Χριστοῦ οὐκ ἔχει, οὗτος οὐκ ἔστιν αὐτοῦ, εἰ δὲ Χριστὸς ἐν ὑμῖν...εἰ δὲ τὸ πνεῦμα...οἰκεῖ ἐν ὑμῖν), and when the same *termini technici* (cf. in the Hermetic writings ἐν θεῷ γίνεσθαι) are constantly employed, this certainly may be explained first of all from the fact that the basic idea of the relationship of the two worlds to each other is the same, but this agreement is hardly accidental. Where the very word appears along with the idea, the appropriation is almost certain.

If I proposed to give an exhaustive portrayal of the idea of the πνευματικός, I should here have to take up the matter of asceticism, which Paul explicitly represents not as a prescription that came to him from Christ, but as a gift of the Spirit. It too is found in Hellenistic mysticism and is indissolubly connected with the belief of the mysteries. But I have attempted to sketch the basic outlines in the *Historia monachorum und Historia Lausiaca* (Göttingen 1916), and an exhaustive presentation would require a new book.

I prefer to take another look at another internal contrast that reminds us of how strong at the same time is the Jewish feeling in Paul, which heretofore has not been touched upon and indeed has elsewhere been systematically excluded from the investigation. In that feeling there is rooted, above all, the concept of the ἐκκλησία, which of course is likewise heightened to a mystical level. I cannot here picture how great has been the effect of Paul's following the example of the Jewish synagogue by not connecting the leadership of the individual ἐκκλησία, which indeed always is it- 33 self the complete earthly counterpart of the entire heavenly church, with the possession of special gifts of the Spirit, πνευματικά (they are to serve the church, not to rule in it); nor is it possible for me here to show how the basically Hellenistic worship service, which he so vividly pictures in I Cor. 14, can evolve back into the more sober, much more Jewish worship of the Διδαχὴ τῶν ἀποστόλων; the tradition must steadily gain in strength as compared to that of the continuing revelation, and the leader of the community must become the guardian of the tradition. But I must at least deal briefly with the struggle of the same apostle, who often appears to place such enormous value upon γνῶσις, against its

over-valuation, because a hurried treatment of the crucial passage once brought upon me from the theological side the bitterest and most widely publicized attack.[18] I must do this all the more because even the struggle against Hellenistic ideas shows how far Paul compromised with them and how heavily he himself was influenced by them.

Paul's hymn of love (I Cor. 13) has prompted some doubts and misgivings in two respects. Capable exegetes have declared that they are unable to understand what is its connection with its context, the passage about the πνευματικά (spiritual gifts), and it has been curious to everyone that at the conclusion, instead of love, which up to that point has been the sole topic, a triad πίστις, ἐλπίς, ἀγάπη suddenly appears and is emphasized by the addition, stressing the number, of τὰ τρία ταῦτα (only these three, and at the same time: these well known three). Obviously there must be a *formula* behind this--it is the only one in the undoubtedly Pauline epistles--but up to this time no explanation has been found to account for its being cited, so that even a philologist like Corssen (*Sokrates*, 1919, pp. 18ff.) disputes the formula-character, without giving any consideration to the τὰ τρία ταῦτα. Perhaps one could add as a third aporia the fact that quite without any obvious reason for doing so, Paul appears, in the very middle, to turn from love to the spiritual gifts (προφητεῖαι, γλῶσσαι, γνῶσις). According to him, they, like all that is partial, will pass away when that which
384 is perfect appears;[19] but πίστις, ἐλπίς, ἀγάπη, on the contrary, will *remain* (μένει). For a natural and straightforward interpretation this could only mean that they will remain even in the hereafter; the contrasting prospect is (ἐκ)πίπτει, καταργηθήσονται, παύσονται (one may compare II Cor. 3:11: τὸ καταργούμενον διὰ δόξης--τὸ μένον ἐν δόξῃ).[20] Even this as-

sertion is for the first two so astounding, particularly in the light of other of Paul's declarations,[21] that he must certainly mean them here in a different sense, namely as parts of our very nature. Among the perishable πνευματικά, γλῶσσαι and προφητεῖαι are only briefly cited, so that in a lengthier, ingenious argument Paul can prove that in the hereafter the γνῶσις θεοῦ will cease, because it is partial and only a beholding δι' ἐσόπτρου ἐν αἰνίγματι. Some have offered the explanation that "from this point in his exposition onward, the problem of knowledge arises for the apostle and does not leave him even to the very end", without telling us how Paul can here come to the "problem of knowledge" in the first place and what he intends to accomplish with it. Such an explanation in essence only replaces the ancient and appropriate expression with a modern and inappropriate one, without explaining anything. If we take the context as our point of departure, an intentional and systematic polemic against the overestimation of the πνευματικά and especially of γνῶσις in chapters 12-14 is unmistakable. Paul has earlier indicated that the Corinthians are especially proud of the gift of γνῶσις and have forgotten brotherly love (8:1ff.). Now he does not mean to rebuke the striving for the πνευματικά (chapters 12ff.), but warns against placing too high a value upon them. In spite of the diversity of gifts (χαρίσματα), all the members of the community form one body, which God fits together. We do not know whom he values most highly. At first the προτιμᾶν, the *dignatio*, is only doubted. The gifts (prophecy, miraculous powers, speaking in tongues) are intended for the benefit of the whole community and are to be judged according to what they accomplish and what they mean for the whole community; they do not give to the individual bearer any inner and "abiding" worth. Besides this, Paul

knows a still higher way, and he shows this way in the hymn to love. Then he turns back once again to the χαρίσματα with the admonition, "so strive after the πνευματικά, but be especially zealous for love"; of the two gifts that are mentioned in chapter 13 only briefly, speaking in tongues, which is esteemed by the Corinthians above all else, is by far the lesser, because it does not serve the brethren, and prophecy is the loftier. He does not deal with γνῶσις any more at all; even previously it is mentioned only in 12:8, and it evidently is disposed of in chapter 13 within the hymn to love. The necessity of this chapter for the context is clear; it is not clear, however, why πίστις and ἐλπίς here, in *contrast to* γνῶσις, are suddenly combined with ἀγάπη into an indissoluble unity. The explanation suggesting that they might earlier have been combined, and indeed even combined with γνῶσις, in a formula known and cited by Paul's *opponents*, and that Paul here wanted to strike out *only the last-named* element and therefore had to set his own three-part formula in opposition to a four-part formula, was at first only an uncertain conjecture. It was occasioned by the fact that such a four-part formula actually is found in a later pagan author, Porphyry (Ad Marcellam 24): τέσσαρα στοιχεῖα μάλιστα κεκρατύνθω περὶ θεοῦ, πίστις, ἀλήθεια, ἔρως, ἐλπίς. πιστεῦσαι γὰρ δεῖ ὅτι μόνη σωτηρία ἡ πρὸς τὸν θεὸν ἐπιστροφή, καὶ πιστεύσαντα ὡς ἔνι μάλιστα σπουδάσαι τἀληθῆ γνῶναι περὶ αὐτοῦ, καὶ γνόντα ἐρασθῆναι τοῦ γνωσθέντος, ἐρασθέντα δὲ ἐλπίσιν ἀγαθαῖς τρέφειν τὴν ψυχὴν διὰ τοῦ βίου. ἐλπίσι γὰρ ἀγαθαῖς οἱ ἀγαθοὶ τῶν φαύλων ὑπερέχουσιν. στοιχεῖα μὲν οὖν ταῦτα καὶ τοσαῦτα κεκρατύνθω. Pagans too could regard πίστις (cf. above, p. 293), ἔρως or even ἀγάπη (cf. *Nachrichten d. Gött. Ges. d. Wissensch.* 1917, p. 131), and ἀλήθεια or γνῶσις as divine powers. Even before Porphyry, Clement of Alexandria (Strom. VII 57.4) offers a similar

386

enumeration: καί μοι δοκεῖ πρώτη τις εἶναι μεταβολὴ σωτήριος ἡ ἐξ ἐθνῶν εἰς πίστιν, δευτέρα δὲ ἡ ἐκ πίστεως εἰς γνῶσιν, ἡ δὲ εἰς ἀγάπην περαιουμένη ἐνθένδε ἤδη φίλον φίλῳ τὸ γινῶσκον τῷ γινωσκομένῳ παρίστησιν.[22] This is so similar to the quotation from Porphyry, in fact, that we must assume the same source for both of them, and the only question remains whether Clement abridged it or Porphyry expanded it; neither Clement (in this passage) nor Porphyry can be explained accordingly from Paul or--as Corssen has attempted anew--exclusively in his own terms. A further observation appears by way of supplement. In the two writings *De praemiis et poenis* and *De Abrahamo*, Philo offers a system of two triads of virtues or spiritual powers: one for the πρακτικὸς βίος, consisting of ἐλπίς, μετάνοια, and δικαιοσύνη, and one for the θεωρητικός, consisting of πίστις, χαρά, and ὅρασις (in Philo the regular substitute for γνῶσις; cf. above, p. 403). Here also, as is shown by the introduction of χαρά as a divine power, there are underlying Hellenistic influences, so that it would be unjustifiable *a priori* to doubt the existence of a three-part or four-part Hellenistic formula already in the time of Paul. A worthwhile hint from J. Geffcken[23] once suggested to me in what circles one should look for such a formula. The Oracula Chaldaica, a writing

387 highly esteemed by Porphyry, significantly influenced by Persian mysticism but exhibiting no trace of Christian influences, offer as πηγαία τριάς three divine powers, πίστις, ἀλήθεια, and ἔρως, and laud them πάντα γὰρ ἐν τρισὶ τοῖσδε κυβερνᾶταί τε καὶ ἔστιν. Hope was also mentioned: ἐλπὶς δὲ τρεφέτω σε πυρίοχος (W. Kroll, *Breslauer philolog. Abhandl.* VII 1.26 and 74; Migne, PSG 122, 1152a). One need only compare the wording of Porphyry to see that thereby any attempt to derive Porphyry from Paul or to explain him

solely in terms of his own work is definitively barred. I should only doubt whether the oracles are used directly or exclusively; the expression ἐλπίσιν ἀγαθαῖς τρέφειν τὴν ψυχὴν διὰ τοῦ βίου in Porphyry can, as Prof. Jaeger has kindly taught me, have been influenced in part by a recollection of Aeschylus' Prometheus 536: ἡδύ τι θαρσαλέαις τὸν μακρὸν βίον τείνειν ἐλπίσι, φαναῖς ἀλδαίνουσαν θυμὸν ἐν εὐφροσύναις. I first examine the few Oriental documents of Iranian mysticism that are available to us up to the present. That Soghdian fragment M. 14 in Berlin from which I took (above, p. 290, n. 6) the quite ancient enumeration of the five elements as likenesses of the "new man" appears to offer, among distinctions that are quite similar, very ancient, and wholly unaffected by Christianity, a division of "religion's δόξα" (the power or the splendor of religion?) into love, faith, perfection, knowledge, and a fifth attribute or power that unfortunately cannot yet be identified. To a certain extent the division into five parts corresponds to the division into five parts of the spiritual "members" of the light-deity in the Fihrist (Flügel, *Mani*, p. 86): love, faith, fidelity, generosity (the Arabic reading is not entirely certain), and wisdom.[24] Thus this is the earliest Oriental formula accessible to us. From the main text of the Manichaean

388 confession of sin (A. v. Le Coq, "Chuastuanift," *Abhandl. d. Berliner Akad.* 1911, p. 16, line 13) there is preserved in the eighth fragment an enumeration of the seals that is similar, but it names only *four*: "We believed in Zärvan the god, in the sun- and moon-god, in the god of strength and in Burχane: we relied upon them and became *auditores*. We have stamped upon our hearts the four light-seals; one is *love*, which is the seal of Zärvan the god; the second is *faith*, which is the seal of the sun- and moon-god; the third

is *fear* (of god), which is the seal of the fivefold god (Ohrmazd, or Primal Man); the fourth is *wise knowledge*, which is the seal of Burχane. If we, my God, should have been prompted to turn our understanding and our heart away from these four gods, if we should have expelled them from their places, if the divine seals should have been injured, now, my God, purging ourselves from sins we plead, 'Manastar hirza!'" It will be seen that, like the σφραγίς in Hellenistic belief, the seal of the god here is a sign that the particular deity holds property rights over the man. The number of the seals is arranged according to the number of the gods. Le Coq, who at that time was not yet acquainted with M. 14, conjectured, in the second revision (*Journal of the Royal Asiatic Society* 1911: "Dr. Stein's Turkish Khuastuanift from Tun-Huang," p. 300), that the enumeration must originally have corresponded to the five spiritual "members" of the deity in the Fihrist. Since we know that this number five corresponds to the ancient number of the elements and was reduced in the late Hellenistic period to four, this conjecture has become certain and the process clear. The four-seal teaching gives the second oldest (Hellenistic) form of the formula. It does not go back to Mani. In the Fihrist the numbering of the seals as three is explicitly attributed to him (Flügel, pp. 95 and 289), and the entire western tradition confirms this. Doubt on this point is impossible. And strangely, even that confession of sin has the number three alongside the four seals in the conclusion that is extant only in Dr. Stein's copy (*Journal of the Royal Asiatic Society* 1911, p. 298, lines 319ff.; it follows immediately after p. 26 of the Berlin publication): "On account of the ten Commandments, the seven Alms, the three Seals do we hold the name of Auditores; to act their actions we are unable."

The inference is that only in this passage does Mani himself again speak to us; the earlier passage is adopted from an earlier ritual, as something similar is to be observed frequently in the mythological teaching of the Turfan fragments. The three seals are always identified as *signaculum oris, manuum, sinus*. The formula probably is taken over from the Jewish sphere (Deut. 30:14: ἔστιν σου ἐγγὺς τὸ ῥῆμα--the commandment--σφόδρα, ἐν τῷ στόματί σου καὶ ἐν τῇ καρδίᾳ σου καὶ ἐν ταῖς χερσίν σου αὐτὸ ποιεῖν). But precisely corresponding to it is a quite ancient Persian division according to thoughts, words, and works (e.g., Yasht 22);[25] these together form the whole personality (*daena*, there meaning person, not religion), and the soul is led to heaven by three stages of good thoughts, words, and works, as to hell by the stages of evil thoughts, words, and works (in the Mandaean texts the seven stages of the vices, i.e., planets, of the Babylonians have entered in place of these). In the Arda Viraf, chapter 2, three initiatory potions enable the soul to pass through these stations. They cleanse the soul for the passage. It was an obvious thing to give a seal to the soul for each (in the Mandaean texts actually "the seal" is demanded of the soul in each stage). Here the seal testifies that this part of the man is closed to sin and has remained pure. In the Manichaean confession of sin there also follows immediately after the enumeration of the *four* seals a section on the ten commandments, of which man has to keep three with the mouth, three with the heart, three with the hands, and one with his entire being (the *daena*); according to the testimony of the Fihrist this passage comes from Mani; the mention of the *three* seals in the conclusion thus refers to this passage. As a curious thing I should mention further that Philo (De paen. 183), citing the passage from Deuteronomy,

explicitly adds that according to symbolic (and thus pneumatic) interpretation, στόματι, καρδίᾳ, καὶ χερσί means nothing other than λόγοις καὶ βουλαῖς καὶ πράξεσιν, and even adds, in repetition: λόγου μὲν στόμα σύμβολον, καρδία δὲ βουλευμάτων, πράξεων δὲ χεῖρες, ἐν οἷς τὸ εὐδαιμονεῖν ἐστιν. His spelling out so fully what is self-evident sug-

90 gests the conjecture that for the "mystical" exposition he is using a Hellenistic-Iranian source. The Iranian development which we have traced out here shows itself to be entirely untouched by Christianity.

The passage in Porphyry must go back to an Iranian source; thus Porphyry's own choice of the term στοιχεῖα περὶ τὸν θεόν cannot have been accidental. Thus he did *not* use the Chaldaic oracle, but another Hellenistic source, which assumed the number four for the material elements as well as for the spiritual elements of God; if they are united, then man is deified. The translation of the Oriental text was not particularly a happy one; Porphyry himself, if he had drawn directly from it, perhaps would have said στοιχεῖα θεοῦ or θεῖα, as the author of the Colossian epistle (above, p. 342) also more correctly would at least have spoken of μέλη ἐπίγεια (in contrast to οὐράνια as in Paul). But a western language cannot at all fully give expression to the fluid ideas of Oriental mysticism; it is not surprising that even in authors with conceptual resources in abundance, unsatisfactory translations are produced.

The result of the lengthy study now appears to me to be, with respect to Paul, the following: there is nothing to hinder the assumption that he actually found such a formula already present in Corinth. It is not surprising that he had not earlier refuted the formula. For him, after all, faith and love stand at the center of religious feeling in a sense

altogether different from that of the Hellenistic προσήλυτος. He had also experienced hope within himself as a vital divine power and had once commended it, as he did elsewhere with other good qualities, alongside faith and love (I Thess. 1:3; cf. 5:8), though of course without himself intending to coin a formula. Elsewhere, in his relationship to the community he himself bases his claim on γνῶσις, but as he encounters it in the new Hellenistic converts' striving for independence, he senses what separates him from them, and senses that lofty and imperishable divine powers are quite differently at work within himself. He also becomes vaguely aware of the altogether different territory which they occupy. Thus he develops his

391 case, by extolling love in an ardent but systematically constructed outpouring. He has earlier contrasted love with γνῶσις; for him, whether as love for God or love for one's brother, it flows from the same source. This power is imperishable, while the power to attain revelations is intended only for our poor earthly life. When he mentions faith and hope along with love, this is accounted for by his consideration of the formula that is being held up before him, and is justified by the vague feeling that, in a way altogether different from γνῶσις, these two qualities belong to the essential powers of the καινὸς ἄνθρωπος, the Χριστὸς ἐν ἡμῖν; in fact, he has just indicated that one can be a Christian without γνῶσις. This is un-Hellenistic, and yet is genuinely Christian and authentically Pauline. Nowhere does the apostle come so close to us as in this *battle against Hellenism.*

In the *Nachrichten der Göttinger Gesellschaft* 1916, pp. 395ff., I have given a detailed rationale for my interpretation of the thought-context of the thirteenth chapter and have demonstrated the linguistic offences in Harnack's article directed against the historians of religion (*Sitzungsber.*

d. Preuss. Akad. 1911, pp. 132-33). I am highly pleased that so keen an interpreter as H. Lietzmann in the second edition of his commentary has followed me; I have never expected agreement from all those who come after me and on all details, and I am not suprised at such feats of interpretation as making μένει mean "does not come to grief". Only when even a philologist like P. Corssen breaks out in the passionately elevated statement that "the sacred forces of faith, hope, and love do not stem from the musty atmosphere of a pagan mystery religion" may I feel some sense of astonishment. If this is intended only to deny that those forces have played a role even in pagan religions, it still is demonstrably incorrect; indeed, they could not be absent from any religion. But if the statement is intended to attribute to me the assertion that Paul transposed these forces from the mystery religions into Christianity, I only affirm that in the passages under attack (*Historische Zeitschrift* 1916, p. 191, and *Nachr. d. Gött. Ges.* 1916, p. 368) I have expressed the opposite with

392

the greatest emphasis. I have spoken about the *composition of a formula*, and thus about the *formation of a system*,[26] which according to my view Paul found already at hand, adopted, and filled with his own contents, but now, when the struggle has shown him the peril involved in it, has altered. To me this was evidence of how far Paul went, in conceptual formulation, in accommodation to Hellenistic feeling, and what difficulties and conflicts, long observed from the theological side but not explained, necessarily resulted for him from this accommodation, conflicts that he, like all those caught in the transition between two ages, did not succeed in resolving without residue.

Did Paul actually succeed in forcing the refractory part of the Corinthian community to submit? And, if they yielded

out of fear of a magical power residing in the πνευματικός, could the submission continue, and could it be of any worth? I acknowledge that I readily accept many main features of the picture that E. Schwartz (*Charakterköpfe aus der antiken Literatur*, second edition, II) has sketched of Paul the missionary to the Gentiles and church leader. His strongest impact in these regards rests upon what he preserved from Judaism. The πνευματικός only founds θίασοι, hardly continuing congregations, and least of all a church, no matter how passionately he may strive to do so. Even Paul the teacher is not the founder of later Christianity in the measure that is often claimed for him. Otherwise the message of the earthly life and the teaching of the founder Jesus never would have been able to appear alongside the Pauline γνῶσις as it did, once the necessary distance for the formation of a *religious* tradition had been gained. Nevertheless in my judgment this 393 γνῶσις remains, alongside and even beyond the mysticism of the final redactor of the Fourth Gospel, the bearer of the strongest influence that Hellenism ever exerted upon Christianity. Its most consequential influences lie in the origin, not in the further course of development. On this point Bousset is correct.

NOTES

1. ἐν πειθοῖ and ἐν ἀποδείξει are intended to correspond to each other. To the first member there is added (because of 1:17) an explanatory phrase in the instrumental case, σοφίας λόγοις; in the case of the second member, this more specific definition is connected as a genitive to ἀπόδειξις; nevertheless the hearer is intended to sense σοφίας λόγοι as a contrast to πνεῦμα καὶ δύναμις (δυνάμει πνεύματος); later on, πνεῦμα is indeed regarded as in contrast to σοφία, just as δύναμις is here to λόγοι.

2. One may think of the discourse of the pagan in Minucius 11.7, where we should read: *vellem tamen sciscitari, utrumne <sine corporibus an> cum corporibus et corporibus quibus, ipsisne an innovatis, resurgatur. sine corpore? hoc quod sciam neque mens neque anima nec vita est. ipso corpore? sed iam ante dilapsum est; alio corpore? ergo homo novus nascitur, non prior ille reparatur.*

3. Earlier I wrote in verse 45 ὁ ἄνθρωπος--ὁ 'Αδάμ (tradition: ὁ πρῶτος ἄνθρωπος 'Αδάμ, as well as ὁ πρῶτος ἄνθρωρος and ὁ πρῶτος 'Αδάμ), and in the continuation ὁ ἔσχατος 'Αδάμ (tradition: ἔσχατος 'Αδάμ, ὁ ἔσχατος ἄνθρωπος, or ὁ ἔσχατος κύριος--thus Marcion). I now recognize in both places explanatory additions that arose because verse 21 was no longer understood. Corresponding to this is only the pairing: ὁ πρῶτος Ἄνθρωπος and ὁ ἔσχατος. But I note explicitly that for the following statements nothing depends on this version.

4. *Gött. Gel. Anz.* 1924, p. 47; Reitzenstein-Schaeder, *Studien zum antiken Synkretismus*, 1926, p. 26.

5. It is utterly absurd to think that the idea of a class of souls arises out of a Platonic idea and fills the Orient.

6. Karppe, *Les origines du Zohar*, pp. 76, 77. The antiquity of the idea is demonstrated by the Christian counterparts in Excerpta ex Theodoto 72 and 78; cf. *Poimandres*, p. 78 (above, p. 384).

7. Above, p. 14; more fully stated in Reitzenstein-Schaeder, *op. cit.*, Part I, chapter IV. The basic idea is

found precisely thus in the purely pagan parts, which are universally acknowledged: here too there are two Anthropoi.

8. The concept is bound to have been familiar to the community of Apollos, the disciple of John, and in another form also to the Petrine community as well. Hence Paul could employ the word here.

9. *Kyrios Christos* (ET, Nashville, 1970), p. 163; cf. p. 149.

10. Reitzenstein-Schaeder II, pp. 306-7.

11. Part I, pp. 193, 194.

12. The texture of the body causes ἀγνωσία and, since it is the κακία, is the support and foundation of ἀγνωσία; the body is the cunning enemy which, when it pampers us, hates us, and thus would love us if it caused us distress (Scott, II 186, 187, has a different view).

13. Reitzenstein-Schaeder II 321. It is itself essentially the soul that is given by God.

14. In this there is something reminiscent of the Hermetic idea that the body is the enemy which δι' ὧν μισεῖ, φιλεῖ (VII 2; cf. above, p. 449).

15. Contra H. Lietzmann, *Handbuch zum Neuen Testament* 9, second edition, p. 147.

16. In the book which I published jointly with Prof. Schaeder I have attempted to show, by means of numerous examples, how ancient this concept is in the Orient.

17. Cf. the Mithras liturgy 6.4: ἕλκε ἀπὸ τῶν ἀκτίνων πνεῦμα τρὶς ἀνασπῶν.

18. Cf. v. Harnack, *Preuss. Jahrb.* 164.1.

19. The argument is contrived: that which is imperfect, when it becomes perfect, will cease to be (instead of: cease to be imperfect). What applies to the gifts that serve only for edification of the community, γλῶσσαι and προφητεῖαι (they are superfluous in the hereafter), is transferred by Paul to γνῶσις, which elsewhere has a different meaning for

him (of course it still is for him a kind of seeing); it too is partial, and hence it too must pass away.

20. The assertion that Paul is speaking only of love for one's neighbors collapses of its own weight here. In the light of the commandment with which he was acquainted, ἀγαπᾶν θεόν, it could not be justified on linguistic grounds. Nor in terms of content is it tenable: for him, love of God (or of Christ) and love of neighbor form a unitary energy of the soul (above, pp. 473-74).

21. II Cor. 5:7: διὰ πίστεως περιπατοῦμεν, οὐ διʼ εἴδους (i.e., ὄψεως; for comparable language, cf. Corp. Herm. X 5: κατακοιμίζονται εἰς τὴν καλλίστην ὄψιν); Rom. 8:24: ἐλπὶς δὲ βλεπομένη οὐκ ἔστιν ἐλπίς. ὃ γὰρ βλέπει τις, τί καὶ ἐλπίζει; there is a forcible transfer from the last item to the first two of the attribute which in the ordinary sense and usage does not belong to them at all.

22. The system repeatedly recurs in his works; one becomes a pneumatic ἑνώσας τὴν γνῶσιν, πίστιν, ἀγάπην, εἰς ὧν ἐνθένδε (III 69.3; Philo offers some instructive counterparts).

23. Cf. now his book, *Der Ausgang des griechisch-römischen Heidentums*, p. 271. On the matter I should add: from the lists which I have published in *Nachr. d. Gött. Ges.* 1916, p. 386, and 1917, p. 130, it is evident, and is essentially understandable, that in the apostolic era πίστις and ἀγάπη frequently appear in combination, though any sort of combination with ἐλπίς understood as a virtue is very rare; where such a combination is introduced, as a rule there is an obvious misunderstanding of the text. The appearance of the three as women's names could never attest a triadic formula in Christianity and, since throughout the Greek territory of this time a number of virtues appear as women's names (among them Elpis quite frequently appears in pagan usage, Agape occasionally, and Pistis in the sense of "faithfulness" is altogether possible), it is entirely without significance for this question. Even the Roman martyr Sophia, whose three daughters, at first unnamed (Ruinart, second edition, p. 619), in the East later are called Pistis, Elpis, and Agape, could at the most prove something against Harnack's assertion; evidently in this giving of names a tetrad is in mind: σοφία (for γνῶσις), πίστις, ἐλπίς, and ἀγάπη. One must actually marvel at how little continuing influence was at first exerted by the formula, which occurs in Paul only once, but in such a powerfully captivating passage.

24. Cf. Appendix XIII (it is earlier than Philo).

25. It also appears very early on Indian soil.

26. A comparison that naturally would not fit at all points would be conceded. To trace the canon of the four cardinal virtues or of the four elements to a particular man does not imply the assertion that this man invented these virtues or these elements, and this tracing is not refuted by the proof that the words that are involved also occur elsewhere individually or in varying combinations. If a philosopher teaches that "there are not four but five elements", or that "there are not four but seven major vices", I may be permitted to examine how he arrives at this alteration; in the second case this is clear, and in the first case it is subject to dispute; but the fact that the word αἰθήρ occurs even earlier still does not suffice for a fully decisive conclusion.

XVII.

The Technical Language of the Gnostics

The passage from Paul (II Cor. 2:14) cited on page 79, above, reads as follows: τῷ δὲ θεῷ χάρις τῷ πάντοτε θριαμβεύοντι ἡμᾶς ἐν τῷ Χριστῷ καὶ τὴν ὀσμὴν τῆς γνώσεως αὐτοῦ φανεροῦντι δι' ἡμῶν ἐν παντὶ τόπῳ, ὅτι Χριστοῦ εὐωδία ἐσμὲν τῷ θεῷ ἐν τοῖς σωζομένοις καὶ ἐν τοῖς ἀπολλυμένοις, οἷς μὲν ὀσμὴ ἐκ θανάτου εἰς θάνατον, οἷς δὲ ὀσμὴ ἐκ ζωῆς εἰς ζωήν. καὶ πρὸς ταῦτα τίς ἱκανός; οὐ γάρ ἐσμεν ὡς οἱ πολλοὶ καπηλεύοντες τὸν λόγον τοῦ θεοῦ, ἀλλ' ὡς ἐξ εἰλικρινείας, ἀλλ' ὡς ἐκ θεοῦ κατενώπιον τοῦ θεοῦ ἐν Χριστῷ λαλοῦμεν. The picture, to which the idea of the triumph completely gives way (cf. Wissowa in Lietzmann), is gradually re-formed; first the *aroma* is thought of only as the bearer and mediator of the γνῶσις; here the γνῶσις is also our thank-offering to God, as in the Hermetic prayer (above, p. 365); in the second part, the aroma (and its bearer) is the φάρμακον τῆς ἀθανασίας, the means of salvation, the ointment (the idea is Hellenistic, but it has also passed over into the Talmud; cf. the commentaries). Connected with the φάρμακον is the idea that the same means brings life to one, and death to another. The transition from the first, simple idea of εὐωδία to the second, φάρμακον, is not difficult in itself: the aroma of life is necessarily a life-bringing breath. The conclusion shows that Paul is using the figure for the κήρυγμα, pneumatic discourse in the truest and fullest sense (he heaps up the words: ἐκ θεοῦ κατενώπιον τοῦ θεοῦ ἐν Χριστῷ).

The two figures recur frequently in the same connection and with the same usage. In an outpouring entirely composed, one might almost say patched together, of Pauline reminiscences, Ignatius admonishes the Ephesians (chapters 15ff.) to hold to pure doctrine and to guard against κακὴ διδασκαλία. He begins thus: ὁ λόγον Ἰησοῦ κεκτημένος ἀληθῶς δύναται καὶ

394 τῆς ἡσυχίας αὐτοῦ ἀκούειν, ἵνα τέλειος ᾖ ...... πάντα οὖν ποιῶμεν ὡς αὐτοῦ ἐν ἡμῖν κατοικοῦντος, ἵνα ὦμεν αὐτοῦ ναοὶ καὶ αὐτὸς ᾖ ἐν ἡμῖν ὁ θεὸς ἡμῶν, ὅπερ καὶ ἔστιν καὶ φανήσεται πρὸ προσώπου ἡμῶν, ἐξ ὧν δικαίως ἀγαπῶμεν αὐτόν. μὴ πλανᾶσθε, ἀδελφοί μου· οἱ οἰκοφθόροι βασιλείαν θεοῦ οὐ κληρονομήσουσιν (he combines I Cor. 3:16-18 with 9 and 10). εἰ οὖν οἱ κατὰ σάρκα ταῦτα πράσσοντες ἀπέθανον, πόσῳ μᾶλλον, ἐάν τις πίστιν θεοῦ ἐν κακῇ διδασκαλίᾳ φθείρῃ, ὑπὲρ ἧς Ἰησοῦς Χριστὸς ἐσταυρώθη. He becomes material (ῥυπαρός) and falls into eternal fire, as does anyone who listens to him. Then follow the parables in chapters 17 and 18: διὰ τοῦτο μύρον ἔλαβεν ἐπὶ τῆς κεφαλῆς αὐτοῦ ὁ κύριος (what is meant can only be his anointing to be the Christ; the anointing of the dead is ruled out by the very language of the expression), ἵνα πνέῃ τῇ ἐκκλησίᾳ ἀφθαρσίαν. μὴ ἀλείφεσθε δυσωδίαν τῆς διδασκαλίας τοῦ ἄρχοντος τοῦ αἰῶνος τούτου, μὴ αἰχμαλωτίσῃ ὑμᾶς ἐκ τοῦ προκειμένου ζῆν. διὰ τί δὲ οὐ πάντες φρόνιμοι γινόμεθα λαβόντες θεοῦ γνῶσιν, ὅ ἐστιν Ἰησοῦς Χριστός; τί μωρῶς ἀπολλύμεθα ἀγνοοῦντες τὸ χάρισμα, ὅ πέπομφεν ἀληθῶς ὁ κύριος; Περίψημα τὸ ἐμὸν πνεῦμα τοῦ σταυροῦ, ὅ ἐστιν σκάνδαλον τοῖς ἀπιστοῦσιν, ἡμῖν δὲ σωτηρία καὶ ζωὴ αἰώνιος. In the last words Ignatius has already used I Cor. 1:17ff., οὐ γὰρ ἀπέστειλέν με Χριστὸς βαπτίζειν ἀλλ' εὐαγγελίσασθαι. Now, with the verbatim quotation ποῦ σοφός, ποῦ συζητητής (I Cor. 1:10) he passes over to the mystery that he has to proclaim: since the ascension of Christ the new aeon has begun. His description agrees, I note in pass-

ing, in almost every feature with the earliest texts of the Mandaeans' book of the dead: unnoticed by Ruha and the Seven (the archons) the Anthropos has come down to earth; when he leaves the earth again, it loses its light; everything is shaken and bursts; Ruha and the Seven lament that the end of their dominion and the decline of the world has arrived. But back to the parables. The fragrance that Christ brings with him brings ἀφθαρσία to his people (ἐκκλησία was said only because of the connection with the preceding, where the οἶκος θεοῦ is the ἐκκλησία). That they are to be anointed with it is first indicated by the form of the contrast μὴ ἀλείφεσθε δυσωδίαν, and again, the contrast to it is actually formed by λαμβάνετε τὴν γνῶσιν θεοῦ (be anointed with the γνῶσις θεοῦ) ὅ ἐστιν Ἰησοῦς Χριστός. It is difficult here to avoid thinking of the fact that Manda d'Haije, the Anthropos of the Mandaeans, is called γνῶσις θεοῦ. Christ then is explicitly identified in neuter terms as τὸ χάρισμα (in a condescending way; yet on closer examination, the conjectural reading χρῖσμα is not necessary); indeed, heathen mysticism also calls γνῶσις the χάρισμα of God (above, p. 366). But the figure changes again; the curious expression τὸ ἐμὸν πνεῦμα τοῦ σταυροῦ, which apparently is modeled after Paul in I Cor. 1:18, ὁ λόγος ὁ τοῦ σταυροῦ, calls for an explanation. One may hardly think of the πνεῦμα λεκτικόν of the magical papyrus (above, p. 394); but πνέῃ ἀφθαρσίαν has preceded it, and thus the fragrance itself is the breath (πνοή or πνεῦμα), and the fragrance signifies the κήρυγμα, the ἐπαγγελία or διδασκαλία (cf. among later writers, the fragrance of the cross and the oil of the cross). The fact that it is also called σωτηρία καὶ ζωὴ αἰώνιος can no longer be surprising; only the equating of διδασκαλία and μύρον or εὐωδία will, I fear, evoke contradiction. And yet this itself is formula-like. In Hippolytus'

account of the Naassenes (102.14 W.) we read: καὶ ἐσμὲν ἐξ ἁπάντων ἀνθρώπων ἡμεῖς Χριστιανοὶ ἐν τῇ τρίτῃ πύλῃ ἀπαρτίζοντες τὸ μυστήριον (baptism in the heavenly Euphrates) καὶ χριόμενοι ἐκεῖ ἀλάλῳ χρίσματι, ἐκ κέρατος ὡς Δαβίδ, οὐκ ὀστρακινοῦ φακοῦ, φησίν, ὡς ὁ Σαούλ, and (83.5): ἡ γὰρ ἐπαγγελία τοῦ λουτροῦ οὐκ ἄλλη τίς ἐστι κατ' αὐτούς, ἢ τὸ εἰσαγαγεῖν εἰς τὴν ἀμάραντον ἡδονὴν τὸν λυόμενον κατ' αὐτοὺς ζῶντι ὕδατι καὶ χριόμενον ἀλάλῳ κρίσματι. An ἄλαλον χρίσμα can only be an instruction without words; here there is transferred to God what is often said of man, whose most sacred address to God is the θεία σιγή (cf. in Ignatius above τῆς ἡσυχίας αὐτοῦ ἀκούειν, and on ἡσυχία for σιγή, Ign. Eph. 19.1; of course a πνεῦμα ἄλαλον is something entirely different). Only now do I regard the connections of the passage from Ignatius as clear, and I mention only in passing that whereas he promises the Ephesians καὶ φανήσεται πρὸ προσώπου ἡμῶν, the Acts of Thomas (chapter 27, p. 142 Bonnet) portray a mystery in which the anointing is actually performed, and in fact immediately after baptism (one manuscript has even preserved the label of χρῖσμα); its effect is that the ones baptized see God, and indeed they see him as a young man with a blazing torch in his hand, as the sun-god (Mithras) is represented in the mysteries of Apuleius. Of course there is connected with this the instructive discourse which Bousset (*Zeitschr. für die neutestamentl. Wissensch.* 1917, pp. 1 and 8) has splendidly explained; only he might have identified its basis not as Manichaean, but as an earlier epiclesis that had only been appropriated by Mani (because of Ignatius, I mention that in the revision Christ is called τὸ χάρισμα τὸ ὕψιστον and is equated with γνῶσις, ἡ τὰ μυστήρια ἀποκαλύπτουσα τὰ ἀπόκρυφα). In the Hermetic literature, too, teaching and especially prayer always effects the full

vision of God. Later on for the Manichaeans Jesus is the one who brings γνῶσις, and of course is also the moon-god.

Before I draw the conclusions, I cite yet a third enigmatic passage, I John 2:20ff. The author warns that the end of the ages has come: the antichrist is already approaching, and there are many antichrists; they have gone out from us, but they do not belong to us: καὶ ὑμεῖς χρῖσμα ἔχετε ἀπὸ τοῦ ἁγίου καὶ οἴδατε πάντα. οὐκ ἔγραψα ὑμῖν ὅτι οὐκ οἴδατε τὴν ἀλήθειαν, ἀλλ' ὅτι οἴδατε αὐτήν, καὶ ὅτι πᾶν ψεῦδος ἐκ τῆς ἀληθείας οὐκ ἔστιν. τίς ἐστιν ὁ ψεύστης εἰ μὴ ὁ ἀρνούμενος ὅτι 'Ιησοῦς οὐκ ἔστιν ὁ Χριστός; οὗτός ἐστιν ὁ ἀντίχριστος, ὁ ἀρνούμενος τὸν πατέρα καὶ τὸν υἱόν. πᾶς ὁ ἀρνούμενος τὸν υἱὸν οὐδὲ τὸν πατέρα ἔχει. ὁ ὁμολογῶν τὸν υἱὸν καὶ τὸν πατέρα ἔχει. ὑμεῖς ὅ ἠκούσατε ἀπ' ἀρχῆς ἐν ὑμῖν μενέτω. ἐὰν ἐν ὑμῖν μείνῃ, ὅ ἀπ' ἀρχῆς ἠκούσατε, καὶ ὑμεῖς ἐν τῷ υἱῷ καὶ ἐν τῷ πατρὶ μενεῖτε. καὶ αὕτη ἐστὶν ἡ ἐπαγγελία ἥν αὐτὸς ἐπηγγείλατο ἡμῖν, τὴν ζωὴν τὴν αἰώνιον. ταῦτα ἔγραψα ὑμῖν περὶ τῶν πλανώντων ὑμᾶς. καὶ ὑμεῖς τὸ χρῖσμα, ὅ ἐλάβετε ἀπ' αὐτοῦ, μενεῖ ἐν ὑμῖν καὶ οὐ χρείαν ἔχετε ἵνα τις διδάσκῃ ὑμᾶς, ἀλλ' ὡς τὸ αὐτοῦ χρῖσμα διδάσκει ὑμᾶς περὶ πάντων, καὶ ἀληθές ἐστιν καὶ οὐκ ἔστιν ψεῦδος, καὶ καθὼς ἐδίδαξεν ὑμᾶς, μενεῖτε ἐν αὐτῷ. The χρῖσμα imparts full γνῶσις, but is therewith equated both in language and in essence with the ὅ ἠκούσατε ἀπ' ἀρχῆς. But at the same time it also appears to be seen as the person of the proclaimer; indeed, he is the Logos. There is an obvious reference to John 15:4ff., μείνατε ἐν ἐμοί, κἀγὼ ἐν ὑμῖν; indeed, if I read it correctly, to 14:6ff. also, ἐγώ εἰμι ἡ ὁδὸς καὶ ἡ ἀλήθεια καὶ ἡ ζωή, where Christ in fact is also characterized as γνῶσις. It is arbitrary here to interpret χρῖσμα as πνεῦμα and to think of the ancient consecration of prophets, and it destroys the sense of the entire passage if we think of a cultically performed sacrament. The formula-like equation

97

of the proclamation at baptism with the χρῖσμα fully explains the passage, and the comparison with Ignatius confirms the interpretation, even down to details (Paul's words in II Cor. 1:12, ὁ δὲ βεβαιῶν ἡμᾶς σὺν ὑμῖν εἰς Χριστὸν καὶ χρίσας ἡμᾶς θεός, ὁ καὶ σφραγισάμενος ἡμᾶς καὶ δοὺς τὸν ἀρραβῶνα τοῦ πνεύματος ἐν ταῖς καρδίαις ἡμῶν perhaps will support this explanation better than the explanation of the χρῖσμα as πνεῦμα, but the expression here has become totally devoid of pictorial import).

The three passages, which serve to interpret each other, exhibit a distinctive development of the style of pneumatic discourse. It is true that the first one (II Cor. 2:14) seems strange to us; the fact that the figure is constantly changing shows that Paul does not start from the idea and only later seek the appropriate pictorial form for it; no, from the very outset he thinks in pictorial and figurative terms, and he presupposes that his readers are able to think likewise; hence the figure is also re-shaped along with the idea. It is altogether a different matter with Ignatius; he evidently is employing a fixed stylistic instrument of pneumatic discourse. It requires the hardly comprehensible, allegorical designations (cf. τὸ ἐμὸν πνεῦμα τοῦ σταυροῦ) and a fixed typology. It is a form of sacral speaking in tongues, which constantly poses problems for the hearer and is not meant to be understood by the unbeliever, the authentic counterpart to allegorical or pneumatic exegesis, indeed, actually only a consequence of it: if in the sacred tradition the πνεῦμα is constantly speaking in allegories which only the favored person understands, so must the πνευματικός do the same, in order to validate his claim. The cultic language and the magical practice of many peoples offer something similar. Because in the particular myth the disk of Horus is the most costly sac-

rifice, later on in the cult any valuable sacrificial gift is called the disk of Horus, without any more thought of the myth itself; or the pictorial representation of the sun, for example, provides the expression for the mysterious mythological narrative in magic: κάνθαρος ὁ πτεροφυὴς ἀπεκεφαλίσθη (Dieterich, *Jahrb. f. Phil.* Suppl. XVI, p. 796); or symbol and interpretation are intermingled, as in the Mandaean story of the white eagle (Johannesbuch, chapter 73). The prayer, the truly pneumatic part, especially favors sudden changes from one figure to another, first in the epicleses, and then also in the explication; if for the Mandaean God is the planter and the builder, the two figures will easily intermingle, as the thought of the suppliant turns to one or the other. What is at first an individual creation easily hardens, especially in Oriental religions, into a formula; in prophetic discourse it was re-shaped into artistically elaborated allegory (as in Ezekiel), and now this allegory becomes a traditional legacy and is transferred from one body of material to another and from one religion into another (one may think of the Shepherd of Hermas). Different and yet somewhat similar, it would appear, is the development of the secret language of the alchemists. Here too the transition from the individual creation to a formula is easily traced out. Out of the myths related in the ancient writings and the explanatory glosses on them there arise formulas, i.e., code words. The cosmic egg (ᾠόν) and its parts survived in quite general usage; certainly more rarely there remained δράκοντος χολή (Berthelot in the alchemist lexicon 6.23; cf. 15.8, from the myth of the battle with the dragon, which I have explained in the Festschrift for Fr. C. Andreas), πηλὸς Ἡφαίστου (Berthelot 13.2), Ὄσιρις (12.9), ἀετίτης λίθος (5.20), and Ἡλίου χαῖται (7.19). Others stem from ancient sacrificial prescriptions, which were

"pneumatically" misinterpreted (γάλα βοὸς μελαίνης in 6.15; θαλλοὶ φοινίκων in 8.6). The formulas of the ancient language of riddle also make their contribution (λίθος ὁ οὐ λίθος). A favorite is the easily recognizable reinterpretation of actual mysteries (ἱερὸς γάμος, renewal, rebirth, raising of the dead), of which instructive examples are afforded by the writing (cf. the examples above, p. 398) which I published in the *Nachrichten d. Gesellschaft d. Wissenschaften*, Göttingen 1919, pp. 1ff. In connection with the similarity of this secret language with the mystical-theological language the existence of such lexicons has a certain interest for the philologist; they serve the reader, by affording him a compilation of the possibilities of interpretation; they also
399 serve the writer, by giving him a choice among such formulas that are incomprehensible to the uninitiated person. One can also learn the pneumatic language, like any other language. Actually there must have been such compendia available quite early for Christian and Jewish mysticism, and I could wish for a more knowledgeable person to investigate the late remnants of this literature. Not only would pneumatic exegesis thereby come into fuller light, but pneumatic discourse as well, both of them, indeed, essentially Oriental constructions. That slipping from one figure to another that makes it so difficult for us to understand them is in deliberate imitation of prophetic utterance, which intends to have its effect by means of disconnected individual images and words. Hence the language of mysticism or of gnosis follows a development similar to that of the language of alchemy, from the free and individual construction to the scholastic formula. For a formula such as ἄλαλον χρῖσμα we must search for an interpretation, as well as for δράκοντος χολή. Only the aids for the search are more abundant in the former case.

Ignatius wishes to speak in this kind of artificial language when he undertakes to prove to the συμμύσται Παύλου that through his martyrdom, which is already beginning, he has become a pneumatic, and thus the true gnostic and Παύλου μύστης: Paul provides the foundation, but he does some new creating; but his imitation remains tedious and tortured, and particularly impoverished in thought. The author of the first epistle of John bears the same relationship to the Gospel of John as does Ignatius in this passage to Paul. Hence the formula-language is for him still more firmly fixed, but also, of course, more simple. For the interpretation of this language one must stick to the code words, as for example in 3:9, σπέρμα αὐτοῦ ἐν αὐτῷ μένει, one must focus on the concept μένει ἐν ὑμῖν. The σπέρμα θεοῦ is also, Hellenistically speaking, the ζωή (e.g., Corp. herm. XIV 10), and for him the latter again is Jesus or the divine in us, the λόγος τῆς ζωῆς (1:1). I readily believe that he uses the figurative expression without giving it much thought, as the alchemist does his γρῖφοι, and I place this interpretation of mine over against the explanation in the *Sitzungsber. d. Berl. Akad.* 1915, p. 541, which goes contrary to the language. For *Paul* neither a definite striving for style nor any compulsion of a formula is discernible. To be sure, for his figures he utilizes Hellenistic mystery perspectives, but he creates freely. Only a few more words on this substantive part.

In the Iranian tradition the awakening of God's Ἄνθρωπος, who is sleeping because he is sunken in matter, is accomplished either by means of the brief magical utterance (thus in the Zarathustra hymn) or by means of the detailed instruction (a lengthy κήρυγμα, as in the Manichaean liturgy), or by virtue of the fact that the divine envoy causes him to smell the fragrance of life and employs a means to that end

(Theodore bar Konai). The awakening always corresponds to the revival of the dead god. Nevertheless the actual cultic action in the awakening will have to assume somewhat different features from the representation of the awakening in verbal form. We have a description of such a cultic action from the Phrygian mysteries in Firmicus Maternus, De errore prof. rel., chapters 22ff. It is originally similar to the fitting together of the members of the dead (i.e., sleeping in the night, and indeed deceased) deity in the Egyptian daily cult (Morin, "Cult divin journalier en Egypte," *Annales du Musée Guimet* XIV 70ff.). The cult of the dead in various places must have known something similar. A newly added feature, however, when this cultic action became a mystery in our sense of the word, is the use of the ointment which was applied in reviving the deity (the φάρμακον τῆς ἀθανασίας; cf. Diodorus I 25, Griffith, *Demotic Magical Papyrus*, pp. 131, 133; and the alchemistic writing translated from the Aramaic, above, p. 398) to anoint also the *mystai* who were present, in order to maintain a participation in the destiny of their deity. A brief proclamation is pronounced in that connection. If one keeps in mind the necessary distinctions, this cultic action also can lead us into an understanding of the word of Paul. The description reads thus: *nocte quadam simulacrum in lectica supinum ponitur et per numeros digestis fletibus plangitur. deinde cum se ficta lamentatione satiaverint, lumen infertur. tunc a sacerdote omnium qui flebant, fauces unguentur, quibus perunctis sacerdos hoc lento murmure susurrat:* θαρρεῖτε, μύσται, τοῦ θεοῦ σεσωσμένου· ἔσται γὰρ ἡμῖν ἐκ πόνων σωτηρία. *quid miseros hortaris* <*ut*> *gaudeant, quid deceptos homines laetari conpellis?.....idolum sepelis, idolum plangis, idolum de sepultura proferis, et miser, cum haec feceris, gaudes. tu deum tuum liberas, tu iacentia lapidis membra conponis, tu insensibile*

401

corrigis saxum. tibi agat gratias deus tuus, te paribus remuneret donis, te sui velit esse participem: sic moriaris, ut moritur, sic vivas, ut vivit. nam quod olore perunguentur fauces.....unguentum hoc reserva mortuis, reserva morituris ......aliud est unguentum, quod deus pater unico tradidit filio, quod filius credentibus divina numinis sui maiestate largitur. Christi unguentum inmortali conpositione conficitur et spiritalibus pigmentorum odoribus temperatur. hoc unguentum a mortalibus laqueis putres hominum artus exuit, ut sepulto primo homine ex eodem statim homine homo alius felicius nascatur. Firmicus is acquainted with I John 2:18ff. and only re-interprets it to some degree. The πνευματικὸν χρῖσμα of the Christian faith gives the true inner resurrection, while the σωματικὸν χρῖσμα of the belief in Attis at most gives the ἀφθαρσία σώματος, but at the same time eternal corruption. By means of this point, which of course Firmicus is the first to introduce, the idea is sharply distinguished from the Pauline idea. Nevertheless, even the vivid portrayal of the cultic action offered to us by Firmicus can render clearer to us the presuppositions of the apostle's figurative language and can thereby contribute to the understanding of that language.

XVIII.

The Dual Awareness in Romanticism

What I intend by the comparison perhaps can best be illustrated by the rich essay by P. Hensel, "Das Schauerliche bei E. Th. A. Hoffmann," in the *Frankfurter Zeitung* 1907, No. 130 I. Hensel places a significant development in Hoffmann's use of the marvelous and in his feeling in the period of Hoffmann's relocation in Berlin. "The earlier separation of reality into spatially distinct areas of the ordinary and the marvelous has ended. The two realities are interwoven, and sometimes one, sometimes the other seizes man, who in this way...is a citizen of two worlds....The student Anselm knows very well that he, stuffed in a glass bottle, stands alongside other fellow-sufferers on a shelf in the study of
402 the archivist Lindenhorst; his companions in misfortune, on the other hand, ridicule him, who, standing on the bridge over the Elbe, utters sighs of lamentation, and they leave well enough alone with respect to the archivist's specimen bottles in the Linke Bath." Thus Lindenhorst himself is the king of spirits, but with just as much reality, again, nothing more and nothing less than the mysterious archivist, the faithful functionary, in whom Rector Paulmann and the colleagues note nothing remarkable other than a bit of tenseness. As children we all lead such a double life and have the ability constantly to transform reality into miracle. But only for a few is this ability preserved in adolescence, and then it shows its power primarily to a person in love. Poets and artists enjoy that ascent of their very nature into the realm

of genius and inspiration for a longer time. But the majority of those who are earlier blessed forget their love for a stuffed animal, forfeit their native rights in the land of the genies, the kingdom of miracle, and end up in the big glass bottles, where they are very cozy and comfortable. But those who do not let themselves be driven out and who all through their lives look into the world through big eyes of amazement and wonder, the artists, employ what they have to proclaim about the world in which they live to awaken in others the recollection that they too were once at home in that world. It would be rewarding to trace out how it is in essence Hoffmann's most highly personal experience and feeling that prompted him to portray even the favored persons themselves as "hybrid creatures"; how the two sides of his nature bring it about that he, the exemplary, faithful, and zealous official, to a certain degree wants to strip off the robe of office only in the evenings, borne by the spirits of wine and food into his real kingdom, and as the king of spirits, which he is according to the other side of his nature, wishes to appear among kindred spirits; and how in this solution of the problem, which is to find an adjustment between his own "I" and the world, the dualism between them is not overcome, but is introduced into the "I" itself. Precisely because he refrains from settling the issue, Hoffmann can elevate that second part of his "I" into the superhuman, and

*03 the autonomy of the imagination increases excessively. In a time of strain and dissatisfaction, the extremely intense stimulation of religious yearning and imagination obviously was bound to exert an infinitely more profound effect than this over-excitement of a merely esthetic feeling. But even the shadowy reflection can give us a little assistance toward understanding that all-powerful movement that invaded the West

from the Orient. Above all, it can show how the contrast between an ordinary, drab outward life and a rich inner life paves the way for such an exaggeration of the feeling, and to this extent can be useful for the understanding of a personality like that of Paul, though of course we shall never fully achieve that understanding.

XIX.

The Meaning of the Self

The work of a comparative *history* of religions, as I am attempting to practice it here on a narrowly limited body of material, naturally has a close connection with the folklorist treatment of the pre-history of religions. The former, however, moves in the opposite direction; it does not take as its starting-point uncultured and arrested peoples, of whose history and reciprocal influences we know nothing, the so-called primitives, but aspiring and alert nations that are in contact with each other; moreover, it uses as a foundation a discernible and developed form of these religions and, moving gradually backward from that form, strives to identify, by means of comparisons, the general and the distinctive presuppositions and driving forces in the religions. The main tool in this process must be the language, and the work purely philological. To a person for whom, as is true for me, the Oriental languages are closed, in spite of all the help of friends only the outlines at most will be discernible; such a person can only help to formulate the task, not fulfill it himself; but perhaps he can show what he hopes to derive from it for his own science and for those that are closely related to it.

I should like to begin with a word of thanks and a confession. When as a young student of theology, after searching about for a long time I transferred to classical philology, I was first of all attracted by the altogether differently structured art of interpretation which I encountered here in a

master like Johannes Vahlen. In my youthfully exuberant enthusiasm, I was filled with the conviction that here at last fixed guidelines, and indeed, as I believed then, unassailable rules were offered to me, as to how one had to press on from the tradition to the word of the author and from the latter to the meaning and to the life of feeling. In my promotion to the doctor's degree, which was then still a ceremonial occasion, I expressed the conviction that I would owe only to this instruction whatever I could achieve in my chosen science. Life has led me into areas other than those of my teacher; but I owe to him the fact that when I once occupied myself with a single verse from Paul (I Cor. 2:14), I sensed that it was necessary to work my way into the entire pattern of his train of thought and his rhetoric, in short, his language; and that in turn has prompted this book and has posed for me the inquiry into the Oriental and the Greek elements in the thought and feeling of Paul. I have not been able to strike out the interpretations of broader contexts which were written down at that time, primarily for my own uses; they form the necessary foundation for all the rest. In spite of the continuing inadequacy of my acquaintance with the theological literature, I still have a lively sense of how greatly theological interpretation has changed since my student days, and indeed even since this book first appeared (Note: this appendix was added in the second edition of this book), and has drawn nearer to our philological interpretation; but it is hoped that because of the intentional subordination of the interpretation to historical investigation, it still will have something distinctive to offer. Because everything that we have by way of intellectual possession, and especially everything that we owe to the ancient cradle of world civilization, Asia, has passed through the Greek and the Roman spheres, and because our lan-

guage and with it our concepts have been thus formed, and down to the present time we have been influenced only by peoples who have passed through the same schooling, classical philology is the servant of all the sciences and, for me, for precisely that reason the queen of the sciences. An actual intellectual history without it and the auxiliary tools that it affords remains without foundation, helpless and inadequate. The word always forms for us the point of departure; and the task is to press on through from the word to an understanding of the concept or the perspective, first of all in the individual language, and then in a group of national languages that are bound together by racial commonalty or historical connection.

A number of languages translate the Greek pronoun αὐτός with a substantive. Thus the Indian, for which I briefly cite from Oldenberg's exemplary presentations (*Vorwissenschaftliche Wissenschaft: Die Weltanschauung der Brahmana-Texte* 1919, p. 86; cf. *Lehre der Upanishaden*, pp. 52-53): the word *atman* is etymologically related to *Atem* (Translator's note: the German word "Atem" means "breath"); it denotes "the self", especially in contrast to what is not the self, and it refers to the actual person in contrast to kinfolk, possessions, and the outside world in general; within the actual person it denotes the body as a whole, in contrast to the individual members (Oldenberg, pp. 87.1, 88), or the parts (p. 101);[1] further, it identifies what is inward, the essential, the *vivifying*, the dominant, over against what is external, non-essential, dominate. The fact that the gods originally were *atman*-less signifies that they were originally mortal. Here we are already at the boundary of the exaltation that then makes the *atman* the *invisible* power that is at work in the senses, but also in thought (Oldenberg, p. 88); the further development into

the self of the consciousness, which is one and the same in us and in the cosmos, the latter in fact originally representing a vivified body, a man in his totality, need not concern us any further here.

Obviously there is here an underlying sense of duality and separation, and yet again of the belonging-together or even of the union of two things, and there is no religion where we would expect to find it more surely than in the

406 Iranian. The invisible, celestial world and the mundane world, God and the soul, are indeed such counterparts. The assumption of a heavenly body, the strange idea, still unclear to us, of the Fravasi, all point in that direction. The σῶμα τέλειον[2] in the Mithras liturgy, which consists of the primal elements of the elements that form us in turn; or the virgin who in the Yasht 22 encounters the soul of the devout as its counterpart, because, to put it briefly, she consists of the soul's virtues; or the idea of Gayomard, prevalent in the Damdad-Nask, who passes away in matter, but as the soul, the inner and dominant part, arises again in the men who spring forth from the earth--it is hoped that the reader will recall all these. In the Greek magical prayer it is the ἴδιος δαίμων, and another translation, probably τελεία φύσις, "our perfect nature", is offered by the Arabic Hermetic writing from which I was permitted, thanks to H. Ritter's kindness, to cite some fragments.[3] In the Naassene Preaching it is the Anthropos, and thus Gayomard, or, in a neuter designation, the Logos, the inner man, or the Psyche, the divine nature, which holds sway in the cosmos as the total soul, and in the individual man as the individual soul.[4] The τέλος is the uniting of the two, in this world in the "vision", and hereafter in a complete merging. For the feeling Porphyry gives us an explanation in the expression, which would have been strange to any

Greek and yet gives an uncommonly sharp focus, for the vision ἀναδρομή and σύμφυσις πρὸς τὸν ὄντως ἑαυτόν.[5] He actually is acquainted with Persian perspectives and has also found the concept already present in his own Syrian mother-tongue, for the Aramaic word *qnuma*, which is often found in translations for αὐτός, fluctuates in meaning among φύσις, ὑπόστασις, and *persona*, and can even appropriate the concept of the body; it is that which is *one's own*.

)7 It will be good right here to note the little bit that I have been able to learn about the Oriental languages in this matter. In the Turkish, about which W. Bang and A. v. Le Coq have instructed me at my request, the corresponding word is *öz*, which Prof. Bang would relate etymologically to the root *ö-*, "to think, consider, recall"; he suggests that it was formed from that root just as *uz*, "expert, virtuoso", is formed from *u-*, "to be able". In Mongolian there is a corresponding word *beye*, that is explained as *corps, chair, personne, figure esprit, forme, moi, nature, naturel*; and in Manchurian, body, person, essence, *self*, capital, member. Prof. Sieg tells me that this variation in meaning and this pronominal usage could be traced even into the Tokharian language.

Now the word *grev*, which appears so frequently in the Manichaean literature, must have developed in quite the same direction; it too signifies body, figure, but above all the self, an altogether suprasensual being. It is identified in the Chinese Manichaean tractate as *notre nature primitive lumineuse*, our father and our mother, and at the same time as our δόξα; and if the Mithras liturgy offers the best explanation for this, for the words *grev hasenag* the best explanation probably is offered by that term cited by Philo (Quaestiones in Exodum II 46; above, p. 343), for which the translator of the Armenian text offers us two expressions to choose between,

anima principalis or *spiritus principis*. Regardless of whether Philo[6] here used the word ψυχή (soul of the primal man, the all-soul) or πνεῦμα, still it is demonstrated that the Oriental concept was already firmly established before the beginning of the Christian era. For Philo it is related to the μεταβολή of the human soul--since its father and mother are the theme, I could better say "of the human self"--into the divine, for which one can only name one father (God himself). A similar transformation is portrayed by the Hermetic tractate XIII, the λόγος τῆς παλιγγενεσίας. Here too the divine being, whose parts are enumerated and who is different from and yet the same as man, is called υἱὸς θεοῦ, but also of course the Logos, as indeed ἐλλόγιμος also appears for ἔννους (in the mys-

408 tical sense) in the Tractate XII of the Hermetic corpus, which exhibits Iranian influence.

It is instructive that in this connection this tractate[7] itself also offers for the same concept another Greek word, namely ψυχή, and at the same time interprets it as νοῦς. In §9 it proves that the ἐλλόγιμοι are not subject to εἱμαρμένη, in the following words: ὁ νοῦς τούτου (i.e., of God, or of the Aion who was previously named) ἀγαθός ἐστιν, ὅ<σ>περ ἐστὶν αὐτοῦ καὶ ψυχή· τούτου δὲ τοιούτου ὄντος οὐδὲν διαστατὸν τῶν νοητῶν (all νοητά form a unity), ὡς εἶναι (mss. οὖν) δυνατὸν νοῦν, ἄρχοντα πάντων καὶ ψυχὴν ὄντα τοῦ θεοῦ, ποιεῖν ὅπερ βούλεται.....πάντων ἐπικρατεῖ ὁ νοῦς, ἡ τοῦ θεοῦ ψυχή, καὶ εἱμαρμένης καὶ νόμου καὶ τῶν ἄλλων πάντων· καὶ οὐδὲν αὐτῷ ἀδύνατον, οὔτε εἱμαρμένης ὑπεράνω θεῖναι (thus Flussas; mss. read ὑπεράνωθεν οὖν) ψυχὴν ἀνθρωπίνων, οὔτε ἀμελήσασαν, ἅπερ συμβαίνει, ὑπὸ τὴν εἱμαρμένην θεῖναι (thus Flussas; A reads εἶναι, MC οὖν). It should be obvious that what God elevates above *heimarmene* or subjects to it is not the soul but the self of man; similarly, the νοῦς θεοῦ is not the ψυχὴ θεοῦ, which

apparently is asserted three times,[8] but the Self of God; the ψυχὴ θεοῦ in fact corresponds to the ψυχὴ ἀνθρωπίνη, and the tractate begins thus: Ὁ νοῦς, ὦ Τάτ, ἐξ αὐτῆς τῆς (thus A; lacking in MC) τοῦ θεοῦ οὐσίας ἐστίν, εἴ γέ τίς ἐστιν οὐσία θεοῦ.--<εἰ δέ τίς ἐστιν> καὶ ποία τις οὖσα τυγχάνει, οὗτος μόνος ἀκριβῶς, αὐτὸς (mss. αὐτόν; Tiedemann excises this) οἶδεν.--ὁ νοῦς οὖν οὐκ ἔστιν ἀποτετμημένος τῆς οὐσιότητος τοῦ θεοῦ, ἀλλ' ὡς περιηπλωμένος, (mss. ἀλλ' ὥσπερ ἡπλωμένος) καθάπερ τοῦ ἡλίου τὸ φῶς (mss. τὸ τοῦ ἡλίου φῶς); cf. XIV 9: ὁ γὰρ θεὸς ἓν μόνον πάθος ἔχει, τὸ ἀγαθόν.....τοῦτο γάρ ἐστιν ὁ θεός, τὸ ἀγαθόν. VI 2: ἡ οὐσία τοῦ θεοῦ, εἴ γε οὐσίαν ἔχει, τὸ καλόν ἐστι, τὸ δὲ καλὸν καὶ ἀγαθόν ἐστιν. His substance or motivation is the good; thus the νοῦς, which is good, is his Self. The magician (see above, p. 392) speaks precisely thus: σὺ εἶ ἡ ψυχὴ τοῦ δαίμονος (an intensified

9 form: the self of the self) τοῦ Ὀσίρεως, in his imitating the Egyptian usage, and immediately thereafter adds: σὺ εἶ τὸ πνεῦμα τοῦ Ἄμμωνος. This sufficiently explains the fact that Paul (above, p. 431) can regard νοῦς and πνεῦμα as identical (for him, both are simply what is innermost in a person); in this he is only following the use of religious language in the Hellenistic world.

A σύμφυσις such as Porphyry alludes to is mentioned in the Avesta Yasna 49.5: "He, o Mazdah, is happiness and fulness, whoever has united his *daena* with Vohu Mana being well cognizant of Armaiti through Asha, and with all those in Thy Kingdom, o Ahura."[9] For Porphyry, but for the Indians also (cf. Bhagavad-Gita XI 52-55), it is attained in the vision. The so-called Poimandres (above, p. 12) offers a portrayal of the process. The heavenly Νοῦς (Vohu Mano) appears to the prophet, bestows upon him through the vision, full γνῶσις and therewith immortality as well, and remains forever with him,

safeguarding him against all κακία; he has become ἔννους. Here νοῦς and ψυχή are the two parts in God that belong together, as in man; they are his essence, which consists of φῶς and ζωή. Thus the νοῦς of God enters into man (or is awakened in him). The utterly un-Greek division of these parts provides still further assurance that an Iranian source actually underlies this passage. Bartholomae gives us the following meanings of the Persian word *daena*: "1. Religion; 2. inner being, spiritual I, individuality; frequently incapable of translation." How the two concepts can be brought together is still so inadequately clarified that some scholars are inclined to predicate two words that only have a similar sound but are completely independent of each other. It appears to me that the still inadequate analysis of the Oriental concept of the "Self" rules out that interpretation. The passage from the Avesta from which I started can only mean, "whoever has incorporated into his own Self the 'good mind',

410 the Self of the god".[10] Thus it corresponds exactly to the presentation and the feeling found in the Poimandres and is fully explained by the Poimandres. We gain an impression of ancient Iranian piety. Thus taken externally, *daena* here signifies the Self as the νοῦς. Its heavenly counterpart here bears the half-mythological name. In Yasht 22 the soul of the devout encounters its image, which has earned its brilliant beauty through the good thoughts, words, and deeds of the soul, and which says, "I am your *daena*". The two are united, and a divine being emerges, which then is venerated as Ohrmazd. Here also the simple, and indeed self-evident, interpretation appears to me to be: "your Self". I see no difficulty in the fact that the word is used one time to speak of the human part, and the next time of the divine part. That fact is grounded in the concept itself, the idea that the

two are really the same. I am unable also to admit the validity of the objection, brought out by Cursetji Pavri once again in another connection, that *daena* cannot signify the soul since it sometimes appears alongside the word *urvan*, and the latter denotes the soul, and therefore *daena* must be distinguished from it. In this passage, *daena* indeed does not denote merely the soul, but the self, of which the "soul" appears as the content; as I have stressed repeatedly, everything depends on the function of the word. Any religious language that is not artifically distilled from a philosophical system or from a textbook on dogmatics, thus losing its religious character, employs various words for the same feeling, because no one of them fully exhausts the feeling, or because the change in expression is required by the rhythm
11 of the discourse or by the combination of ideas. A string of such designations, that always are only approximations, especially in prayers, then becomes customary--one may think, for example, of τήνδε ἀξίωσιν, τὴν λιτανίαν, τὴν προσύφωσιν, τὴν ἀναφορὰν τοῦ πνεύματος τοῦ λεκτικοῦ (above, p. 394)--and therefrom, in the Orient, there develop first formulas, and then systems. In the Greek formulation of the Manichaean doctrine of the soul the ψυχή, as is well known, is also νοῦς, ἔννοια, φρόνησις, ἐνθύμησις, λογισμός.

Hence it is easy to answer the question of how the same word, "the self", can have as its content one time νοῦς, and another time ψυχή, while in the Poimandres God and man consist of νοῦς and ψυχή, which correspond to a similar duality, φῶς καὶ ζωή; either of the two parts can stand for the whole, can represent our entire spiritual/intellectual, i.e., invisible, part, because they form an indissoluble unity. It is clear that in this context the νοῦς, because for the Oriental it is only the thought that is directed toward the

awareness of deity, the knowledge of God, can also signify religion (of the individual). But that spiritual/intellectual, i.e., invisible, element in us, whether it is life or thought, is, in fact, according to the most ancient view not an individual possession, but something impersonal, and for that very reason divine. In the Persian context we see: the primal man brings life and the knowledge of God into the world, and bequeaths them to those who come after him, who again are thought of only as the one people, the "tribe of souls". The religion as a whole is the soul, and it is immortal, because it is divine. It is the form in which the belief in immortality first is adopted by Judaism. In spite of the re-shaping, the primitive conception continues to exert its influence on down into the later period.

Now it is quite compatible with this interpretation, and indeed it serves only to confirm the interpretation, that the newly discovered Turfan fragments speak, in connection with evil or with the demon, of a *monuhmed*, and that this word, which certainly signifies a (religiously oriented) *power of thought*, something similar to the νοῦς, is connected with the soul of the good and, coupled with the adjective "great", denotes the soul of the primal man (or Ohrmazd) or the world-soul. Moreover, the Avesta in fact speaks of the *daena* of the evil--even he must have a self--, and parts of the Avesta that have been lost taught that Gayomard appears as the first and the leader of the resurrected ones. Just as the ψυχή stands alongside the νοῦς, so alongside the *monuhmed* stands the *giyan* (late Persian *dzan*, a word that like the Greek ψυχή frequently means "life"[11]); the two are set in connection with each other. Further, no difficulty is occasioned by the fact that in the amplifying additions to the song of Zarathustra (above, p. 56) the "heavenly Self" addresses the

412

prophet still sojourning on earth as "O, my body", since soul and body, like the two "selves", form a unity; no difficulty is occasioned, I say, if we have only correctly understood that religious concept of the self, which is so foreign to us, in its inevitable development.

I have been able to offer these propositions, whose imperfections I myself sense very keenly, only as a hypothesis, a task for those versed in the languages. Hence I am under obligation to add what constrains me to offer this hypothesis; that is, what riddles it would readily and naturally solve; what it explains. Is it not puzzling that the man for whom the immortality of our souls affords the foundation of the new religion and of his own proclamation, Paul, never uses the term which was so common in that time, ἀθάνατος ψυχή, indeed, that for him the word ψυχή is connected with the idea of something lower, earthly, perishable? There is no other explanation for this than that he is unacquainted with, or does not recognize, our concept of the soul, i.e., the Greek concept common in Greek since Plato. For it he substitutes πνεῦμα, thus the πνεῦμα ἐν ἡμῖν, but this πνεῦμα is--it may be said openly--something incomprehensible to us. It is the

3

πνεῦμα θεοῦ, but the conception must widely diverge from what we make of "the Spirit" or "the Spirit of God":[12] it has a μορφή, has brilliance or consists of brilliance, is a garment, transforms us (μετασχηματίζει), is substantial, indeed, like the visible man, has a body and members; like this visible man it must grow and become complete; it is the ἔσωθεν ἄνθρωπος.[13] Bousset offers the only solution comprehensible to me: it is the Χριστὸς ἐν ἡμῖν. But how can one bring these two conceptions together? That it is the Anthropos, the Adakas of the Mandaeans, allows us still only vaguely to discern a part of the way that the explanation must traverse. And on

the other hand, it is again a religious capacity for knowledge, a knowledge about God and from God, the νοῦς (I Cor. 2:16). It is in us, and yet again it has its own existence in "God's world". Moreover, in other, mostly non-Pauline passages, λόγος[14] appears for the concept νοῦς, and it appears to combine within itself the two elements or essential attributes of deity, light and life.

At the outset we are given some help along the way by the observation of Prof. Schaeder (Reitzenstein-Schaeder II, p. 299) that Mani conceived of the soul as material; indeed, it is light; and if this is true of the soul, then it is true of God also, of course. He cannot at all comprehend the full concept of the immaterial. As far as Mani is concerned, this much is clear and uncontestable. If the system of the Poimandres is actually taken from an early Persian writing, the same also holds true for that writing, for God and the divine man in us consist of light and life, and the divine world consists of elements which correspond to our own. Ostanes, at the beginning of the fifth century B.C., appears to have believed something similar. When he equates the (planetary) spheres, the

414 ἀγέλαι, with the *Amesha-Spentas* (above, p. 231, n. 58), he shows the continuing influence of the ancient Iranian list of elements in spite of all Zarathustra's reinterpretation. But in view of the inadequate linguistic compilations which I offered above, the question must after all be expanded and deepened: did Oriental thought, before it was influenced by the Greeks, even know the concept "immaterial" at all? The division between visible and invisible emerges in many places very early; people even speak of an ἀόρατον φάος. But it, like the νοῦς and the God of the Stoa,[15] remains material; they are indeed "essence". Thus that curious development in the Oriental languages, for which "the Self" is a being, from the attachment

to the body and to the visible manifestation of a whole all the way to the idea of the invisible and uniting force which then can be designated as life, consciousness, spirit, can be understood to some degree. Paul then used this Oriental concept, which offered such a variety of conceptual possibilities and in the mysteries even made them vivid, to render comprehensible to himself and to others his belief in the resurrection and his consciousness of being related to Christ. Moreover, for him the "Christ in me" must *necessarily* have merged with the πνεῦμα, the new Self, and the "life" in him.

Let us stop for a moment and see whether we could make still further gains here. The fact that this Self as the νοῦς, as religious knowledge, is also religion, would immediately account for the interpretation of Christ, which appears particularly in Jewish Christian communities, as *anima mundi*, i.e., as the primal man. The fact that it can also be called "Logos" lets us comprehend the speculations of Philo: in connection with him we could not speak of a Logos-doctrine, but of an Anthropos-speculation, which in fact is demonstrable in the Judaism of this period.[16] And the fact that this "Self" moreover is connected with the community of the believers; the Pneuma or Christ is bestowed only within that community; the church is his body and he as τὸ ἡγεμονικόν is its head,--all this would require no further explanation. But what about the idea of the ἀθάνατος ψυχή of the individual, the individual soul? It is not ruled out, even for the Oriental, and in a certain sense it is even required in the belief of the mysteries. But it could attain the dominant position which it holds in our religion only through the *Greek* concept of the ψυχή, with which individuality is necessarily bound up. The concept of the πνεῦμα loses in

meaning or is limited to the church; Χριστὸς ἐν ἐμοί becomes a mere formula, lacking in perspectival content, for submission to him; and the *Greek* concept of the soul re-shapes the faith. For an Augustine, all else retreats in the face of the two basic ideas of "God" and "the soul", i.e., the individual soul--this because Paul's influence is so all-powerful, because the idea of the church has such a powerful effect upon him, and because his veneration of Christ is so profound. His path to Christianity led him through ancient philosophy; this had an influence, not upon his dogmatic conviction, but upon what was most peculiarly his own, his piety, which now continues to exert its own influence.

But back to the main track of our investigation! At least in *one* passage we can determine with certainty Paul's relationship to the Oriental or Hellenistic belief in the "Self", namely in the account of the vision which is supposed to offer a guarantee of his ἐξουσία and γνῶσις, and we owe to Albrecht Dieterich our thanks that we are able to do this. I refer to the portrayal, discussed above on pp. 86-87 and 469, of his being caught up into the third heaven. Here I no longer place the emphasis on the individual words such as ἁρπαγέντα,[17] nor upon the fact that the concept, broadly explained in the Mithras liturgy, of the Self as the τέλειον σῶμα, which sums up in itself the five divine members or elements as a whole and imparts the revelation to us, is *presupposed* here; what seems important to me is rather the fact that here Paul speaks of a consciousness/self within him, which is different from him and yet is bound up with him. According to his present feeling it still is not the Χριστὸς ἐν αὐτῷ[18]--for whom such an exaltation into the third heaven would have no significance; quite soberly, in discourse that is not at all metaphorical, he pictures to what lofty heights and what mysterious power it

416

brought a divine being that lives in him, in order to use the threat of this being's power to constrain the community to be submissive to him. Anyone who takes offense here only for reasons of style has never sensed the aim and meaning of this part of the epistle. For this reason I have found it necessary to analyze those sections. Anyone who actually interprets it has, in my judgment, a choice only between two explanations: either Paul is a charlatan and a fraud (γόης), or he has actually appropriated a Hellenistic mystery-feeling, and Christianity was actually influenced by Hellenistic mystery-religion so near to its origins. There is a certain intrinsic justification in the fact that Christianity's early opponents always viewed the matter thus;[19] they still were unable to discern the immense differences. When I really attempt even only in some measure to make vivid for myself the religion of a man like Paul, his life of feeling, I cannot at all pass over such a passage. To me it gives irrefutable testimony of how strong in him is that dual feeling whose religious presuppositions I have traced out in the main part of this book and for which I felt obliged to offer a faint counterpart from the more
17 recent past in the preceding appendix; for to us--and not to philologists alone--the understanding of this kind of feeling has been almost totally lost, although it still exerts an influence--not understood, to be sure--in individual poets and theologians even down to the present.

NOTES

1. In spite of that, Oldenberg has some reservations against the translation "body": even where that translation seems to be suggested, it has to do, in the final analysis, with the self as contrasted with the non-self. It appears to me that here an earlier idea is involved, which sees the individual only in the body, as Wackernagel has demonstrated from Homer for old Greek thought. The best example is offered by the very ancient maxim that "man is twenty-one-fold, for he has ten fingers, ten toes, and the self" (above, p. 349, n. 1).

2. There the individual parts (elements) form the contrast.

3. Reitzenstein-Schaeder I, pp. 112-13.

4. Cf. the Martyrdom of Peter (above, p. 210): ὁ γὰρ πρῶτος ἄνθρωπος, οὗ γένος ἐν εἴδει ἔχω ἐγώ.

5. Above, p. 296, n. 1. This is reminiscent of the μεταμορφοῦσθαι in the vision in Paul's context (and still more of Rom. 6:5, σύμφυτοι; cf. the context there).

6. Cf. Philo's De plantatione 18, 19, where we find the words νοῦς, ψυχή, and πνεῦμα (πνοή), and the concept of the invisible man who nevertheless has a form.

7. In the actual text the language is almost entirely religious, but even in ancient times critical comments were interspersed by a philosophically schooled reader, for example in the introduction quoted below.

8. Scott of course excises it all three times, because he is unacquainted with Oriental conceptions or is not willing to recognize them.

9. The translation is taken from the dissertation, written under the direction of Prof. Jackson, by Cursetji Pavri, "The Zoroastrian Doctrine of a Future Life," New York 1926, p. 30. This passage in the dissertation gives *iza* and *azuitis* as the words in the text translated as "happiness" and "fulness", and comments that they are taken in a personal sense here. The duality evidently corresponds to the duality of the beings that are united. Pavri translates the word *daena* as "conscience".

10. It is not insignificant that Corp. herm. XII emphasizes ὁ τοῦ θεοῦ νοῦς ἀγαθός ἐστιν and sees the οὐσία τοῦ θεοῦ in the ἀγαθόν. Through this ἀγαθὸς νοῦς man enters into the kingdom of God and thereby is delivered from all κακία, and hence also from εἱμαρμένη. He is *united* with the divine: οὐδὲν γάρ ἐστι διαστατὸν τῶν νοητῶν, and he himself has become νοητόν. I am not looking for the mysteries-belief in the tractate or in the passage from the Avesta, but I see how that belief could, and indeed must, have been attached to these writings. The Ἀγαθὸς δαίμων who appears here as the god of revelation, is Vohu Mano, the Poimandres of the first tractate. But I cannot write a commentary on the Hermetic document here.

11. One may think of Poimandres §17: ὁ δὲ Ἄνθρωπος ἐξ ζωῆς καὶ φωτὸς (the divine components) ἐγένετο εἰς ψυχὴν καὶ νοῦν, ἐκ μὲν ζωῆς ψυχήν, ἐκ δε φωτὸς νοῦν. The etymology appears to confirm this. One time in a review I allowed myself to be led astray into explaining *giyan* as the animal soul, though I did not do this in the treatment of the goddess Psyche or in the work on the Iranian redemption-mystery (see the latter book, p. 38). Of course Augustine offers the occasion for this; but we are unable to say whether Augustine correctly understood Mani or what name Mani gave to the προσφυῆς ψυχή (an admittedly earlier term). Life itself is divine.

12. The passages cited above, on p. 454, which any reader can abundantly expand upon brief reading, suffice for proof of this assertion.

13. To him the σῶμα πνευματικόν is a self-evident, necessary concept (I Cor. 15:48; cf. above, p. 440). This way of conceiving it cannot arise out of the Hebrew word *ruach*.

14. Here I only recall the names Adakas (Adam) the Word and Adakas the God among the Mandaeans (cf. above, p. 15).

15. In light of the statements of M. Pohlenz, the question may be raised whether there is not an Oriental feature continuing to exert an influence here in the Stoa.

16. Likewise in connection with the prologue to the Fourth Gospel. I am unable to judge to what extent the usage of *Memra* also exerts an influence (Reitzenstein-Schaeder II, pp. 315-16) and how the usage itself is to be explained.

17. Livy XXXIX 13.13: *raptos a diis homines, quos machinae inligatos ex conspectu...abripiant.* Philo, De vit. cont. 12 Cohn: ὑπ' ἔπωτος ἁρπασθέντες οὐρανίου...μέχρις ἂν τὸ ποθούμενον ἴδωσιν.

18. Only later is it equated with the "Christ who speaks in him". Here he still senses it as something special, as in I Cor. 5:4: τὸ ἐμὸν πνεῦμα σὺν τῇ δυνάμει τοῦ κυρίου 'Ιησοῦ (above, p. 462. It inflicts the κόλασις). I shall certainly consider the fact that both statements were written in a time of conflict and were directed to a Hellenistic community, and therefore can only one-sidedly set forth the convictions of the author. But in my judgment it must actually be a part or a form of his convictions.

19. This is shown even in such minor items as the question of the proconsul in the trial of the Scillitan martyrs: *quae res in capsa vestra?* He naturally was thinking of the *cista mystica* and was disappointed to hear the answer: *libri et epistulae Pauli viri iusti.*

XX.

On the Developmental History of Paul

Ed. Schwartz, in his "Charakterköpfe", has delineated with marvelous sharpness what growing up in a Hellenistic environment and thinking in the Greek world-language meant for Paul's intellectual horizons. The character of the little book made it impossible for him to point out the details and particularly to point to the lexical circle in which the apostle's language was rooted. Hence Paul could at first appear to him as inwardly altogether a Jew. It was precisely at this point that my investigation was designed from the very outset to begin, and to prove that Paul therefore strove earnestly *also* to become a Hellene to the Hellenes. I can understand that, as long as one began with the assumption that Paul could have gained his acquaintance with Hellenistic piety only in Tarsus before his conversion, even Dieterich's brilliant discoveries were received in theological circles with the greatest reserve. Those discoveries appear to demand the almost unthinkable assumption that while he was still a Jew, Paul possibly had been initiated into two or three mystery religions or at least had become acquainted with the language and perspectives of their communities in personal intercourse. This assumption was no longer required once we had proof of the existence of a religious literature of edification and revelation for the mystery religions and hence of the existence of a mystical language for the Hellenism of Paul's time. Of course Philo alone could have sufficed for this proof and for the solution of the puzzle. He speaks of the mysteries

with abhorrence and revulsion, and yet he himself extraordinarily often employs the language of the mysteries, is strongly influenced by their perspectives, and assumes that his readers are familiar with them. He testifies, as we now know from other sources also, that in large circles of the Diaspora, Judaism actually had begun to blend with Hellenism or with

418 Oriental religions. Here a sizable movement, which corresponded to the general religious development in the Near East and which was violently suppressed in the homeland, was functioning without restriction. It is understandable that the same elements that wrought the fundamental re-shaping of the Judaism that was faithful to the Law emerge still more clearly here: Persian piety; Babylonian belief in fate, which had long been bound up with the Persian piety; and "magical", outwardly Hellenized cultic forms. Moreover, it is understandable that the opposition to a Judaism restricted to the nation could in some places be intensified to extraordinary sharpness. To this Jewish-Gnostic movement--we may be permitted to sum up the necessarily diverse manifestations under a single label--belongs also the baptist movement that is connected with the name of John; again, connected with it in a way that is not yet entirely clear is Mandaeism, and numerous later Jewish Christian sects or individual works like the Odes of Solomon, the Johannine literature, or the Pseudo-Clementines also exhibit a contact with it. By virtue of its very origin, indeed, infant Christianity was bound to find a footing most readily here. We know that here the Jewish messianic hope not only had lost its national and political character, but had also been re-shaped into a theological idea, though to be sure a less-than-clear one, an idea of an emissary of God who, traveling through the world either invisibly or in human form--according to a widely held view apparently also in the figures

of various men--preserves the knowledge of God, and thus life itself, in the world; his departure then brings about the collapse of the world, but in the judgment of the world that is bound up with that event, he saves those who belong to him. The combination with the belief in the decline of the world, a final judgment, and a renewal of the world, and the name of this being, who is thought of as exalted above all the prophets or as holding sway in them--*bar nasha* or Enosh or Adam, Greek Ἄνθρωπος--shows that in the last analysis it is related to the Persian Gayomard. The latter, at least according to the later belief in Zarathustra, continues to work, like Zarathustra himself, in the Saoshyant, the redeemer, who is born of the virgin of his seed; according to the earlier

419 view, he is the first of the resurrected ones, who leads his tribe into the new world. It seems to me that the derivation of the whole idea from this doctrine is hardly subject to dispute any longer, since A. Goetze[1] has demonstrated its basic features as already existing in the fifth century B.C.

Certainly we shall never be able fully to elucidate the inner experience of an actual conversion--not even where we have as many accounts as in the case of Augustine or Luther, and thus even less in the case of Paul. And yet every historian will have to undertake the task for himself. A theologian whom I highly esteem, Johannes Weiss, once expressed the opinion that he could comprehend it only if Paul had been personally acquainted with Jesus during the latter's lifetime, and now in the conversion experience recognized him. I would counter by saying that it far more readily becomes comprehensible to me if Paul was already acquainted with this idea of the emissary when he experienced the profoundly moving vision; it gave him the assurance that this idea is correct, the conviction that redeemed him, that the preaching of a God who in-

deed seeks sinners and unworthy people, is the truth. No one can offer *proof* for such an assumption; we can only demonstrate that it is intrinsically possible, and that it can actually serve to explain what otherwise is hardly understandable. This assumption also makes it possible for me in some measure to understand the fact that after his first instruction by a Hellenistic Christian, without further investigation of the life of that Jesus, Paul went for two years into solitude in the Arabian territory south of Damascus. The significance of the fact that he then joined a Hellenistic community has rightly been so strongly emphasized by Heitmüller (*Zeitschr. f. ntl. Wissenschaft* XIII, 1912, pp. 320-21) and Bousset (*Kyrios Christos* 1913; ET 1970). The major influence must have been exerted upon him by the language and cultus of that community, not by the cultus or the forms of expression of the original community. Finally, from the moment he consciously undertook to prepare himself for preaching to the Ἕλληνες he must have begun a systematic study of their religious language and of the world as they perceived it, which then was necessarily deepened in the continuing association with the communities. The importance of this language and
420 this perception of the world for a full understanding of the epistles addressed to the Hellenistic communities will have to be conceded from the very outset. The attempt also to connect with this the more profound distinctions in the understanding of the new doctrine which is grasped while still in its formative stages is intrinsically justified.

Even if we believe that Paul borrowed from that Hellenistic religious literature nothing more than the language, individual images and concepts, this still indeed is of immeasurable significance. After all, word and image, having assumed an independent status, continue to have their impact,

awakening new ideas, demanding inferences and justification of their use, and creating new concepts and ultimately dogmas. But word and image also exert, especially in the religious life, an influence back upon the one who utters them himself; precisely because they can never totally coincide with the religious thought, and only match the original religious feeling in a wholly inadequate fashion, they influence both thought and feeling, not only in the appropriation but even in the very creation of the latter. As rarely as this is stressed, I see precisely herein the justification of the philological labor in the area of the *history* of religions; it is necessary, for what is involved in these linguistic investigations is much more than language and words alone. Our religious feeling is wordless, but its conceptual elaboration and arrangement in our thought is done in words. The Greek word πνεῦμα, in light of the historical development of its usage, allows and even demands ideational connections that are entirely different from those of the Hebrew *ruach* or the Aramaic *rucha*. The Greek word, as we have seen, can denote what is innermost in man, his Self, the invisible and yet effectual in him as well as in God, and yet again it signifies the spiritual nature that survives after the material life has ended. We must start out from this Greek word if we wish to comprehend Paul's Christology in terms of its origin and development and to make clear how it was received among Greek-speaking people. Bousset, to be sure, in his last work took a long step toward the recognition of this mysterious development when he sought to locate the apostle's basic feeling in the declaration, ὁ δὲ κύριος τὸ πνεῦμά ἐστιν; 421 but now it is our obligation to justify, in terms of the history of language, that step and to continue it. Only with the instruments of his language could even a Paul render compre-

hensible his tremendous religious experience and make it the foundation of his belief; the pre-condition is provided by the conceptual world of his time, not by our own dogmatically developed concepts and systems. Only thus does Paul come alive for us. The demand that Christ should be perfected in us, and the feeling that Paul himself no longer lives, but that Christ lives in him, only acquire their full meaning when we start out from the ideas which have produced that language and which continue to function latently in it. Of course a boundary must at once be drawn: those ideas and that language *make possible* and *form* the thought even of a Paul about his religious experience: it has its force and its origin in the overwhelming constraint of total surrender to the one who has brought inward liberation to him through the revelation of a God who searches out the sinner. This ultimate and innermost element of the life of feeling, which we can only intimate and can never fully express in words, is everywhere what is creative and lasting; its setting, which is determined by thought-form and form of language, is only the collaborative and changeable; to use Paul's terms, the latter is the ψυχικόν, and the former is the πνευματικόν. But for our labors the apostle's warning must always apply: ἀλλ' οὐ πρῶτον τὸ πνευματικόν, ἀλλὰ τὸ ψυχικόν, ἔπειτα τὸ πνευματικόν.

Let us trace out this perspective somewhat further with respect to the example which we earlier selected. It is understandable that a Jewish community that is predominantly Aramaic-speaking, even though it is also strongly influenced by Iranian belief and permeated with Greek elements, must express a similar feeling differently, that it is not acquainted with a concept of πνευματικός, and that from the Hebrew concept *ruach* it gains only the idea of a momentary visitation

from God which indeed Paul also preserves in the idea of ἐν πνεύματι λέγω, but cannot connect it in that form with the person of Christ. The Old Testament idea of a pouring-out of the *ruach elohim*, the presupposition of which is precisely the external separation from the Χριστός, here gives
•22 the form of expression for the same inner need. It is understandable that people overcome the diversity in these forms of expression, so long as the demand for a system takes a subordinate place to feeling; but it is also understandable that the diversity has decisively influenced the development of later dogmatics, because the *ruach elohim* in the feeling of that time again can assume the place of "the emissary" and this basic concept still survives in the thought of the later period.[2]

Hence philological labor on the original documents of our religion necessarily comes under the same laws to which it is subject in relation to the primary documents of other religions also, and will inevitably have to combine historical consideration with the consideration of the psychology of religion.[3] In spite of the distinctions and contrasts, in keeping with Söderblom's insistence everything that we call religion becomes for the philologist a unitary entity which he must treat in uniform fashion. The sphere of philological labor does not extend to the ultimate origin; it can approach the very innermost personality and the experience of the individual man only by intimation and inference, but all the shaping and formulation, from the choice and the coining of the words onward, is subject to its consideration; it seeks to become acquainted with a small part of the unending fabric of reciprocal influences between nation and nation, and between person and person. Some say, "Philology is looking for cases of borrowing; it wants to explain and account

for things." Of course; otherwise it would not be a science, and would not have the history of the life of the spirit as its object. However, it does not propose to explain the religion itself, but its outward form and formulation, its σῶμα ψυχικόν, as I have earlier called it; and precisely where philology proves that a borrowing has taken place, it seeks to identify what is individual about the re-shaping. I may repeat here an example that was cited earlier. I am convinced that for the elaboration of his interpretation of Christ, Paul used a conception, already present in both Hellenistic and Palestinian Judaism, but ultimately stemming from the Iranian sphere, of the divine Anthropos as the bearer of the true religion. But I have already earlier emphasized three major differences, and now I stress them again. That Anthropos did not die, and for Paul the fact that Christ, himself innocent, suffered the death of a criminal stands at the center of the religious feeling; that other Anthropos has no connection with our sins, and for Paul the conviction that his own sins made this death necessary and that he himself has been set free from his sins by that death forms the very foundation; finally, the other Anthropos indeed worked on earth, ascended, and will come again, but Christ has arisen from the dead and has shown himself to Paul himself. This is for him the actual content of his message; the ardor of religious feeling that binds him to his Lord can only be explained from this perspective, not from the doctrine of the Anthropos. In spite of the borrowing, his religion remains new and his very own. Precisely here I sense that dogma, the formula of the language as well as of thought, still belongs to the σῶμα ψυχικόν. In the basic attitude of the soul, the piety itself, far more than in the dogma, lies the individuality and originality of a religious personality; that piety can only appropriate what finds points

423

of contact within itself, indeed, what is already present in germ, and it shapes everything, consciously or unconsciously, to its own norms. Thus also at all times authentic piety cannot lie in a literal adherence to formulas that have arisen conditioned by the times and by the individual; it is not general or universal property, but always more or less an individual possession.

If that σῶμα ψυχικόν possesses such a rare capacity to persist that the number of basic religious ideas and images can remain surprisingly small through all the changes of the times, a major reason for this lies in the fact that they 24 never fully express the feeling, the piety itself, and in every time, indeed in every individual person, they can undergo a deepening, an evaluation, or an interpretation that varies from instance to instance. Indeed, we see this also with respect to the dogmas that arise out of these expressions. I was amazed when, in my "Weltuntergangsvorstellungen", I was obliged to trace out how for a long time the dogma of Christ's descent into hell appears to form the chief point of the Christian faith and how far it now is pushed to the periphery of the faith even for its most passionate defenders; for a great many it has been pushed even beyond the periphery. The philological treatment of the history of religions can, by tracing the earthly form, the σῶμα ψυχικόν, of religion in its development, contribute to the increase of our understanding of the actual kernel, the σῶμα πνευματικόν, and thereby to the preservation of religion ever new and vital. The old master of our discipline in German Protestantism, Hermann Usener, once posed this task for philology in the reestablishment of the *Archiv für Religionswissenschaft* (VII, 1904, p. 32); and an unforgettable Strassburg theologian, H. I. Holtzmann, has called for the collaboration of our discipline in this effort in the conclu-

sion to his presentation of the Christian religion (*Kultur der Gegenwart*, Teil I, Abt. 4, 1906, p. 713). I am filled with deep concern now when I see in Protestant theology, and not in theology alone, a passionate struggle against historical examination and research, which among younger people only too often becomes hostility to "scholarship". Theology and historical study appear to me to be indissolubly bound together with the emergence and the basic idea of our Protestantism. When people now seek to secure for Protestantism an external initiative or even political influence in the narrowing and the creating of uniformity with which the dominance of formulas always is essentially connected, then I fear that they are overlooking the fact that its inner strength has always consisted in the fluidity of its outer boundaries and the possibility that whoever might seek in his own way a relationship to our religion and its tradition might be counted as belonging to it. I should almost believe that the latter kind of person has been its most effective champion. I began these studies, which were intended to point to a source of our historical knowledge which at that time was still too little noted, not to edify, but neither with the purpose of destroying. I do not surrender the hope that in them too there is confirmed the observation, often made in other areas, that honest scholarly labor certainly can temporarily stir up contention, but that in the long run it cannot divide, but only unite.

NOTES

1. "Persische Weisheit im griechischen Gewande," *Zeitschr. f. Indologie und Iranistik* II, 1923, pp. 60 and 167. Also Reitzenstein-Schaeder 1926.

2. I cannot go into this concept here, and shall only indicate that it seems to me that here Bousset goes somewhat too far in his separation of the Hellenistic-Christian and the Jewish-Christian view, though his suggestions are altogether worthy of consideration and are quite helpful. He was unable adequately to assess the Jewish contribution even in the Hellenistic doctrine of the God Anthropos and the basic Iranian ideas.

3. Only when the religio-psychological consideration would overstep its boundaries and claim the formulation or even the dogma as object of experience and of inner feeling would philology have to object, since it reserves for historical consideration alone the history of the forms of language and thus also of the forms of thought.

INDICES

I. INDEX OF SUBJECTS

II. INDEX OF PASSAGES CITED

A. From Jewish and Christian Literature

B. From Secular Literature

III. INDEX OF WORDS

A. Greek

B. Latin

C. Other Languages

IV. INDEX OF SCHOLARS CITED

D1032615